PROCEEDINGS

39th Annual Conference

of the

AMERICAN COUNCIL ON CONSUMER INTERESTS

March 31 - April 3
Lexington, Kentucky

Teresa A. Mauldin
Editor

Copyright 1993

ISSN 0275-1356

Distributed by

ACCI
240 Stanley Hall
University of Missouri
Columbia Missouri 65221
(314) 882-3817

CONTENTS

Invited Lecturers/Special Speakers

Refereed Papers

Refereed Poster Abstracts

Special Topics and Invited Papers

Workshops/Panel Discussions

Graduate Student Papers

Roundtables

AUTHORS INDEX TO THE 1993 PROCEEDINGS

xiv

xv

FROM THE EDITOR

The 39th Annual Conference of the American Council on Consumer Interests was held in Lexington, Kentucky, March 31-April 3, 1993. A wide variety of topics was discussed by consumer professionals from education, business, and government. Skip Laitner, of Economic Research Associates, presented the Colston E. Warne Lecture. Biotechnology was the focus of the Esther Peterson Policy Forum.

Forty-seven manuscripts were submitted for consideration as refereed papers with 30 accepted for presentation (46% rejection rate). Papers covered a wide variety of topics including health care issues, environmental concerns, time allocation, expenditure patterns, consumer behavior, complaint behavior and response, and financial issues.

Of the 25 poster abstracts submitted 19 were accepted for presentation (24% rejection rate). Poster topics focused on health care issues, consumer behavior, financial management, and child custody and support.

There were numerous special topic sessions, invited paper sessions, workshops, panels, and roundtable discussions at the conference. These sessions focused on issues such as demand side management, child care, consumer expenditures, environmental claims in advertising, taxpayer literacy, international consumer issues, effective teaching in the consumer area, home-based businesses, and current status of the profession. In addition, this year a special invitation went out to graduate students to submit manuscripts which were reviewed by other graduate students.

Presenters at the conference were invited to submit manuscripts or abstracts to be included in this publication. This was the second year that manuscripts were submitted on disk in a reduced sized font. This procedure has allowed us to make a few changes in the presentation of manuscripts in this publication, specifically, the running header indicating the publication and year. We hope that this change will be helpful. This year, in addition, the organization of the publication has changed with refereed papers first, followed by refereed poster abstracts, special topics and invited papers, workshops and panel discussions, and finally graduate student session and roundtable discussion abstracts.

The program chairs, Richard Widdows and Gong-Soog Hong, are to be commended for their hard work in putting together an informative program. A particular thank you goes to Gong-Soog for stepping in when Rick had the opportunity for traveling to participate in an international project.

Lexington, Kentucky is an exciting and beautiful city in the spring but the special events and the basketball fever truly got the blood "racing." Many thanks to Ray Forgue and Mary Ellen Edmondson for the excellent accommodations and for being superb hosts.

I wish to extend a special thank you to Virginia Haldeman for taking the big leap of moving this publication into 20th century technology. This change will continue to help future editors make improvements in this publication. In addition, Virginia has been a wonderful support person providing the guidance a new editor needs so much. A very special thank you goes to Anita Metzen who also has been patient in answering my many questions along the way. I would like to express appreciation for the assistance of my department secretaries, Susan Brooks and Linda Toney. And, finally a very special thank you to my student worker Shronda Hill for all her extra special efforts.

Teresa Mauldin
University of Georgia

1993 ACCI CONFERENCE CHAIRS

Program Chairs: Richard Widdows, Gong-Soog Hong, Purdue University

Poster Chair: Sharon Burns, The Ohio State University

Local Arrangements Chairs:
Ray Forgue, Mary Ellen Edmondson, University of Kentucky

1993 Conference and Poster Reviewers

Mohamed Abdel-Ghany, University of Alabama
Anne Bailey, Miami University of Ohio
Peter Basiotis, USDA
John Brady, University of Utah
W.Keith Bryant, Cornell University
David Bunting, Eastern Washington University
Margaret Charters, Syracuse University
Glennis Couchman, Oklahoma State University
Ann Coulson, Kansas State University
Carol Denson, University of Delaware
Roger Dickinson, University of Texas
Julia Dinkins, USDA
Richard Feinberg, Purdue University
Cynthia Fletcher, Iowa State University
Karen Folk, University of Illinois
Virginia Haldeman, University of Nevada
Janice Heckroth, University of Pennsylvania
Gong-Soog Hong, Purdue University
Jutta Joesch, University of Utah
Dixie P. Johnson, Purdue University
Phyllis Johnson, University of British Columbia
Virginia Junk, University of Idaho
Bob Kerton, University of Waterloo
Jane Kolodinsky, University of Vermont
Barbara DeLuca, University of Dayton

Julia Marlowe, University of Georgia
Teresa Mauldin, University of Georgia
Rob Mayer, University of Utah
Mary McRee, Purdue University
Carol Meeks, University of Georgia
Manouchehr Mokhtari, University of Maryland
James Morrison, University of Delaware
Bill Passero, Bureau of Labor Statistics
Dorothy Price, Washington State University
Deanne Sharpe, University of Alabama
Karen Stein, University of Delaware
Pat Tengel, University of Maryland
Christine Vogel, Vogel Associates
Harold Wattel, Hofstra University
Rob Weagley, University of Missouri
Mary Winter, Iowa State University
Jing-Jian Xiao, University of Rhode Island
Cathleen Zick, University of Utah

Student Reviewers:
Sharen A. DeVaney, The Ohio State University
Deana Grobe, Oregon State University
Aimee Prawitz, Louisiana State University
Xiang Y. Zhong, Purdue University

THE AMERICAN COUNCIL ON CONSUMER INTERESTS

ACCI was established in 1953. Over these past 40 years, numerous professionals have contributed their time and energies to serve the ACCI membership in leadership positions.

1992-1993 Board of Directors

President:	Jeanne Hogarth, Cornell University
Vice-President/Pres. Elect:	Barbara Slusher, University of Missouri-Columbia
Treasurer:	Brenda Cude, University of Illinois
Immediate Past President:	Loren Geistfeld, The Ohio State University
	Patricia Bonner, Eastern Michigan University
	Margaret Charters, Syracuse University
	Raymond Forgue, University of Kentucky
	Jane Kolodinsky, University of Vermont
	John Kushman, University of Delaware
	Jane Schuchardt, U.S. Department of Agriculture
	Norman Silber, Hofstra University
Executive Director:	Anita Metzen, University of Missouri-Columbia

Standing Committee Chairs

Career Opportunities:	Marilyn Chase, SUNY-Plattsburg (92-95)
Consumer Education:	Josephine Swanson, Cornell University (91-94)
Development:	Rader Hayes, Marquette University (91-94)
Finance:	Robert Weagley, University of Missouri (90-93)
Future Directors:	Marlene Stum, University of Minnesota (92-93)
Int'l Consumer Affairs:	Margaret Charters, Syracuse University (92-95)
JCA Policy Board:	Carole Makela, Colorado State University (90-94)
Membership:	Scott Maynes, Cornell University (92-95)
Research:	Robin Douthitt, University of Wisconsin (91-93)
Exhibits:	Joan Kinney, University of Wisconsin (92-95)
Applied Consumer Economics Award:	Ramona Heck, Cornell University (91-94)
Distinguished Fellows Award:	Jean Bowers, (90-93)
Steward M. Lee Award:	Rosella Bannister, Eastern Michigan University (90-93)
Student Research Award:	Peter Basiotis, USDA, (91-94)

THE 1993 COLSTON E. WARNE LECTURE

Ricardian Land: The Forgotten Piece of the Economic Development Puzzle

John A. "Skip" Laitner[1]

I travel a great deal. In all of my trips I try to pull out some new insights or ways of helping me understand the way the world works. Several years ago I was invited to Topeka, Kansas to give a presentation to the annual meeting of the Mid-America Regulatory Commissioners. At the time I was living in Lincoln, Nebraska and decided that rather than fly, I would take the longer drive down and learn something about the countryside.

It was about ten o'clock in the morning when I pulled into the town of Blue Rapid, Kansas, looking for a place to grab a cup of coffee. Like many midwestern towns, there was only one small restaurant on the town square, and it was filled to morning capacity as the farmers and business people gathered for their morning coffee and conversation. When I walked into the cafe, there was only one spot left for me to sit, and that was at the end of a long cafeteria table across from an old burly farmer who was impassively sipping his own cup.

After a few moments of uncomfortable silence we finally began some idle conversation. This eventually led to his asking me what I did for a living, to which I replied, "I'm an economist on my way down to give a talk in Topeka." He grunted in a rather disgusted way and I said, "I take it you don't think too much of economists." He thoughtfully muttered, "Nope. Them, lawyers and bureaucrats are about the lowest form of species on earth."

At that pronouncement I gulped and meekly hoped, "You don't really believe that, do you? Everything on this God's earth has some sort of value. Surely even economists and lawyers." After a doubtful moment, he looked at me out from under his Kent Feed Seed Cap and said, "Yeah, as a form of protein I suppose they'd make a good feed supplement for my cattle."

You can imagine my discomfort at this point. But there was also the hint of a twinkle in his eye and I calmly replied, "Well, you know there are just enough of us economists, lawyers and bureaucrats that if you went that far, the price of your corn would probably drop pretty dramatically. You wouldn't want that to happen would you?"

"Naw," he dolefully replied. "I suppose I'd rather have the higher grain prices, as bad as they

are." And right then and there I swore I would do everything to keep the price of corn and wheat just as high as I possibly could!

Just as I had no idea that my own well-being was so closely tied to the price of corn, there are some fundamental changes in our economy that are closely tied not so much to the price of feed grain as to some significant changes in our natural resource base. In the next 90 minutes I have with you this morning, I hope to share some of my thoughts — hopefully in ways that help create some new understanding about the role of natural resources, what classical economists call Ricardian Land, in the economic process. I then want to share what I think are some new ways we need to redefine the economic process.

Consider that in the next 90 minutes that I will speak and answer your questions, Americans will add another 750,000 tons of carbon-dioxide to the atmosphere. We will lost another half million tons of top-soil through wind and water erosion. In that same 90 minute period, we will import about 380,000 barrels of oil and dump 40,000 more used car tires into our landfills.

At that same time, about five plant and animal species will become extinct from the earth and we will lose about 7,000 acres of world forests. Some 15,000 more people will be added to the world's population. All of this in just the next 90 minutes.

Bernard Reimann, a management professor at Cleveland State University, recently noted that the "difference between the intelligent person and the stupid person is that the intelligent person can put together seemingly unrelated pieces of information and create a new whole." (Teitelbaum, 1992, page 104) In that spirit, let me ask you to seriously consider think through a critical economic link — one between the losses and impacts I've just described, and the fact that the annual per capita growth of the world economy is actually declining. (Brown, 1993, page 16).

Defining Our Terms

To begin our exploration of this issue, let me offer two critical definitions. The first is Economic Activity. I define economic activity as

---

[1]Founder and Principal,
Economic Research Associates

the process of providing the material goods and services for consumption — hopefully in ways that enhance the personal, cultural and spiritual development of our family, community and society. In other words, economic activity is the process of directing the flow of material goods toward a larger, non-material goal.

I define, in turn, Economic Development as the set of actions or policies designed to sustain economic activity — given changes in population, expectations, technology, and resource constraints. With this definition we can begin to see the first hint of how resources might actively fit within the context of economic development. First, we want to maintain economic activity in ways that meet rising expectations and a growing population. Second, we must better understand and address the issues of technological change and changes in the quality and availability in our natural resource base.

The variety of constraints in the exploitation of natural resources are growing. This is true whether we must desalinate more water to meet the needs of residents and visitors in the U.S. Virgin Islands; whether we are confronted with diminished old growth forests; or whether we have to drill another 5,000 feet for new supplies of natural gas.

Underpinning the growing resource constraints is the inherently inefficient use of those resources. From start to finish — from the mining, processing and fabrication of resources into useful consumer goods, to the consumption, and, finally the disposal of resulting wastes, we obtain as little as 15 to 20 percent use of those resources. In fact, our research strongly suggests that the growing inefficiency of resource consumption constrains economic activity and is a major cause of the worldwide economic downturn.

But if resources are so vitally important to the economic process, why isn't this extreme level of inefficiency more apparent to us either as consumers, or as producers? We can point to the problem of public goods, or to our nation's appalling lack of understanding about basic environmental processes. We can also talk about the notion of our throw-away society, as well as about the poverty and isolation of basic economic theory. It is that last, the isolation of economic theory, that I want to explore in more detail with you during my remaining time.

Desert Wisdom

Despite my close call in Blue Rapids, Kansas I continue to travel a good deal and in recent years I have found myself doing more and more work in Arizona. Although I have never really given myself the time to absorb the sense of it, I have long been fascinated by what Joseph Wood Krutch called "the desert phenomenon." (Krutch, 1954)

The lure of the desert has been tugging on my mind for many years. In 1986 I decided to spend more time in Arizona's Sonoran Desert — not simply to be in the desert, but to learn more of the phenomenon itself. Somehow I have been fascinated by the lessons of the desert and how the wisdom of desert living might help me think through the basic tenets of economic theory.

I am not a stranger to the desert. In fact, much of my growing up was spent hiking the Superstitions, the Santa Catalinas and the Saguaro National Monument. My father was one of the construction workers who built the Glen Canyon Dam. I remember clearly the frequent hikes taken in the area, crawling through many of the canyons and regions now known as Lake Powell. On several occasions, I have hiked the Grand Canyon.

What I saw as a young man was an interesting, although apparently unrelated, collection of rock formations, flora and fauna. Strange, I thought, that so many wondrous things could survive in such an inhospitable environment.

What I didn't see, and what I have begun to appreciate only in the last few years, is that the desert is a highly organized, integrated Community of Life. The flora and fauna are not just surviving, they are flourishing. They flourish so successfully because they have adapted to, helped shape and become a part of the desert. When exploring any part of the desert, one cannot examine the wildlife apart from the vegetation, nor the vegetation apart from the soil. Each would lose its identity and meaning without the other elements that comprise its living environment.

I came to the desert in search of new metaphors for my work in economic policy. For any number of reasons, I believed that a "greater diversity of theory is needed in economics to supplement the conditioned expectations of formal economic theory." (Hall, 1986, page 34).

Recalling the lure of the desert within my imagination, I instinctively felt there were new lessons to be learned — about my chosen discipline of economics and, more importantly, about the role of cooperation, diversity and integration.

Life in the desert yields a rich set of metaphors to guide the development of our institutions. This is true whether they are businesses, communities or governmental agencies. Let me be clear on this point, however. I do not look to the entire desert as my single metaphor. Rather, I look to the desert for those aspects of the metaphor which might catalyze new thoughts, which might help me learn, and which might help me introduce new lessons into the work I do within the public policy arena.

Insights from the Sonoran Sentinel

Perhaps the best-known symbol of the Sonoran Desert is the giant saguaro cactus. Looming over 35 feet tall and weighing two to three tons, this desert sentinel seems to lend a quiet but majestic presence throughout the desert floor. The saguaro stands remarkably human-like, an individual among a hundred species of plants. Yet to talk of the saguaro apart from its environment is to shut out a full understanding of its uniqueness.

The saguaro is a close family member to reptiles, birds, insects and plants alike. With its massive interior, the giant cactus provides a stable temperature that is cooler than the outside air. Its spines offer protection. Its fruit is a source of nourishment.

The saguaro is a living condominium to gila woodpeckers, cactus wrens and white- winged doves. From a vantage point on top of the cactus, a hawk is able to scan the area for prey. At the same time it is able to keep a watchful eye on its young.

The ant, the packrat, the javelina pig, the fox and the skunk, are all are attracted to the roughly 200 delicious fruits that the saguaro produces each year. The Tohono O'otam (meaning the Desert People) and now their descendants, the Papago Indians, have used the same fruits to make syrups, preserves and ceremonial wines.

With so great a feast that is so freely given to its many "family members", one wonders how the saguaro can be expected to reproduce its own species. Its secret lies in the sheer number of seeds generated within each fruit, seeds which help assure the replacement of the parent cactus. Within a 100-year productive cycle more than 40 million seeds are produced by a single plant. So highly prized are these seeds by the desert wildlife that only one seed in 40 million is expected to survive its parent.

Despite this enormous bounty and giving, the number of saguaro plants remains constant from year to year. The evidence, then, suggests that both cooperation and survival are a part of this desert patriarch's way of life. But the survival of the desert family is not a one way street. The saguaro also benefits from the same family that it supports.

Starting from a single seed, the saguaro faces a multitude of dangers, ranging from winter frost and searing heat, to hungry animals and frequent drought. Those plants which do survive are likely the ones which grow in the shadow of a "nurse" plant.   These neighboring plants offer the surviving cactus at least partial protection from the environmental extremes.

At 50 to 60 years of age the saguaro begins to flower. This usually occurs in the month of May, and then for only a very brief 24-hour period. Nectar bats, insects and birds take their fill of the saguaro blossoms and — as they flit from one plant to another -- the pollination process is completed.

The saguaro is a succulent which stores water within its massive stem. Its extensive root system is designed to absorb large amounts of surface water as quickly as possible. The waxy film secreted on its surface reduces the loss of precious moisture.

The saguaro spines do more than protect the plant from unwanted intruders. They offer shade. The large surface-to-air ratio of the spines helps to dissipate heat from the plant much like the radiator in a car. At the same time, the spines offer a break against the desiccating winds. During the night, they help condense what little moisture is in the air so that it can be collected by the root system once the water beads and falls to the desert soil.

The Curious and the Diverse

The presence of the saguaro highlights a complex network of supportive and exploitive mechanisms among the desert species. It is but one example of the remarkable diversity of plant and animal life found in the desert. Indeed, the profusion of life, color and textures found in the desert belies the popular myths surrounding the apparent harshness of the environment. Consider the boojum, a plant whose name was inspired by the Lewis Carroll poem, "The Hunting of the Snark".

Many see the odd-looking boojum as an upside-down turnip that looks more like a refugee from the world of Dr. Seuss than a thriving desert plant. Although it looks more primitive than efficient, the boojum has a remarkable capacity to make the most out of the little rainfall and other nutrients that come its way. In fact, the boojum "is actually a highly advanced form of life and belongs very much to the world" of the Sonoran Desert. (Helms, 1980, page 33)

Another example of the diversity found in the Sonoran Desert is the kangaroo rat. Instead of constructing a massive irrigation project to bring needed water into its home, this efficient little rodent lives without ever having to drink a single drop of water! Thanks to the animal's well-developed kidneys, its urine and feces are highly concentrated to minimize the loss of water. The moisture content of its burrow is maintained by the humidity within its breath. What new water it does require can be metabolized from the plants and seeds it eats.

The ocotillo is yet another desert inhabitant that turns efficiency into a livelihood, in spite of an otherwise inhospitable desert environs. A relative of the boojum, it can grow a full crop of leaves within 48 hours of a rainfall. Once the moisture is gone, the leaves are shed just as quickly as they were grown. The ocotillo can produce its leaves in any month. Depending upon the rainfall and warmth, it can run through several leafing cycles within a single year. The frequent shedding of leaves is far from a wasted effort.

The leaves become nutrients to be absorbed by the soil for use by future plants and animals.

Lessons from Convergent Evolution

What are the lessons these desert dwellers hold for the economic and business disciplines? The question can best be answered by drawing from yet another example of the desert metaphor — the concept of convergent evolution. This theory suggests that in the desert, the similarities in appearance are poor indicators of whether or not plants are related to one another. While the South African aloe plants have similar adaptations to those of the Sonoran agave family, the two have lineages that are quite unrelated.

The vegetative parts of both the aloe and the agave plants are mostly the product of the few adaptive mechanisms available to a given environmental stress. In other words, there are only a limited number of ways to gather and store water. Thus, both plants rely on their extensive roots systems and their ability to store water within their leaves.

Flowers, by contrast, are the evolutionary result of intricate relationships with the animals that pollinate them. Because of a dynamic two-way interaction, flowers are structurally more complex than the stem and root system of a plant. The basic patterns of flowers are usually recognizable even when they change in the evolutionary process. Thus, the distinctive lineages of the aloe and the agave are revealed in the differences of their flowers and fruits, not in the similarity of their vegetative parts.

In a similar way, the similarity of prices between two commodities does not reveal the full costs of their respective production and consumption. Other measures are required to complete this "rest of the story." Such measures might include, for example, how many Kilocalories (Kcal) of energy, or how many tons of water, air and soil were consumed and/or wasted in the process of producing the two commodities. One early illustration of this point is the work completed in the 1970's by Cornell University researcher, David Pimentel.

Pimentel found, for example, that the quantity of fuel needed to grow a kilogram of corn decreased by 105 Kcal from 1959 to 1970. Consistent with economic theory, an independent review of market prices in that same period (measured in constant dollars) showed that, indeed, the prices paid for a bushel of corn fell in response to this apparent gain in efficiency.

But Pimentel's research also showed that in the same period, the energy needed to both manufacture the farm equipment and support the work of the farm laborer actually increased by 143 Kcal per kilogram of corn. In other words, a 105 Kcal decline in direct energy consumption was offset by a 143 Kcal increase in the total indirect energy requirements -- a net increase of 38 Kcal to produce a kilogram of corn. (Hall, 1986, page 46.)

At the same time that the total energy requirements for corn production were climbing, the energy costs to produce energy also increased. By 1970 it took 30% more energy to produce a barrel of oil equivalent than it did in 1959. This made the energy subsidy of corn production even more costly.

The full costs of energy consumption were not at all obvious in looking at the price of corn in 1970. Therefore, the opportunity costs of different choices in the nation's farm and energy policies could not be fully known. As one group of writers recently noted, "neoclassical economics has ignored almost totally the physical, geological and biotic underpinnings of economic production." (Hall, page 34.) The question is, can we afford to ignore this issue?

Economics in Isolation

Yet, the failure of neoclassical economic theory goes well beyond the faulty estimation of prices. By focusing solely upon the market relationships between households and business firms, traditional economic theory treats marketplace exchanges as if they take place apart from the intricate web of life symbolized, earlier, by the saguaro cactus. Coordinated and measured only by a dollar transaction, neoclassical economic theory treats people and firms as if they operate in isolation from the very world which sustains them.

To say that it "costs" $2.50 per bushel of corn without including the full set of impacts associated with producing it, is to limit the understanding of what a dollar means to both the consumer and the producer. With commodity prices that yield incomplete information, alternative methods of growing or consuming corn cannot be fully evaluated. Hence the isolation of economics fails us.

To put this perspective in more concrete terms, agriculture again offers an illustration. Presently, the U.S. economy requires six billion tons of raw materials and energy to produce the vast amount of food and manufactured goods consumed each year. Total solid waste products exceed 7.3 billion tons annually. Thus, the products we consume each year are dissipators of resources, rather than carriers for the next user. (Pawley, 1983) This is a level of waste that represents a striking contrast to the interactive network of life that flourishes in the desert.

It should take little convincing that the prices we pay for food do not even begin to reflect the magnitude of this consumptive imbalance. The reason for the disparity between consumption and waste becomes especially clear when we learn that topsoil losses account for as much as 4.0 billion tons of the annual U.S. total solid waste output. In the present economic arrangement, soil is treated as a free or inconsequential good. Nowhere is the enormous waste of topsoil reflected in the price of corn sold in the marketplace. It is almost as if the market, through a purposefully incomplete pricing picture, is trying to limit how the earth's resources are to be used.

Without better information about the full impacts of our transaction, our choices are limited in two ways. First, incomplete prices narrow the range of alternatives under consideration. Many options that are otherwise available to us are simply not seen as feasible. We might, for instance, think that our only water supply option is to build a large irrigation project rather than switch from present cropping patterns to a mix of hardier plants indigenous to the environment.

Second, while the price of corn may justify the switch to a cropping pattern that lowers the direct fuel cost of farm operations, it does not pick up the indirect energy losses, the increased thermal and air pollution costs, and the chemical threat to soil bacteria which are necessary for long-term plant survival.

Ad Hoc Remedies

What remedies might be employed to help us evaluate our transactions within the context of the web? There are at least three possibilities. More can be added, and all might be improved upon — especially as we grapple with new metaphors to help reshape our social and economic framework. I refer to them as ad hoc remedies because our present understanding of both the importance of metaphor and the impacts of consumption is incomplete.

The lack of better metaphor, coupled with our incomplete knowledge of the consequences of current consumption patterns, prevent the certainty of a permanent course of action. Still the lessons are sufficiently clear to warrant consideration of these interim remedies.

A. Expressing Democratic Purposes in Economic Terms

To start, we must change the way we express our economic concepts. For example, the production function is the economist's recipe for how the output of the economy is related to the mix of resources available for use. In simple notation it invariably is written as

$$Q = F(K,L). \qquad (1)$$

The variable Q represents the level of output expected for a given economy while F stands for the phrase, "is a function of." The physical stock of plant and equipment, called capital, is represented by K. The work force, or Labor, is L. The expression reads, "the output of an economy is a

function of the capital and labor used to produce needed goods and services."

The most obvious improvement to be made at this point is to acknowledge a more active role of natural resources, R, in the economic process than is generally conceded. In this regard we sometimes find

$$Q = F(K,L,R). \qquad (2)$$

This newer version of the expression reads, "output is a function of capital, labor and resources." Still, the production and consumption of material goods creates other impacts which ought to be explicitly accounted for in the evaluation. These include disruptions, D, in the interaction of the web; and waste, W, which all too often is manifested by pollution, P, of one variety or another.

By accounting for these impacts, we are given a better sense of how the present mix of technology constrains future choices. Given these new impacts, the expression might become

$$Q = F(K,L,R,D,W,P). \qquad (3)$$

Even now, the notation still reads that output is "a function of" an isolated and non-integrated set of things. The implicit assumption is that the production function operates independently of values and choices.

But recall what it is we ask from the output of our economy. It is not merely to produce goods and services for the sake of consumption. Rather, it is to provide for the material well-being of our community (society) in a way that enhances our personal and cultural development.

Presumably these goals are to be pursued in a manner that reflects a democratic society. If that is, indeed, the case, then we can substitute the variable C, which represents the purposes of the community, for F. Instead of limiting our expression to a statement that output is merely a function of a some set of isolated or unrelated factors, we finally arrive at an expression something like

$$Q = C(K,L,R,D,W,P). \qquad (4)$$

This last expression might read: "Output is catalyzed by community goals and values which employ the mix of capital, labor and resource factors available to it, and which generate waste, environmental disruptions and pollution in ways that tend to limit future choices."

In this context, the role of economic output takes on a whole new meaning. In a similar way, other economic expressions can begin to capture the democratic purposes to which resources should be applied. They can also incorporate the full realm of technology, resources and impacts which affect those democratic purposes. Finally, better choices can be made as to how the mix of technologies and resources can be fashioned to achieve the full complement of community goals.

B. Ad Hoc Improvements in the Pricing Signals

Market arrangements now depend upon the price signal to coordinate the allocation of resources. As already discussed, prices fail as an effective allocation mechanism for any number of reasons. While better institutional arrangements (other than price signals) may be required, until those arrangements are in place, people should be at least be receiving an ad hoc or interim message about the impacts that present consumption has on the environment and on the economy.

One such strategy lies in the regulated utilities arena. On the one hand, we must ensure that the price of electrical or natural gas consumption reflects the full external costs of consumption. In this way, the customers would realize the true impacts that current usage will have on tomorrow's economy. Our work indicates that for each kilowatt-hour (kWh) of consumption there is an associated environmental cost of about 1.5 to 4.0 cents per kilowatt-hour. Similarly, it appears that for each kWh not conserved through the more efficient use of electricity, we lose about 2.0 cents of income to the economy.

If today's inefficient mix of technologies is costing us about 6.0 cents per kWh in combined environmental and economic losses, these impacts should be incorporated into the price of electricity. With this information, consumers can decide how to rationalize their consumption before they are locked into an environmental or economic impact they didn't want and didn't know was coming. (The technique to evaluate such impacts is discussed in Laitner, 1988.)

On the other hand, we don't want to lock people into a pattern of consumption that cannot be changed should higher price signals be issued. In other words, the demand for energy must be kept elastic by giving people the ability to adequately respond to price signals.

Maintaining an elastic demand implies two things. First, technical assistance must be provided to consumers for them to know how they can change energy usage patterns. Second, consumers must be given the financial ability to make that change. Both can be done by pooling the revenues generated by the energy surcharge into an efficiency fund to be used for such purposes.

As more and more people take advantage of efficiency opportunities, the external costs, by definition, will diminish over time. The surcharge will be reduced. This mechanism then becomes a means to both reflect the larger costs of energy consumption as well as a way to provide consumers with the means to respond to those impacts.

(Laitner, 1988) Similar arrangements should be explored and advanced in other areas of economic policy.

C. Expanding the Notion of Diversity

A third remedy is to draw lessons from the diversity which exists within the biological arena, but which too often is poorly understood. Returning to Arizona for our example, researchers have learned that early inhabitants of the Sonoran Desert used some 450 species of plants growing there as food sources. The plants also provided shelter, medicine, tools and weapons. Compare that to the fact that, presently, the most important staple foods grown in the world are limited to only seven crops — wheat, rice, corn, barley, soybeans, common beans and potatoes.

In Arizona today, agriculture accounts for almost 80% of total water consumption. None of the food crops which are now grown there are native to the desert. All of the present crops require enormous amounts of water. The public subsidies which are needed to anchor the construction of new water supply facilities have become a source of major controversy. Meanwhile, the common, water-efficient mesquite provides an easily harvested and nutritious pod that is edible without having to be cooked. The ironwood and the paloverde also produce a large source of nutritious seeds.

While these and many other potentially new crops are not competitive with the modern cropping patterns of today, a re-evaluation of the pricing institution and the rewriting of the production function might help restore them to their prehistoric usefulness. Failing that, research and development policies should be emphasized to accelerate the commercial viability of these new (old) crop resources.

One means of encouraging the return to the diverse resources currently being overlooked may be to encourage the ethic of self-sufficiency within communities. Current development theory focuses heavily on export-led activities. In sustaining the trade flow, resources not available to the community are imported. Just enough work is done on those imported resources to add sufficient value to sustain local businesses at which point they are exported.

If some consumer product is not immediately available to the community, these finished goods are also imported — regardless of (and oblivious to) the hidden impacts or the alternative choices. Little effort is expended to see what presently available materials might be fashioned into useful goods for use within the community. A recent course I took reinforced this point. Its very long title was, "Energy-Efficient Owner-Built Homes for Under $20,000 Using Recycled Materials."

The instructor had participated in the

construction of more than 200 low-cost dwellings. Yes, they were efficient. But they were also comfortable homes and aesthetically pleasing. In one of his lectures the instructor noted that among the most impressive homes built around the turn of the century in Nebraska were known as rammed-earth dwellings.

Instead of importing timber products from the Pacific Northwest or the Southeastern states, families relied on compacted dirt. In the nicer earthen homes, despite the uncomfortable image conjured up by the term rammed earth, there was no evidence to tell of their peculiar construction. Nor was there any discomfort in how people lived compared to life in the more conventional dwellings.

In the early 1900's Nebraskans began to abandon the rammed earth shelters in favor of the more typical wooden structures, in part because of a growing snob-appeal. Yet the wooden homes offered no better shelter than rammed earth dwellings. In many cases they were a poorer shelter, especially in terms of their temperature and humidity comfort levels.

As a result of this shift in construction materials, Nebraska now imports a large amount of timber harvested at a significant environmental and economic cost. This is all the more ironic since — when viewed in a different context — the state has most of the indigenous resources needed to construct a comfortable and affordable housing stock. The environmental impact is likely to be minimal compared to the extensive harvesting that now occurs in the forests of the Pacific Northwest.

Unfortunately, most people associate self-reliance with a sharply negative image, even as topsoil losses continue to mount, landfill costs rise, pollution impacts increase and pecuniary interests displace community values. For this reason, the value of self-reliance as a development option is greatly underestimated. The many local resource options available within any community are, therefore, lost.

The Need for New Metaphors

A number of writers have noted that we are an economy in transition. Economic volatility, uncertainty and complexity are manifestations of that transition. But this preoccupation with change may be masking the emerging patterns of interconnectedness (Luke, 1986).

The basic tenets of neoclassical economics are founded upon the notion of separation -- that the household is separate from the firm, that the firm is separate from the community, and that all are separate from the environment. By definition, then, current economic theory is not equipped to handle the dimension of problems whose solutions imply an explicit integration of goals, constraints and choices into the economic process. "Without

the ability to temporarily forget what we know, our minds remain cluttered up with ready made answers." (von Oech, 1983, page 10)

In such a circumstance, the conscious search for new metaphors can become part of the ad-hoc planning process, shaking our consciousness as a community so we can learn of new ways to shape our institutions. Part of that learning process is to open ourselves up to new ideas in the hope that new solutions will emerge. As Keynes aptly noted, "the difficulty lies not in the new ideas, but in escaping the old ones." (Keynes, 1936, page viii)

References

Brown, L., et al (1993). State of the world. New York: W.W. Norton and Company.

Hall, C.A.S., et al (1986). Energy and resource quality: The ecology of the economic process. New York: John Wiley and Sons.

Helms, C.L. (1980). The sonoran desert. KC Publications.

Keynes, J.M. (1936). The general theory.

Laitner, S. (1988). Designing energy strategies to incorporate external costs into public policy: Where 'LES' is more. Proceedings of the National Regulatory Research Institute's Sixth Biennial Research Information Conference.

_____.(1991, October). Environmental costs of energy uses. Report for the Missouri Environmental Improvements and Energy Resources Authority as part of its statewide energy plan, Jefferson City, MO.

_____.(1993, March). Prefiled testimony of John A. Laitner. Before the Connecticut Department of Utility Control, Docket No. 92-11-11, filed on behalf of the City of Hartford, CT.

Luke, J.S. (1986). Managing interconnectedness: The need for catalytic leadership. Futures Research Quarterly, (Winter).

Pawley, M. (1983). Building for tomorrow: Putting waste to work. San Francisco, CA: Sierra Club Books.

Teitelbaum, R.S. (1992, November 2). The new race for intelligence. Fortune.

Von Oech, R. (1983). A whack on the side of the head. New York: Warner Books.

The Esther Peterson Consumer Policy Forum on
Biotechnology and the Consumer
The Food and Drug Administration Perspective

Eric Flamm, Food and Drug Administrtion[1]

The following is a transcription of the presentation by Eric Flamm from the FDA's Office of Biotechnology, a component of the Commissioner's Office involved with the development and writing of food biotechnology policy.

I would like to thank ACCI for inviting me to participate in this forum. I will give a very brief overview of what FDA's regulatory and legal authority is for foods and food safety and then show how we've used that authority to regulate biotechnology-derived food products. Then I'll discuss some of the comments we have had from consumers on that policy and how we addressing those comments. I would be very interested to hear from you on how we might be able to better address those concerns.

Under the Food Drug and Cosmetic Act, FDA has both pre-market and post-market authority over food. The pre-market regulatory authority covers food additives, those substances that are added to food intentionally, such as sweeteners or preservatives added to processed foods. If a substance meets the definition of food additive, it is required to get regulatory approval by the FDA before it can be marketed.

A caveat to the definition of a food additive is that if the substance is "generally recognized as safe" (GRAS) the substance doesn't meet the definition of a "food additive." A food additive is something intentionally added to food that is not generally recognized as safe. Congress added that caveat so that FDA would not have to regulate substances that were already commonly used in food and known to be safe--salt and pepper for example. The GRAS exclusion also means we don't have to regulate things like tomatoes in vegetable soup, which technically would meet the definition of a food additive.

If a company is marketing or plans to market a new substance that is going to be added to food, the firm has to make that decision on its own. It has that burden, responsibility, and freedom to decide, on its own, whether the substance meets the definition of a food additive--Is it a food additive or is it GRAS? And generally it is a fairly easy decision; either it is something that's already commonly used in food, or it isn't.

But often times the substance may be a modification of something that is commonly accepted for use in food, and then the question is whether this modification is significant enough to consider it as a different substance. When companies aren't sure about whether these differences are significant, they consult with the FDA and ask our opinion. Sometimes, for various reasons, they may ask us to affirm their product as GRAS. To do that they present a petition similar to that for a food additive, and ultimately we write a regulation affirming this product is GRAS if it meets all of the appropriate criteria. There are a lot of market pressures as well as legal pressures that keep manufacturers very conservative, because it's not a good thing to be told you are illegally marketing an unapproved food additive. Firms have to take their products off the market, and there's a lot of bad publicity. So FDA ordinarily does not have problems in this pre-market approval area.

The second oversight mechanism, FDA's authority to take adulterated food off the market, is the primary method by which FDA regulates whole foods. This is the authority the FDA uses for removing fish that is contaminated with mercury, or cornmeal contaminated with aflatoxin, or potatoes that have unsafe, high levels of natural toxicants that potatoes ordinarily produce. This post-market authority of FDA's puts a legal duty on manufacturers to ensure that any food product they market is safe. The responsibility has to be on the manufacturers because it would be impossible for FDA to test the safety of every tomato and every piece of fish, although we do perform inspections. The burden is on industry to ensure that their products are safe.

The pre- and post-market authorities are the essential ways the FDA has of assuring the safety of food. Another relevant aspect of food law is the labeling requirements. Here the law places certain limitations on what the FDA is allowed to require in labeling and as well as certain requirements as to what it must require in labeling. Basically, foods have to be labeled with a common or usual name and the labeling must reveal all information that is materially significant in light of representations made or implied about the food or in light of consequences that may arise from the use of that food. Clearly, there can be some subjectivity as to what information should be considered "materially significant," but the

---

[1]Office of Biotechnology, F.D.A.

question has to be addressed within the constraints imposed by the law.

What issues are raised by biotechnology-derived foods and how does FDA apply its regulatory authority to those foods? Last May, FDA published a policy statement on foods from new plant varieties. This policy is for plants developed with any technique, but most people are interested only in the aspects that apply to the biotechnology-derived foods. If a new substance is introduced into food, by genetics or by breeding, that substance meets the "added" part of the definition of a food additive. So it is considered to be a new substance added to food. Now the next question is: is that substance GRAS or not? If it's not generally recognized as safe, then it is a food additive and it must be approved by FDA. On the other hand, if the product is of a class of substances that are generally accepted for use in food, then it is exempt from the definition and does not have to come to FDA for approval.

As it happens, with genetic engineering, what you're doing is moving genes into plants and genes encode proteins. So basically what you're adding to food with genetic engineering are new proteins. Now, proteins as a class do not raise food safety concerns. That does not mean that there are not individual examples of proteins that may be dangerous. But as a class, proteins are digested, they are metabolized, and they don't raise food safety issues. There are anywhere from 100,000 to 1,000,000 different proteins in foods. Of all proteins known, only a handful are orally toxic. So, unlike many of the chemicals added to processed food, proteins are not novel substances whose safety is unknown or whose potential interactions with other chemicals in food is unknown.

In its policy statement, FDA describes the kinds of information necessary to establish that a protein is safe, providing an elaborate flow chart with explanatory text. Basically the kinds of information needed is: a protein of a type that is already found in food? Do you know the function of that protein? Does the function of the protein, in any way, raise food safety issues? If you don't know what the function of that protein is, then you are required to come to FDA and go through a food additive approval process. But if you do know what the function is, and it's a function that is found in other proteins in food and does not raise any food safety issues, and, if that protein will not be in high levels in the food, (if it's an enzyme that is going to be there trace amounts, enough to modify how the plant grows but not enough to make any difference in the food products from that plant) then the marketers are not required to consult with FDA, It is just another protein that raises no issues.

Nevertheless, the FDA has strongly encouraged companies to meet with us to discuss their new developments to make sure that there are no unresolved issues. In fact companies are routinely consulting with us. At this point there are very few companies that have products that are anywhere near coming to market, so there aren't that many companies ready to meet with FDA. But the FDA has met with companies who are very early in their development process, who want to find out if their product is one that is going to raise concerns or not. That is the food additive aspect of biotech food products.

The post market or adulteration aspect of the FDA policy addresses the potential problems of inadvertent increases in levels of natural toxicants or decreases in levels of nutrients. Here also the policy statement contains elaborate guidelines describing the kinds of tests and monitoring a company needs to do to ensure that its food is as safe and wholesome as others like it. This section puts developers on notice that their products have to meet certain standards of safety. The guidance is to a large extent a description of the practices breeders routinely follow when developing new plant varieties. If, for example, a plant is of a type that has toxicants associated with it at a significant level, or that are significant toxicants in and of themselves, then companies have to monitor their new variety to make sure the levels of toxicants are in the normal range. In many ways this really is a concern more for traditional breeders than for the genetic engineers, because with some kinds of traditional breeding, there is a greater likelihood of inadvertently introducing higher levels of toxicants. In any case, this is a concern for all breeders and, it's always been a concern for breeders. Again the FDA has an elaborate guidance policy so that breeders know what is considered to be standard practices for them to use to ensure that their products are in compliance with general safety standards and don't raise any new safety issues.

Just to recap, we have a food policy that says if you put something unusual or that raises any safety questions into foods, it must be approved by FDA. In general it is likely to be very rare for genetic engineers to put something unusual into food, despite the fact that one can move genes between all sorts of organisms.

The one thing that is fairly specific to genetic engineering is the ability to move proteins between different food groups, for example moving a peanut protein into a tomato. If you are allergic to peanuts, that raises some very obvious concerns. In such a case, FDA's policy requires that the tomato be labeled as containing peanut protein, unless the sponsor can demonstrate conclusively that he did not transfer a protein responsible for the peanut's allergenicity. I would like to stress that nobody that the FDA is aware of is moving peanut proteins around, and that they would clearly have to be out of their minds to do so.

The general policy regarding potential transfer of allergens is that if one moves a protein from a commonly allergenic food to another food, the new food must be labeled as containing protein from the donor food. The only exception is if the sponsor can show that the transferred protein is not responsible for the donor food's allergenicity, or that when expressed in the new food it is not allergenic. There are about 100,000 genes in a plant. Each gene codes for a protein. Of these approximately 100,000 proteins, most of which are not in the food part of the plant or are there at very low levels, only a few will be responsible for the food's allergenicity. So, unless one is moving a gene coding for one of the predominant proteins in the food, it is very unlikely that he would be transferring an allergen. Nevertheless, special labeling will be required for such food unless the sponsor can demonstrate that the food has not acquired the allergenicity of the donor food.

Now, moving to labeling in general, as I mentioned earlier, labeling has to reveal all information that is materially significant in light of potential consequences of the use of that food, or in light of representations made or implied about that food. That is a strict requirement, but it is also a very limited requirement. For example, the FDA can't require a label to say whether unionized labor was used in the production of a particular corn plant. The FDA has never found that the kind of breeding technique used to develop a new variety is materially significant, because it does not give any information about the quality of the food that is being developed. It doesn't tell whether there is something new in the food or if the food has a new quality to it. Therefore FDA's labeling policy currently does not require mandatory labeling simply because genetic engineering techniques were used in the development of a food crop.

On the other hand, if the food is really different, for example if one were to modify canola oil so that it has a high level of saturated fat (so that one could use it, for example, in candy bars), we would not allow the manufacturer to say he is using canola oil. Because that modified canola oil does not meet what one expects for canola oil, the manufacturer would need to have a different name, or need to say "high saturated fat canola oil," or something on that order. Thus, if the food itself is changed significantly, labeling will be required.

The FDA has received some 3,300 comments on this policy and 90 to 95 percent of those comments have come from consumers. The 5 to 10 percent of comments that have come from academics in the field and from industry have been positive, very supportive, saying that it is a scholarly policy, that it really makes a lot of sense. But as I mentioned, 90 to 95 percent of the comments are not from those groups. Most of the comments from the consumers have been quite negative. They want mandatory special labeling for foods derived from genetically engineered plants, without apparent regard for whether the food is altered in any

significant way by the modification. Many comments requested that there products receive mandatory pre-market approval by FDA. Not surprisingly, not everyone is aware of the GRAS exemption and that Congressional action would be required to alter it. There were also many comments requesting mandatory notification to FDA of the intent to market foods derived from genetically engineered plants. Some comments expressed concerns about allergenicity. Others raised potential religious or ethical issues--if a gene is transferred from an animal to a vegetable, does that change the nature of the vegetable such that people who are kosher or follow Moslem strictures or are vegetarians would violate their beliefs by eating this vegetable? We are still in the process of reviewing and analyzing all the comments. Presently, we think that of all the issues raised, allergenicity and labeling can best profit from further discussion. We are expecting to publish notices in the Federal Register requests for information on specific aspects of the allergenicity and labeling issues.

The labeling notice should be published in the next month or so. It probably will contain a discussion of the legal strictures on labeling, in particular the kinds of information that FDA can and cannot require to be revealed through labeling. It may also discuss how FDA has dealt with other labeling issues, such as those posed by irradiated foods and protein hydrolysates. Ultimately, we hope to use the information we receive to identify specific issues that will be the focus of a public meeting to be announced in the future.

We are not as far along in drafting the notice about allergenicity, but expect to follow the same general strategy. We likely will publish a notice describing some of the allergenicity issues on which we want comments. We would then review the responses and use them as the basis on which we would hold a public scientific meeting with a panel of prominent food allergists. We hope thereby to receive the most current scientific recommendations on how best to minimize the potential for allergenicity problems that may be associated with foods derived from new plant varieties.

Of special interest to this audience, I think, is the question of how does FDA meet consumer demands and expectations within our legal framework and within the strictures of the scientific information that exists about these products. Many people do not understand or trust science or scientists in general; they often don't trust government scientists in particular, and they especially don't trust industry scientists. They also often don't trust the government process. We were not helped by having our policy announced by Vice-President Quayle as a deregulatory measure, something we had no control over.

Our policy was developed exclusively by FDA scientists, and the FDA sees it as actually a very strong regulatory policy. FDA easily could have made the argument that with breeding, a substance is added only to the first generation plant. Thereafter, it is made by the plant itself with no human intervention. However, the FDA instead said that new substances introduced by breeding meet the "added" part of the food additive definition. If they are not generally recognized by the relevant community of scientific experts as safe for use in food, they are food additives requiring pre-market approval. However, I have great difficulty convincing non-scientists that the FDA policy actually encompasses and focuses on those aspects of the molecular techniques that raise any scientific concerns whatsoever.

So the question remains, how does one enlist public confidence in a policy that covers an area that is very controversial and very difficult to understand. Most people do not have the scientific background, nor the time or interest, to really understand the scientific issues that the FDA policy addresses. They therefore have to take on faith what we or someone else tells them about the policy.

Many people distrust scientists because they know examples where scientists have been wrong or have distorted the truth. Clearly the tobacco industry has people who represent themselves as scientists, who say that there is a correlation but no causation between cigarette smoking and cancer. Because "genetic engineering" raises all kinds of associations in people's minds, few of which are positive, many people are often very willing to believe the worst about our policy.

What I would like to leave you with is that we believe that our policy is a very strong policy. It applies the same standards to substances added to food through breeding as apply to chemicals added to processed food. The policy focuses on those aspects of foods from new plant varieties for which safety issues exist. We see no reason to believe that the use of molecular techniques in breeding will lead in any way to a decrease in the safety or wholesomeness of the food supply.

The Esther Peterson Consumer Policy Forum on
Biotechnology and the Consumer
The Private Sector Perspective

Karen Marshall, Monsanto[1]

The following is a transcription of the presentation by Karen Marshall from Monsanto's Agricultural Group, working in environmental and public affairs. Her work at Monsanto focuses on biotechnology, with responsibility for public relations to support Roundup-tolerant crops in the U.S. and Canada; she also works with food issues associated with genetically-modified plants. Ms. Marshall's presentation included slides.

I can guarantee you, as a member of industry, we believe we are regulated. We have a whole group of people who work primarily, if not totally, to fulfill regulatory needs. In addition to the FDA, many of our products we also must go through EPA for certain aspects, and we are regulated by the USDA as well, so we know Washington intimately.

I have been on many platforms and never had the word canola used before I speak. And here is Eric Flamm this morning talking about canola. For those of you who don't know, this is, indeed, canola. These little black seeds are full of a very good oil that is becoming increasingly popular in the U.S., Canada and Japan. The gorgeous little flowers are canola blossoms and, if you have ever traveled through canola territory in Europe where they call it oilseed rape, when it's in bloom, you know it's one of the prettiest fields you can ever imagine. Canola is just one of a variety of plants that Monsanto is improving through biotechnology.

Today I'd like to give you a little bit of background in biotechnology from a totally unscientific viewpoint because, as you heard from my background, I am not a scientist. I come to biotech from the public relations perspective, trying to explain it to the consumer. I'm going to talk a bit about what we're doing in biotechnology, simply to give you an idea of the wide range of products that are in the pipeline.

I'd really like to reemphasize what was said about the fact that most products are years away from even possibly being available to consumers. We are in the early stages of figuring out how to talk to consumers and discovering which products will eventually find a place on the kitchen table. And I think it is important to understand that each product brings its own set of issues, its own set of consumer manifestations.

Now I'm sure for most of you, if you're typical consumers--and we're all consumers--you do not think of Monsanto as a food company. There are people inside Monsanto who do not think of us as a food company. For years, I've been trying to convince them that it was imperative that we begin to think of ourselves as not just as the partner of the farmer, but also as a food company that must see a product through, in essence, to the final consumer.

Our biotechnology work is in two areas. Monsanto has a company called Searle, which is a pharmaceutical company. Biotechnology as it applies to food is centered in the Agricultural Company. Monsanto has been in the food business for years. NutraSweet is one of our companies. But beyond that, we also provide a lot of ingredients that are used in the food industry. We keep the cake mix from caking in the box and we keep your seafood fresh when it's on the trawler before it gets to the processing plant.

While we believe biotechnology is going to make us partners in tomorrow's harvest, we have to learn to think in the ways that consumers think; farmers are not our only customer anymore.

What is biotechnology? It sounds very new, high tech. This is probably part of our problem with consumers, but the roots of today's biotechnology are centuries old. We like to use corn as an example of how breeding through the centuries has taken corn from a rather inedible wild corn, which is still grown in Guatemala, to corns that we take for granted today--popcorn, field corn, and sweet corn. I'll bet some of you can remember when the corn was grown fairly close to the house and your mother would put on the pot of boiling water and you practically shucked it (the corn) on the run to the kitchen because it was only sweet and wonderful if you cooked it immediately. Today, we can get really great sweet corn in grocery stores after it has survived the transportation period. And that is just the result of plant breeding.

If we look at that as a basic background of what biotechnology is, then let's define the word. Just split it in half: bio means living, biology, the science of life. And technology is merely the tools and the techniques that allow us to put that to practical use. But then we get into genetic

---

[1]Agricultural Group, Monsanto

engineering. Do we call it biotechnology or do we call it genetic engineering? Genetic engineering is the phrase most often used inside the companies to talk about the new biotechnology. We're really taking about what has been done for many years and we like to think of this as the next logical application.

Most of us talk about biotechnology and the agriculture sector. But this pie chart slide represents what is our best guess as to where, by the year 2000, products from biotechnology and genetic engineering are likely to net out. You can see that human therapeutics, drugs to protect human life from disease, is the biggest sector. And many of those are already in the marketplace. Human insulin is a perfect example of that. There is probably research going on in biotechnology to handle about any illness or disease that is facing humanity. Diagnostics are everything from the home pregnancy test to tests to measure levels of antibiotics in products. Specialty products are things like yeast for bread and beer making and improved rennet for cheesemaking. Environmental biotech products are those wonderful things like the microbes that can eat oil slicks. I think that is an awfully small sector for the potential, but that is not where the emphasis is right now. And then you see the agriculture sector--not really the big part compared to how much emphasis we place on it in the public.

At Monsanto we are developing crops in all of these areas, and this is part of our problem. If you look at all of the things that we are dealing with, it's very hard to think of biotechnology per se. Issues that go with insect resistance are not necessarily the issues that go with herbicide tolerance, and certainly not the same issues that go with an improved tomato. And yet we are forced into lumping them together.

A lot of the crops we are working on are (improved) more for agronomic traits than for consumer benefits. For example, the Colorado potato beetle is really a problem for potato growers. In some areas of the country, the beetle has almost decimated their ability to grow potatoes. Today there aren't very many good options for controlling this beetle. If any of you garden at home, you probably have been faced with some pests along the way, and the product many of you probably use is b.t., bacillus thurengiensis. Basically, this is a natural protein that is very toxic to specific targets. In this case, we are working on potatoes by inserting the b.t. that controls the potato beetle. It doesn't control the green peach aphid, which is another problem in the potato industry; it controls only the beetle. But we think that can be a major benefit.

Those of you who garden also know that one problem with b.t., when you apply it externally, is that the next rain washes most of it off. You have to keep applying it, but this insect resistance is actually the potato protecting itself. What you get, ultimately, is just a great potato, the same potato you've been eating all along. This truly is a b.t. potato; it's from one of our field trails. We don't eat it yet because it's still in research, but we do cook it to see what it looks like. With b.t. what we hope we'll get is an answer to insect problems and that processors will get a stable supply. Farmers and processors both will benefit. Will consumers know the difference? No. They are going to get just the same potato, in essence, that they've always had. And so this carries with it that kind of consumer issue; the benefit is not directly for consumers.

In the lobby at our research facility at Monsanto, we have two potato plants in a display and we have to replace them every week. One has been made resistant to the potato beetle and the other is just an average potato plant. We put Colorado potato beetle larva in the container (with the plants) and by the end of the week, the one plant, our plant, will have little spots to show you where the beetle took a bit and didn't like it. Actually, it freezes its digestive system and it dies. And the other plant has these bugs sitting on what's left of the leaves. Virtually in a week they can strip them bare. That's why we have to keep changing the plants. Ten days is too long; you don't have any kind of demonstration.

This is a bollworm. Before I came to Monsanto, I thought it was the boll weevil that was the real problem to the cotton grower. They said, no, it has just been made famous by song. But bollworms and caterpillars really do great damage to cotton crops and, at this stage, the growers must spray very heavily with insecticides to control the bollworm and other lepidopterans. Last year in some areas, for example, the bollworm was such a problem that it was not unusual for a cotton farmer to spray 14 to 15 times just to control this little worm. Without insecticide treatment, the bollworm can virtually strip a cotton plant in a week or less.

Cotton sounds like the most innocuous of the consumer products because you don't think you eat cotton. But it does have its own food component. Cotton meal is used, cottonseed oil is a favorite of the snack food industry, and cotton lint is used in ice cream for emulsification. Cotton is probably the most "consumer friendly" of the products that have no direct consumer benefit--other than the fact that farmers hopefully can spray less.

And this gives you an idea of the difference between a cotton boll that has been attacked by the bollworm and the cotton boll that has not. You can see the difference it makes for the grower in terms of how much cotton he'll get out of his planting. About eight million U.S. acres are infested by the bollworm and about half of that is what we call economically damaged, where it really does destroy the crop. So we think fewer sprays are good for the farmers and we think it is good for the environment. An issue here, however, is the concern raised that if you're putting b.t. in lots of things, could we end up having resistance to b.t., will b.t. stop being effective? Nothing comes without an issue.

These are potato plants and another area where we are working--to try to cut virus and disease in potatoes. How many of you have seen a potato that has those little brown veins in them? That's a virus and it probably won't hurt you, but you probably cut it out. The processing industry to a great extent does that too, so it's a major problem in terms of how much product is wasted.

And while virus is something that we deal with in this country, it's really a major problem in the Third World. It has devastating effects there. Some people say, "So what are you doing to do for the Third World with this biotechnology? Is this really going to feed the millions?" It can, but it's not automatic because the plants they grow are not necessarily the same plants that we do.

Florence Wambugu is a researcher from Kenya, a Ph.D. spending three to five years with Monsanto. She is trying to find a sweet potato that is virus resistant. Sweet potatoes and cassava are major crops, or could be, in much of Africa. But currently sweet potatoes don't meet the potential. They're fine carbohydrate sources, but about 50 percent of the crop is lost to virus. And so we're hoping that Dr. Wambugu will be able to take our technology and find a sweet potato that she can take back to Kenya and work with there. It's our contribution and we are working with government agencies to support this effort as well.

Sweet potatoes really can be a major source of revenue for the Kenyans as well as good for their diet. One great thing about sweet potatoes is they will grow where other things won't. In very bad drought conditions, the sweet potato will still flourish. Farmers love to grow their corn, but they can plant sweet potatoes among the corn rows and, if the drought hits and the corn dies, they can still have their sweet potatoes. They can also be stored in the ground; that will protect them from theft and rodents. And one thing that I think is really important to remember about this technology is that it is in the seed. For once we are not trying to export some kind of technology that requires big tractors, lots of fertilizers, lots of chemicals and lots of technical know how. No matter how subsistence the level, the farmer knows how to plant a seed or plant a tuber.

Now, back to canola. Many people would like to see farmers use no chemicals, no herbicides. Where herbicides are concerned, we really don't think there are good alternatives right now and, until we have those, it's a question of how to help farmers control weeds that compete with crops. You can go out and you can pull them by hand, but that gets a little tough if you have a 500-acre spread. And weeds really do compete with the crops for

solid and water and nutrients and sunlight. Why not just cultivate more? Frankly, with new soil conservation mandates, farmers couldn't do it if they wanted to. The more they run that cultivator across the field, the more they are causing soil run off and all kinds of erosion damage.

We are also working with soybeans that we are engineering to be able to tolerate our herbicide Roundup. We've chosen Roundup for a variety of reasons. It has a good environmental profile; it's classified category E by the EPA, which means it's never been shown to cause cancer. Farmers like it and it's effective. But if you have ever used Roundup on the cracks in your driveway, you know it has this one limiting factor--it can't tell a crop from a weed from your rosebushes. So, basically what we are trying to do is engineer plants that will ignore Roundup so you can spray it after the crop is up. The advantage is that you don't spray until you know you need it. Now you have to spray it ahead of time, as kind of an insurance policy in case weeds come along later.

This brings up the consumer issue, raised mostly by environmentalists who want totally sustainable agriculture, that we are encouraging farmers to remain reliant on herbicides. But, as I said earlier, there is not another good answer at this stage.

Now I'd like to talk about the areas where we are working that most consumers think of when they think of biotechnology. And that's basically the things that they will be able to touch and feel and see and eat as a whole food, the ones that are being developed for processing qualities or taste qualities.

We're working on potatoes that have higher starch content. I'm always a little reluctant to talk about this product, because it's the one that excites the media more than anything else, and it's way down in the pipeline. It will be years before we have a product that is commercially viable. But I'd like to give you an idea of the potential of biotechnology for consumers.

Potatoes have a high water content and when you are transporting potatoes, you are carrying a lot of water around the country; that's one issue. And when you fry potatoes, and frankly we fry them more than anything else, you displace the water with oil. But if you could make a potato that is consistently higher in starch--and that is a big issue; you can do it somewhat with regular breeding programs, but you can't get a consistently higher starch potato--when you fry it, it takes less oil and it absorbs less oil. So the possibilities are exciting, but we are not there yet.

We would all like a tomato in January that tastes as good as what we get out of our garden in August. I'm not sure that will ever be possible actually, because when you can pluck one out of your back yard, and have the satisfaction that you grew it yourself and it's still warm with the sunshine and tastes wonderful, that has all kinds of aesthetic properties. But a number of companies are working on tomatoes that taste better, taste closer to home grown year around.

I don't think there is a person alive in America today who hasn't heard about Calgene's FlavrSavr tomato. They (Calgene) are likely to be the first with a tomato on the market. Their technology is somewhat different from ours, but the concept is the same--to try to give you a better tasting tomato year around.

If you have ever wondered why tomatoes taste so bad in January, it's because they have to pick them green because they simply can't get them to your store without turning to mush otherwise. When we talk about vine-ripened, we mean allowing them to stay on the vine longer. If they get to that pink stage, then they pretty much have developed their flavor profile. If you pick them at this green stage, you can gas them with ethylene and they become red, but they never really develop the profile that you think of as a good tomato.

The real question is will consumers accept foods from biotechnology? I believe so, and there is some research that supports my opinion. That is not to say that I think it will be easy. What is Monsanto doing to ensure that the consumer will understand that genetically-modified foods, at least in most cases, food that are really no different or not significantly different from the foods they already have or, in some cases, will be better? It's a hard call.

We have guidelines. We have to satisfy ourselves as a company, first, that we are really comfortable with what we're doing. And one of the things that is basic to us is that we will take the time to do it right. There will be lots of experiments along the way. Our goal is to keep working at it until we bring products to the market that we think are the products that are right and well done. I mean, you may know how to move a trait, but that doesn't mean it's the product you want to develop.

We follow stringent testing guidelines and we have to be sure that the science is right. We start with the guidelines for regulations around the world as our minimum and then build on top of that.

We review the work internally on a regular basis. I may work on soybeans and we have scientists who are devoted to potato sciences, or who are devoted to canola. But we bring in other groups of people, from other parts of the company, on a regular basis to review. Are we using the right tests? Are we following the right criteria? Are we asking the right questions? And are we really looking beyond the pure science in terms of what are the issues out there?

And then we set up external panels. We have a physicians panel, for example; physicians, social scientist and nutritionists. We show them our tests and say, "Okay, what questions aren't we answering?" We are trying to lay a foundation that will allow us to at least feel comfortable and hope that we can explain to consumers that it's being done right. We've invited ethicists in too.

When we decided as a company to go into biotechnology in the late '70s, we built a facility to do this research at the edge of St. Louis County. Since 1984, we've had thousands and thousands of people come through that facility. And that's part of our program to try to listen to consumers--which is sometimes hard because most consumers don't really understand the technology. And we try to share information. We really are trying to be open. We've had people visit who don't like our technology as well as people who think it's really the answer to their problems. We are trying to understand how to talk to consumers, how to explain biotechnology so that you are not making it a throw away and at the same time making it understandable at various levels. We still have a long way to go in that effort. We learn every day. We've been learning for years.

I would really welcome any suggestions from you. You deal with consumer issues all the time. If you have ideas of what we should be doing, what we might be doing, what you think we are doing wrong, we'd like to hear and keep the dialogue going. Thank you.

The Esther Peterson Consumer Policy Forum on Biotechnology and the Consumer: Biotechnology and the Consumer Interest

Robin A. Douthitt, University of Wisconsin, Madison[1]

An Invited Presentation at the Annual Conference of The American Council on Consumer Interests Esther Peterson Policy Forum

Biotechnology is a technology developed in the early 1970s that allows humankind to create living cellular matter that never before existed! It has provided scientists with a powerful tool to engineer some of the most startling scientific advances in our modern world. One of the technology's most successful applications has been creation of synthetic chemical compounds that in their natural form are extremely scarce, and thus very expensive. For example, recombinant DNA processes enable us to produce synthetic insulin that is now readily and economically available for diabetes treatment.

More controversial, however, has been the technology's use in agricultural plant and animal applications. Environmentalists worry about the unique properties of these newly created microorganisms to reproduce and mutate (Krimsky, Bergman, Connell Shulman & Wilker, 1989). Consumers worry about potential health risks as synthetically produced plants and animals make their way into the food chain (Hansen, 1990). The government is worried about all of the above as they strive on ever more limited budgets to keep up with the industry's fast paced developments and to promulgate regulations that protect us from future risks that even scientists know little or nothing about (Kraus, Malmfors, & Slovic, 1992).

What I would like to focus on today is consumer risk perception and biotechnology. My remarks largely represent a synthesis of published consumer risk perception research. The full citations and credit for previous research will be provided in my paper to be published in the conference proceedings.

Scientists are consistently irritated that consumers worry about the "wrong" risks (Sandman, 1989). Their frustrations intensify when for example consumers associate a higher health risk with riding in an airplane than riding in their own cars without wearing seat belts. These scientists brand consumers as irrational. For example, in 1983 during hearings on construction of a nuclear electrical generating facility in the state of New York a psychologist testified that fears of local residents should not be considered by the state regulatory officials because "the fear they feel is out of proportion to the actual risks, which are in many cases known to these people. This is phobic thinking" (Freudenburg, 1988). At the same time of course, after so much as telling consumers they are ignorant and phobic, scientists cannot understand why consumers are losing confidence in their standing as authority figures in the field of risk assessment.

Many persist in arguing that consumers "irrational" behavior is merely a manifestation of an informationally imperfect market and that consumer risk education is the key to changing their perceptions. As many of you know, I have had a long standing interest in the economics of information. I strongly believe in Steven Salop (1978) and E. Scott Maynes principle that accurate information is both a scarce and valuable resource to the economy and society. However, many facets of consumer information processing remain great mysteries in the world of social science research. For example, although you all simultaneously hear these presentations, each of you will leave today with widely different perceptions about our messages. Should my message conflict with a deeply held belief, you will very likely discount what I have to say. However, if my message is consistent with your personal belief system, you will likely embrace it.

Thus, it should come as no surprise that different consumers, when offered the same risk information will process that information in different ways. Smokers perceive the risks associated with smoking differently than non-smokers. Sun worshipers perceive less risk associated with sun bathing than those who do not. And a recent study has found that even the scientists (toxicologists) who conduct risk assessments for industry see chemicals as more benign than their counterparts in academia and government (Kraus, Malmfors, & Slovic, 1992)!

There is however a growing literature that identifies other mediating factors critical in understanding consumer risk perception. These factors are referred to as "outrage" factors. Outrage factors and perceived risk are positively correlated; that is, consumers underestimate hazards of risk that are low outrage and overestimate the hazard of risk that is high-outrage (Sandman, 1989).

[1]Professor, Consumer Science

Risk psychology thus indicates that consumers associate greater perceived risk with involuntary (versus voluntary), with exotic (versus familiar), with dreaded (versus not dreaded), with focused in time and space (versus diffuse), and with morally relevant (versus irrelevant) risk exposure. Those who refuse to account for such factors when dealing with consumer risk perceptions risk igniting consumer outrage and thus are themselves contributing to the problem of consumer misperception. Again a good example can be found in a nuclear regulatory case study (Sandman 1989).

A small community, nervous about the location of a low-level radiation waste site in their town, held public hearings where government officials were to address local citizen concerns. A bus driver who drove by the waste site several times a day, asked for a dosimeter to monitor his radiation exposure. The regulatory agency hotly refused his request on the grounds there was no measurable exposure. They argued it would be "bad science" to "take such foolish objections seriously."

Our recent experiences with recombinant bovine growth hormone (rbGH), a biotechnological application, also demonstrates the effects of outrage factors on consumer risk perception. rbGH is the synthetic form of the growth hormone found naturally in the pituitary of a cow. Subcutaneous applications of the substance in cows may increase their milk production by 15-25 percent. However, in rbGH's commercial development, industry never considered consumer response to the product's use. Given that farmers, not consumers make the choice to use the technology (an involuntary risk), given that biotechnology is considered by most an exotic technology (versus familiar), and given that some consumers hold deep moral beliefs that any kind of human interference with the "natural order" is wrong (versus irrelevant moral issue), manufacturers should have known that there would be a need to address consumer concerns. Instead the industry insisted that rbGH is "good science" and that anyone who would say otherwise is irrational, phobic, or both.

Industry will continue to build citizen outrage if they ignore biotechnology's psychological reality. Consumers will become more outraged over "acceptable" risks. As long as biotech firms manage low hazard risks information in genuinely outrageous ways, consumers WILL CONTINUE TO MOBILIZE AGAINST THEM (Sandman, 1989).

Thus, simply providing risk information about biotechnology is not the solution to this complex problem. As much attention must be paid to consumer perception of risk as to scientific variables. Ignoring consumer concerns, or worse yet, labeling them as irrational and discounting them, is guaranteed to create hostility and will ultimately stand in the way of successful product acceptance (Hance, Chess, & Sandman, 1989).

Another critically important element in understanding biotechnology and consumer risk perception is understanding the role of consumer confidence in the government's ability regulate health risks. Over the last decade consumer confidence has fallen. In 1980 (Heimbach, 1981) only 10 percent of consumers were very worried about food safety. By 1990 (The Food Marketing Institute) 20 percent of consumers had doubts that the food in their supermarket was safe. While by 1991 (van Ravenswaay & Hoehn, 1991) 25 percent of households had doubts. Given this increased concern about food safety it is not surprising that by 1990 (Research Alliance, 1990) 36 percent of consumers rated the Food and Drug Administration (FDA) as only fair or poor at keeping unsafe products off the shelf. About 46 percent of consumers rated the FDA fair or poor in monitoring products to ensure they are safe.

The U.S. Congress, Office of Technology Assessment (1992) has stated that, "Public acceptance or rejection of new food products produced via biotechnology will determine the commercial success of these products. Public... level of confidence in agencies responsible for ensuring the safety of the products will be of paramount importance." If consumer loss of confidence can be tied to perceived decline in faith in regulatory enforcement, action should be taken. When government regulators are not trusted, the products they guarantee will not be accepted. Thus it is not only consumers who are hurt by this loss of confidence. When consumers chose to reject safe new products because they have lost confidence in regulator's ability to protect them, manufacturers will suffer as well.

In this sense it is in both the producers AND the consumers interest that we have agencies with strong regulatory powers to ensure that consumers once again feel confident in delegating risk assessment to the regulators. Manufacturers may not like the bureaucratic process associated with establishing food safety standards and new product approval protocols, but in the long run that process may be preferable to consumers with imperfect and possibly inaccurate information making their own risk assessments in the marketplace.

References

Chess, C. (1989). Risk Communication and Public Participation. In Proceedings: Ninth Annual Gulf of Mexico Information Transfer Meeting. New Orleans, (December), 225-228.

Food Marketing Institute (1990). TRENDS: Consumer Attitudes in the Market Place. Washington, D.C.: Food Marketing Institute.

Freudenburg, W. R. (1988). Perceived Risk, Real Risk: Social Science and the Art of Probabilistic Risk Assessment. Science, 242, 44-49.

Hadden, S. G. (1991). Regulating Product Risks Through Consumer Information. Journal of Social Issues, 47 (1), 93-105.

Hance, B., Chess, C., & Sandman, P.(1989). Setting a Context for Explaining Risk.Risk Analysis, 9 (1), 113-117.

Hansen, Michael K. (1990). Biotechnology and Milk: Benefit or Threat? An Analysis of Issues Related to bGH/bST Use in the Dairy Industry. Mount Vernon, NY: Consumer Policy Institute: Consumer's Union.

Heimbach, J. (1981). Yesterday, Today, and Tomorrow: Consumer Perceptions of Food Safety. Washington D.C.: Division of Consumer Studies, Bureau of Foods, U.S. Food & Drug Administration (unpublished paper).

Kraus, N., Malmfors, T. & Slovic, P. (1992). Intuitive Toxicology: Expert and Lay Judgements of Chemical Risks. Risk Analysis 12(2), 215-232.

Krimsky, S., Bergman,K., Connell, N., Shulman,S., & Wilker, N. (1989). Controlling Risk in Biotech. Technology Review (July), 62-70.

The Research Alliance. Marketing Research and Counseling Service. (1990). Consumer Reactions to the Use of BST in Dairy Cows. (Research Rep No. 9095-02). Arlington, Virginia.

Salop, S. (1978). Parables of Information Transmission in Markets in The Effect of Information on Consumer and Market Behavior. American Marketing Association. Andrew A. Mitchell Ed. Carnegie-Mellon University.

Sandman, P. (1989). Hazard Versus Outrage in the Public Perception of Risk, in Effective Risk Communication Ed. V. Cavello, D. McCallum and M. Pavlova. New York: Plenum, 45-49.

U.S. Congress, Office of Technology Assessment. (1991). U.S. Dairy Industry at a Crossroad: Biotechnology and Policy Choices. (Special Report OTA-F-470) Washington, DC: U.S. Government Printing Office.

U.S. Congress OTA. (1992). A New Technological Era For American Agriculture. (OTA-F-474). Washington, DC: U.S. Government Printing Office.

van Ravenswaay, E.O. & Hoehn, J.P. (1991). Consumer Perspectives on Food Safety Issues: The Case of Pesticide Residues in Fresh Produce. East Lansing MI: Department of Agricultural Economics, Michigan State University, Staff Paper No. 91-20.

Two Challenges: Life and Informationally Imperfect Consumer Markets Reflections of a Consumer Economist

E. Scott Maynes, Cornell University[1]

E. Scott Maynes is the 1993 Distinguished Fellow. The following is an outline of his presentation to the membership.

I. Life

   A. A Cartoon As Parable--Figure 1

      1. Charles Addams: "Honk, if you believe in Reincarnation!!"

      2. The moral: If--like me--you are a skeptic, it is your belief that, at best, you have but one life to live. The lesson: "Make the best of it!"

   B. What Is Life's Goal?

      1. The maximization of lifetime utility. Of course!! But what does it mean? I offer my interpretation.

      2. Friendships: personal and professional!!

      3. Memories: a set of experiences that, in retrospect, give you satisfaction for the rest of your life. A personal example: a 1950 canoe trip that lasted two weeks and took us down the Connecticut River, 430 miles from top to bottom!

         a. From age 70, what strikes me about my collection of significant memories is the large number that come from my early years.

      4. Professional achievement, e.g., ACCI's

"Distinguished Fellow" award. It tells me that my colleagues recognize and appreciate what I have tried to do professionally.

      5. Success for your family, and especially the feeling that you have contributed as much as possible to them and that they have done reasonably well in terms of their goals.

      6. The feeling, hopefully well grounded, that you may have contributed something positive to others: your students, your friends, organizations to which you belong, your profession, to society in general.

   C. The Means

      1. As a guiding principle, the equal development of Mind, Spirit, and Body. (This I owe to Springfield College and the YMCA.)

      2. Interpreted:

         a. Mind. The development of your mental capacities hardly needs commendation to this group.

         b. Spirit, and its development imply, for me:

            (1) The development and refinement of one's values, i.e., "criteria of desirability" (Williams, 1968).

            (2) Lifelong efforts to see that your behavior embodies your values.

         c. Body. The development and continuance of physical capacity implies a regime of diet, exercise, rest, self-control, etc. that maximize your ability to perform. Neglect your body and you will be in no position to maximize lifetime satisfaction.

            (1) Naps: A helpful, healthful secret.

---

[1]Emeritus Professor, Consumer Economics and Housing

(a) <u>Whenever</u> you are feeling physically or mentally weary, don't fight it: nap!! For 15 minutes, half an hour, even an hour.

(b) The payoff: you will feel so refreshed, so able to make difficult decisions that your net output per work period will have increased.

(c) In case your office lacks a sofa, there is <u>always</u> a suitable, private site. See me for tips on where to nap at the University of Minnesota, Cornell, Consumers' Association (London), Federal Trade Commission.

(d) There is now considerable research, documenting the efficacy of napping. For a nontechnical summary, cf. <u>New York Times</u>, September 12, 1989, p. C1.

(e) Napping is uncommon in most of the institutions we inhabit, especially for juniors.   In my following my advice, you may invoke my Senior Status as your authority!

3. <u>The Open Mind</u>

a. I have never encountered a <u>new person, idea, job, situation</u> from whom or which I did not learn, positively or negatively.

b. Sometimes these new things were scary in the extreme and induced feelings of inadequacy.

c. My advice: seek new things. you will learn; you will grow in your capacity to deal with the new and the unexpected.

II. <u>The Greatest Market Failure of All: Informationally Imperfect Consumer Markets-- Figure 2</u>

Prelude: Why this topic? In my view it is of paramount importance to all consumers and all families. My "case" for this topic was first made 20 years ago (Maynes, 1976). Many pieces have been added in the interim. Here I seek to

pull together all the old pieces and to add something new.

A. <u>The Appalling Fact</u>

1. <u>Most</u> local markets for <u>most</u> consumer goods are characterized by a <u>near-zero correlation between price and quality.</u>

a. This was Loren Geistfeld's conclusion based on his masterful review article of 5 years ago. (Geistfeld, 1988).

b. But the situation is worse than Geistfeld painted it.   Why? Because his analysis did not take into account the impact of price discrimination in the form of coupons, discounts, the results of bargaining.   All these increase price dispersion without affecting quality.

Figure 2
<u>The Market For Panty Hose, Ithaca, N.Y., April 4-10, 1988 by Gail Leopoid, Margo Shatz, Leslie Topiol</u>

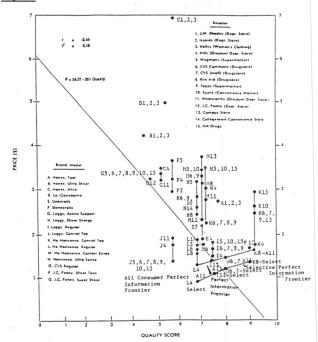

2. The implication: all of us can lose large shares of the purchasing power of our income.

a. But the ones who stand to lose the most are the ignorant and the otherwise disadvantaged.   They won't or can't search extensively and/or effectively.

b. Do recall: income earned as HH purchasing agent is better than ordinary income: it is not taxed.

(1) Benjamin Franklin's maxim: a penny saved is a penny earned.

(2) Scott Maynes' maxim (for the 21st century!): a dollar saved is two dollars earned.

B. My Claim to Your Attention

1. I have new things to say.

2. This is a problem for:

a. Consumer educators: you must grapple with what meaningful advice you can give for shoppers in these kinds of markets.

b. Consumer researchers:

(1) This is a serious obstacle to consumer wellbeing.

(2) You--both friends and foes-- will want to assure yourselves that my analysis is correct and that informationally imperfect markets constitute a real problem and not just a statistical illusion.

c. Family Economists. If my analysis is correct, the use of income or income/needs (Duncan, 1983) as a measure of economic wellbeing is not justified.

C. The Critical Concept: Quality

1. Defined: "The extent to which a variety of a product, a brand-retailer combination, provides the service characteristics (comfort, durability, safety, etc.) that the consumer desires." Mathematically, as a first approximation, quality is a weighted average of characteristics. Cf. Maynes, 1976.

2. Quality is measured cardinally, i.e., a quality score denotes by how much Variety A is better than Variety B.

a. The reason: consumers spend money that is cardinal, i.e., one dollar is four times as large as a quarter. If Variety A costs 25% more than B, it is natural and appropriate to ask by how what

percent A is better than B.

3. Something new. Quality is assessed under the twin assumptions of full understanding and full information (FU/FI).

a. Full understanding interpreted. The assessor of quality understands how things work, e.g., the caliper brakes of a 10-speed bicycle.

b. Full information implies assessments made under the best information possible, e.g., a laboratory test showing that Bicycle A stops in 25 feet under standard conditions.

c. Why should we prefer FU/FI assessments of quality? Because it is only under these conditions that preferences can be assumed to be "true" and stable.

4. The controversial assumption: that all consumers will accept FU/FI assessments of quality as correct. More carefully, consumers will accept the ordering of quality scores as correct while recognizing that the relative magnitudes denoted by quality scores are subject to error. (Cf. II-E-3 regarding the latter assertation.)

5. Possible Objections to This Assumption

a. Different tastes (preferences): Yes, these exist, but:

(1) We will prepare and disseminate quality data only for "standard" products, e.g., VCR's, not for products whose characteristics are intrinsically different, e.g., houses, or subjective, e.g., paintings.

(2) Most of the hypothesized differences in preferences resolve themselves into preferences for different "products." (Cf. Maynes, 1976 for a detailed discussions of the concept of product.)

(a) Example. An colleague at the FTC, when asked why she had three 10-speed bicycles, answered plausibly: "I have one each for commuting, touring, and racing."

(b) Another example: a professional photographer seeks different characteristics in single-lens reflex cameras than an enthusiastic amateur. This implies that FU/FI evaluations of the quality of single-lens reflex cameras would differ as between (1) professionals and (2) amateurs.

b. Different weights. [If you are already familiar with and understand (Curry and Faulds, 1986) or Curry (1988), skip to c.]

(1) Curry and Faulds (1986) concluded that weights do not usually affect quality scores.

(2) In arriving at this conclusion they derived the conditions under which weights "matter." Applying these conditions to 355 non-automotive product tests from Stiftung Warentest, they concluded that, under a strict interpretation of their conditions, weights "mattered" in 2 percent of tests and, for a less stringent interpretation, an additional 12 percent of tests.

c. Different characteristic scores. How likely is it that, under FU/FI, different consumers will assign different characteristic scores?

(1) Consumers Union, our FU/FI source for inputs to characteristic scores, bases its published assessments on four types of information:

(i) laboratory tests;

(ii) controlled use tests, e.g., taste tests of orange juice;

(iii) surveys of users for products/services where performance seems transparent, e.g., settlements of auto insurance claims;

(iv) engineering or other expert judgments.

(2) Few consumers who read that Consumer Reports assigned Bicycle A a score of 8 on a 0 to 10 scale while B was scored 7, would in evaluating A and B reverse CR's judgment.

(3) Generalizing this, one would expect consumers to accept Consumer Reports' characteristic scores as their own.

d. Omitted Characteristics

(1) Consumers Union, on whom we rely for quality assessments, excludes from its quality assessments the following types of characteristics:

(a) intrinsically subjective characteristics, e.g., the appearance of a camera;

(b) characteristics for which valid tests cannot be devised, e.g., the durability of some products;

(c) characteristics of retailers, e.g., friendliness, locational convenience.

(2) The effect of the first two omissions (subjective and untestable characteristcs) is not likely to be large since it is CU's practice to confine its quality assessments to products whose most relevant characteristics are objective and testable.

(3) Retailer characteristics.

(a) The omission of one retailer characteristic-- locational con-venience-- is important and may be utility-conferring and lead to rational purchases above the PIF. The effect of locational convenience will be variable: what is convenient for you may be inconvenient for me.

(b) Other characteristics of retailers, e.g., decor, choice, generous "return" policies, etc., may be summarized and appraised under the "Good Guys/Bad Guys" hypothesis. "Good Guys" are retailers who offer many ancillary services that consumers want and are willing to pay for; "Bad Guys" offer fewer such services. On a price-quality map one would expect the varieties sold by Good Guys to appear high above the PIF with a small price variance while, contrariwise, the offerings of Bad Guys should be close to or on the PIF, also characterized by a small price variance.

(i) Table 1 tests the Good Guys/Bad Guys hypothesis. For each variety of a product sold, the retailer price ratio may be defined as the ratio of the price charged by this retailer for this variety to the corresponding Frontier Price, i.e., the PIF price for that level of quality. Thus a Retailer Price Ratio of 1.00 indicates that this variety is on the PIF; higher prices are expressed as multiples of the Frontier Price, e.g., 1.50. Table 1 displays Retailer Price Ratios for sellers of single-lens reflex cameras in Ann Arbor, Michigan. The results require no formal analysis. There are neither Good Guys nor Bad Guys. Instead, most retailers offer both "high" and "low" prices for various levels of quality. This analysis has been reproduced many times, invariably yielding the same picture.

(ii) For an alternative view suggesting that there are "retailer effects" on prices, even though small, cf. (Geistfeld and Key, 1991).

e. Conclusion: FU/FI consumers will accept our quantifications of Consumer Reports' published quality data as their own, except for an adjustment to take account of the undoubted utility-conferring effect of locational convenience.

Table 1
Test of Good Guy/Bad Buy Hypothesis

Type of Store	Number of Prices	Retailer Price Ratios	Low/High
Camera specialists:			
Quarry Photo (Campus Store)	12	1.00, 1.05, 1.35, 1.36, 1.91, 2.33, 2.37, 2.49, 2.50, 3.01, 5.21, 5.50	1.00, 5.50
Quarry Photo (Stadium Boulevard)	10	1.00, 1.20, 1.53, 1.91, 2.04, 2.24, 2.37, 3.01, 4.43, 5.20	1.00, 5.20
Lobby Hobby	10	1.29, 1.35, 1.70, 1.78, 1.79, 1.92, 2.17, 2.74, 2.80, 4.06	1.29, 4.06
Purchase Camera	4	1.45, 1.96, 1.97, 2.42	1.45, 2.42
Lafayette Radio-TV	4	1.53, 2.10, 2.67, 3.66	1.53, 3.66
Sun Photo	4	1.27, 2.36, 2.58, 3.55	1.27, 3.55
Mean number of prices = 7.33, mean low = 1.26, mean high = 4.07, mean range = 2.81			
Discount houses:			
Big George	7	1.020, 1.15, 1.78, 2.15, 2.22, 3.50, 4.16	1.00, 4.16
Century House	4	1.53, 2.07, 2.53, 3.66	1.53, 3.66
K-Mart	2	1.00, 3.53	1.00, 3.53
Meijers' Thrifty	5	1.43, 1.48, 2.09, 2.11, 3.22	1.43, 3.22

Table 1 continued

State Discount   2   2.06, 4.68   2.06, 4.68

Mean number of prices = 4.00, mean low = 1.40,
mean high = 3.85, mean range = 2.46

Department stores:

Sears	3	1.00, 1.87, 4.11	1.00, 4.11
Hudson's	6	1.28, 1.80, 2.17, 2.35, 2.89, 4.44	1.38, 4.44
J.C. Penney	4	1.29, 1.40, 3.17, 3.55	1.29, 3.55
Montgomery Ward	4	1.33, 1.52, 1.87, 3.40	1.33, 3.40

Mean number of prices = 4.25, mean low = 1.25,
mean high = 3.85, mean range = 2.63

Drug, variety stores:

Maple Village Pharmacy	5	1.18, 1.70, 1.73, 2.26, 4.00	1.18, 4.00
Arbor Drugs	3	1.00, 1.66, 3.80	1.00, 3.80
Lucky Drugs	2	1.78, 4.25	1.78, 4.25
Cunningham's (Plymouth Mall)	2	1.66, 3.85	1.66, 3.85
Cunningham's (Westgate)	2	1.73, 4.11	1.72, 4.11
Cunningham's (Arborland)	2	1.66, 4.11	1.66, 4.11
Cunningham's (Georgetown)	2	1.73, 4.11	1.73, 4.11
Richardson's Pharmacy	2	1.70, 3.86	1.70, 3.86
Mindell's Pharmacy	1	1.57	
Stadium Pharmacy	1	2.02	
Ivory Photo	1	1.57	

Mean number of prices = 2.18, mean low = 1.59,
mean high = 3.65, mean range = 2.52

D. The Central Artifact: The Price-Quality Map

   1. Same old thing:

      a. Your Goal: the Perfect Information Frontier.

   b. The rationale: why pay more for a given level of quality?

   c. Where on the PIF? Consumer Sovereignty gives the answer: it depends upon your preferred trade-off between price and quality.

2. Something New: the PIF is a region, not a line.

   a. Cf. Figure 2, a price-quality map for panty hose.

   b. Note the shaded area. This represents prices that are accessible for some, but not for all consumers.

   c. The explanation. Some consumers, but not all, initiate or take advantage of price discrimination, in the form of discounts, coupons, sales to special groups, and--especially for more complex products--the outcome of bargaining.

3. Something New: Potential Losses in Informationally Imperfect Markets

   a. Old hat. You pay too much for a given level of quality. For example, you buy C1, C2, or C# for $6.95 instead of L4-All for $1.15, an "overpayment" of 5.70 for a given quality.

      (1) By these devices, some consumers will be able to purchase L4-Select, L11-Select, and K8-Select as well as other prices that lie below PIF-All.]

   b. New: for a given price, you receive less quality. For example, for a price of $2.95 you buy F2 with a quality score of 56 instead of K15 with a quality score of 92, thus suffering a quality loss of 39 percent [= (92- 56)/92].

      (1) Since quality scores are, in essence, measures of utility, you have lost 39 percent of the utility purchasable for $2.95, or in dollar equivalents, $1.15 (= $2.95 x 39%).

   c. New: the "wrong" trade-off between price and quality, i.e., not the trade-off you would have selected under FU/FI conditions.

(1)   Example: How many of us intending to buy L-4-All would stick to this choice if we knew that we could buy K8-All, achieving a 67 percent improvement in quality (= 92/57) for only a $0.25 increase in price ($1.60 vs. $1.35)?

d. New: the "wrong" features or accessories. Again, not the features or accessories you would have selected under FU/FI conditions.

E. Problems and Lessons for Consumer Researchers and Educators

1. The Consumers Unions of the world, in most advanced countries--USA, UK, Germany--give us mostly ordinal assessments of quality.

a. Blobs: 0   0   0   0   0

(1)   We believe we understand the 5-point equal-interval scale.

(2)   But the CU's ordinarily fail to tell us the critical information: by how much 0 is better than 0.

b. They list varieties "in order of estimated overall quality." Again, they withhold the critical information: by how much is A better than B.

c. As Table 2 shows, 59 percent of the product tests published in Consumer Reports in 1992 were ordinal while 41 percent were, appropriately, cardinal.

Table 2

Cardinal Vs. Ordinal: Consumer Reports' Product Tests, 1992

	Number of Tests	Percent of Tests
Quality Reported Cardinally:		
Numerical Quality Scores	72	41%
With Blobs	17	10%
Without Blobs	6	3%
Bar Charts		
With Blobs	25	14%
Without Blobs	24	14%
Quality Reported Ordinally:	105	59%
Ordered by Overall Quality		
With Blobs	70	40%
Without Blobs	6	3%
Not Ordered by Overall Quality: But Blobs	29	16%
Total Product Tests	177	100%

d. Ironically, most of the CU's utilize cardinal quality scores for most of their prepublication scoring of quality. Then they convert these to the ordinal forms in which they are published.

e. The back of our professional hand to the CU's for not publishing all the cardinal quality data they manufacture.

f. This means that ordering of quality on price-quality maps, based on CU's published data, is robust. The cardinal comparisons, however, involve guesswork.

2. The Slope of the Perfect Information Frontier

a. The shape of the PIF is a crucial bit of information for consumers.

(1)   If it consists of a single point--and I have seen many that do--or if the slope is minimal, then the marginal cost of obtaining the best quality is little as long as the consumer can locate the lowest price. (On

Figure 1, when will the consumer "know" that he has found K8 and not K15?)

b. Economists are inclined to interpret the PIF as a cost function for quality, e.g., how much does it cost to "produce" a higher quality?

    (1) Presumably this illusion arises from their use of the simple models of intermediate microeconomics where the firm is both primary producer and retailer of its product.

    (2) In the real world there are likely to be several steps between production and retail sales: producer, distributor, wholesaler, retailer. At each stage prices are set; at each stage price discrimination is possible.

    (3) In a seminal article some years ago, Alfred Oxenfeldt listed 20 different goals of price-setting, each of which could result in a different price for a given set of conditions (Oxenfeldt, 1973). Given different parameters, the same principle could give rise to different prices. Add to this the different prices resulting from the initiation of price discrimination by either seller or buyer, and we have a vast array of prices for the same variety or for the same product. Given this chain of decisions, it is clear that no simple relation exists between the "production" of quality and the slope of the PIF.

3. Two research topics of paramount importance:

a. The efficiency of consumption;

b. The blueprint for or recognition of an effective local consumer information system.

4. The efficiency of consumption.

a. I call the attention of Family Economists to the fact that such

commonly used measures of economic wellbeing as income and the income/needs ratio denote potential economic wellbeing. To determine the actual distribution of economic wellbeing, one must take into account how well households spend their income.

    (1) More specifically, to what extent do different kinds of households purchase above the PIF? What is the dollar value of losses suffered because of above-PIF purchases? How are these distributed?

b. These questions cry out for persuasive answers.

c. As far as I know, these questions have not been addressed. A closely related concern is the question; do the poor pay more? See the classic (Caplovitz, 1967) and the much more persuasive (Hall, 1983). Hall shows that the stores in which the poor purchase are inferior with respect to price, quality, extent of choice, and cleanliness. But no one has documented how well or how poorly the poor fare within this inferior environment.

d. The efficiency of markets.

    (1) In addition to exploring the efficiency of consumers, one may ask whether markets are "efficient."

    (2) A perfectly competitive market is perfectly efficient. By assumption, consumers possess and act upon FU/FI information regarding price and quality. Hence, there exists a single low price for each level of quality.

    (3) I call your attention to a seminal paper by Ratchford and Gupta (1990) which presents a model that, for the first time, spells out the effects of search under different conditions, on the price-quality correlation. See (Hjorth-Andersen, 1992), (Maynes, 1992), (Geistfeld, 1993) for critiques and to

(Ratchford and Gupta, 1992) for a rejoinder.

5. The local consumer information system

a. Informationally imperfect consumer markets have existed for a long, long time. It was (Oxenfeldt, 1950) whose work first revealed the low rank correlation between quality and list (not actual) price. Oxenfeldt's pioneering effort was replicated in the very first issue of the Journal of Consumer Affairs by (Friedman 1967). Friedman hoped to assist consumer educators by uncovering a positive relationship between price and quality, thus validating the price-as-an-indicator-of-quality algorithm. Instead, his paper confirmed the near-zero rank correlation between price and quality My study with Assum (Maynes and Assum, 1982) utilized price-quality maps to document the near-zero correlation between cardinal measures of quality and actual prices. Thus, we have known for a long time, with progressively better research confirmation, that most local consumer markets for most goods are informationally imperfect.

b. It is clear that existing institutions have not repaired this failure. Not CU. Not any of the organizations of the Consumer Movement.

c. For a long time many people have proposed and experimented with different versions of a "local consumer information system" that would provide consumers with the information they needed to land on the PIF. Or, better, that would improve consumer markets so that, for most goods, cardinal quality is highly correlated with actual prices. My list of attempts:

> 1974--Robert Krughoff started the Washington Consumers'Checkbook (1974 on). Checkbook, published quarterly, now has 52,000 subscribers in Washington and 30,000 in the San Francisco area where it has reproduced itself as the Bay Area Checkbook.

> Maynes, Vivian, Morgan, and Duncan, 1977--A call for and blueprint of a local consumer information system. Alas, a workable system has yet to emerge.

> 1978--The British developed Prestel as a general consumer information system in which consumers can call

on their home receiver information stored in a central computer. Cf. (Maynes, 1982) for a definitive evaluation of Prestel as a consumer information system, (Maynes, 1983) and (Widing and Talarzyk, 1983) for summaries of Prestel. Cf. (Mayer, 1989) for an assessment of the consumer information possibilities of the French videotex system, Teletel.

1992--(Snider and Ziporyn, 1992) propose and--cockily--forecast the development of Independent Consumer Information Centers that will distribute buying advice produced by government supported CU-like testing organizations. These Consumer Information Centers, the authors rashly assert, will ultimately displace conventional marketing and advertising. For a critical review, cf. (Maynes, 1993)

F. My Challenge to Your All

Beat me out in:

1. Teaching consumers to fare better in informationally imperfect markets;

2. Documenting the efficiency of consumption;

3. Blueprinting and/or developing a workable consumer information system--a billion dollar idea!!

References

Caplovitz, D. The Poor Pay More. New York: The Free Press, 1967.

Curry, D. J. (1988). The concept of quality: new insights, unanswered questions, 111-142, in E. S. Maynes and ACCI Research Committee, eds., The Frontier of Research in the Consumer Interest. Columbia, MO: ACCI.

Curry, D. J. and Faulds, D. J. (1986). Indexing produce quality: issues, theory and results, Journal of Consumer Policy, 13 (1), 134-145.

Duncan, G. J. (1983). Years of Poverty, Years of Plenty. Ann Arbor: Institute for Social Research.

Friedman, M. P. (1967). Quality and price considerations in rational consumer decision making, Journal of Consumer Affairs, 1 (1), 13-23.

Geistfeld, L. V. (1988). The price-quality relationship: the evidence we have, the evidence we need, 143-172, in E. S. Maynes et al, eds., The Frontier of Research in the Consumer Interest. Columbia, MO: ACCI.

_____ (1993). Price, quality, and market efficiency, Consumer Policy Review, 3 (1), 4-10.

_____ and Key, R. J. Assocation between market price and seller/market characteristics, Journal of Consumer Affairs, 25 (1), 57-67.

Hall, B. F. (1983). "Neighborhood differences in retail food stores: income vs. race and age of population, Economic Geography, 59 (3, July), 282-295.

Hjorth-Andersen, C. (1992). Alternative interpretations of price-quality relations, Journal of Consumer Policy, 15 (1), 71-82.

Mayer, R. N. (1989). Against all odds: the state of Videotex in France, 629-633 in T. K. Srull, ed., Advances in Consumer Research, Vol. 16. Provo, UT: Association for Consumer Research.

Maynes, E. S. (1976). The concept and measurement of product quality, 529-560, in Nestor E. Terleckyj, ed., Household Production and Consumption. New York: National Bureau of Economic Research.

_____ (1982). Prestel In Use, A Consumer View. London: National Consumer Council.

_____ (1983). Prestel in use: lessons for Americans, 275-279, in K. P. Goebel, ed., Proceedings of ACCI, 1983. Columbia, MO.

_____ (1992). Salute and critique: remarks on Ratchford and Gupta's analyais of price-quality relations, Journal of Consumer Policy, 15 (1), 83-96.

_____ (1993). Review of Snider and Ziporyn (1992), Review of Industrial Organization, forthcoming in 1993.

_____ and Assum, T. (1982). Informationally imperfect consumer markets; empirical findings and policy implications. Journal of Consumer Affairs, 16 (1), 62-87.

_____, Vivian, W., Morgan, J. N., Duncan, G. J. (1977). The local consumer information system, a missing institution? Journal of Consumer Affairs, 11 (1), 17- 33.

Oxenfeldt, A. (1950). Consumer knowledge: its measurement and extent, Review of Economics and Statistics, 32 (4), 300-314.

_____ (1973). A decision-making structure for price decisions, Journal of Marketing, 32 (4), 48-53.

Ratchford, B. T. and Gupta, P.(1990). On the interpretation of price-quality relations, Journal of Consumer Policy, 13 (4, December), 389-412.

_____ (1992). On estimating market efficiency, Journal of Consumer Policy, 15 (3), 2975-294.

Snider, J. and Ziporyn, T. (1992). Future Shop, How Future Technologies Will Change the Way We Shop & What We Buy. New York: St. Martin's Press.

Washington Consumers' Checkbook (1974 on). Washington: Center for the Study of Services.

Widing, R. E. II and Talarzyk, W. W. (1983). Introduction to Videotex: where it stands, 259-268, in K. P. Goebel, ed., Proceedings of ACCI, 1993. Columbia, MO.

Williams, R. M., Jr. (1968). The concept of values, in D. M. Sills, ed., International Encyclopedia of the Social Sciences. New York: Macmillan.

Determinants of Search for Grocery Items: An Empirical Assessment of the Economics of Information Theory

Rosemary J. Avery, Cornell University[1]

This paper examines the usefulness of Stigler's (1961) economics of information theory in the study of pre- and in-store search for grocery items. Data used in the analysis were collected in Columbus, Ohio in 1990. Results indicate that Stigler's theory provides a better fit for consumer's pre-store rather than in-store search. Pre-store search was found to be motivated by cost-benefit considerations. In-store search was found to be motivated by time, energy and mobility constraints.

Introduction

One of the major theories dealing with the determinants of consumer search is the theory first proposed by George Stigler (1961) called the economics of information. The basic premise of this theory is that markets are characterized by a frequency distribution of prices. According to Stigler, rational consumers search to obtain sufficient information to make optimal purchases. He proposes that search comes at a cost to the consumer, primarily in terms of the "price" (opportunity cost) of their time. Furthermore, Stigler proposes that increased search yields diminishing marginal returns, and that rational consumers will continue to search only as long as the marginal benefits of search (in terms of reduced price or increased quality) are greater than the marginal costs of search.

One of the limitations of applying Stigler's theory to the direct study of consumer search behavior is the fact that it does not explicitly incorporate many non-economic factors identified in other disciplines as having a major impact on search behavior, e.g., purchase involvement (Slama and Tashchian, 1985) and social visibility of the purchase (Feick and Price, 1987). Another reason for its lack of application in other disciplines is the ambiguity of its theoretical predictions in less structured purchase situations. Examples of such situations would be those for frequently purchased, low ticket items and non-durable goods, e.g., grocery purchases. In these markets the marginal benefits of search for each individual item are negligible, yet the accumulated benefits in the category of purchases may be substantial. In addition, empirical evidence indicates that in these markets other non-economic considerations, such as convenience of purchase, may well be more important (Claus and Hardwick, 1972). Another

limitation of Stigler's theory is that it is essentially a single time period model and does not take account explicitly of the fact that frequency of purchase might result in accumulated price information which will carry over into future time periods and reduce search costs in that time period. On the other hand, if prices vary substantially over time in these markets, it is unclear what the implications of Stigler's theory would be in terms of consumer search.

Application of Theoretical Concepts to the Grocery Market

Costs and Benefits of Search

The grocery market is a highly competitive market characterized by many sellers, a high degree of price dispersion and intensive price and product advertising. Individual product items in this market usually carry a low unit price, although the accumulated expenditure on all grocery items constitutes a substantial proportion of the consumer's monthly expenditure.[1]

Search in this market is a two-stage process. Search occurs both prior to selecting a seller (pre-store search) and after a particular seller has been identified (in-store search). Pre-store activities include search activities such as reading advertisement, clipping coupons and processing this information in terms of shopping lists. In-store search activities include price and product comparisons, search for special deals and couponed items.

The consumer's costs of search in this market is high due to the fact that grocery shopping is a complex, and extremely time and energy consuming activity (Ackerman, 1989). Time costs of search in this market are high due to the duration and frequency of purchase situations. Consumers with a high opportunity cost of time (i.e., high wage rate/high income) experience relatively higher costs of search in this market. In addition, constraints on a consumer's time created by, for example, employment and other time commitments, further increase the costs of search.

Grocery items are purchased on a frequent and regular basis. However, the accumulation of market specific information is difficult due to the complexity of the task (i.e., the multiplicity of item prices to be identified and remembered), the instability of prices, and the intensity of price

[1]Assistant Professor,
Consumer Economics and Housing

dealing (i.e., specials, quantity discounts, rebates and coupons). The complexity of grocery shopping adds to the cost of search. In fact, the task of obtaining complete price information is so costly in this market that consumer's tend only to form general price impressions and act on that basis (Ackerman, 1989). Consumer's cognitive costs of search may differ due to varying abilities in identifying, assessing and exploiting information that is obtained in this market. Education and market experience may contribute substantially to lowering the cost of search in this market (i.e., they increase the efficiency of search).

Empirical evidence indicates that, due to the relatively high time costs of search in this market, consumers may trade off monetary benefits of search for non-price related aspects of the purchase situation. These aspects may include factors such as **service quality** (breadth and depth of product offering and checkout service) and **convenience of location** (Ackerman, 1989; Goldman and Johansson, 1978) both of which lower the consumer's time cost of purchase.

Non-Economic Factors Influencing Supermarket Search Activity

Empirical evidence exists that suggests that grocery shopping is a unique purchase category in that it is intricately related to family roles and ego identity of consumers (Feick and Price, 1987; Slama and Tashchian, 1985; Zeithaml, 1985). This involvement has been found to have an impact on their search and purchase behavior. Traditional supermarket shopping behavior for these "involved" shoppers include activities such as clipping coupons, budgeting, searching the newspapers for special prices, composing shopping lists, and talking to friends about products, places to shop and other facets of the market (Slama and Tashchian, 1985). In addition, involvement has been linked to several demographic characteristics of the consumer. Slama and Tashchian (1985) report higher involvement of females, greater involvement when young children are in the home, and suggest that other factors such as marital status, age, education and income of the consumer will be related to purchase involvement.

Conceptual Model

Consumer search in the grocery market is assumed to include antecedent (pre-store) and point of purchase (in-store) search activity. Pre-store search activity is undertaken to obtain price and product information, to select desired items, and to select retail outlets for purchases. In-store search activity is undertaken to ensure that pre-selected items are in fact optimal given the product offering and prices of the chosen retail outlet.

Search activity is assumed to be motivated by three underlying factors. The first of these factors is the **costs of search**. These costs of search include time, money, and transportation.

Consumer's time costs will be affected by the availability of time for grocery shopping. The availability of time will be determined by alternative time commitments such as employment, household production and other structured leisure activities. These commitments effectively raise the "price" of time in grocery shopping by limiting the supply of time to the consumer. Monetary resources will affect consumer's cost of search by raising the opportunity cost of their time in grocery shopping. Limitations on mobility and the availability of transportation will raise the cost of search to the consumer.

The second factor affecting search is the consumer's **perceived benefits of search**. If consumers perceive that prices vary substantially in the market and that significant price reductions can be obtained by canvassing a variety of sellers, it is expected that a higher level of search will be undertaken. On the contrary, if consumers perceive that the market is fairly competitive, and/or that there is a high level of advertising in that market which functions to reduce price dispersion, it is expected that the level of consumer search will be reduced.

The third factor proposed to affect search will be the **involvement of the individual** in the activity of grocery shopping. Grocery shoppers who are involved in the grocery purchase activity, i.e., who enjoy the activity, who view themselves as "expert" shoppers and see the activity as part of their role definition, are predicted to undertake more search than consumers who are not as involved in the grocery purchase activity.

Hypotheses

H1: Consumer search for grocery products is a two-stage process and factors affecting search will have a differential impact on search at each of these stages.

H2: Constraints of the availability of time in shopping will raise the consumer's perceived price of time in grocery shopping and will be negatively related to the level of search.

H3: The consumer's opportunity cost of time will be negatively related to the level of search.

H4: Transportational constraints will raise the cost of search for the consumer and will be negatively related to level of search.

H5: Consumer perceptions of high price dispersion in the grocery market will increase the perceived benefits of search and will be positively related to level of search.

H6: Consumer involvement in the grocery purchase activity will be positively related to level of search.

Data and Sample

Data used in this study were collected in Columbus, Ohio during 1990. The data were obtained as part of a larger study of grocery shopping behavior designed and funded by The Ohio State University (Department of Marketing) and collected by Spencer Research Associates of Columbus, Ohio. The study consisted of a telephone interview and follow-up mail survey administered to a random sample of households in the Columbus metropolitan area.

Telephone interviews and mail surveys were completed by the primary grocery shopper in the household. Telephone interviews were completed with 600 respondents and the response rate to the mail survey was 62 percent. Matching these two surveys resulted in a usable sample of 373 respondents. Missing data on variables used in this analysis were imputed using multiple regression techniques.

Description of the sample

The majority of primary grocery shoppers were female (84.7%), married (60.6%), employed full-time (51.5%), owned a car (87.1%), and lived either without children or with children older than 10 years (74.8%). Fifty-four percent of sample households had an annual (before tax) income of $25,000 or more. The mean age of females in the sample (39.8 years) was slightly higher than male respondents (35.8 years). Male respondents worked significantly longer hours in paid employment (41.5 hours) than female respondents (37.8 hours), but no significant differences were found in their mean years of education (14.2 years for females and 14.9 years for males). Significant differences were found in the household size of married versus non-married respondents. The average household size for married respondents was 3.04 persons compared with 1.76 for non-married respondents.

A comparison of the sample statistics with Census data for the Columbus Standard Metropolitan Statistical Area (SMSA) in 1990 indicates that the sample over-represents higher income and larger households. To correct for this bias and enable the results of this study to be generalizable to the Columbus grocery market, data weights were created (using a raking procedure) which matched the sample with Census data on household size and income. All analyses reported in this study were estimated using these sample weights.

Descriptive Information on Supermarket Shopping Behavior and Motivations

The majority of respondents were store loyal in the sense that they either shopped at one supermarket all the time or only occasionally at another store. Only 21.7 percent of respondents regularly shopped around for their grocery items.

The primary motivation for choosing a supermarket was found to be location (43.7%) and prices in the store (22.0%). Despite the reported store loyalty, 42.9 percent of respondents were found to compare prices across different stores at least once per month or more frequently, and 82.3 percent of respondents regularly compared prices of items in their supermarket they patronize on a regular basis. The majority of respondents (77.5%) read advertisements for supermarket items on a regular basis in order to check items on special at different stores and, to compare prices or to shop specials at their primary store. In addition, a high percent of respondents reported using several other shopping techniques such as clipping coupons (81.2%), scanning shelves to seek specials (78.0%), using a shopping list (76.7%), buying when an item is on special (68.1%), using a weekly shopping routine (53.6%), using a weekly dollar budget (44.2%), waiting to buy an item until it goes on special and, using a weekly time budget (32.7%).

Empirical Measures

Dependent variables: pre- and in-store search behavior

The telephone and mail survey instruments included several questions about respondent's pre- and in-store supermarket search activities. The questions that focussed on **pre-store search activity** included activities such as: budgeting, making lists, reading advertisements, clipping and swapping coupons, talking to friends about specials, and identifying store specials. A set of dummy variables was created for each of the above mentioned questions to indicate if the respondent undertook that activity. A measure of pre-store search activity was obtained by summing these values.

The questions focussing on **in-store search activity** included activities such as: searching for specials at different stores, number of prices usually compared in the store, comparison of brands and sizes of items in the store, scanning the shelves for other information. A set of dummy variables was created for each of the above mentioned questions to indicate the respondent's extent of involvement in that activity. A measure of in-store search activity was obtained by summing these values.

Independent Variables

The telephone and mail surveys provided two types of measures on the resources and constraints of the respondent, actual observed and perceived costs of search. The observed measures on the respondent's time resources included: weekly hours of employment; weekly time commitments to structured non-work activities such as education, religious activities, volunteer work, organizational participation, and sporting activity; and, weekly hours of household work, excluding shopping time. The measure of constraints on the respondent's monetary resources used in this study was yearly household income. Two measures of respondent's mobility constraints were available in the data set, age of respondent and whether they owned a car or not.

In addition to these measures, the mail survey provided responses to a set of attitude statements regarding consumer's perceived resource constraints, perceived benefits of search, and purchase involvement on a 5-point Likert scale. Measures on these items were factor analyzed using the SAS factor algorithm and an orthoginal varimax rotation. Seven factors were retained using the discontinuity criterion (Rummel, 1979). Factor scores from this procedure were estimated and used as independent variables in the analysis for the purpose of comparison with the objective measures of these concepts.

Control Variables

In addition to the variables of interest in this study, a set of control variables was included in this analysis to account for variation in the amount of pre- and in-store search activity resulting from household situational factors which have been reported by Zeithaml (1985) to affect grocery purchase activity. The following control variables were included in the empirical model: a variable to indicate if the respondent was married; a variable indicating the total number of persons living in the respondent's household; a variable to indicate if respondent had children less than ten years old living in the household; and, a variable to indicate the gender of the respondent.

Estimation Methods

Two alternative specifications of the models for pre- and in-store search were estimated. In the first specification of the model the observed levels of resource constraints were entered into the model. In the second specification estimated factor scores indicating perceived resource constraints were entered into the model. Both specifications of the model were estimated using the SAS general linear models algorithm.

Results and Discussion

Pre-Store Search Activity

Both models explaining pre-store supermarket search activity were significant at the .01 level. The R^2 for the models were .18 and .16 respectively (Table 1). Amount of committed non-work time was found to significantly decrease pre-store search activity. This results suggest that pre-store search might be driven by the availability of free time, i.e., that pre-store search may be undertaken at times regarded by the individual as "free" or leisure time, and that limits on this free time in turn limits the amount of pre-store search undertaken by the individual. Pre-store search activity is therefore not competing for the work time of the individual. These results may be explained by the fact that much pre-store search activity is done in the home. Time does not need to be "set aside" for specific search activities. It

is interesting that neither employment hours, nor household production time were found to be related to pre-store search. The fact that employment hours and time spent in household production were not significant in explaining pre-store search support the hypothesis that pre-store search is regarded by the consumer as a leisure time activity rather than completing for other productive time. In addition, the measure of perceived time constraints used in the second specification of the model was not significant in explaining pre-store search. This result further supports the hypothesis that pre-store search is a free-time activity rather than time that competes for other productive activities.

In considering the impact of monetary constraints on pre-store search it should be remembered that the two alternative measures of the concept used in the analysis would be predicted to have opposite effects. Higher levels of household income would be predicted to negatively related to amount of search, the reason being that the marginal cost of search is higher and the marginal value of a dollar saved by search would be less for these individuals. On the other hand the measure of perceived budget constraints would be predicted to be positively related to pre-store search as higher factors score are indicative of lower perceived levels of monetary resources. Results of the analysis using household income as a measure of resource constraints support Stigler's theory. Household income was found to be significant and negatively related to pre-store search. However, counter intuitive results were obtained when using the measure of perceived monetary constraints. Individuals who perceived a higher level of constraints on their resources were found to undertake less pre-store search. In interpreting this result it should be remembered that the pre-store search variable was created to indicate breadth of pre-store search and not depth of search. It may be that perceived budget constraints might lead an individual with tight budget constraints to undertake one pre-store search activity intensely, e.g., intense couponing to save money. This effect would not be picked up in this analysis. However, it is interesting to note that higher perceived budget constraints lead to a less variety in pre-store search activities.

Mobility constraints would be predicted to increase the cost of search and therefore decrease the amount of search undertaken by the individual. The reason for this prediction is that mobility constraints put a higher cost on between-store shopping activity and, therefore, reduce the value of cross-store price/quality comparisons. As predicted, results indicate that perceived mobility constraints significantly decreased pre-store search activity. However, in the alternative specification of the model the variables age and car ownership were not found to be related to pre-store search. It would appear that perceived mobility constraints do in fact reduce search activity, but that these constraints are neither age/energy related, nor do they relate to store accessibility via car transportation.

Table 1
Regression Results: Pre- and In-Store Search Activity

Variable	Model: Pre-Store Search				Model: In-Store Search			
	Model A[1]		Model B[2]		Model C[3]		Model D[4]	
	Coefficient	S.E.	Coefficient	S.E.	Coefficient	S.E.	Coefficient	S.E.
INTERCEPT	4.022**	0.944	3.308**	0.409	6.467**	0.626	4.746**	0.293
Pre-Store Search Activity					0.077*	0.034	0.095**	0.035
Resource Constraints: Time								
Hours of employment	0.001	0.007			-0.002	0.005		
Committed non-work time	-0.041**	0.012			-0.012	0.008		
Household production time	0.010	0.011			0.009	0.007		
Perceived time constraints			3.943	5.378			-9.566**	3.543
Resource Constraints: Money								
Household income	-0.021**	0.006			0.006	0.004		
Perceived budget constraints			13.634**	5.139			2.496	3.417
Resource Constraints: Mobility								
Age of respondent	-0.006	0.010			-0.036**	0.007		
Respondent owns a car	0.433	0.398			0.124	0.258		
Perceived mobility constraints			-13.433**	5.225			10.516**	3.472
Perceived Benefits of Search								
Factor A	17.798**	4.770	16.739**	4.722	2.894	3.149	0.353	3.163
Factor B	10.132*	4.747	11.721**	4.720	-5.837*	3.093	-7.427**	3.134
Perceived Purchase Involvement								
Factor C	5.532	4.886	5.994	4.912	2.279	3.169	1.617	3.241
Factor D	-10.786*	5.127	-7.285	5.081	-0.362	3.340	0.615	3.354
Control Variables								
Respondent is married	0.174	0.337	0.006	0.308	0.058	0.218	0.131	0.203
Household size	0.257*	0.133	0.218	0.130	-0.001	0.087	0.076	0.086
Young children in home	0.290	0.398	0.701	0.379	-0.071	0.186	0.167	0.251
Respondent is female	1.111**	0.358	1.208**	0.354	-0.076	0.235	-0.089	0.236
F-Statistic	5.62**		6.27**		4.17		3.31**	
R^2 adjusted	0.18		0.161		0.149		0.100	

[1] Model of pre-store search using actual measures of resource constraints
[2] Model of pre-store search using perceived measures of resource constraints
[3] Model of in-store search using actual measures of resource constraints
[4] Model of in-store search using perceived measures of resource constraints
* indicates that coefficient is significant at .05 level
** indicates that coefficient is significant at the .01 level

Variables measuring perceived benefits of search were found to be significantly and positively related to the number of pre-store search activities in both specifications of the pre-store search model. This result lends strong support to Stigler's theory. If consumers perceive that the payoff to search is high they should be more willing to invest in search activities for price and quality information in such a market.

Involvement in the activity of supermarket shopping was found be negatively related to pre-store search activity in one specification of the model and insignificant in the other. This result is puzzling and contrary to results from other studies suggesting that involvement with a particularpurchase category significantly explains search behavior in that category. A possible explanation for this result may be that individuals who regard themselves as interested in grocery shopping or good sources of information on price/quality aspects of grocery shopping may already have a large stock of accumulated human capital at their disposal. This stock of information would reduce the need to invest in pre-store search.

Females in this study were found to engage in significantly more pre-store search activities than their male counterparts. This result would indicate that, despite the increased involvement of males in supermarket shopping over the past decade, this involvement has not extended beyond the actual in-store purchase activity. In addition, individuals shopping for larger families were found to make larger investments in pre-store search. If it is assumed that larger family size is associated with larger weekly grocery expenditure, such families would stand to reap higher benefits form their pre-store search and this results would be predicted. Marital status and the presence of young children in the home were not found to be significantly related to the number of pre-store search activities engaged in.

In-Store Search Activity

Both specifications of the model explaining in-store supermarket search activity were significant at the .01 level. The R^2 for the models were .15 and .10 respectively, indicating that the specification of the model using actual levels of resources provided a better fit for the data (Table 1). The amount of pre-store search undertaken by the individual was found to be significant in explaining in-store search activity. Individuals who undertook a greater variety of pre-store search activities were found to search more in the store situation. This result would indicate that pre-store search is a complement rather than a substitute for in-store search, and that individuals who search more before coming into the store also are more likely to search for price/quality information while they are in the store. This results suggests a positive dependency between the two stages of the search process. For example, it may be that pre-store search activity

such as clipping coupons requires additional search in the store to locate the couponed item or to compare the couponed price to the price of other sale items.

Amount of time allocated to paid work, household production and other committed non-work activities was not significant in explaining in-store search activity. However, individuals who perceived their lives as rushed and pressured were found to undertake significantly less in-store search. This result indicates that perceived, rather than actual, time constraints are salient determinants of in-store search for the consumer. These perceived time constraints may emanate from the fact that grocery shopping is a less desirable or physically tiring activity, and may lead consumer to choose grocery stores close to home, those with speedy check-out facilities, wide aisles and adequate parking.

Neither measures of monetary constraints were significant in explaining the amount of in-store search activity. It was hypothesized that consumers with higher levels of household income would undertake less search activity due to their relatively high cost of time and/or lower marginal value of a dollar saved by search. On the other hand, higher perceived monetary constraints were hypothesized to increase search efforts due to the high marginal value of a dollar saved. However, these results would indicate that while budget constraints operate at the pre-store level motivating a cost benefit analysis of search activity, income constraints are not salient determinants of in-store search behavior.

Perceived constraints on the individual's energy level, health and ability to get around were found to significantly increase in-store search activity. People who are physically limited in their ability to travel to many stores might substitute greater in-store product and price comparisons for pre-store comparisons (which does not benefit them since they cannot travel to alternative stores). At the same time age of the individual was found to significantly decrease this same search activity. It may be that older shoppers find in-store search physically tiring and prefer to search in the comfort of their own homes.

A seemingly counter intuitive result is that individuals who perceive high benefits to search in the grocery market were found to undertake significantly less in-store search activity. It may be that in the mind of the consumer these search benefits are defined in terms of between store price/quality variability rather than in-store price/quality variability, i.e., that the benefits of search are significantly reduced once one enters the grocery store. If this is the case, once a grocery store has been selected for purchase the consumer does not have the motivation actively search further, but becomes a price "taker" rather than expend further effort in search.

Neither purchase involvement nor demographic characteristics of the individual were found to be significant in explaining in-store search activity. As stated previously, highly involved grocery shoppers may have an accumulated stock of human capital regarding price/quality information in this market that would reduce the need for further search activity. The lack of significance of respondent's gender on the amount of in-store search supports findings from previous studies that have indicated a higher level of involvement of males in in-store food shopping over the past few decades.

Conclusions

Results of this study support the hypothesis that pre- and in-store search are separate yet related stages in the search for grocery items. Furthermore results indicate that pre-store search complements in-store search activity rather than substituting for it, i.e., consumer who accumulate price/quality information before they enter the store are more likely to be active searchers in the store. In comparing empirical results from the models of pre-store and in-store supermarket search activity it appears that factors that determine search at these two stages of the process are different. From the results of this study it is clear that **pre-store search** appear to be motivated by a cost/benefit reasoning, and is limited by the availability of committed non-work time. Perceived benefits of search were found to be a strong motivator of pre-store search activity, while perceived mobility constraints were found to be associated with reduced pre-store search effort. These mobility-constrained consumers may view themselves a "price takers" from their local (albeit convenient) supermarket and, therefore, perceive reduced benefit of search for information regarding stores they cannot visit. On the other hand, in-store search activity appear to be driven by perceived time, energy and mobility constraints. In evaluating these results in terms of Stigler's economics of information theory, it appears that pre-store search activity more closely follows the traditional cost/benefit model, but that this model might be less applicable to in-store search processes.

One of the more interesting findings from this study is the differential impact of consumer's perception of their resource constraints compared with objective measures of those constraints which are so often used in studies of this kind. For example, hours of employment are often used in studies to indicate constraints on leisure time. However, in this study committed non-work time was found to be the relevant time constraint for pre-store search. Furthermore, measures of factors affecting mobility used in previous studies have included ownership of a car and access to public transport. In this study it appears that mobility factors such as health and level of energy were more salient determinants of search.

A surprising result from this study is that the individual's reported involvement with grocery shopping was found to be only weakly associated with pre-store search activity. results of this study do not support the literature that suggests personal involvement is related to irrational levels of search. While there is evidence that females are still more active pre-store searchers, the gender difference in search is not evident in their in-store search behavior.

In undertaking further work in this area, researchers should focus on obtaining better measures of search to include not only type of activity undertaken, but the intensity of search effort in these activities. Furthermore, comparisons of search patterns for durable and non-durable items would provide interesting insights into the applicability of rational economic theory to different categories of consumer expenditure.

References

Ackerman, Norleen M. (1989). Money resources, time demands, and situational factors as predictors of shopping time. Journal of Consumer Studies and Home Economics, 13, 1-19.

Becker, G. S. (1965). A theory of the allocation of time. The Economic Journal, 75, 493-517.

Claus, J.R. & Hardwick, W. G. (1972). The Mobile Consumer: Automobile Oriented Retailing and Site Selection. Ontario: Collier-Macmillan.

Feick, L. F., & Price, L. L. (1987). The market maven: A diffuser of marketplace information. Journal of Marketing, 51(1), 83-97.

Goldman, Arieh & Johansson, J. K. (1978). Determinants of Search for Lower Prices: An Empirical Assessment of the Economics of Information Theory. Journal of Consumer Research, 5, 176-186.

Rummel, R.J. (1970). Applied Factor Analysis. Evanston: Northwestern University Press.

Slama, M. E., & Tashchian, A. (1985). Selected socioeconomic and demographic characteristics associated with purchasing involvement. Journal of Marketing, 49(1), 72-82.

Stigler, G. J. (1961). The economics of information. The Journal of Political Economy, 69, 213-225.

Zeithaml, V. A. (1985). The new demographics and market fragmentation. Journal of Marketing, 49(3), 64-75.

Endnote
1. Food (including alcohol) expenditure accounted for 19.4 percent of total consumption of U.S. consumer units in 1986-87 (U.S. Department of Labor, Bureau of Statistics).

Impact of Information on Consumers' Concerns About Technological Innovations: The Case of BST

Barbara J. Slusher, University of Missouri-Columbia[1]
Kefan Zhang, University of Missouri-Columbia[2]

Stigler's information search theory is the framework for investigating the impact of different types of information on consumer attitudes toward the use of an innovative food production process in the dairy industry. It is found that consumer concerns are significantly alleviated by information from authority figures while concerns increase when consumers are given initial technical information, which involves high processing costs. Highly educated consumers are less likely to use information, especially authority information, to change their attitude toward BST. Poorly educated consumers are more likely to use authority information to alleviate concern about BST. Those who have prior awareness of BST and those who consume more milk in their households are more significantly impacted by authority information; they use authority information to alleviate concern. In general, the more information consumers have about BST, especially authority information from truthworthy sources, the greater the decline in the initially high concerns about BST.

Introduction

In contemporary markets, consumers experience abundant choice while suffering from both information overload and lack of useful information, all at the same time. With increasing technological development and complexity of consumer markets, search and comprehension of information becomes increasingly difficult for consumers. It may be impossible for consumers to know and understand products well enough to make truly informed decisions, especially for innovative products which are highly technical.

Given this situation, the question becomes: Do consumers search and attempt to understand information before they make decisions about innovations? Some studies indicate that consumers do not understand information, at least in the same way that the informants intended (Jacoby, 1977). Other studies show that consumers simply do not desire more information, either because it will increase confusion or they perceive prohibitive processing costs (Cox, 1990).

There is an alternative to information which requires extensive processing costs; consumers can rely on the judgment of authority figures. Consumers can put their trust in these authorities, thereby accepting or rejecting innovations on the basis of this trust.

This study investigates the use of technical and authority information by consumers when they are forming attitudes toward an innovative product. The goal of this study is accomplished by investigating consumers' reactions to the use of bovine somatotropin (BST) in milk production.

BST is a genetically produced product that can boost a cow's milk production by 10 to 25 percent when injected into cows. It is a protein hormone which is also naturally occurring in cows. The Food and Drug Administration has not given full approval for commercial use of BST; however, they have asserted that milk produced with BST is safe for human consumption and it is experimentally on the market. Consumers Union has asked for extensive additional research before FDA makes a final judgment about approval. Jeremy Rifkin and his group, Foundation for Economic Trends, continue their campaign against approval. And, the chemical companies which developed BST technology actively seek approval. As a result, consumers are being given BST information from several groups, some with opposing opinions.

Because of the highly technical nature of BST and because it is viewed as a fairly controversial issue, consumers' reaction to BST based on their use of technical and authority information is appropriate to accomplish the objectives of this study.

The specific objectives of this study are to: 1) describe the initial level of awareness about biotechnology and genetic engineering and consumers' concern level about use of this technology, 2) assess the extent of change in consumers' concern level at different stages of information exposure to technical and authority information about BST, 3) assess whether consumers with prior knowledge of BST react to information differently than people without prior

---

[1]Assistant Professor
Consumer and Family Economics

[2]Ph.D Graduate Candidate
Consumer and Family Economics

knowledge; and, 4) identify characteristics of consumers who are more likely to use authority information for technological innovations.

Theoretical Framework

In Stigler's (1961) information search model, consumers only engage in information search to the point that the marginal benefit of search is equal to the marginal cost of search. Applying this concept to the BST issue, consumers will choose a type of search activity which will equate the expected benefits with the expected costs.

The expected benefits of BST information search are defined as the potential benefits to the consumer of using BST in milk production. BST usage can potentially result in new attributes and economic gains. Hence:

Expected Benefits = f(New Attributes,
                      Economic Gain)

Because there is no reason to believe that the functional form is nonlinear, the benefit equation can be written as:

Expected Benefits = A1 (New Attribute)
        + A2 (Economic Gain)   (1)

where A1 and A2 denote the direction or sign as well as the magnitude of the relationship.

Let us assume that BST-produced milk will be labeled when it is put into the market. (This is a realistic expectation as a high percentage of consumers are demanding such labeling (Douthitt, 1990; Slusher, 1990.) With labeling, there will be BST-produced milk and nonBST-produced milk. The only different between these two products is that one is from cows injected by BST and the other is not. Would the BST label indicate to the consumer additional new attributes? Even BST proponents say the attributes of milk produced in this manner are unchanged. Opponents warn of potential safety problems. At best then, BST usage is judged safe for human consumption as the composition of the resulting milk is unchanged. Therefore, we can conclude that BST usage has no potential benefits to consumers in the form of new attributes, except now milk has a label denoting whether it is or is not produced with BST supplements.

What about economic gains? The price of milk is currently low and it might be lower yet if BST is used in the dairy industry. BST usage will increase milk production which leads to a greater supply of milk. According to supply and demand theory, in this case if the demand is constant (the best case scenario), the price of milk will be lower after introducing BST. This result will happen if there is no government intervention in the form of price controls. As a result, consumers may benefit from a lower price.

Since BST-produced milk has not been put into the market yet, this economic benefit is not certain, or perhaps even more probable. If there is an economic gain for consumers, it will be a function of lower milk prices and of household milk demand. If demand declines due to safety and other concerns, then the potential economic gain is reduced or possibly eliminated altogether.

Because BST-produced milk provides nothing different than nonBST-produced milk, there are no new attributes to milk; the only difference is the BST-produced label. The impact of having a BST label on milk depends on consumers' attitudes toward BST usage. Two factors likely affect consumer attitudes toward BST: 1) Milk has long been viewed as a pure and nutritional food, and 2) Contemporary consumers have greater awareness of nutritional attributes than consumers have had in the past due to more nutritional education and media coverage of diet-related diseases. Higher nutritional consciousness may lead to lower risk taking in food consumption, especially when there are many alternative foods. Therefore, consumers who are given the information that milk, which in their perceptions is pure and natural, is being produced "somehow artificially" are likely to have negative attitudes about the resulting product. If this is true then the sign of A1 in Equation (1) will be negative. The magnitude of A1 will measure the level of consumers' attitudes.

As mentioned above, the magnitude of economic gain (see Equation (1)) has a lot to do with government policy. If the free market prevails and milk prices are lowered, consumers who continue to purchase milk will have economic gain. Consumers who reduce their milk consumption have less gain, and those who switch to alternative products do not gain anything from BST per se. Consequently, A2 will take either a positive value or zero. A2 is defined as the amount of milk purchased during a certain time period.

The expected cost of BST information search is a function of the cost of search activity and the efficiency of search activity. The cost equation can be written as:

Expected cost = f(Cost of Search,
            Efficiency of Search)   (2)

Research indicates that consumers are generally not seekers of information about technological innovations. This would be especially true if the product associated with that new technology is not on the market yet. Consistent with past research, let's assume that consumers do not specifically search for BST information. BST information is a by-product of other information searches or it is obtained from general life activities, eg reading the newspaper. Therefore, the cost of search for BST information is no different from the cost of general information search. In fact, the cost of search cannot be specifically attributed to BST information search. Then, the remaining cost is the efficiency of search activity.

The efficiency of search activity is defined as the speed with which consumers can process and comprehend information. People with high efficiency will process information faster and more accurately. People with low efficiency will process more slowly or they may be incapable of processing and comprehending information with their current human capital skills. Consumers can gain higher efficiency by studying and acquiring more knowledge and skills.

A new technology, such as BST, by its very nature, is unfamiliar to consumers. Information processing efficiency is lower for all consumers who face unfamiliar information, as contrasted to familiar information. Moreover, the controversy surrounding BST has provided consumers with conflicting information. Therefore, consumers have to overcome unfamiliar, highly technical terminology, and screen conflicting information in order to form their own judgment. Hence, the efficiency of search activity is most important in evaluating the total cost in the case of BST.

Given expected benefits and search cost functions, consumers choose search activities in order to equate the two equations. Equation (1) and equation (2) can be combined to explicitly show how consumers make decisions. Assuming that expected benefits are constant across consumers, the combined decision equation is:

Expected Benefit = Expected Cost
= f(Cost of Search,
Efficiency of Search)   (3)

Since the efficiency variable has a positive value, with higher efficiency reducing total costs, the equation can be rewritten as following:

Expected Benefits = Cost of Search
- Efficiency of Activity   (4)

There are two types of information search activities which consumers can use. The first type is when consumers actively screen and process technical information in order to make judgments themselves. The second type of activities is to seek authorities who can be trusted to make a judgement for you. On the basis of this trust consumers allow authorities to determine whether they accept or reject the innovation. The underlying rationale for using the second type of search activities is that the authority has greater efficiency in screening and processing this technical information. By using an authority's judgement, consumers' efficiency level is increased and the total cost is reduced. As a result, the marginal cost is equal to the marginal benefit. The condition in equation (4) holds.

Rational consumers will choose information search activities to match their efficiency levels to the expected benefits. If the expected benefit is high, consumers can afford some investments in human capital to increase their efficiency of search. This can be time and effort spent in trying to understand the new information. When the expected benefit is low, such as the case of BST, consumers cannot justify learning and processing cost. As a result, consumers with poor processing skills are more likely to use authority judgments if they are forced to make a choice.

Methodology

Sample and Data

Data collected in 1990 from a randomly selected sample of households listed in telephone directories from across the state of Missouri were used. Mail and telephone methods were used to collect information from the main grocery shopper of households. Fifty-eight percent of the 456 households contacted by phone provided information, including information on their food consumption attitudes and patterns. The resulting sample size was 219.

The telephone interview involved a series of questions asking respondents' attitude about BST usage after providing an item of BST related information. Specifically, respondents were asked, "If you learned ..., would you be concerned?" Both technical information and authority information were provided. See Table 1 for the specific information provided and the order of presentation. Because concern levels were assessed after each piece of information, the degree of attitude change which occurred as a result of that bit of information can be measured. Respondents who did not answer any one of the above questions were excluded from the study. This reduced the sample size to 166.

The study methodology controlled for respondents' information search, including the amount and type of information. Prior awareness of BST was assessed and used in the analysis, thereby controlling for information search prior to the survey.

Seventy percent of sample respondents were female. Respondent ages varied from 18 to 99 years, with a mean of 49.9 years. Modal household size was two members with 2.8 being the mean. There was wide representation of educational and income levels. All respondents purchased and used milk in their households, but to varying extent and purposes.

Measurement

Respondents' initial concern level is assessed by a three-item index. The items asked whether the respondent has concerns about using biotechnology for plants, animals, and in the food industry, with the response scale being no, not sure, and yes. After receiving bits of information about BST (see Table 2) for specific information), the change in respondents' level of concern about BST was repeatedly assessed. Change in attitude could either be positive or negative; concern could be either increased or decreased. In the case of authority information, this would reflect either trust or distrust in the expert or authority.

Table 1
Conceptual variables and their measurement

Conceptual Variable	Operational Variable	Coding
Efficiency of infor processing	Educational Level Studied Nutrition & Foods Age Age Squared	continuous 1 No 2 Yes Years
Stock of info	Prior awareness BST	1 Unaware 2 Aware
Cost of search	Type of information	Technical Authority
Information usage	Change in concern about BST after bits of Information	Quantity Change 0=Concern Increased 1=Concern Decreased
Economic gain	Milk consumption	gallons/wk

Analysis

Paired t-tests are used to assess the change in concern levels after information is provided. Subsample comparisons are done for those who have prior awareness of biotech and BST and those who are unaware of biotech and BST until the time of the survey. Technical and authority information are also grouped (inverting scales so they are in similar direction), with further testing for significant change in concern level.

Multiple regression is used to identify the factors which explain the magnitude of change in concern level after all information is provided. Logistic regression analysis is used to examine the factors that influence the probability of using authority information. Both regression models include: educational level, prior awareness of BST, whether food and nutrition has been studied, age, age squared, and milk consumption.

Age and age squared are included to reflect the cumulative effect that experience can have on information processing efficiency. The squared term is included as it is thought that the relationship is, in fact, a curvilinear one. Information processing efficiency will increase with age up to a point, then it will decrease.

Results and Discussion

Of the 219 respondents, 42% indicate they have heard or seen something about the use of BST in the dairy industry prior to the survey. Similarly, 40% indicate they know what biotechnology or genetic engineering is, but most cannot give even a general definition. The assessment of the initial level of concern about the use of biotechnology and genetic engineering in the plant, animal, and food industry finds 27% without any concern and 20% having concerns about use in all three areas, and the remainder having mixed reactions. Table 2 shows that the initial assessment of concern about BST in particular found that near half of the respondents say they either definitely or probably are concerned about using genetic engineering in milk production. Some (15%) are unsure while 36% are either definitely or probably not concerned. Table 2 gives full information about the level of concern after each bit of information.

TABLE 2
Percentage Distribution of Respondents' Concern level for Different Types of Informations (n=219)

	Definite Not	Prob Not	Not Sure	Prob Yes	Def Yes
Technical information					
1. Would you be concerned if you learned that **genetic engineering** has provided dairy farmers a way of **increasing milk production**?	10%	26%	15%	37%	12%
2. Would you be concerned if you learned this process involved **injecting cows** with **synthetic somatotropin** which also is **naturally occurring** in cows?	5%	17%	15%	34%	29%
3. Would you be concerned if you learned the production process involved **daily injections** of a **growth hormone**, with the resulting **milk** being **unchanged**?	9%	25%	15%	30%	21%

Table 2(Continued)
Authority Information

4. Would you have concerns if you learned that the **FDA approved** milk produced with BST, a growth hormone, as safe for human consumption?	9%	30%	12%	30%	19%
5. Would you have concerns if **USDA scientists** said BST-produced milk was safe and does not harm cows?	11%	32%	13%	30%	14%
6. Would you have concerns if you learned **Jeremy Rifkin**, head of a **non-profit group** called Foundation of Economic Trends, **opposed** this method?	13%	21%	30%	25%	11%

Table 3 shows the t-test results for the change of respondents' concern level following each bit of information, and for information grouped into technical and authority information. The change in concern level is significant for all bits of technical information and for one of the three bits of authority information. Respondents' concern level increased significantly after they were told "..the process involved injecting cows with synthetic somatotropin which also is naturally occurring in cows." Remaining information decreased their level of concern, especially the information that the resulting milk would be unchanged and that scientists confirmed that BST-produced milk is safe and the cow is unharmed (which has not been scientifically verified yet, incidently). In general, technical information increases respondents' concern while authority information decreases their concern level. Scientists seem to be the most trustworthy authority for these respondents; their attitudes are not significantly changed by assurances from the Food and Drug Administration that the technology is safe. Nor are they significantly alarmed when told that Jeremy Rifkin, who heads a non-profit group called Foundation for Economic Trends, opposes this technology.

There is no significant difference in respondents' change in concern as a result of having prior awareness of BST, except for their reaction to FDA's potential approval of BST. For that particular information, those without prior awareness of BST significantly used FDA approval to alleviate concern.

Across the complete sample, 3.9% of respondents reduced their level of concern while 96.1% increased their level after given all technical information. After the authority information, 65.3% of respondents's reduced their concern level while 34.7% increased their concerns.

The results in Table 3 indicate that the amount of information respondents received makes a difference in changing consumers' attitudes. The first initial bits of information increased concern, while the remaining information alleviated concern, although to varying degrees.

Table 3
T-TEST Results for Change in Concern level Across Different Types of Information: Whole Sample and Between Respondents Awareness and Unaware of BST

	All Sample	Aware vs Unaware	
Change result of:	MEANS	SD	T-STAT[1]
Question 1	1.23 (16.52)**	.07	.92
Question 2	.49 (5.70)**	.09	1.20
Question 3	-.37 (-4.14)**	.09	.32
Question 4	-.06 (-.61)	.10	2.54**
Question 5	-.21 (-3.15)**	.07	.95
Question 6	-.01 (-.10)	.10	1.09

	All Sample	Aware vs Unaware	
Change result of:	MEANS	SD	T-STAT
Technical infor (Q1-2-3)	4.32 (23.89)**	.18	.05
Authority Infor (Q4-5-6)	-.84 (-5.08)**	.16	-1.66

[1]T-statistics for the whole sample are in the parenthesis
** Significant at a .01 level
* Significant at a .05 level

Table 4 shows the results of the multiple regression analysis on the total change that occurred from respondents' initial reaction to 11 biotechnology through the provision of authority information. While the study is not very successful in terms of explaining variance in the change of concern level (adjusted R^2 = .09), the model is significant. The significant negative sign of education indicates that those with higher information processing abilities are less likely to use the information provided to change their attitude about BST.

Logistic regression results are shown in Table 5. The dependent variable is measured as categories of respondents: 1. who increase their concern level as a result of authority information (coded 0), and 2. who decrease their concern level as a result of authority information (coded 1). (Note--this is change after receiving all technical information.) The variable which

Table 4

Multiple Regression Analysis of Factors Explaining Change in Concern About BST As Result of Both Technical and Authority Information

	COEFFICIENTS	SD	T-STATISTICS
INTERCEPT	1.38	1.78	.77
EDUCATION	-.53	.19	-2.86**
AWARENESS	-.99	.54	-1.83
FOOD STUDY	-.27	.38	-.72
AGE	-.03	.06	-.48
AGE-SQUARED	.0005	.0007	.80
AMOUNT OF MILK	.69	.20	.56

R-squared=.09
F-TEST ON SIGNIFICANCE OF THE MODEL=2.51**

** significant at a .01 level
* significant at a .05 level

significantly decreases the probability that respondents use and trust authority information to alleviate concerns about BST is educational level, ie. more highly educated respondents have less trust in authority information than do poorly educated respondents. Variables which significantly increase the probability that respondents use authority information to alleviate concern are household milk consumption and prior awareness of BST. Those who have some knowledge of the BST controversy or who are more highly impacted by it are more trustful of authority information.

TABLE 5

LOGISTIC ANALYSIS OF FACTORS EXPLAINING HOW RESPONDENTS REACT TO THE AUTHORITY INFORMATION
(0=Concern Increased-No Trust,
1=Concern Decreased-Trust)
(N=157)

VARIABLES	PARAMETERS	ASYMPTOTIC STANDARD ERROR
INTERCEPT	-.58	1.10
EDUCATION	-.42**	.13
AWARENESS	.78*	.36
STUDY FOOD	-.15	.31
AGE	-.004	1.04
AGE-SQUARED	.00003	.0003
AMOUNT OF MILK	.29*	.14

Log-likelihood Statistic 188.65**

** Statistically significant at the .01 level.
* Statistically significant at the .05 level.

CONCLUSION

This study assesses the impact of different types of BST information on consumers' concern level about use of the technology. Most technical information increases the concern level. Consumers rely on authority information, especially from scientists, to alleviate fears. This is especially true for those who are less educated, presumably those with poor information processing skills. Study results suggest that consumer concerns can be somewhat alleviated by providing more information.

The only way to solve the consumers' problem with information overload and lack of real information is to provide sufficient, accurate, and needed information in a format which has low search costs. This is especially true for products of a highly technical nature. Information processing costs are high, especially for consumers with poor processing skills; therefore, authority information is needed. Consumers must have confidence in the authority, however, if the information is to have the intended impact. This study indicates that educated consumers may lack faith in the FDA, which was established as a watchdog for consumer welfare. Nor, do educated consumers have confidence in the judgments of non-profit groups which again purport to be watchdogs for consumer welfare. USDA scientists are the authorities which still have the ability to affect their attitudes about BST.

Acknowledgements

Contribution from the Missouri Agricultural Experiment Station Journal Series Number 11899.

References

Cox, L. J., Mcmullen, B. S., & Garrod, P. V. (1990). An Analysis of the Use of Grades and Housebrand Labels in the Retail Beef Market. Western Journal of Agricultural Economics, 15(2), 245-253.

Douthitt, R. A.(1990). Biotechnology and Consumer Choice in the Market Place: Should There Be Mandatory Product Labeling? A Case Study of Bovine Somatotropin and Wisconsin Dairy Products. In R.N. Mayer (Ed.), Enhancing Consumer Choice: Proceeding of the Second International Conference on Research in the Consumer Interest(pp. 97-104). Columbia, MO: ACCI.

Jacoby, J., Chestnut, R. W., & Silberman, W. (1977). Consumer Use and Comprehension of Nutrition Information. Journal of Consumer Research, 4(September), 119-128.

Jr, Jose Encarnacion (1990). Consumer Choice of Qualities. Economica, 57(Feb), 73-89.

Slusher, B. J. (1990). Consumer Acceptance of Food Production Innovations: An Empirical

Focus on Biotechnology and BST. In R.N. Mayer
(Ed.) Enhancing Consumer Choice: Proceedings
of the Second International Conference on
Research in the Consumer Interest(105-116).
Columbus, MO: ACCI.

Stigler, G. J. (1961). The Economics of
Information. The Journal of Political Economy,
Vol LXIX (June), 213-225.

Consumer Information and Changing Preference for Fats and Oils: Estimation of Implicit Prices

Dong-Kyoon Kim, The Ohio State University[1]
Wen S. Chern, The Ohio State University[2]

The expenditure share form of hedonic price is developed for estimating the consumer values of three nutrient fats using time series data. The model incorporates cholesterol information. Regression results show evidence of changes in consumer preference induced by health information in the consumption of cooking and salad fat and oils.

Introduction

Since 1950's, the consumption of such vegetable oils as soybean oil and corn oil have been increasing, while the consumption of such animal fats as lard has been declining in the end use category of cooking and salad oils, as shown in Figure 1. This trend of replacing animal fats by vegetable oils can be also observed in total consumption of fats and oils. These consumption patterns may be attributed to the consumer's concern about health and diet. Many medical and dietary studies have shown a positive relationship between intake of saturated fat and cholesterol level and the relationship between cholesterol and the risk of heart disease. Therefore, the medical profession, nutrition scientists and public health agencies have recommended that people should reduce consumption of fats, and especially saturated fat and cholesterol. Above all, dietary animal fats and vegetable oils are among the major sources of saturated fat and cholesterol. Among three major end-uses of fats and oils, the one for cooking and salad dressing is more directly connected with household choice problem in fats and oils consumption. Therefore, the consumption of fats and oils for this end-use is selected to examine the changing consumption pattern.

Based on many continuing medical and dietary studies, increasing health information has been released or given to consumers by media, consumer education groups, physicians, and advertising by food companies. Those information may induce structural changes in the consumption of cooking and salad fats and oils. To quote Capps and Schmitz:

"Information about saturated fats and cholesterol in the diet appears to be the major explanation for structure change, albeit other reasons include unprecedented economic shocks in the 1970s, increases in participation in the labor force by women, and changes in income distribution, age distribution, and racial composition." There have been many studies to analyze the impact of product information on food consumption. Most of them used commodity demand model (Brown and Schrader, 1990, Chang and Kinnucan, 1991, Chern, Loehman and Yen, 1992).

The objective of this paper is to examine the changing consumption pattern of cooking and salad fats and oils using a characteristics demand model rather than a good demand model. Specifically, using hedonic price equations, consumer implicit values (hedonic prices) of saturated, monounsaturated and polyunsaturated fats are estimated for five fats and oils: corn oil, cottonseed oil, peanut oil, soybean oil, and lard. The Consumer Good Characteristics Model (CGCM) developed by Ladd and Suvannunt (1977) extended and redefined in terms of budget share. In addition, the model is modified to incorporate cholesterol information to examine its impacts on the consumer values of characteristics.

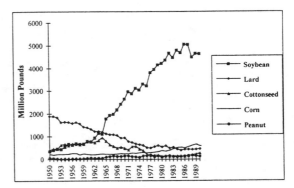

Figure 1
Consumption Trend of Five Cooking and Salad Fats and Oils.

---

[1]Graduate Research Associate, Department of Agricultural Economics and Rural Sociology.

[2]Professor, Department of Agricultural Economics and Rural Sociology.

The major hypotheses to be tested in this study include i) consumers place a higher value for unsaturated fats (polyunsaturated and monounsaturated) than saturated fat and ii) consumer health information affects the valuation of three nutrient fats. For these testings, a moving regression procedure is employed for a fifteen-year interval from 1950 to 1990.

Methodology and Model Specification

Houthakker (1951-52) and Theil (1951-52) were among the first to incorporate product characteristics into utility maximization process. Later, Lancaster (1966, 1971) developed the theoretical model of what is now known as the characteristics model. Lancaster's model embodied three important assumptions, which have been examined by Lucas (1975), Hendler (1975), and Ladd and Zober (1977). The assumptions in Lancaster model are i) linear consumption technology (LCT) implying a fixed ratio of characteristics to products, ii) utility being independent of the distribution characteristics among products (IDC) i.e., utility depends only on the amount of characteristics and not from product sources, and iii) non-negative marginal utility (NNMU).

Suvannunt (1973), and Ladd and Suvannunt developed the CGCM without the three assumptions concerning the Lancaster's original model. The CGCM yields two testable hypotheses: i) for each product consumed, the price paid by the consumer goods equals the sum of the marginal monetary values of the product's characteristics, where the marginal monetary value of each characteristic equals the quantity of the characteristic obtained from the marginal implicit price of the characteristic, and ii) consumer demand functions for goods are affected by characteristics of the goods. It has been extended further by Adrian and Daniel (1976); Terry, Brooker and Eastwood (1985); Eastwood, Brooker and Terry (1986); Morse and Eastwood (1989). These empirical works have focused on food and nutrition demand analysis. The specific model used in this study is based on the CGCM with some modifications because the CGCM is most suitable for food and nutrition demand analysis.

This paper tries to analyze changes in consumption pattern for cooking and salad fat and oils in the presence of health information. Following the Lancaster's framework, a consumer chooses a bundle of goods which maximize his utility by consuming characteristics (c_i's) of those goods, subject to a household budget constraint. Total amount of utility depends on total amount of characteristics that products possess, not products themselves. In the presence of consumer health information, the classical assumption of perfect information and constant tastes does not hold any longer. Consumer's preference is assumed to change when additional information is being accumulated. A change in preference is defined as a change in the parameters of a utility function, which are assumed to depend on consumer's state of

knowledge as well as other factors. Assuming n products and m characteristics, the utility function of a representative consumer is shown as:

$$U = U(C_1, C_2, \ldots, C_m; S(N)) \qquad (1)$$

where C_i = total amount of the ith characteristic consumed by the consumer from the consumption of all products. S is a state variable which is a function of consumer information. The level of ith characteristic is a function of the quantities of goods consumed and the quantities of characteristics obtained from the good :

$$C_{ij} = C_{ij} (q_1, \ldots, q_n, C_{1i}, \ldots, C_{mi}; S(N)) \qquad (2)$$

where C_{ij} = the amount of characteristic j per unit of ith good and q_i = the quantity demanded of good i.

Assuming that the consumer has a limited and constant money income (M), the budget is

$$M = \sum_{i=1}^{n} p_i q_i + r \qquad (3)$$

where r is the household expenditure for all other goods. The consumer's decision is to maximize the utility derived from characteristics which are obtained from the consumption of q's. The utility maximization problem can be expressed as:

$$Max \ L = U + \lambda \ (M \sum_{i=1}^{n} p_i q_i + r) \qquad (4)$$

The first order conditions are

$$\frac{\partial L}{\partial q_i} = \sum_{j=1}^{m} \left(\frac{\partial U}{\partial C_j} \right) \left(\frac{\partial C_j}{\partial q_i} \right) - \lambda p_i + 0$$

$$\frac{\partial L}{\partial r} = \frac{\partial U}{\partial r} - r = 0$$

$$\frac{\partial L}{\partial \lambda} = M - \sum_{i=1}^{n} p_i q_i - r = 0 \qquad (5)$$

Since is the marginal utility of income, Eq. (5) can be expressed as

$$p_i = \sum_{i=1}^{m} \left(\frac{\partial C_j}{\partial q_i} \right) \left[\left(\frac{\partial U}{\partial C_j} \right) / \left(\frac{\partial U}{\partial M} \right) \right] \qquad (6)$$

where $(\partial U/\partial C_j)/(\partial U/\partial M)$ is the marginal rate of substitution of income for j^{th} characteristic or implicit price paid for the jth characteristic by the ith product and $(\partial C_j/\partial q_i)$ is the marginal yield of the jth product characteristic by the ith product. Assuming that the marginal implicit price is constant, and if a linear form is selected, Eq. (6) becomes

$$p_i = \alpha_i + \sum_{j=1}^{m} h_{ij}s_{ij} \qquad (7)$$

where $(\partial C_j/\partial q_i)$ and $(\partial U/\partial C_j)/(\partial U/\partial M) = h_{ij}$.

A realistic assumption employed in this specification is that the consumer values of various fats do not vary among commodities: there exists only one implicit price of a characteristic in the market. Under this assumption, the hedonic prices are restricted as

$$h_{1j} = h_{2j} = \dots h_{nj} = h_j \qquad (8)$$

This means that the consumer value of jth characteristic is equal across commodities in the market. Under the condition of Eq. (8), Eq. (7) becomes

$$p_i = \alpha_i + \sum_{j=1}^{m} h_j S_{ij} \qquad (9)$$

This study deals with three nutrient fats as common characteristics. Each fat and oil is composed of the three fatty acids in constant ratio over time, although all fats and oils have different compositions of nutrient fats. This constant ratio over time induces multicollinearity among explanatory variables. As an attempt to overcome the problem of multicollinearity, the implicit price equation is modified to become an expenditure share equation. The expenditure share form avoids the multicollinearity problem and still allows the identification of the hedonic prices.

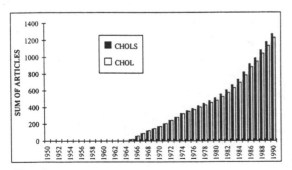

Figure 2
Cholesterol Information Indices (CHOLS and CHOL), 1950-1990.

Furthermore, it often encounters less problem of heteroscedasticity than the expenditure form. Specifically, Eq. (9) can be rewritten as an expenditure equation as:

$$p_i q_i = \alpha_i q_i + \sum_{j=1}^{m} h_j s_{ij} q_i \qquad (10)$$

The expenditure share equation can be obtained from (10) as:

$$W_i = \frac{p_i q_i}{\sum_{i=1}^{n} p_i q_i} = \frac{\alpha_i q_i + \sum_{j=1}^{m} h_j s_{ij} q_i}{\sum_{i=1}^{n} \alpha_i q_i + \sum_{i=1}^{n} \sum_{j=1}^{m} h_j s_{ij} q_i}$$

for i=1, ..., n and j=1, ..., m (11)

where W_i is expenditure share of good i.

Since the amount of consumer information about cholesterol has changed during the sample period, the accumulated information may have effected the consumer's taste and preference. These impacts have been modeled by incorporating a linear or quadratic time trend variable as done in Cowling and Rayner (1970), Ethridge and Davis (1982), and Brorsen, Grant and Rister (1984). However, an index based on publications of medical research articles related to cholesterol seems to be a better proxy of the amount of consumer information than time trend variable.

Brown and Schrader developed the cholesterol information index (CHOL) which is the sum of medical journal articles supporting a link between cholesterol and arterial disease minus the sum of articles questioning the link. They constructed the index for 1966-1988, using Medline data base. We have updated it to 1990. The use of this index is justified on the basis in that medical research papers provide basic materials for most of public or professional information released by media, public education agencies, or used by physicians and commercial advertising.

The differing effects of negative and positive information can be easily found in the psychology and marketing studies, providing evidences that the negative information is more powerful in influencing impression than a positive one. Osgood, Suci and Tannenbaum (1957) found that equally polarized positive and negative information did not have a balancing effect on impression formation; rather, the direction of influence favored the negative information. Several marketing studies (Arndt and Wright, 1974) have found a greater reliance on negative information. In this paper, only the number of articles supporting the link (CHOLS) is used as a proxy for consumer information rather than the CHOL, because there has been evidences of relatively greater impact of negative vis-a-vis positive information and, furthermore, there exist no clear and reliable measure of relative weights of the impacts. The CHOLS had increased steadily from 1966 to 1976, followed by more dramatic increases from 1982 to 1987, shown in Figure 2.

The CHOLS is incorporated into the model to capture changes in consumer taste due to changing consumer information (N). The information is assumed to affect the consumption of characteristics only through consumer's subjective valuation of characteristics (implicit prices) because the ratio of characteristics in a product does not change over time. In this context, the implicit price (h_i) is specified as

$$h_i = h_i^* (1 + c_i \cdot N) \qquad (12)$$

where N is the CHOLS as a proxy of consumer health information.

Then, the expenditure share equation incorporating consumer health information can be specified by substituting Eq. (12) into Eq. (11) ;

$$W_i = \frac{\alpha_i q_i + \sum_{j=1}^{m} h_j^* (1 + c_j \cdot N) s_{ij} q_i}{\sum_{i=1}^{n} \alpha_i q_i + \sum_{i=1}^{n} \sum_{j=1}^{m} h_j^* (1 + c_j \cdot N) s_{ij} q_i}$$

$$(13)$$

This is the empirical model to be estimated in this study. In order to allow for time lag in information dissemination, the cholesterol information index is lagged for one year.

Data

Annual data from 1950 to 1990 are used for this study. Both quantity and price data were collected for crop years beginning October 1. The quantity data include only the end use for cooking and salad dressing. The quantity data were collected by the

Bureau of the Census. The price data were compiled by the Economic Research Service of USDA. The nutrient ratios composed in these fats and oils under investigation are presented in Figure 3. The ratio of saturated fat is the highest in lard. Over 85% of corn oil and soybean oil is composed of unsaturated fat. In the case of peanut oil, monounsaturated fat is the largest component. Lard has the smallest ratio of polyunsaturated fat among them.

Estimation Results

The above nonlinear model, Eq. (13) is estimated by maximum likelihood procedure assuming additive and normally distributed errors. The Davidson-Fletcher-Powell method is used as a nonlinear estimation algorithm. The regression coefficients, h_i's, are consumer values (unit=cents/lb) of nutrient fats. As mentioned, the nonlinear regression was run for a 15-years interval during 1950-1990. Totally, there were fourteen regression runs. Some of estimation results are presented in Table 1. The trends of implicit price estimates of nutrient fats and the impcts of consumer information on implicit prices are present in Figures 4 and 5, respectively.

First of all, a likelihood ratio test is conducted to check the significance of information variable for the full sample, 1950-1990. The estimation with three information coefficients produces significant estimates for three implicit prices and for information coefficients of saturated and polyunsaturated fats at the 1% level, and of monounsaturated fat at the 10% level. Under the restriction of no information effect, all the implicit price estimates are significant at the 1% level. The likelihood ratio test statistic is 24.29 which is enough to reject the null hypothesis of no information effect at the 1% level. This hypothesis test result supports the following explanation of changes in consumer preference.

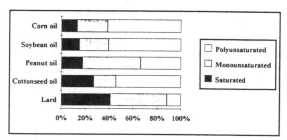

Figure 3
The Composition of Fatty Acids by Product.

Table 1
Selected Estimated Coefficients for Several Time Periods.

Parameters	1954-1968	1962-1976	1966-1980	1976-1990
H_s^a	11.837***	16.554***	19.456***	24.054***
H_m	11.197***	17.133***	20.635***	26.130***
H_p	12.834***	17.963***	23.657***	25.722***
C_s	-0.0045	-0.0018**	-0.0025*	-0.0008***
C_m	-0.0076***	0.0024	0.0124*	-0.0004*
C_p	-0.0052**	0.00002	0.0030	-0.0005***
A_1	1.2851*	2.6256**	6.1528**	-0.3684
A_2	0.1288	0.2584	4.5124**	0.3469
A_3	1.7024*	2.0342*	1.7460	5.4791***
A_4	-0.5119	-2.2848**	-7.7646**	-2.3558**
A_5	-0.8820	-2.2592**	-5.3361**	-1.0874
L.L.F.	207.44	209.24	212.5549	231.5812

[a] the subscript letters, s, m, p, indicates saturated fat, monounsaturated fat and polyunsaturated fat, respectively, and the subscript numbers indicates corn oil, cottonseed oil, peanut oil, lard and soybean oil in order; * indicates significant at the 10% level; ** indicates significant at the 5% level; *** indicates at the 1% level.

All the implicit price estimates are positive and significant at 1% significance level. As shown in Figure 4, until the 1964/1978 period, implicit prices of all three fats are comparable with average prices. Since the 1952/1972 period with the exception of the 1964/1978 period, the implicit price of saturated fat has been lower than those of unsaturated fats. Above all, from the 1966/1978 to the 1970/1984 periods, the differences in implicit prices became much greater between saturated fat and two unsaturated fats. And since the 1972/1986 period, monounsaturated fat became the most valued fat.

Based on the CHOLS, the consumer health information was first to accumulate in 1966. As shown in Figure 5, the results show that there had been no information effect on the implicit prices, and the implicit price of unsaturated fats had not always been higher than those of saturated fat until the 1958/1972 period. From the 1960/1974 period, consumer information began to influence on consumers' subjective valuation of three nutrient fats. The consumer information made unsaturated fats more valued and saturated fat less valued until the 1970/1984 period. The impacts of consumer information on implicit prices had been the strongest in the period of 1968/1982. The most obvious pattern of changing in consumer taste was in the periods from 1964/1978 to 1970/1984. In those periods, consumers gave much higher values on unsaturated fats than on saturated fat. As a final phase of the changes in the periods from 1972/1986 to 1976/1990, consumer information are not effective any more, but the implicit prices of unsaturated fats have been higher than those of saturated fat.

In summary, the estimation results of both implicit price estimates and the information coefficient estimates shows gradual changes in consumer preference in favor of unsaturated fats over saturated fat and these changes appeared to begin in the mid-1960s. Furthermore, the results show that the consumer health information induced the changes in consumption pattern of cooking and

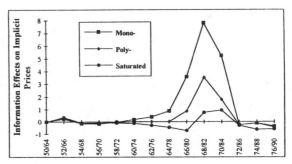

Figure 5
Estimates of Consumer Health Information Coefficients.

salad fat and oils. Both sets of estimates show a very similar changing pattern.

Net Fat Value (NFV)

In order to separate the values of fat characteristics from other characteristics such as taste or other nutrients, the net fat value (NFV) is calculated. The NFV is defined as;

$$NFV_i = \sum_j \hat{h}_j \cdot S_{ij} \cdot q_i \qquad (14)$$

where $\hat{h}_j$ is an estimate of implicit price. Thus, the NFV is the sum of values of fat characteristics. This measure is comparable with an average price of the product because the primary assumption of the hedonic price equation is the price of a product is the sum of the marginal monetary values (implicit price) of the product's characteristics (Ladd and Suvannunt). The ratio of the NFV to price represents the relative importance of the characteristic. It may be, in turn, used as a measure of consumer preference of characteristics for a particular product consumption.

Using the implicit price estimates, aggregate NFV of five cooking and salad fat and oils is approximately 65% of average price of five fat and oils. This indicates that a consumer weighs 65% of prices on nutrient fats. In other words, nutrient fats are valued by a consumer by 65% of the product price. Also, the NFV is calculated for each fat and oils. The results show that the NFV is high for soybean oil (85%), cottonseed oil (83%) and corn oil (71.5%), and low for peanut oil (38%) and lard (63%). The percentages are approximate values by taking the average in every time period of estimation. Therefore, in the case of peanut oil, there may be other characteristics such as taste, whose implicit prices were not accounted for in the present model.

Summary and Conclusion

The modified hedonic price equations in the expenditure share form are used for estimating of the implicit prices of three nutrient fats. The

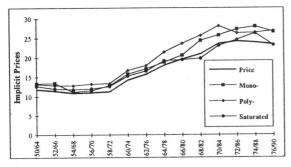

Figure 4
Estimates of Implicit Prices of Nutrient Fats.

study focuses on examining whether changes in consumption pattern of cooking and salad oil took place during the study period, and whether the consumer health information had an impact on consumer valuation of nutrient fats. The estimates of implicit prices are all significant, and show that the implicit values for unsaturated fats are much higher than saturated fat from mid-1960 to mid-1986, implying changes in consumer taste in the consumption of cooking and salad fat and oils. These changes were shown to be caused by dramatic increases in available cholesterol information from 1982 to 1987. Specifically, the impact of consumer health information began to be captured, firstly, in the implicit prices of unsaturated fats from the 1962/1972 period. As it were, during the 1960s and 1970s, it was mostly on the implicit price of saturated fat. In recent years, the impacts of information has been found in all three nutrient fats. These findings suggest that the consumer was only concerned about saturated fat in the 1960s and 1970s. However, the health concern changed consumer preference of consuming less fats in the 1980s. These preference changes are evident from the negative values of information coefficients estimated for all periods since the 1972/1986 period. The estimates of the NFV show that the consumer may value other characteristic such as taste for peanut oil.

In conclusion, the satisfactory results of this study support that an expenditure share form of hedonic price specification is a useful model when there is a problem of severe multicollinearity, especially in case that the ratios of characteristics are constant over time. Above all, this study provides strong evidence of changing consumer preference caused by the accumulation of consumer health information. The results of this study suggest that valuable information can be provided to consumers in selecting food, through public education or other means. Further endeavor and investigation to improve the model specification as well as the empirical results are currently in progress.

Acknowledgements

Research was sponsored by the Farm Income Enhancement Program at the Ohio State University. The authors express gratitude to Thomas Sporleder for his support of this study.

References

Adrian, J., & Daniel, R. (1976). Impact of socioeconomic factors on consumption of selected food nutrients in the United States. American Journal of Agricultural Economics, 58, 31-38.

Arndt, J. (1968). Word-of-mouth advertising and perceived risk. In H.Kassarjian & T. Robertson (Eds.), Perspectives in Consumer Behavior. Illinois: Coleview.

Blackley, p., Follain, J.R., Jr., & Ondrich, J. (1984). Box-cox estimation of hedonic models: How serious is the iterative OLS variance bias? Review of Economics and Statistics, 66, 348-353.

Brown, D.J., & Schrader, L. (1990). Cholesterol information and shell egg consumption. American Journal of Agricultural Economics, 72, 548-555.

Brorsen, B.S., Grant, W.R., and Rister, M.E. (1984). A hedonic price model for rough rice bid/acceptance markets. American Journal of Agricultural Economics, 66, 548-555.

Cassel E., & Mendelsohn, R. (1985). The choice of functional forms for hedonic price equations: Comments. Journal of Urban Economics, 18, 135-142.

Chang, H.S., & Kinnucan, H.W. (1991). Advertising information, and product quality: The case of butter. American Journal of Agricultural Economics, 72, 1195-1203.

Chern, W.S., Loehman, E.T., & Yen, S.T. (1992). Information, health risk beliefs, and the demand for fats and oils. Department of Agricultural Economics and Rural Sociology, The Ohio State University.

Cowling, K, & Rayner, A.J. (1970). Price, quality and market share. Journal of Political Economy, 78, 1293-1309.

Eastwood, D.B., Brooker, J.R., & Terry, D.B. (1986). Household nutrient demand: Use of characteristics theory and a common attribute model. Southern Journal of Agricultural Economics, 18, 235-246.

Ethridge, D.E., & Davis, B. (1982). Hedonic price estimation for commodities: An application to cotton. Western Journal of Agricultural Economics, 7, 293-300.

Halvorsen, R., & Pollakowski, H.O. (1981). Choice of functional form for hedonic price equations. Journal of Urban Economics, 10, 37-49.

Hendler, R. (1975). Lancaster's new approach to consumer demand and its limitations. American Economic Review, 65, 194-199.

Houthakker H. (1951-52). Compensated changes in qualities and quantities consumed. Review of Economic Studies, 19, 155-164.

Jordan, J.L., Shewfelt, R.L., Prussia, S.E., & Hurst, W. C. (1985). Estimating implicit marginal prices of quality characteristics of tomatoes. Southern Journal of Agricultural Economics, 17, 139-145.

Ladd, G.W., & Zober, M. (1977). Model of consumer reaction to product characteristics. Journal of Consumer Research, 4, 89-101.

Lancaster, K.J. (1966). A new approach to consumer theory. Journal of Political Economy, 74, 132-157.

Lancaster, K.J. (1971). Consumer demand: A new approach. New York: Columbia University Press.

Lucas, R.E.B. (1975). Hedonic price functions. Economic Inquiry, 13, 157-178.

Morse, S.C., & Eastwood, D.B. (1989). A theoretical and empirical investigation of the hedonic price equation for foods. University of Tennessee Agriculture Experiment Station Bulletin 666.

Osgood, C.E., Suci, G.J., & Tannenbaum., P.H. (1957). The measure of meaning. Urbana, IL: University of Illinois Press.

Putnam, J.J. (1990). Food consumption, prices, and expenditure, 1967-1988. USDA-ERS, Statistical Bulletin No. 804. Washington, D.C.

Suvannunt, V. (1973). Measurement of quantities and prices of product qualities. Unpublished Ph.D. Dissertation, Iowa State University.

Terry, D.E., Brooker, J.R., & Eastwood, D.B. (1985). Characteristic theory and household demand for food nutrients. University of Tennessee Agriculture Experiment Station Bulletin 639.

Theil, H. (1951-52). Qualities, prices and budget inquires. Review of Economic Studies, 19, 129-147.

U.S. Department of Agriculture (1972). U.S. fats and oils statistics 1950-1971. USDA-ERS Statistical Bulletin N. 489. Washington, D.C.: Economic Research Service.

U.S. Department of Agriculture (1980). U.S. fats and oils statistics, 1963-1978. USDA-ERS Statistical Bulletin No. 631. Washington, DC: Economic Research Service.

U.S. Department of Agriculture (1983). Statistics on oilseeds and related data, 198=65-1982. USDA-ERS Statistical Bulletin No. 695. Washington, DC: Economic Research Service.

U.S. Department of Agriculture. Dairy: Situation and outlook yearbook. Washington, D.C.: Economic Research Service.

U.S. Department of Agriculture. Oil crops: Situation and outlook yearbook. Washington, D.C.: Economic Research Service.

U.S. Department of Commerce. Current industrial reports: Fats and oils production, consumption and stock. Washington, D.C.: Government Printing Office. Various issues.

U.S. Department of Agriculture (1979). Composition of food: fats and oils raw, processed, prepared. Agricultural Handbook No. 8-4. Science and Education Administration.

Wright, P. (1974). The harassed decision maker: Time pressures, distractions and the use of evidence. Journal of Applied Psychology, 59 (5), 555-561.

Consumer Expenditure Pattern Differentials
Between Working-Wife and Non-Working Wife Families

Hui Wang, The University of Alabama [1]
Mohamed Abdel-Ghany, The University of Alabama [2]
Deanna L. Sharpe, The University of Alabama [3]

Data from the 1989 Consumer Expenditure Survey were analyzed in an attempt to provide answers for the following two questions: (1) How do working-wife families' average and marginal propensities to spend compare with those of nonworking-wife families, and (2) To what extent are those propensities affected by the differences in families' characteristics? The results indicate that consumption patterns of the working-wife and nonworking-wife families are different. The major part of the differences is due to the differences in the sociodemographic characteristics of the two groups.

Since World War II, the increased participation of married women in the American labor force has been recognized. Reasons cited for this change include use of labor-saving household appliances, growth of commercial services, decreasing family size, and the availability of jobs which make it easier for women to be employed outside the home (Long, 1958).

Change in the productive role of married women has generated much interest among professionals regarding the effect of wife's labor force participation on household consumption patterns. Wives' earnings can improve their families' level of living by increasing discretionary consumption. Or, wives' earnings may help their families maintain an existing level of living when husbands' real earnings fall because of a cut in work hours, job relocation, or the ravages of inflation. Whatever the reason for wife's employment, families with two earners generally have higher levels of income than families with one earner. In 1988, median income among families with both husband and wife employed was $40,422, substantially higher than the median of $26,652 among families in which the husband was the only earner (U.S. Department of Commerce, 1990).

When a wife becomes employed, her family still needs to maintain a minimum level of home produced goods and services and leisure time. Whether the overall quality of life of that family increases, decreases, or remains constant depends on the value of the nonmarket production given up and on the availability of market substitutes for that production. Many employed wives purchase time-saving goods and services to successfully combine dual productive roles (Foster, 1979).

Previous research indicates that, although American women have the major responsibility for consumption activities (Metzen & Helmick, 1975), their relative power in household money management is enhanced when employed outside the home (Blood & Wolfe, 1960). The greater decision-making power held by working wives could contribute to differing patterns of household consumption between families who have a wife employed outside the home versus families who do not (Bilkey, Massaro, & Meehan, 1962). Working-wife families have job-related expenses such as clothing, transportation, and childcare. Usually considered nondiscretionary, these expenses would not result from a working wife's increased decision-making power. Differences in expenditures for nonjob-related items, however, suggest the working wife may have input into household expenditure decisions. Whatever the underlying causes, consumption differences suggest that wife's labor force participation may affect the allocation of financial resources in her household.

The purpose of this paper is to seek answers to these questions:
1. How do working-wife families' average and marginal propensities to spend compare with those for nonworking-wife families?
2. To what extent are those propensities affected by the differences in families' sociodemographic characteristics?

Review of Literature

The relationship between wives' labor force participation and household consumption expenditures has received considerable attention. Researchers have questioned whether wives' labor force participation would lead to an increase in consumption expenditure to offset fewer hours devoted to household production activities. Findings have varied. Several researchers have concluded that, all else equal, the employment

[1] Former Graduate Assistant, Consumer Sciences

[2] Professor, Consumer Sciences

[3] Assistant Professor, Consumer Sciences

status of the wife was not significant in explaining purchase decisions for time-saving household durables or other major expenditures (Foster, Abdel-Ghany, & Ferguson, 1981; Nickols & Fox, 1983; Strober & Weinberg, 1977, 1980; Weinberg & Winer, 1983). Other researchers, however, have found wife employment to be positively associated with net expenditure on consumer durables (Hafstrom & Dunsing, 1965; Mallan, 1968; Schaninger & Allen, 1981). Wife employment has also been found to be positively associated with expenditures for personal care, domestic services (Vickery, 1979), gasoline, shelter, food away from home, women's apparel, and child care (Deweese & Norton, 1991; Jacobs, Shipp, & Brown, 1989; Yang & Magrabi, 1989). Bellante and Foster (1984) found differing expenditure levels between working-wife and nonworking-wife families except for personal care and domestic services.

In contrast to previous studies, Bryant (1988) noted wife's work hours had a negative and significant impact on durable goods expenditures and concluded that durables and wife's home time were complements. However, Bryant's sample of durable goods included many durables related to leisure activities versus time-buying or time-saving activities.

Other researchers have concluded that expenditure level differences between working-wife families and nonworking-wife families are associated with role overload of the wife (Reilly, 1982), level of wife wages (Weagley & Norum, 1989), or household income level (Rubin, Riney, & Molina, 1990).

Theory and Relevant Variables

Theoretical Rationale

In the household production model, the household invests in capital assets (savings), capital equipment (durable goods) and capital embodied in its "labor force" (human capital of family members). Like the business firm, the household engages in production using labor and capital. The household is assumed to seek maximization of utility subject to resource and technological constraints (Michael & Becker, 1973).

Michael and Becker (1973) suggest that a wife's labor force participation should be positively associated with expenditures on time-saving-services since the workweek for employed-wives is much longer than that for nonworking-wives (Vanek, 1974). Although all households face roughly the same prices for market goods and services, the value they assign to time differs substantially. Compared to nonworking-wife families, working-wife families are more likely to substitute time-saving goods for home production.

Standard demand theory (Friedman, 1976) posits a positive relationship between income and the purchase of goods and services, except in the unusual case of an inferior good. Galbraith (1973) and Mincer (1960) postulate that, holding total family income constant, the consumption to income ratio will be smaller in working-wife families than in nonworking-wife families. Based on the observation that family consumption requires highly labor-intensive administration, Galbraith posits a smaller durables' expenditure to income ratio for working-wife families compared to nonworking-wife families. Mincer, however, regards purchase of durables as a form of saving and suggests a larger durables' expenditure to income ratio instead.

Duesenberry's (1967) relative income hypothesis provides a useful approach to explain the relationship between wives' labor force participation and household consumption. For most wives, the economic motivation to work is closely related to husbands' earnings. When a nonworking-wife family finds a gap between own income and consumption levels and those of comparable families, the wife is likely to work. So, at the relevant wage rate, sufficient income to close the income-consumption gap is obtained. If wives have very low market wage rates, wives' labor supply may not be forthcoming despite presence of an income-consumption gap relative to their life-cycle comparison group. The effort required by the wife to reduce the gap is deemed too arduous and not worth the lost home production. Once the wife is employed, working-wife families find that although they may have the same aggregate income as their nonworking-wife families, they are different consumers from those other families. These differences may lead to working-wife families having a higher consumption to income ratio than nonworking-wife families to maintain parity regarding the durables' expenditures to income ratio.

Theoretical Model

Linear regressions were used to estimate marginal propensities to spend for working and nonworking-wife families. The functional forms were based on the linear expenditure system, i.e. marginal and average propensities to spend are nonnegative and each add up to one.

In this study, total consumption expenditure was used as a proxy for the income variable for several reasons. The permanent income hypothesis suggests that total expenditures are an appropriate measure of income since families can better control expenditures than income in the short run. Total consumption expenditure has been used as a proxy for income (Chen & Chu, 1982) and has been shown to give a better fit than income in models designed to predict expenditures in a number of expenditure categories (Prais & Houthakker, 1971). In this study, total expenditure is defined as the sum of household expenditure on: food away from home, food at home, alcohol, housing, apparel services, transportation, health, entertainment, personal care, reading, education, tobacco, miscellaneous, and personal insurance.

Discussion of Variables

To control for the presence of a husband and for husband employment, this study selected married couples with or without children where the husband worked 40 or more hours per week. To control for differences in wife employment, the sample was divided into two groups, based on the employment status of the wife.

Wife's labor force participation is defined as the number of hours a wife worked outside or inside the home to earn money. Non-employed wives had 0 hours labor force participation per week. Full-time employed wives worked 40 or more hours per week in paid employment. Wives who worked between 1 and 39 hours per week were omitted from this study.

Dependent Variables

The dependent variables are household consumption expenditures for: food at home, food away from home, alcohol and tobacco, housing, apparel service, transportation, health, entertainment, personal care, reading and education, miscellaneous, and personal insurance. Each of these expenditure categories sums several related expenditures. The specific components of each expenditure category used in this study are delineated in the Bureau of Labor (1989) Interview Survey Public Use Tape Documentation.

Independent Variables

The independent variables include total consumption expenditure, age and education of the wife, race, family size, and region of residence. Use of total consumption expenditure has been discussed.

Wife age can often track life-cycle events and explain differences in family consumption expenditures (Bellante & Foster, 1984). In this study, wife age is a categorical variable. Young wives are under age 25 or between 25-34. Middle-aged wives are in the age groups: 35-44, 45-54, and 55-64. Older wives are aged 65 or older.

Previous expenditure studies control for education of the wife (Abdel-Ghany & Foster, 1982; Bellante & Foster, 1984). The relationship between wife's education and family consumption expenditure has been found to be significant but complex (Abdel-Ghany & Foster, 1982; Hafstrom & Dunsing, 1972). Higher educational levels may be associated with increased efficiency in nonmarket production. This increased efficiency is positively related to household real income, which should, in turn, increase expenditures on services (Michael, 1972; Michael & Becker, 1973). A family with more educated members could achieve higher levels of consumption (which could lead to increased net worth) with a given amount of resources than a family of similar composition, but with less educated members. Thus, education is included to control for differences in efficiency. In this study, education of the wife is a categorical variable: less than high school education, high

school graduate, some years of college education, and college graduates or more.

Previous research indicates black families spend more on clothing and less on food away from home than non-black families (Alexis, 1962). This result suggests that varying patterns of consumption might result from different tastes of families of different races. In this study, race is categorized into white and nonwhite using race of the respondent. If the respondent is white, the family is defined a white family even if the spouse is nonwhite.

Family size is the actual number of members in the household. Holding income constant, as family size increases, a greater proportion of income must be used to satisfy present consumption needs of the family.

Differences in consumption may arise because of climate-related variations and cultural differences (Hassan, 1974; Michael, 1972). Region of residence of the survey participant is included to control for regional differences in consumption patterns. Due to limitations in the original data, in this study, region is indicated by the dummy variables urban northeast, urban midwest, urban south, and urban west. Rural area is the omitted category.

Statistical Procedure

Linear regressions were used in estimating the marginal propensities to spend for working and nonworking-wife families. To determine whether the differences in expenditure patterns reflected by these regression results are statistically significant, the Chow test (Chow, 1960) was used. This test indicates whether the same regression function could be represented by the same regression plane for the working and nonworking-wife groups. The procedure tests equality of entire sets of regression coefficients in each expenditure function for the working and nonworking-wife groups.

Average propensities to spend were calculated for each sample point and then averaged over the sample. The t-test was used to test for statistically significant differences between the average propensities for the working and nonworking-wife groups.

Source of Data and Characteristics of the Sample

Most previous research on expenditure patterns has used data from the 1960s or 1970s. One contribution of this study is that the data are relatively current. The 1989 Consumer Expenditure Interview Survey (U.S. Department of Labor), is part of an ongoing survey conducted by the Bureau of the Census for the Bureau of Labor Statistics. This survey provides the most extensive national household expenditure data available in the United States. In addition to expenditure data, information is collected on household characteristics and income. Expenditure data used in this study are quarterly but have been annualized by multiplying by four.

Sample Characteristics

The sample was weighted to more accurately represent population characteristics. As Table 1 indicates, there were 3847 full-time working-wife families, and 1592 nonworking-wife families in this study.

Table 1
Selected Characteristics of the Sample, 1989-1990

Characteristics	Full-time Working-Wife Families (n=3847)	Nonworking-Wife Families (n=1592)
Age of wife	%	%
Under 25	6.9	6.7
25 to 34	32.8	24.0
35 to 44	31.7	26.1
45 to 54	19.4	19.3
5 to 64	8.0	15.6
65 and over	1.2	8.2
Education of wife	%	%
Less than high school	10.3	27.4
High school graduates	39.5	37.7
Some college	39.8	29.8
College graduate	10.4	5.1
Race		
White	89.0	91.3
Other	11.0	8.7
Region of the Country		
Urban Northeast	15.1	18.6
Urban Midwest	21.2	18.9
Urban South	30.0	24.5
Urban West	16.6	19.5
Family Size	3.25	3.63

The majority of full-time working-wives (33%) were between the ages of 25 and 34. The highest percentage (26.1%) of nonworking wives was the 35 to 44 year old age group.

An almost equal number of full-time working wives and nonworking wives had completed high school (40% and 38%, respectively. But, among wives with college degrees or more, 10.4% were full-time working wives and 5.1% were nonworking wives.

White families accounted for 89.0% of full-time working-wife families and 91.3% of nonworking-wife families. In both the urban northeast and the urban west, nonworking-wife families slightly outnumbered full-time working-wife families. In the urban midwest and urban south, the opposite result was obtained. The average number of family members was 3.63 for nonworking-wife families and

3.25 for full-time working-wife families.

The average dollar expenditures of nonworking-wife families and full-time working-wife families are reported in Table 2. Working-wife families generally spend more money than nonworking-wife families. The average total expenditures were $36,792 for full-time working-wife families and $30,718 for nonworking-wife families per year. Compared to nonworking-wife families, full-time working-wife families spent less on food at home and health but more on food away from home, alcohol and tobacco, housing, apparel service, transportation, entertainment, personal care, reading and education, miscellaneous, and personal insurance.

Table 2
Expenditures of Working-Wife and Nonworking-Wife Families, 1989-1990

Expenditure Categories	Full-Time Working-Wife Families (n=3847)	Nonworking Wife Families (n=1592)
Total expenditures	$36,792	$30,718
Food at home	3,760	4,134
Food away from home	1,730	1,328
Alcohol and tobacco	622	527
Housing	11,210	9,535
Apparel service	2,005	1,506
Transportation	7,852	6,231
Health	1,414	1,581
Entertainment	2,074	1,642
Personal care	324	272
Education and reading	710	625
Miscellaneous	361	231
Personal insurance	4,473	3,105

Results and Discussion

Marginal propensities and average propensities to spend by expenditure category of working-wife and nonworking-wife families are reported in Table 3. Computed F-ratios for the Chow test for all expenditure categories are all statistically significant at the .01 level. Thus, the estimated parameters of the separate regressions for the working-wife and nonworking-wife families are significantly different from those of the pooled regression for a given expenditure category. Therefore, we conclude that consumption patterns of the working-wife and nonworking-wife families are different.

The marginal propensity to spend for any expenditure category measures the net effect of change in family's total consumption on its expenditure in this category by holding other sociodemographic factors constant. Because of the additive property of the linear function, the sum of the marginal propensities to spend for all expenditure categories for either the working-wife or the nonworking-wife families equal unity.

A comparison of all marginal propensities to spend shows how working-wife and nonworking-wife families will allocate a given change in the total expenditure to different categories. The general pattern of the marginal propensities to spend as presented in Table 3, indicates that working-wife families are expected to distribute more of their higher expenditures to transportation, entertainment, education and reading, and personal insurance. The nonworking-wife families are expected to allocate more of their expanded budget to food at home, food away from home, alcohol and tobacco, housing, apparel service, health, personal care, and miscellaneous expenditures.

Table 3

Marginal Propensities and Average Propensities to Spend by Expenditure Category of Working-Wife and Nonworking-Wife Families, 1989-1991

Expenditure Category	Marg. Propensity		Avg. Propensity	
	W-W Families	NW-W Families	W-W Families	NW-W Families
Food/home	.019	.029	.131	.181
Food away/home	.043	.045	.047	.041
Alcohol & tobacco	.007	.009	.021	.026
Housing	.208	.247	.326*	.330*
Apparel service	.045	.047	.056	.048
Transportation	.420	.366	.167***	.151***
Health	.022	.043	.046	.057
Entertainment	.108	.082	.041	.038
Personal care	.003	.004	.011	.010
Educ. & reading	.029	.027	.013	.014
Misc.	.011	.016	.100	.005
Pers. insurance	.085	.084	.130**	.101**

* not significant on .05 level
** not significant on .01 level
*** not significant on .001 level

The average propensities to spend calculated for each sample unit are presented in Table 3. The average propensities to spend for housing, transportation, and personal insurance were the only ones that did not differ significantly between the working-wife and nonworking-wife families. Although these average propensities were not statistically significant, their estimated marginal propensities were higher and statistically significant for the nonworking-wife families. This result suggests that nonworking-wife families have much stronger inclination to spend more on housing, transportation, and personal insurance when their income increases, ceteris paribus.

To discover the extent to which working-wife and nonworking-wife families' average propensities to spend are affected by their differences in sociodemographic characteristics a procedure was adapted and employed similar to that used by Bell (1974) in analyzing black-white wives' labor force participation differentials. The basic technique involves estimating what the nonworking-wife

group's propensities would be if it retained its own consumer behavior but had the working-wife group's sociodemographic characteristics. By substituting the working-wife group's equation, the resulting average propensities to spend were derived and are shown in Table 4.

The average propensities for food at home, alcohol and tobacco, housing, health, personal care are lower than those obtained from the original nonworking-wife group. But, average propensities to spend for food away from home, apparel service, transportation, entertainment, education and reading, miscellaneous expenditures, and personal insurance were higher. The differences between the average propensities presented in Table 4 are all significant at least on the .05 level. Thus, to answer the second question raised in this paper, if the nonworking-wife families had the sociodemographic characteristics of the working-wife families, their expenditure pattern would be different.

It is evident that the average propensities to spend for the nonworking-wife group became closer to those of the working-wife group when the nonworking-wife group assumed the sociodemographic characteristics of the working-wife group. Thus, it can be concluded that the major part of the differences in spending patterns between the working-wife and nonworking-wife families is due to the differences in the sociodemographic characteristics of the two groups. Stated in other terms, controlling for sociodemographic characteristics of both groups would tend to decrease spending differences between the two groups.

Table 4

Average Propensities to Spend by Expenditure Category: The Effect of Differences in Families' Characteristics

Expenditure Category	Nonworking-Wife Characteristics & Nonworking-Wife Behavior	Nonworking-Wife Characteristics & Working-Wife Behavior
Food at home	.181	.136
Food away from home	.041	.043
Alcohol & tobacco	.026	.023
Housing	.330	.317
Apparel service	.048	.049
Transportation	.151	.199
Health	.057	.048
Entertainment	.038	.050
Personal care	.010	.009
Education & reading	.014	.018
Miscellaneous	.005	.008
Personal insurance	.101	.103

Implications

This paper presents information on expenditure patterns of working-wife and nonworking-wife families, which provides valuable input for policy makers. Public policies in the areas of taxes and specific family-oriented programs affect family expenditures. These policies and programs impact differentially on families with different number of earners. Understanding the consumption patterns of working-wife and nonworking-wife families identified in this study inform the decision making processes of such policies and programs.

References

Abdel-Ghany, M., & Foster, A. C. (1982). Impact of income and wife's education on family consumption expenditures. Journal of Consumer Studies and Home Economics, 6, 21-28.

Alexis, M. (1962). Some negro-white differences in consumption. American Journal of Economics and Sociology, 21, 11-28.

Bell, D. (1974). Why participation rates of black and white wives differ. The Journal of Human Resources, 9, 465-479.

Bellante, D., & Foster, A. C. (1984). Working wives and expenditures on services. Journal of Consumer Research, 11, 700-707.

Bilkey, W. J., Massaro, V. G., & Meehan, J. P. (1962). The structural effects on consumer disbursement of wives working. Review of Economics and Statistics, 44, 221-224.

Blood, R. O., Jr. & Wolfe, D. M. (1960). Husbands and wives: The dynamics of married living. Glenco, IL: The Free Press.

Bryant, W. K. (1988). Durables and wives' employment yet again. Journal of Consumer Research, 15, 34-47.

Chen, Y. P., & Chu, K. W. (1982). Household expenditure patterns: The effect of age of family head. Journal of Family Issues, 3(2), 233-249.

Chow, G. C. (1960). Tests of equality between sets of coefficients in two linear regressions. Econometrica, 28, 591-605.

Deweese, G., & Norton, M. J. T. (1991). Impact of married women's employment on individual household member expenditures for clothing. The Journal of Consumer Affairs, 25(2), 235-257.

Duesenberry, J. S. (1967). Income, saving, and the theory of consumer behavior. New York: Oxford University.

Foster, A. C. (1979). Wife's earnings as a factor in family net worth accumulation. Ph.D. Dissertation, University of Missouri.

Ann Arbor, Michigan: University Microfilm, No. 80-02356.

Foster, A. C., Abdel-Ghany, M., & Ferguson, E. E. (1981). Wife's employment - Its influence on major family expenditures. Journal of Consumer Studies and Home Economics, 5, 115-124.

Friedman, M. (1976). Price theory. Chicago: Aldine Publishing, 12-64.

Galbraith, J. K. (1973). Economics and the public purpose. Boston: Houghton Mifflin Company.

Gauger, W. H., & Walker, K. E. (1980). The dollar value of household work. Information Bulletin 60, Ithaca, New York: New York State College of Human Ecology, Cornell University.

Hafstrom, J. L., & Dunsing, M. M. (1972). Satisfaction and education: A new approach to understanding consumption. Home Economics Research Journal, 1, 4-12.

Hassan, Z. (1974). Household expenditure patterns in Canada. Canadian Journal of Agricultural Economics, 22(2), 61-78.

Jacobs, E., Shipp, S., & Brown, G. (1989). Families of working wives spending more on services and nondurables. Monthly Labor Review, 112, 15-23.

Long, C. D. (1958). The labor force under changing income and employment. A study by the national bureau of economic research. Princeton: Princeton University Press.

Mallan, L. B. (1968). Financial patterns in households with working wives. Ph.D. dissertation, Northwestern University. Ann Arbor, Michigan: University of Microfilms, No. 60-1887.

Metzen, E. J., & Helmick, S. A. (1975). Secondary workers earnings and their impact on family income adequacy. Home Economics Research Journal, 3, 249-259.

Michael, R. T., & Becker, G. S. (1973). On the new theory of consumer behavior. Swedish Journal of Economics, 75, 378-396.

Michael, R. T. (1972). The effect of education on efficiency in consumption. National Bureau of Economic Research, Occasional Paper No. 116, New York: Columbia University.

Mincer, J. (1960). Labor supply, family income and consumption. American Economic Review, L(2), 574-583.

Nickols, S. Y., & Fox, K. D. (1983). Buying time and saving time: Strategies for managing household production. Journal of Consumer Research, 10, 197-208.

Prais, S. J., & Houthakker, H. S. (1971). The analysis of family budgets. Cambridge, MA: The University Press.

Reilly, M. D. (1982). Working wives and convenience consumption. Journal of Consumer Research, 8, 407-418.

Rubin, R. M., Riney, B. J., & Molina, D. J. (1990). Expenditure patterns differentials between one-earner and dual-earner households: 1972-1973 and 1984. Journal of Consumer Research, 17, 43-52.

Schaninger, C. M., & Allen, C. T. (1981). Wife's occupational status as a consumer behavior construct. Journal of Consumer Research, 8, 189-196.

Strober, M. H., & Weinberg, C. B. (1977). Working wives and major family expenditures. Journal of Consumer Research, 4, 141-147.

Strober, M. H., & Weinberg, C. B. (1980). Strategies used by working and non-working wives to reduce time pressures. Journal of Consumer Research, 6, 338-348.

Strober, M. H. (1977). Wives' labor force behavior and family consumption patterns. The American Economic Review, 67(1), 410-417.

U. S. Department of Commerce (1990). Statistical abstract of the United States. Washington, D.C.: Government Printing Office.

U. S. Department of Labor, Bureau of Labor Statistics (1989). Consumer Expenditure survey: 1989, Interview Survey Public Use Tape and Documentation.

Vanek, J. (1974). Time spent in housework. Scientific American, 231, 116-120.

Vickery, C. (1979). Women's economic contribution to the family. In R. E. Smith (Ed.), The subtle revolution: Women at work (pp. 159-200). Washington, D.C.: The Urban Institute.

Waldman, E., & Jacobs, E. E. (1978). Working wives and family expenditures. Paper presented to annual meeting of the American Statistical Association. San Diego, California.

Weagley, R. O., & Norum, P. S. (1989). Household demand for market purchased, home producible commodities. Home Economics Research Journal, 18, 6-18.

Weinberg, C. B., & Winer, R. S. (1983). Working wives and major family expenditures: Replication and extension. Journal of Consumer Research, 10, 259-263.

Yang, S. J., & Magrabi, F. M. (1989). Expenditures for services, wife's employment, and other household characteristics. Home Economics Research Journal, 18(2), 133-147.

Self Selection and
Wage Gaps between Genders and Races

Xiaojing Jessie Fan, The Ohio State University[1]

Using data from the 1979-1990 NLSY, this study investigated whether self selection was equally important for different gender and race groups, why there were differences, if any, and how and to what extent could it explain the wage gaps between genders and races. Findings suggest that both systematic differences in decision making between genders and races, and the perceived overall low probability of labor force participation by the employers for their female employees are the key factors in understanding the wage gaps.

Introduction

It has been documented regularly in both time-series and cross-sectional data that white men's average wage rate is considerably higher than that of white women, black men, and black women. Various attempts have been made to explain the wage gaps using human capital related variables such as education attainment, training and work experience, and structural component variables of the labor market such as area and region (Mincer, 1974; Corcoran, 1978; Corcoran & Duncan, 1979; Nah & Rudd, 1992; Minor & Rudd, 1992). However, most of the wage gap studies have not been very successful in terms of explanatory power. Researchers consistently found that adjustments for these skill and labor market differences still left white men at a considerable advantage (Corcoran & Duncan, 1979; Nah & Rudd, 1992; Minor & Rudd, 1992).

In recent years, models involving selectivity problems have received considerable attention in economic literature. In wage offer studies, it has been widely recognized that self selection could affect the market wage rate, because individuals with a higher probability of being in the labor force may share some common characteristics which can not be solely captured by traditionally used variables. Self selection may affect the market wage rate in two general ways: objective and subjective. The objective way is that individuals who tend to be in the labor force may be systematically different from those who are not. Some working people may view career success as one of the most important goals in their life and are willing to put a lot of effort in their work, while people with a low probability of being in the labor force usually have less work attachment. The subjective way is more from the employers' side. As Becker (1975) suggested, when an employee is perceived to have a higher probability to drop out

of the labor force, firms are usually less willing to invest in his or her human capital, mostly in the form of job training and promotion. In long run, his or her wage rate will be lower than others who are perceived to have a higher probability of staying in the labor force. Furthermore, firms may be less willing to hire persons with a higher likelihood of labor force withdrawal. Therefore, the wage rate of the individuals with a low probability of labor force participation may be depressed due to their own and others' decisions.

While self selection is widely used in wage offer studies, to my knowledge, it has not been considered in wage gap researches. The purpose of this study was to investigate whether self selection was equally important for different gender and race groups, why there were differences, if any, and how and to what extent could it explain the wage gaps between genders and races after controlling the effects of human capital, occupation and location.

Review of Literature

Numerous variables and theoretical relationships have been postulated regarding factors influencing wages and earnings such as human capital variables, socio-demographic characteristics and labor market components (Jones & Pack, 1989).

Using PSID data, Corcoran & Duncan (1979) found that wage advantages enjoyed by white men can not be explained solely or even primarily by superior qualifications or more attachment to the labor force. Even after adjusting for an extensive list of qualification and attachment measures, more than two-thirds, one-half, and two-fifths of the wage gaps between white men and black women, white women, and black men, respectively, remained unexplained.

In their study of the male-female wage gap, Nah & Rudd (1992) examined the impact of marital status on the wage rates of married men, single and married women, who exhibit strong labor force attachment. Using NLSY data, their findings showed that the wage rates of single and married women who worked full time, continuously lag about the same amount behind those of married men, other things equal. Their analysis explained about sixty and thirty percent of wage gaps between married men and

---

[1]Ph.D candidate,
Family resource management

single women, married women, respectively.

Also using NLSY and NLS, Minor & Rudd (1992) tried to identify and compare factors affecting wage rates of young black and white men in a recent year, as well as to determine whether these factors have changed since the mid 1970's. Their wage gap analysis indicated that in 1989 differences in the characteristics of the two groups of men accounted for about two-thirds of the observed wage gap, while in 1976 differences accounted for only about 45%.

Only one study (Nah & Rudd, 1992) estimated the probability of labor force participation. However, the inverse-Mill's ratio, which represents self selection bias, turned out to be insignificant in the wage offer equation and was not included in the wage gap analysis.

Theoretical Background

The fundamental theoretical background of wage offer and wage gap analysis is human capital theory (Becker, 1975). It suggests that the market wage rate is determined by the productivity of the labor. Since worker characteristics such as education attainment, work experience, labor force attachment, on-the-job training, and health can act as an indirect measure of productivity, it is generally recognized that higher education attainment and more on-the-job training can enhance an individual's earning capacity (Becker, 1975).

As Becker (1975) pointed out, many workers increase their marginal productivity by learning new skills and perfecting old ones on the job, and thus improving their capacity of earning. Becker divided on-the-job training into general and specific training. Completely general training increases the marginal productivity of trainees by exactly the same amount in the firm providing the training as in other firms, while specific training increases the productivity more in the firm providing the training than in other firms.

Because general training can raise their future wages, the trainees are willing to pay for the cost by receiving wage rates below their current productivity during the training period. However, specific training is different. If training is completely specific, the wage an employee could get elsewhere would be independent of the amount of training he/she had received. A plausible argument is that the wage rate paid by the training firm would also be independent of training given a competitive labor market. Thus the firm would have to pay for specific training costs, for no rational employee would pay for training that did not benefit him/her, and the firm would collect the return from such training in the form of larger profits resulting from higher productivity.

Becker introduced a crucial concept in understanding specific training: the likelihood of labor turnover. Suppose a firm had paid for the specific training of a worker who quit the job, its capital expenditure would be partly wasted, for no further return would be collected. Therefore, the firm's willingness to pay for specific training should closely depend on the likelihood of labor turnover. Becker suggested that firms paying for specific training will take into account possible turnover when they make the investment decision. Furthermore, by recognizing that the likelihood of a quit is not fixed but depends on wages, they will offer higher wages after training than could be received elsewhere to reduce the likelihood of labor turnover.

Since training is usually a combination of general and specific training, the likelihood of labor turnover plays an important role in determining the quantity and quality of training an employee can receive. An individual with a high probability of turnover would receive less on-the-job training, and therefore, face a lower long term wage rate than an individual with a low probability of turnover.

It is usually perceived that women have a higher probability of labor force withdrawal because of their family responsibilities, especially child rearing. Statistics also show that black men have a considerably lower probability than white men. If self selection is important in determining market wage rate, we can expect the differences in self selection between genders and races to explain the wage gap to some extent.

Analytical Framework

The analysis in this study consisted of three major parts. The first part was a standard Heckman two-stage selectivity model, for the purpose of getting good estimates of the self selectivity and its impact on market wage rate. The second part was a wage gap analysis using white men's wage offer structure as the standard to investigate how much of the wage gap could be explained by self selection. In order to further illustrate the discrepancy between white men's wage and others, the last part presented a simulation of the relationship between work experience and market wage rate for different gender and race groups.

Heckman's two-stage selectivity model

In 1974, Heckman considered a model of labor supply in which wages and hours worked were the two endogenous variables. Following Maddala (1983), the model consisted of the market wage equation

$$W = \beta_0 + BX + u_1 \qquad (1)$$

and the shadow wage equation

$$S = \gamma_0 + \Gamma Z + \eta H + u_2 \qquad (2)$$

where X and Z were vectors of exogenous variables which included human capital variables, demographic variables and labor market characteristics. Heckman assumed that hours worked (H) adjust, so that S=W.

Hence, from equation (1) and (2), we get

$$H = \frac{\beta_0 + BX - \gamma_0 - \Gamma Z}{\eta} + \frac{u_1 - u_2}{\eta} \qquad (3)$$

If H>0, the person is in the labor force, and we observe H and W. If H=0, the person is not in the labor force. For those individuals who are not in the labor force, we have

$$\frac{u_1 - u_2}{\eta} < \frac{\gamma_0 - \beta_0 + \Gamma Z - BX}{\eta} \qquad (4)$$

or

$$u_1 - u_2 < \gamma_0 - \beta_0 + \Gamma Z - BX \qquad (5)$$

because η is expected to be positive. By defining $Var(u_1 - u_2) = \sigma^2$, we have

$$Prob(H \leq 0) = \Phi\left(\frac{\gamma_0 - \beta_0 + \Gamma Z - BX}{\sigma}\right) = \Phi(\tau_0 + TY) \qquad (6)$$

where $\Phi(.)$ is the standard normal distribution function, Y is a vector of exogenous variables which possibly consists of the variables in X and Z. If we transform hours of work H to a binary variable with H=1 if the observation is in the labor force, and H=0 if not, Equation (6) becomes the probit equation we estimate in the first-stage.

By further denoting

$$\Delta = \tau_0 + TY \qquad (7)$$

the conditional mean of the error term u_1 is:

$$E(u_1 | H > 0) = E\left(u_1 \Big| \frac{u_1 - u_2}{\sigma} > \Delta\right) = \frac{\sigma_1^2 - \sigma_{12}}{\sigma} \frac{\phi(\Delta)}{1 - \Phi(\Delta)} \qquad (8)$$

Thus, the market wage offer equation can be written as:

$$W = \beta_0 + BX + \frac{\sigma_2^2 - \sigma_{12}}{\sigma} \frac{\phi(\Delta)}{1 - \Phi(\Delta)} + v = \beta_0 + BX + \theta\lambda + v \qquad (9)$$

where $\lambda = \phi(.)/(1 - \Phi(.))$, and is usually referred to as the inverse Mill's ratio in risk literature. Equation (9) is the basis of the second-stage wage offer equation in this analysis.

Therefore, the expected value of the market wage can be decomposed into two parts:

$$E(W | H > 0) = \beta_0 + BX + E(u_1 | H > 0) \qquad (10)$$

where the last part is due to self selection bias.

While the applications of selectivity models have gained much popularity in labor economics literature, little attention has been given to the interpretation of the results. As Dolton & Makepeace (1987) and Huang & Raunikar (1990)

correctly pointed out, the estimated coefficients from equation (9) do not represent the complete marginal effects of the independent variables, if these variables were a subset of independent variables included in the selection equation (6). It follows that the conventional approach for assessing marginal effects from the estimated coefficients of equation (9) is incorrect and will provide misleading interpretation of the results. Following Huang et al. (1990), the conditional marginal effect of independent variable X_i can be expressed as

$$\partial E(W | H > 0) / \partial X_i = \beta_i + \theta[\partial\lambda / \partial X_i] = \beta_i - \tau_i\theta[(TX)\lambda + \lambda^2] \qquad (11)$$

by assuming X=Y, for simplicity, and using the fact that

$$\partial\lambda / \partial X_i = \frac{[\Phi(.)\partial\phi(.)/\partial X_i - \phi(.)\partial\Phi(.)/\partial X_i]}{[\Phi(.)]^2} = -\tau_i I \qquad (12)$$

and

$$\partial\Phi(TX)/\partial X_i = \tau_i\phi(.), \quad \partial\phi(TX)/\partial X_i = -\tau_i TX\phi(.) \qquad (13)$$

To better serve the purpose of this study, special attention was given to the first-stage probit analysis. While all available variables that can be related to decision making in labor force participation were entered into the initial model, only significant variables were kept in the final model, so that the estimated self selection term would not be affected by model misspecification.

In the second-stage wage offer analysis, hourly wage rate was converted into logarithmic form to reduce the hetroskedesticity of the error term, and to capture possible nonlinear relationships between dependent and independent variables. A full model(1) was estimated first with all available related variables. Interaction terms between education and work experience were considered since, the reward from experience can be different for different education levels. Then, stepwise regressions were performed and only significant variables selected remained in the reduced model(2), except the self selection variable λ, which stayed in the model regardless of its significance. F tests were performed to make sure it was not worthwhile to keep insignificant variables in the model(2). The reduced model was reestimated and if λ was still not significant, a final model(3) was run without this self selectivity term. Model(2) (if λ was significant) or model(3) (if not) were used in the following wage gap analysis and simulations.

Wage Gap Analysis

By assuming all individuals face the same market wage offer structure (eg. white men's wage offer equation), we can plug in women's and black's characteristics in white men's wage offer equation, and find out how much of the wage gaps can be explained by differences in their characteristics. This technique was used in most of the wage gap studies. The rationale behind it is that if there was no discrimination in the market and the wage rate was determined only by individual qualifications regardless of gender and race, most of the wage gaps should be explained by the differences between characteristics of these groups. If a large percentage of the wage gap can not be explained, as was the case in most of the previous studies, then either there were some qualifications remain unaccounted for, or there was discrimination in the wage offer market. A main purpose of this study was to treat self selection as a previously unaccounted for qualification and investigate to what extent it can explain the wage gaps between genders and races.

Simulation

Since the results of the wage gap analysis suggested that a large proportion of the wage gap was attributable to self selection bias, an attempt was made to identify the role of systematic differences (objective) and statistical discrimination (subjective) in explaining wage gaps. While controlling all occupation, personal characteristics and labor market characteristics, simulations were run to illustrate the relationship between work experience and wage rate for the four gender and race groups. The rationale behind this is that if there were no subjective effects, individuals with a lower probability of labor force participation can get the same training opportunity as others, the reward from their work experience should be the same as those with a high probability of labor force participation. Simulations were done on a married individual, with one child less than 6 years old, living in an urban area but not SMSA and not in the south. Three education levels were considered: high school, college, and graduate education, with occupation wages equal to the mean of the occupational median wages for the corresponding educational category.

The Data

Data for this study were from the 1979-1990 National Longitudinal Survey of Youth (NLSY). It was conducted by the Human Resource Center of Ohio State University. The initial sample had 12686 cases who were first interviewed in 1979 and every year thereafter. After deleting noneligible cases and cases with missing data on dependent and independent variables, the remaining sample size was 8917, including both individuals in the labor force and out of labor force. Since previous studies suggested that the wage offer equation and labor supply decision differ substantially between different gender and race, the sample was disaggregated into four subsamples: white male, white female, black male, and black female. For estimation of the wage offer equation, an individual must not have been enrolled in school at the interview time. To avoid given undue weight to atypical observations, the hourly wage rate had to be greater than or equal to $1 and less than or equal to $40 to be eligible for the sample.

A list of definitions of the variables is presented in Table 1.

Table 1
Definitions of Variables

Name	Description
LOGWAGE:	log of hourly wage rate in 1990
HIGHSCH:	high school education (12-15 years)
COLLEGE:	college education (16 years)
GRADUATE:	graduate education (>16 years)
ENROLL2:	currently enrolled in high school
ENROLL3:	currently enrolled in college
LNWKEXP:	log of work experience (1,000 hours)
MARRIED:	marital status:1=married, 0=others
FAMSIZE:	family size
NOKIDLT6:	number of children less than 6
HEALTHPM:	health limitation
PROWORK:	attitude toward women working
EXOGY:	exogenous income ($1,000)
URBAN:	area: 1=urban, 0=rural
SOUTH:	region: 1=south, 0=other regions
SMSA:	SMSA: 1=center of SMSA, 0=others
UERATE:	local unemployment rate
MEDIWAGE:	occupational median wage
COLLBARG:	collective bargaining

Results and Discussion

First-stage probit analysis

In Table 2 the marginal effects of the first-stage probit analysis are presented for the four gender and race groups. These marginal effects of X_i was calculated using the following formula (Maddala 1990):

$$\partial P/\partial Z_i = \gamma_i \phi (\gamma_0 + \Gamma Z) \qquad (14)$$

where P was the probability to be in the labor force.

For women and black men, formal education has the largest marginal effects on their probability of labor force participation. On the average, an individual with a college degree was about 20%, 23% or 31% more likely to be in the labor force than one who had less than high school education, for white women, black men, and black women, respectively, holding other things equal. If an individual had some graduate level education, the increase in the probability of labor force participation was even larger. On the negative side, having children less than 6, and having health problem reduce the probability of white women's labor force participation about 10% each. For black men, having a health problem reduces their probability of labor force participation about 16% percent on average, holding other things equal. Thus, a health problem has the single most important negative effect on black men's probability of labor force participation. For black women, having children less than six years old lowers their probability of labor force participation about 8%, holding other things equal. For white men, no single variable has a very big marginal effect on their probability of labor force participation.

Table 2
Estimates from Probit Analysis:
Dependent Variable: Whether R was in labor force[a]

Explanatory Variables	W. Male mar. eff.	W. Female mar. eff.	B. Male mar. eff.	B. Female mar. eff.
HIGHSCH	0.0391	0.1034	0.1050	0.1302
COLLEGE	0.0768	0.2032	0.2321	0.3064
GRADUATE	0.0954	0.3240	0.3613	0.5625
ENROLL2	-0.0941	-0.3033	-	-
ENROLL3	-0.0258	-	-	0.1235
LNWKEXP	0.0350	0.1277	0.1089	0.1747
MARRIED	0.0498	-	0.1525	0.1088
FAMSIZE	-0.0081	-	-	-
NOKIDLT6	-	-0.1324	-	-0.0775
HEALTHPM	-	-0.1180	-0.1599	-
PROWORK	-	0.0428	-	-
EXOGY	-	-0.0022	-0.0015	-0.0043
URBAN	0.0253	-	-	-
SMSA	-0.0324	-	-	-
SOUTH	-	-0.0375	-	-
UERATE	-0.0087	-0.0278	-	-0.0498
INTERCEPT	0.3873	0.6888	-0.4333	0.0754
Cragg-Uhler R^2	0.2158	0.3009	0.2453	0.3753
Sample Size	3218	3210	1230	1259

[a] all coefficients are at least statistically significant at $\alpha=0.10$ level

Second-stage wage offer equation estimation
After deleting missing data and ineligible data, about 75% of those who were employed at the interview time were left in the estimation of the wage offer equations. Because this sample was fairly young and in a small age range (25-33), and also because age was highly correlated with work experience, age did not show significance in any of the four equations and was therefore dropped out of the model.

One feature of this model was the measurement of occupation. The conventionally used eight occupation categories have been criticized by many researchers because the categories do not really capture the occupational differences. This can be a reason why many wage offer studies found occupation to be not very significant while it should be based on common knowledge. In this study, another sample was drawn from the twelve year NLSY data. To obtain maximum sample size for each occupation category, observations were entered into the sample if the hourly wage rate and the census occupation coding were observed. Thus some of the wage observations may be for the same individual, but for different years, and possibly for different occupations. All wage rates were inflated or deflated to 1983/1984 dollars using the consumer price index. A median wage rate was estimated for each census three digit occupation and this occupational median wage was then used as an index of occupation differences in the wage offer equation. Not surprisingly, white men hold the highest paid occupations, on average. In 1983/84 dollars, white men's mean occupational median wage was about $8.01, which was about 113% of the average median wage for occupations held by black females. White women were in occupations generally better paid than black men and black women.

The results of the estimated wage offer equation for white men and black men are summarized in Table 3. Lambda, which represents the self selection bias, was very significant for these two groups, both in the full model and the reduced model. This indicates that the self selection effect, indeed, exists and can significantly affect the market wage rate for white and black men. Since the traditional male role is to be financially responsible for the family, men who don't work usually have big differences from men who are in the labor force, especially in term of career goals, work attachment, and responsibility. However, for females, things are different. The regression results for white and black females, presented in Table 4, suggest that self selection was not significant in females' wage offer equations, indicating that females who were in the labor force might not be systematically different from those who were not working, or, possibly, they were not perceived or treated differently from those who were not working. One possible reason is that the motivation of females to be in the labor force can be very different. It can be high career goals, which are usually related to high human capital, or it can be just having to work to earn a living. Some women with good qualifications may find their home productivity higher than their market productivity, and with plenty of exogenous income to support them, they may choose to stay home rather than work outside. Since women's labor force participation decisions are more complicated than men's, and overall, women have a lower rate of labor force participation, it is rational for firms to expect them to have a higher risk of labor turnover than men, thus they are at a disadvantage in equal opportunity for training and getting good jobs.

Table 3
Estimated Wage Rate Equations for White Men and Black Men: Dependent Variable: LOGWAGE (t-value in parenthesis)

Explanatory Variable	White Men	Coefficients	Black men	
	Model(2)	Mar. Eff.	Model(2)	Mar. Eff.
HIGHSCH	-	0.0688	-	0.0712
COLLEGE	-	0.1350	-	0.1574
GRADUATE	-	0.1678	0.2709 (2.769)***	0.5159
LNWKEXP	-	0.0615	0.0480 (1.757)*	0.1219
LNWKHIGH	0.0354 (3.792)***	0.0354	-	-
LNWKCOLL	0.1082 (7.701)***	0.1082	0.0801 (3.450)***	0.0801
LNWKGRAD	0.1419 (6.775)***	0.1419	-	-
URBAN	0.0956 (4.675)***	0.1401	0.0896 (2.456)***	0.0896
SOUTH	-0.0977 (-5.453)***	-0.0977	-0.1413 (-5.015)***	-0.1413
SMSA	0.0838 (2.863)***	0.0268	-	-
MEDIWAGE	0.0899 (19.171)***	0.0899	0.1152 (13.005)***	0.1152
COLLBARG	0.1696 (7.931)***	0.1696	0.2007 (6.610)***	0.2007
LAMBDA	-0.8228 (-7.109)***		-0.4449 (-4.0179)***	
INTERCEPT	1.479 (28.213)***		1.1899 (10.089)***	
Adj. R^2	0.3488		0.3895	
F-value	133.274***		60.822***	
Sample Size	2224		751	

*** statistically significant at α=0.01 level
** statistically significant at α=0.05 level
* statistically significant at α=0.10 level

Since individuals with different education levels may have different returns from work experience (Becker, 1975), education dummies were used not only as intercept dummies, but also as slope dummies in the form of interaction terms with the logarithm of the work experience. In the full model(1), some of the human capital variables exhibited insignificance because of multicollinearity. The reduced model(2) for men and model(3) for women, selected by stepwise regression, more efficiently captured the relationship between wage rate and human capital. Therefore, the following wage gap analysis and simulation were performed utilizing the results of model(2) for men and model(3) for women, and their corresponding marginal effects.

Table 4
Estimated Wage Rate Equations for White Women and Black Women:Dependent Variable: LOGWAGE (t-value in parenthesis)

Explanatory Variable	White Women	Coefficients	Black Women	
	Model(2)	Model(3)	Model(2)	Model(3)
HIGHSCH	-	-	-	-
COLLEGE	0.3390 (8.539)***	0.3506 (9.445)***	0.4131 (5.705)***	0.3666 (6.031)***
GRADUATE	0.4639 (9.254)***	0.4811 (10.569)***	0.4716 (4.656)***	0.3960 (5.044)***
LNWKEXP	0.0664 (3.621)***	0.0730 (4.425)***	0.1165 (3.401)***	0.0893 (3.525)***
LNWKHIGH	0.0550 (4.252)***	0.0575 (4.576)***	0.0657 (2.912)***	0.0570 (2.671)***
LNWKCOLL	-	-	-	-
LNWKGRAD	-	-	-	-
URBAN	0.1089 (4.984)***	0.1099 (5.041)***	0.1307 (3.283)***	0.1291 (3.245)***
SOUTH	-0.0592 (-3.024)***	-0.0606 (-3.105)***	-0.1374 (-4.637)***	-0.1396 (4.720)***
SMSA	-	-	0.0525 (1.580)*	0.0535 (1.610)***
MEDIWAGE	0.1168 (21.290)***	0.1169 (21.319)***	0.1044 (11.971)***	0.1044 (11.965)***
COLLBARG	0.1281 (4.503)***	0.1279 (4.498)***	0.1386 (4.442)***	0.1383 (4.433)***
LAMBDA	-0.0464 (-0.412)	-	0.1358 (1.181)	-
INTERCEPT	0.8277 (12.035)***	0.7898 (15.492)***	0.7008 (5.111)***	0.8321 (10.378)***
Adj. R^2	0.4021	0.4022	0.4357	0.4253
F-value	129.455***	145.581***	48.508***	53.710***
Sample Size	1720		642	

*** statistically significant at α=0.01 level
** statistically significant at α=0.05 level
* statistically significant at α=0.10 level

Wage Gap Analysis
The wage gap analysis was conducted using white men's wage offer equation as the comparison group. If the argument about why self selection is not significant in women's wage offer equations is correct, then men's wage offer equations may be the ones with wage offer truly based on individual self selection differences instead of overall probability.

The results of the wage gap analysis are summarized in Table 5.

Table 5
Wage Gap Analysis Using White Men Wage Equation

	White Women vs. W. Men	Black Men vs. W. Men	Black Women vs. W. Men
	Percent	Percent	Percent
Total Gap	100.00%	100.00%	100.00%
Single Factor Explained			
Human Capital	-5.00%	10.16%	1.72%
Location	1.42%	2.59%	3.95%
Occupation	21.96%	30.16%	25.79%
Col. Bargaining	5.56%	-6.24%	-3.06%
Self Selection	**77.00%**	**47.67%**	**46.68%**
Total Explained	100.00%	84.33%	74.51%

Figure 1
Simulation: High School Education

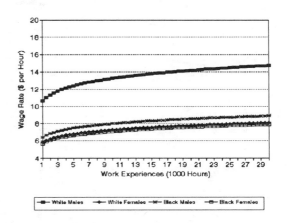

For the sample used in this study, the mean wage rate for white male was $11.20. For white female, black male and black female, it was $9.18, $8.94, $8.13, respectively. For the wage gap between white women and white men, all of the gap was explained, and 77% of it was attributable to differences in self selection. For black men and women, total explained gap was about 84% and 75%, respectively, with more than half of the explained gaps attributable to differences in self selection bias.

On average, measurable human capital differences (including formal education and work experience) account for about -5%, 10% and 2% wage gaps between white men and white women, black men, and black women, respectively. Only black men's formal education was considerably less than white men and picks up a noticeable amount of the wage gap.

As expected, occupational differences pick up about 22%, 30% and 26% of the wage gaps between white men and white women, white men and black men, and white men and black women. Engaging in jobs where collective bargaining was involved does help blacks a little bit, especially black men.

Figure 2
Simulation: College Education

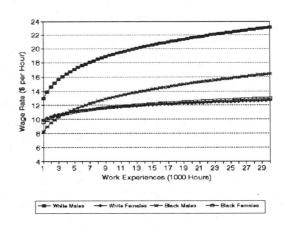

Simulation
    If females do get less training opportunities due to their overall low probability of labor force participation, the relationship of their work experiences and wage rate will be different from those of the males. It can be expected that the reward from the work experience will be lower for women than for men, since for the same amount of work experience, women will accumulate less human capital than men because of less training. Figure 1, 2 and 3 illustrate the simulation results of the individual described in the analytical framework section, with education at high school, college and graduate school level, respectively.

Figure 3
Simulation: Graduate Education

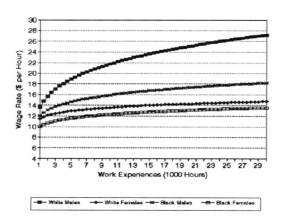

For all three education categories, white men have the highest beginning wage rate and gain the highest return from their work experiences. The differences in return from work experience is bigger for all individuals with graduate and college education than for high school graduates. For individuals with graduate education, the beginning wage rate is reasonably close between genders and races, but along with increases in work experiences, the wage gap is getting bigger and bigger, especially between women and white men. The simulation for college graduates showed the similar pattern. In general, we can conclude that the higher the education level, the closer the beginning wage rate between genders and races, but the differences between the slopes of the wage rate curves is greater.

The simulation results confirm our hypothesis that women and also black men get less rewards from the same amount of work experiences, holding other things equal.

Conclusion

Based on the above analysis, the three questions proposed at the beginning of the paper can be answered.

The marginal effect of selectivity bias on market wage rate was different for white men, white women, black men and black women. It was significant in men's wage offer equations, but not in women's wage offer equations. The size of the marginal effect was greater for white men than for black men.

Possible explanations for the differences follow: (1) There exists systematic differences in terms of work attachment, career goals, and other attitude characteristics between genders and races, which will affect their market wage rate; (2) In conformation of Becker's theory about the relationship of on-the-job training and the likelihood of labor turnover, firms' perception of

high labor force withdrawal risk may lead them to be less willing to invest in female and also black men's job training, and thus depress the long run wage rates of females and blacks; (3) In both white and black women's wage offer equations, self selection was not significant. This indicates the possibility that there are large variations in terms of women's decision making about labor force participation. Those who are in the labor force may not necessary have higher qualifications than those who are not. On the other hand, statistical discrimination may well exist. Since the future labor force participation status is less predictable for females than for males, the training opportunity of those who are in the labor force might be depressed by the overall low probability of labor force participation of the group in which they belong, so that individual differences are no longer important. The simulation results of relationships between market wage rate and work experience for different groups further confirm that females get less return from the same amount of work experience than white males, holding other things equal.

The term λ , which represents the self selection bias, accounts for a large percentage of the wage gaps between genders and races. It is not clear what proportion of the gap is attributable to systematic differences and what proportion to statistical discrimination. Further studies are needed to explore this.

Policies such as tax incentives may be implemented to encourage employers to provide equal training opportunities for their female employees. More studies should be done to investigate the true long run likelihood of labor force withdrawal of working females with different characteristics. Accurate information should be provided to the employers so that their evaluation of the likelihood of labor turn over of the female employees could be more fact-based.

References

Becker, G.S. (1975). Human Capital : A Theoretical and Empirical Analysis, Chicago: University of Chicago Press.

Corcoran, M. & Duncan, G. (1979). Work History, Labor Force Attachment, and Earning differences between Races and Sexes. Journal of Human Resources. 14, 3-20.

Heckman, J. (1976). The Common Structure of Statistical Models of Truncation, Sample Selection and Limited Dependent Variables and a Simple Estimation for Such Models. Annal of Economics and Social Measure. 5, 570-579.

Heckman, J. (1979). Sample Selection Bias as a Specification Error. Econometrica. 47, 153-161.

Jones, J.E. & Pack, C.J. (1989). The Effect of Human Capital, Socioeconomic, and Labor Market Factors on Wages. Home Economics Research Journal. 18, 110-125.

Maddala, D.S. (1983). Limited-Dependent and Qualitative Variables in Econometrics. Cambridge: Cambrige University Press.

Mincer, J. & Polachek, S. (1974). Family Investments in Human Capital and Earnings of Women. Journal of Political Economy. 82(2), 576-608.

Miner, J. & Rudd, N.M. (1992). Human Capital and Wage Differentials of Young Black and White Men. Unpublished Dissertation. The Ohio State University, Columbus, Ohio.

Nah, M. & Rudd, N.M. (1992). The Male-Female Wage Gap: A Test of Becker's Hypothesis." Unpublished Dissertation. The Ohio State University, Columbus, Ohio.

Household Food-Away-From-Home and Frozen Food Consumption and Prices of Wives' and Husbands' Time: A Disaggregated Cross-Sectional Analysis

Frank F. Chiang, Cornell University[1]

In this study, Becker's time allocation model, Heckman's selection bias-corrected technique, and Tobit model were applied to analyze the prices of wives' and husbands' time on the possibility and magnitude of making FAFH and frozen food purchases. The results of this study show that households with higher wife's and husband's offered wages tend to have a larger FAFH consumption.

In the last three decades, married women participation in the labor force has increased dramatically. In 1960, the labor force participation rate of married women was approximately 31.9 percent. By 1988 it had risen to 56.7 percent. Consequently, American married women decreased their non-market time (household work and leisure activities). For example, by 1967 the average amount of time spent by married women in household work activities was about 6 hours/day (Bryant, 1986). It had fallen to about 5 hours/day by 1975 (Hill, 1985).

This phenomenon has attracted much attention and concern from researchers. Numerous studies have investigated the relationships between wives' employment and several components of consumption (e.g. automobile, housing, and home appliances, etc.). In addition, a number of studies analyze the relationships between the time allocation and the wives' employment. Several studies (Prochaska and Schrimper, 1973; Redman, 1980; Kinsey, 1983; Lippert and Love, 1986; Bryant, 1988) show that the increasing employment of wives has resulted in changes in their consumption of goods and services, and in their household production time.

As married women have become an important part of the labor force participation, the implications from Becker's (1965) household production theory are more relevant. Becker provided a new theory of household economics, i.e. households are producers of non-market commodities rather than simply consumers of market goods and services. When the time of working wives becomes more valuable as earnings increase, working wives generally decrease their time on home work activities, particularly food preparation. Thus, the demand for substitutes for the home work activities, such as home appliances (microwaves and dish-washing machine, etc.), frozen foods, and FAFH, becomes greater. Especially, frozen foods and/or FAFH might be chosen as substitutes for the preparation of meals at home because of time-savings, convenience, and variety.

The sales figures of frozen foods support the above argument. More and newer frozen foods are introduced into the food market from frozen vegetables to frozen-prepared plate dinners and entrees. Russel (1985) indicated that 3.3 billion dollars were spent in frozen-prepared plate dinners and entrees in 1984. Thus, frozen foods are expected to be a significant item in the household menu and play an important role in the food industry in the future.

This study tries to examine the price of wives' and husbands' time not only on household production activities but also on food consumption behavior and patterns. Does wives' working status affect FAFH and frozen food consumption? Do the wives' and the husbands' wage rates affect expenditures on FAFH and frozen food? Are there different results when using disaggregated food items instead of aggregated food items? This study is motivated by these questions.

The principal focus of this empirical analysis is to examine the relationships between household FAFH and frozen food consumption and the prices of wives' and husbands' time. In other words, this study is to estimate the influence of the values of wives' and husbands' wages, and household socioeconomic characteristic factors on FAFH and frozen food expenditures. To model demand for FAFH and frozen foods appropriately it is necessary to address the characteristics of the household relating to the household's time allocation, resource allocation behavior, age composition and other demographic characteristics.

This study utilizes cross-sectional data generated from the 1987 Bureau of Labor Statistics Expenditure Diary Survey (Consumer Expenditure Survey) to analyze the consumption of FAFH, and frozen foods (frozen meals and frozen/preparation food other than meals). In order to obtain better explanations for the occurrence of zero expenditures and to improve model specification, the use of the limited dependent variables model will be investigated. Also, the measurements of the values of non-working wives' and non-working husbands' times are derived using a technique by Heckman (1979).

Specific research objectives include the

---

[1]Graduate Student,
Consumer Economics and Housing

following: (1) to specify a model for relating wives' employment and wage, and household socioeconomic factors to household expenditures on FAFH and frozen food consumption, and (2) to examine the relationships between the household FAFH and frozen food consumption and the price of wives' and husbands' time.

Literature Review

The literature review for this study falls into three parts: first, a review of past studies concerned with the relationships between wives' employment and several components of consumption; second, studies that have introduced Heckman's technique to estimate offered wages in the related analysis; and finally, studies that have dealt with the specification of censoring regression models will be explored.

Consumption and Wives' Employment

Several studies have examined the homemaker's time allocation and expenditures on durables and purchasing of time-saving goods and services incorporating household characteristics with their models. Most of studies started with the conventional consumption theory and Becker's (1965) theory of time allocation. It is assumed that households maximize their utility through the consumption of combinations of goods and services.

For durable goods, there are two hypotheses relating to the relationship between durables consumption and wives' employment: first, most married females' employment responds to and tends to offset transitory movements in other components of family income (Mincer, 1962; Bryant, 1988); second, the durables and wives' home time are complements in home activities (Galbraith, 1973; Bryant, 1988). The implication of the first hypothesis is that the portion of working wives' earnings spent on durables is greater than that of other income. And the second hypothesis indicates that durables and wives' time are used together in household activities. Thus, durables expenditures increase with wives' employment. A number of studies (Strober and Weinberg, 1977, 1980; Bryant, 1988) have shown that durables expenditures and working wives' time are substitutes in the household activities although the statistical evidence is weak.

Regarding the purchase of time-saving goods and services, Yang and Magrabi (1989) investigated the relationship between the wives' employment status and expenditures for purchased services, specifically, FAFH, child care, and domestic services. They specified the purchase of services as a function of the wife's employment status (quantitative and qualitative information), education of wife, age of wife, household income, and other socio-demographic factors. A Tobit model was used in their analysis. Their results indicated that the amount of time the wife spent on work was positively related to expenditure on child care services, but not other services. Redman

(1980) used the 1972-73 and 1973-74 Nationwide Survey of Consumer Expenditures data to examine the impacts of women's time allocation on expenditure for FAFH and prepared foods. She found that a positive relationship between wives' employment and prepared food, but not the FAFH.

Not much econometric evidence exists to support strongly the positive relationship between female employment and consumption patterns. There are several reasons to explain this result: (i) problems in the model specification and estimation, (ii) aggregate data versus disaggregate data, i.e. total food expenditures and single item or sub-group food items, and (iii) change of household structure, i.e. the increase of single-parent households.

Selection Bias-Corrected Technique

Observations on earnings per hour of work is not available from the data set for those wives who were not paid labor force participants. This creates a sample selection problem. Generally, a technique originally outlined by Heckman (1979) to derive offered wages is used to measure the value of earnings for those who did not report a market wage. Here, two estimation equations were used to derive the wife's and husband's hourly offered wages by using Heckman's technique: a labor force participation (probit equation), and an offered wage equation. The estimation procedures are: first, use a probit model on the whole sample to derive a measure of the selection bias; second, use an OLS model with the workers only sub-sample to estimate the coefficients of the offered wage equation via selection bias-corrected regression (Killingsworth, 1983).

Censoring Regression Models

All the above studies used cross-sectional data on individual households' expenditures on durables and several other goods and services. With data from individual households, one can expect a portion of the observations on the expenditures to be zero, especially on durables and frozen foods. In order to obtain better explanations of the occurrence of zero expenditures and to improve model specification, the use of the limited dependent variables models is necessary. Maddala (1983) has provided excellent reviews of the literature pertaining to the specification and estimation of models that fall within the limited dependent variable. However, brief illustrations of the Tobit model are provided.

The Tobit model was originally developed by Tobin (1958) and has been widely applied to censored data. The Tobit model is a one-step decision method. In other words, it assumes that the decision to consume a certain good and the quantity to consume are decided at the same time. The Tobit model is defined as follows:

$$y_i^* = x_i\beta + \epsilon_i \qquad \epsilon_i \sim N(0, \sigma^2) \qquad (1)$$
$$y_i = y_i^* \qquad \text{if } y_i^* > 0$$
$$= 0 \qquad \text{otherwise}$$

where y_i is the ith individual household's observed expenditure on FAFH or frozen foods in this study and y_i^* is the ith household's desired or optimal expenditure and can be the solution of the utility maximization subject to household budget. The vector x_i consists of explanatory variables, β is a vector of unknown coefficients, and ϵ_i is a vector of independently and normally distributed random variables with mean zero and variance σ^2. For the ith household it is known that if $y_i > 0$ then $y_i^* > 0$, however it is possible that $y_i = 0$ and $y_i^* > 0$ for frozen foods purchased prior to the survey period.

Theoretical Model

In this section, a theoretical model is provided. Traditional consumer demand theory assumes that households attempt to maximize utility from the services or goods purchased in the marketplace, given a budget constraint. The quantities purchased by a household are supposed to be optimal quantities, i.e. quantities determined by maximizing utility function under a budget constraint (Phlips, 1974).

In this study, the household production theory of Becker (1965) was applied. He assumed that households use non-market time (T_i) and market goods (q_i) via the "production functions" f_i to produce more basic commodities (Z_i). Hence, the modified demand system can be specified as follows:

$$\text{Max. } U = U(Z_1, Z_2, ..., Z_i) \quad i=1, 2, .., n \quad (2)$$

where U is the utility function satisfying general restrictions.

$$\text{s.t. } g(Z_1, Z_2, ..., Z_i) = Z \quad (3)$$

where g is an expenditure function of Z_i and Z is the bound on resources.

The production function f_i to produce the commodities Z_i can be defined as

$$Z_i = f_i(q_i, T_i; HC) \quad (4)$$

where q_i is a vector of markets goods, T_i is time inputs to produce commodity Z_i, and HC is the household characteristics that affect the household production and consumption capabilities.

The goods constraint can be specified as

$$\textstyle{_1\Sigma_n} P_i \cdot q_i = Y = T_w \cdot W + V \quad (5)$$

where P_i is a vector of market price for market goods q_i, Y is money income, T_w is a vector of time spent at work, W is a vector of the wage rate, and V is other income.

The time constraint is defined as

$$\textstyle{_1\Sigma_n} T_i = T - T_w \quad (6)$$

where T is total time available. T_i is a function of T_w. We assumed that if T_w is increasing then T_i is decreasing.

Hence, we can rewrite the maximization utility function as

$$\text{Max. } U = U(Z_i) \equiv U(q_i, T_i; HC) \quad (7)$$
$$\text{s.t. } \Sigma P_i \cdot q_i = Y \quad (8)$$
$$\Sigma T_i = T - T_w$$

The analysis reduces to finding a maximum of $U(Z_i)$ subject to the restriction, money income and time (equation (8)). The solution to equation (7) and (8) will be the form

$$q_i = h_i(P_i, W, Y, HC) \quad i = 1, 2, ..., n \quad (9)$$

Equation (9) is a set of n derived Marshallian demand functions that is obtained by solving the first order conditions. Generally, this relationship is referred to as an Engel curve (Deaton and Muellbauer, 1980). The quantity of each commodity purchased is represented as a function of income (wage income plus other income), own price and the prices of substitutes and complements, and the household characteristics. Hence equation (9) is the demand function.

Demand for frozen food is a subset of total demand for q_i which can be expressed in terms of expenditure as functions of Y and HC (Kinsey, 1983),

$$EXP = \Sigma P_i \cdot q_f = h_f(W, Y, P_f, HC) \quad (10)$$

where EXP is household expenditures for FAFH or frozen food items.

Generally, one can assume that there is an interior solution in the utility maximization function that implies that the household purchases some quantity of each and every commodity. However, in survey data some households reported that they did not purchase the commodity in question or they reported consumption to be zero during the survey period. In this situation, those households that report a zero expenditure represent a corner solution.

Consider further the discrete choice in utility maximization. We Introduce a binary value variable D_i such that $D_i = 1$ if $q_f > 0$ and $D_i = 0$ if $q_f = 0$. That is

$$q_f = h_f(Y, W, P_f, HC) \quad \text{if } D_i = 1 \quad (11)$$
$$= 0 \qquad\qquad\qquad \text{if } D_i = 0$$

In order to estimate the demand functions as specified in equation (11), maximum likelihood methods can be applied.

Data and Variables

In this section the data set and variables are introduced. The present study used the data from the 1987 diary survey of the Consumer Expenditure Survey (CEX), Bureau of Labor Statistics, U.S. Department of Labor, 1990. This diary survey collected the data on two consecutive one-week periods. In this study, first-week expenditures on foods were used rather than second-week expenditures, and only those households containing married couples were selected. In addition, those households that contained incomplete information such as missing

Table 1
Definition of Variables for CEX DATA, 1987.

Variables	Definitions
FROZFOOD	Weekly frozen food items expenditures (in dollars)
FAFH	Weekly FAFH expenditures (in dollars)
AGE_WIFE	Age of wife
AGE_HUSB	Age of husband
EDUCA1_WI	= 1 if wife completed H.S.
EDUCA2_WI	= 1 if wife not completed college
EDUCA3_WI	= 1 if wife has college or more education
EDUCA1_HU	= 1 if husband completed H.S.
EDUCA2_HU	= 1 if husband not completed college
EDUCA3_HU	= 1 if husband has college or more education
EXPE_WIFE	= AGE_WIFE - years of wife's education - 6
EXPE_WIFE^2	= EXPE_WIFE*EXPE_WIFE
EXPE_HUSB	= AGE_HUSB - years of husband's education - 6
EXPE_HUSB^2	= EXPE_HUSB*EXPE_HUSB
HRWAGE_OW	Wife's hourly offered wage
HRWAGE_OH	Husband's hourly offered wage
NONEARN	Household's annual nonearning income (in thousands)
NWHITE_W	= 1 if wife is non-white
NWHITE_H	= 1 if husband is non-white
CHILD05	= 1 if household has aged 0-5 children
CHILDREN	Numbers of children
HOMEOWNER	= 1 if household owns the house
NORTHEAST	= 1 if household resides in the Northeastern urban areas
MIDWEST	= 1 if household resides in the Midwestern urban areas
SOUTH	= 1 if household resides in the Southern urban areas
WEST	= 1 if household resides in the Western urban areas
HHSIZE	Numbers of person in household
HHSIZE^2	= HHSIZE*HHSIZE
AGED1	Proportion of household 0-12 yrs old
AGED2	Proportion of household 13-18 yrs old
AGED3	Proportion of household 41-60 yrs old
AGED4	Proportion of household over 60 yrs old

values on income and other household characteristics were also deleted. The data were composed of the individual household's expenditures on FAFH and frozen foods along with the information about the household's economic and demographic characteristics. The resulting sample consisted of 2675 households (observations).

Household weekly expenditure on FAFH and frozen foods served as the dependent variables, respectively. In this study, household expenditures of frozen foods are the sum of the weekly expenditure of all frozen food items, and household expenditures of FAFH are the sum of the weekly expenditure of all FAFH items. Expenditure was defined in terms of dollars. The variables used to explain food consumption included age of wife, education of wife, wife's and husband's hourly offered wage, household annual nonearning income, race of wife, number of children, household size, household size squared, region, and household age-composition. The dependent and explanatory variables are defined in Table 1. Also, the descriptive statistics for the variables used in the models are listed in Table 2.

Table 2
Descriptive Statistics for the Variables Used in the Models.

Variable	Mean	Standard Deviation
FROZFOOD	.99	2.57
FAFH	29.31	30.08
AGE_WIFE	43.37	15.37
AGE_HUSB	46.08	15.86
EDUCA1_WI	.42	.49
EDUCA2_WI	.23	.42
EDUCA3_WI	.18	.39
EDUCA1_HU	.34	.47
EDUCA2_HU	.21	.41
EDUCA3_HU	.25	.44
EXPE_WIFE	25.15	15.88
EXPE_WIFE^2	884.65	977.71
EXPE_HUSB	27.60	16.41
EXPE_HUSB^2	1030.95	1079.68
HRWAGE_OW	6.32	2.04
HRWAGE_OH	7.58	2.32
NONEARN	4.86	8.75
NWHITE_W	.09	.29
NWHITE_H	.09	.28
CHILD05	.25	.43
CHILDREN	.95	1.19
HOMEOWNER	.78	.42
NORTHEAST	.17	.38
MIDWEST	.22	.42
SOUTH	.24	.43
WEST	.22	.42
HHSIZE	3.14	1.23
HHSIZE^2	11.35	9.68
AGED1	.17	.22
AGED2	.06	.14
AGED3	.24	.34
AGED4	.19	.36
WORK_WI	.55	.50
WORK_HU	.82	.38

The variable representing the educational level of wife was measured in four levels: education less than high school, high school graduate, some college education, and college graduate or more. The two classifications of race of wife used were white and non-white. Five classifications of region were specified--Rural, Northeast, Midwest, South, and West.

Generally, households with different sizes, and age-composition have different consumption patterns. In order to make the comparisons across households of different sizes and composition suitably, equivalence scales are sometimes used to account for differences. However, when the equivalence scales are incorporated into the model, it usually increases the complexities and involves the use of specialized functions (Reynolds, 1989). Hence, this study treats the household age-composition variables simply. There are five age groups to represent household composition effects: age less than 13, age 13 to 18, age 19 to 40, age 41 to 60, and age over 60.

In this study, the wife's and husband's hourly offered wages were introduced into the model. These wages were estimated from the offered wage equations.

Experience variables (EXPE_WIFE, EXPE_WIFE^2, EXPE_HUSB, and EXPE_HUSB^2) were obtained from age and education variables. For example, for those wives who have a high school degree, their experience will be equal to their age - years of education - years of preschool, i.e. age - 12 - 6. In this study, the number of years for education less than high school (including not completed high school), some college education, and college graduate or more are coded as 10, 13, and 16, respectively.

Empirical Analysis

The estimation results of nonworking wives' and husbands' hourly offered wages, and the Tobit model in the analysis are described in this section. The principal hypothesis of this study is that the prices of wife's and husband's time are associated with FAFH and frozen foods expenditures. The expected signs of these two prices are positive. The higher the offered wage, the more valuable his (her) time. Hence, FAFH and frozen foods become substitutes for home prepared meals. Theoretically, the wage effect has two effects: income effect and substitution effect.

Offered Wage Imputation

The estimation of wives' and husbands' offered wages followed Heckman's sample selection correction procedures. The estimated offered wages are assumed to be a function of education, experience, race, and residential region.

Mathematically, the market wage equations can be defined as,

WORK =f(age, education, household annual (12) unearned income, children, household size, residential region, home ownership)

LN(WAGE) =f(education, experience, (13) experience squared, race, region, LAMBDA)

First of all, we derive the correction variable LAMBDA by estimating a labor force participation equation (12), which is a probit model, using the total sample. For the results of the probit model see the first column of Table 3. and Table 4.

Table 3
Parameter Estimates of the Wives' Labor Force Participation and Offered Wage Equation.

Variables	Probit	Offered Wage
Dependent Variable	Employment Status	Hourly Wage
CONSTANT	1.9714 (10.773)[a]	.9346 (8.932)
AGE_WIFE	-.0405 (-14.337)	
EDUCA1_WI	.4160 (5.104)	.2256 (3.328)
EDUCA2_WI	.5065 (5.573)	.3548 (4.889)
EDUCA3_WI	.7127 (7.355)	.7749 (10.129)
EXPE_WIFE		-.0348 (6.668)
EXPE_WIFE^2		-.6305*10^{-3} (-5.616)
NONEARN	-.0281 (-6.672)	
NWHITE_W	.1196 (1.254)	-.1050 (-1.762)
CHILD05	-.7357 (-9.867)	
HHSIZE	-.0890 (-3.587)	
NORTHEAST	.2029 (.214)	.2255 (3.675)
MIDWEST	-.0194 (-.217)	.2385 (4.146)
SOUTH	-.0728 (-.818)	.2797 (4.866)
WEST	-.0830 (-.913)	.3209 (5.449)
HOMEOWNER	.1366 (1.956)	
LAMBDA		.0165 (.183)
N	2675	1466
R^2		.15
Adj. R^2		.14
Log-Likelihood	-1495.8	
X^2	692.08	

[a] t Statistics are in parentheses.

LAMBDA is then included in the market wage equation (13) which is estimated on the subsample of working wives and husbands.

The resulting coefficients were used to calculate the offered wages for the whole sample (see the second column of Table 3. and Table 4.).

Statistical Results

Presented in Table 5. are the results of the Tobit models. The LIMDEP mainframe version was used in the estimations. In the case of frozen food consumption, significant coefficients include NWHITE_W AND HHSIZE. Households with a white wife and larger size tend to have a stronger intention to purchase frozen foods than others.

Table 4
Parameter Estimates of the Husbands' Labor Force Participation and Offered Wage Equation.

Variables	Probit	Offered Wage
Dependent Variable	Employment Status	Hourly Wage
CONSTANT	4.0728 (11.773)[a]	1.2539 (11.933)
AGE_HUSB	-.0607 (-13.803)	
EDUCA1_HU	.3041 (2.983)	.1587 (2.394)
EDUCA2_HU	.4496 (3.438)	.3010 (4.141)
EDUCA3_HU	.9509 (7.203)	.4482 (6.389)
EXPE_HUSB		.0401 (5.864)
EXPE_HUSB^2		-.806*10^{-3} (-5.437)
NONEARN	-.0558 (-11.850)	
NWHITE_H	-.0570 (-.390)	-.0905 (-1.225)
CHILD05	-.5381 (-3.129)	
HHSIZE	.0371 (.798)	
NORTHEAST	-.0226 (-.159)	.2428 (3.282)
MIDWEST	.0269 (.201)	.3342 (4.822)
SOUTH	.0346 (.261)	.2224 (3.221)
WEST	.1031 (.748)	.2002 (2.859)
HOMEOWNER	.1479 (1.253)	
LAMBDA		-.3981 (-2.847)
N	2675	2194
R^2		.12
Adj. R^2		.11
Log-Likelihood	-587.10	
X^2	1346.2	

[a] t Statistics are in parentheses.

The positive and significant household size coefficient is consistent with the expectation that the larger household size is likely to purchase more frozen foods than those having smaller household size. The variables of wives' and husbands' offered wage rate, HRWAGE_OW and HRWAGE_OH, are not significant in frozen food consumption model, although, the signs of these two variables are all positive as expected from theory. Hence, there is no strong evidence to support positive relationships between the prices of wives' and husbands' time, and the consumption of frozen food according to the results of this study.

Table 5
The Estimated Tobit Model of Frozen Food and Food-Away-From-Home Expenditures.

Variables	Frozen Food	FAFH
CONSTANT	-15.3869 (-7.256)[a]	-27.6943 (-4.151)
AGE_WIFE	-.0218 (-.543)	-.0872 (-.668)
EDUCA1_WI	.0190 (.026)	9.1094 (3.841)
EDUCA2_WI	.4514 (.482)	10.8857 (3.584)
EDUCA3_WI	-.3619 (-.191)	3.6106 (.597)
HRWAGE_OW	.2755 (.786)	2.9437 (2.607)
HRWAGE_OH	.2870 (1.865)	2.1628 (4.297)
NONEARN	.0457 (1.650)	.0779 (.822)
NWHITE_W	-2.8928 (-3.592)	-6.6488 (-2.849)
CHILDREN	-1.1287 (-1.398)	-7.5445 (-2.661)
NORTHEAST	-.4749 (-.590)	1.6792 (.645)
MIDWEST	-.3172 (-.398)	1.3732 (.532)
SOUTH	-.2482 (-.302)	2.8148 (1.064)
WEST	-.0765 (-.085)	2.9672 (1.020)
HHSIZE	2.7498 (2.438)	8.4678 (2.325)
HHSIZE^2	-.1799 (-1.330)	-.2020 (-.457)
AGED1	2.8055 (.741)	-12.3669 (-.953)
AGED2	3.8258 (1.149)	14.2681 (1.225)
AGED3	1.5572 (1.247)	-4.9252 (-1.221)
AGED4	1.8126 (.960)	-3.9802 (-.652)
Sigma	7.3957 (29.778) (65.774)	31.6308
Log Likelihood	-2893.0	-11443.0

[a] t Statistics are in parentheses.

In the case of FAFH consumption, the results are encouraging. The significant coefficients include EDUCA1_WI, EDUCA2_WI, HRWAGE_OW, HRWAGE_OH, NWHITE_W, CHILDREN, and HHSIZE. Households with noncollege graduate wife, higher wife's and husband's offered wages, white wife and larger household, tend to have a stronger intention to purchase FAFH than others. The reason for the positive and significant household size coefficient is same as in the case of frozen food consumption.

The variables of wives' and husbands' offered wage rate, HRWAGE_OW and HRWAGE_OH, are highly significant in the FAFH model. In addition, the signs of these two variables are all positive as expected. Hence, strong evidence supports positive relationships between the prices of wives' and husbands' time, and the consumption of FAFH according to the results of this study.

In this study, not only the price of wives' time, but also the price of husbands' time is incorporated into the model. However, the results are different between the two types of goods. In comparing the results from the two Tobit models, the coefficients, HRWAGE_OW and HRWAGE_OH, in the case of frozen foods are much smaller than those in the case of FAFH, i.e., 0.2755 vs 2.9437 and 0.2870 vs 2.1628. One way to explain this result is that the income effect on FAFH consumption is greater than the income effect on frozen food consumption since the cost of FAFH is much more expensive than the frozen prepared meals.

Summary and Conclusions

In this study, Becker's time allocation model, Heckman's selection bias-corrected technique, and Tobit model were applied to analyze the prices of wives' and husbands' time on the possibility and magnitude of making FAFH and frozen food purchases. Data used for the study are from the 1987 diary survey of the Consumer Expenditure Survey, Bureau of Labor Statistics, U.S. Department of Labor. The data were comprised of individual household expenditures on FAFH and frozen foods along with information about the household's economic and demographic characteristics.

FAFH and frozen food expenditures were specified as a function of age of wife, education of wife, wife's and husband's hourly offered wage, household annual nonearning income, race of wife, number of children, household size, household size squared, region, and household age-composition. This study suggests that there is no strong evidence to support the positive relationships between the prices of wives' and husbands' time, and the consumption of frozen food. However, households with higher wife's and husband's offered wages tend to have a larger FAFH consumption according to the results from this study.

Another proxy measurement for the prices of wives' and husbands' is the shadow wage approach instead of the offered wage. The shadow wages might give us another explanation in determining the household's consumption behavior. In addition, a comparison between dual parent households and single parent households is needed in further research.

References

Becker, G. (1965). A theory of the allocation of time. Economic Journal, 75, 493-517.

Bryant, W. K. (1986). Technical change and the family: An initia foray. In R.E. Deacon & W.E. Huffman (Eds.), Human Resources Research, 1887-1987 (pp. 117-126). Iowa State University: College of Home Economics.

Bryant, W. K. (1988). Durables and wives' employment yet again. Journal of Consumer Research, 15, 37-47..

Deaton, A., & Muellbauer, J. (1980). Economics and Consumer Behavior. Cambridge: Cambridge University Press.

Galbrian, J.J. (1973). Economics and the Public Purpose, Boston, MA: Houghton Mifflin.

Heckman, J.J. (1979). Sample selection bias as a specification error. Econometrica, 47, 153-61.

Hill, M.S., (1985). Patterns of time use. In F. T. Juster & F. P. Stafford (Eds.), Time, Goods, and Well-Being (Chap. 7). Ann Arbor: Survey Research Center, Institute for Social Research, University of Michigan.

Kinsey, J. (1983). Working wives and the marginal propensity to consume food away from home. American Journal of Agricultural Economics. 65:10-19.

Lippert, A., & Love, D.O.. (1986). Family expenditures for food away from home and prepared foods. Family Economics Review, 86(3), 9-14.

Maddala, G.S. (1983). Limited-Dependent and Qualitative Variables in Econometrics. New York: Cambridge University Press.

Mincer, J. (1962). Labor force participation of married women: A study of labor supply. Aspects of Labor Economics-- A Conference of the University-National Bureau Committee for Economic Research, report, National Bureau of Economic Research, Princeton, NJ: Princeton University Press.

Phlips, L. (1974). Applied Consumption Analysis. Amsterdam: North-Holland.

Prochaska, F., & Schrimper, R.A. (1973). Opportunity cost of time and other socioeconomic effects on away-from-home food

Consumption. *American Journal of Agricultural Economics*, 55(4), 595-603.

Redman, B.J. (1980). The impact of women's time allocation on expenditure for meals away from home and prepared foods. *American Journal of Agricultural Economics*, 62(2), 234-237.

Reynolds, A. (1988). *An Econometric Analysis of Fresh-Winter Vegetables Consumption: Extensions of the Tobit Model*. Dissertation, University of Florida.

Strober, M. H., & Weinberg, C.B. (1977). Working wives and major family expenditures. *Journal of Consumer Research*, 4, 141-47.

_____, (1980). Strategies used by working and non-working wives to reduced time pressures. *Journal of Consumer Research*, 6, 338-48.

Tobin, J. (1958). Estimation of relationships for limited dependent variables. *Econometrica*, 26, 24-36.

U.S. Department of Labor, Bureau of Labor Statistics. (1987). *Consumer Expenditure Survey*: (Interview Survey/Diary Survey), Washington: U.S. Government Printing Office.

Zick, C.D., & Bryant, W.K. (1983). Alternative strategies for pricing home work time. *Home Economics Research Journal*, 12, 133-44.

The Diversity of Income and Net Worth of the Elderly

Lucy Xiang Y. Zhong, Purdue University[1]
Patricia M. Titus, Purdue University[2]
Dixie Porter Johnson, Purdue University[3]

The present study examined the diversity in the financial status of the elderly, using the 1983 Survey of Consumer Finances. Income and net worth were used as the measures of financial status. Six characteristics were used to measure diversity: retirement status, age, race, sex, education and marital status. N-factor factorial designs were created. The effect of one independent variable was obtained controlling for the others. The results show that education, retirement status, and marital status were significant indicators of both income and net worth. In addition, age, sex, and race were significant in explaining the differences in net worth.

Introduction

During the last several decades, the economic status of the aged population as a whole has improved substantially (Grad, 1984; Hurd & Shoven, 1982; Minkler, 1989; Radner, 1986, 1988; Rich, 1983; Schulz, 1988). The poverty rate for the elderly has decreased and real income has risen significantly. Compared to younger households, the elderly have higher asset holdings and a higher rate of homeownership. Social Security benefits for the elderly have increased in real terms, whereas inflation-adjusted wages have declined (Congressional Budget Office, 1988). Pension plans and Medicare have also contributed to the improvement of the well-being of the elderly.

Although the elderly as a whole are better off, they are not a homogeneous group. Researchers have suggested that younger elderly versus older elderly, retired versus nonretired and married couples versus widowed women differ substantially in their economic position (Abbott, 1977; Burkhauser, Holden, & Myers, 1986; Radner, 1986; Taeuber, 1988).

Heterogeneity is one of the most important characteristics of the elderly to emerge from research. Culter (1991) stated that as people age, they become more dissimilar. There is a substantial diversity among the 31 million elderly. They are men and women, blue collar and white collar, urban, suburban and rural, young-old and old-old, whites and nonwhites. Zitter (1991) suggested that the older population was the most diverse of all age groups. As may be expected, their income levels and financial assets differ substantially.

The definition of economic status used to assess the financial well-being of the aged is very important and can have a significant impact on that assessment. Income is one of the most important criteria. However, income is not the only source contributing to the economic welfare of the aged. Radner (1988) pointed out that a complete assessment of the economic status of the elderly requires data about both wealth and income. But relatively little research has considered both wealth and income due to the lack of complete data. The objective of this study is to assess the financial status of the elderly, using the 1983 Survey of Consumer Finances. The diversity among the elderly will be explored. Both income and net worth will be used to examine the financial status.

Review of Literature

The elderly have the right and privilege to retire. The establishment of pension plans and various other governmental programs encourage them to retire. However, factors such as wage/salaries, education, occupation, financial variables and health are closely related to the retirement decision. High earnings create the expectation of high levels of post-retirement consumption and are associated with elements of job satisfaction. Mitchell and Fields (1982) concluded that higher wages resulted in late retirement. Education attainment may reflect a "taste" for work. Burkhauser (1980) found that years of schooling were inversely related to the probability of accepting early Social Security benefits. Duggan (1984) discussed three reasons

[1]Doctoral Student, Consumer Sciences and Retailing

[2]Assistant Professor, Consumer Sciences and Retailing

[3]Associate Professor, Consumer Sciences and Retailing

why education is directly related to labor force participation of older workers. First, the motivation to seek higher education often leads people to work longer than their less-educated counterparts. Second, higher education is associated with higher wages and better working conditions. Last, higher levels of education make it easier for older workers to find jobs.

Social psychological variables also affect retirement behavior. Quinn (1978) analyzed the relationship between job characteristics and the likelihood of early retirement. He found that early retirement was more likely from jobs with undesirable attributes such as high stress, monotony and great physical demands. Other studies show that retirees who work tend to be well educated, white-collar rather than blue-collar workers and self-employed (Duggan, 1984; Parnes & Less, 1983; Skoglund, 1979).

Economic factors also affect the retirement decision. Atchley (1988) concluded that individuals whose perceived financial resources in retirement as less than their perceived economic needs are expected to continue working to maintain their income level if physically able to do so (Atchley, 1988). Post-retirement employment apparently increases retirees' earnings and therefore, this group of individuals tends to have much higher earnings than the retired aged.

If the retired and the nonretired aged are grouped together, the total mean and median income for "the aged" is increased. This makes the financial situation in terms of income look better than it actually is for retired people and worse than it actually is for the employed. However, most research does not separate the nonretired from the retired for two reasons (Schulz, 1988). Most of the data do not provide for such a breakdown. In addition, given the data, it is difficult to set a cutoff line for the retired and nonretired. Schulz (1988) suggests a three-category tabulation --- full-time workers, part-time and unemployed workers, and the fully retired. In this study only two categories: the fully retired and the employed, are examined.

The life-cycle theory developed by Modigliani and Brumberg (1954) predicts that individuals save until retirement and then dissave after that point. The model implies that as the aged get older, their income and net worth will decline. Radner (1986) also suggested that in the aged population, as age increases, the size and composition of the family, labor force participation, and income types and amounts received differ substantially.

Traditionally the elderly are defined as those age 65 and over. However, this traditional definition is not adequate (Cutler, 1991). The multiple needs for products, service and medical care are not characterized accurately by a single denotation of 65 and over. The elderly in their

80s and 90s spend a large percentage of their income on medical care (Culter, 1991; Schulz, 1988). Schulz (1988) also reported that persons over age 84 were nearly twice as likely to be below the poverty level (21.3 percent) as those age 65 to 74 (11 percent). This is because the very old tend to have lower incomes than the average 65 year old due to asset depletion, erosion of pension income through years of inflation, and declining health and the related expenditures (Clark, 1990). Also, the elderly over 85 are more likely to have children who are retired or deceased, implying less family income available for intrafamily transfers to aged parents (Clark, 1990). In addition, the individuals age 65 and age 75 may have been working under different Social Security or pension laws. Age is another independent variable in the present study.

Life expectancy differs substantially, with women living longer than men on average. This creates a problem as people age --- there will be more widowed women than widowed men. The current study intends to investigate the economic status of people 65 years and older. As people age, the number of families with a female head tends to increase. Therefore, gender differences appear to be very important for the purpose of this study. Traditionally female households tend to have lower income and wealth than male households because of differences in education, work experience and other factors. Access to highly rewarding professional jobs, dominated for many years by men, continues to be out of the reach of most working women (Sokoloff, 1988; Bielby & Baron, 1986). Nor have women made inroads into well-paying jobs in the skilled trades which typically offer both security and pensions (Morgan, 1991). Five out of the ten top occupations of women are still sales clerks, secretaries, bookkeepers, cashiers, and typists (Kahne, 1985; Wellen & Peck, 1990).

Pensions are one of the important outcomes of labor-force participation. Currently retired women are significantly less likely than men to receive pensions (Morgan, 1991). When they receive pensions, the amount continues to be lower than that of male retirees (Packard & Reno, 1980). In 1984, two-thirds of individuals receiving pension benefits were men. On average, men aged 65 to 69 received $639 per month compared to $348 for women of the same age (Statistical Abstract, 1991). In 1984, 64 percent of women workers were in jobs where their employer offered a pension plan, but only 39 percent were vested in a pension plan, compared to 50.3 percent for men (Statistical Abstract, 1991). This difference exists, in part, because until recently, only 22 percent of adult women had ten years or more on their current job, a common minimum tenure to achieve vesting (Statistical Abstract, 1991).

Ethnicity is an important factor in understanding the aged population (Kravitz,

Pelaez, & Rothman, 1988). According to the projection of the U.S. Bureau of the Census, the elderly white population as a percentage of total elderly will decrease from 89.8 percent in 1990 to 78.7 percent in 2050 while the elderly black population will increase from 8.3 percent to 14 percent (Statistical Abstract, 1991). Although the percentage of the black elderly is increasing, their economic status is still worse than whites. Abbott (1977) reported 30 percent of the black elderly depended on public assistance payments versus 7 percent of white elderly. Another study also concluded that twice as many black aged, compared to white aged, needed medical and dental care but had delayed treatment because of financial problems (Shanas, 1977). The present study, due to sample constraints, groups race into whites and nonwhites.

Human capital theory states that education and on-the-job training help individuals to acquire specific skills and to improve their ability to obtain and assimilate information (Becker, 1975; Schwartz & Thornton, 1980; Welch, 1970). In addition, education helps individuals to perceive and understand changing conditions and to respond effectively. Becker (1975) views education as an investment in human capital which is similar to industry's investment in physical capital. The incentive to invest depends on the expected rate of return.

Morgan and David (1963) assessed the effect of education on income by controlling for other factors such as occupation, sex, race, and age. They found education, especially graduating from college, to be the main factor affecting income. Wolfle and Smith (1956) also suggested that education, mainly college graduation, is the major factor determining income. College graduates earn significantly more than non-college graduates. In addition, they concluded that the increase in income compensated for the costs of college and the delays in entering the work force.

Peck and Couchman (1987) noted that high educational levels increase the likelihood of employment, post-educational employment, and higher earnings. The mean monthly pension income of a person with a college degree was $950 compared to high school graduate who received a mean monthly pension income of $550 in 1980 (Szinovacz, 1982).

Marital status is another variable studied in the present study. As noted earlier, women on average have longer life expectancies than men, thus affecting marital status of the elderly. In 1988, two in three white men 75 years and older were married while two in three white women that age were widows (Taeuber 1988). Zitter (1991) pointed out that women over 65 years old are more likely to be widowed than married. This relationship is even more dramatic for women over age 75: approximately 50 percent of them live alone. It was projected that by the year 1995 more than three-fifths of women over age 75 will live by themselves.

A study conducted by Holden (1988) concluded that married women are economically better off than the women living alone although the former typically live in a larger household with higher consumption needs. She analyzed the Census data in 1980 and reported that while the personal income (after adjustment to family size) of married women was lower than that of single women, the poverty rate for married women was only 7 percent, versus 30 percent for women living alone. The higher personal incomes of women without husbands were far less than is necessary to achieve a level of economic well-being equivalent to that enjoyed by women whose husbands were alive.

Traditionally, the death of a husband often marks the point of economic reversal for the surviving wife. Burkhauser et al. (1986) reported that the change in marital status was the most important factor affecting the economic status of elderly women.

Ross, Danziger and Smolensky (1987) used the 1950 through 1980 decennial U.S. Census data to track individual birth cohorts. They determined that the transition from wife to widow led to a sharp and permanent decline in economic well-being.

The purpose of this research is to examine the diversity in the financial status of the aged using the 1983 Survey of Consumer Finances data. Income and net worth are used to measure financial status. The elderly are separated into subgroups by retirement status, age, sex, race, marital status and education.

Based upon the findings of the literature review, the following hypotheses are tested. All analyses are carried out controlling for other factors.

H1a: The employed elderly have higher income than the retired elderly.
H1b: The employed elderly have higher net worth than the retired elderly.
H2a: Elders ages 65-69 have higher income than those ages 70-74. Elders ages 75 and over have the lowest income.
H2b: Elders ages 65-69 have higher net worth than those ages 70-74. Elderly ages 75 and over have the lowest net worth.
H3a: Male elderly headed households have higher income than female headed elderly households.
H3b: Male elderly headed households have higher net worth than female elderly headed households.
H4a: Elderly whites have higher income than elderly nonwhites.
H4b: Elderly whites have higher net worth than nonwhites.
H5a: Elderly married couples have the highest

income, followed by separated/divorced/never married. The widowed elderly have the lowest income.

H5b: Married couples have highest net worth, followed by separated/divorced/never married. The widowed elderly have the lowest net worth.

H6a: Income increases with education attainment.

H6b: Net worth increases with education attainment.

H7: There are interactions among independent variables.

Methodology

The data for this study were from the 1983 Survey of Consumer Finances. The Survey was jointly sponsored by the Board of Governors of the Federal Reserve System and several other government agencies and administered by the Economic Behavior Program Division of the Survey Research Center at the University of Michigan (Avery, Elliehausen, & Canner, 1984). Personal interviews were conducted with the head of the household; in the case of a married couple, this was the person most knowledgeable about the family's finances (Avery et al., 1984). The person interviewed was encouraged to consult financial records and other family members to provide complete and accurate information. A multi-stage probability sampling design was used to select a sample representative of all families in the continental United States, excluding those on military bases. The survey includes 3,824 area probability respondents and a high income sample. To create the sample for this analysis, households with a head of age 65 and over were selected from the original data set. The high income sample was not used in this study. The respondents with negative income were deleted. The sample was weighted to an area probability sample. This resulted in a sample size of 546 elderly.

Household income was measured by summing the dollar amounts of wages and salaries; income from professional practice, business, or farm; income from IRAs and municipal bonds; taxable interest income; dividend income; sales of stocks/bonds or real estate; rent, trust income, or royalties from investment; workers or unemployment compensation income; child support and alimony; gifts and inheritance; food stamps, SSI, welfare, and other public assistance; retirement, annuity, pension; disability income and other income.

Net worth consisted of paper assets such as financial assets and cash value of whole life insurance, house, value of other properties, gross market value of vehicles, business with and without management interest, present value of private pension and present value of social security minus total liabilities on assets. Analytical procedures

In this study, it was expected that the difference in the mean levels of one independent variable would depend on the different levels of the other independent variables. Therefore, N-factor factorial designs were performed to simultaneously control for other variables. The mean of the response variable was compared over the levels of any one of the independent variables controlling for the others. Moreover, both main effects and interactions could be obtained through a factorial design.

SAS General Linear Models (GLM) procedure was used instead of analysis of variance (ANOVA) because of unbalanced cell sizes. In addition, multiple comparison procedure was performed to identify the groups which were significantly different. Contrast estimates were used to show the significance of one variable across all levels of the other variables.

Results

Five hundred forty-six elderly persons met the criteria of this study. Table 1 outlines the demographics of the respondents. The mean income of the fully retired was less than half of the mean income of the employed: $15,469 versus $36,417. The mean net worth of the retired was a little more than half that of the employed: $219,106 versus $389,780. The mean income for the age group 65-69 was $23,796, compared to $18,367 for age 70-74, and $11,360 for age 75 and over. The mean net worth for age group 65-69 was $287,164, compared to $264,425 for age 70-74, and $169,566 for age 75 and over. Compared to nonwhites who had a mean income of $7,332, whites had more than twice the mean income, $19,058. The same was true for net worth: whites with $257,281 compared to nonwhites with $97,554. Female households had less than half of the income of male households: $9,123 versus $21,509. Their net worth was also less than half that of male households: $127,881 versus $287,753. The separated/divorced/never-married households had the lowest income and net worth, compared to married couples and widowed households. Income and net worth increased as educational levels increased. Individuals with the highest education level (college degree) had the highest income ($44,931) and net worth ($507,059), compared to those with lowest education (grade 0-8) who had an income of $8,808 and net worth of $135,998.

Table 2 presents the results of the General Linear Models procedure for income. Education, retirement status, and marital status were statistically significant indicators of income amounts across all levels of other independent variables. However, age, race, and sex did not have a statistically significant effect on income amounts after controlling for other factors. In addition, the interaction between education and retirement status, education and age, education and sex, and retirement status and age, were statistically significant.

A contrast statement shows that college

graduates had significantly higher income than all of the other educational groups (p<.001). The employed and the retired differed greatly in their income amounts. Married couples differed from separated/divorced /never married at the .05 level and from the widowed at the .10 level.

Table 1
Mean income and net worth by demographic variables

Variable		Income ($)	Net worth ($)	n	(%)
Retirement Status:	Retired	15,469	219,106	495	(91)
	Employed	36,417	389,780	51	(9)
Age:	65-69	23,796	287,164	179	(33)
	70-74	18,367	264,425	155	(28)
	75 +	11,360	169,566	212	(39)
Race:	Whites	19,058	257,281	470	(86)
	Nonwhites	7,332	97,554	76	(14)
Sex:	Male	21,509	287,753	366	(67)
	Female	9,123	127,881	180	(33)
Marital Status:	Married	23,727	314,618	301	(55)
	S/D/N-M	8,934	111,948	64	(12)
	Widowed	9,950	146,252	181	(33)
Education:					
	Grade 0-8	8,808	135,998	222	(41)
	Grade 9-12	13,872	210,933	94	(17)
	H.S.diploma	16,423	251,574	108	(20)
	Some college	27,688	322,329	58	(11)
	College degree	44,931	507,059	64	(12)

Table 2
Results of GLM procedure for income

Source	DF	F value
EDUCATION	4	25.40 ***
RETIREMENT STATUS	1	16.45 ***
MARITAL STATUS	2	2.84 *
AGE	2	2.24
SEX	1	2.01
RACE	1	1.00
EDUCATION * RETIREMENT	4	5.44 ***
EDUCATION * AGE	8	1.78 *
EDUCATION * SEX	4	2.49 **
RETIREMENT STATUS* AGE	2	4.78 **

*** Significant at the .001 level.
** Significant at the .01 level.
* Significant at the .10 level.

Table 3 presents the results of the General Linear Models procedure for net worth. Education, retirement status, marital status, age, sex, and race were all statistically significant. This contrasts with previous results when explaining income; age, race, and sex were not significant.

The interactions between education and retirement status, education and age, retirement status and age were significant; the interaction between education and sex was not.

Table 3
Results of GLM procedure for net worth

Source	DF	F Value
EDUCATION	4	27.82 ***
RETIREMENT STATUS	1	26.95 ***
MARITAL STATUS	2	7.87 ***
AGE	2	2.43 *
SEX	1	3.11 *
RACE	1	4.58 **
EDUCATION * RETIREMENT	4	10.53 ***
EDUCATION * AGE	8	8.64 ***
RETIREMENT STATUS* AGE	2	5.68 **
EDUCATION * SEX	4	1.90

*** Significant at .001 level.
** Significant at .01 level.
* Significant at .10 level.

A contrast statement shows that the net worth of the individuals with a college degree and some college differed from the other three levels (grade 0-8, 9-12, and high school diploma). Individuals age 70 to 75 had significantly higher net worth than individuals age 65 to 69. Male households had significantly higher net worth than female households. Whites had significantly higher net worth than nonwhites.

Discussion

The results show that the elderly were economically diverse. Both measures of economic status, income and net worth, differed substantially among subgroups.

Education was one of the most important indicators of their economic status. College graduates had significantly higher income and net worth than individuals who did not have a college degree. The results support the postulation that the return on investment in education is substantial.

Individuals with some college had significantly higher net worth than those with less education, but it was not significant for income amount. Also from grade 0-8, grade 9-12 to high school graduates, the income and the net worth increased as education attainment increased. However, the difference was not significant.

The hypothesis about retirement status is also supported by the results. The employed elderly had much higher income and net worth than the retired. The results support the contention by Schulz (1988) that earnings contributed most to the higher income of the employed. In addition, the employed had higher accumulated net worth probably because the employed are better educated and have been working in better-paid positions

(Duggan, 1984; Parnes & Less, 1983).

Married couples compared to ever-married and never-married persons had the highest income and net worth. It was expected that the widowed elderly would have the lowest income and net worth. However, the results show that the separated/divorced/never married elderly were the most vulnerable sector. Compared to the separated/divorced/never married households, the widowed elderly may inherit property from their spouses. Also, the Social Security laws guarantee that after a husband's death, the wife's benefits are raised from 50 percent to 100 percent, which may increase the income and net worth of the widowed households.

The results demonstrate that basically both income and net worth show the same trend by subgroups of the elderly. However, compared to the income measurement, net worth differentiates more subgroups. Although certain groups do not differ significantly in income, their amount of net worth differs. Therefore, it may be concluded that net worth can provide a more precise picture of the diversity among the elderly.

Conclusions and Implications

The 1983 Survey of Consumer Finances was utilized to assess the diversity in financial status of the elderly in a cross-sectional design. Financial status was measured by income and net worth. The results from factorial designs and contrast comparisons demonstrate that income differences and net worth differences existed among the aged population.

Educational attainment, retirement status, and marital status were significant in explaining differences found in both measures of the financial status of the elderly. The income of individuals with the highest level of education was five times that of their counterparts with the lowest educational level. The net worth of individuals with the highest educational attainment was four times that of persons with the lowest educational attainment. Retirement status was also closely related to economic well-being of the aged. The retired were still in a relatively worse financial situation when compared to the employed. The employed aged were better off from both earnings and asset accumulation.

The research finding on marital status supports the hypothesis that married couples were better off than other types of households. An unexpected finding was regarding the separated/divorced/never-married households and the widowed households. It was hypothesized that the widowed households were the most vulnerable sector. However, the results show that the separated/divorced/never-married households had the lowest income and net worth.

Age, race and sex were also examined in this study. Although the mean values of income and net worth differed greatly among these subgroups, the effects were not statistically significant for income after controlling for other factors.

One of the reasons that age was not a significant factor for income may be that the range of age subgroups was too narrow, only five years apart. Future research should try other dividers if sample sizes allow.

Minority groups such as blacks, Hispanics, and Asians are culturally and economically diverse. The current study had to group them together because of the small sample sizes. The grouping results in a loss of information about each subgroup. Future studies should investigate the minorities by subgroups.

Gender differences may be closely related to other characteristics such as education, occupation and age. Therefore, after controlling for other factors, the effect of sex on income was not significant.

There are several limitations in this study. Underreporting of income and net worth amounts is an important problem in financial surveys. Studies show that in the Current Population Survey, property income was underestimated by more than 50 percent (Radner, 1987). In addition, underreporting differs by age and rises as age increases (Radner, 1982). The current study did not adjust for underestimates. Thus, underreporting could deflate the mean income and net worth.

In dividing the elderly into subgroups, cell sizes were very small, decreasing the reliability of the findings. A larger sample of elderly is recommended for future research to allow investigation in more detailed grouping of race, employment status and marital status.

Future research should also consider using income and net worth per capita to obtain the estimates adjusted for household sizes. As noted above, only financial assets were used. Further research should include the value of home and other properties.

The diversity of the financial status of the elderly, as measured by income and net worth, suggests that policy makers may want to consider the varying impact of proposed and existing policies related to the elderly.

The results by race are mixed. Controlling for other factors, income by race did not differ significantly in 1983; but net worth did. Further research in this area should be given high priority because of the projected increase of minority groups as a percentage of the elder population in the United States (Statistical Abstract, 1991).

The importance of education cannot be overemphasized. Policies related to access to education are critical as educational attainment affects households throughout their life cycle. The present study measures this impact in the later years; but the time for intervention is at a much earlier stage of the life cycle.

When education is controlled, the financial status of separated/divorced/never-married households may in part be related to employment patterns not directly measured in the present study. Irregular or part-time employment affects not only income but also future retirement benefits. Laws governing vesting are critical, as well as regulations that facilitate the offering of pension plans by employers.

Acknowledgement

The authors would like to thank Dr. Richard Widdows for his helpful comments in the earlier version of this manuscript and the Federal Reserve for providing the data for the analyses.

References

Abbott, J. (1977). Socioeconomic characteristics of the elderly: Some black-white differences. Social Security Bulletin, 40(7), 16-42.

Atchley, R. (1988). Social forces and aging: An introduction to social gerontology. Belmont, CA: Wadsworth.

Avery, R. B., & Elliehausen, G. E. (1985). 1983 Survey of Consumer Finances: Technical Manual and Codebook. Board of Governors of the Federal Reserve System.

Avery, R. B., Elliehausen, G. E., & Canner, G. B. (1984). Survey of consumer finances, 1983. Federal Reserve Bulletin, 44(1), 3-15.

Becker, G. S. (1975). Human capital (2nd ed.). New York: Columbia University.

Bielby, W. T., & Baron, J. N. (1986). Men and women at work: Sex segregation and statistical discrimination. American Journal of Sociology, 91(1), 759-799.

Burkhauser, R. V. (1980). The early acceptance of social security: An asset maximization approach. Industrial and Labor Relations Review, 33(4), 484-492.

Burkhauser, R. V., Holden, K. C., & Myers, D. A. (1986). Marital disruption and poverty. Department of Economics. Nashville, TN: Vanderbilt University.

Clark, R. L. (1990). Income maintenance policies in the United States. Handbook of Aging and the Social Sciences, 3rd ed. Binstock, R. H. & L. K. George (Eds.). San Diego: Academic Press. 382-397.

Congressional Budget Office (1988). Trends in family income: 1970-1986. Washington DC: U.S. Government Office.

Culter, N. E. (1991). Happy birthday to the gerontology 5,000. Journal of the American Society of CLU & ChFC, 44(6), 23-25.

Grad, S. (1984). Incomes of the aged and nonaged, 1950-82. Social Security Bulletin, 47(6), 3-17.

Holden, K. C. (1988). Poverty and living arrangements among older women: Are changes in the well-being of elderly women understated? Journal of Gerontology, 43(1), S22-S27.

Hurd, M., & Shoven, J. B. (1982). Real income and wealth of the elderly. American Economic Review, 72(5), 314-318.

Kahne, H. (1985). Not yet equal: Employment experience of older women and older men. International Journal of Aging and Human Development, 22, 1-11.

Kravitz, S. L., Pelaez, M. B., & Rothman, M. B. (1988). Delivering services to elders: Responsiveness to populations in need. In Bass S.A., E.A. Kutza, & F.M. Torres-Gil (Eds.). Diversity in Aging. Glenview: IL: Scott, Foreman. 47-71.

Lopata, H. Z., & Norr, K. F. (1980). Changing commitments of American women to work and family roles. Social Security Bulletin, 43(6), 3-14.

Minkler, M. (1989). Gold in gray: Reflections on business's discovery of the elderly market. The Gerontological Society of America, 29(1), 17-23.

Mitchell, O.S., & Fields, G.S. (1982). The effects of pensions and earnings on retirement: A review essay. In Research in Labor Economics Vol.15. Ehrenberg, R.G. (Ed.). Greenwich, CT: JAI Press. 115-155.

Modigliani, F. & Brumberg, R. (1954). Utility analysis and the consumption function: An interpretation of cross-section data. In Kurihara K.K. (Ed.). Post-Keynesian Economics. New Brunswick, NJ: Rutgers University. 388-436.

Morgan, L. A. (1991). Economic security of older women: Issues and trends for the future. Growing old in America (4th ed.). B. B. Hess, & E. W. Markson (Eds.). New Brunswick, NJ: Transaction. 275-292.

Morgan, J., & David, M. (August, 1963). Education and income. Quarterly Journal of Economics,

423-437.

O'Rand, A., & Henretta, J. C. (1982). Delayed career entry, industrial pension structure, and early retirement in a cohort of unmarried women. American Sociological Review, 47, 365-373.

O'Rand, A. M., & Krecker, M. L. (1988). Pension, unions and small firms: Trends in pension protection in the workplace. Proceedings of Annual Scientific Meeting of the Gerontological Society of America. San Francisco. 314-340.

Packard, M. D., & Reno, V. P. (1980). A look at very early retirees. In Issues in Contemporary Retirement, R. Ricardo-Campbell, & E. P. Lazear (Eds.). Stanford, CA: Hoover Institution. 243-265.

Parnes, H. S., & Less, L. (1983). From work to retirement: The experience of a national sample of men. Columbus, OH: Ohio State University.

Peck, C. J., & Couchman, G. M. (1987). Work history patterns of midlife women. Paper presented at the meeting of the American Home Economics Association. indianapolis, IN.

Quinn, J.F. (1978). Job characteristics and early retirement. Industrial Relations, 17(10), 315-323.

Radner, D. B. (1982). Distribution of family income: Improved estimates. Social Security Bulletin, 45(7), 13-21.

Radner, D. B. (1987). Money incomes of aged and nonaged family units, 1967-84. Social Security Bulletin, 50(8), 9-28.

Rich, S. (1983, August 19). Census finds elderly's after-tax income higher than average. The Washington Post.

Ross, C. M., Danziger, S., & Smolensky, E. (1987). Interpreting changes in the economic status of the elderly, 1949-1979. Contemporary Policy Issues, 5(4), 98-112.

Schulz, J. H. (1988). The economics of aging (4th ed.). Dover: Auburn House.

Schwartz, E., & Thornton, R. (1980). Overinvestment in college training? The Journal of Human Resources, 15(1), 121-123.

Shanas, E. (1977). National survey of the aged. Final Report to the Department of Health and Human Services.

Skoglund, J. (1979). Work after retirement. Aging and Work, 2, 103-112.

Sokoloff, N. J. (1988). Evaluating gains and losses by black and white women and men in the professions, 1960-1980. Social Problems, 35(1), 36-53.

Statistical Abstract of the United States. (1991, 111th ed.). U.S. Department of Commence, Bureau of the Census.

Szinovacz, M. (1982). Women's retirement. Beverly Hills, CA: Sage.

Taeuber, C. (1988). Diversity: The dramatic reality. In Bass, S. A., E. A. Kutza, & P.M. Torres-Gil (Eds.). Diversity in Aging. Glenview, IL: Scott, Foreman. 1-45.

Welch, F. (1970). Education in production. The Journal of Political Economy, 78(1), 35-59.

Wellen, P.D., & Peck, C.J. (1990). Effects of human capital factors on income and net asset amounts of older women. Home Economics Research Journal, 19(2), 107-119.

Wolfle, D., & Smith, J.G. (1956). The occupational value of education for superior high-school graduates. Journal of Higher Education, 27(4), 201-232.

Zitter, M. (1991). Older population: Most diverse of all American age groups. Healthcare Financial Management, 42(12), 38-42.

Elderly and Out-Of-Pocket Home Care: Are Expenses Financially Catastrophic?

Marlene S. Stum, University of Minnesota[1]
Jean W. Bauer, University of Minnesota[2]
Paula J. Delaney, University of Minnesota[3]

Are out-of-pocket home care expenditures a source of financial catastrophe among disabled elderly persons? Using data from the 1984 National Long Term Care Survey this study used 3 definitions of catastrophic out-of-pocket home care expenses to examine expenditure-to-ability to pay concepts. The extent and characteristics of elderly in this sample with catastrophic expenses varied widely depending upon the definition utilized. Implications for long term care policy development and cost-containment are discussed.

Policymakers continue to strive to provide quality long term care to older Americans at costs that are less financially burdensome for individuals or society. Health policy and delivery systems are struggling to address this goal within the shifting realities of people living longer after the onset of chronic disease and disability, aging of the baby boom cohort, dramatic growth in the number of individuals 85 years and older, and preference for community-based care (Rowland & Lyons, 1991). Of all groups in society, the elderly are most likely to utilize health care services and incur catastrophic health care costs (Feder, 1991; Holden & Smeeding, 1990). Varied policies have been proposed and debated to reduce the risk of incurring catastrophic health care costs by the elderly or their families.

While catastrophic, or financially burdensome, costs have been the center of attention, the meaning of "catastrophic" has rarely been consistent. Some research and policy discussions have focused on "catastrophic" high costs incurred for a variety of health care services (e.g. hospital, physician, nursing home) and the resulting private burden via out-of-pocket expenditures (Schwartz, Naierman, & Birnbaum, 1978; Wyszewianski, 1986). Such studies consistently find that a small proportion of the population are high users and account for the majority of health care expenditures (Liu, Manton, & Liu, 1985; U.S. Health and Human Services, 1982). Few studies and policy discussions have focused on "catastrophic" as health care costs relative to a person's financial resources or ability to pay (Feder, Moon, & Scanlon, 1987).

In this study, the question of whether home care expenses are financially catastrophic is examined using three definitions of "catastrophic" and a sample of disabled elderly with out-of-pocket home care expenditures. Catastrophic definitions are developed on the assumption that burden is a function of expenditures relative to ability to pay. Characteristics of elders meeting the varied definitions of "catastrophic" are contrasted to help understand potential target elderly when addressing private financial burden.

A limited number of studies have examined non-institutionalized long term care costs alone or as a portion of total out-of-pocket health care expenditures (Liu, Manton & Liu, 1985). No studies examined catastrophic home care costs by comparing expenditures relative to an ability to pay. Current gaps in public and private programs increase the risk of financial insecurity for elderly incurring long term care expenses, especially from community-based care (Feder, 1991). Paid home care is one means of helping individuals with routine and often repetitive tasks of daily living. Home care services can range from social (homemaker/chore assistance, aid with bathing and toileting) to health related services (nursing and nurses aides, monitoring of medication).

As long term care policy develops and cost-containment is debated, it is essential to clarify the definition of "catastrophic" and understand patterns of home care expenditures. Public policy issues that will affect some of our most vulnerable citizens will depend upon the different conceptions of what constitutes a catastrophic long term care expenditure.

Literature Review

Defining Catastrophic Costs

Despite the interest in catastrophic health care costs and cost-containment, there appears to be no consensus among policymakers or researchers as to what constitutes catastrophic health care expenditures for an individual or a family. Wyszewianski (1986) suggested that definitions of catastrophic are generally either: 1) "high cost" when expenses exceed a specified amount regardless of source of payment or ability to pay; or 2)

---

[1]Assistant Professor, Family Social Science

[2]Associate Professor, Family Social Science

[3]Graduate Student, Family Social Science

"financially catastrophic" when expenditures are large in relation to ability to pay. Schwartz, Naierman & Birnbaum (1978) examined catastrophic illness episodes in which a person incurred $5000 or more of medical expenses in a calendar year. Policy proposals commonly use high cost definitions by recommending coverage for persons with annual health expenditures in selected services above a certain dollar amount (Feder, Moon & Scanlon, 1987).

Financially catastrophic definitions vary according to what is included as resources or ability to pay. Wyszewianski (1986) suggested that ability to pay is determined by the extent of third party coverage and other resources available to pay for care. Specifically, ability to pay for health care should consider total financial resources (third-party coverage, income, accumulated assets) minus total nonhealth, nondiscretionary expenditures. Most research and policy proposals, however, only consider third-party coverage and income (Wyszewianski, 1986). Third-party coverage is considered when out-of-pocket expenditures are focused upon, thereby deducting the amount covered by any third party.

A majority of the research did not conceptually define financially catastrophic but operationalized the concept as a ratio of out-of-pocket expenditures to family income (Berki, 1986; Berki, Wyszewianski, Magilavy, & Lepkowski, J.M., 1985; Coughlin, Liu, & McBride, 1992). Berki (1986) specifically referred to expenditures for medical care becoming financially catastrophic when endangering a family's ability to maintain its customary standard of living and compared the ratio of out-of-pocket expenditures to family income. Coughlin, Liu, and McBride (1992) recognized the importance of other family financial resources beyond income on ability to pay, but their data were limited to income.

Policy proposals and programs are more likely to recognize other resources or variations in the obligations people face. For example, the Medicaid program takes into account certain assets as well as differences in obligation by recognizing family size. A catastrophic illness program in Maine had qualifications of exceeding costs equal to 30% of net income plus 10% of net worth over $20,000 (Wyszewianski, 1986). Moon (1977) and Holden & Smeeding (1990) emphasized the importance of considering both income and liquid and illiquid assets when examining the economic well-being of individuals over 65 years of age.

High cost and catastrophic expenditure definitions also differ on the specific thresholds for burdensome outlays. At what point do expenditures become burdensome? Wyszewianski (1986) suggested that if the focus is cost containment a threshold should capture the group accounting for the disproportionate amount of expenditures. Current federal income tax policy suggests that a logical threshold is when out-of-

pocket health care expenses exceed 7.5% of adjusted gross income. Researchers typically included 10-20% as the catastrophic threshold (Feder, Moon & Scanlon, 1987; Wyszewianski, 1986).

Characteristics of Elders With Catastrophic Expenses

Who is more likely to have catastrophic health care expenses? Income has consistently been found to be a distinguishing variable, with lower income and below poverty families and elderly more likely to have catastrophic health care expenditures (Berki, 1986; Berki, et al., 1985; Kovar, 1986; Thomas & Kelman, 1990; Wyszewianski, 1986). Coughlin, Liu and McBride's (1992) results suggest that out-of-pocket expenses for drugs and physician services were more likely to be catastrophic for the poor, whereas out-of-pocket expenses for nursing home and hospital services were likely to be burdensome regardless of income level. Individuals with catastrophic health care expenses are also more likely to experience a lack of third party coverage, whether private insurance or public programs such as Medicaid (Berki, 1986; Berki, et al., 1985; Thomas & Kelman, 1990; Wyszewianski, 1986).

Personal characteristics associated with catastrophic burdens have included living arrangement (living alone); marital status (one person families); age (over 65 years); race (Blacks), and education (higher) (Berki, et al, 1985; Kovar, 1986; Coughlin, Liu, & McBride, 1992; Rossiter & Wilensky, 1982; Thomas & Kelman, 1990). Health status and the impact of need also appear to be significantly related to catastrophic expenses. Individuals with catastrophic burden are more likely to report greater need for health care as reflected in prior nursing home use, poor self assessed health, and greater functional limitations or disabilities (Collins & Stommel, 1991; Coughlin, Liu, & McBride, 1992; Kovar, 1986; Thomas & Kelman, 1990).

Methodology

Data Source and Sample

Data used in this analysis are from the 1984 National Long Term Care Survey (NLTCS) conducted by the Bureau of the Census and sponsored by the Department of Health and Human Services. The 1984 NLTCS is the second-wave in a longitudinal survey of the personal characteristics and use of health-related services by non-institutionalized disabled elderly in the United States, a sub-group at risk of long term care expenses. This dataset provided the best and most recent home care expenditure data available at the time to address the research questions. The 1982 NLTCS interviewed a random sample of Medicare enrollees with the presence of one or more limitations in activities of daily living (ADLs) or instrumental activities of daily living (IADLs) lasting 3 months or longer. The 1984 community-dwelling sample (N=5934) consists of respondents from 1982 who were re-interviewed, individuals who turned 65 between 1982 and 1984, and individuals screened out in 1982 but who now met the chronically disabled criteria. Further methodological details concerning the 1982 and 1984 surveys and sampling procedures have been described elsewhere (Macken, 1985; Manton, 1988).

A subsample of respondents (N=859) reporting out-of-pocket expenditures for home care help with ADLs, IADLs, or nursing services provided the sample for this study. A majority of the sample was female (74%), White (92%), widowed (56%) or married (30%), and between the ages of 75 to 84 (45%) or 65-74 years (30%). Forty percent had 9-12th grade education levels and 36% had 8th grade or less education. A majority of home care users had fairly high levels of functional ability, no prior nursing home use (84%), and perceived their health as good (31%), fair (31%) or poor (26%). The most frequent family size was one member (54%), followed by 2 (36%). Just over half of the sample (53%) had no children within 60 miles, and 25% had at least one. A majority (76%) reported no unpaid helpers. Elderly in this sample lived in both rural (55%) and urban (45%) locations and were distributed fairly evenly across the four major census regions.

Operational Definitions

Financially Catastrophic. In this study, the focus was on identifying elderly who had "financially catastrophic" home care expenses rather than "high cost" home care. Three different approaches were utilized to calculate a person's ability to pay. While an overwhelming majority of studies have only considered family income as ability to pay, in this study family income was adjusted for selected non-discretionary expenses, and the availability of wealth (assets and home equity) was considered. In Catastrophic Definition 1, a ratio was calculated of out-of-pocket home care expenditures to family income minus shelter and food costs (see Table 1). Total out-of-pocket home care expenditures were calculated by adding the actual dollar amounts reported by the respondent in the last month for home care assistance with ADLs, IADLs or nursing services. Family income versus per capita income was utilized based on the assumption that family members pool their resources. All sources of monthly earned and unearned income for all family members were summed to create total family income. Shelter and food costs are basic necessities and a consistent measure was possible for all persons in the sample. Shelter cost was based on the reported monthly home mortgage payments or rent value. Homeowners with no outstanding mortgage and non-cash renters were assigned a value of zero for shelter cost. Food cost was calculated for each household using the United States Department of Agriculture (USDA) monthly cost of food at home estimate (low-cost plan, January 1984).

Individuals were considered to have financially catastrophic expenses when the expenditure-to-adjusted income ratio was greater than .10 or greater than -.20. This meant that catastrophic included households for whom home care expenses were 10% or greater than their adjusted income (a positive ratio); and households for whom shelter and food costs were greater than income, therefore leaving no income to cover home care expenditures (a negative ratio). Other studies of health care expenditures to income have not adjusted income and therefore have not had the potential for negative ratios. The catastrophic thresholds of .10 and -20 are arbitrary, but were selected given common use in the literature of ratios greater than 10% as catastrophic (Berki, 1986; Feder, Moon, Scanlon, 1987; Wyszewianski, 1986). A larger margin of error was allowed for individuals with a negative ratio because food costs were imputed.

In Catastrophic Definition 2, as recommended by Moon (1977) and Holden and Smeeding (1990), wealth was included in determining an elderly person's ability to pay. Respondents who met the threshold for expenditures-to-adjusted income and also reported no assets (savings accounts, certificates of deposit, stocks, bonds, mutual funds, etc.) were considered to have catastrophic expenditures. While it would be ideal to consider the dollar amount of assets available, the amount of missing data limited the focus to whether assets were or were not reported as available.

Catastrophic Definition 3 added a home equity threshold to the equation as an additional indicator of wealth and ability to pay. Home equity was calculated by taking reported home market value less the outstanding mortgage with both coded into identical proportional scales (range 2.0 to 20.0). Home owners with no mortgage were assigned a mortgage value of 0.0; renters were assigned a home equity value of 0.0. Respondents meeting all criteria for Definitions 1 and 2 and reporting home equity less than the sample median of 3.5 (equivalent to $20-35,000) were considered to have financially catastrophic home care expenditures. Holden and Smeeding (1990) recommended including home equity and utilized the median value as measures of financial insecurity for individuals 65 years and older.

Explanatory Variables. Based on the literature three types of individual characteristics were selected which are likely to influence whether elderly persons experience catastrophic home care costs relative to ability to pay. The Andersen and Newman (1973) behavioral model of health services utilization identifies similar characteristics of individuals and categorizes them into: a) predisposing factors (personal characteristics which exist prior to health need and influence use and resources such as gender, marital status, race, education); b) need factors (health status serving as stimulus for home care use, including self-report, functional limitations, prior medical use; and c) enabling factors (family social support and community resources). Table 1 displays definitions, coding, means and standard deviations for all catastrophic definitions and explanatory variables.

Table 1
Catastrophic and Explanatory Variables Mean, Standard Deviation and Coding Algorithm

Variable		M	SD	Coding Algorithm
Financially Catastrophic				
Def (1) $\dfrac{\text{Out-of-Pocket Expenditures}}{\text{Income-(Shelter Cost + Food Cost)}}$		.45	.49	0 = No, 1 = Yes
Def (2) $\dfrac{\text{Expenditures}}{\text{Income-(Shelter Cost + Food Cost)}}$	and No Assets	.11	.32	0 = No, 1 = Yes
Def (3) $\dfrac{\text{Expenditures}}{\text{Income-(Shelter Cost + Food Cost)}}$	and No Assets and home equity ≤ median	.09	.28	0 = No, 1 = Yes
Predisposing Characteristics				
Age		79.06	7.57	Actual # of years
Gender			.44	0=Male, 1=Female
Marital Status			.64	1=Married, 2=Widowed 3=Divorced, Separated, Never Married
Race			.28	1=White, 2=Other
Education		10.35	3.74	Actual # of years
Need Characteristics				
Functional Ability		.72	.27	Index based on weighted ADLs & IADLs 0-1 range with 1=highest functional ability
Perceived Health		2.72	.98	1=Excellent, 2=Good, 3=Fair, 4=Poor
Prior Nursing Home Use Ever			.37	1=Yes, 2=No
Enabling Characteristics				
Family				
Size		1.65	.95	Actual # of household members
Helpers		.34	.71	Actual # of unpaid helpers
Unpaid Helper Days		.56	1.74	Actual # of unpaid helper days
Children		.82	1.14	Actual # of children within 60 minutes traveling time
Community				
Population Density			.50	1=rural, 2=urban
Census			1.02	1=northeast,2=north central,3=south,4=west

Note: Means have been deleted for categorical variables

Analysis

   To address the question of whether home care expenses for disabled elders were financially catastrophic, frequency distributions were calculated for each definition of catastrophic. Profiles of elders who met each catastrophic definition were then compared with those who did not met catastrophic definitions using chi-square analyses or two-tailed pooled variance t-tests for significant differences (p≤ .05).

Findings

Extent of Financially Catastrophic Home Care

   Disabled elderly reported average monthly out-of-pocket expenditures for home care of $173 (1984 dollars). Home care expenditure levels were highly skewed as one-half made out-of-pocket payments of $32 or less per month, whereas only 10% reported paying more than $496 per month.
Home care expenditure patterns were similar to other types of health care service expenditures with a small percent of individuals accounting for the greatest proportion of the total out-of-pocket expenditures.

   The percentage distribution for the ratio of out-of-pocket home care expenses to adjusted income was as follows: greater than -.21 (9.0%), -.20 to -.01 (2.8%), 0 to .05 (41%), .06 to .10 (13.8%), .11 to .20 (10.1%), .21 to .50 (11.7%), .50 to 1.0 (4.3%), 1.01 and greater (7.3%). The mean ratio of expenditures-to-adjusted income was .125 and the median .05. When using Catastrophic Definition 1, 45% (N=369) of the disabled elderly would be considered to have catastrophic expenditures. Adding no assets in Catastrophic Definition 2, 11.5% (N=94) of the sample had catastrophic expenditures. The percentage qualifying is reduced to 8.8% (N=72) when home equity is added in Catastrophic Definition 3.

Characteristics of Elderly With Catastrophic Expenses

   Predisposing, need, and enabling characteristics of elderly with financially catastrophic expenditures and elderly without catastrophic expenditures were compared to determine which variables emerge as significantly related to elderly using each of the catastrophic definitions. At least one variable from each predisposing, need, and enabling category was significantly related to elderly meeting Catastrophic Definition 1 (p≤05). Elderly in this catastrophic group were more likely older, more disabled or with less functional ability, had prior use of a nursing home, and were from larger households than elderly not meeting this definition of catastrophic expenditures.

   When elderly with and without catastrophic expenditures are compared using Catastrophic Definitions 2 and 3, predisposing variables were more likely significant with only one enabling variable and no need variables significantly related. Elderly meeting Catastrophic Definition 2,

were more likely than their non-catastrophic counterparts to be divorced, separated or never married; Black or Hispanic; less educated; and receive more unpaid helper days from family members. Elderly meeting Catastrophic Definition 3 differed from elderly in Catastrophic 2 only in regards to gender; they were more likely to be male.

Discussion

   Few studies on catastrophic costs among the elderly have examined out-of-pocket long term care costs relative to a person's ability to pay. Questions regarding the extent to which home care expenses are financially catastrophic and for whom were addressed in this study. Because the sample was a select subgroup of the aged population, those with functional limitations, results from this study are not generalizable to the entire elderly population. On the other hand, analysis of this sample presents an informative picture of a subset of the elderly population that is most vulnerable to long term care costs and most likely to be targeted in publicly financed long term care programs. Expenditure data were limited to a time period of one month and may be high or low relative to annual expenditures or episodes of care expenditures for any respondent. In addition, given the data is from 1984, changes in home care coverage, supply, acceptance, and the ability of elders to pay, need to be taken into account.

   In this sample of disabled elderly the extent to which out-of-pocket home care expenses were financially catastrophic depended markedly on how "financially catastrophic" and, specifically, ability to pay was defined. As ability to pay was expanded beyond adjusted income to include assets and home equity the extent to which home care expenses appeared a problem for most individuals was greatly reduced. Almost half of the sample (45%) were defined as having catastrophic expenses when adjusted income was considered, whereas closer to one-tenth (11% to 8.8%) were defined as having financially burdensome problems when wealth was also considered.

   The sample spent on average 12.5% of their adjusted income just on home care expenses, with a majority (54.8%) falling between and 0 and 10%. The average ratio in this study is similar to average proportions of selected health care expenses to family income (non-adjusted) found for other elderly and non-elderly populations (Kovar, 1986; Thomas & Kelman, 1990). Clearly, the total number considered to be financially catastrophic depends on the threshold selected (>10%, 20%, 30% of income).

   The results in this study also reinforce the shifting profile of elderly with catastrophic expenses as definitions for financially catastrophic are varied. Such findings reinforce the importance of the definition used in establishing public policy. No single variable nor any one of the three categories (predisposing, need, enabling) was significantly related to all three definitions of catastrophic expenses. If elderly are targeted on the basis of Catastrophic Definition 1, need, age, and household member size would appear relevant. Need variables had the strongest relationship and perhaps higher expenses are the driving force behind the catastrophic burden of these elders. In comparison, if elders are targeted on the basis of Catastrophic Definitions 2 or 3 when wealth is considered, elderly with less chance to accumulate high incomes or wealth would be targeted (minorities, less educated, divorced, separated, or never married). For this group an inability to pay is perhaps behind their catastrophic burden. In addition, elders meeting Catastrophic Definitions 2 and 3 are also receiving a great deal of help from informal sources.   Such results refute the presence of a substitution effect between paid and unpaid home care. The quantity of informal help received is related to home care expenditures and not the number of helpers nor the number of children living nearby.

Implications

As long term care policy continues to be debated, questions regarding catastrophic expenses for an aging population and the role of private and public resources must be clarified and understood. The lack of public and private insurance coverage for home care has led to many questions regarding the financial burden for elders. Defining what is financially catastrophic for a diverse elderly population is not obvious. As this study suggests, a clear distinction as to the meaning of financially catastrophic private costs requires that definitions should explicitly address: a) the definition of ability to pay; b) the threshold level for financial burden; c) the unit of observation (individual or family); d) the time span of expenditures; and e) the health care services included in expenditures. Unforeseen and unintended policy outcomes could be minimized if each of these elements was more carefully understood and held consistent with broader societal values and objectives.

In this study of home care expenditures incurred in one month, the results clearly reinforce the importance of definitions of ability to pay. The definition(s) used to determine whether home care expenses are financially catastrophic will directly and indirectly impact elders, their family members, and society. Which ratio definition best assesses an elderly consumer's ability to handle home care expenses? The answer is a question of values and whether one is looking at cost-containment from an individual or societal perspective. Persons who believe that individuals should save during the working years to protect themselves against potential financial risks in retirement and old age, as well as policy makers wanting to limit state or federal budgets for long term care, would most likely argue for Definitions 2 and 3. Persons who believe that individuals should not have to spend their life savings on long term care, whether nursing home or home care, would most likely argue that Definition 1 is most appropriate.

Should all or part of an individual's wealth such as assets and home equity be spent on long term care expenses, transferred to family members, or passed on as inheritance? Discussions of what is financially catastrophic, especially for an elderly population, should reflect consensus about the types of resources that a person can and should use in defraying the costs of care. Dilemmas regarding ability to pay are not new to many family members and financial planning professionals struggling with decisions on nursing home costs and transferral of assets to qualify for Medicaid (Bacon, Ceitman, Ahmad, & Ainina, 1989).   The promotion but relatively limited use of reverse home mortgages to assist in paying for long term care suggests certain societal and individual trends (Jacobs & Weissert, 1986). Ethical dilemmas about equity, justice, and other social values will only escalate for family members and society as long term care needs of an aging population tangle with differences in ability to pay.

Not only do varied catastrophic definitions play a role in understanding the current extent of and estimates of cost-containment problems, such definitions also influence which elders will be targeted. The varied profiles of elderly with catastrophic expenses which emerged in this study reinforce the need to more fully understand the role predisposing, need, and enabling variables play in catastrophe and burden. Additional empirical information on characteristics of persons incurring specifically defined catastrophic home care costs using varied data sources would be useful as policy reform occurs.

Many long term care policy proposals currently focus on defining catastrophe from a medical not an economic sense. For example, having problems with 3 or more ADLs is frequently included as eligibility criteria for home care (The Pepper Commission, 1990; Rowland & Lyons, 1991). While research does suggest that elderly with more functional limitations are more likely to have higher expenditures, ability to pay concepts are ignored in strictly medical definitions. Equity issues related to medical need and ability to bear the financial burden should be discussed in relation to each other as policies and programs develop. The challenges of providing quality long term care at costs that are less financially burdensome will no doubt expand with the aging population as a consumer issue in the next century.

References

Andersen, R., & Newman, J.F. (1973). Societal and individual determinants of medical care utilization in the United States. Milbank Memorial Fund Quarterly, 51(1), 95-124.

Bacon, P., Ceitman, L., Ahmad, K., & Ainina, M. (1989). Long-term catastrophic care: A financial planning perspective. Journal of Risk & Insurance, 56(1), 146-154.

Berki, S.E. (1986). A look at catastrophic medical expenses and the poor. Health Affairs, 15(4), 138-145.

Berki, S.E., Wyszewianski, L., Magilavy, L.J., & Lepkowski, J.M. (1985). Families with high out-of-pocket health services expenditures relative to their income, (Final report). Washington, D.C.: U.S. Dept of Health & Human Services.

Collins, C., & Stommel, M. (1991). Out-of-pocket expenditures by family caregivers of dementia patients residing in the community. Home Health Care Services Quarterly, 12(4), 29-43.

Coughlin, T.A., Liu, K., & McBride, T.D. (1992). Severely disabled elderly persons with financially catastrophic health care expenses: Sources and determinants. Gerontologist, 32(3), 391-403.

Feder, J. (1991). Paying for home care: The limits of current programs. In D. Rowland & B. Lyons (Eds.), Financing home care: Improving protection for disabled elderly people (pp. 27-50). Baltimore, MD: Johns Hopkins University Press.

Feder, J., Moon, M., & Scanlon, W. (1987). Medicare reform: Nibbling at catastrophic costs. Health Affairs, Winter, 5-20.

Holden, K., & Smeeding, T. (1990). The poor, the rich, and the insecure elderly caught in-between. The Milbank Quarterly, 68(2), 191-219.

Jacobs, B., & Weissert, W. (1986). Helping protect the elderly and public against catastrophic long-term care costs. Journal of Policy Analysis & Management, 5(2), 378-383.

Kovar, M. G. (1986). Expenditures for the medical care of elderly people living in the community in 1980. Milbank Quarterly, 64(1), 100-132.

Liu, K., Manton, K.G., & Liu, B.M. (1985). Home care expenses for the disabled elderly. Health Care Financing Review, 7(2), 51-58.

Macken, C. (1985). Descriptive profile of the functionally impaired aged living in the community: Findings from the 1982 long-term care survey. (Draft Report). Baltimore, MD: Office of Research and Demonstrations, Health Care Financing Administration.

Manton, K. (1988). A longitudinal study of functional change and mortality in the United States. Journal of Gerontology, 43(5), S153-161.

Moon, M. (1977). The measurement of economic welfare. New York: Academic Press.

Rossiter, L. F., & Wilensky, G. R. (1982). Out-of-pocket expenditures for personal health services, (data preview 13). Washington, D.C.: U.S. Dept of Health & Human Services.

Rowland, D., & Lyons, B. (1991). The elderly population in need of home care. In D. Rowland & B. Lyons (Eds.), Financing home care: Improving protection for disabled elderly people (pp. 3-26). Baltimore, MD: Johns Hopkins University Press.

Schwartz, M., Naierman, N., & Birnbaum, H. (1978). Catastrophic illness expense: Implications for a national health policy in the United States. Social Science & Medicine, 12, 13-22.

The Pepper Commission (1990). Recommendations to the Congress: Access to health care and long-term care for all Americans. March 2, 1990; Rpt. 27-427. Washington, D.C.: U.S. Government Printing Office.

Thomas, C., & Kelman, H.R. (1990). Unreimbursed expenses for medical care among urban elderly people. Journal of Community Health, 15(2), 137-149.

Wyszewianski, L. (1986). Financially catastrophic and high-cost cases: Definitions, distinctions, and their implications for policy formulation. Inquiry, 23(4), 382-394.

Predictors of Health Care Use by the American Indian Elderly

Gong-Soog Hong, Purdue University[1]

This study examined the factors influencing the health care use by the American Indian elderly in a rural environment. One hundred and thirty-seven Indian elders in White-Eagle and Pawnee tribes in Oklahoma were interviewed. Tobit analysis shows that physical health status, the number of disability days, education, employment status, and perceived access difficulty to health care services have significant effects on physician-visits. Findings indicate that need factors as well as enabling factors play the major roles in the use of physician services by the American Indian elders.

The over-all health status of the American Indian population currently remains far below that of general population in the United States. In 1988, the American Indian mortality rate for alcoholism was 438 percent greater, for tuberculosis was 400 percent greater, for diabetes was 155 percent greater, and for accidents was 131 percent greater than the U. S. population (Department of Health and Human Services, 1991).

The health status of the American Indian elders is even worse than the general Indian population. In fact, it is believed that Indian elders experience worst health condition among all ethnic groups in the U.S. Being Indian, being elderly, and living in rural area is considered to be the most disadvantageous position in American society (Seori and Seori, quoted in Cook, 1989).

The most prevalent illnesses among the American Indian elderly are arthritis, diabetes, tuberculosis, and otitis media (American Association of Retired Persons, 1987; Department of Health and Human Services, 1991; Congress of the U. S., 1986). About 50 percent of Indian elderly are suffering from arthritis. Hearing problems and poor eye-sight are also reported by more than 50 percent of Indian elderly. Over a half of Indian elderly are under medication because of the existing health problems (National Indian Council on Aging, 1986). These illnesses lead to higher levels of functional limitations for daily activities and mortality. According to the National Indian Council on Aging (1980), about 71 percent of American Indians aged 65 and over experience mild-to-severe limitations in their ability to perform activities of daily living.

One way to improve the health status of the American Indian elderly is to promote the use of health care services when needed. It is easy to assume that the American Indian elders are well-taken care of by the federal government since the Indian Health Services provides free health care services for all Indian population in the U.S. But, existence of health care facilities and services does not guarantee utilization of the services. Equal availability does not mean an equal use of the services. Some are more likely to and others are less likely to use them depending on the social, demographic, and health conditions. However, little empirical study has been done to understand the pattern of health care use among the American Indian elderly. This study investigates the factors affecting the use of physician services by the American Indian elderly in a rural area.

Conceptual Framework

Andersen's (1968) behavioral model provides three important factors to predict the use of health services: predisposing, enabling, and need. Predisposing factors are individual characteristics which affect the propensity to use health services. It includes socio-demographic characteristics such as age, gender, occupation, ethnicity, etc. Enabling factors represent individual's ability to use health services in time of need. It is a condition that either facilitate or hinder the use of health services and includes health insurance, income, family resources, etc. Need factors are conditions that require medical attention such as perceived health problems, functional limitations, etc.

The model has been applied to elderly population to predict the patterns of health services use. The existing literature consistently shows that need factor is the best predictor of health care use, and enabling and predisposing factors have little predictive power. Evashwick (1984) observed that need factors measured by functional limitations and physical health conditions were the most important predictors of the use of physician services, home care, ambulatory care, and hospital services among elderly persons. Coulton and Frost (1982) found the perceived need for health care has the most strong effect on the use of mental health care. Coulton (1982) and Wolinsky, Coe, Miller, Predergast, Greel, and Chavez (1983) also reported that the variance in health care use was explained the most by the need factor: the nutritional risk was the most important predictor of the use of physician and emergency room services, and the occurrence of hospital episodes for

---

[1]Assistant Professor, Consumer Sciences & Retailing

noninstitutionalized elderly. A similar finding was also reported by Frederiks, Wierik, Visser, and Sturmans (1990), which showed that the more the functional limitations, the higher the utilization of health care services.

Little study, however, has been done to examine the pattern of health care use by minority elderly in the context of Andersen's model. It might be argued that the model would not apply to minority elderly to predict the use of health services because of their different cultural backgrounds and social experiences in American society. This study examines how the Andersen's model apply to the use of physician services by American Indian elderly.

Data and Methods

Procedures. Oklahoma is an ideal place for the study of the American Indian elders because of large Indian population in the State. North Central rural area of Oklahoma was chosen as a study site where two Indian Health Service clinics serve five native Indian tribes (i.e., Osage, Otto, Pawnee, Iowa, and White-Eagle). Two Indian tribes, White-Eagle and Pawnee, were selected for the sampling of the elderly based on the tribal population size and tribal willingness to cooperate with the proposed research. There are no "reservations" per se in Oklahoma due to the uniqueness of land policy, but still most of the tribal members live together in certain locations. White-Eagle tribe resides near Ponca City , which is located 105 miles north of Oklahoma City, Oklahoma. Pawnee tribe resides in Pawnee, which is located about 80 miles Northeast of Oklahoma City. Ponca City and Pawnee are within 20 minutes-drive.

A survey instrument was developed to accomplish the study objective. It contains information on demographic characteristics, socio-economic status, health status, health care use, health attitudes, and living conditions of the elders.

Data Collection. The computer lists of Indian elders who were members of the White-Eagle and Pawnee tribes were obtained from the tribal offices. It was the most up-to-date computer lists of tribal members available through Bureau of Indian Affairs. It contained the information of 159 and 101 elders from White-Eagle and Pawnee tribes respectively. All elders in the computer lists were contacted individually by the native Indian interviewers. Many elders did not live in the addresses provided by the computer lists. A few elders refused to be interviewed based on their beliefs that most researchers exploit the American Indians for their academic purposes.

The American Indian Interviewers were selected to be sensitive to the native Indian culture based on previous experience in data collection, tribal background, and familiarity with the study sites. Tribal officers were involved in the selection process of the interviewers. General training was given to the interviewers prior to data collection.

The data were collected from 137 Indian elders aged 55 and older, seventy-eight elders from Ponca and fifty-nine from Pawnee tribe. Age 55 was chosen because American Indians have shorter life expectancy than the general population. Personal interviews were conducted by trained American Indian interviewers who were also members of either Ponca or Pawnee tribe.

Model and Estimation. The Andersen's (1968) conceptual model of health care utilization, which consists of predisposing, enabling, and need components, is employed to examine the factors affecting physician-visits: predisposing factors include age, gender, marital status, drinking, smoking; enabling factors include family income, education, employment status, informal caregiver, and perceived access difficulty; and need factors include physical health, mental health status, and the number of disability days. The analytic model is presented in Figure 1. Tobit analysis was employed for the model estimation since about 30 percent of the respondents has no physician-visits during 6 months prior to the survey. Tobit analysis is appropriate when missing or zero observations exist for the dependent variable (Maddala, 1983).

Figure 1
Conceptual Framework

Predisposing Factors
  Age
  Gender
  Marital Status
  Drinking
  Smoking

Enabling Factors   --> Health Care Use
  Family Income
  Education
  Employment Status
  Informal Caregiver
  Perceived Difficulty

Need Factors
  Physical Health
  Mental Health
  Disability Days

Variables. The dependent variable is the use of physician services. It is measured by the number of visits made to see doctors during the past six months. The mean value of physician-visits is 3.4. Independent variables are grouped into three categories: predisposing, enabling, and need.

Predisposing Factors. Age is a continuous variable and it ranges from 55 to 89. Gender is a dummy variable, 1 if male and 0 if female. The

Table 1
Measurements of Variables

Variables	Measurement	Mean	SD
Dependent:			
Physical visits	number of visits last 6 months	3.36	7.94
Independent Variables:			
Need Factors			
Physical Health[1]	sum of health problems	5.78	4.29
Mental Health[2]	Index	32.80	5.16
Disability Days	# restricted days/last 6 months	11.44	17.68
Enabling Factors:			
Family Income	mean monthly income during last 6 months	699.88	389.52
Education	years of education	10.50	1.52
Employment Status	dummy variable =1 if employed	0.22	0.41
Informal Caregiver	dummy variable = 1 if present	0.80	0.30
Perceived Access Difficulty to Health Care[3]	continuous variable	1.40	1.29
Predisposing Factors:			
Age	continuous variable	66.23	8.43
Gender	dummy variable = 1 if female	0.66	0.47
Marital Status	dummy variable = 1 if married	0.40	0.49
Drinking	dummy variable = 1 if drink	0.17	0.38
Smoking	dummy variable = 1 if smoke	0.24	0.43

[1]Measured by the sum of existing health problems
[2]The sum of 10 areas of feelings measured ordinarily.
[3]The sum of difficulty areas, long wait, getting appointment, communications and transporation.

sample consists of 91 female elders and 46 male elders. Marital status is also a dummy variable, 1 if married and 0 if non-married. Fifty-six elders are currently married and 81 elders are not married (i.e. divorced, separated, widowed or never married). Drinking is a dummy variable, 1 if currently consumes alcohol, 0 if not. Smoking is also a dummy variable, 1 if smoke, 0 if not smoke.

Enabling Factors. Family income is measured by the sum of all sources of income during last 6 months (i.e., earnings, rental income, income tribal benefits, Social Security benefits, SSI, etc.). Education is measured by the number of years of formal education and the mean value is 10.5. Employment status is a dummy variable, 1 if employed (full or part time) and 0 if not employed. In this study, 35 or more hours per week is defined as full time employment. Less than 20 hours of work per week is considered as part time employment. Informal caregiver is measured by the presence of someone who provides help to maintain average daily life. The services provided for the elders are cleaning, cooking, laundry, shopping, transportation, etc. It is a dummy variable, 1 if caregiver present and 0 if not. Access difficulty is the sum of all difficulties reported by the elder: getting appointment, long-wait, transportation, and communication.

Need Factors. Three components of health status (i.e., physical health, mental health, and disability days) are included. The physical health status is measured by the sum of the presence of 22 health problems such as eye, ear, arthritis, diabetes, kidney, and others. The mental health status is measured by 10 items expressing feelings (i.e., unhappy, sad, depressed, etc.). Each item is measured ordinally: very often, fairly often, hardly ever, not at all. The mean value is 32.6 and it ranges from 10 to 40. The higher value represents the better mental well-being. Disability days[1] are measured by the number of days that an individual restricts his/her usual activities because of illness or injury in the past six months. Table 1 presents the summary of all variables.

Results

Most Indian elders in Ponca and Pawnee tribes receive their medical services from the Indian Health Service (IHS). Ninety-two percent of the elders receive their health care services from IHS, 3 percent receive from hospital emergency room, and 2 percent of the elders receive from private physicians. These results indicate that the IHS is the major source of health care for the elderly in these two tribes. Cunningham and Schur (1991) reported the IHS or tribal facility is usual source of health care for the American Indians in the U.S.

Table 2
Results of Tobit Analysis for the Use of Physician Service

Variables	Estimated Coefficient	Standard Error
Need Factors:		
Physical Health	0.068**	0.027
Mental Health	-0.001	0.021
Disability Days	0.006*	0.003
Enabling Factors:		
Family Income	-0.0001	0.0001
Education	0.230**	0.086
Employment Status	0.537*	0.277
Informal Caregiver	-0.176	0.289
Perceived Difficulty	0.183*	0.081
Predisposing Factors:		
Age	-0.001	0.014
Gender	-0.054	0.219
Marital Status	-0.147	0.251
Drinking	0.172	0.230
Smoking	0.149	0.288
Log likelihood ratio	-68.02	
N	137	

*significant at 0.05
**significant at 0.01

As Table 2 shows, health status is significantly related to the use of physician services by the American Indian elderly. Both physical health condition and the number of disability days have statistically significant effects on the use of health care service. The elders with more physical health problems tend to visit physicians more often than those with less physical health problems. Elders with more days of restricted usual activity because of sickness tend to see physicians more than those with less restricted activity days. Mental health status does not show statistically significant effects on the physician-visits. Health conditions have major effects on the use of physician services by Indian elders.

Of the five enabling factors, education, employment status, and perceived access difficulty have significant effects on physician-visits. Educated elders are likely to use more physician services than the less educated. This may be explained by the fact that educated individuals are likely to be more health conscious and efficient in maintaining good health (Auster, Leveson, & Saracheck, 1969; Leigh, 1983). Educated individuals are also more likely to be informed about health care system (Pauly & Satterwaite, 1981). Employed elders tend to see physicians more frequently than the not-employed. This is contrary to the expectation that employment may limit available time for the physician-visits, thus results in fewer visits. It may indicate that employed elders are more mobile with their own cars than the not-employed, which will allow them to visit physicians more often. They may be also more sensitive to their health conditions because of their duty in employment and tend to use more preventive care. Elders who perceive more access difficulty to physician-visits tend to visit physicians more often than those who perceive less access difficulty. This is inconsistent with common sense that people with access difficulty are less likely to visit physicians. What the result is suggesting is that elders with more physician-visits tend to experience more difficulty in seeing the physicians.

Family income and informal caregiver do not have significant effects on the use of physician-visits. The lack of significant effect of informal caregiver is contrary to the existing literature which indicates that elders with informal caregivers are less likely to use formal health care services because of substitution effect. None of the predisposing factors (i.e., age, gender, marital status, drinking, and smoking) has significant effect on physician-visits.

Conclusions

The main contribution of the study is the empirical examination of physician-visits by the American Indian elderly. This study, the first systematic attempt to address the use of physician services, provides empirical knowledge about the determinants of the use of physician services among the American Indian elders.

The findings show that predisposing factors have relatively weak effects, whereas need and enabling factors play the major role in health service utilization. These results are consistent with the existing literature on health service utilization, where predisposing factors have little effects and need factors have the major effects on the utilization of health services (Wolinsky et al., 1983). It indicates that the Anderson's model is just as useful in predicting the use of health services by the American Indian elderly as elderly population in general.

Additionally, it is important to recognize that no geriatric care is available at IHS. Elderly American Indians are deliberately discriminated in health care since they are less likely to be productive in the labor market than younger Indians who have more market potentials (Subcommittee on Health and Environment, 1984; Hena, 1990). Discriminatory policy against elderly will add more difficulties in getting adequate health care among elders. Establishing geriatric care programs for the elderly could enhance the accessibility of health care.

Generalization of this study is limited to rural Indian elders of White-Eagle and Pawnee tribes in Oklahoma because the sampling was limited to those two tribes. It is not certain whether or not a similar pattern will emerge in other situations such as urban Indian elders, other tribes in different states. Future research should address these issues to advance our understanding of Indian elderly health care.

References

American Association of Retired Persons (1987). A profile of older Americans (No. PF 3049 (1187) D996). Washington, D.C.: American Association of Retired Persons.

Anderson, R. (1968). A behavioral model of families' use of health services. National Bureau of Economic Research, Research series 25.

Auster R., Leveson, I., & D. Saracheck. (1969). The production of health, an exploratory study. The Journal of Human Resources. 4(4): 411-436.

Congress of the United States, Office of Technology Assessment (1986). Indian Health Care. OTA-H_290. Washington D. C.: U.S. Government Printing Office.

Cook, C. (1989). Problems of American Indians. Hispanic and Indian Elderly: America's Failure to Care, Comm. Pub. No. 101-730. Washington, D.C.: U.S.Government Printing Office.

Coulton, C. & Frost, A. (1982). use of social and health services by the elderly. Journal of Health and Social Behavior, 23: 330-339.

Cunningham, P. & Schur, C. (1991). Health Care Coverage: Findings from the Survey of American Indians and Alaska Natives. Research Findings 8. U.S. Department of Health and Human Services. AHCPR Pub. No.91-0027.

Department of Health and Human Services (1991). Trends in Indian Health 1991. Washington D. C.: Indian Health Service.

Department of Health and Human Services (1990). Indian health service: regional differences in Indian health, 1990. Washington D. C.: Indian Health Service.

Evashwick, C., Rowe, G., Diehr, P. & Branch, L. (1984). Factors explaining the use of health care services by the elderly. Health Services Research, 19(3):357-382.

Frederikn, C., Wierik, M., Visser, A. & Sturmans, F. (1990). The functional status and utilization of care of elderly people living at home. Journal of Community Health, 15(5):307-317.

Hena, J. (1990). Statement of The National Indian Council on Aging. Presented at the Commissioner's Forum on the Reauthorization of the Older Americans Act. Denver, Colorado.

Leigh, J. (1983). Direct and indirect effects of education on health. Social Science Medicine. 17(4): 227-234.

Maddala, G.S. (1983). Limited-dependent and Qualitative Variables in Economics, New York:Cambridge University Press.

National Indian Council on Aging (1986). Research Project to Derive Information on the Health, Housing, and Safety Status of Indian Elders. Albuquerque, New Mexico.

National Indian Council on Aging (1980). May the Circle be Unbroken A New Decade. Albuquerque, New Mexico.____

Pauly, M. & Satterwaite, M. (1981). The pricing of primary care physicians' services: t test of the role of consumer information. Bell Journal of Economics, 12(2): 488-506.

Subcommittee on Health and the Environment (1984). Indian health Care: an overview of the federal government's role. Comm. print 98-Y. Washington D. C.: Government Printing Office.

Wolinsky, F., Coe, R., Miller, D., Prendergast, J., Greel, M. & Chavez, N. (1983). Health services utilization among the n noninstituionalized elderly. Journal of Health and Social Behavior. 24: 325-337.

Endnotes
1.   This definition is adopted from National
       Center for Health Statistics Health Interview
       Survey Procedure   (U.S.   Department   of
       Commerce, National Technical Information
       Service, 1975).

Risk-Benefit Analysis of Cigarette Smoking:
Public Policy Implications

Rachel Dardis, University of Marlyand[1]
Thomas Keane, U. S. Department of Transportation[2]

The objective of this study was to investigate the benefits and risks from smoking over the lifetime of the individual. Benefits were based on willingness to pay for cigarettes while risks were based on changes in life expectancy and medical costs. The estimated risk-benefit ratios were high. For the average smoker, they ranged from 0.94 to 2.38 for a five percent discount rate and from 0.30 to 0.75 for a ten percent discount rate.

Introduction

The impact of cigarette consumption on consumer welfare has been recognized since the seventeenth century. However, the relationship between health and cigarette consumption was not investigated to any great extent until the twentieth century. Researchers concluded that the three major smoking-related diseases were cancers, cardiovascular diseases and respiratory system diseases (Oster, Colditz and Kelly 1984). According to the 1979 Surgeon General's Report cigarette smoking was the "single most important preventable environmental factor contributing to illness, disability and death in the United States" (Surgeon General 1979, p. vii). A recent study by the Office of Technology Assessment estimated that there were 314,000 smoking related deaths in 1982 while the number of life years lost was 5.3 million (Office of Technology Assessment 1985). The total costs to society was $65 billion or $2.17 per package of cigarettes.

Domestic cigarette consumption has declined in the past two decades due to a variety of factors. They include "continued large hikes in cigarette wholesale prices, prospects for higher taxes, more and more social smoking restrictions, declining social acceptability of tobacco use in the United States and antismoking activities" (Grise 1991, p. 31). However, 29 percent of men and 23 percent of women still smoke in the United States (National Center for Disease Control, 1992). Thus, the societal costs of cigarette smoking are likely to remain high in the future.

Existing antismoking policies in the United States mean that the individual is responsible for the decision to smoke or not to smoke. It is of interest, therefore, to examine the positive and negative consequences of cigarette smoking from the perspective of the individual. Of particular importance in such a comparison is the fact that the benefits and risks from smoking are incurred at different points in time. The individual, who smokes, incurs benefits immediately while the negative consequences of smoking or risks are incurred many years in the future (American Cancer Society 1980). Thus, the individual's subjective rate of time preference will play a role in assessing the risks from smoking.

The purpose of this study was to investigate the benefits and risks from smoking over the life of the individual. Benefits are based on the individual's willingness to pay for cigarettes while risks are based on changes in life expectancy due to smoking and the medical costs of smoking related diseases. The results of this analysis should assist in evaluating the risks posed by cigarette smoking and provide insight on the impact of delayed or postponed risks on consumption decisions which yields immediate benefits.

Procedure

The analysis was confined to male smokers due to data availability. It was assumed that the individual in this study began smoking at the age of 20 in the year 1955 and continued to smoke at the same rate throughout his lifetime. Three smoking levels were used - light, average and heavy and each level resulted in different benefits, life expectancies and medical costs for the individual. According to the data reported by the American Cancer Society (1980) the health consequences of smoking do not begin to take effect until at least six years after smoking commences. Therefore, there were no differences in life expectancy or medical costs for smokers and nonsmokers from age 20 to age 25.

Procedures for estimating changes in life expectancy and medical costs due to smoking are discussed in the first two sections while the benefits from smoking and risk-benefit analysis are discussed in the two final sections. All benefits and risks were measured in constant 1980 dollars and were discounted to the year 1955 using 5 per-

[1]Professor, Department of Economics

[2]Operations Research Analyst,
 Federal Highway Administration

cent and 10 percent discount rates. Justification for these rates is based on previous studies in the literature (Dardis, Davenport, Kurin and Marr 1983, Garner and Dardis 1987) and recent surveys on the discounting of human lives (Cropper and Portney 1992). Respondents in one of these surveys were asked to choose between a program which would save lives immediately and one that would save lives in twenty-five years. The twenty-five year period is appropriate in view of the long latency period for many smoking related diseases. Respondents considered "6 lives saved 25 years in the future as equivalent to 1 life saved today" resulting in an implied discount rate of 7.4 percent (Cropper and Portney 1992, p. 3).

Changes in Life Expectancy Due to Smoking

The change in life expectancy due to cigarette smoking for light, average, and heavy smokers is given in the following equation:

$$\sum_{t=a+1}^{n} (P_a^t - S_a^t) \qquad (1)$$

where

P_a^t = probability that a nonsmoker aged a will survive to age t,

S_a^t = probability that a smoker aged a will survive to age t,

a = age 20, the age when the individual started smoking, and

n = maximum life expectancy of the individual.

Data on survival probabilities for nonsmokers and three groups of smokers (light, average, and heavy) were obtained from the American Cancer Society (1980) for five year age intervals from age 25 to age 100. These data were combined with data from U.S. Life Tables to yield five year survival probabilities from age 20 to 100. Annual survival probabilities within each five year period (eg. P_{30}^{31}) were then obtained based on the assumption that survival probabilities were constant within each five year period.

Expected Medical Costs from Smoking

Expected medical costs were based on the probability of death in year t due to smoking and the associated medical costs. The probability of death in year t was based on different survival probabilities for smokers and nonsmokers over time using data from the American Cancer Society (1980). Average medical costs were based on three major smoking related diseases - Lung Cancer (LC), Coronary Heart Disease (CHD) and Chronic Obstructive Pulmonary Disease (CHPD). These diseases were selected because they had the clearest links with cigarette smoking (Oster, Colditz and Kelly 1984).

Data from the study by Oster, Colditz and Kelly (1984) provided information on the probability of the individual living 1,2,...,n years after the onset of a disease and its annual medical costs. Annual medical costs were converted to the year of death using 5 and 10 percent discount rates and multiplied by their respective probabilities to yield medical costs over the duration of the disease. The relative importance of each disease was then used to obtain average medical costs for the three smoking related diseases. The relative importance was 40 percent for LC, 41 percent for CHD and 19 percent for CHPD (Surgeon General, 1989). It was assumed the probability of contracting more than one disease was zero following the procedure used by Oster, Colditz and Kelly (1984).

The present value of expected medical costs from smoking was then given by

$$\sum_{t=a+1}^{n} EMC_t / (1+i)^{t-a} \qquad (2)$$

where

EMC_t = expected medical costs in year t, or (AMC) (M_t)

AMC = average medical costs for the three smoking related diseases

M_t = probability of death in year t due to smoking, and the other terms are as defined earlier.

Benefits from Smoking

Benefits were based on willingness to pay for cigarettes and are measured by the area under the demand curve. The willingness to pay for a certain quantity, Q_t, may be broken into two components- actual expenditures on cigarettes (P_tQ_t or EX_t) and the consumer surplus from being able to purchase the quantity Q_t for a price P_t (Keane 1993).

Consumer expenditures in year t (EX_t) were based on the three smoking levels identified in the report of the American Cancer Society (1980). Light smokers consumed 10-19 cigarettes per day while average and heavy smokers consumed 20-39 cigarettes and 40 or more cigarettes a day respectively. Values of 15, 30 and 40 cigarettes per day were used for the three groups. The average price of a cigarette pack from 1955 to 1990 was based on price/quantity data for 51 states (Tobacco Institute 1990). An increase of 4.3 percent per year was used for the years 1991 to 2000 based on consultation with individuals in the Bureau of Labor Statistics and the Tobacco Institute. Prices for the years 2001 to 2035 were assumed to equal the price in the year 2000. It should be noted that any bias concerning assumptions of future prices is likely to be small due to the fact that expenditures were discounted to 1955.

The second component is consumer surplus (CS_t). It is the triangular area about the price line (P_t) and is estimated assuming a linear demand curve and inserting values for the price elasticity of demand E_t ($\Delta Q/\Delta P$) (P_t/Q_t). Then,

$$CS_t = \frac{1}{2} \Delta P \Delta Q \qquad (3)$$

$$= \frac{1}{2} (\frac{P_t}{E_t})Q_t \qquad (4)$$

$$= \frac{1}{(2E_t)} (P_t Q_t) \qquad (5)$$

Price elasticities of demand for all smokers were based on reviews of demand studies by Andrews and Franke (1991) and Wood (1989). Three values were selected based on these studies. They were -0.40, -0.54 and -0.68. These three values were assumed to represent the demand by average smokers who consume 20-39 cigarettes per day. They account for the majority of smokers (57 percent) according to the Surgeon General's report (1989). Light and heavy smokers account for 24 percent and 19 percent of smokers respectively. It was assumed that demand was more inelastic for heavy smokers and values equal to one half the values for average smokers were used. Values for light smokers could then be obtained based on the relative importance of the three smoking groups.

The present value of benefits from smoking is given by

$$\sum_{t=a+1}^{n} S_a^t (EX_t + CS_t)/(1+i)^{t-a} \qquad (6)$$

Risk-Benefit Analysis

A comparison of risks and benefits requires that all components be measured in constant dollars and discounted to the year 1955. This has already been done for medical costs and benefits. The final risk component, the change in life expectancy due to smoking, may also be measured in dollars and discounted if a dollar value is attached to a life year. As Weinstein and Stason note "the reason for discounting life years is precisely that they are being valued relative to dollars and since a dollar in the future is discounted relative to a present dollar, so must a life year in the future be discounted relative to a present dollar (Weinstein and Stason 1977, p. 716).

The mortality risk from smoking is given by

$$V \sum_{t=a+1}^{n} (P_a^t - S_a^t)/(1+i)^{t-a} \qquad (7)$$

where V = value of a life year and the second term is the change in discounted life years.

Two life year values of $25,000 and $50,000 were used in this study based on previous research. Two studies provided information on life year values. Zeckhauser and Shepard reported values ranging from $14,500 to $94,250 ($1980). Garner and Dardis (1987) obtained a net cost of approximately $25,000 ($1980) per life year saved for males undergoing in-center dialysis, which was the dominant treatment for End Stage Renal Disease patients. This value is an appropriate lower bound because society has elected to defray the costs of such treatments.

Life values from wage and consumer market studies were also used to generate life year values (Fisher, Chestnut, and Violette 1989). There was considerable variation in the life values reported which ranged from $0.45 million to $8.0 million ($1980). Life values from the four consumer market studies ranged from $0.46 million to $0.61 million and were converted to life year values assuming a remaining life expectancy of 34 years for the population at risk and 5 and 10 percent discount rates. Life year values ranged from $21,000 to $28,000 for a 5 percent discount rate and from $36,000 to $48,000 for a 10 percent discount rate.

Results

The change in discounted life years due to smoking, which is used to estimate the mortality risk, is given in Table 1. The values are less than one in all instances reflecting the long latency period of smoking-related diseases and the impact of discounting. This may help to explain why individuals continue to smoke in spite of repeated health warnings.

The mortality risk is given in Table 2. It varies in order of importance with the discount rate, life year values and smoking intensity. Mortality risks range from $14,450 to $48,600 for a 5 percent discount rate and from $2,475 to $9,250 for a 10 percent discount rate.

Table 1. Change in Discounted Life Years Due to Smoking

Discount Rate	Smoking Intensity[a]		
	Light	Average	Heavy
5%	0.578	0.652	0.972
10%	0.099	0.111	0.185

[a]Based on average number of cigarettes smoked per day.

Table 2. Mortality Risk from Smoking: ($1980)

Discount Rate	Value of a Life Year	Smoking Intensity		
		Light	Average	Heavy
5%	$25,000	14,450	16,300	24,300
	$50,000	28,900	32,600	48,600
10%	$25,000	2,475	2,775	4,625
	$50,000	4,950	5,550	9,250

Table 3. Present Value of Expected Medical Costs from Smoking: ($1980)

Discount Rate	Smoking Intensity		
	Light	Average	Heavy
5%	678	760	1,062
10%	165	186	300

Table 4. Present Value of Total Risks from Smoking: ($1980)

Discount Rate	Value of a Life Year	Smoking Intensity		
		Light	Average	Heavy
5%	$25,000	15,128	17,060	25,362
	$50,000	29,578	33,360	49,662
10%	$25,000	2,640	2,961	4,925
	$50,000	5,115	5,736	9,550

Table 5. Present Value of Benefits from Smoking: ($1980)[a]

Discount Rate	Price Elasticity of Demand	Smoking Intensity		
		Light	Average	Heavy
5%	Low	7,691	18,163	36,784
	Average	6,736	15,551	29,972
	High	6,201	14,012	25,965
10%	Low	4,178	9,916	20,389
	Average	3,659	8,487	16,613
	High	3,368	7,647	14,392

[a]Differences between estimates for a given smoking intensity are due to change in consumer surplus when the price elasticity of demand changes.

Table 6. Risk Benefit Ratios for Smoking

Discount Rate	Value of a Life Year	Price Elasticity of Demand	Smoking Intensity		
			Light	Average	Heavy
5%	$25,000	Low	1.97	0.94	0.69
		Average	2.25	1.10	0.85
		High	2.44	1.22	0.98
	$50,000	Low	3.85	1.84	1.35
		Average	4.39	2.15	1.66
		High	4.77	2.38	1.91
10%	$25,000	Low	0.63	0.30	0.24
		Average	0.72	0.35	0.30
		High	0.78	0.39	0.34
	$50,000	Low	1.22	0.58	0.47
		Average	1.40	0.68	0.57
		High	1.52	0.75	0.6

The present value of expected medical costs from smoking is given in Table 3. Values are considerably lower than those obtained for morality risk and range from $165 to $1,062.

The present value of total risks from smoking are given in Table 4. The range of values is similar to those obtained for mortality risks since the medical costs are small. The smallest risk occurs for a light smoker, a $25,000 life year value and a 10 percent discount rate while the highest risk occurs for a heavy smoker, a $50,000 life year value and a 5 percent discount rate.

The present value of benefits from smoking are given in Table 5. Benefits vary according to the discount rate, price elasticity of demand and smoking intensity. Smoking intensity has the greatest impact in this instance followed by the discount rate and the price elasticity of demand. Benefits range from $3,368 to $7,691 for light smokers compared to values of $14,392 and $36,784 for heavy smokers.

Risk-benefit ratios for smoking are given in Table 6. They vary from 0.24 to 4.77 depending on the discount rate, the value of a life year, the price elasticity of demand and smoking intensity. Again, the discount role has a major impact. The fact that risk-benefit ratios are higher for light smokers than for heavy smokers is not surprising since the increase in benefits when smokers switch from light to heavy smoking is considerably greater than the increase in risks. This is due to the fact that risks are discounted more heavily since they occur in the future whereas benefits are distributed over the life of the individual.

The following discussion is confined to the results for the average smoker who accounts for nearly three fifths of the population. Risk-benefit ratios for this group range from 0.94 to 2.38 for a 5 percent discount rate with higher values reflecting higher life year values and higher demand elasticities. This means that every dollar of benefits yields a risk or loss ranging from 94 cents to $2.38 which might be considered a very high risk tax. The ratios decline when a 10 percent discount rate is used and range from 0.30 to 0.75.

It is of interest to compare the results of this study to an earlier study which examined the risks and benefits for a variety of consumption activities (Dardis et al. 1983). Compact and subcompact automobiles were found to be the highest risk consumer products in this study which used a 10 percent discount rate and a life value of $459,000 ($1980). This is equivalent to a life year value of $48,000 assuming the average driver would live 34 more years. The results of this study were used to estimate risk-benefit ratios for automobiles based on a unitary price elasticity of demand for automobiles. They were 0.14 for compacts and 0.20 for subcompacts. For purposes of comparison risk-benefit ratios for the average

smoker were re-estimated using a life year value of $48,000. They ranged from 0.55 for a low price elasticity of demand to 0.72 for a high price elasticity of demand. Thus, the risks from smoking are considerably greater than the risks from driving though automobiles might be considered as more essential than cigarettes. This result conflicts with the conclusion of Lowrance that risks are more likely to be acceptable when exposure is essential rather than a luxury (Lowrance 1975, p. 87). However, they are in keeping with Starr's comments that we are more tolerant of risk we impose on ourselves as opposed to risk imposed by others (Starr 1968).

Discussion

The results of this study indicate that the risk-benefit ratios from smoking are relatively high. For the average smoker, they range from 0.94 to 2.38 for a 5 percent discount rate and from 0.30 to 0.75 for a 10 percent discount rate. The individual's time preference rate has a major impact as well as the value of a life year.

There are several possible explanations for the continuance of smoking in spite of the high risk-benefit ratios. First, the individual faces uncertainty about the adverse consequences of his actions in that he may not live long enough to acquire a smoking-related disease or may never get such a disease. As a result the individual may either disregard the risk entirely, in which case the risk-benefit ratios become zero, or may use discount rates which are higher than 10 percent. Either response would provide individuals with a more favorable risk-benefit ratio and one closer to other consumption activities.

A second explanation for the continuance of smoking is that some individuals may lack information concerning the health consequences of smoking. Breslow (1982) examined surveys of the American public concerning cigarettes and concluded that a significant percentage of the public was still not clear on the hazards. The level of awareness had undoubtedly increased over time and has contributed to a reduction in smoking in the United States as well as in other developed countries (Grise 1991, Surgeon General 1989).

The addictive nature of cigarettes smoking may also play a role. The 1989 report of the Surgeon General notes as follows:

In 1964, tobacco use was considered habituating. A substantial body of evidence accumulated since then, and summarized in the 1988 Surgeon General's Report has established that cigarettes and other forms of tobacco use are addicting. Given the prevalence of smoking, tobacco use is the nation's most widespread form of drug dependency (Surgeon General 1989, p. 21).

In this context it is important to note that most cigarette smokers do not start out expecting to become addicted. Jaffe and Kanzler (1979, p. 6) suggest that both cigarette smokers and opiate and alcohol users may gradually lose "the capacity to change" and "while the user may want to believe she/he can stop at any time, the behavior indicates that this is not the case." According to a 1979 survey (DHEW 1979) 50 percent of teenagers who smoke think they will not be smoking five years from now. Thus, smokers may only consider the benefits from smoking initially and disregard the risks since such risks can be reduced to a considerable extent by quitting (Oster, Colditz and Kelly 1984). However, once the individual has become addicted the ability to quit diminishes and smoking continues in spite of unfavorable risk-benefit ratios. The addictive nature of cigarettes means that voluntary risk has been replaced by involuntary risk. Thus, it is no longer a question of willingness to pay but rather of necessity to pay. Involuntary risk may have an unfavorable risk-benefit ratio since the individual is no longer free to choose between consumption or abstinence based on perceived risks and benefits. Society, in turn, should be less tolerant of this activity since it has changed from a voluntary risk to an involuntary risk (Starr 1968).

Two major policies to reduce smoking include education and information programs and higher prices for cigarettes through excise or sales taxes. The impact of educational and price policies will vary according to the individual's risk response, time preference rate, and patterns of smoking behavior. Higher prices would not only discourage consumption but would also provide revenue to fund educational programs. Higher prices are likely to be particularly effective for adolescents since they have not yet become addicted to nicotine and have more income severe constraints.

The fact that excise and sales taxes provide additional revenue and also discourage smoking has undoubtedly stimulated recent increases in federal and state taxes. The federal excise tax was increased by four cents to 20 cents in 1991 while eleven states and the District of Columbia increased taxes an average of 5 cents a pack. According to Grise (1991, p. 27) "many cities and other local governments also tax cigarettes and four-fifths of the States now impose sales taxes on cigarettes." However, sales taxes vary. While the national average is 24 cents it ranges from 2.5 cents a pack in Virginia to 46 cents a pack in Hawaii. It is only 5 cents a pack in North Carolina. Will (1992, p. C7) criticized the recent Virginian decision not to raise cigarette taxes though he recognized that "taxing cigarettes when tobacco is the state's largest cash crop may be hazardous to political health." He noted that the revenue from the cigarette sales tax in California, which was increased to 35 cents, was used to fund "tobacco education, medical care, and research" and that "the percentage of Californians smoking has

declined 17 percent." Similar results occurred in Canada where federal and provincial taxes have increased the price of a pack of cigarettes to $5.50.

Finally, this study examined the consequences of smoking from the perspective of the individual so that only the individual risks from smoking were considered. However, smoking also imposes costs on others. These external costs include passive smoking, house fires, and medical costs borne by the State and Federal Governments and hence the taxpayer. Such costs are far greater than the tax revenues received from cigarettes (Keane 1993). Thus, both smokers and non smokers have a great deal to gain from a reduction in this high risk consumption activity.

References

American Cancer Society. (1980). Dangers of Smoking, Benefits of Quitting. New York: American Cancer Society.

Andrews, R. L. & Franke, G. R. (1991). The determinants of cigarette consumption: a meta analysis. Journal of Public Policy and Marketing. 10(1), 81-100.

Breslow, L. (1982). Control of cigarette smoking from a public policy perspective. Annual Review Public Health. 3, 129-151.

Cropper, M. L. & Portney, P. R. (1992). Discounting human lives. Resources. 108, 1-20.

Dardis, R., Davenport, G., Kurin, J. & Marr, J. (1983). Risk-benefit analysis and the determination of acceptable risk. Journal of Consumer Affairs. 17(Summer), 38-56.

Fisher, A., Chestnut, L. G. & Violette, D. M. (1989). The value of reducing risks of death: a note on new evidence. Journal of Policy Analysis and Management. 8(1), 88-100.

Garner, T. & Dardis, R. (1987). Cost-effectiveness analysis of end-stage renal disease treatments. Medical Care. 25(1), 25-34.

Grise, V. N. (1991). Outlook for tobacco. Outlook '92. Washington, DC: U.S. Dept. of Agriculture.

Jaffe, J. H. & Kanzler, M. (1979). Smoking as an addictive disorder. In N. A. Krasnegor, (Ed.) Cigarette Smoking as a Dependence Process. Washington, DC: National Institute of Drug Abuse.

Keane, T. (1993). Risk-benefit analysis of cigarette smoking: public policy implications. M.S. Thesis. University of Maryland, College Park, MD.

Lowrance, W. D. (1976). Of Acceptable Risk. Los Altos, CA: William Kaufman.

National Center for Disease Control. Office of Smoking and Health. (1992). Personal communication.

Office of Technology Assessment. (1985). Smoking-Related Deaths and Financial Costs. Washington, DC: Office of Technology Assessment.

Oster, G., Colditz, G. A. & Kelly, N. L. (1984). The Economic Costs of Smoking and Benefits of Quitting. Lexington, MA: Lexington Books.

Starr, C. (1968). Social benefit versus technological risk. Science. 165, 1232-1238.

Surgeon General. (1989). Reducing the Health Consequences of Smoking, 25 Years of Progress: A Report of the Surgeon General. Washington, DC: U.S. Dept. of Health and Human Services.

Surgeon General. (1979). Smoking and Health: A Report of the Surgeon General. Washington, DC: U.S. Dept. of Health, Education, and Welfare.

Tobacco Institute. (1990). The Tax Burden on Tobacco, Historical Compilation, 25. Washington, DC: The Tobacco Institute.

U.S. Department of Health, Education and Welfare. (1979). Teenage Smoking: Immediate and Long Term Patterns. Washington, DC: U.S. Department of Health, Education and Welfare.

Weinstein, M. C. & Stason, W. B. (1977). Foundations of cost-effectiveness analysis for health and medical practices. New England Journal of Medicine. 296, 716-726.

Will, G. F. (1992). Tobacco road. Washington Post. February 16, C7.

Wood, R. (1989). The Role of habit in cigarette consumption. Doctoral dissertation. University of Maryland, College Park, MD.

Zeckhauser, R. & Shephard, D. (1976). Where now for saving lives?. Law and Contemporary Problems. 40 (Autumn), 5-45.

Impact of Water Regulation on Consumer Well-Being

Joyce Shotick, Bradley University[1]
Robert Scott, Bradley University[2]

As concern for environmental quality increases, consumers demand more regulation. However, environmental regulation has both benefits and costs, which ultimately reach the consumer. The purpose of this project was to identify direct and indirect costs and benefits that would result from proposed environmental regulation. A cost benefit analysis was conducted to determine the social net gain.

Protection of natural water resources is currently a major public issue that affects everyone. Over half of the U.S. population receives its drinking water from underground water wells (Drinking Water, 1990) and the average adult consumes about two liters of water a day (Health Advisory, 1988). In order to maintain and improve the quality of our natural resources, the U.S. and state governments established the Environmental Protection Agency (EPA). The EPA's emphasis for the 1990's will be on pollution prevention such as eliminating the risk of highly toxic contaminants leaking into underground water systems (The Quality of Life Concept, 1973). The Safe Drinking Water Act of 1974 commissioned the EPA to monitor contaminant levels in community wells (Cothern, 1986).

The growing awareness that environmental quality has substantial impact on consumer well-being is generating demand for environmental regulation. This demand for regulation is drawing consumption economists into designing and evaluating regulation. The positive and negative effects that environmental regulation has on the quality of life need to be assessed by consumption economists who are trained in consumer well-being.

The purpose of this paper is to identify the costs and benefits associated with regulation designated to protect natural underground water resources and their impact on consumers. As part of the process of proposing specific legislation, the EPA must study the economic effects of such legislation on consumers and businesses, as well as the natural environment (Shechter, 1985). Enactment of such regulation depends, in part, upon the resulting net economic gains or losses to society.

Proposed Environmental Legislation

Prevention and early detection of chemical leakages or spills by chemical facilities are major EPA objectives. Enacting standards for handling and storing chemicals is the principle method of preventing contamination.

The study of the impact of a regulation is called the "economic impact study" (EcIS). The EcIS entails calculating the specific costs that targeted businesses and communities would incur. Also, quantitative and qualitative benefits to society must be determined. Through this cost-benefit analysis, net social gains or losses due to implementing such regulations can be estimated. The economic theory upon which the EcIS is based implies that the gains from the most recent regulation must be greater than or equal to the cost of compliance in order for the regulation to be beneficial to society (Samuelson and Nordhaus, 1989).

Docket R89-5 was a proposed regulation in the state of Illinois regarding potential contamination of underground water from facilities processing or storing dangerous chemicals (Gallagher, Scott and Garbade, 1991). This regulation required monitoring groundwater at chemical production facilities, the closure of landfills, land treatment facilities, and surface impoundments within a vicinity referred to as a " setback zone" of a water source. Also, building new facilities within the setback zone was prohibited.

The environmental regulation may consist of cease and desist orders to businesses that are overtly polluting the natural environment. Or, the regulation may merely require businesses to provide additional protective devices to contain hazardous chemicals. For either purpose, the environmental regulation is proposed and enacted to ensure the maintenance of the natural environment.

Model for Assessing Economic Impact

Although EcIS studies in the past calculated the costs to businesses, the specific affects to consumers were never analyzed. Therefore, the following model was developed to provide a visual construct for clarity in direction of such

---

[1]Instructor, Finance and Quantitative Methods

[2]Professor, Economics

research. The model depicts the flow of costs and benefits from proposed environmental regulation to consumers' well-being. This model is illustrated in Figure 1. The process begins with consumers demanding environmental regulation for protection of nearby natural resources. The EPA responds to the demands by proposing necessary regulation in communities where potential hazards may occur.

Figure 1
Impact of Environmental Regulation on Consumers and Businesses

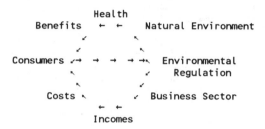

Protection of the environment has several positive impacts on consumers. Both quantitative and qualitative benefits are listed in Table 1. One major qualitative benefit is aesthetic nature of the environment, to which no monetary value has been attached. Another qualitative aspect is the disturbance of the ecosystem. Animals and plants would be impaired if their drinking or food supplies are damaged. This would give rise to a chain reaction in the ecosystem which would ultimately affect consumers.

Table 1
Quantitative and Qualitative Benefits of Drinking Water Regulation

QUANTITATIVE BENEFITS	QUALITATIVE BENEFITS
Avoided Health Care Costs	Aesthetic Aspect of Natural Environment
Avoided Loss of Income	Insured Functioning of Ecosystem
Avoided Loss of Household Production	Maintained Land Value

Maintaining water resources implies that human health would be maintained. Good health is obviously crucial to consumer well-being (Williams and Hafstrom, 1986), however, monetizing this benefit is complex. Consumers depend upon good health to allow them to find employed work as well as to perform domestic work in order to provide goods and services that are necessary for the household. Thus avoided medical costs, avoided loss of income, and avoided loss of ability to work in the household were the measurable benefits to consumers.

On the other hand, enacting environmental regulation has profound impacts on the business sector. There are direct and indirect costs of compliance for the business firms, that are stated in Table 2. These costs to businesses are transferred to consumers in terms of higher prices or loss of income if the firms should decide to minimize or shutdown its facility. Additionally, if businesses were to reduce production or shutdown, wage earners from those businesses would be laid-off, and these consumers would experience a drastic reduction of their level of consumption.

Table 2
Direct Costs to Businesses and Indirect Costs to Consumers Due to Drinking Water Regulation

DIRECT COSTS INCURRED BY BUSINESSES	INDIRECT COSTS INCURRED BY CONSUMERS
Closure of Specified Facilities	Loss of Income
Construction of Containment Walls	Possible Relocation to Seek Employment
Monitoring Systems	Higher Prices for the Product

Research Methods

Assessing the impact of the regulation for each type of facility was a difficult task because both the costs and benefits of this regulation varied tremendously by type of facility and its location. Therefore, those facilities for which the costs and benefits had the highest potential of underground water contamination were selected for detailed study via a scenario approach using Monte Carlo simulation (Mansfield, 1980). This approach was selected because specific quantitative data necessary for the cost-benefit analysis could be obtained.

Based on engineering analysis of chemical contaminations, a probability of a contamination incident was determined. Then the Monte Carlo procedure scanned a 20 year period in which a contamination incident could occur and a random event was generated. The size of the population that could be affected was a random variable that was also generated by Monte Carlo. For a given population, the number of people who would contract an illness from contaminated drinking water was randomly generated.

The type and extent of such illnesses are dependent upon the chemical contaminants in the water and the period of consumption. Potable water may have low concentrations of naturally-occurring and man-made chemicals and still be safe for human consumption. The EPA has established acceptable levels of chemicals that may be present for safe consumption (Cothern, 1986). In the event that chemical contamination exceeds the acceptable level, adverse health effects in the community would occur. The range of potential chemicals and their associated health impairments have been determined by the U.S.EPA (Drinking Water, 1990).

Nine various illnesses were identified with the consumption of chemically contaminated water. The results of such potential hazards are assembled in Table 3. The most severe illness was determined to be cancer and the least severe illness might be dermatitis. Health care costs associated with specific illnesses were estimated using Diagnostic Related Group costs furnished by the Health Care Financing Administration (National Cost Estimates, 1988). The average hospital costs were stated for each case as well as the total costs. The total costs included hospital care, physician care, and at home care. For example, an individual who developed gastrointestinal problems could face medical costs of $12,776, on average. Depending upon the population of the community, total medical costs to consumers with these problems could be tremendous.

Table 3
Direct Avoided Medical Costs Associated with Various Illnesses

Illness	Average Hospital Costs for Each Case	Total Costs for Each Case
Cancer	$12,680	$32,513
Kidney Damage	$ 5,008	$12,841
Lymphoma	$ 4,631	$11,874
Gastrointestinal	$ 4,982	$12,776
Renal Failure	$ 7,290	$18,692
Liver Damage	$ 6,382	$16,363
Chronic Poisoning	$ 5,336	$13,682
Methemoglobinemia	$ 3,695	$ 9,474
Dermatitis	$ 2,733	$ 7,008

Based on the number of persons affected, the costs of medical treatment and loss of income was calculated and discounted to present value. For each scenario, 10,000 iterations of the Monte Carlo procedure were conducted. Then a statistical expected value of avoided costs were calculated. The sum of these costs, which would be avoided if the regulation was implemented comprised the quantitative benefits.

Results

The costs of all facilities was estimated by the environmental engineers. However, the benefits derived from the regulation were calculated for three specific types of facility. Thus the cost-benefit analysis was conducted on those types of facilities.

Cost Analysis
The total anticipated costs are comprised of direct and indirect costs to businesses and consumers. Costs of complying with the regulation imposed on the businesses are the direct costs and indirect costs that would be incurred by consumers and workers of these businesses. These results are displayed in Table 4. This study encompassed the

effects of this regulation on businesses over a twenty year period. Therefore, present value of the costs were estimated.

Table 4
Costs of Compliance by Facility Type and in 1990 Dollars (In Thousands of Dollars)

Facility Type	Number Affected	Total Cost
Underground Storage	54	$ 4,649
Surface Impoundments	59	$19,996
Road Oil	5	$ 119
Ag Chemical	54	$ 6,080
Landfill	5	$ 3,980
Land Treatment	5	$ 0
De-Icing	27	$ 1,207
Waste Piles	43	$ 294
Totals	252	$36,325

The direct compliance costs consisted of the initial and on-going costs that the specified businesses would incur. The legislation specified that some facilities would be required to close down and others would have to invest in prescribed containment and monitoring systems. For example, it was found that an average agricultural chemical facility will spend $15,000 initially and $8,000 annually to meet these proposed regulations.

The indirect costs consist of secondary effects to consumers and the labor force. It was assumed that some of the direct costs would be passed along to consumers in the form of a price increase for the product or service offered by that facility. For the average Illinois grain farmer, this was estimated to increase his cost of production. This may cause marginal farmers to terminate their farm businesses.

Additional indirect costs consisted of loss of employment to workers of the targeted facilities designated to be closed. The loss of a business in a small community may result in financial hardship for all members of that community. Loss of employment due to compliance costs would financially and emotionally erode consumer well-being (National Cost Estimates, 1988).

Benefit Analysis
The benefits resulting from improved protection of groundwater quality are the costs that the regulation would help both consumers and businesses in the State of Illinois to avoid. The major benefit of this regulation to consumers would be the prevention of illnesses that might occur due to water contamination.

Three facilities, surface impoundments, agricultural chemical plants, and landfills would incur over 80% of the direct total costs of implementing this regulation. Because of the complexity of estimating the benefits of protection from a particular leakage of chemicals into the water wells, those three facilities were analyzed in detail.

The sum of benefits from the regulation directed at these facilities totaled 1.285 million dollars (see Table 5). These are only the quantitative benefits, and loss of life is not included in this analysis, as was directed by the State of Illinois.

Table 5
Costs and Benefit Comparison for Selected Facilities (Present Value in Thousands of 1990 Dollars)

Facility Type	Total Compliance Cost	Total Benefit Amount
Surface Impoundment	$19,995.8	$ 603.9
Agricultural Chemical	$ 6,080.1	$ 639.3
Landfill	$ 3,980.0	$ 41.8
Totals	$30,055.9	$1,285.0

Cost-Benefit Comparison
The quantitative results of this economic impact study are displayed in Table 5. The total compliance costs to the selected businesses were $30 million, whereas the total benefits to the communities were estimated to be $1.28 million. The costs of implementing this regulation were estimated to far exceed the quantitative benefits.

There are three explanations for this difference. First, no value on the loss of life due to water contamination was incorporated into the quantitative analysis. Secondly, the Monte Carlo procedure is based on averages. There is no way of predicting the magnitude of a severe contamination incident. Finally, the ecological impact as well as other qualitative factors were not quantified. These could be areas of future research.

Based in part by these estimates, the Illinois EPA decided to enact this regulation. The difference between costs and benefits of this regulation is the premium that the State of Illinois is willing to pay for social insurance. Policymakers decided that preventing the loss of life and other qualitative aspects were worth 28.8 million dollars. The premium for social insurance will be an important issue to study in the future as more regulation is proposed.

Economic-Environmental Implications

Maintaining our drinking water has implications that reach far into the future. The avoidance of polluting an underground water supply may have benefits that cannot be anticipated. For example, some pollutants retain their dangerous potency for hundreds of years. Many generations from now will have to suffer with the effects of those pollutants.

Technological progress is imperative to achieve economic growth. Often technology is accompanied by pollutants which must be discarded. Therefore it is important for analysis of regulation to be conducted so that economic activity can continue without seriously impairing our natural environment. A balance between technological progress and environmental maintenance must be achieved.

By protecting our water source, the required supply of potable water can be insured. The quality and price of water would remain such that all consumers would be able to purchase what is necessary for their well-being. Additionally, regulation to maintain the quality of air, lakes and oceans must be evaluated.

Quantitative analysis is important to prevent overregulation. However, qualitative benefits must not be overlooked in a cost benefit analysis. Maintaining natural resources is important to consumers, but maintaining a balance of regulation and economic impact is also important to our society.

References

Cothern, C.R. (1986). Estimating risk to human health. Environmental Science and Technology, 20, 111-116.

Cothern, C.R. (1986). Techniques for the assessment of carcinogenic risk due to drinking water contaminants. Critical Reviews in Environmental Control, 16(4), 357-399.

Gallagher, D., Scott, R.C. & Garbade, J. (1991). Prepared for Illinois Department of Energy and Natural Resources, Office of Research and Planning. Economic Impact Study of Regulations for Activities within Setback Zones and Regulated Recharge Areas (Docket R89-5).

Mansfield, E. (1980). Statistics for business and economics. New York: W.W. Norton Co.

Samuelson, P.A. & Nordhaus, W.D. (1989). Microeconomics. New York: McGraw-Hill Book Co.

Shechter, M. (1985). Economic aspects in the investigation of groundwater contamination episodes. Ground Water, 23, 190-197.

Williams, F.L. & Hafstrom, J.L. (1986). Compendium of quality of life research. Urbana, IL: Illinois Agricultural Experiment Station.

_____. (1990). Drinking water. Environmental Protection Agency Journal, 16(5), 22-25.

_____. (1988). Health advisory. Washington,

D.C.: Office of Drinking Water.

_____. (1973). <u>The quality of life concept: a potential new tool for decision-makers</u>. Washington, D.C.:   Office of Research and Monitoring.

_____. (1988).   <u>National cost estimates</u>. Washington, D.C.: Office of the Actuary.

Does It Cost More to Buy "Green"?

Brenda J. Cude, University of Illinois at Urbana-Champaign[1]

Consumers are becoming increasingly interested in assessing the environmental impacts of their decisions. Yet, the popular view that it costs more to buy the environmentally preferred choice may deter some consumers from acting on their concerns. The purpose of this study was to determine whether a price differential exists between so-called greened up products (environmentally improved versions of established products) and their alternatives. Prices were collected in 28 supermarkets in a large midwest state.

Consumers are becoming increasingly interested in assessing the environmental impacts of their purchase, use, and disposal decisions. In a 1990 survey, nearly 90% of consumers said they considered the environmental impact of the products they buy and over one-half have decided not to buy a product because they worried about the environmental impact of the product or package (Hager, 1990).

Marketers have responded by introducing new "green" products and redesigning existing products and packaging. In 1991, green products accounted for 7% of all household product sales, 7% of all health and beauty aid sales (Green MarketAlert, 1992a), 6% of total food sales, and 3% of annual beverage sales (Green MarketAlert, 1992b). Sales of green products as a percent of the total are expected to increase to 10% or more in each of the four categories by 1996 (Green MarketAlert, 1992a & 1992b).

Response by consumers to environmental marketing has been mixed. Polls (Hartman, 1992; Roper Organization, 1990; Roper Organization, 1992;) estimate that no more than 23% to 26% of the population considers itself to be an environmentalist. Up to one-half of our population continues to respond to environmental issues with either negativism or apathy (Roper Organization, 1992).

One reason consumers commonly cite for not "buying green" is that environmentally responsible products cost more. Over one-half of the respondents in the Roper Organization's (1990) poll indicated that the higher price of more environmentally responsible alternatives was a factor in explaining why they don't do more for the environment. In Roper's 1992 poll, nearly half of all Americans would not pay any additional money to

buy eight products offering environmental benefits. In fact, public opinion polls (Gerstman & Meyers, 1989; Hartman, 1992; Roper Organization, 1990; Roper Organization, 1992) have assumed that the green alternative is more expensive since a standard question for such polls is, "How much more would you be willing to pay for a more environmentally conscious product?"

This article examines the issue of whether it is reality or myth that green alternatives are more expensive. It reports the results of a price survey in one state in which alternatives making environmental claims were compared to more traditional choices. Implications for educators are also identified.

Review of Literature

A review of literature uncovered very limited evidence to substantiate the popular opinion that environmentally responsible products are higher in price than alternatives. However, the idea that there is a significant price differential appears often in the popular press (Manning, 1991; Roha, 1991; Wang, 1991). One article reported that it would cost the typical family about $155 more a year to buy "green" toilet paper, dishwasher soap, and laundry detergents (Williams, 1991). However, no information is available about how or where prices were collected or how the "green" alternatives were selected.

Ligon (1991) compared the prices of 15 products in one of three categories:

1. bulk versus single-serving packages,

2. disposable versus reusable or recyclable packages, and

3. excessively packaged products versus products in little or no packaging.

The data yielded few surprises. The five items priced in bulk were from 22% to 459% more expensive in single-serving packaging. Bulk was apparently simply defined as packaging other than single serving; for example, one price comparison was between individually wrapped sugar packages and a 5-pound bag of sugar. Thus, this portion of the study appears to merely confirm a variation on the numerous previous studies (see Cude & Walker, 1984, for example) that have examined the unit prices of larger versus smaller sizes.

[1]Associate Professor, Division of Consumer Sciences

In the second category, prices of disposable versus recyclable packages were examined. For example, prices for microwaveable popcorn versus popcorn in a recyclable container were compared. The price differential in this category ranged from 29% to 180%; a pound of coffee in premeasured filters was 71% more expensive than a pound of coffee in a metal can and 50 filters.

The third category compared the prices of excessively versus minimally packaged products. The researcher did not define "excessively" packaged but included the following comparisons in this category: produce shrink wrapped on a polystyrene tray versus unpackaged produce, microwaveable rice versus a 10-pound bag, and a disposable camera versus a roll of film. Again, the excessively packaged products cost more; the price differentials ranged from 24% to 1531%.

Although Ligon addressed interesting questions, the study has numerous limitations. First, prices were collected at a single store at only one point in time. The author's categories were not defined nor is it clear why certain products were appropriate examples of their categories. While it is true that basing purchase decisions on the lowest unit price not only saves the consumer dollars but also is often an environmentally conscious decision, the study does not address the issue of whether products promoted for their environmental benefits are indeed more expensive.

Carl Frankel (1991), editor of Green MarketAlert, has identified two categories of products touting environmental benefits: deep-green and greened up. "Deep-green" products have built their very identities around their claimed environmental virtues. Examples include biodegradable and compostable diapers, some household cleaners, unbleached coffee filters, and some health and beauty products. Most deep-green products have captured relatively small market shares. In 1991, Frankel (Green MarketAlert, 1992a, 1992b) estimated that deep-green products have no more than 2% of the market share for household products, foods, and beverages, and 4% of total health and beauty aid sales.

In most categories, far more products touting environmental benefits are "greened up"--environmentally improved versions of established products (Green MarketAlert, 1992b). Examples include concentrated laundry products and recycled bath tissues. Greened up products have captured relatively impressive market shares. For example, by the end of 1992, powder concentrated detergents had captured 55% of all detergent sales, up from 35% just 1 year earlier (Bird, 1993).

Another important distinction between deep-green and greened up products is that greened up products are more likely to be in national distribution. The relatively smaller market shares of deep-green products suggest higher distribution and marketing costs per unit than for greened up products. Also, manufacturers of deep-green products tend to be too small to achieve economies of scale (Wang, 1991). Therefore, one might expect deep-green products to be less available to consumers and more expensive to buy than greened up products.

Research Objectives

This research had two objectives. The first was to determine whether a price differential exists between greened up products and their alternatives (other than deep-green products) and, if so, the magnitude of that price differential. Greened up products were selected as the focus of the study primarily because they were more likely to be found in supermarkets than deep-green products.

The second objective was to determine whether greened up products are available to consumers in both large and small stores and, if so, whether the price differential varies with the size of the store. One might expect smaller stores to be less likely to stock greened up products and/or to price them higher. Smaller stores are more likely to be independent stores or small "Mom and Pop" stores. Compared to larger stores, smaller stores tend to stock fewer items and may be unable to charge the lower prices of larger stores. Also, to the extent that managers of smaller stores view products claiming environmental benefits as specialty items, they may be less likely to stock such items.

Procedures

Ideally, the products selected for the study would be ones in which an option was available which was clearly environmentally superior to the alternatives. However, environmental superiority is not easily defined (see, for example, Consumer Reports, 1992). Therefore, for the purposes of this study, the comparison was between product options claiming a green edge and alternatives not making a claim.

Nine products were selected for price comparison. The criteria for selection were that the product was readily available in both large and small supermarkets[1] and that there was at least one greened up brand alternative being marketed as more environmentally conscious. Comparisons were made for the following products;[2] the greened up choice is in italics:

Laundry detergent - Liquid, concentrated powder, and regular powder

Fabric softener - Fully constituted liquid and concentrate[3]

Paper towels, napkins, toilet tissue, and facial tissue - With and without a recycled content claim

Coffee filters - <u>Unbleached</u> versus no claim

Cleaning products - In a <u>recycled plastic</u> bottle versus a conventional plastic bottle; in an aerosol can versus a <u>trigger spray bottle</u>

Feminine hygiene products - <u>With</u> and without a <u>biodegradability claim</u>

Data collection procedures were carefully defined to reduce variation across data collectors. For each of the "conventional" alternatives (i.e., fully constituted liquid fabric softener), one to three brand names were selected for data collection. To insure availability at as many stores as possible, brands selected were ones widely advertised nationally (<u>Advertising Age</u>, 1990). The goal was to identify at least one brand likely to be found in all stores to be included in the survey. For example, Tide was selected as the brand name for comparison for laundry detergent. Prices were collected for Tide liquid, Tide concentrated powder, and Tide regular powder detergent. Package sizes and other descriptive information (e.g., regular absorbency) were defined for each of the conventional alternatives.

Brand names, package sizes, and other descriptive information were also defined for the majority of the green alternatives in each of the product categories. Brands were selected based on surveys of local stores. Because there are a multitude of brands of recycled paper products, data collectors were given a list of brand names they might encounter and were asked to record information about <u>any</u> paper product making a recycled content claim.

Price differentials may reflect differences in a variety of factors in addition to environmental merit, including demand, packaging, advertising, and quality. Every attempt was made to control for as many of the factors as possible. Different forms of the same brand were compared for three products (fabric softener, detergent, and furniture cleaner). For two other products (household cleaner and tampons), the comparisons were between two brands that dominate the markets.

Data collectors were instructed to select a fairly large, "normal" supermarket in their community (not a convenience or specialty store). They also recorded the store size and noted any special promotion in the store related to environmental concerns such as a shelf labeling program or a program to collect grocery bags.

Data collectors were recruited through the Cooperative Extension Service. Information about the project was distributed throughout the state and volunteers were requested. The 27 individuals who volunteered to collect data consisted primarily of professional home economists; nine were volunteers or community workers under the supervision of a professional.

Results

Prices were collected from 28 supermarkets in July 1991 in a large midwest state. The supermarkets were well distributed geographically throughout the state and represented both urban and rural locations.

The stores from which data were collected were fairly equally divided across four size categories. Eight were 50,000 square feet or larger while six were smaller than 10,000 square feet. Seven stores were 10,000 to 25,000 square feet and seven were 25,000 to 49,999 square feet in size.

Price differentials are reported in Table 1 as mean percentages. They were computed by averaging the percent difference between the price of the green alternative and the price of the conventional choice.

Objective 1

Laundry detergent. The prices per load of concentrated powder ("ultra") detergents, liquid detergents, and regular powder detergents were compared. On the average, the concentrated alternative cost 18% less per load than the liquid detergent and 24% less than the regular powder detergent. The concentrated alternative was, on the average, 5.6 cents less per load than liquid detergent (21.7 cents compared to 27.3 cents). The "ultra" detergent was 6.7 cents less per load than regular powder detergent. At the largest stores, the "ultra" detergent was 9% less expensive per load than liquid on the average and 26% less per load than regular detergent. The differentials were 22% and 23%, respectively, at the smallest stores. The concentrated detergent was less expensive per load than either the liquid or the regular powdered detergent in all but one of the price comparisons made. The greatest variation in the price differences was between ultra and liquid detergents in the largest stores.

Fabric softener. On average, the concentrated refill was 58 cents cheaper than the 64-ounce container, a cost savings of 19%. The concentrate was the same price as or less expensive than the 64-ounce container at each of the 27 stores that stocked both items. On average, the price differential across the stores was as little as 6 cents and as much as $1.04.

Recycled paper products. Prices for paper towels and toilet tissue were compared per 10 square feet. Paper napkins and facial tissues were priced per 10 items. For each of the four paper products, the mean price of the option claiming recycled content was lower per unit of measure than the mean price of the option not claiming recycled content. In stores with both a recycled and a nonrecycled choice, the recycled option was more expensive in only 5 of the 56 comparisons for paper towels and 11 of the 60 toilet tissue price comparisons; the recycled option was the less expensive choice for paper napkins in all but 3 of

Table 1.

Mean Percent Price Difference between Greened Up and Conventional Options.

Comparisons	<50,000 sq ft			25,000-49,999 sq. ft.			Store Size 10,000-24,999 sq. ft.			>10,000 sq. ft.			All Stores		
	n	% Price Diff.	s.d.	n	% Price Diff.	s.d.	n	% Price Diff.	s.d.	n	% Price Diff.	s.d.	n	% Price Diff.	s.d.
Concentrated Powder Laundry Detergent[a] *versus*															
Liquid	8	-9.1%	35.0	6	-18.2%	9.5	7	-25.0%	5.4	4	-22.3%	2.7	25	-17.9%	20.7
Regular Powder	7	-25.7	8.7	6	-22.3	10.6	7	-23.3	11.6	2	-23.3	0.8	22	-23.8	9.4
Concentrated Fabric Softener[b] *versus*															
Regular Liquid	8	-20.7	4.7	7	-16.5	8.2	7	-17.0	9.1	5	-20.6	5.6	27	-18.6	7.0
Recycled Paper Towels[c] *versus*															
Brand 1 Not Recycled	7	-34.6	18.4	7	-39.0	10.7	7	-39.9	21.7	9	-39.1	17.9	30	-38.2	16.9
Brand 2 Not Recycled	6	-13.0	11.6	7	-6.4	16.1	6	-22.3	22.6	8	-27.5	19.7	27	-17.6	19.0
Recycled Toilet Tissue[d] *versus*															
Brand 1 Not Recycled	8	-16.4	32.1	8	-32.3	16.1	9	-21.3	23.2	5	-35.8	21.9	30	-25.3	24.2
Brand 2 Not Recycled	8	-21.5	27.3	8	-17.4	27.4	9	-19.8	28.1	5	-32.1	24.8	30	-21.7	26.2
Recycled Facial Tissues[e] *versus*															
Brand 1 Not Recycled	3	-31.7	9.4	5	-21.7	5.6	4	-24.3	23.6	4	-34.8	12.7	16	-27.5	14.0
Brand 2 Not Recycled	3	-27.6	12.0	5	-24.5	5.1	4	-26.2	26.1	2	-33.3	0.7	14	-26.9	14.0
Recycled Paper Napkins[d] *versus*															
Not Recycled	5	-11.6	13.0	7	-12.1	12.1	5	-14.6	17.6	·	—	—	17	-12.7	13.3
Unbleached Coffee Filters[e] *versus*															
Brand 1 *versus* No Claim	9	+44.4	58.8	6	+40.7	20.3	7	+56.4	57.0	2	+50.9	65.3	24	+47.5	48.7
Brand 2 *versus* No Claim	8	+48.0	66.4	6	+109.5	86.5	5	+82.8	86.1	3	+63.4	49.5	22	+74.8	74.5
Household Cleaner in Recycled Plastic Bottle *versus*															
Virgin Plastic Bottle	7	+4.8	5.9	5	-0.2	6.8	5	-3.2	12.8	2	-9.1	12.9	19	-0.1	9.4
Furniture Cleaner in Trigger Spray Bottle *versus*															
Aerosol Container	6	-4.9	8.2	4	-10.2	6.8	5	-3.5	5.6	4	-2.2	8.0	19	-5.3	7.0
Tampons Claiming Biodegradability *versus*															
No Claim	5	-3.3	12.8	6	-9.9	10.8	4	-11.6	21.3	3	+4.7	4.1	18	-6.0	13.8

[a] Price per load.
[b] Price comparison between 64 oz. of regular and 2.5 oz. of concentrated (equals 64 oz. reconstituted)
[c] Price per 10 sq. ft.
[d] Price per 10 tissues/napkins.
[e] Price per 100.

the 17 comparisons and in all but 2 of the 30 comparisons for facial tissues.

The mean percent difference in prices ranged from 13% for paper napkins to 38% for one brand of paper towels. Recycled toilet tissue and facial tissue were, on the average, 22% to 27% less expensive than options not claiming recycled content. However, compared to the other product categories the standard deviations were relatively large for recycled paper products, especially toilet tissue.

Coffee filters. "No bleach added" is a common environmental claim made for coffee filters. The mean prices of two popular brands that make that claim were $1.24 and $1.54, respectively, per 100 filters. The mean price of the 14 brands that did not make an environmental claim was $1.04 per 100. In stores that stocked both bleached and unbleached coffee filters, unbleached Brand 1 was more expensive than the bleached version in 20 of 24 comparisons; unbleached Brand 2 was more expensive than the bleached version in 21 of 22 comparisons. The mean price differentials were 47% (Brand 1) and 75% (Brand 2). However, the standard deviations were larger for coffee filters than for any other product category.

Cleaning products. Two household cleaners were compared, one marketed in a recycled plastic bottle and the other in a conventional plastic bottle. The mean prices of the two were virtually the same at $1.61 for the product in the recycled plastic bottle and $1.63 for the product in the conventional bottle.

Prices were also compared for a furniture cleaner marketed in an aerosol can and the same brand in a trigger spray bottle. The mean price of 14 ounces in the aerosol spray was $3.04 compared to $2.87 in the trigger spray bottle, a difference of 5%.

Feminine hygiene products. Prices were compared for one brand that made a biodegradability claim and one that did not. For a 40-count box of regular tampons, the mean price of the brand making the environmental claim was $5.64 compared to $5.82 for the brand that made no environmental claim. Overall, the mean price differential was 6%.

Objective 2

The second objective was to determine if green alternatives were available in small as well as large stores and, if so, if the price differential between alternatives varied by store size. The data consistently indicated that green alternatives were available in stores in each of the four size categories. The majority of the stores in each size category sold concentrated detergent and fabric softener, recycled paper towels, and biodegradable tampons. Regardless of size, stores were least likely to sell recycled facial tissue. Compared to larger stores, smaller stores were less likely to stock recycled toilet tissue and paper

napkins, unbleached coffee filters, and household cleaner in a recycled plastic bottle.

Also, the price differentials between the conventional and the green alternatives were quite a bit larger in the smaller stores than in the other stores. Across all of the data collected, the mean price difference in the two largest store size categories was 6%, compared to 9% in stores 10,000 to 24,000 square feet and 17% in the smallest stores.

Summary and Discussion

In summary, coffee filters was the only product category in which the "green" alternative was consistently more expensive per unit. However, this product category was unique in two respects. It was the only category in which the products not making a green claim were more likely to be store brands or generics rather than nationally advertised brands. Also, Brand 2, a brown coffee filter, might be considered a deep-green brand; Brand 1, which claimed to use a chlorine-free bleaching process, was closer to the greened up concept.

The consistent and significant price advantage of concentrated fabric softener and laundry detergent over conventional alternatives should provide added incentive to consumers who want to reduce the amounts of packaging waste they generate. And, the price advantage rather than the environmental benefits of reduced packaging may explain the rapid increase in market share for concentrates. However, the price advantage of concentrated detergent would rapidly disappear if consumers who doubt the cleaning ability of only 4 ounces used far more than recommended. The price advantage of recycled paper products over nonrecycled options was somewhat unexpected and is contrary to the expectations of some consumers (Cude, 1991). However, other consumers believe the quality of recycled paper products to be consistently lower than that of nonrecycled choices and would expect recycled paper products to be less expensive (Cude, 1991).

Implications for Educators
and Future Research

Consumers identify a variety of reasons to explain why they choose not to incorporate environmental concerns in their purchase decisions. This research suggests that at least one of those reasons, that buying green costs more, may not be valid. However, it is not clear that all of the greened up options included in the study are environmentally superior to their conventional alternatives. Future researchers are challenged to replicate the study after developing an operational definition of "green" that would be widely accepted.

Educators could replicate this research as a class project or with local community organizations. Future research projects should include deep-green options as well as a greater variety of greened up products with data collection in multiple retail outlets, including hardware stores, discount retail stores, mail order catalogs, and garden supply centers as well as supermarkets.

References

Advertising Age. (1990, May 21). Brands, products & services by ad spending, pp. 26-27.

Bird, L. (1993, January 5). Detergent industry spins into new cycle. The Wall Street Journal, pp. B1, B4.

Consumer Reports. (1992, November). Are you a green consumer?, pp. 704-707.

Cude, B.J. (1991, November 13). Testimony before the Environmental Protection Agency, Public hearings on use of the terms recycled and recyclable and the recycling emblem in environmental marketing claims.

Cude, B. & Walker, R. (1984). Quantity surcharges: Are they important in choosing a shopping strategy? Journal of Consumer Affairs, 18(2), 287-295.

Frankel, C. (1991). Industry's response to green consumerism: What it has done, what more it can do. In Proceedings of the National Environmental Labeling Conference (pp. 159-167). Media, Penn.: Pennsylvania Resources Council.

Gerstman & Meyers, Inc. (1989, October). Consumer solid waste management: Awareness, attitude, and behavior study. New York: Author.

Green MarketAlert. (1992a, March). Green MarketAlert's green product market forecasts, 1991-1992: Part 1: Household products and health and beauty aids, pp. 1-6.

_____. (1992b, April). Green MarketAlert's green product market forecasts, 1991-1992: Part 2: Food and beverage markets, pp. 1-5.

Hager, M. (1990, March/April). What you can do to save the earth. Consumers Digest, pp. 62-66.

The Hartman Group. (1992, January). The Hartman environmental marketing report. Newport Beach, Calif.: The Hartman Group.

Ligon, P.J. (1991, November). Isolating the cost of excessive packaging. BioCycle, pp. 68-70.

Manning, A. (1991, June 27). A store for those who buy in to ecology. USA Today, p. 6D.

Roha, R. (1991, May). It's not easy shopping green. Changing Times, pp. 67-68.

Roper Organization Inc. (1990, July). The environment: Public attitudes and individual behavior. Racine, Wis.: S.C. Johnson & Son, Inc.

Roper Organization Inc. (1992, July). Environmental behavior, North America: Canada, Mexico, United States. Racine, Wis.: S.C. Johnson & Son, Inc.

Wang, P. (1991, September). Going for the green. Money, pp. 98-102.

Williams, C. (1991, June 23). The price of the green. Chicago Tribune, p C1.

Endnotes

1. While price comparisons could also have easily been made among products sold in hardware stores, this research limited its focus to items sold in supermarkets.
2. Batteries and light bulbs were eliminated from the comparisons because the researcher discovered that neither item was routinely available in supermarkets. Trash bags were also eliminated because an alternative claiming environmental superiority was not always available.
3. The concentrate on the market at the time of the study was designed to be diluted with water; "ultra" fabric softeners were not yet available.

Households' Perceptions of the Severity of an Environmental Crisis and Decision-Making Surrounding the Adoption of Conservation Activities

Walter L. Ellis, University of New Hampshire[1]

This study ascertains whether households' perceptions of the severity of an environmental crisis are related to their decisions to adopt conservation activities. Data came from a 1990 Washington Post poll. An OLS multiple regression found households who perceived the world currently to be facing an environmental crisis to report adopting conservation activities. This perception was found to be a more consistent predictor of households' decisions to adopt conservation activities than were sociodemographic factors.

Introduction

There is growing concern among many environmentalists and policy makers that problems with the environment are worsening. In fact, for the first time in this century a June 1992 Earth Summit was held in Rio de Janeiro to address problems with the environment. The apparent reduction of the earth's ozone layer, global warming, and solid and hazardous wastes are among the most pressing problems that may be contributing to the problems with the environment (Holdgate, 1991; Knox, 1991; Davis, 1990; Wirth, 1990; Begley, 1988; & Russell, 1987).

Conservation is the key to mitigating problems with the environment. However, conservation remains little practiced (DeYoung, 1985-86). Driving less can help reduce the emissions of carbon monoxide and other toxic air pollutants. Yet, it is estimated that the number of motor vehicle miles travelled by individuals doubled from one trillion in 1970, to two trillion, in 1990 (Wilson, 1991).

Recycling is seen by many as an excellent way to handle the nation's waste problems (Knox, 1991; Belsie, 1990; Williams and Duxbury, 1987). It can reduce solid waste by 15 to 50 percent (Forester, 1988). However, while states have set an arbitrary recycling goal of 25 percent of their waste (Belsie, 1990; Thomas, 1988), the nation is currently recycling at the rate of only 10 percent or less (Knox, 1991).

Households' perceptions of the severity of an environmental crisis may be related to their decisions to adopt conservation activities. The purpose of this study, therefore, is to ascertain whether or not households' perceptions of the severity of an environmental crisis are related to their decisions to adopt conservation activities. The objectives of this study are to: 1) ascertain households' perceptions of the severity of an environmental crisis, and 2) ascertain whether or not households' perceptions of the severity of an environmental crisis are related to their decision-making relative to the adoption of specific conservation activities.

Conservation is crucial to the environment. Thus, it is critical that environmental/consumer educators have a working knowledge of research on households' perception of the severity of an environmental crisis and decisions that result regarding the adoption of conservation activities. The understanding of such research could aid them in developing strategies and educational programs to help reduce any barriers to households' adoption of such activities.

Review of Literature

Earlier researchers have focused on individuals who express concern about environmental problems and issues. Researchers have found among other factors that being white and female are positively associated with environmental concern (Taylor, 1989; Lowe & Pinhey, 1982); urban residence is positively associated with environmental concern (Van Liere & Dunlap, 1980; Mohai & Twight, 1987; Lowe & Pinhey, 1982); and agricultural families and family income were negatively associated with environmental concern.

Information regarding the relationship of education and age to environmental concern is not clear. Several researchers have found education to be positively associated with environmental concern (Lowe & Pinhey, 1982; Van Liere & Dunlap, 1980; Tognacci, Weigel, Wideen, & Vernon, 1972). Research by Samdahl and Robertson (1989) found education to be the reverse.

Several researchers have found age to be negatively associated with environmental concern (Van Liere & Dunlap, 1980; Mohai & Twight, 1987; Tognacci et al., 1972; Lowe & Pinhey, 1982). Research by Samdahl and Robertson (1989) again found the reverse. Van Liere and Dunlap (1980) and Samdahl and Robertson (1989) report that in general, sociodemographic factors can not effectively explain variation in environmental concern because the predictive ability of coefficients for these factors is quite low.

---

[1]Assistant Professor, Department of Family and Consumer Studies

Political ideology has been found to be an important variable in expressing environmental concern. Van Liere and Dunlap (1980) found those politically liberal to be positively associated with environmental concern. Political conservatism has been found to be negatively associated with environmental concern (Lowe & Pinhey, 1982).

More recently, researchers have defined environmental concern as the extent to which individuals perceive that their own health and personal well-being are directly threatened by environmental problems. Research by Baldassare and Katz (1992) found perceived environmental threat to be highest among younger residents, women, liberals, and democrats. They also found that residents who perceived environmental problems as a threat to their health and personal well-being significantly engaged in overall environmental practices and, specifically, recycled, limited their driving, conserved water, and purchased environmentally safe products.

Research Hypothesis

The current study examines another critical dimension of environmental concern, that is, the extent to which households' perceive the world currently to be facing an environmental crisis. It is hypothesized that households who perceive the world currently to be facing an environmental crisis will be more likely to adopt specific conservation activities than households who view the word "crisis" to be too strong a word to describe the current situation.

Methodology

Data

The data used in this study were obtained from a 1990 Washington Post poll which centered on environmental issues. Adults aged 18 and over living in households with telephones in the 48 contiguous states and the District of Columbia were selected by random digit dialing. Within the household, the respondent selected was the adult living in the household who last had a birthday and who was at home at the time of the interview. The sample consisted of 1,016 respondents.

The respondents were asked if they thought the world currently is facing an environmental crisis, or if they felt that the word "crisis" is too strong a word to describe the current situation. Respondents were also asked if they thought problems with the environment are exaggerated. In addition, respondents were asked if they had done anything specifically to improve the environment such as limiting their driving to ease air pollution, regularly participating in a community trash recycling program, cutting back on the amount of water they use around the house, or stopping the use of certain products because they were environmentally harmful. Sociodemographic information on respondents was also collected.

Descriptive Statistics

The majority (92 percent) of respondents were white. Over half (52 percent) of the respondents were females. A third of the respondents lived in small towns. A third of the respondents were between the ages of 31 and 44. The most likely (41 percent) level of education completed was high school. The majority (58 percent) of respondents were full-time workers.

The greatest proportion (41 percent) of respondents earned between $30,000 and $50,000. Over half (52 percent) of the respondents identified with the working class. The respondents were most likely (41 percent) to describe their political orientation as moderate. Conservatives (26 percent) and liberals (24 percent) were almost evenly divided.

Respondents were concerned with environmental problems. Three-fourths of the respondents believed that problems with the environment are not exaggerated. Well over half (58 percent) of the respondents perceived the world currently to be facing an environmental crisis. This finding is comparable to research by Baldassare and Katz (1992) who found 60 percent of their residents to perceive the personal threat of environmental problems as "Very Serious."

Reported frequencies of adopting conservation activities were high. Over two-thirds (66 percent) of the respondents regularly participated in a community trash recycling program, 48 percent limited their driving to ease air pollution, 75 percent cut back on the amount of water they use around the house, and 77 percent stopped using certain products because they were environmentally harmful. These findings are comparable with other studies of environmental concern. Research by Baldassare and Katz (1992) found 68 percent of their residents to often recycle, 76 percent to often conserve water, 51 percent to often purchase environmentally safe products, and 35 percent to often limit their driving to reduce air pollution. An April 1991 Gallup Poll found 86 percent of the American public to recycle, 46 percent to cut back on the use of their cars, 68 percent to cut back on their water use, and 68 percent to avoid buying or using aerosol sprays (Hueber, 1991).

Data Analysis

An Ordinary Least Squares (OLS) multiple regression procedure was used to: 1) ascertain households' perceptions of the severity of an environmental crisis, and 2) ascertain whether or not households' perceptions of the severity of an environmental crisis are related to their decisions to adopt specific conservation activities. The purpose of the OLS multiple regression is to estimate the independent effect of each sociodemographic variable on perceptions of the severity of an environmental crisis when all other sociodemographic variables in the equation are constant.

Only sociodemographic variables that have been found to be important in the environmental concern literature were included in the OLS regression equation. All variables were entered into the equation simultaneously using the force entry option in the Statistical Package for the Social Sciences (SPSS Inc., 1983). The standardized regression coefficient was used to describe the effects of the variables.

Findings and Discussions

Objective 1

The first objective was to ascertain households' perceptions of the severity of an environmental crisis. The data are reported in Table 1. Blacks and females were likely to perceive the world currently to be facing an environmental crisis. Alternatively, whites and males were likely to view the word "crisis" to be too strong a word to describe the current situation of the environment.

Blacks' perception that the world currently is facing an environmental crisis is not surprising given the fact that they are likely to experience "environmental racism" (Mohai & Bryant, 1992). Blacks are exposed to a disproportionate share of environmental hazards (Bullard, 1992; Mohai & Bryant, 1992; Taylor, 1992). For instance, blacks and other minorities are four times more likely than white residents to live within one mile of a commercial hazardous waste facility (Mohai & Bryan, 1992).

Females' perception that the world currently is facing an environmental crisis may be due in part to the fact that they are concerned about environmental problems. Females are more concerned than males about environmental issues such as air pollution and hazardous waste (Blocker & Eckberg, 1989). Moreover, females have been found to perceive air pollution as being a threat to their health and personal well-being (Baldassare & Katz, 1992).

Table 1
OLS regression of factors influencing households' perception that the world currently is facing an environmental crisis

Factors	
Conservative	-.02
Education	.03
Black	.07*
Urban	.03
Female	.10*
Age	-.02
Rural	.05
Liberal	-.01
Income	.01

R^2 =   .02
F   = 2.05
*   = $p \leq .05$

Objective 2

The second objective was to ascertain whether or not households' perceptions of the severity of an environmental crisis are related to their decision-making relative to the adoption of specific conservation activities. The data are reported in Table 2. Households who perceived the world currently to be facing an environmental crisis were likely to adopt all of the positive conservation activities. Alternatively, households who viewed the word "crisis" to be too strong a word to describe the current situation were less likely to adopt these activities. This finding supports the research hypothesis.

Households who viewed the word "crisis" to be too strong a word were three times as likely to agree with the statement "Problems with the environment are exaggerated" than households who perceived the world currently to be facing an environmental crisis (41 percent and 12 percent, respectively). Thus, households who viewed the word "crisis" to be too strong a word may have felt that the adoption of conservation activities was not warranted. As indicated in the correlation matrix in Table 3, this belief was found to be negatively associated with each of the conservation activities.

Summary

Blacks and females perceived the world currently to be facing an environmental crisis. Alternatively, whites and males viewed the word "crisis" to be too strong a word to describe the current situation of the environment. Households who perceived the world currently to be facing an environmental crisis adopted all of the positive conservation activities. Alternatively, households who viewed the word "crisis" to be too strong a word to describe the current situation did not adopt these activities.

Implications for Environmental/Consumer Educators

The preservation of the environment is dependent on conservation. Households' perceptions of the severity of an environmental crisis were found to be a more consistent predictor of their decisions to adopt conservation activities than were sociodemographic factors. This finding is comparable to research by Baldassare and Katz (1992) who found personal environmental threat to be a better predictor of overall environmental practices than were demographic variables and political factors.

It is imperative that environmental/ consumer educators direct environmental education programs to that segment of the public, particularly males, who took the less drastic view of the environment by viewing the word "crisis" to be too strong a word to describe the current situation of the environment. There is some uncertainty surrounding the race finding. There may be a spurious

Table 2

OLS regression of factors influencing households' decisions to adopt conservation activities

Conservation Activities

Factors

	Recycle	Limit driving	Stop using harmful products	Cut water
Conservative	-.05	.01	.01	-.01
Education	.09*	-.03	.07*	.05
World facing crisis	.07*	.07*	.16*	.07*
Urban	-.06**	.06**	-.06*	-.01
Black	-.01	-.01	.01	-.02
Age	.06*	.11*	.03	.07*
Female	.01	.06*	.06**	.07*
Rural	-.01	.03	-.02	-.01
Liberal	.04	.04	-.01	-.01
Income	.01	-.06**	.01	-.06**
R²	.02	.04	.04	.02
F	2.40	3.83	3.84	2.15

* = p ≤ .05
** = p ≤ .1

Table 3

Pearson correlation matrix of the belief that problems with the environment are exaggerated and households' decisions to adopt conservation activities

"Problems with environment exaggerated"

Conservation activities

Recycle	-.08*
Limit driving	-.02
Stop using harmful products	-.10*
Cut water use	-.03

* = p ≤ .05

relationship due to the small sample size of black households.

Households who took the less drastic view of the environment were found to be nonadopters of conservation activities. Thus, these households are taking a passive role in the preservation of the environment. The passive role could be due in part to the fact that these households tended to believe that problems with the environment are not serious.

However, problems with the environment are serious. For instance, it has been estimated that the average individual produces in the home approximately one ton of waste per year, some of which is hazardous (Williams & Duxbury, 1987). While the generation of solid waste is expected by some to increase 20 percent by the year 2000, disposal capacity is decreasing (Forester, 1988).

It is crucial that environmental/consumer educators devise a strategy to make the seriousness of problems with the environment more apparent. One approach would be to incorporate fear appeals in the content of their environmental education programming. Research by Hine and Gilford (1991) found respondents who were exposed to an antipollution fear appeal to exhibit a higher verbal commitment to responsible environmental behavior than respondents who were not exposed.

Another approach for environmental/ consumer educators would be to advocate for more stringent environmental policies. Research by Lansana (1992) found recyclers to prefer a mandatory recycling program. However, as of 1992, only 38 states have recycling goals or mandates (Scarlett, 1992). While mandated recycling may do little to educate the public about waste management (Scarlett, 1992), it can send the message that solid and hazardous wastes are a serious problem.

Environmental/consumer educators have taken either the crisis management approach or the long-term view approach to preserving the environment. Regardless of the approach, if problems with the environment are to be dealt with effectively, then it is imperative that all households, including those who view the word "crisis" to be too strong a word to describe the current situation of the environment, make affirmative decisions to adopt conservation activities.

References

Baldassare, M. & Katz, C. (1992). The personal threat of environmental problems as predictor of environmental practices. Environment and Behavior, 24(5), 616-661.

Begley, S. (July 11, 1988). The endless Summer?

Newsweek, 18-20.

Belsie, L. (1990). Recycling abounds across America. Christian Science Monitor, 8.

Blocker, T. & Eckberg, D. (1989). Environmental issues as women's issues: General concerns and local hazards. Social Science Quarterly, 70(3), 586-593.

Bullard, Robert D. (1992). In our backyards. EPA Journal, 18(1), 11-12.

Davis, Trenton G. (1990). Learn to think globally. Journal of Environmental Health, 27-28.

DeYoung, R. (1988-89). Exploring the difference between recyclers and nonrecyclers: The role of information. Journal of Environmental Systems, 18, 341-351.

Dunlap, Riley E. (1991). Public opinion in the 1980s: Clear consensus, ambiguous commitment. Environment, 33(8), 9-37.

Forester, William S. (1988). Solid waste: There's a lot more coming. EPA Journal, 14(4), 11-12.

Hine, Donald W. & Gilford, R. (1991). Fear appeals, individual differences, and environmental concern. Journal of Environmental Education, 23(1), 36-41.

Holdgate, Martin W. (1991). The environment of tomorrow. Environment, 33(6), 14-20, 40-44.

Hueber, G. (April 1991). Americans report high levels of environmental concern, activity. The Gallup Poll Monthly, 6-12.

Knox, Robert J. (1991). Toxic overload: The waste disposal dilemma. Journal of Environmental Health, 53(6), 15-17.

Lansana, F. (1992). Distinguishing potential recyclers from nonrecyclers: A basis for developing recycling strategies. Journal of Environmental Education, 23(2), 16-23.

Lowe, George D. & Pinhey, Thomas K. (1982). Rural-urban differences in support for environmental protection. Rural Sociology, 47(1), 115-128.

Mohai, Paul & Bryant, B. (1992). Race, poverty, and the environment, EPA Journal, 18(1), 6-8.

Mohai, Paul & Twight, Ben W. (1987). Age and environmentalism: an elaboration of the buttel model using national survey evidence. Social Science Quarterly, 68(4), 798-815.

Russell, M. (1987). Environmental protection for the 1990s and beyond. Environment, 29(7), 12-15, 34-3

Bamdahl, Diane M. & Robertson, R. (1989). Social determinants of environmental concern: specification and test of the model. Environment and Behavior, 21(1), 57-81.

Scarlett, L. (1992). A forum: Will the U.S. recycling approach work? EPA Journal, 18(3), 42-45.

Statistical Package for the Social Sciences. (1983). SPSSX. New York, NY: SPSS Inc.

Taylor, D. (1992). The environmental justice movement. EPA Journal, 18(1), 23-25.

Taylor, D. (1989). Blacks and the environment: Toward an explanation of the concern and action gap between blacks and whites. Environment and Behavior, 21(2), 175-205.

Thomas, Lee M. (1988). The environmental challenges of our cities. EPA Journal, 14,(4) 2-3.

Tognacci, Louis N.; Weigel, Russell H.; Wideen, Marvin F.; Vernon, D. (1972). Environmental quality: how universal is public concern? Environment and Behavior, 4(1), 73-86.

Van Liere, Kent D. & Dunlap, Riley E. (1980). The social bases of environmental concern: A review of hypotheses, explanations and empirical evidence. Public Opinion Quarterly, 44(2), 181-197.

Williams, M. & Duxbury, D. (1987). Managing household hazardous wastes, EPA Journal, 13(3), 11-13.

Wilson, Richard D. (1991). Motor vehicles and Fuels: The strategy. EPA Journal, 17(1), 15-17.

Wirth, Timothy E. (1990). Conservation is the key, Journal of Environmental Health, 25.

Consumer Support for Policy Legislation on the Use of Recombinant Bovine Growth Hormone

Deana Grobe, Oregon State University[1]
Robin Douthitt, University of Wisconsin-Madison[2]

This study examines consumer support for policy legislation on the use of rbGH treated herd milk. Results suggest that consumers who had health concerns were willing to support both the labeling of treated herd milk, and a temporary ban on the sale of rbGH treated herd milk. The results also suggest that higher income consumers were more supportive of labeling and a temporary ban on rbGH treated herd milk.

Introduction

Biotechnology came into existence in 1973 when two scientists successfully isolated a gene and inserted it into another gene, creating living cellular material. It allows particular sequences of DNA to be "isolated, manipulated, and re-introduced into many different kinds of living things" (Post, 1982). The biotechnological "tool" used to manipulate DNA is recombinant DNA (rDNA).

As early as 1920 the naturally occurring bovine growth hormone (bGH) had been shown to increase milk production. However the number of pituitary glands needed to extract bGH to increase milk production was not cost effective. The advent of recombinant DNA technology in 1973 made it possible to produce a synthetic bovine growth hormone (rbGH) which could be injected into lactating cows to increase milk production. Approval has not been granted for its use, but commercial application to the Food and Drug Administration for approval of the synthetic hormone has sparked controversy. Farmers, producers, policy makers and consumers are debating whether there exist differences between the synthetic bovine growth hormone (rbGH) and the natural bovine growth hormone (bGH). For its manufacturers, rbGH offers a product to increase the dairy industry's milk production efficiency. However, concentration on the market's supply-side did not adequately prepare rbGH's manufacturers for the potential impact of consumers' skepticism toward rbGH. Deep rooted consumer beliefs that milk is a pure, wholesome product--an image fostered by advertisement by the National Dairy Board--has created an obstacle to acceptance of rbGH use.

This paper will examine consumer support for regulation of rbGH treated herd milk. A public policy model is applied, hypothesizing that risk-averse consumers would be willing to support policy legislation.

Literature Review

With the media bombardment of new, previously undetected technological threats to human health, consumers are "asking more questions about food quality and safety" (Huang, 1991). Many of the new questions can be attributed in part to 1) persistent problems historically to the introduction of "ill-considered" technologies, imposing dangerous products onto consumers (Hermann, 1982), and 2) erosion of consumer confidence through a mistrust in regulatory agencies.

Since the passage of the Pure Food Bill Act in 1906, legislation has often reacted to public demand after "dramatic revelations" of dangers and risks have sparked public opinion and awareness of a particular problem (Hermann, 1982). In recent decades, new technologies are emerging in the food industry to help eliminate such dangers as fat, cholesterol, sugar, salt and caffeine in our diet. However, these new food technologies do not come without risk, and little evidence exists to support the disappearance of these new technological risks (Hermann, 1982). The public will continue to be exposed to risks, and will establish individual tolerances to acceptable practices and risks.

Studies have shown a loss of consumers confidence in the ability of regulatory agencies to protect the safety, wholesomeness, and nutritional quality of the food supply (Harlander, 1991). Polls have shown decreasing consumer confidence in the safety of food throughout the end of the 1980's and early 1990's (van Ravenswaay & Hoehn, 1991). In 1989, evidence on consumer food safety confidence found a 10-15% decrease in "very" or "mostly" confident consumers. By 1990, less than 70% of respondents were "completely" or "mostly" confident that food was safe, a 15% decrease in confidence since 1989 (van Ravenswaay & Hoehn, 1991).

Biotechnology is certainly a complex science and one that consumers find difficult to understand. Because of this complexity, consumers

---

[1]Graduate Student, Family Resource Management

[2]Professor, Consumer Science

must feel that they can place a great deal of trust in either regulators or manufacturers and users. If the use of rbGH is unregulated, or if consumers perceive it as being unregulated, the authority and trustworthiness of not only the risk communicator but also the farmer and manufacturer is of the utmost importance. Farmer reluctance to accept the technology and previous manufacturer or industry safety errors will seriously undermine consumer trust.

This result may reflect the consumer's loss of confidence in regulators' ability to protect them in the market. Historically, federal regulators strategized to "eliminate or control food hazards rather than labeling the products and letting consumers decide whether to buy the product," (Harris, Padberg & Capps, 1991). However, with loss of consumer confidence in regulators' abilities to adequately protect them from risks (Harlander, 1991) consumers are increasingly either demanding that they be provided with risk information so that they can make their own assessments or engaging in a personal risk management strategy that involves curtailing their consumption of a suspect product.

Secondly, in light of regulators' reluctance to indicate through labeling whether or not milk has come from a treated herd, consumers face an involuntary risk exposure since rbGH use is a producer level decision. This problem is unsurmountable unless government reconsiders its role in this area. Previous research has shown that consumers would purchase more treated herd milk if given a choice than if an involuntary risk is imposed upon them. With involuntary risks, product criteria are determined not by the final consumer, but rather by some controlling body like producers (Starr, 1969).

In deciding whether to support specific policies or legislation, one would expect consumers to be in favor of a regulation if that particular regulation increases their utility, where "utility" is the "satisfaction that a person receives from his or her activities" (Nicholson, 1990). Therefore, we can suggest that consumers who are fearful would want to secure an acceptable risk level in order to increase their utility. That is, these consumers will be risk-averse to rbGH-treated herd milk because they would like to have more certainty about the risks presented to them. Through this framework, a hypothesis is posed that risk-averse consumers would be willing to support either (1) a temporary ban or (2) labeling legislation to ensure an acceptable risk in the products they purchase. The purpose of this analysis is to find out what factors influence consumers' willingness to support these specific policy legislation. Whether consumers expressed concerns about future health effects, income, and education were included as explanatory variables in the models.

Data

The data used in this analysis were collected via telephone survey administered to 1,056 randomly selected Wisconsin households. Interviews were conducted with the adult person who made most of the household food purchase decisions. The interviews were approximately 7 minutes in length and took place between February 26 and may 9, 1990. The survey response rate was 69.2 percent (Douthitt, 1991).

Only respondents who were aware of the rbGH controversy (89% of entire sample) were asked to respond to the entire survey. Other respondents were only asked demographic questions. Milk purchasing respondents were asked about the quantity of milk they purchased, the average price they paid, and how much they were willing to pay for non-treated herd milk, if they had a preference. Thus, the subsample used in this analysis consists of respondents who (a) were the primary food purchasers for their family, (b) were aware of rbGH issues, (c) purchased milk, and (d) reported complete data. The final subsample size was 801.

Models

In Wisconsin, the government has tried to address consumer concerns and the potential negative economic effects on farmers of rbGH with two different strategies: a temporary moratorium on the sale of products from treated herds and product labeling. Therefore, opinions of these policy strategies were asked of respondents and are the only two included in this analysis.

Equation (1) represents the model to estimate consumer support for legislation to label fluid milk from rbGH treated herds,

$$SUPPLAB = \beta_0 + \beta_1 HEALTHCON + \beta_2 INCOME + \beta_3 EDUC + \epsilon \quad (1)$$

where labeling support is operationalized as SUPPLAB, an indicator variable equal to one if the respondent supported labeling of milk from cows treated with rbGH. Whereas, the independent variables are: HEALTHCON, an indicator variable equal to one if the respondent expressed concern over discovery of future ill-health effects related to the use of rbGH; and the control variables INCOME, equal to (1) if the respondents' household income was over the state median of about $30,000; and EDUC, a continuous variable measuring highest grade of school completed.

The question on support for labeling (SUPPLAB), asked whether the respondent supported or opposed legislation that would require labeling of dairy products that used milk from cows treated with rbGH. The independent variables in the model provide measure of factors that may effect an increase in support for labeling legislation. HEALTHCON measures the concern for future discovery of ill-health effects. If consumers are concerned about future health effects, they will be more willing to support labeling. Thus, it is hypothesized that HEALTHCON will positively influence SUPPLAB, as an increase in health concern increases support for labeling. HEALTHCON is an indicator variable equal to (1) if there was a concern for health, (0) otherwise.

Income was included in the model as it is hypothesized that when family's economic status increases the opportunity cost of an accident would increase, so one might expect these consumers to be more risk-averse, thus more willing to support labeling legislation. McGuirk et al., (1990) found the income level of $20,000 to $50,000 were the most worried about health effects and were the most skeptical of the government.

Education was included into the model as it is hypothesized that highly educated individuals tend to be more aware of the issue and most likely to act on these concerns, implying a positive influence in supporting labeling legislation. Educated consumers may also be more aware of the milk price support system, realizing the economic benefits to small dairy farms if support for policy legislation occurred.

Equation (2) represents a model to estimate consumer support for a temporary ban on the use of rbGH,

$$BAN = \beta_0 + \beta_1 HEALTHCON + \beta_2 INCOME + \beta_3 EDUC + \epsilon \quad (2)$$

where support for a temporary ban is operationalized as BAN, an indicator variable equal to one if the respondent supported a temporary ban of milk from cows treated with rbGH. The question asked respondents whether they strongly agree, agree somewhat, disagree somewhat, or strongly disagree with placing a temporary ban on the sale of rbGH in Wisconsin.Whereas, the independent variables are again, HEALTHCON, INCOME, and EDUC.

Table 1
Definition of Policy Variables

Dependent Variables

SUPPLAB - Equal to (1) if support labeling of dairy products; (0) otherwise;
BAN - Equal to (1) if agree to place a temporary ban on the sale of rbGH treated herd milk in Wisconsin; (0) otherwise.

Independent Variables

HEALTHCON - Equal to (1) if concerned about the future discovery of ill-health effects; (0) otherwise;
INCOME - Equal to (1) if income is over the state median of about $30,000; (0) otherwise;
EDUC - Respondents' highest grade in school.

Analysis

Since the dependent variables in this and the subsequent model is dichotomous, probit regressions were run. Results are presented in Table 2.

The two variables, HEALTHCON and INCOME, were found to be statistically significant in both regressions. As indicated by the marginal effect of HEALTHCON, if respondents expressed concern about future discovery of ill-health effects, the probability that support for labeling is expressed increased by 24%, and the probability for support of a temporary ban is expressed increased by 33%. This result is consistent with the expectation that consumers who had health concern were willing to support both the labeling of treated herd milk and a temporary ban on the sale of rbGH-treated herd milk.

Table 2
Probit Results for Policy Legislation

Regression 1: SUPPLAB

Variable	Parameter Estimate	Standard Error	T ratio	Marginal Effect
CONSTANT	-.591652	.352342	-1.679	
HEALTHCON	1.23663	.118606	10.426	24%
INCOME	.203446	.112978	1.801	4%
EDUC	.272860E-01	.260274E-01	1.048	1%

Log Likelihood -365.40
Chi-square 112.74˙

Regression 2: BAN

Variable	Parameter Estimate	Standard Error	T ratio	Marginal Effect
CONSTANT	-.506625	.338395	-1.497	
HEALTHCON	1.21451	.117243	10.359	33%
INCOME	.242788	.106649	2.277	7%
EDUC	.633154E-02	.248545E-01	.255	0%

Log Likelihood -411.28
Chi-square 113.26˙

Similarly, as indicated by the marginal effect of INCOME, if annual income is greater than $30,000 (INCOME equals 1), the probability that the respondent expressed support for labeling legislation increased by 4% (significant only at the 10% level) and support for a temporary ban increased by 7%. The result is consistent with the hypothesis that higher income consumers would be more risk-averse, because they have a higher opportunity cost if an accident occurred, and are thus more willing to support labeling legislation.

Finally, education is insignificant in the model. This may be a reflection of the collinearity between income and education. Another study (Kaiser, Scherer, & Barbano, 1992) which analyzed consumer support for policy effects of rbGH found that consumers who supported labeling of rbGH also had the largest potential milk-consumption response.

Discussion and Conclusions

The public policy model hypothesized that risk-averse consumers will be willing to support policy legislation. Results suggest that consumers who had health concern were also willing to support both the labeling of treated herd milk and a temporary ban on the sale of rbGH-treated herd milk.

This result may reflect the consumer's loss of confidence in regulators' ability to protect them in the market. Harris, et al., proposes an alternative approach to eliminating or controlling food hazards by providing options to consumers with respect to risks, but also providing them with information for choosing among options (Harris, et al., 1991).

One possible solution is to create a stronger risk communication, which in theory should "calm unwarranted fears if consumers appear to be more worried about a risk than the facts suggest is appropriate" (Groth, 1990). When considering whether a risk communication strategy for rbGH is appropriate, it is important to balance expert assessments of product risk and consumer beliefs about products risks (Hadden, 1989). An effective risk communication strategy must both cover objective data on actual risk while recognizing the powerful role of consumer beliefs in determining perceived risk. A mechanism needs to be established so all parties can communicate their concerns. Once consumers are involved in the process of risk assessment, they will feel more in control and will increase their trust in the parties involved. Finally, scientists and other parties need to understand how consumers understand risks and the role of beliefs (Groth, 1990). Displaying the facts so consumers will understand can increase consumer trust in experts.

Secondly, in light of regulators' reluctance to indicate through labeling whether or not milk has come from a treated herd, consumers face an involuntary risk exposure since rbGH use is a producer level decision. This problem is insurmountable unless government reconsiders its role in this area. Hadden talks about labeling as one of the "least aggressive" forms of government policies: by providing information it is "merely a mechanism for perfecting a marketplace in which information is not that easy to obtain" (Hadden, 1991). Harris, et al., point out there are some positive effects of labeling legislation: a) the public will understand the level of health hazards, b) it will deter the distribution of irresponsible information, c) consumers are better able to choose among risks, and d) there will be a greater perception of the safety of the food supply leading to an openness and cooperation between consumers, food industry leaders, and regulators (Harris, et al., 1991). Thus, a strategy of labeling would enable consumers to choose among risks. Legislation could either pass a bill to label rbGH treated herd milk, or label rbGH-free milk allowing consumers who want more certainty to continue consuming the milk they believe is pure. Farmers would be certified depending on the type of milk they were producing. Passing legislation to place a temporary ban on rbGH treated milk would allow time to adequately test the product and provide information to consumers.

The results of this study are important as they provide an interesting insight into the lack of consumer confidence toward the documentation presented through scientific findings. These findings provide policy strategy to decrease the risk felt by consumers toward rbGH technology. However, this paper is not without limitations. To combat limitations within the policy model, it would be interesting to probe into concerns about milk price support systems, and consumers' trust in regulatory agencies. Evaluating consumers' thoughts on government policies and agencies may tap into another reason for support of policy legislation.

References

Douthitt, R. A. (January, 1991). A consumer's perspective on proposed commercial use of the recombinant bovine growth hormone. LaFollette Issues, University of Wisconsin-Madison.

Groth, E. (September, 1990). Communicating with consumers on food safety and risk issues. Food Technology, 32-34.

Hadden, S. G. (1989). A citizen's right to know: Risk communication and public policy. San Francisco: Westview Press.

Hadden, S. G. (1991). Regulating product risks through consumer information. Journal of Social Issues, 47(1), 93-105.

Harlander, S. (May, 1991). Social, moral and ethical issues in food biotechnology. Food Technology, 152-159.

Harris, W. D., Padberg, D. I., & Capps, O. (1991). Food labels: Is time to consider adding food safety information. Choices, Fourth Quarter, 34-37.

Hermann, R. (1982) The consumer movement in historical perspective. Reprinted in Aaker, D. A., and Day, G. (1982). Consumerism search for the consumer interest. 4th (ed.) New York: Press.

Huang, C. L. (Fall, 1991). Attract consumers for the wrong reasons. Choices, 18-21.

Kaiser, H., Scherer, C. & Barbano, D. (April,

1992).   Consumer perceptions and attitudes toward bovine somatotropin. Northeastern Journal of Agricultural Resource Economics, 10-19.

Miller, H., & Ackerman, S. (March, 1990). Perspective on food biotechnology. FDA Consumer, 8-13.

Nicholson, W. (1990). Intermediate microeconomics. 5th (ed.) Dryden Press.

Post, L. A. (May, 1982). Laying the groundwork: The techniques and applications of recombinant DNA technology. Biotechnology and the environment: The regulation of genetically engineered organisms used in the environment. Proceedings of the Seventeenth Annual Conference on the Environment.

Starr, C. (September, 1969). Social benefit versus technological risk: What is our society willing to pay for safety? Science, 165, 1232-1238.

van Ravenswaay, E. & Hoehn, J. P. (1991). Consumer perspectives on food safety issues: The case of pesticide residues in fresh produce. Department of Agricultural Economics. Michigan State University.

An Analysis of Factors Influencing Sources and Amounts of Adolescents' Income

Carol B. Meeks, The University of Georgia[1]

This study examined factors influencing the sources and amounts of income adolescents receive. There were 1834 adolescents. Allowance amount increased with age and family income and decreased with number of children. Being paid for helping at home decreased with age of the adolescent. White adolescents were more likely to be paid for work at home than black adolescents. When paid, older adolescents received slightly more per month than younger adolescents. Living in a nonmetro area or the South increase the amount adolescents were paid for work at home. Being older, white, in a larger family and living outside the South all increased the likelihood of the adolescent being employed in the marketplace.

Whether adolescents should receive an allowance or not is controversial. So is the idea that adolescents obtain income from earnings by working in the marketplace. Little recent research exists which examines adolescents' income.

Educators often recommend that children and adolescents be given an allowance to provide them with experiences for handling money (Dunsing, 1956). The allowance should provide a continuing experience and increasing responsibility for financial needs. Parents in Marshall's (1964) study also reported giving children an allowance as a relatively easy or frictionless way to handle children's spending money.

The alternative to receiving an allowance is to earn money in the marketplace. The typical high school student today holds a part-time job (Bachman, 1983; Peters, 1989). Employment was argued to provide adolescents with a real world environment, putting them in contact with a wider range of people of different ages and income levels. It teaches practical skills including responsibility and the value of money.

Today's children are receiving more money than in the past, beginning at younger ages and rising rapidly as they enter elementary and middle school. About 60 percent of all children receive an allowance (McNeal 1990). Other sources of income include gifts and earnings. "Overall, 83 percent of children's money comes from home, while 17 percent comes from outside the home" (McNeal 1990). Obviously as children become adolescents this will shift somewhat.

Stipp (1988) reported that children's main income sources are spending money (65% get some from their parents), an allowance (58%), and money as a birthday present (61%). Children from less affluence families have more spending money than children from affluent families (Stipp 1988). Children in nontraditional households are more likely to get spending money, get larger allowances, and among 9-to-11-years old, they are more likely to earn their own money.

Early research by Rogerson and Whiteford (1960) had found that the most common source of money for ninth graders was earnings and irregular amounts of money (dole). Receiving money by the dole method was related to sex, social status, and size of community (Rogerson & Whiteford 1960). The size of community in which the subject lived tended to be significantly related to the amount of money received. Dunsing (1956) reported that irregular-earnings were received by 61 percent of the sample; allowances by 31 percent and dole by 8 percent.

Hollister, Rap & Goldsmith (1986) reported that sixth grade girls were more likely to receive an allowance than sixth grade boys. Boys were more likely to earn money. Dunsing (1956) reported similar findings. Marshall and Margruder (1960) found that there were no differences in knowledge of the purchasing power of children who received an allowance and those who received spending money in other ways. Marshall (1964) also found no differences in financial knowledge and responsibility between children given an allowance and those not given an allowance.

The purpose of this research is to examine sources and amounts of income received by adolescents. Specifically this study seeks to determine whether individual and family characteristics make a differences in whether an adolescent receives an allowance, is paid for work performed at home, or earns money in the marketplace and the amount of support received from the family. Future research will examine adolescent expenditures.

Method

Data

The sample of 12 to 18 year old adolescents in this study was drawn from the National Survey of Families and Households. This survey included interviews with a probability sample of 13,017 respondents. The sample included a main cross-section sample of 9,643 households plus a double sampling of blacks, Puerto Ricans, Mexican

[1]Professor and Head,
  Housing and Consumer Economics

Americans, single-parent families and families with stepchildren. One adult per household was randomly selected as the primary respondent. Data on the adolescent were provided by this respondent. Interviews were conducted between March 1987 and May 1988. The survey was composed of both an interview component as well as self-administered questionnaires.

Subjects

There were 1,834 adolescents between the ages of 12 and 18 in the sample (Table I). Of these, 52.6% were males and 47.4% were females. The adolescent sample consisted of 70.5% whites, 20.2% blacks, 8.2% Spanish Americans and 1.1% others (Asians, American Indians). Mean age of the adolescents was 15 years. Mean number of children per household was 3.0 while mean household income was $31,699. The family structure in which these adolescents lived included 63.4% in families with two parents, 29.8% in single-parent families and 6.9% in other family structures such as no parent in the household. In the sample, 73.0% lived in metro areas as compared with 27.0% in nonmetro areas. Regional distribution included 18.3% in the Northeast, 26.0% in the Northcentral, 38.2% in the South and 17.5% in the West.

Variables

The adolescents in the sample could receive income from three possible sources: an allowance provided by the family, payment for extra jobs done around the house (not included in the allowance), and earnings from other sources such as a regular job, paid babysitting, or other occasional work. Respondents provided the amount of the allowance and the amount paid extra for work around home. These two variables were added to determine the total amount of income the adolescent received from the family. Amount of earnings was not collected in the study.

The above dependent variables were analyzed using the following independent variables: sex, age, and grade of the adolescent, race, family structure, number of children in the family, family earnings, metropolitan and regional location. Age of the adolescent and family earnings were continuous variables. Sex and metropolitan location were dummy variables.

In the discriminant analysis, each of the following variables were coded into 0,1 categories with 1 being the item specified. The omitted discriminator is noted for each variable. Race categories were white, black, and other. Black was the omitted variable. Number of children was subdivided into only child families, families with 2 or 3 children, or families with more than 3 children. Only child was the omitted variable. Grades were grouped as mostly A's, A's & B's, mostly B's, B's & C'S, mostly C's, and C's or lower. Mostly C's was the omitted category. Family structure included two-parent, single-parent, or other. Single-parent was the omitted category. For region, South was the omitted

region. Northeast, Northcentral and West were included. The grade that the adolescent attended in school was rejected as a variable since it was highly correlated with age. Multicollinearity among the remaining predictors was not a problem.

In the analysis of variance, race was coded as white, black, or other. Number of children was a continuous variable. Household structure was coded as two-parent, single-parent or other. Region and grades were categorical variables including all the categories specified above. Thus, coding of several variables differed somewhat from the discriminant analyses. No variables were omitted.

Analysis

The three binary dependent variables were analyzed with discriminant analysis. Discriminant analysis is a statistical technique which may be used to classify cases into a particular group based on the information carried by the discriminating variables (Klecka, 1980).

The variable coefficients represent the amount of change in an adolescent's position on that function if its score on the corresponding variable changed by one unit. To determine where any individual adolescent would be classified, their raw score on each predictor variable is multiplied by the associated classification function coefficient. These products are summed and added to the constant.

For the discriminant analyses, the sample was randomly split into two groups. One group, the developmental sample containing 90% of the subjects, was used to obtain the discriminators that were significant. The results from this analysis were then validated on the other 10% of the sample to see how well they discriminated.

An analysis of variance using SAS-GLM was performed on amount of allowance, amount paid for jobs around the house and the sum of these two variables.

Findings

Approximately half (51.8%) of the sample received an allowance with 32.7% being paid extra for work at home (Table II). Income was earned in the marketplace by 58.5% of the adolescents. The average allowance was $34.48 per month and the average amount paid for helping at home was $16.71 for mean of $36.05 of support provided by the family.

Sources of Income

Quality of Predictions. Of key importance in discriminant analysis is how well the variables selected as discriminators predict behavior of the adolescents. Results are reported for both the developmental and validation samples.

In the developmental sample, the discriminating variables correctly classified 64.1%

Table 1.

Discriminant Analysis of Income Sources

Variables	Allowance*** Partial R^2	F^a	Paid jobs at home*** Partial R^2	F^a	Market Earnings*** Partial R^2	F^a
Sex	0.000	0.03	0.002	3.65	0.000	0.05
Age	0.034	55.00***	0.036	58.47***	0.050	80.42***
Race						
White	0.002	2.39	0.028	44.73***	0.046	75.16***
Other	0.001	1.45	0.001	2.14	0.002	3.64
Grades						
Mostly A's	0.001	2.17	0.000	0.02	0.001	1.93
A's & B's	0.000	0.08	0.002	2.65	0.000	0.00
Mostly B's	0.002	2.56	0.002	2.96	0.000	0.02
B's & C's	0.000	0.05	0.003	4.85*	0.003	4.79*
C's or <	0.000	0.09	0.001	1.62	0.000	0.10
Children						
2-3	0.000	0.00	0.000	0.00	0.004	6.88**
> 3	0.001	1.76	0.002	2.58	0.000	0.02
Family Structure						
Married	0.001	2.19	0.001	0.90	0.000	0.39
Other	0.000	0.00	0.001	1.36	0.002	2.29
Family Income	0.002	2.54	0.010	15.55***	0.000	0.36
Metro	0.009	14.10***	0.000	0.29	0.002	3.36
Region						
Northeast	0.004	5.67*	0.000	0.02	0.004	6.81**
Northcentral	0.000	0.62	0.001	1.47	0.011	16.62***
West	0.000	0.13	0.003	4.32*	0.016	24.84***

   * p<.05
  ** p<.01
*** p<.001
  [a] Multivariate [F]

of the adolescents as receving allowance and 58.9% as not receiving an allowance. In the validation sample, 53.7% of the adolescents were correctly classified as receiving an allowance where as 64.8% were correctly classified as not receiving an allowance. These finds suggest the predictors have merit but the lack of consistency weakens support for their use.

In the developmental sample, the discriminating variables correctly classified 67.6% of the adolescents as being paid for jobs at home and 62.7% of those with were not paid extra for working at home. In the validation sample, 58.1% of the adolescents were correctly classified as receiving pay for jobs at home whereas 66.9% were correctly classified as not being paid for jobs at home. These findings support the use of the variables as discriminators.

In the developmental sample, the discriminating variables correctly classified 69.4% of the adolescents who had earnings from work in the marketplace and 62.8% of those with did not. In the validation sample, 69.5% of the adolescents were correctly classified as receiving market earnings while 70.9% were classified correctly is not receiving market earnings. This suggests the variables are equally good at predicting employment and no employment in the marketplace.

Predictor Variables. In addition to knowing how well the discriminant function differentiates between members of the groups studied, the contribution of the individual predictor variables to that success is also important. All of the overall equations were significant (Table 1).

Variables found to discriminate between those

Table 2

Discriminant function coefficients for income sources

Variables	Allowance		Paid jobs at home		Market Earnings	
	Yes	No	Yes	No	Yes	No
Constant	-50.42	-46.61	-45.88	-49.34	-51.46	-46.70
Sex	6.19	6.16	6.15	6.32	6.12	6.13
Age	4.41	4.20	4.14	4.37	4.50	4.24
Race						
White	3.43	2.99	2.79	2.14	4.40	3.36
Other	7.80	7.26	7.08	7.49	6.50	6.99
Grades						
Mostly A's	4.01	4.47	4.65	4.93	5.30	4.95
A's & B's	6.06	6.26	6.35	6.81	6.74	6.58
Mostly B's	3.75	4.18	4.36	4.89	4.70	4.56
B's & C's	6.15	6.41	6.54	7.12	6.49	6.64
C's or <	4.96	5.23	5.33	5.42	5.80	5.50
Children						
2-3	6.00	5.78	5.71	6.02	6.26	5.94
> 3	4.74	4.40	4.30	4.80	4.38	4.38
Family Structure						
Married	0.69	0.90	0.96	0.67	1.04	1.01
Other	-0.87	-0.73	-0.70	-1.12	-0.09	-0.46
Family Income	0.00	0.00	0.00	0.00	0.00	0.00
Metro	7.08	6.66	6.51	6.55	6.11	6.38
Region						
Northeast	3.33	3.00	2.88	2.81	3.28	2.89
Northcentral	2.75	2.68	2.64	2.46	3.42	2.83
West	2.98	2.94	2.91	2.50	4.07	3.23

adolescents who received allowances and those who didn't were age, metropolitan location and northeast region. The gap between whether an adolescent received an allowance or not increased with age (Table 2). Adolescents in metro areas were more likely to receive an allowance than those in nonmetro areas. Living in the Northeast as opposed to the South, also meant the adolescent was more likely to receive an allowance.

For the equation on payment for jobs at home, age, family income, being white, receiving B's and C's, and location in the western region were all significant classification variables. The gap between being paid for work at home or not increased with the age of the adolescent. Older adolescents were less likely to be paid for work around the home than younger adolescents. White adolescents were more likely to be paid for work at home than black adolescents. Adolescents who make

B's & C's in school were less likely to be paid for work at home than adolescents who make all C's. Location in the Western region compared with the South resulted in adolescents being more likely to be paid for work at home.

Earning income in the marketplace was predicted by age, race, B's and C's, 2 to 3 children in the family, and location in another region other than to the South. As would expected, older adolescents were more likely to have market earnings. White adolescents were more likely than Blacks to have market earnings. Adolescents in two or three children households were more likely to be working for pay than only children. Location outside the South also resulted in adolescents being in the workplace.

Table 3.

<u>Analysis of Variance for Types and Amounts of Income Received by Adolescents</u>

Source[a]	Allowance		Paid jobs at home		Total Family Support	
	Type III Sum of Squares	F Value	Type III Sum of Squares	F Value	Type III Sum of Squares	F Value
Sex (1)	1848.47	1.92	247.24	1.26	141.09	0.14
Age (1)	99333.61	103.04***	5790.68	29.50***	85965.09	84.40***
Race (2)	585.49	0.30	238.46	0.61	680.08	0.33
Grades (6)	1305.24	0.23	823.89	0.70	3569.13	0.58
No. of Children (2)	5907.27	3.06*	533.43	1.36	3418.30	1.68
Family Structure (1)	3751.06	3.89*	0.44	0.00	4626.38	4.54*
Family Income (1)	3750.76	3.89*	472.19	2.41	3907.77	3.84*
Metro (1)	0.00	0.00	1094.99	5.58*	179.09	0.18
Region (3)	6593.37	2.28*	2551.24	4.33**	13879.57	4.54**
Equation		7.16***		3.90***		6.31***
Equation DF	18,741		18,486		18,963	
R^2		.15		.13		.10

*Degree of freedom in parenthesis

Amount of Income

Several variables contributed to significant differences in the amount of the allowance that an adolescent in the study received (Table 3). As age increased one year, the amount of the allowance increased by $6.35. As the number of children in the family increased, the amount of the allowance decreased by $1.33. Adolescents in two-parent households received $32.44 per month compared with adolescents in one-parent households who received $35.87 per month. As family income increase by $10,000 the amount of the allowance increased by .55.

The amount paid for work performed at home varied significantly by age, metro location and region. As age increased by one year, the amount paid the adolescent per month increased by $1.86. Metro adolescents received an average of $15.93 per month compared with $19.35 for nonmetro adolescents. Adolescents in the South received $21.78 per month on average compared with $17.05 in the Northeast, $17.69 in the Northcentral region and $14.77 in the West.

The total amount of income given to the adolescent by the family varied significantly by age, family structure, family income, and region. As age increased by one year, the amount of support increased by $5.11. As the number of children increased by one, the amount of income decreased by $1.28. As family earnings increased by $10,000, adolescent income increased by .44. Adolescents living in the South had more total income provided by the family ($42.67) than adolescents living in any other region.

Fewer adolescents in this study received an allowance than might have been expected based on earlier research. Market earnings was received by close to 60 percent of the sample which is similar to other findings.

Age of the adolescent which ranged from 12 to 18 was significant in every equation. The older the adolescent the greater the likelihood they received an allowance and the higher the amount. Perhaps parents recognize that ability to manage money increases as does the needs of the adolescents. Younger adolescents were more likely to be paid for work at home but older adolescents earned slightly more per month. Total amount of income given to the adolescent increased with age. Older adolescents were also more likely to be employed in the marketplace. Given the age requirements for employment this is not surprising.

Family income did not influence receipt of an allowance but did influence the amount of the allowance. Family income significantly increased the probability and amount paid for work at home and the total amount of income the adolescent received from the family. It was expected that higher income families with more resources would provide adolescents with more support.

Adolescents in one-parent families received a significantly higher allowance and total support per month from the family than adolescents in two-parent families. Adolescents in one-parent families may be responsible for more purchases that adolescents in two-parent families. They may also be responsible for performing more work at home.

The amount of the allowance decreased as family size increased. Adolescents in larger families were more likely to be employed in the marketplace.

White adolescents were more likely to be paid for work at home than black adolescents and were more likely to be employed in the marketplace. The latter may be due to limited job opportunities for black adolescents.

Metro/nonmetro location was a key variable. Adolescents in metro areas were more likely to receive an allowance than adolescents in nonmetro areas but there was no significant difference in the amount. Although metro/nonmetro location was not significant in being paid for work at home, adolescent living in nonmetro areas were paid significantly more than those living in metro areas. There may be more work to be performed in nonmetro areas than metro such as larger lots to care for.

Region had a significant impact in several equations. It is assumed that region is capturing variations in economic and cultural conditions.

This study looked at one portion of the economic situation of adolescents - sources and amount of income, particularly income provided by the family. The data suggest that half the adolescents do not have the opportunity to manage financial resources. There also seems to be a difference in philosophy held by parents with some families providing adolescents with an allowance and some paying extra for jobs performed at home but not doing both. Further research into the relationships between experiences by adolescents and adult financial skills needs to be explored.

Acknowledgement

"The National Survey of Families and Households was funded by a grant (HD21009) from the Center for Population Research of the National Institute of Child Health and Human Development. The survey was designed and carried out at the Center for Demography and Ecology at the University of Wisconsin-Madison under the direction of Larry Bumpass and James Sweet. The field work was done by the Institute for Survey Research at Temple University."

Research support was provided by the United States Department of Agriculture through the Georgia Agricultural Experiment Station under Southern Regional Project S206.

References

Bachman, J.(1983). Premature affluence: Do high schools students earn too much? Economic Outlook, (Summer), 64-67.

Dunsing, M.(1956). Spending money of adolescents. Journal of Home Economics, 48(6), 405-409.

Helmick, S. & Jurich, A.(1981). Employment behavior of adolescent family members. Home Economics Research Journal, 10(1), 21-31.

Hollister, J., Rapp, D. & Goldsmith, E.(1986). Monetary practices of sixth-grade students. Child Study Journal, 16(3), 183-191.

Marshall, H.R. & Magruder, L.(1960). Relations between parent money, education practices, and children's knowledge and use of money. Child Development, 31, 253-284.

Marshall, H.(1964). The relation of giving children an allowance to children's money knowledge and responsibility and to other practices of parents. The Journal of Genetic Psychology, 104, 35-51.

McNeal, J.(1990). Children as consumers." American Demographics, 12, 36-39.

Peters, J.(1989). Youth clothes-shopping behavior: An analysis by gender. Adolescence, 24(95), 575-580.

Rogerson, L. & Whitford, E.(1960). Money experiences of ninth-grade pupils. Journal of Home Economics, 52(1), 44-45.

Stipp, H.(1988). Children as consumers. American Demographics, 10, 26-32.

Estimated Income Elasticities for Usual Expenditures on Food at Home and Away from USDA's 1989 Continuing Survey of Food Intakes by Individuals and Diet and Health Knowledge Survey

P. Peter Basiotis, U.S. Department of Agriculture[1]

Data from 1,850 U.S. Households from USDA's 1989 Continuing Survey of Food Intakes by Individuals and Diet and Health Knowledge Survey, were utilized to estimate income elasticities for usual expenditures on food at home and food away from home. These expenditures and the probability of positive expenditures on food away from home were regressed on several characteristics available in the combined data sets. Most notable were self reported valuations of food characteristics such as food safety, nutrition, price, and taste.. The estimates suggest similar income elasticities to those reported by previous researchers; and a positive impact of "taste" on expenditures on food at home and a negative such impact of "price" and "nutrition."

Introduction

Food consumption expenditures as a proportion of all household expenditures rank third after housing and transportation expenditures in the U.S. (Yang). It is clearly important to understand the nature of factors affecting food expenditures. Several studies have been published in the last two decades addressing these issues. As with almost all econometric studies, studies of food expenditures have been limited by the available data, the state of economic theory, and the availability of practical econometric tools.

Several past studies have demonstrated the link between sociodemographic and economic factors and food consumption expenditures (e.g., Hama & Chern; Smallwood & Blaylock; Basiotis, Brown, Johnson & Morgan; Morgan; Capps & Havlicek; Morgan, Johnson, Lee & Goungetas). Being economic studies, their primary focus was on estimating and reporting income elasticities.

The present study was motivated by several factors:

1. The availability of USDA's 1989 Continuing Survey of Food Intakes by Individuals (CSFII) and its concomitant Diet and Health Knowledge Survey (DHKS) data.

2. The desire to estimate income elasticities for Food At Home (FAH) and Food Away From Home (FAFH), and compare them to those previously reported in the literature.

3. The availability of self reported valuations of such food characteristics as:

a. Food Safety

b. Nutrition

c. Price

d. Taste

e. Storage Life, and

f. Ease of Preparation.

This last set of factors is available for the first time for households in combination with substantial amounts of economic and other data from a nationally representative sample. Thus the results may be of interest to those at all levels of the food chain, nutritionists and nutrition educators, some government agencies, public health professionals, academics, and the public.

Theoretical Issues and Statistical Model

Applied econometric models of demand for food are typically guided by economic theory, usually either classical or household production theory. Choice of the appropriate theoretical framework can be very important for estimation because severe statistical biases may result if the researcher does not choose prudently. In practice, however, the researcher is usually limited by the available data. This has resulted in approximately the same set of available variables being included in such models regardless of theoretical framework. (Basiotis).

A consequence of this is that, depending on choice of theoretical framework, a given available variable may be thought of as being a proxy for several unrelated and unobservable economic variables. For example, the observed variable "age" can stand as a proxy for human capital in the form of experience. It affects the demands for FAH and FAFH through its effects on the household production function. It can also be thought of as proxy for preferences unique to cohorts. As such it would affect the demand for food through the utility function in either theoretical framework. As an additional example, the presence of children could be a proxy for

---

[1]Economist, Human Nutrition Information Service.

preferences (affecting the utility function), availability of time (affecting the opportunity cost of time), or availability of household labor performed by older children.

Thus, interpretation of estimated coefficients will be affected by choice of theoretical framework. However, assuming that the same observable (proxy) variables are included in the analysis, the estimates themselves will not be affected by choice of theoretical framework.

These observations are relevant to the present study since the availability of the food characteristics valuation variables allows for a somewhat less restrictive model specification. The specification employed here was guided by household production theory, and previous studies of FAH and FAFH and thus, estimated coefficients should be interpreted accordingly. Specifically, expenditures on FAH and FAFH, and the probability of positive usual food expenditures on FAFH were each related to household income, household size, the above mentioned food characteristics valuations, and a number of other sociodemographic characteristics. Theoretically, because about one fifth of the households reported no expenditures on FAFH for the two months prior to the interview, econometric methods such as Ordinary Least Squares (OLS) should not be used since the resulting parameter estimates could be biased and inconsistent (Tobin; Fomby et al., Amemiya). However, for this study, use of Ordinary Least Squares (OLS) was thought appropriate based on past findings with this type of truncated variable (Yang; Yang and Basiotis; Frazao).

More generally, the theoretically appropriate econometric technique depends on the assumptions regarding behaviors that generate "zero" expenditures on FAFH. An excellent discussion of the complex issues involved can be found in Blaylock and Blisard. Nevertheless, the two food expenditure models were estimated by OLS and the probability of positive usual expenditures on FAFH was specified as a Probit model estimated by Maximum Likelihood, all using the Limdep version 5.1 statistical software package (Greene).

Data and Variables Definitions

Data from USDA's 1989 Continuing Survey of Food Intakes by Individuals (CSFII) and Diet and Health Knowledge Survey (DHKS) were used in this analysis. The CSFII collected dietary and other information on U.S. households and individuals within sample households. At approximately four weeks following the interview, the person deemed the main meal planner was interviewed by telephone regarding his or her awareness of links between diet and disease, and on related topics. In particular, the respondent was asked to report on a scale of 1 ("Not Important") to 6 ("Very Important") his or her valuation of food characteristics when shopping for food. These

were: product safety, nutrition, price, how well the food keeps, ease of preparation, and taste. In addition to these variables, the other independent variables included in the model were annual household income (including the food stamp bonus income if applicable) and its square, household size, and its square, single person household, presence of child up to eighteen years of age, distance from the store, self reported food sufficiency status, food stamp program and/or WIC participation, headship, employment and education status of head(s), who the main meal planner is, geographic region, race, urbanization, tenancy status, housing unit type, and presence of pregnant female in household.

Limitations

As in all applied econometric studies, several limitations must be borne in mind when interpreting the results reported here. To begin with, the nature of the study was exploratory. Household production theory and past analyses on the demand for food guided model specification and selection of variables. Thus the possibility of committing gross errors was reduced.

Several problems remain, however. A major limitation is that the OLS model specification may not be an appropriate statistical tool for analyzing expenditures on FAFH. (Cragg; Haines, Guilkey & Popkin; Lin). Analysis was done on an equation-by-equation basis, as opposed to a more appropriate systems approach. As market prices were not available, region/urbanization differences were used as proxies for price variation. Given the size and number of these limitations, results should be interpreted with caution.

Results

Estimated means and regression coefficients are shown in Table 1. The estimated marginal propensities to consume out of household income at the sample mean are 0.042 and 0.020 for FAH and FAFH, respectively. Again at the income and food expenditures sample means, these marginal propensities translate to income elasticities of 0.28 for FAH, and 0.60 for FAFH. These estimates are in wide agreement with previously estimated food expenditures income elasticities.

Reporting that, when grocery shopping, food safety is a very important issue was not found to be statistically associated with any of the three models shown in table 1. Those who considered nutrition very important when shopping for food were estimated to spend about $4.57 less per week than those who did not report nutrition as being very important, ceteris paribus. They were also less likely to have expenditures on FAFH. Those who considered price to be very important tended to spend about $6.40 less on FAH per week. Storage longevity and ease of preparation did not appear to be associated with expenditures on FAH and

Table 1.
Summary Table of Means and Regression Coefficients Estimating Relationships between Usual Food Expenditures at Home and Away, the Probability of Positive Food Expenditures Away from Home, and Several Household Characteristics; 1989 CSFII and DHKS (N=1,799).

INDEPENDENT VARIABLE	MEAN	USUAL FOOD EXPENDITURES ON FOOD AT HOME (MEAN=$64.85 PER WEEK) COEFFICIENT	P-VALUE	USUAL FOOD EXPENDITURE AWAY FROM HOME (MEAN=$14.39 PER WEEK) COEFFICIENT	P-VALUE	PROBABILITY OF POSITIVE FOOD EXPENDITURE AWAY (MEAN PROPORTION=0.79) COEFFICIENT	P-VALUE
Constant	1.0000	26.9356	0.0029	2.24751	0.6077	0.272220	0.3666
Household annual income including FSP bonus (per week)	$433.64	0.485684e-01	0.0000	0.212887e-01	0.0000	0.872316e-03	0.0000
Household annual income squared		-0.818747e-05	0.0001	-0.161162e-05	0.1043		
Household size	2.6359	16.9396	0.0000	1.44202	0.3126	-0.787974e-01	0.0560
Household size squared		-0.661295	0.0169	-0.110238	0.4140		
"Very important when shopping for food:* Food safety	0.73819	2.92244	0.1955	0.345735	0.7461	0.368670e-02	0.9712
Nutrition	0.64480	-4.57092	0.0274	-0.921562	0.3610	-0.195552	0.0381
Price	0.60812	-6.41231	0.0020	-1.37313	0.1592	-0.377556e-01	0.6764
Keeping well	0.60089	0.493493	0.8032	-1.63569	0.1070	-0.496296e-01	0.6020
Ease of preparation	0.40078	-2.59866	0.1821	1.72032	0.0638	0.670120e-01	0.4273
Taste	0.76042	5.52424	0.0131	-0.563593	0.6057	0.661261e-02	0.9476
Single person household	0.26626	-4.61779	0.2207	-1.73439	0.3416	-0.231290	0.0925
Child 1 to 18 years of age present	0.41412	-2.70621	0.4102	-1.02595	0.5174	0.384093	0.0038
Distance from the store (in miles)	4.0887	-0.112752	0.3451	-0.625204e-01	0.2713	0.592128e-02	0.3069
Self reported food supply: Not enough to eat	0.43357e-01	-8.09158	0.0565	-2.70060	0.1860	-0.539254	0.0007
Household is receiving foodstamps	0.12451	-0.647792	0.8141	-2.02658	0.1602	-0.297440	0.0112
Household has member(s) on WIC	0.45581e-01	2.28635	0.6191	0.551503	0.7873	0.354530	0.0728
Headship: Male head only	0.10951	-2.79280	0.6827	8.36025	0.0098	0.178530	0.4951
Female head only	0.32740	-7.09591	0.2394	4.18586	0.1446	-0.105642e-01	0.9632
Employment Status: Male head (if present) employed part-time	0.51695e-01	3.73455	0.3904	2.91561	0.1537	0.374478	0.0796
Male head (if present) employed full-time	0.38521	0.787184	0.7593	-0.248987	0.8245	0.105806	0.3620
Female head (if present) employed part-time	0.12118	0.406253	0.8578	1.92246	0.1545	0.357761	0.0110
Female head (if present) employed full-time	0.26014	1.89696	0.4172	2.03370	0.0629	0.138005	0.1971
Education: Male head (if present) high school	0.47360	3.19234	0.2108	2.51613	0.0384	0.187450	0.0835
Female head (if present) high school	0.60589	-1.00191	0.6589	0.689235	0.5282	0.400149	0.0000
Male head (if present) college	0.12173	-6.77943	0.0396	1.48726	0.3540	0.267055	0.1646
Female head (if present) college	0.11451	6.13746	0.0522	-1.02974	0.5089	-0.254135	0.1062
Main meal planner: Female head	0.58699	-13.9715	0.0201	2.55722	0.3820	-0.299116	0.1970
Male head	0.72262e-02	-10.8402	0.3050	12.2782	0.0145	-0.335627	0.4352
Region: Midwest	0.22568	-13.8123	0.0000	-2.32685	0.0632	0.614548	0.0000
South	0.39133	-8.29004	0.0007	-1.27873	0.2661	0.226587	0.0218
West	0.17510	-5.38610	0.0529	-1.71622	0.2003	0.441174	0.0003
Race: Black	0.12729	3.95378	0.1674	-1.67478	0.2239	0.220558	0.0616
Other	0.41690e-01	1.87360	0.6761	-1.66114	0.4408	-0.220537e-01	0.9080
Urbanization: Suburban	0.41857	1.59912	0.4600	1.46813	0.1467	0.206891	0.0258
Nonmetropolitan	0.29127	0.894187	0.7010	-1.92648	0.0795	-0.155040e-01	0.8734
Tenancy status: Rent	0.37799	0.687841	0.7410	-1.65473	0.0981	-0.168357	0.0603
Occupy without payment	0.23902e-01	1.21070	0.8161	-3.35507	0.2223	-0.344861	0.1231
Housing unit type: Group quarters	0.12785e-01	18.5036	0.0166	2.91698	0.4392	-0.181049	0.5542
Rooming house	0.61145e-02	11.3256	0.3144	1.68775	0.7486	4.83528	0.9898
Pregnancy status: pregnant person in household	0.22235e-01	0.278095	0.9158	-1.77158	0.5483	0.179382	0.5535

Adjusted R-squared		0.36	0.26	
Chi-squared(38)				326.23

FAFH, nor the likelihood of having positive expenditures on FAFH. Those respondents who considered taste to be very important spent an average of $5.50 more per week on FAH. Because of space limitations, the remaining estimates are presented in table 1 without any discussion.

Summary and Conclusions

An exploratory model of expenditures on FAH, FAFH, and the likelihood of households reporting positive expenditures on FAFH in the 2 months prior to being interviewed were estimated. Income marginal propensities and elasticities at the sample mean values were computed. These were in general agreement with marginal propensities and elasticities reported in previous studies.

A novelty of the present study was the inclusion of self reported valuations of selected food characteristics when grocery shopping. As might be expected, those concerned with food prices reported about ten percent lower weekly expenditures on FAH. Those who reported valuing taste had about eight percent higher expenditures on FAH per week. Somewhat surprising was the estimate that those who value nutrition very much had about seven percent lower FAH expenditures per week. One explanation may be that those respondents are more nutrition oriented and better educated, and thus more efficient, food shoppers. Confirmation of this speculation will have to await analyses of those respondents' diets.

Even though the analysis was guided by past research on food consumption, and the estimated income elasticities were similar to those found previously, a number of limitations remained. These were discussed at some length earlier. Because of those limitations, however, results should be viewed with some caution.

References

Amemiya, T. (1985). Advanced econometrics. Cambridge, Mass: Harvard U. Press.

Basiotis, P.P., Brown, M., Johnson, S.R. & Morgan, K.J. (1983). Nutrient availability, food costs, and food stamps. American Journal of Agricultural Economics. 65(3), 685-693.

Basiotis, P.P. (1991). Estimated income, age, and selected demographic characteristics elasticities for food groups from USDA's 1985 and 1986 Continuing Survey of Food Intakes by Individuals. In V. Haldeman (Ed.), The Proceedings of the American Council on Consumer Interests 37th Annual Conference, 286-292.

Blaylock, J.R., Blisard, W.N. (1991). Consumer demand analysis when zero consumption occurs: The case of cigarettes. (Technical Bulletin Number 1792). Washington, D.C.: Economic Research Service, U.S. Department of Agriculture.

Capps, O. Jr., & Havlicek, J. Jr. (1984). National and regional household demand for meat, poultry, and seafood: A complete systems approach. Canadian Journal of Agricultural Economics, 32, 93-101.

Cragg, J.G. (1971). Some statistical models for limited dependent variables with application to demand for durable goods. Journal of Econometrics, (39), 29-44.

Frazao, E. (1992). Food Spending by Female-Headed Households. (Technical Bulletin Number 1806). Washington, D.C.: Economic Research Service, U.S. Department of Agriculture.

Fomby, T.B., Hill, C.R., & Johnson, S.R. (1984). Advanced econometric methods. New York: Springer-Verlag.

Greene, W. (1989). LIMDEP. Graduate School of Business, New York University.

Haines, P.S., Guilkey, D.K., & Popkin, B.M. (1989). Modeling food consumption decisions as a two-step process. American Journal of Agricultural Economics. 71, 543-552.

Hama, M.Y., & Chern, W.S. (1989). Food expenditure and nutrient availability in elderly households. Journal of Consumer Affairs. 22(1), 3-19.

Lin, T.F., & Schmidt, P. (1983). A test of the Tobit Specification Against an Alternative Suggested by Cragg. Review of Economics and Statistics. 65, 174-77.

McDonald, J.F., & Moffitt, R.A. (1980). The uses of Tobit analysis. Review of Economics and Statistics. 62, 318-21.

Morgan, K.J., Johnson, S.R., Lee, Y.Y & Goungetas, B.P. (1985) Use of 12 groups in foods in households differing in size, income and receipt of food stamps. Journal of Consumer Studies and Home Economics. 9, 113-131.

Morgan, K.J. (1986). Socioeconomic factors affecting dietary status: An appraisal. American Journal of Agricultural Economics. 68, 1240-1252.

Smallwood, D., & Blaylock, J. (1981). Impact of household size and income on food expenditure patterns. (ESCS Technical Bulletin Number 1650). Washington, DC: U.S. Department of Agriculture,

Tobin, J. (1958). Estimation of relationships for limited dependent variables. Econometrica, 26, 24-36.

Yang, H.W. (1990). Expenditures on food away from home by U.S. low-income households - 1985/86. (Unpublished Master's Thesis), College Park,

MD: Department of Textiles and Consumer
Economics, University of Maryland-College
Park.

Yang, H.W. & Basiotis, P.P. (1989). Expenditures
on food away from home by low-income
households: analysis using USDA's 1985 and
1986 Continuing Survey of Food Intakes by
Individuals (CSFII) Data. Paper Presented at
the Annual American Agricultural Economics
Association Meeting, July 31-August 3,
Knoxville, Tennessee.

Reservation Wages: An Empirical Test of Alternative Measures

Tak Chee Puang, University of Missouri[1]
Edward J. Metzen, University of Missouri[2]

Reservation wage rates obtained by two procedures for wives in Malaysian households are compared. Estimated rates for both employed and non-employed wives are very low relative to both the mean market wage rate of the employed wives and the mean self-reported reservation wage rate of the non-employed wives. The mean self-reported reservation wage rate seems more realistic than that obtained by statistical estimation.

Introduction

The purpose of this research is to present a comparison of statistically determined estimates of reservation wages with subjects' own reported reservation wage rates for a sample of female heads of household in Malaysia.

A reservation wage rate is the market wage rate that, at the margin, would entice a non-employed person to choose to work in the marketplace. The reservation wage rate becomes a matter of central importance when estimating the value of a homemaker's time. For non-employed persons, the reservation wage rate is a measure of the marginal value of home time. For such persons, the value of their time at home, or reservation wage, is greater than the market wage offered to them. The reservation wage is different from the potential market wage a non-employed person might command; conceptually, the reservation wage must be below the potential market wage, or else the individual would take market employment at the higher rate -- assuming that jobs at the higher rate are available to the individual.

For individuals who work in the marketplace, the value of their time in market employment is at least equal to the marginal value of their time at home.

It would be conceptually unsound to assign a zero potential wage rate or reservation wage rate for homemakers. The homemaker engages in household production, but could also produce some level of market goods and/or services. Researchers in earlier times estimated homemakers' potential market wage rates by assigning employed persons' wage rates to non-employed persons who had

characteristics similar to those of the employeds. Heckman (1974) challenged this implicit assumption that the proclivities of people who are not employed are the same as those of people who are employed, given the same measured characteristics. Heckman developed a system for estimating homemakers' potential market wage rates that adjusts for the unobserved differences between workers and non-workers (differences in propensities toward housework, for example).

The first step in the Heckman technique is to estimate the probability of an individual participating in paid market work. This estimation is based on the entire sample in the data set; probit analysis is used to estimate the probability of participation or non-participation. The probit equation generates a value for each observation for a derived variable, lambda. This variable is then included with the other explanatory variables in the wage equation for the employed women. The purpose of the lambda variable is to correct for selectivity bias that may be present in the sample. The statistical significance of the coefficient on the lambda variable is the test for presence of selectivity bias.

The Heckman technique imposes a restriction in calculation of the lambda variable. There must be at least one variable in the probit equation on the probability of being employed in step 1 that is not included in the wage rate equation in step 2 (Maddala, 1987). A collinearity problem is created if the identical set of variables is included in the two equations.

Literature Review

Ferber and Green (1985) utilized the Heckman procedure to estimate the potential market wage rates of two samples of homemakers, from the Illinois Panel and from the Panel Study of Income Dynamics, and compared these estimates with respondents' own estimates of their potential market wage rates. They found the mean econometrically-estimated potential wage rate to be lower than the mean homemakers' own estimated potential wage rate in both samples. They suggested that "the data adjusted for selection bias may not be useful for the opportunity cost approach to valuation of housework," and pointed

---

[1]Institutional Research Analyst, Office of Research

[2]Professor and Chair, Consumer and Family Economics

out that "women who choose to be full-time homemakers may be out of the labor market because of a higher reservation price rather than lower potential earnings."

Zick and Bryant (1983) noted that potential wage rates provide only a lower limit of the price non-employed individuals place on their home time. They extended the procedure to estimate homemakers' reservation wages conceptualized as the opportunity cost of home time, for a sample of wives from the NE-113 project, An Interstate Urban/Rural Comparison of Families' Time Use. (The methodology is described by Zick and Bryant, and below). This technique was also utilized by Pappalardo (1987), who compared statistically derived estimates of reservation wage rates with subjects' own stated rates for a sample of Cornell University students; she found the estimated mean to be substantially below the mean for respondents' declared rates. Duncan (1992) followed the same procedure to estimate reservation wage rates for young women using data from the 1987 survey of the Young Women's Cohort of the National Longitudinal Surveys of Labor Market Experience. The resulting estimates were very substantially higher than the value of wives' time in the household calculated by the housekeeper cost method. Duncan (1992, 168) reported that "the reservation wage estimates exhibited marked sensitivity to the specification of the model."

Theoretical Formulation

Estimation of The Reservation Wage as an Opportunity Cost Measure

A system of equations is utilized to obtain estimates of the opportunity cost of home time for both working and non-working women (Heckman, 1980). This system is comprised of a wage offered equation, a wage asked equation, and a market clearing equation :

WAGE OFFERED (Market Wage)
$$W = \alpha_0 + \alpha_1 A + e_1 \qquad (1)$$

WAGE ASKED (Reservation Wage)
$$W^* = \beta_0 + \beta_1 B + \beta_2 h + e_2 \qquad (2)$$

MARKET CLEARING
$$W \geq W^* \qquad (3)$$

In Equation 1, A represents a vector of factors determining the homemaker's market wage rate. B in Equation 2 is a vector of home productivity characteristics, while h is the hours not spent in home-related activities. This formulation assumes that the homemaker's hours not spent in home-related activities reflect hours worked in the market place. Hours worked are assumed to affect W^* but not W; thus hours worked is included in Equation 2, but not in Equation 1.

The reservation wage rate, W^*, is unobservable and thus cannot be estimated directly. However,

for those women who worked, market wage rate is assumed to equal reservation wage rate, $W = W^*$. Thus Equations 1 and 2 can be equated to derive an hours worked equation.

$$h = \frac{1}{\beta_2}(\alpha_0 + \alpha_1 A - \beta_0 - \beta_1 B) + \frac{e_1 - e_2}{\beta_2} \qquad (4)$$

The parameters of Equation 2 are retrieved from the estimated coefficients in Equations 1 and 4. Vector A includes a variable not included in vector B, a general characteristic of systems of equations. The variable excluded from vector B should ideally be an intervally scaled variable which affects the market wage rate but not the reservation wage rate. An example of such a variable would be the regional unemployment rate.

Alternative Specification

A straight-forward alternative to the estimation procedure outlined above is to simply ask individuals to specify their reservation wage.

Empirical Specification of the Estimation Procedure

Variables selected for the models, hypothesized to be associated with probability of being employed, market wage rate, hours employed, and reservation wage rate, and the hypothesized direction of their association, are shown in Table 1.

The empirical models are as follows:

WAGE OFFERED:

$$\begin{aligned} W = &\ a_0 + a_1 \ (WSEDUC) + a_2 \ (WIAGE) \\ &+ a_3 \ (WIAGE2) + a_4 \ (WUNION) \\ &+ a_5 \ (CHINESE) + a_6 \ (INDIAN) \\ &+ a_7 \ (AREA) \qquad (5) \end{aligned}$$

WAGE ASKED:

$$\begin{aligned} W^* = &\ b_0 + b_1 \ (WSEDUC) + b_2 \ (WIAGE) \\ &+ b_3 \ (WIAGE2) + b_4 \ (WUNION) \\ &+ b_5 \ (CHINESE) + b_6 \ (INDIAN) \\ &+ b_7 \ (WILL) + b_8 \ (NO\ KID) <7) \\ &+ b_9 \ (HSALARY) + b_{10} \ (TRANSP) \\ &+ b_{11} \ (HOMECAP) + b_{12} \ (HOMEOWN) + \\ &+ b_{13} \ (ELECT) + b_{14} \ (ROOMS) \\ &+ b_{15} \ (HOUSSIZE) + b_{16} \ (AWHOURS) \qquad (6) \end{aligned}$$

MARKET CLEARING:

$$W = W^* \qquad (7)$$

Table 1
Variables and Hypothesized Effect in Models.

Variable	Definition	Descrp Stat.		Variable Effect on:			
				Prob Emp (Probit)	Ln WR	Ave Hrs Work /wk	Ln Res WR
		Freq	%				
EMP	0 = wife employed	408	43.7				
	1 = wife not employed	526	56.3				
AREA	0 = rural	540	57.8				
	1 = urban	394	42.2	-	+	-	
WUNION	0 = non union membership	890	95.3				
	1 = union membership	44	4.7	+	+	-	+
RACE	MALAY (ref)	465	49.8				
	CHINESE	361	38.6	+	+	+	+
	INDIAN	108	11.6	+	+	+	+
WIFE's PHYS DISABILITY	0 = No	755	80.8				
	1 = Yes	179	19.2	-		-	-
HOME OWNERSHIP	0 = owned	478	51.2				
	1 = not owned	456	48.8	-		+	-
ELECTRICITY	0 = Yes	579	62				
	1 = No	355	38	+		+	-
		Mean	S.D.				
WSEDUC	Wife's education level	0.9	0.9	+	+	-	+
WIAGE	Wife's age	33.6	8.2	?	+	-	+
WIAGE2	Wife's age sq.	1194	561				
NO. KIDS < 7	# of children < 7 years	1.5	1.2	-		-	+
HSALARY	Husband annual salary	3828	5642	+		-	+
INDEX OF TRANSP VEHICLES	Ownership of: car=150, hv truck=150, lt.truck=150 motorbike=60, bicycle=10	67.3	89.7				
HOUSEHLD	# hh equip: sew mach, elec iron, ceil fan, elec iron, ovennette, gas cooker, elec stove, fridge, air con, wash mac	2.6	3.2			+	?
HOUSSIZE	# in household	6.5	2.7			-	+
ROOMS	# of rooms	3.1	1.5			-	+
JOBFT	ease obtain FT job: 1=v.easy, 2= fairly easy, 3=depends, 4=fairly diff 5 = v. diff.	4	1.3	-			
JOBPT	ease obtain PT job: 1=v. easy, 2= fairly easy, 3=depends, 4=fairly easy , 5 = v. diff.	3	1.4	-			

AVERAGE HOURS WORKED:

$$\begin{aligned}
\text{AWHOURS} &= c_0 + c_1 \text{ (WSEDUC)} + c_3 \text{ (WIAGE)} \\
&+ c_3 \text{ (WIAGE2)} + c_4 \text{ (WUNION)} \\
&+ c_5 \text{ (CHINESE)} + c_6 \text{ (INDIAN)} \\
&+ c_7 \text{ (AREA)} + c_8 \text{ (WILL)} \\
&+ c_9 \text{ (SKIDAGE1)} + c_{10} \text{ (HSALARY)} \\
&+ c_{11} \text{ (TRANSP)} + c_{12} \text{ (HOMECAP)} \\
&+ c_{13} \text{ ((HOMEOWN)} + c_{14} \text{ (ELECT)} \\
&+ c_{15} \text{ (ROOMS)} + c_{16} \text{ (HOUSSIZE)} \qquad (8)
\end{aligned}$$

The coefficients for the variables in equation 6 are derived from the coefficients for those variables in equations 5 and 8 3 . However, the coefficient for hours worked (AWHOUR) in equation 6 is derived from the coefficients on place of residence (AREA) in equations 5 and 8. AREA is the identifier (omitted) variable, hypothesized to affect wage offered but not value of home time.

Data Source

The data used in this analysis are from the Malaysian Family Life Survey 1976-1977, a panel study with data collected by interview in three waves four months apart. The survey was conducted by RAND Corporation in collaboration with the Agency for International Development. Sample size is 1171 households who responded to all three rounds of survey. The subsample used to conduct the analysis presented here consists of 934 cases which were in all three survey rounds; were of the Malay, Chinese, or Indian race; had non-zero total family income; had a married woman in the household; had relevant information on her husband; had an employed husband. Household is defined as the people who eat and sleep in the house, including immediate family members and other relatives. The unit of analysis is the primary female in the household. Women who earned any money during the survey year is classified as employed (n=526); 408 women were not employed for pay at any time during the year. Market wages are comprised of cash and the value of in-kind payments, before any deductions. Wage rates are calcuated from reported earnings and reported work time. Reservation wage rates were reported in response to the question, "What rate of pay would you have to earn before you would take a job outside the home?" Monetary values presented in this paper are quoted in Malaysian dollars.

Results of Analysis

The LIMDEP program was utilized for the Probit and OLS analyses. Results of the probit analysis of characteristics associated with being employed are reported in Table 2. Wife's age is positively associated with being employed, at a decreasing rate. Chinese and Indian women are more likely than Malay women to be employed. With other factors controlled, urban wives are less likely to be employed than those living in rural areas. The presence of young children deters women from employment.

As expected, husband's salary, which is considered wife's unearned income, is negatively related to her labor force participation. Wife's education, wife's disability, transportation resources, and wife's judgment regarding ease of attaining a full-time or part-time job were not statistically significant.

The multiple regression analyses on the wage asked and wife's hours worked equations are conducted on only the 526 cases in which the wife was employed in the marketplace. The calculated coefficients for the estimated reservation wage

Table 2

Parameter Estimates for the Probability of LaborForce Participation (Employed and Nonemployed Wives)[a]

	Maximum Likelihood Estimate
CONSTANT	-1.91***
WSEDUC	-0.08
WIAGE	0.15***
WIAGE2	-0.002***
WUNION	
Non Union (ref)	
Union Membership	1.22***
RACE	
MALAY (ref)	
CHINESE	0.32***
INDIAN	0.36***
AREA	
RURAL (ref)	
URBAN	-0.33***
WIFE's PHY> DISAB.	
NO DISAB. (ref)	
WILL (DISAB)	-0.06
NO. KID < 7 yrs	-0.11***
HSALARY	-0.00002***
JOBFT	0.02
JOBPT	-0.03
INDEX OF TRANSPORT	-0.0004

[a] N=934
*** $p < = 0.01$

equation are then applied to all 934 households. The results of the estimated values for the wage asked, hours worked, and reservation wage equations are presented in Table 2. Consistent with the standard human capital model, the wage equations are estimated in semilog form (Porath, 1970).

Results from the first regression in Table 2 show that education, age, race, and union membership are significantly related to the log value of the wage rate for employed women. The variable lambda is also statistically significant, reflecting differences in characteristics between employed and non-employed wife. In the second

Table 3
Parameter Estimates for Wife's Market Wage, and Hours Worked, and the Calculated Reservation Wage Rate Equations
(t Statistics in Parentheses)

	LNWWR [a]	AWHOURS [a]	Cal. LN(RWR) [b]
CONSTANT	-4.636***	54.939	-4.658
	(-4.393)	(1.247)	
WSEDUC	0.389***	-0.498	0.390
	(6.005)	(-0.318)	
WIAGE	0.139***	-1.531	0.139
	(2.643)		
WIAGE2	-0.002***	0.024	-0.002
	(-2.316)	0.795)	
UNION MEMBER	1.245***	-6.599	1.247
	(4.307)	(-0.511)	
CHINESE	0.389***	0.907	0.389
	(3.327)	(0.199)	
INDIAN	0.755***	3.908	0.754
	(4.666)	(0.754)	
URBAN	0.002	5.434	
	(0.017)	(1.197)	
PHYSICAL DISABILITY		0.886	-0.0004
		(0.444)	
NO. KID<7 YRS		-0.121	0.00005
		(-0.076)	
HSALARY		0.0004	-0.0000002
		(1.430)	
INDEX OF TRANSPORT		-0.005	0.000002
		(-0.423)	
HOME PROD. CAPITAL		0.831**	-0.0003
		(2.152)	
OWN HOME		1.988	-0.0008
		(1.178)	
NO ELECT		3.680	-0.0015
		(1.830)	
ROOMS		0.608	-0.0002
		(0.930)	
HOUSSIZE		0.165	-0.00007
		(0.433)	
LAMBDA	0.938**	-28.473	-
	(2.240)	(-1.316)	
AVE HRS WORKED\WK			0.0004
R [2]	0.232	0.141	

[a] n =526   [b] N=934   *** p < = 0.01.   ** p < = 0.05

regression, which is the hours worked equation, home production capital is the only statistically significant variable; as expected, it is positively associated with hours worked. R2s for both equations are modest, a result consistent with results of similar analyses (Duncan, 1992; Ferber and Green, 1985; Pappalardo, 1987; Zick and Bryant, 1983).

The third regression equation in Table 3 shows the derived coefficients utilized to predict a reservation wage rate for all women in the sample. The predicted values from the reservation wage equation were converted from log values into dollars for subsequent analysis.

Comparison of Reported Reservation Wage Rate and Estimated Reservation Wage Rate

Table 4 presents the mean actual wage rate and the mean estimated reservation wage rate for the workers, and the reported reservation wage rate and estimated reservation wage rate for the women not employed in the marketplace. The mean actual hourly wage rate for employed wives ($0.88) is very substantially higher than the mean estimated reservation wage rate ($0.33). While theory supports a reservation wage rate below the market wage rate for employed persons, the estimated reservation wage rate seems low in relation to prevailing market wages. For the non-workers, the mean estimated reservation wage rate ($.26) is slightly lower than that for employed women, but only about one-third of their mean reported reservation wage rate ($0.75).

Table 4
Estimated Mean Wife's Hourly Wages for Workers and Non-Workers (in Malaysian Dollars)

	N=526		Non-Workers N=408	
	Actual Wage	Est. Res. Wage	Rept. Res. Wage	Est. Res. Wage
Mean	$0.88	$0.33	$0.75	$0.26
S.D.	$1.40	$0.41	$0.53	$0.29
Median	$0.50	$0.22	$0.63	$0.21

The Pearson correlation between the reported wage rate and estimated reservation wage rate for non-employed women is .44, indicating that not only are the mean values for these two measures quite disparate, but their degree of association across cases is also modest. The correlation between actual wage rate and estimated reservation wage rate for employed workers is .61.

Discussion

For employed women, the empirical data support the logic that the mean market wage rate is greater than the mean estimated reservation wage rate. However, the estimation procedure derives a mean reservation wage rate that seems unrealistically low, relative to prevailing market wages.

For the non-employed women, the mean estimated reservation wage rate is slightly lower than that of the employed women, and substantially below their own self-reported mean reservation wage rate. Both are below the average market wage rate of employed women.

The data suggest that the estimation procedure attributes reservation wage rates to both employeds and non-employeds which are inconsistent with existing conditions. Surely the dynamics of labor markets would have narrowed the very substantial gap between existing market wages and the estimated reservation wages. The non-employeds' mean self-reported reservation wage rate, which approaches the mean market wage rate for employed women, would seem to be the more valid measure.

The fact that the non-employeds' reported reservation wage rate is somewhat lower than the mean market wage rate of the employeds may, at first impulse, suggest that at least some of the non-employed women are behaving irrationally because they are not in market employment. However, it may be the case that the non-employeds do not have the particular characteristics necessary to attain jobs which pay more than their reservation wage, or that jobs which would pay more are simply not available in locations that make it feasible for these women to take employment. Under such a condition, the data are not inconsistent with theory. Given the relative difficulty of obtaining either a full-time or part-job reported by these women, a scenario of unavailability of jobs at wage levels above their reservation wage rates seems a realistic interpretation of the data.

As with any reported data, it is possible that the declared reservation wage rate may be biased either upward or downward. On the other hand, there is also the possibility that the estimated reservation wage rate is a biased approximation of the true reservation wage rate. A reported reservation wage rate takes into account the unmeasured personal tastes and other factors that are not represented in the data set. This fact is important because it is unlikely that the estimation equations take into account every factor which determines an individual's reservation wage rate. Some may argue that the Heckman technique, in correcting for selectivity bias, accounts for such intrinsic characteristics as taste for work. Others may suggest that asking subjects to specify their reservation wage rate results in more valid data via intuitive incorporation of those factors by respondents.

Which then, is the preferred approach to the reservation wage question -- statistical estimation or direct inquiry? In the present analysis, the reported reservation wage rate is a more realistic reflection of prevailing conditions than the reservation wage rate obtained via the estimation procedure. Analysis of the merits of reported and estimated reservation wage rates continues to present an important conceptual challege for researchers. In absence of better empirical support for the estimation procedure than exists to date, we strongly recommend that if individuals' reservation wage rates are of interest, the prudent approach is to simply ask them to declare their reservation wage rate themselves.

REFERENCES

Duncan, K. (1992). The value of time in household works : Estimate from the NLS data. In V. Haldeman (Ed.), The Proceedings of the American Council on Consumer Interests 38th Annual Conference, 163-170.

Ferber, M. & Green, C. (1985). Homemakers' imputed wages: Results of the Heckman technique compared with women's own estimates. Journal of Human Resources, 20(1), 90-99.

Heckman, J. (1974). Shadow wages, market wages, and labor supply. Econometrica, 42(4), 649-694.

Heckman, J. (1980). Sample selection bias as a specification error with an application to the estimation of labor supply functions. In J. Smith (Ed.), Female Labor Supply, 207-208. Princeton University Press.

Maddala, G.S.(1987). Limited Dependent and Qualitative Variables in Econometrics, 232, Cambridge University Press.

Pappalardo, J. (1987). Ghostbusting: In search of the reservation wage. In V. Hampton (Ed.), The Proceedings of the American Council on Consumer Interests 33rd Annual Conference, 43-48.

Porath, B. (1970). The production of human capital over time. In W. Hansen (Ed.), Education, Income and Wealth,. 35, Boston: NBER.

Spence, M. (1973). Job market signaling. Quarterly Journal of Economics, 355 - 374.

Zick, C. & Bryant, K. (1983). Alternative strategies for pricing home work time. Home Economics Research Journal, 12 (2), 136-137.

Endnotes
[1]The coefficent b_{16} in Equation 6 is identified from coefficents a_7 and c_7 in Equations 5 and 8. The coefficents for Equation 6 may be retrieved as follows:

$$b_0 = a_0 - c_0 * b_{16}$$
$$b_1 = a_1 - c_1 * b_{16}$$
$$b_2 = a_2 - c_2 * b_{16}$$
$$b_3 = a_3 - c_3 * b_{16}$$
$$b_4 = a_4 - c_4 * b_{16}$$
$$b_5 = a_5 - c_5 * b_{16}$$
$$b_6 = a_6 - c_6 * b_{16}$$
$$b_7 = - c_8 * b_{16}$$
$$b_8 = - c_9 * b_{16}$$
$$b_9 = - c_{10} * b_{16}$$
$$b_{10} = - c_{11} * b_{16}$$
$$b_{11} = - c_{12} * b_{16}$$
$$b_{12} = - c_{13} * b_{16}$$
$$b_{13} = - c_{14} * b_{16}$$
$$b_{14} = - c_{15} * b_{16}$$
$$b_{15} = - c_{16} * b_{16}$$
$$b_{16} = - a_7/C_7$$

Are 800 Number Offerings Meeting the Needs of all Consumers?

Dr. Kathleen Morrow, Syracuse University[1]
Dr. Clint Tankersley, Syracuse University[2]

There has been tremendous growth in the use of 800 numbers by businesses over the past decade in an attempt to build a relationship with their customers. The effectiveness of these systems depends somewhat on what kinds of consumers use them and how satisfied they are with the interaction? These results of an exploratory study on 800 usage indicate that while usage is high, it varies across demographics. Most users are satisfied with the service they received.

Introduction

As direct marketing has moved into the high-tech arena, telecommunications - or telemarketing - has become an essential tool for many corporations. Direct marketers are finding that by combining 800 numbers or 900 numbers with the more traditional methods of advertising, such as print or television, they are generating sales faster than when television or print media are used alone (Unkel, 1991; Stern, 1991).

Telemarketing or telecommunications also permits better consumer communications by allowing for two-way interacting and an immediate feedback mechanism. Telemarketing, if properly designed and well executed can meet consumer needs in a timely fashion and at the point-of-need in the decision making process. Well-trained telephone representatives who staff a company's 800 lines, for example, not only humanize a large corporation's usual faceless image, but may also provide product information, handle complaints, and also sell add-on products to consumers or direct them to local retailers or distributors for a final purchase decision.

Cost, along with a way to build relationships with consumers, are among the reasons why this growth in telemarketing, has occurred. A telephone call costs an average $2.50 in comparison to an average letter cost of over $10.00 - $50.00 or a personal sales visit of over $200.00. If an order can be placed, or a complaint resolved in a more efficient manner, it is a win-win situation and the needs of both the consumer and the corporation are being met.

While the use of 800 numbers has grown significantly in recent years, very little academic research has been done on its usage by consumers. Our exploratory study attempted to determine: 1. Do consumers use 800 numbers? 2. How do they use 800 numbers? 3. Does this usage vary across demographic characteristics and 4. Are customers satisfied with their use of 800 numbers?

Previous marketing studies have determined that by and large, American consumers have found the inbound 800 numbers easily accessible and non-threatening (Smith, 1991). The "customer care" programs have found acceptance and in fact have become the standard of doing business from the small family-owned business to the GE Answer Center's 250 telephone operators who receive approximately three million calls a year. (Stern, 1991).

Gronmo (1987) predicts that the strategies position of consumers, i.e. consumers' ability to advance their own interests in relation to other groups in society, will be weakened as the new technologies become more commonplace. At the same time the strategic position of the more powerful commercial and institutional actors is likely to be strengthened. This means that consumers are increasingly bombarded with greater quantities of information, in a more targeted fashion in an accelerated time frame. Companies must be careful about equating quantity of information with quality of information. Although some researchers have found that as consumers are provided with increasing amounts of information relevant to a specific purchase decision, they make more efficient purchases, others find that if consumers are provided with "too much" information, overload occurs. (Geise, 1985; Sproles, 1978; Maholtra; Keller, 1987).

The challenge then is for organizations to meet consumer needs in a much more effective manner as they design and implement the various communication technologies. Combined with touchtone technology such as voice mail and automated attendant systems, telemarketing is both a time efficient and cost efficient way to meet consumer needs, whether those needs are placing an order, obtaining a bank balance or requesting a piece of literature.

A 1988 study surveyed company use of 800 lines

---

[1]Associate Professor, Retailing/ Consumer Studies

[2]Associate Professor, School of Management

and found that 50 percent of the respondents were using 800 numbers for customer feedback, compared with 38% in a 1983 study by the same research firm (Chadwick, 1991). This explosion in growth will provide tremendous amounts of consumer feedback to organizations. If companies learn to use this computer feedback in a positive and ethical manner, this can be a real advantage for organizations are using the data both as a measurement of consumer satisfaction, and identification of quality control problems, input into the design of new products and the redesign of existing products (Chadwick, 1991).

A TARP study found that 50 percent of large businesses use 800 numbers for customer service (TARP 1988). To get a perspective on the growth, one has to remember that it has only been 25 years since the toll-free 800 number was first introduced. During that time, it's growth has been from seven million calls in 1967 to over 10 billion in 1991. It is now over a $6 billion a year industry (Lefton 1992).

Methodology

A self-administered questionnaire was mailed to a random sample of 5,000 customers of a major Northeast utility which is a supplier of both natural gas and electricity. The sample was randomly selected from their list of over 1.8 million customers. The cover letter stated that this was a study on their use of 800 numbers being conducted by a university and requested their cooperation. A total of 845 usable surveys were returned, a response rate of 17%. While this is not an exceedingly high response rate, it seems reasonable for an initial exploratory survey and the subject under study. The demographics of the respondents closely matched their distribution in the general population.

The questionnaire asked consumer about their usage of 800 numbers and their satisfaction with the most recent transaction. Usage was measured several ways. First, a general question asked usage on an often/seldom/never scale. Respondents were then asked to quantify how many times in the past 6 months they have used an 800 number, from 0 to 10 or more times. Next, they were asked to relate number of times used to contact specific organizations such as a bank, airline/car rental, mail order company, etc. They were then questioned concerning what they like and disliked about 800 numbers. The final questions asked their satisfaction with how the most recent call was handled.

The data were analyzed by tabulating the aggregate numbers and then running a Chi-Square test on each question versus the demographic characteristics of the respondents (sex, occupation, age, income level). Significant differences across categories are noted on the tables.

Results

The results of the study are first presented in aggregate form to present a picture of how the population, in general, uses and perceives 800 numbers. These results are then analyzed and discussed across demographic characteristics, showing the differences in usage and perceptions of various segments of the market. Usage results are discussed first, followed by likes and dislikes, and then satisfaction.

Consumer Usage

The general usage results (Table 1) indicate that slightly over half of the respondents (51.5%) often use 800 numbers, while only 3% say they never use them. These values are consistent across gender groups. There are significant differences in usage (.01 level) across occupation, age, income and education levels. The biggest users were upper managers (80% said they often used 800 numbers) compared to blue collar, student and retired who predominantly said they seldom use 800 numbers (66%-44%). These groups' response for often use were only in the upper 30% range. With age groups, those below 26 and above 55 used 800 numbers less frequently. There was a direct relationship between income levels and usage, with 71% of the top income level ($81,000+) responding often vs. 34% for the lowest group (under $20,000). This trend continued with the educational level, with 65% of college graduates often using 800 numbers compared to 12% of those with only some high school.

Table 1
General 800 Number Usage
(only selected categories are presented to demonstrate differences between categories)
Per Cent Responding

Variable	Often	Seldom	Never	Significance
Gender	52%	45%	3%	n.s.
Occupation				.01
Blue Collar	32	66	2	
Upper Mgmt.	80	20	0	
Retired	38	44	8	
Homemaker	47	48	6	
Student	38	62	0	
Age				.01
18-25	46	49	5	
35-40	61	39	0	
55-60	43	52	5	
71-75	33	47	11	
Income (000's)				.01
under $20	34	57	9	
43-50	58	41	1	
51-61	67	32	1	
over 81	71	29	0	
Education				.01
Some H.S.	12	73	15	
Some college	53	45	2	
College grad.	65	33	2	

The results become even clearer when usage is quantified into either 0, less than 5, 5 - 9, and 10 or more times used within the last six months. Here (Table 2), there are significant differences across all demographic variables. Males tend to use them more, 50% vs. 38% for females in the 10 or more category. Upper management had 80% response that they used 800 numbers 10 or more times compared to 17% for blue collar workers. Middle age groups, 41 - 54, had the highest usage, while those over 65 had the least. The lowest income group had 38% uses under 5 times and 29% over 10, compared to the highest group 1% checked over 10, while 8% checked under 5. A major change seemed to occur at the $50,000 income level with higher income showing higher usage. On education, 57% of those with only some high school used 800 numbers less than 5 times, while 54% of those with a college degree used them more than 10 times.

Table 2
Usage of 800 Numbers
Per Cent Responding

Variable	>10	5-9	<5	0	Significance
Total	44%	25%	27%	4%	
Gender					.01
Female	38	30	28	4	
Male	50	19	27	4	
Occupation					.01
Blue Collar	17	27	48	8	
Upper Mgmt.	80	16	5	0	
Retired	32	19	42	8	
Homemaker	31	34	30	5	
Student	33	33	25	8	
Age					.01
18-25	46	26	33	6	
41-45	54	16	26	3	
61-65	42	19	33	5	
71-75	30	25	40	5	
Income (000's)					.01
Under 20	29	24	38	9	
43-50	46	26	25	2	
51-60	62	26	12	0	
Over 81	71	21	8	0	
Education					.01
Some H.S.	17	14	57	12	
Some Coll.	45	26	26	3	
Grad. Sch.	54	27	18	1	

In analyzing specific uses (Table 3), the most frequent uses were for requesting information (65%), ordering products (63%) and making reservations (37%). There were no usage differences between males and females. Heavy users for requesting information tended to be students (blue collar was lowest) and those with at least some college education. With regards to ordering products, while all occupations were high, 91% of upper level managers checked this category compared to only 49% of the retirees. Consumers under 66, making over $51,000 and highly educated were the heaviest users of 800 numbers for ordering products or services. Those using 800 numbers for

reservations were college educated managers or professionals with upper incomes.

Table 3
Specific Uses
Per Cent Responding

	Request Information	Make Reservation	Make Complaint	Order Product
Total	65%	37%	16	63%
Occupation				
Students	83	38	8	67
Blue Collar	53	23	19	60
Upper Mgt.	70	66	23	91
Retired	62	28	16	49
Age				
18-25	68	30	19	70
41-45	69	46	17	69
71-75	59	30	22	52
Income (000's)				
Under 20	59	16	19	51
43-50	69	51	14	62
51-61	71	45	21	76
Over 81	73	79	14	86
Education				
Some H.S.	48	8	15	46
Some College	71	36	18	66
Grad. School	72	55	16	72

When specific organizations and number of times contacted were asked, ordering from a mail order company was the most frequently checked response, followed by airlines and banks. The frequency of response then drops drastically before getting to utilities, insurance and credit card companies.

Likes and Dislikes About 800 Numbers
There were many more positive responses concerning the use of 800 numbers than negative responses (see Table 4). While 85% responded to what they liked, only 43% responded negatively. Consumers like to use 800 numbers because they don't cost anything (86%) and they are convenient (53%). A major negative comment was that they don't like being put on hold (25%). A strong finding was that the majority of respondents preferred 800 number offerings with an easy to recall number (i.e. 800-333-3000) (75%) rather than a word (i.e. 800-Niagara) (25%). These likes and dislikes were consistent across all demographic categories.

Table 4
Likes & Dislikes With Using 800 Numbers

Likes:	Fast	Conven.	Talk to Person	Handled By Person	Doesn't Cost
n = 721	36%	54%	34%	24%	87%

Dislikes:		Impersonal		Put On Hold	
n = 359		3%		25%	

Satisfaction With Recent Call

The respondents were generally satisfied with how their most recent call was handled (Table 5). Eighty-nine percent checked that they were pleased, while 7% indicated that they felt the person answering the phone didn't have the information to answer their request and 4% felt that the person didn't care. While there were not many statistically significant differences across demographic variables, there were some variations in satisfaction. Females were slightly (91% vs. 86%, .05 level) more satisfied than males. Students, those in a trade and retirees were the least satisfied. With regards to age, 41 - 61 were the most satisfied, while those 71 and over were the least. The older consumers were the most likely to feel the person on the phone didn't care about them.

Table 5
Satisfaction With Use
Per Cent Responding

	Pleased	Didn't Know	Didn't Care	Signif.
Total	89	7	4	
Gender				
Female	91	5	4	.05
Male	86	10	5	
Occupation				n.s.
Blue Collar	87	9	9	
Upper Mgmt.	93	5	2	
Retired	84	9	7	
Homemaker	92	4	4	
Student	82	5	14	
Age				n.s.
18-25	82	9	9	
41-45	95	5	0	
61-65	85	6	9	
71-75	77	11	10	
Income (000's)				n.s.
Under 20	82	11	7	
43-50	91	6	3	
51-60	94	4	2	
Over 81	92	4	4	
Education				.05
Some H.S.	75	14	11	
Some Coll.	89	9	3	
Grad. Sch.	93	4	4	

There also seemed to be a direct relationship between income and education and satisfaction. The lower income groups felt that the person didn't know the information they needed (10%) or didn't care (7%). Those with only some high school felt the person didn't know (14%) or didn't care (11%), compared to college graduates, who had percentages of 4% for both negative responses.

Discussion and Implications

The major findings of this exploratory study were that while a majority of the respondents frequently use 800 numbers (over five times a month), usage varies across socioeconomic/ demographic variables. Heavy users have higher education and income levels and hold more professional types of positions. Major uses of 800 numbers were for requesting information, ordering products and making reservations. Consumers seem to be satisfied with their use of 800 numbers as few had strong dislikes and most were pleased with their most recent call. Companies should note that consumers with lower educational levels and lower income levels seemed to show a lower satisfaction level. This pattern may be in response to the fact that businesses have less effective communication with these consumers and therefore are not able to develop specific call expectations for this type of consumer.

Similarly, older consumers show a slightly lower satisfaction level. Again, this may be due to a lack of realistic expectations but also may be combined with a distrust of the use of computers and related technology.

The variation of results in usage and satisfaction substantiates the caveats suggested by Chadwick (1991) on using 800 numbers to collect consumer data/feedback. Building a customer database is important, but if 800 numbers are only reaching a select group of consumers, making inferences from talking to them may not be indicative of the typical product/service customer. Companies must be careful about their usage of the 800 number information and data gathered.

The results show that when consumers call an 800 number, they call with a very specific goal to be met, i.e., order goods, make an airline reservation or check a bank balance. This pattern of behavior should indicate that 800 number operations should be designed with the user needs in mind. The design should allow consumers to enter and move through the system to obtain the desired service or information quickly and directly.

An issue needing further research and action relates to increasing the usage among low users. Low users were identified as lower income, lower education, non-managerial or professional and either below 26 or over 55 years old. This correlated with findings by McEwen (1978) who concluded that toll-free numbers eliminate barriers to information seeking, but do not reach consumers who are not information seekers. If companies want to build relationships with these types of customers, educational programs must be designed to inform low users of the value of 800 numbers to them. Value for this group probably means the ability to solve problems or get information easily. This means targeting communications to this group stressing the ease and value of use.

Finally, as with any customer/company interaction, the nature of the interaction greatly affects the perception of the outcome. If an 800 number is being used to enhance relationships or image, those representing the company must be well trained, not only from an information perspective, but also on interpersonal skills. The study indicated that older customers and those with lower incomes had the greatest perception that the company representative either didn't know the information they wanted or didn't care about them. Either of these responses is detrimental to building a customer relationship.

Consumers and consumer affairs organizations will need to work together to design systems and networks to provide the information the consumer needs from the organization that is best able to provide that information. All this networking must work effectively and in a timely fashion. The marketplace will, in the future, reward those businesses who provide relevant and accurate information to the consumer. (Sandbach, 1967).

References

Chadwick, K.G. (1991). Some Caveats Regarding the Interpretation of Data from 800 Number Callers. Journal of Consumer Marketing, 8 (4), Fall.

Giese, T.D. & Weisenberger, T. M. (1985). The Perception and Use of Consumer Information Sources. Journal of Education for Business, (October), 38 - 43.

Grimm, C., Cottrell, R. & Jenks, M. (1990). Customer Service 800 Numbers: Recent Research and New Developments. MOBIUS (February), 31 - 35.

Gronmo, S. (1987). The Strategic Position of Consumers in the Information Society. Journal of Consumer Policy, 43 - 67.

Keller, K.L. & Staelin, R. (1987). Effects of quality and quantity of information on decision effectiveness. Journal of Consumer Research. 14, (September).

Lefton, T. (1992). Toll-free Turf Wars. Adweek's Marketing Week, (January 27), 28 -29.

Malhotra, N.K. (1982). Information Load and Consumer Decision Making. Journal of Consumer Research, 8, (March), 419 - 430.

McEwen, W.J. (1978). Bridging the Information Gap. Journal of Consumer Research, 4, 247 - 251.

Sandbach, W. (1971) Consumerism's Role in Marketing Strategy. Sales Management, (November 15), 39 - 40.

Smith, J. A. (1991). The New Frontier. Direct Marketing, (July), 61 - 63.

Sproles, G.B., Geistfeld, L.V. & Badenhop, S. B. (1978). Informational inputs as influences on efficient consumer decision-making. The Journal of Consumer Affairs, 12 (1), 88 - 103.

Stern, A.L. (1991). Telemarketing polishes its image. Telemarketing, (June), 106 - 110.

TARP. (1988). 800 numbers for customer service: a 1988 profile. SOCAP/TARP Study. (Spring).

Unkel, M. (1991). Telepromotions: when to use 800 and 900 numbers. Telemarketing, (September), 82 - 85.

Determinants of Consumer Credit Card
Repayment Patterns

Lien-Ti Bei, Purdue University[1]

This study investigates three credit card repayment patterns, namely revolvers, partial revolvers, and non-revolvers, which are defined as original responses for holders of bank or retail store cards, based on the 1983 Survey of Consumer Finances. Multivariate logistic regression analysis is used in this study to determine the probability of repayment patterns by households' socio-demographic, financial, and attitudinal characteristics. The results show that financial and attitudinal factors are the most important determinants.

American households' credit-card debts have been growing for many years. The amount of outstanding balances on credit cards per family have increased from $649 to $1,472 (measured in constant 1986 dollars) from 1970 to 1986 (Canner, 1988). Actually, households' credit-card debts were steadily increasing after 1986. The median credit-card debt of families holding rose from $600 to $900 (in 1989 dollars), and the proportion of families carrying such debts increased from 37 percent to 39.9 percent between 1983 and 1989 (Kennickell & Shack-Marquez, 1992).

Not only the amount of credit-card debt has increased, the proportion of household holding credit cards has also expanded during the same time period. Credit cards have been widely held by American families. The proportion of families holding at least one type of credit card has grown from 51 percent to 71 percent between 1970 and 1986. Retail store cards were the most frequently held type of card in 1986, with 62 percent of all families holding such a card. The most dramatic increase has occurred in the holding of bank cards, which were the second widely held in 1986, from 16 percent to 55 percent over the time period (Canner, 1988).

Retail store cards and bank cards show a common characteristic: the opportunity to revolve the credit card debt. Many researchers attribute the successful increase of the revolving credit card to its flexible repayment terms (Heck, 1983; Canner, 1988), interest-free grace periods (Canner & Cyrnak, 1986), and convenience (Luckett & August, 1985; Canner & Cyrnak, 1986). Therefore, two types of credit card usage patterns by consumers can be identified: for financial needs through installments and for convenience in transactions (Canner & Cyrnak, 1986). These two credit card usage patterns create three types of repayment patterns for the credit card outstanding: always revolving, partial revolving, and never revolving in the 1983 Survey of Consumer Finances. Consumers, who always revolve credit card debt and hardly ever pay the amount of credit card bills in full, can be named as revolvers; whereas consumers, who never revolve credit card debt and always pay full bills, can be called non-revolvers. Some consumers at the middle stage, who sometimes pay full amount or always pay some bills in full, are partial revolvers.

The purpose of this study is to investigate the determinants which contribute to the probability that a consumer with bank or store cards will be primarily a revolver, partial revolver, or non-revolver. The characteristics of revolvers and partial revolvers are important to credit issuers. The profits of card issuers depend in large part on generating interests from the outstanding debt of revolvers. The more monthly payments consumers do not pay in full, the more profits card issuers earn. On the other hand, some consumers revolve credit card debts because of their financial difficulties, which means higher risk for creditors. Hence, the probability of a consumer being a revolver and partial revolver, related to their characteristics, provides a useful information concerning potential risks and profits for card grantors.

Understanding the determinants of being a revolver, partial revolver, or non-revolver is also important for social-economists. Only revolving credit debt represents the true consumer credit-card burdens. The credit for convenience purposes may inaccurately inflate the growth of consumer debt (Luckett & August, 1985). Therefore, subtracting non-revolvers' debts from the total consumer debt is useful to investigate the actual households' credit burdens and their repayment abilities. Revolvers who have problems paying full credit debts usually tend to go bankrupt, resulting in social loss. The results of this study can provide further insight on financial and economic characteristics of consumers who potentially have payment problems.

The Determinants of
a Revolver or Non-Revolver

The first objective of this article is to determine factors related to being a revolver, partial revolver, or non-revolver. To perform the

[1]Master Student, Consumer Sciences
and Retailing

objective of this study, a model of credit card repayment patterns is used similar to Canner and Cyrnak's (1986) model. They study household credit card usage patterns by selected family characteristics and develop a logistic model to estimate the probability of a household's usage pattern, using the data of the 1983 Survey of Consumer Finances. In their model, the dependent variable is convenience, which is a dummy variable dividing households into two groups: convenient users who always pay the full amount of credit card bills, and financial users who hardly ever or sometime pay bills in full. However, the 1983 survey data provide three payment categories of bank or store credit card holders: those who hardly ever, those who sometimes or for some cards, and those who almost always pay the total amount due each month. There is no theoretical reason that consumers with sometime full payments will tend to be revolvers or non-revolvers, so they can be a single group, neither revolver nor non-revolver. Thus, it is a premise in this study that the dependent variable has three ordinal categories consistent with the original data.

Canner and Cyrnak (1986) assume that the probability of being a convenience user is a function of financial, socio-demographic, and attitudinal variables. In their model, financial factors are 1982 family income, ratio of monthly debt payments plus monthly rent payments for non-homeowners to monthly income, and ratio of liquid assets to 1982 income. Demographic variables are education level, age, and race of household head, and race multiplied by 1982 income. Attitudinal factor is an index constructed by summing the number of positive responses about possible reasons for borrowing. All their independent variables are included in this study, except the variable of race multiplied by 1982 income. They employ this variable to represent the interaction between race and income. However, it is not significant in their results, and the Pearson correlation coefficient for race and income is only 0.05 in the present study. Thus, this interaction variable is excluded from the model. Another change is that their attitudinal factor is substituted by adopting the direct answer to consumers' general attitude toward credit cards in this model.

Variables indicated above have the same hypotheses as those in Canner and Cyrnak's model. Income is proposed to have a positive relationship with the ability to pay the credit card debt (Canner & Cyrnak, 1986; Slocum & Mathews, 1970; Mandell, 1972). The ratio of liquid assets to income is hypothesized to be positively related to the probability of being a non-revolver, whereas the ratio of monthly payment to income is negatively related to that probability (Canner & Cyrnak, 1986). Age is hypothesized to be positively associated with the probability of achieving full payments, according to the life-cycle theory (Ando & Modigliani, 1963; Thurow, 1969). During the 20 to 35 age period, a household is faced with problems of raising and building a family. So, the family

consumption is higher, related to the family income when a household head is young. After 35 years of age, a household's income may begin to exceed expenditures for current consumption. Therefore, a household's repayment ability increases as the family head ages (Canner & Cyrnak, 1986; Mandell, 1972). Whites are found to be positively related to being non-revolvers in Canner and Cyrnak's (1986) study. Household heads with high educational level are assumed to have a greater probability of being non-revolvers compared to low educational household heads (Canner & Cyrnak, 1986; Mandell, 1972).

Moreover, the model tested in this study controls for five more demographic factors and one more financial factor than the model used by Canner and Cyrnak: family size (i.e., the total number of persons in household), presence of a child under eighteen years of age, marital status, occupation, sex of household head, and the consumer loan payment problem. Family size and presence of children are related to the stage of family life cycle (Heck, 1983), also associated with family consumption expenditures (Thurow, 1969). It is probably the case that large families with children are faced with heavier financial needs and higher potential payment problems (Heck, 1983).

Sullivan and Fisher (1988) identify the characteristics of consumers who missed or fell behind scheduled debt repayments. They report that a greater proportion of women have debt payment difficulties than men. However, they also argue that the sex of household head incorporated family life-cycle. Hence, the gender of household head is added in the present model to test the relationship between gender and credit card repayment difficulties, controlling for other variables.

Canner and Luckett (1990) apply multivariate techniques to approach the determinants of household loan payment performance. Their results show that the marital status of household head is significantly related to a household's loan payment performance. Households with married and single heads have a higher probability without any missed or late payment than separated or divorced head, when controlling for other variables. Thus, the marital status is included in this credit repayment pattern study, and presented as a dummy variable: 1 is separated or divorced, and 0 is others. Canner & Luckett (1990) also examine the relationship between the occupation of household head by twelve categories and loan payment problems. Here, occupation is a dummy variable (1 represents professional workers or managers, 0 is others).

Credit grantors usually view consumers with records of late loan payments as risky creditees, because those consumers may have financial problems and also hardly pay the revolving card debt in full. So, the consumer loan payment problem is added into the model as one of the financial variables to examine whether it actually is related to the revolver/non-revolver status. Chart 1 presents the definitions of all variables used in

Chart 1
Variable Definitions

INDEPENDENT VARIABLES

SOCIO-DEMOGRAPHIC
AGE - age of household head
FAMILY SIZE - total number of persons in household
CHILDREN - presence of a child under 18 years of age   1: if household has children under 18;
                                                        0: if not.

MARITAL STATUS - marital status of household head   1: divorced or separated;
                                                        0: others.

OCCUPATION - job category of household head   1: professional worker or manager;
                                                        0: others.

SEX - the gender of household head.   1: male;
                                                        0: female.

EDUCATION - the educational level of household head   1: 0-8 grades;
                                                        2: 9-12 grades;
                                                        3: high school diploma;
                                                        4: some college;
                                                        5: college degree.

RACE - race of household head   1: white;
                                                        0: non-white.

FINANCIAL
LOAN-PROB - the consumer loan payment problem   1: sometimes delayed or missed payments
                                                        0: all paid as scheduled or no loan

INCOME - 1982 family income (dollars)
LIQUID/INCOME - ratio of liquid assets to 1982 family income
PAYMENT/INCOME - ratio of monthly debt payments plus monthly rent payments for non-homeowners
         to monthly income

ATTITUDINAL
ATTITUDE - general credit attitude   1: good idea or good in some ways
                                                        0: bad idea

DEPENDENT VARIABLES

PAYMENT PATTERN (Model 1) - payment patterns for retail store and bank credit cards
        2 : always pay full amount credit card bills
        1 : sometimes pay full amount or always pay some bills in full
        0 : hardly ever pay full amount of bills
PAYFULL (Model 2-1) - payment patterns for store and bank cards
        1: always pay full amount credit card bills
        0: others
PAYSOME (Model 2-2) - payment patterns for store and bank cards
        1: sometimes pay full amount or always pay some bills in full
        0: others
PAYHARD (Model 2-3) - payment patterns for store and bank cards
        1: hardly ever pay full amount of bills
        0: others

---

this study. Since the dependent variable, the repayment pattern, contains three levels, the ordinal Logistic regression analysis is suggested as an appropriate technique for analysis (Aldrich & Nelson, 1988).

The second objective of this study is to determine distinctive household characteristics for each type of credit repayment patterns: non-revolvers who always pay full amount of credit card bills, partial revolvers who sometimes pay full amount or always pay some bills in full, and revolvers who hardly ever pay full amount of bills. Therefore, three separate models are developed for three repayment patterns. Independent variables in this part are the same as those in the first model. The definitions of the three dependent variables are also listed in Chart 1. The binary logistic regression is used to examine these three models.

Empirical Tests

Data are from the 1983 Survey of Consumer Finances conducted by the Survey Research Center of

Table 1
Ordinal Logistic Regression Results
Model 1: Three Types of Credit Card Repayment Patterns

Independent Variable	Mean Value	Parameter Estimate	Standard Error	Wald Chi-Square	
Constant 1		-0.71	0.33	4.74	*
Constant 2		0.62	0.33	3.60	*
SOCIO-DEMOGRAPHIC VARIABLES					
Age	46.32	0.01	0.00	10.39	**
Race	0.89	0.32	0.13	5.83	*
Education	3.55	0.04	0.04	1.06	
Family Size	2.79	-0.10	0.05	4.87	*
Children	0.42	0.01	0.13	0.01	
Marital Status	0.12	-0.08	0.15	0.27	
Occupation	0.39	0.08	0.10	0.55	
Gender	0.79	0.08	0.13	0.34	
FINANCIAL VARIABLES					
Loan-Problem	0.11	-1.00	0.14	52.07	**
Income	33.01	0.00	0.00	5.33	*
Liquid/Income	0.50	0.88	0.10	77.72	**
Payment/Income	0.18	-1.01	0.21	22.51	**
ATTITUDINAL VARIABLE					
Attitude	0.81	-0.46	0.11	16.78	**

Criteria for Assessing Model Fit
       -2 Log Likelihood $\chi^2 = 469.08$ **
Concordance   71.6%
Score Test for the Proportional Odds $\chi^2 = 19.94$

*significant at .05 level.
**significant at .01 level.

the University of Michigan. The survey sample consists of 3,824 randomly selected U.S. households. A total of 2,224 households holding at least one bank or retail store card, without negative income and uncertain attitudes toward credit cards, are analyzed in this study. Within these households, 1,059 are non-revolvers, 584 are partial revolvers, and 581 are revolvers.

Pre-test

The interactions within independent variables have been tested before applying logistic analysis. None of the Pearson correlation coefficients between each pair of variables is greater than 0.75. Therefore, no variable representing interaction is included in models.

Three Types of Credit Card Repayment Patterns

Table 1 presents the results of the ordinal logistic regression. Three credit card repayment patterns are analyzed as ordinal responses. The premise assumption of three parallel types of credit card repayment patterns is accepted as measured by the chi-square value of 19.94. It

supports that sometimes paying credit card bills in full can be viewed as a middle pattern between long-term revolver and non-revolver. Also, the model fit is significant at 0.01 level.

The age of household head and family size are significantly related to credit card repayment pattern. As the age of household head increases, the probability of paying full credit card bills increases. On the contrary, family size is negatively associated with the probability of paying credit card bills in full. These two results are consistent with the life-cycle theory. The race of household head is also a significant variable. Whites are more likely to pay credit card bills in full than blacks, Hispanics, and others.

The proportions of revolvers, partial revolvers, and non-revolvers by sex and marital status of household heads, without the consideration of other variables are illustrated in Table 2. Women are more likely to be long-term revolvers than men. Also, separated or divorced

Table 2
Credit Card Repayment Patterns by Gender and
Marital Status of Household Head

Characteristics	Non-revolver	Partial Revolver	Revolver	Chi-Square
Male	46.79	27.40	25.81	5.72*
Female	50.75	21.94	27.31	
Separated & Divorced	40.58	27.54	31.88	7.48*
Married, Single, & Widowed	48.61	26.08	25.31	
All Households	47.62	26.26	26.12	

* significant at .05 level.

household heads are more likely relative to other marital status to revolving credit card debts. However, sex and marital status are not significant in multivariate analysis (shown in Table 1). The present study supports that gender and marital status of household head incorporate other household characteristics (Sullivan and Fisher, 1988) which dominate the credit card repayment patterns. Moreover, there is no evidence that other demographic variables, such as the presence of children under eighteen, occupation, and educational level of household head, are related to credit card repayment pattern when controlling for other variables.

All financial variables are significantly associated with credit card repayment patterns. Consistent with the hypotheses, the repayment pattern of a household with higher income or higher ratio of liquid assets to income is more likely to be a non-revolver. It is obviously that households with higher income or more liquid assets have greater ability to pay the full amount of monthly credit card bills. The ratio of monthly debt payments plus monthly rent payments for non-homeowners to monthly income is negatively related to being a non-revolver. In addition, households with consumer loan payment problems tend to hardly ever pay the full amount of credit card bills. It is probably the case that loan payment problems are associated with the family financial difficulty, so those households have to revolve their credit card debts. This result reveals why credit grantors use late payment records to reject credit card applicants. Creditors tend to accept the possible association between bad payment records and financial problems, then reject those credit applicants due to minimizing business risk.

Not unexpected, a negative attitude toward credit cards is highly related to being a non-revolver. For households with problems of paying bills in full, revolving credit cards help them solve the payment difficulty. On the other hand,

consumers who have a positive attitude toward credit cards may use credit cards more frequently and rely upon credit cards more easily.

Special Characteristics for Each Pattern of Repayment

The next step is to examine each type of credit card repayment pattern to find out its special characteristics. Three multivariate logistic models are developed for three patterns: non-revolvers who always pay full amount of credit card bills, partial revolvers who sometimes pay full amount or always pay some bills in full, and revolvers who hardly ever pay full amount of bills. The results are illustrated in Table 3 to Table 5. These three models all fit at the 0.01 level.

The significant variables for being a non-revolver (shown in Table 3), contrasting to other two repayment patterns, are the same as those in the previous ordinal logistic model. The finding is not surprised because roughly half of the bank and retail credit card holders were non-revolvers contributing the characteristics in these two models.

However, a closer analysis for partial revolvers (presented in Table 4) indicates their distinctive characteristics. Compared with long-term revolvers and non-revolvers, households with consumer loan payment problems and lower ratio of liquid assets to income are more likely to be partial revolvers. Also, a positive attitude toward credit cards is positively and significantly related to being a partial revolver. This is acceptable because a partial revolver may have only temporal payment difficulty, but not actually rely upon credit cards long term.

The further multivariate logistic analysis for revolvers (shown in Table 5) identifies that

Table 3
Multivariate Logistic Regression Results Model 2-1: Characteristics for Non-Revolvers

Independent Variable	Parameter Estimate	Standard Error	Wald Chi-Square	
Constant	-0.44	0.37	1.44	
SOCIO-DEMOGRAPHIC VARIABLES				
Age	0.01	0.00	7.72	**
Race	0.42	0.16	7.05	**
Education	0.01	0.05	0.02	
Family Size	-0.12	0.05	4.77	*
Children	-0.06	0.15	0.15	
Marital Status	-0.11	0.17	0.46	
Occupation	0.08	0.11	0.48	
Gender	0.01	0.15	0.01	
FINANCIAL VARIABLES				
Loan-Problem	-1.01	0.18	30.87	**
Income	0.00	0.00	5.20	*
Liquid/Income	0.85	0.10	68.23	**
Payment/Income	-1.09	0.26	18.14	**
ATTITUDINAL VARIABLE				
Attitude	-0.53	0.12	18.84	**

Criteria for Assessing Model Fit		
-2 Log Likelihood	χ^2 = 422.93	**
Concordance	74.0%	

*significant at .05 level **significant at .01 level.

Table 4
Multivariate Logistic Regression Results Model 2-2: Characteristics for Partial Revolvers

Independent Variable	Parameter Estimate	Standard Error	Wald Chi-Square	
Constant	-1.39	0.38	13.50	**
SOCIO-DEMOGRAPHIC VARIABLES				
Age	-0.01	0.00	1.65	
Race	-0.12	0.15	0.57	
Education	0.08	0.05	2.17	
Family Size	0.05	0.05	0.77	
Children	0.15	0.15	0.94	
Marital Status	0.16	0.18	0.80	
Occupation	0.04	0.12	0.10	
Gender	0.19	0.16	1.45	
FINANCIAL VARIABLES				
Loan-Problem	-0.31	0.16	3.66	*
Income	-0.00	0.00	1.23	
Liquid/Income	-0.45	0.10	19.07	**
Payment/Income	0.03	0.11	0.06	
ATTITUDINAL VARIABLE				
Attitude	0.37	0.14	7.29	**

Criteria for Assessing Model Fit		
-2 Log Likelihood	χ^2 = 85.36	**
Concordance	60.5%	

*significant at .05 level **significant at .01 level.

Table 5
Multivariate Logistic Regression Results Model 2-3: Characteristics for Revolvers

Independent Variable	Parameter Estimate	Standard Error	Wald Chi-Square	
Constant	-0.18	0.39	0.20	
SOCIO-DEMOGRAPHIC VARIABLES				
Age	-0.01	0.00	4.95	*
Race	-0.26	0.15	2.85	
Education	-0.08	0.05	2.04	
Family Size	0.08	0.06	2.04	
Children	-0.07	0.16	0.17	
Marital Status	0.00	0.18	0.00	
Occupation	-0.11	0.13	0.77	
Gender	-0.18	0.16	1.23	
FINANCIAL VARIABLES				
Loan-Problem	1.05	0.15	49.69	**
Income	-0.00	0.00	4.06	*
Liquid/Income	-1.03	0.16	39.77	**
Payment/Income	0.68	0.24	8.45	**
ATTITUDINAL VARIABLE				
Attitude	0.31	0.14	4.74	*

Criteria for Assessing Model Fit
         -2 Log Likelihood χ^2 = 286.13   **
Concordance   73.2%

*significant at .05 level.
**significant at .01 level.

age of household heads is negatively and significantly associated with the probability of being revolvers. Moreover, the four financial variables are all significant. Households with lower income, lower ratio of liquid assets to income, higher ratio of monthly payments to income, or other consumer loan payment problems, are more likely to always revolve their credit card debts. Also, credit revolvers tend to posit more positive attitude toward credit cards.

CONCLUSION AND SUGGESTION

The assumption of three types of credit card repayment patterns is accepted. It means that the partial revolvers should be seen as a middle stage between long-term revolver and non-revolver.

It was proved in this study that financial and attitudinal variables are more able to indicate consumers' repayment patterns than socio-demographic variables. "Attitude" is significant in all models. Almost all of the financial variables are strongly associated with credit card repayment patterns. The relationship between loan payment problems and credit card repayment patterns, which has not tested in previous studies, significant in this study. These findings imply that most households revolve their credit card debts because of the financial needs, but not only due to their positive attitudes toward credit card. Conversely, their positive credit attitudes may be attributed to that the flexible payment of credit cards solve parts of their financial problems.

The age of household head is significant in all models, except for the test of the partial revolver. This result supports the life-cycle theory. Another variable regarding the life-cycle theory, family size, is only significant in the ordinal model and associated with being a non-revolver.

A closer analysis for each type of repayment patterns provides some further insights. These two groups donate potential profits and risk for creditors. Households having other consumer loan payment problems, lower income, and lower ratio of liquid assets to income tend not pay credit card bills in full.

Distinguishing partial revolvers is useful for creditors because this group of consumers are lower risky than always revolvers, and pay more interests to creditors than non-revolvers. However, the consumer's credit card repayment pattern only provides the information of potential profits and risks to creditors. Creditors should consider the trade-off between profits and risks. Furthermore, the profitability of each repayment pattern to creditors are also related to the amount and frequency of using credit card by consumers, which are worth further studying.

The implication for consumer educators is that consumers should learn how to properly use the credit card as a tool to solve their financial problems. Although credit cards have flexible repayment terms, the high interest rates can cause consumers to go bankrupt easily. Consumers should be aware of the interest rate and truly understand it before using credit cards. The relationship between the interest rates of credit cards and repayment patterns is another issue for the future research.

The limitation of this study is that the 1983 survey data is too old to represent households' credit card repayment patterns in 1992. However, the change of repayment pattern over time period can be examined by using the 1989 and 1983 Surveys of Consumer Finances to develop a pooled cross-section time series research.

Acknowledgement

The author would like to thank Dr. Dixie Porter Johnson for her assistance and suggestion in this study, and the Federal Reserve for providing the data.

Reference

Ando, A. & Modigliani, F. (1963). The life Cycle Hypothesis of Saving: Aggregate Implications and Tests. American Economic Review, 55-84.

Aldrich, J. H., & Nelson, Forrest D. (1988). Linear Probability, Logit, and Probit Models. California: Sage Publications, Inc.

Canner, G. B. (1988). Changers in Consumer Holding and Use of Credit Cards, 1970-86. Journal of Retail Banking, 10(1) 13-24.

Canner, G. B. & Cyrnak, A. W. (1986). Determinants of Consumer Credit Card Usage Patterns. Journal of Retail Banking, VII, 1-2, 9-18.

Canner, G. B., & Luckett, C. A. (1990). Consumer Debt Repayment Woes: Insights from a Household Survey. Journal of Retail Banking, 12, 1, 55-62.

Heck, R. K. Z. (1983). Determinants of Credit Card Possession Behavior: A Test for Differences Among Types of Credit Cards. Consumer Economics & Housing, N.Y.S. College of Ecology, Cornell University, 1-47.

Kennickell, A. & Shack-Marquez, J. (1992). Changes in Family Finance 1983-1989: Evidence from the Survey of Consumer Finance. Federal Reserve Bulletin, 78, 1-18.

Luckett, C. A., & August, J. D. (1985). The Growth of Consumer Debt. Federal Reserve Bulletin, June, 389-402.

Mandell, L. (1972). Credit Card Use in the United States. Michigan: Institute for Social Research, University of Michigan.

Slocum, J. W. JR., & Mathews, H. L.(1970). Social Class and Income as Indicators of Consumer Credit Behavior. Journal of Marketing, 34, 69-74.

Sullivan, C. A., & Fisher, R. M. (1988). Consumer Credit Delinquency Risk: Characteristics of Consumers Who Fall Behind. Journal of Retail Banking, 10, 3, 53-64.

Thurow, L. C. (1969). The Optimum Lifetime Distribution of Consumption Expenditures. The American Economic Review, 59, 2, 324-330.

Complaint Channels and Grievance Mechanism Systems in Health Care Institutions

Margaret A. Charters, Syracuse University[1]

This empirical study of a random sample of members of the National Society of Patient Representation and Consumer Affairs was initiated to 1) describe their current roles and levels of power, 2) determine the extent to which they fulfill the formal complaint function in hospitals today, 3) compare 1990 and 1970 models of hospital patient grievance mechanisms and 4) compare the empirically determined patient representative model of information flow about consumer complaints with the Gilly model.

Andreason's exhaustive analysis of the literature in consumer satisfaction and complaining behavior points out that there remain major gaps in our knowledge base. The literature has primarily focused on the determinants of satisfaction and responses to dissatisfaction with exchanges. It has only recently focused on institutional response to voiced dissatisfaction (Andreasen 1988).

Studies in the United States, Canada and the United Kingdom all document lower rates of satisfaction in service than product categories. Andreason concludes that the domain of services is one in which more work is needed. The models reported in his review were much less successful in accounting for complaining behavior with respect to services. He hypothesizes that one reason may be a lack of clarity as to appropriate complaint channels. Bryant asserts "Research must model and investigate empirically firm as well as consumer behavior if we are to be successful in understanding consumer dissatisfaction and complaints" (Bryant 1988 p. 725). An idea of how the entire system works is missing in research on consumer satisfaction and dissatisfaction (Gerner, 1988).

This study of patient representative personnel is an empirical investigation of a major channel (patient representative departments) for receiving complaints and responding to them in health care institutions, a service area.

Background

Patient representatives in healthcare institutions "provide a specific channel though which patients can seek solutions to problems, concerns and unmet needs ...coordinate between departments and recommend alternative policies and procedures" (NSPRCA 1989). The American Hospital Association Guide to the Healthcare Field Code #67 describes patient representatives as "personnel through whom patients and staff can seek solutions to institutional problems affecting the delivery of high quality care and services". The Joint Council for Accreditation of Healthcare Organizations (JCAHO) requirements effective January 1990, go one step further and mandate each hospital to have a mechanism to "receive, respond to complaints and take corrective action when appropriate" (AHA 1990).

Researchers using the information processing model of consumer complaints distinguish between complaint handling and complaint management. Complaint handling is the response to the customer complaint. Complaint management involves decisions about change in policies and procedures to prevent future dissatisfaction for all customers (Fornell and Westbrook, 1979). Gilly draws on and extends this organizational information processing model in her study of the dynamics of complaint management in one hospital (Gilly, 1991). See Figure 1. The study of the roles of patient representatives in healthcare institutions reported here, provides further empirical data to test the Gilly model of information flow about consumer complaints in a service environment.

Figure 1
Information Flows About Consumer Complaints

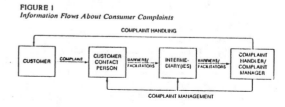

FIGURE I
Information Flows About Consumer Complaints

Many different titles are used for those involved in the formal patient complaint function in healthcare institutions. The most common, currently, is "patient representative". Their professional organization is the National Society of Patient Representation and Consumer Affairs (NSPRCA). Researchers in a study of complaint functions done for the Secretary of Health Education and Welfare's Commission on Medical Malpractice selected the term "patient grievance mechanism" as the most appropriate term to identify the subject of their study (Fry, 1972). This study developed three hypothetical models of patient grievance mechanisms.

---

[1]Associate Professor, Director,
Consumer Studies Program

Model One's objectives were to "relieve top level administrators of the task of resolving "minor" complaints and help keep patients in a positive frame of mind while in the institution" (Fry, 1972 p. 103). This would correspond to the traditional complaint handling model designed to satisfy unhappy customers. Model Two assumed the added responsibility of investigating "matters patients complain about and introducing needed changes into the delivery pattern in an effort to reduce malpractice claims and improve the quality of care" (Fry 1972 p.111). This model includes the information flow included in both the complaint handling and complaint management process as described by Gilly (Gilly 1991 p. 300). Model Three adds an information flow to an external independent office that could "oversee and evaluate the processes used to respond to patient complaints and concerns about medical treatment,". This last model was intended to provide the "objectivity" that mechanisms funded by the institutions they monitor may be unable to achieve. Model One was most frequently used in the hospitals of 1972.

The Study

Objectives

The present study was initiated to: 1) describe the current roles and levels of power of patient representatives, 2) determine the extent to which this position is used to fulfill the formal complaint function i.e. patient grievance mechanism in today's hospitals, 3) determine what model is most frequently used in the hospitals of the 1990's and 4) compare the empirically determined model of patient representative complaint handling in healthcare institutions in this study with the Gilly model of information flows about consumer complaints in one hospital (Gilly,1991).

Methodology

The membership list of NSPRCA of the American Hospital Association formed the population base. A one-third random sample was taken by starting with a numeral from a random numbers table and selecting every third name on the membership list. A five-page questionnaire was mailed in March of 1990 with a follow-up letter and duplicate survey form in April. The survey instrument was piloted with a small group of patient representatives and revised according to their comments. Detailed follow-up interviews were conducted with three of these pilot representatives. A 56% sample response rate was achieved; 181 usable surveys were analyzed.

The institutions included 92% not-for-profit hospitals; (four-fifths private, one-fifth government); 5% for-profit; 3% HMOs. One half were teaching hospitals. Patient representatives are thus more heavily represented in teaching hospitals as the ratio of teaching to non-teaching hospitals is approximately 1:4 in the United States. [Council on Graduate Medical Education; 1990.]

Evaluation And Analysis

Staffing Patterns

Almost one-half (47%) of the institutions studied had only one professional representative on staff; 33% had 2-4; 13% had 5-9 and 7% had 10 or more. Every possible combination of professionals, volunteers, and clerical staff was found. Analysis by total staff size and type of hospital revealed no consistency in staffing patterns.

Reporting Patterns

Patient representatives report to a relatively high level of administration of health-care institutions. Seventeen percent reported directly to a top administrator or CEO type. Almost two-thirds of the patient representatives' supervisors reported to a top officer or the board of trustees. These personnel are favorably positioned to seek solutions to problems as well as report concerns about quality of care. One-half of the patient representatives reported in the general administrative functional stream. Others reported through quality assurance/risk management (13%), nursing/medical (13%), marketing (9%), and finance (2%).

Time Allocations

Complaint investigation and information/referral took on average the largest blocks of time but varied greatly from institution to institution; complaint handling from 2% to 70% and information/referral from 1% to 90%. Grouping activities into broader categories as shown in Table 1 presents an even clearer picture of time allocation.

Table 1
Time Departments Spent on Groups of Activities

Activity	Percent (N=113)					
	0-4	5-9	10-14	15-19	20-49	50+
Complaint Handling 　Complaint Investig. 　Complaint Analysis 　Pat. Questionnaire	21	2	10	5	36	34
Information/Referral 　Information referral 　Prepare Educ Material 　Distribute Pat. 　　Bill Rts.	23	7	13	14	29	14
Risk Mgm./Qual. Assur. 　Risk Management 　Quality Assurance	54	15	11	1	13	6
Liaison 　Physician Liaison 　Community Liaison	79	11	3	3	4	0
Report Writing	44	15	19	3	19	0
Committee Meetings	65	20	11	1	4	0

Complaint Handling

The extent to which patient representatives spend their time in complaint handling reflects the extent to which they can be considered patient grievance mechanisms. On average, complaint activity took 27% of patient representative time; 50% or more of the time of one-fifth of them; less than 10% of the time of only 15% of them. Combining complaint investigation, analysis and patient quality-of-care questionnaire activities, 34% of the departments spent more than 50% of their time handling complaints; 70% spent more than 20% of their time this way.

Whether or not departments spent 50% or more of their time on complaint handling was unrelated to hospital size but was directly related to the number of beds per patient representative.

The types of complaints listed by a weighted average of their frequency are shown in Table 2. Problems of staff attitude and nurse communication were most frequently encountered. Billing was a distant third. Almost every patient representative checked physician communication as a problem; only 40% said it occurred frequently. Non-checklist items mentioned included lost property, room comfort, time waits, bioethical issues and expectations.

Table 2
Frequency of Problem Type

Problem	Percent Frequency				Mean**	Sample	
	Never N/A	1*	2*	3*		No.	%
Staff Attitude	2	2	24	71	2.64	177	98
Nurse Communic.	2	4	26	69	2.60	177	98
Billing/Insur	4	12	30	54	2.33	174	96
Physic Communic.	1	9	50	40	2.28	179	99
Food	8	22	33	37	1.97	166	92
Medical Records	9	31	41	18	1.69	164	91
Scheduling	17	29	35	19	1.56	150	83
Discharge Arr.	19	34	38	9	1.36	146	81
Pharmacist Commun.	27	55	14	2	.95	133	73

*1=Seldom: 2=Occasionally: 3=Frequently
**Mean was calculated using weights Seldom=1,Occasionally=2 and Frequently=3

Information/Referral

Customer contact by patient representatives was not only for the purpose of receiving complaints. Information and referral activities included responding to inquiries, providing information to patients and staff, preparing educational materials, and distributing the Patient Bill of Rights. Either 14% or 43% of the patient representative departments could be called "information/referral" programs depending whether "major focus" is defined as 20% or 50% of time spent.

Risk Management and Quality Assurance

The activity checklist in the survey included both risk management and quality assurance. The lack of a clear definition of these terms makes their relationship to complaint handling unclear, a limitation of the study. One-fifth of the departments spent 20% or more of their time and 6% spent 50% or more of their time on these activities.

Report Writing and Committee Membership

The survey format did not permit allocation of this time to functional areas such as complaint handling. Report circulation and committee participation enhance patient representatives' information brokerage role as a source of power. Forty-four percent of the respondents cited specific policies and/or procedures that had been changed as a result of their reports; 20% felt their reports had minimal or no impact on institutional policy. Committee meetings took, on average, only 3% of department time.

Patient Contact

A Likert-type scale was used to determine the method and frequency of patient contact. Responses are listed in Table 3. Ninety-four percent of the respondents checked personal visit; 59% said contact was made frequently this way. Ninety-one percent listed telephone number; 87% outside mail; 83% switchboard and 78% survey. The listed telephone number was assumed to be the in-house number for the patient representative department.

Table 3
How the Patient Contacts Patreps

Method	Percent					Total Used	
	Never/N/A	1*	2*	3*	Mean*	No	%
Personal Visit	6	3	32	59	2.45	171	94
Listed Number	9	5	24	62	2.39	165	91
Swithboard	17	9	33	40	1.97	150	83
Survey	22	12	27	39	1.84	142	78
Outside Mail	13	20	45	21	1.76	158	87
Comment Cards	41	10	24	24	1.32	107	59
800 Number	90	5	1	4	.19	19	10

*Mean was calculated by weighting
Seldom = 1; Occasionally = 2; Frequently = 3

Types of Power

The power to resolve patient concerns determines the effectiveness of patient representative departments as a patient grievance mechanism, indicating the extent to which they are complaint handlers or complaint managers. Survey participants checked from a list of 30 those acts they were permitted to perform in order to resolve patient complaints. See Table 4.

Table 4
<u>Actions Patient Representatives Can Perform</u>

Actions	Percent
Level 1	
Interview Patients	99
Determine validity of complaint	97
Collect information from staff involved in complaint	96
Explain outcome of grievance procedure to patient	94
Access relevant medical records	93
Access relevant financial records	84
Access relevant accident reports	84
Inspect all premises	83
Level 2	
Recommend corrective action regarding services provided	97
Recommend changes in hospital rules/regulations	95
Recommend change in hospital policy	91
Recommend corrective action regarding physical property	87
Recommend adjustment to patient bills	85
Recommend corrective action regarding financial records	83
Recommend in-service education/staff training for staff	80
Recommend corrective action regarding staff performance	73
Participate in risk management	78
Participate in quality assurance	76
Conduct studies of patient satisfaction	76
Conduct in-service education/training for staff	75
Monitor corrective action	74
Level 3	
Organize an action committee to revise policy	46
Adjust patient bills	43
Order corrective action regarding services provided	33
Order corrective action regarding physical property	29
Order corrective action regarding financial records	29
Require staff attend action committee meetings	21
Order corrective action regarding staff performance	17
Level 4	
Change hospital rules/regulations	12
Change hospital policy	11

Ascending levels of power to respond to complaints are to be able to: 1) <u>collect</u> or <u>access</u> data; 2) <u>recommend</u> corrective action; 3) <u>order</u> corrective action; and, 4) <u>implement</u> change in regulations and policies. Levels 1 and 2 are clearly complaint handling; levels 3 and 4 involve complaint management.

More than 80% of the patient representative departments could perform all actions listed at <u>Level 1</u>. Almost all of them could interview patients, determine the validity of a complaint, collect information from staff and explain the outcome of the grievance procedure to the patient. Only about four-fifths could inspect all premises and access financial and accident reports. More than 80% of the departments could perform at <u>Level 2</u> with the exception of recommending corrective action regarding staff performance (73%). Less than 50% of the departments had <u>Level 3</u> power to

order corrective action in response to complaints. Surprisingly, about 45% of the patient representatives could organize an action committee and adjust bills; less than one-third could order other corrective action. It was unexpected that so many of the patient representative departments had the power to adjust patient bills. Further inquiry revealed that this power is usually limited to adjustments under a pre-determined dollar amount which varies among hospitals. Only slightly more than 10% of departments had <u>Level 4</u> to implement change in hospital regulations or policies.

There appears to be an intermediate level of power between the ability to recommend and the ability to order corrective action. Here the patient representatives can conduct studies, educate, train, monitor recommended action, and participate in activities of risk management and quality assurance. This cluster of actions might be classified as the power to take preventative action. About 75% of the departments performed these actions which lie somewhere between complaint handling and complaint management.

SUMMARY AND CONCLUSIONS

The major roles of patient representatives are responding to complaints or providing information/referral. Combining complaint investigation, analysis and patient quality-of-care questionnaire activities, 34% of the departments spent more than one-half of their time handling complaints; 70% spent more than 20% of their time this way. Information/referral took more than one-half of the time of 14% of the department time; 43% spent more than 20% of their time this way. The types of activities that patient representatives can engage in to respond to complaints reflect four levels of power within the institutions. Most can handle complaints, accessing information and recommending action i.e. complaint handling roles. Less than one-half of the group can order corrective action and slightly more than 10% can change hospital rules and regulations and change policy to prevent future dissatisfaction for all customers, the roles of complaint management. An intermediate set of activities to prevent dissatisfaction are performed by three-quarters of the patient representatives. These can be considered either complaint handling or complaint management depending on the purpose for which they were initiated.

These patterns show that the grievance mechanism model has changed dramatically since 1972. At that time hospitals most frequently used a grievance model that emphasized complaint handling to placate unhappy customers, performing only power level 1 and 2 activities (Fry 1972). This 1990 study describes a hospital mechanism that more closely resembles Model Two of the earlier Fry study indicating a shift toward the combination of complaint handling and complaint management functions to change procedures and systems to increase satisfaction of all customers. There is no evidence in the current study of information flow to an external independent office as recommended in Model Three of the Fry study. However, the new requirements in accreditation standards of JCHAO will provide some external oversight to the grievance processes established. The perception of conflict of interest inherent in patient representative mechanisms funded by the institutions they monitor has been discussed elsewhere (Charters 1992).

Information Flows About Consumer Complaints

Gilly states "Few studies on consumer services discuss how input from customers and customer contact personnel is communicated to managers who can make decisions regarding policies and procedures (Gilly 1991 p.295). She assumes that customer contact personnel and managers are different people (Figure 1).

Gilly's model includes the following steps: 1) Customer expresses a complaint to a customer contact person (boundary spanner); 2) Customer contact person forwards the complaint (if they cannot handle it) to the complaint handler; 3) The complaint handler responds in an attempt to satisfy the customer; 4) The complaint handler passes information to the complaint manager; 5) The complaint manager directs changes in policy/procedure to prevent further dissatisfaction of all customers; 6) Complaint manager conducts followup to ensure complaint resolution.

This study of patient representatives describes the types of managerial action that they can take to solve problems. It shows that patient representatives, the major customer contact personnel in health care institutions, may also be both complaint handlers and complaint managers. The roles described in this study suggest some modification of Gilly's model of information flow about consumer complaints. See Figure 2.

Figure 2
Patient Representative Model

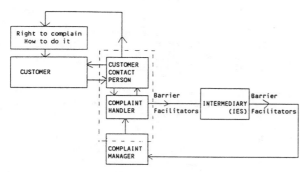

*Patient Representative role indicated by broken line

The information flow in this model begins with the patient representative (as customer contact person) who informs the customer of their right to complain and how to do it. When the customer reports a complaint, it is communicated to the patient representative who in the simplest situation becomes complaint handler and gives the results back to the customer. This sets up a circular flow including further customer feedback if necessary. The Gilly model shows no feedback to the customer by the contact person.

If handling the complaint involves boundary spanning with intermediaries (i.e. working across departments such as nursing or housekeeping) the patient representative as complaint handler proceeds with this process until the complaint is resolved and reports back to the customer for continuous feedback.

If the resolution of a similar type of complaint for all customers requires a change in policy or procedure i.e. complaint management, the patient representatives can either order corrective action or change policy/procedure depending on their power. In either case the information flow goes back through the complaint handler and customer contact person for feedback to the customer. The complaint manager does not communicate directly with the customer contact person in this model.

The major differences in the models appear to be that in the Gilly model the contact person performs the function of boundary spanner while in the patient representative model this is done by the complaint handler. The Gilly model does not provide the customer feedback loops found in the patient representative model. Implementation of new JCHAO accrediting standards may require even further modification of the model in relation to information about "how to complain" and "take corrective action" i.e. influence policy and procedure. It suggests the possibility of expanding the role of the customer contact person even further into the management role.

Fry researchers recommend that patient grievance mechanisms should report to at least the second level of management to give the needed access to all institution departments. Seventeen percent of the patient representatives in this study report to the first level of institutional management; almost two thirds reported to a second level.

Discussion

Hermann (1988) points out the one-sided nature of the main body of CS/D research that focuses on dissatisfaction rather than satisfaction and suggests that consumer researchers would find it very useful to know what attitudes, knowledge and behaviors lead to satisfaction. A commitment to delivering high quality services which not only satisfy consumers but meet or exceed the expectations of customers, achieved by a process of continuous improvement and teamwork is called Total Quality Management (TQM). "This continuous improvement is achieved by problem-solving teams who engage in identifying customer problems, finding solutions and then providing ongoing control of the improved process." (Coate;1990.) The patient representative role as revealed in this study provides non-threatening access to information about patient expectations of quality care and how it is delivered in health care institutions. Their liaison role across departments as boundary spanners is similar to the cross-functional management component of TQM which integrates team activities across divisions to achieve institutional goals. Complaint management rather than just complaint handling is required in the TQM process. Leebov says "a hospital that has no patient representatives has a painfully acute case of top-management myopia." (Leebov 1990 p. 136) The variety of activities performed and the low professional staff to bed size ratios shown for patient representatives in this study are not consistent with widespread high priority for this function.

Excellence in the delivery of services in healthcare environments must address key service components of technical competence, environment, people skills, systems and amenities. Consumer groups include patients, visitors, physicians, employees and third party payers.

Further Research Needed

Consumer researchers are currently beginning to give more attention to the service area and health care issues in particular (Gilly et al,1991; Solnick and Hemenway, 1992); health care providers are beginning to pay more attention to grievance procedures (Charters 1992). New accreditation requirements will accelerate the latter trend (JCHAO).

The complexity of the service environment may require the establishment of a series of grievance mechanisms in any one institution. The extent to which patient grievance mechanisms exist in health care institutions in the United States is not currently known. Gerner (1988) points out that what appears to be missing in the research is a clear idea of how the entire system works. A systematic understanding not only of mechanisms for measuring consumer satisfaction and dissatisfaction but also how providers respond to them is required. Further research into the effectiveness of alternative mechanism models and their patterns of information flow is needed in all service areas, not only healthcare.

References

American Hospital Association (1990). The Joint Commission Accreditation Manual for Hospitals, Sections MA. 1.4.10-MA.1.4.11.4, p. 73.

Andreasen, A.R. (1988). Consumer complaints and redress: What we know and what we don't know. In E.S. Maynes & ACCI Research Committee (Ed.) The Frontier of Research in The Consumer Interest. Columbia, MO: American Council on Consumer Interests.

Bryant, W. K. (1988). Consumer Complaints and Redress: some Directions for Future Research. In E.S. Maynes & ACCI Research Committee (Ed.) The Frontier of Research in The Consumer Interest. Columbia, MO: American Council on Consumer Interests.

Charters, M. A. (in press). The Patient Role and Sources of Power. Hospital and Health Services Administration.

Carmel, S. (1990). Patient Complaint Strategies in a General Hospital. Hospital and Health Services Administration , 35 (2) 277-287.

Coate, L. E.(1990). Implementing Total Quality Management in a University Setting. Oregon State University.

Council on Graduate Medical Education (1990). Supplement:The Financial Status of Teaching Hospitals: The Underrepresentation of Minorities in Medicine.

Fornell, C.(1988). Corporate Consumer Affairs Departments: Retrospect and Prospect. In E.S. Maynes & ACCI Research Committee (Ed.), The Frontier of Research in The Consumer Interest. Columbia, MO: American Council on Consumer Interests.

Fry Consulting Group Inc. (1972). A Study of Patients' Grievance Mechanisms. Prepared for the Secretary's Commission on Medical Malpractice. Washington D.C. U.S. Dept. of Health Education and Welfare. OCLC 788-953-6.

Gerner, J. (1988). Research on Consumer Satisfaction and Dissatisfaction. In E. S. Maynes & ACCI Research Committee (Ed.), The Frontier of Research in the Consumer Interest, (p. 749). Columbia, MO: American Council on Consumer Interests.

Gilly, M. C., William Stevenson, W., & Yale, L. (1991). Dynamics of Complaint Management in the Service Organization, Journal of Consumer Affairs, 25(2), 295-337.

Greyser, S., Judge, J., & Peterson, E. (1986). What is the Role of Consumer Affairs Within the Corporation? Mobius, 5(2), 4-9.

Herrmann, R. O.(1988). Consumer Complaints and Redress: What We Know and What We Don't Know. In E. S. Maynes & ACCI Research Committee (Ed.), The Frontier of Research in the Consumer Interest(p. 727-730). Columbia, MO: American Council on Consumer Interests.

Leebov, W. (1988). Service Excellence. The Customer Relations Strategy for Health Care, American Hospital Publishing Inc.

Leebov, W. (1990). Effective Complaint Handling in Health Care. American Hospital Publishing Inc.

Mailick, M. (1982). Patient Representative Programs: A Social Work Perspective. Social Work in Health Care, 7(4), 40-51.

Maynes, E. S. (1988). Universities as Resources for Consumer Affairs Professionals. Mobius, 7 (2), 25-28.

McLaughlin, C. P., & Kaluzny, A. (1990). Total Quality Management in Health: Making it Work. Health Care Management Review, 15 (3), 7-14.

NSPRCA, (1989) Mission Statement and Strategic Plan. National Society for Patient Representation and Consumer Affairs of the American Hospital Association, Revised 10/89.

Solnick, S. J., & Hemenway, D.(1992). Complaints and Disenrollment at a Health Maintenance Organization. Journal of Consumer Affairs, 26(1).

Shopping Time, Grocery Expenditures, and Coupon Savings: Insights into a Time/Money Tradeoff

Jane Kolodinsky, University of Vermont[1]
JoAnne Labrecque, Universite de Hautes Ecoles Commerciales[2]

This study examines the relationship between shopping time, expenditures on groceries, and coupon savings using a utility maximization model. It incorporates shoppers' preferences for time and shopping, and includes a more exact measure of shopping time by accounting for both travelling and in-store time, and psychological characteristics that may affect shopping behavior.

Forty-nine percent of grocery shoppers want "short waits at the checkout" (Progressive Grocer 1991), 50% want "good (supermarket) layouts for fast easy shopping," and 66% of dual earner households indicate "we have less time to shop than five years ago" (Fram and Axelrod 1990). Time is scarce, and we appear to have less of it. On the other hand, 50% of consumers cite low prices, frequent sales, and availability of specials as important aspects of choosing a supermarket, and 56% indicate that they used cents-off coupons at a higher rate in 1990 than in 1989 (Progressive Grocer 1991). Because consumers are concerned with both money and time when grocery shopping, these statistics raise the question, "What is the relationship of the time-money tradeoff in grocery shopping behavior?"

Review of Literature

Time spent grocery shopping has not been a priority topic for economic research. It is not mentioned in two recent reviews of the household time use literature (Juster and Stafford 1991; Godwin 1991), though a few researchers have examined shopping in the aggregate (Kooreman and Kapteyn 1987; Gershuny 1987). Doti and Sharir (1981) have posited an economic model of grocery shopping in which households consume two composite goods (groceries and non-groceries) and allocate time between work, buying goods, and other leisure, subject to time and budget constraints. Estimates of simultaneous decisions between grocery expenditures and shopping time using a sample of 100 California consumers were obtained using two stage least squares. Dislike of shopping, employment of wife, presence of children, and increased educational attainment decreased the time spent shopping, while increases in expenditures increased shopping time. Employment of wife, increased educational attainment, presence of children, and increases in shopping time all increased expenditures on groceries.

Marketers have been somewhat interested in shopping time. Arndt and Gronmo (1976) developed a model that specified shopping time as a function of structural market conditions, social position, needs, and shopper orientation. Using 3,040 observations from a Norwegian time-budget study, they found that being female and having higher incomes increased time spent shopping. Ownership of a freezer, living close to a grocery store, and working longer hours decreased time spent shopping. Park, Iyer, and Smith (1989) examined the role of store environment and time available for shopping on grocery shopping behavior. Using a two by two factorial design, they selected a random sample of 68 California consumers. Shoppers who felt "time pressure" spent significantly less time shopping, had fewer unplanned purchased, and failed to purchase intended products more often than those who did not feel pressured for time.

Missing from these studies of shopping time is the endogeneity of prices paid for groceries. Price dispersion in the grocery market is well documented. Although consumers may misperceive actual price differences (Maynes and Assum 1982), a distribution of grocery prices can be sustained due to market characteristics including product differentiation not based on objective attributes of quality, size of seller, market concentration, and the proliferation of coupons and other discounts (Conner et al. 1985; Collins 1968; Gallo 1982a). Carlson and Geiseke (1983) examined number of searches (which decrease price paid for groceries) and grocery expenditures. 284 responses were obtained from a 1956 Michigan panel study of food purchases. Two stage least squares estimates revealed that increases in expenditures, income and age increased the number of searches made. Increases in prices, income and age increased expenditures on groceries. Prices paid for groceries fell as the number of searches increased. Kolodinsky (1990) developed a model of price information search that incorporated household production theory (Becker 1965), the economics of information (Stigler 1961), and the idea that time can yield utility directly. Savings from search were endogenously determined. Analysis using a

---

[1]Assistant Professor, Consumer Studies

[2]Assistant Professor, Marketing

sample of 95 dual earner households found increased price savings increases time spent in search. Levendahl (1988) formulated a model of coupon redemption based on utility maximization in which coupons explicitly allow households to obtain discounts on food. Using a sample of 299 New York, Chicago, and Los Angeles households, paper towel purchases were analyzed. Both income and education are positively related to coupon redemption. This evidence supports two hypotheses related the impact of these variables. First, highly educated, higher income consumers may be better shoppers because they more efficient shoppers. That is, they are better able to locate, sort, organize, and cash in coupons. The cost of using coupons is lower. Second, these consumers are more likely to purchase brands for which coupons are available.

Enjoyment spent in an activity has been anecdotally included in discussions of time allocation (Dow and Juster 1980; Wilkie and Dickson 1980). Butler (1991) speaks of Canadian malls as tourist attractions. Prus and Dawson (1991) explore shopping as recreational or laborious. Specific to grocery shopping, both economists and marketers have touched on the idea of time enjoyment. In the economic literature, Doti and Sharir (1981) found dislike of shopping to have negative, albeit not significant, effect on shopping time, while Kolodinsky (1990) found that enjoyment of price information search increased the time spent in the activity. In the marketing literature, Hortman et al. (1990) found pleasant atmosphere oh several segments of shoppers: non-discount store shoppers, non-price sensitive shoppers, the elderly, and even highly price sensitive shoppers. Using a sample of 910 Quebec grocery shoppers, Labrecque (1991) found that shopper preferences for store attributes affected the probability of choosing a store type. Enjoying grocery shopping increased the probability of shopping at more than one store type and shopping at superstores, as opposed to traditional supermarkets.

All these studies have explained in part time use, expenditures, and savings from search. However, most studies used relatively small samples, making the results difficult to generalize. Some studies were either focused on marketing applications, and concentrated more on shopping orientated variables. Other studies were economic applications, and focused more on price, income, quantity relationships without accounting for shopping variables that do not fit neatly into neoclassical microeconomic theory. In addition, shopping time has typically been measured as the time spent in a store, with no regard for travel time to or between stores.

Methodology

Theory
The model proposed to examine grocery shopping time, expenditures and savings has its roots in the work of Doti and Sharir (1981) and Kolodinsky

(1990). It utilizes Stigler's (1961) model in which searching for price information can lower prices paid in a market. However, while Doti and Sharir (1981) used dislike of shopping as a taste shifter in their empirical analysis, they did not explicitly account for it in their theoretical specification. And, while Kolodinsky (1990) explicitly modelled time as a direct source of utility and the endogeneity of prices paid for groceries, the specification accounted only for time spent in price search and "other home produced goods." The utility maximization model accounts for food purchased, time spent shopping, other purchased goods, and leisure other than that provided by grocery shopping. Choices are constrained by the budget, specified as a full income constraint.

$$U = f(X_f, \sum_{i=1}^{N} T_{si}, X_o, L; K) \qquad (1)$$

$$wH + v = P_f(\sum_{i=1}^{N} T_{si})X_f + w\sum_{i=1}^{N} T_{si} + P_o X_o + wL \qquad (2)$$

where
X_f = food purchased
$\sum T_{si}$ = time spent shopping, $i = 1,2...,N$
X_o = other goods, a composite commodity
L = leisure time
K = taste and productivity shifters
w = market wage rate
H = total available time
v = non-wage income allocated to meal production
P_f = price of grocery inputs
P_o = price of other goods

Time is explicitly included in the utility function, and its components include all time related to shopping. Examples are in-store shopping and travel time.

Imposing weak separability allows the derivation of food and shopping time demand without explicitly considering the demand for other goods. The Lagrangian function for this case is written:

$$L = u(X_f, \sum_{i=1}^{N} T_{si}; K) \quad \lambda((wH+ v) - P_f(\sum_{i=1}^{N} T_{si})X_f - w\sum_{i=1}^{N} T_{si}) (3)$$

where $(wH + v)$ equals the portion of total income pre-allocated to purchasing food and spending time shopping. Maximization of (3) reveals the demand equations for food purchased and time spent grocery shopping. Importantly, prices paid for food are endogenous.

Data
Data are from a 1987 study that included 1200 respondents who participated in a mail panel lasting one week. Respondents kept track of expenditures, coupon use and value, travel time, and grocery shopping time in each store they visited during the seven day period. Questions about shopping attitudes and demographics were

TABLE 1. SUMMARY STATISTICS AND HYPOTHESIZED EFFECTS

| | | MEAN | HYPOTHESIZED EFFECT | | |
			COUPVAL	EXP	TIME
LNINC	Nonwage Income	35.498 (16.025)	(?)	(+)	(?)
WAGE	Wage Rate Of Shopper	10.32 (7.00)	(-)	(+)	(-)
AGE	Age Of Shopper	38.45 (11.57)	(?)	(?)	(+)
EDUC	Years Of Education	13.45 (2.44)	(?)	(?)	(?)
GENDER	Percent Male Shoppers	.21 (.40)	(?)	(?)	(-)
LNPERSON	Family size	2.31 (1.57)	(+)	(+)	(+)
KID6	Number Of Children $\leq$ 6	.45 (2.04)	(+)	-	-
KID18	Number Of Children $\geq$ 6 $\leq$ 18	.52 (.85)	(+)	(+)	(+)
PRICE	Chooses A Store Based On Price	.00[a]	(-)	(-)	(?)
QUALITY	Chooses A Store Based On Quality	.00[a]	(?)	(+)	(+)
BR*PR	Interaction Of Price And Brand	.04 (.72)	(-)	-	-
MICRO	Ownership Of A Microwave	.52 (.49)	-	(?)	-
FREEZER	Ownership Of A Freezer	.53 (.50)	(+)	(?)	(?)
AWARE	Shopper Is Price Aware	.00[a]	(+)	(-)	(?)
BRAND	Shopper Is Not Brand Loyal	.00[a]	(-)	(-)	(?)
INDIVID	Shopper Likes Individual Service	.00[a]	-	-	(+)
PARTY	Shopper Likes To Feast	.00[a]	-	(+)	-
BROWSER	Shopper Likes To Shop	.00[a]	-	-	(+)
ACTIVE	Shopper Is Pressed For Time	.00[a]	(-)	(?)	(-)
COUPVAL	Value Of Coupons	.97 (2.84)	-	(?)	(?)
EXP	Weekly Expenditures On Groceries	98.36 (64.11)	(+)	-	(+)
TIME	Weekly Shopping Time, Including Transportation	102.64 (76.37)	(?)	(?)	-

N=580[a] Factor Analyzed Variable

included. A response rate of 79% was obtained, as 950 respondents returned the survey, a rate above the 75% average found when the "total design method is used" (Dillman 1978), and cited as being "not unlike other surveys of this type" (Arndt & Gromno (1976). Because of the detailed nature of the information, a number of respondents did not complete all the information necessary to be included in this particular analysis. Most missing data concerned psychological aspects of shopping. This analysis includes 580 respondents, or 61% of those returned. Determining non-response bias is difficult. Comparison of the respondents compared with non-respondents would be a formidable task, given that non-respondents were classified as so because they did not provide the psychological information. An examination of this group with those that did provide all information based on demographic characteristics including age, gender, education, and family composition showed no significant differences. The final data set is rich with the types of variables needed for the empirical analysis. Table 1 summarizes the variables used in the analysis.

Expenditures are measured as the total spent on groceries for a one week period. Because of the panel nature of the data, actual expenditures were summed, excluding those made in convenience stores, as these are not "major purchases" (Canadian Grocer 1991).

Equation (3) implies that prices paid for food are endogenous and are a function of time spent shopping. The sample includes information on the savings obtained through coupon redemption, used as a proxy variable for prices. As the value of coupons increases, prices paid for individual items decreases. Because our major interest is in the fact that search can yield savings, this is the appropriate variable to measure.

Time spent shopping includes many possible time uses, some of which were outlined in the theory section of this paper. We have explicit information on in-store shopping time and travelling time, which are not accounted for together in previous research.

Two economic variables are measured: non-wage income (LNINC) and wages (WAGE). The wage rate is the hourly wage earned in the labor market by the self-designated major grocery shopper. For those respondents who are not employed in the labor market, Heckman's (1977, 1979) method for estimating the reservation wage rate was used to obtain a value for the wage variable. Non-wage income includes all household income other than that earned as wages by the major shopper. The natural log of income is the variable used. As income increases, expenditures on food increase, but not in a linear fashion, a phenomenon known as Engel's Law (Timmer et al. 1983).

The theoretical specification also indicates

that tastes are important. Demographic variables include age of shopper (AGE), number of persons in the household (LNPERSON), number of younger and older children in the household (KID6 and KID18), education in years, (EDUC), and gender of the major shopper (GENDER). The natural log of household size is the variable used. As the number of persons in a household increases, food expenditures increase, but not in a linear fashion. Also, one would expect more time to be taken to shop for a larger family. However, one would not expect time to increase in a linear fashion. While more items may be purchased, for many items, an increase in quantity is obtained by simply reaching for a larger size. Several variables related to shopping are also included to reflect taste differences. QUALITY, a measure of whether a shopper chooses a store based on quality of items, PRICE, a measure of whether a shopper chooses a store based on price, FREEZER and MICRO, measures of ownership of a freezer and microwave oven are included. Six shopper preference variables related to shopping behavior and time use were formulated. While previous studies have included variables accounting for like or dislike of shopping, (Doti and Sharir 1981; Kolodinsky 1990), several dimensions of shopper preferences may affect shopping behavior. These variables were extracted using factor analysis and varimax rotation on a series of 31 statements describing food shopping and meal preparation activities, along with shopping attitudes and opinions. Varimax rotation is preferred because it produces high loadings on some statements and near zero loadings on others, making interpretation of the factors rather straight forward (Greene et al. 1988). Six factors accounted for 98% of the variance in the 31 statements. The factors identified include: awareness of prices (AWARE), choosing bulk or store brand items most often (lack of brand loyalty) (BRAND), enjoyment of shopping (BROWSER), time savers (ACTIVE), those that prefer individual service (INDIVID), and those fond of gourmet meals and having dinner parties (PARTY). Hypothesized directions of effects of the variables are included in Table 1.

Empirical Specification

The specification of the demand equations must account for the simultaneous determination of prices, time spent shopping and grocery expenditures. It must also account for censored sample bias, as 8% of the sample reported zero expenditures and shopping time, and 63% of the sample did not use a coupon during the survey period. Finally, we are interested in structural equations. Theory indicates that prices and expenditures on groceries, and time spent shopping are simultaneously determined. The structural equations are of the form:

$$Y_i = \alpha_{ij} \sum_{\substack{j=1, \\ i \neq j}}^{2} Y_{ij} + \beta_{im} \sum_{m=1}^{19-2} X_{im} + e \tag{4}$$

TABLE 2. STRUCTURAL EQUATION ESTIMATES

VARIABLE	COUPVAL	EXP	TIME
INTERCEPT	.96 (4.16)	-36.43 (51.59)	1.59 (51.02)
LNINCOME	-1.14 (.58)**	9.17 (5.03)**	-1.24 (5.41)
WAGE	-.07 (.03)**	.11 (.42)	.32 (.44)
AGE	-.002 (.03)	.42 (3.0)*	.65 (.27)***
EDUC	-.1 (.09)	-1.36 (1.13)	.59 (1.21)
GENDER	1.70 (.57)***	-7.52 (2.86)	-1.56 (2.96)
LNPERSON	-1.51 (1.11)	13.95 (6.34)**	-1.24 (5.41)
KID6	.58 (.54)	-	-
KID18	-.73 (.50)*	-1.79 (2.86)	1.62 (0.37)***
PRICE	.18 (.24)	-1.79 (2.86)	-1.59 (2.96)
QUALITY	.71 (.31)**	-1.76 (3.53)	4.03 (3.06)*
BR*PR	.46 (.30)*	-	-
MICRO	-	-1.52 (6.74)	-
FREEZER	-1.88 (.74)***	14.43 (5.50)***	.004 (6.95)
AWARE	-.12 (.55)	-7.09 (3.65)**	7.98 (3.65)**
BRAND	-.78 (.22)***	-7.63 (3.44)**	-2.83 (3.58)
INDVID	-	-	-5.68 (1.21)***
PARTY	-	1.04 (3.55)	-
BROWSER	-	-	-4.78 (3.20)*
ACTIVE	1.40 (.32)***	-4.07 (3.65)	-3.95 (4.42)
COUPHAT	-	.95 (1.58)	6.10 (1.45)***
EXPHAT	.09 (.04)**	-	.20 (.23)
TIMEHAT	.02 (.030)	-.04 (.22)	-
SIGMA	4.94 (.15)***	59.03 (1.80)***	60.87 (1.85)***
LOG LIKELIHOOD	-1689.3	-3058.8	-3080.9
R2	.46	.197	.367

N=580 Standard errors in parentheses. *Significant at ≤ .10 **Significant at ≤ .05 ***Significant at ≤ .01

There are two endogenous and seventeen exogenous variables in each equation, because two of the exogenous variables in each structural equation must not appear in any other equation to insure identification. Given these factors, a two stage Tobit estimator is used (Maddala 1983; Nelson and Olson 1978).

In the first stage, reduced form equations are estimated for coupon value, time spent shopping, and grocery expenditures, expressed as Y_i, for i=1,2,3:

$$Y_i = \gamma_{i0} + \sum_{m=1}^{19} \phi_{im} X_{im}$$

(5)

where X_{im} are independent variables.

Tobit was used to estimate reduced form equations to correct for sample selection bias. Spearman rank correlation tests indicated that heteroskedasticity was not a problem in the expenditure equation. In the second stage, Tobit was used to estimate structural equations.

Results

Results of estimating the structural equations for coupon value (COUPVAL), grocery expenditures (EXPGROC), and shopping time (TIMESHOP) are presented in Table 2.

Coupon Value

As a whole, results are robust, with an R^2 of .46 before iterating and a log likelihood of -1689.3 after. Eleven of the right hand side variables were significant, including Sigma.

Coupon savings are an inferior good. As the price of time increases (WAGE) savings decrease, as expected for a time intensive activity. Female shoppers (GENDER) reap more savings, while presence of older children (KID18) has a negative effect on savings. While shopping for quality (QUALITY) increases coupon savings, shopping for price (PRICE) has no significant effect, although the coefficient is positive. Selecting a store based on price and having a lack of brand loyalty (BR*PR) increase savings. Ownership of a freezer (FREEZER) has the unexpected result of decreasing coupon savings. Some psychological variables influence savings. A lack of brand loyalty (BRAND) decreases savings, while being pressed for time increases coupon savings (ACTIVE). Increases in expenditures (EXPHAT) increase coupon values.

Expenditures

The expenditures equation was less robust than the other two equations, with an R^2 of .17 before iterating an a log likelihood of -3508.8 after. Seven of the independent variables are significant.

Expenditures are a normal good; as income increases (LNINC), expenditures increase. Increases in age (AGE) increase expenditures. The effect of increasing family size (LNPERSON) is positive as is owning a freezer. Psychological variables influence expenditures. Price awareness (AWARE) reduces expenditures, as does choosing bulk items and store brands(BRAND).

Shopping Time

The shopping time equation produced an R^2 of .37 before iterating and a log likelihood of -3080.0 after. It performed in between the other two equations. Eight of the right hand side variables were significant, including Sigma.

Both age (AGE) and presence of older children (KID18) are positively related to time spent shopping. Choosing a store based on quality (QUALITY) increases shopping time. Psychological variables also influence time. Price awareness (AWARE) increases shopping time. Enjoyment of shopping (BROWSER) and preferring individual service (INDIVID) actually decrease shopping time. Increases in coupon value (COUPVAL) increase shopping time.

Discussion

Because this study is the first that examines shopping time, grocery expenditures, and coupon savings in a single simultaneous system, comparison with previous research is difficult. Notwithstanding this, our results are most like the findings of Carlson and Geiseke (1983) with regard to savings and expenditures. Food is a normal good and increases in age are associated with increased expenditures. The relationship between age and expenditures is not unusual because in our study age of respondent ranged from 21 to 68, with the majority of respondents reporting children living in the household. One major difference between the two studies is the result concerning increases in price (decreases in price due to increases in coupon value (COUPVAL). While Carlson and Geiseke (1983) found that increases in prices increased expenditures on food, our results show that increases in coupon savings (decreases in price) have an insignificant, but _positive_ effect on expenditures. Because any price variable contains both a substitution and income effect, our results can be explained by competing directions of the two effects. While more savings decrease prices paid, which should decrease expenditures, decreased prices also lead to more real income. Since food is a normal good, expenditures will increase. In our case, the insignificance can be due to a netting out of the negative price effect and the positive income effect.

The results regarding shopping time and expenditures are as interesting as those regarding savings and expenditures. They are unlike the results of Doti and Sharir (1983), who found that wife's employment and presence of children decreased shopping time, or Arndt and Gromno (1976) who found that longer hours of employment decreased shopping time. The economic explanation for these results is that employment increases the price of time, as do the presence of children. Our results indicate that economic variables (WAGE, LNINC) Do not affect shopping time, perhaps because ALL consumers want shorter waits at the checkout and have less time for shopping (Fram and Axelrod 1990). Regardless of income or working status (price of time), consumers are trying to save time where they can. Our results indicate that having children ages 6-18 in a household increase shopping time but decrease grocery expenditures. One explanation for this is that older children may have different preferences than their parents, and they may have influence in household purchase decisions. This can increase the time it takes to find a particular product in a single grocery store. Or, it can increase travelling time if parents must travel to a particular store to purchase a product desired by children. School age children may also eat away from home more often than younger children (i.e. school lunches), thus decreasing grocery expenditures. This might explain the sign differences on our two included family composition variables as compared to the single variable used by Doti and Sharir (1981). Arndt and Gromno (1976) also found that ownership of a freezer decreased time spent shopping. Our results are positive, albeit insignificant. Because our measure of shopping included travelling time, the discrepancy in results could be that when travelling time is added, we find some consumers making special trips to take advantage of specials at stores they may not normally shop at, while others stock up at one time and don't shop as frequently. The net effect is insignificant. This speculative result is reinforced by the significant positive effect of FREEZER on expenditures. Whereas owning a freezer is supposed to be a means of saving on the food bill in the long run, it appears that in the short run consumers actually spend more. This may be an artifact of the data, which was collected during early November, when consumers may be stocking their freezers for the winter. Doti and Sharir (1981) also found significant positive effects of time on expenditures and expenditures on time. We have the same results for the effect of expenditures on time. However, we obtain a negative, albeit insignificant, effect of time on expenditures. One major reason for this is our inclusion of coupon savings into the analysis. Indeed, increases in coupon savings increase time spent shopping and increases in expenditures increase coupon savings.

With regard to coupon value, we find our results at odds with Levendahl (1988). Whereas he found highly educated and higher income consumers to be more likely to redeem coupons, we found coupon value to be an inferior good, with education having no significant effect. Because Levendahl (1988) used an aggregate income measure as opposed to our separating out the effect of the price of time (WAGE) and non wage income (LNINC), the discrepancy in results even more troubling. Levendahl's measure contained both a price and income effect. In order for the total effect to be positive, a negative price effect had to be offset by a very large, positive, income effect. In our study, we found a negative own price effect (the price of time decreases coupon value) and a negative income effect. One explanation is that because Levendahl measured number of coupons, while we measured coupon value, it is possible that higher income consumers redeem more coupons of less value. This is not highly plausible. The expected result would be that higher income and higher wage persons would redeem fewer coupons of higher value if Levendahl's hypotheses about higher income households being more efficient holds true. A more plausible explanation could be a difference in the attitudes toward coupon redemption between Quebecers versus Americans. Kolodinsky and Labrecque (1992) found a significant difference in the value of coupons redeemed between these two groups. As other studies have found inconclusive evidence as to the effects of income, more research is needed to find a definitive answer to the question, "are coupons savings a normal or inferior good?" Gender is only significant in the coupon value equation. Women have higher coupon values. This result has not been found previously, as Kolodinsky (1990) found gender to be an insignificant variable in the prediction of savings. However, women are no more likely than men to have different expenditures or shopping times. Although women continue to be the major shoppers in the household, men seem to be no less efficient in their time or money expenditures. There is still room to catch up in the area of savings, however.

With regard to psychological variables, only one, enjoyment, has previously been accounted for in the economic literature (Doti and Sharir 1981; Kolodinsky 1990). Our findings are at odds with both of these studies. The question arises, "how can those who enjoy shopping actually spend less time doing it?" Two answers are plausible. First, these persons may be more efficient. They may actually get more shopping done in less time. Second, it may be that persons who enjoy shopping are those who do not feel time pressured by the activity. If the latter is true, more research in the area of enjoyment must be undertaken. Enjoyment must become a choice variable and be simultaneously determined with shopping time, if we believe that time use can influence enjoyment and enjoyment influences time use.

Our study finds other psychological variables to be significant indicators of shopping time, grocery expenditures, and coupon savings. Active shoppers have higher savings. This is at first puzzling. However, these time pressed consumers may have found that using a coupon is the fastest way to obtain savings on their food bills. Kolodinsky (1992) found that consumers spend about 30 minutes per week clipping coupons. Walker and Cude (1983) found that comparison pricing strategies (with the exception of buying the largest size of one brand) required a minimum of 20 and a maximum of 231 price comparisons, which would require a hefty time commitment. Combine the results of these two researchers and the finding that time pressed consumers (ACTIVE) have higher coupon values becomes plausible. This is an area fruitful for future research.

Those who are not brand loyal (BRAND) have lower coupon values. These are the consumers who buy in bulk and choose store brands often. It appears that consumers who use these strategies have chosen them as an alternative to using coupons. These consumers also have significantly lower grocery expenditures, but no significant differences in shopping time, leading to the assertion that for some persons, this strategy works at saving money.

The interaction of a psychological and shopping variable was found significant. Those shoppers who are not brand loyal but choose a store based on price (PR*BR) have higher coupon values. An explanation for this is that there seems to be a proportion of shoppers who use all possible saving strategies, including choosing a store based on price, purchasing store brand and bulk items, and using coupons. Choosing a store based on quality (QUALITY) increased coupon value. It appears that shoppers do equate items for which coupons are available with quality. Combine the findings of Bellizzi et al. (1981), who documented that consumers believe national brands are of higher quality with the fact that coupons are offered most often for national brands (Gallo 1982a) and the explanation becomes clear as to why shoppers of quality have higher coupon values. Shopping for quality (QUALITY) increases shopping time, as these persons are likely to compare merchandise, squeeze fruit and vegetables, and read labels, for example. Awareness of prices (AWARE) decreases expenditures indicating that there are savings associated with price search. This reinforces the findings of Carlson and Geiseke (1983). Finally, a preference for individual service (INDIVID) actually decreases shopping time. This may be explained by the fact that shoppers who prefer individual service may be loyal to a single store, thus decreasing the travelling time portion of shopping time. This is consistent with the findings of Labrecque (1991) who found that being a service oriented shopper decreased the probability of shopping at more than one store type, compared with shopping at traditional supermarkets.

Conclusions

The theoretical specification translates into robust empirical results. And, while a few of the estimated coefficients turned out to be significant in the "wrong" direction, they can be explained using economic theory and combining results found in other studies of shopping behavior. The study has also taken a step forward in the measurement of variables found to be key in the study of the tradeoffs among expending time and money and obtaining savings. Travelling time added to actual in store shopping time gives a more accurate accounting of the time that must be spent in

grocery shopping. And, most of the shopper preference variables included did affect time, expenditures, and/or coupon savings.

There are three limitations with the data that cause a continued problem in the measurement of shopping time. First, we have included only two types of shopping time: travel time and in-store shopping time. Our data set did not include information about the time spent in pre-purchase search, such as reading food ads or clipping coupons. Second, other types of savings need to be measured. Savings from buying in bulk, for example, may be significant. Because the results, even with this measurement error, are so encouraging, data sets that include information about economic variables, time use variables, demographic information, and shopper preferences should be collected in the future so that a full accounting of shopping time can be obtained. Third, the data reflected a random sample of Quebec residents. Results can be generalized only to this province of Canada because of laws regarding store operating hours, which are more restrictive when compared with the rest of Canada and the United States.

Overall, economic and psychological variables not previously included in economic studies of shopping behavior are important in explaining variation in coupon savings, grocery expenditures, and shopping time. We clearly need future analyses that combine these two areas of study in order to better understand the dynamics of shopping behavior.

References

Arndt, J., & Gromno, S. (1976). The Time Dimension of Shopping Behavior: Some Empirical Findings. Advances in Consumer Research, 3, 230-35.

Becker, G. (1965). A Theory of the Allocation of Time. The Economic Journal. 75, 493-517.

Bellizzi, J.A., Krueckebery, H.F., Hamilton, J.R., & Martin, W.S. (1981). Consumer Perceptions of National, Private, and Generic Brands. Journal of Retailing, 57(4), 56-70.

Butler, R.W. (1991). West Edmonton Mall as a Tourist Attraction. The Canadian Geographer, 35(3), 287-95.

Canadian Grocer (1991) Good News/Bad News Year, February, 93, 136.

Carlson, J., Gieseke, R. (1983). Price Search in a Product Market. Journal of Consumer Research, 9, 357-65.

Collins, N.R. (1968). Market Structure and Cost-Price Margins in the Food Manufacturing Industries. Testimony before the Senate Subcommittee on Antitrust and monopoly, Hearings on Economic Concentration, pt. 2.

Conner, J.M., Rogers, R.T., Marion, B.W., & Mueller, W.F. (1985). The Food Manufacturing Industries: Structure, Strategies, and Performance, Lexington MA: Lexington Books.

Dillman, D. (1978). Mail and Telephone Surveys: The Total Design Method. New York: John Wiley and Sons, Inc.

Doti, J.L., & Sharir, S. (1981). Households' Grocery Shopping Behavior in the Short Run: Theory and Evidence. Economic Inquiry, 19 (2), 196-208.

Dow, G., & Juster, E.T. (1980). Goods, Satisfaction with Activities, and Well-Being. Working Paper, Institute for Social Research, Survey Research Center, University of Michigan.

Fram, E., & Axelrod, J. (1990). The Distressed Shopper. American Demographics, October, 44-45.

Gallo, A. (1982a). Coupons: Part I," National Food Review, NFR 18 (Spring), 11-15.

Gallo, A. (1982b). Coupons: Part II. National Food Review, NFR 19 (Summer), 12-26.

Gershuny, J. (1987). Time Use and the Dynamics of the Service Sector. Service Industries Journal, 7(4), 66-71.

Godwin, D. (1991). Spouse's Time Allocation to Household Work: A Review and Critique. Lifestyles: Family and Economic Issues, 12(3), 253-94.

Greene, P., Tull, D., & Albaum, G. (1988). Research for Marketing Decisions. Englewood Cliffs, NJ: Prentice Hall.

Heckman, J. (1977). Sample Selection Bias as a Specification Error. NBER working paper no.172.

Heckman, J.(1979). Sample Selection Bias as a Specification Error. Econometrica, 47(1), 153-60.

Hortman, S. A, Allaway, J. M., & Rasp, J. (1990), Multisegment Analysis of Supermarket Patronage. Journal of Business Research, 21, 209-23.

Juster, F.T., & Stafford, F. (1991). The Allocation of Time: Empirical Findings, Behavioral Models, and Problems of Measurement. Journal of Economic Literature, 24, 471-522.

Kolodinsky, J. (1990). Time as a Direct Source of Utility: The Case of Price Information Search for Groceries. Journal of Consumer Affairs, 24(1), 89-109.

Kolodinsky, J. (1992). Money-Off Coupons and the Consumer: Are They Worth the Effort? Journal of Consumer Studies and Home Economics, 16, 389-98.

Kolodinsky, J., & Labrecque, J. (1992). The Allocation of Time to Grocery Shopping: A Comparison of Canadian and U.S. Households. Paper presented at Household Time Use in the 21st Century, Cornell University.

Labrecque, J. (1991). Store Type Patronage for Grocery Purchases: A Study of the Quebec Market. Unpublished doctoral dissertation, Cornell University.

Levendahl, J. W. (1988). Coupon Redeemers: Are They Better Shoppers? Journal of Consumer Affairs, 22(2), 264-83.

Kooreman, P.,& Kapteyn, A. (1987). A Disaggregated Analysis of the Allocation of Time Within the Household," Journal of Political Economy, 95(21), 223-49.

Maddala, G. S. (1983). Limited Dependent and Qualitative Variables in Econometrica, Cambridge: Cambridge University Press.

Maynes, E.S., & Assum, T. (1982). Informationally Imperfect Consumer Markets: Empirical Findings and Policy Implications. Journal of Consumer Affairs, (Summer), 62-87.

Nelson, F., & Olson, L. (1978). Specification and Estimation of a Simultaneous Equation Model with Limited Dependent Variables. International Economic Review, 19(3), 695-709.

Park, C., Iyer, E., & Smith, D. (1989). The Effects of Situational Factors on In-Store Grocery Shopping Behavior: The Role of Store Environment and Time Available for Shopping. Journal of Consumer Research, 15, 422-33.

Progressive Grocer (1991). Recession Weary Shoppers Stay Loyal to Supermarkets. 58th Annual Report, April, 58-64.

Prus, R., & Dawson, L. (1991). Shop 'til You Drop: Shopping as Recreational and Laborious Activity. Canadian Journal of Sociology, 16(2), 145-64.

Stigler, G. (1961). The Economics of Information," Journal of Political Economy, (June), 213-25.

Timmer, C.P., Falcon, W. & Pearson, S. (1983) Food Policy Analysis. Baltimore: The World Bank.

Walker, R., & Cude, B. (1983). In-Store Shopping Strategies: Time and Money Costs in the Supermarket. Journal of Consumer Affairs, 17(2), 356-69.

Wilkie,   W.,   &   Dickson,   P.   (1980).   Consumer
        Information Search and Shopping Behavior.
        Unpublished research paper.

Consumers' Use of Money-Saving Strategies in the Purchase of Pet Food During an Economic Recession

Vicki R. Fitzsimmons[1]
University of Illinois at Urbana-Champaign

Cents-off coupons, refunds, coupon cross-merchandising, and buying on sale were investigated for pet food purchasing. Consumers made little use of these. Greater use of money-saving strategies was influenced by greater importance of: (a) using a coupon, (b) price, and (c) refund offer. Respondents employed in service and professional, technical, or managerial occupations used money-saving strategies much less frequently than those not employed. Nutrition and pet's preference were most important to consumers.

Background Information

A recurring trend during economic hard times is increased consumer use of coupons, cents-off promotions, refunds/rebates, sweepstakes, and similar offers from companies attempting to maintain customer loyalty despite declining consumer resources (Hume, 1991). The current recession period is no exception with 7.3 billion coupons redeemed in 1990, a 2.8% increase over 1989 (Kerwin, 1991). In a 1990 grocery shopping behavior study, 83% of respondents said they used coupons. Direct Marketing (1991) reports that consumer use of coupons and cents-off promotions is increasing while use of money-back/cash refunds, sweepstakes, and premiums is decreasing. This suggests that consumers want instant gratification through immediate, rather than delayed, savings which seems more likely during economic hard times.

To date, studies of money-saving strategies such as use of coupons and refunds have focused on food shopping in general (see, for example, Avery & Bautista, 1991; Avery & Haynes, 1991; Maynes, 1991; Warme & Maynes, 1991). It is possible, though, that money-saving strategies vary by product. Studies of coupon and refund use by specific products were not found in the literature review for this study.

One particular product is pet food. (Consistent with the industry's usual custom, pet food in this study refers to dog and cat food and snacks.) Examination of use of money-saving strategies related to pet food shopping during an economic recession is especially important because pet ownership is a discretionary purchase. However, once the pet is owned costs ensue. It is possible that consumers perceive the pet food area as one way of reducing costs without sacrificing the satisfaction of other family needs and wants.

The pet food portion of a household's budget can be sizeable. Dogs and cats consumed over $8.6 billion worth of food and snacks in 1991 (Packaged Facts, 1991). The pet snacks category (biscuits, rawhide, etc.) increased 6.3% in sales for 1988 and continues to be a growing section of the supermarket where pet foods usually are purchased (Crispell, 1991). A recent Gallup survey found that Americans on the average spend approximately $1,300 per year for pet food, snacks, health care, toys, and other expenses (Consumer Reports, 1991). Calculated for the whole economy, that totals to more than $70 billion annually.

Of all 1990 U.S. households, 37% had at least one dog; 31% had at least one cat (Packaged Facts, 1991). Both figures were slight increases over 1989. Further, there are approximately 51-58 million dogs and 49-60 million cats in the United States (Crispell, 1991).

Thus, the overall focus of this study is consumers' use of money-saving strategies in the purchase of pet food. Specific objectives were:

1. To investigate the determinants of frequency of money-saving strategies used in pet food purchases.

2. To investigate how the economic recession has affected purchase behavior related to pet food and snacks; e.g., spending less, switching brands, etc.

Previous studies could give guidance in the formulation of hypotheses, but as stated earlier, no studies of money-saving strategies used for pet food purchases were found. This study will provide such baseline data. Studies of coupon use in general might be useful in predicting relationships. For example, Waldrop (1988) reported that coupon use was more likely for homemakers than for other occupational groups and for those with incomes of $30,000 or more than for those earning below $10,000. Warme and Maynes (1991) found that coupon use was low for those who were single, childless, career-oriented, younger than age 32, and in the income bracket of below $10,000 or above $40,000. But, pet food consumers might be somewhat different from the general

---

[1]Associate Professor, Family and
Consumer Economics

shopping consumer so previous studies on coupon use in general food shopping were not used to formulate hypotheses.

Theory, on the other hand, can help to predict relationships. It is assumed that shoppers wish to optimize their resource use. Money-saving strategies can give more utility by decreasing price of pet food. The overall hypothesis, then, was that frequency of money-saving strategies used in pet food purchases is influenced by selected variables, all of which indicate differing utility levels. Number of pets and perceived importance of money-saving strategies are two such variables. Use of money-saving strategies to purchase pet food is likely to increase with number of pets because of the greater utility for consumers with more pets. Perceived importance of money-saving strategies like coupon use and refunding is likely to predict frequency of use. Respondents placing a greater level of importance on such strategies are assumed to do so because of the higher perceived utility from use of money-saving strategies.

Procedures

Sample
The study was conducted in grocery stores/supermarkets in Champaign-Urbana, Illinois. Convenience market and specialty stores were eliminated from the study because of the more specialized nature of items at these stores. To maximize representation of pet food shoppers, a purposive sampling technique was used. There were 15 grocery stores or supermarkets representing 6 different chains in the two cities; one store from each chain was chosen as a data collection site. Further, to ensure a wide sampling of the twin-city grocery store/supermarket population, sites were selected from the north, south, east, west, and center parts of the twin-city area.

Consumers shopping (browsing, making selections) in the pet food aisle during the scheduled interview time were eligible for the study. Although every individual was eligible for the study, not everyone was approached, given the interviewer's constraint of being able to conduct one interview at a time. Further, the study was limited to adults, aged 18 and over. A screening question for age was used to determine eligibility before the respondent was interviewed. All possible interviews were conducted during the scheduled interview times, resulting in 118 completed interviews. Interviewers were unable to obtain 83 interviews because they were interviewing someone else. Six individuals refused to participate.

Data Collection
Data were collected by trained interviewers who used an interview schedule designed by the principal investigator. Interviews were conducted April 30, May 1 and 2, 1992 at varying times of the day. Days chosen included: (a) both weekday and weekend to ensure interviewing individuals who shop only weekdays or weekends and (b) morning, afternoon, and evening hours to avoid possible time-of-day bias in the sample.

Statistical Analysis
Data were analyzed using the IBM-PC and statistical software, SPSS/PC+. Statistical analyses consisted of frequencies and regression tests. Alpha was set at the .05 level of significance.

Variables
Variables measuring specific money-saving strategies were: (a) cents-off coupon use, (b) free coupon use, (c) refund offer use, (d) coupon cross-merchandising use, and (e) purchasing pet food on sale. Coupon cross-merchandising use was measured by asking the respondent the frequency with which he/she buys a product because it has a coupon for another product. (This is a common marketing strategy used by pet food manufacturers.) Respondents were asked to indicate the frequency of use of each money-saving strategy on a scale of: 1=never, 2=seldom, 3=often, 4=usually, and 5=always. Borgatta and Bohrnstedt (1980) suggest this is an imperfect interval scale that is suitable for regression analysis because of the robustness of the regression test.

For the regression analysis, the dependent variable was created by summing responses for all the money-saving strategies. This resulted in an overall measure of money-saving strategies for each respondent. The independent variables consisted of both demographic and social-psychological variables. The demographic variables were: (a) sex, (b) household income, (c) age, (d) number of pets, (e) household size, (f) marital status, and (g) occupation. Social-psychological variables were: (a) importance of price, (b) importance of pet's preference, (c) importance of nutrition, (d) importance of refund offer, and (e) importance of using a coupon. The independent variables were tested for possible multicollinearity by submitting them to a correlation analysis. Criteria to establish high correlation between variables were set at $r \geq .6$.

One independent variable, occupation, was measured on a nominal scale and was converted to a set of dummy variables for use with the regression procedure. The set of dummy variables consisted of: (a) professional, technical, managerial; (b) clerical, sales; (c) blue-collar (skilled and unskilled); (d) service; and (e) not employed (including homemakers, retired, and students). The not employed group was treated as the omitted category in the regression analysis. Each dummy variable was coded 0=absence of trait and 1=presence of trait. For example, the dummy variable, service, was coded: 0=respondent not employed in a service occupation and 1=respondent is employed in a service occupation.

One other independent variable, household income, was converted for the regression analysis.

Because data were collected in income ranges, rather than on an interval scale, income was recoded to a proportional scale with interval properties. The midpoint of each income range was determined and divided by the midpoint of the lowest income range.

Results and Discussion

Sample Characteristics

The average respondent was a married female, 44 years old with an income of $37,618 and a household size of 2.5 persons. Fifty-five percent of all respondents had at least 1 dog, and slightly more than 70% had at least 1 cat. Number of dogs per household ranged from 0 to 12 with 40% of respondents having 1 dog and 12% having 2 dogs. Likewise, 40% of all respondents had 1 cat, and 16% had 2 cats. Households had from 0 to 20 cats. In terms of occupation, respondents typically were employed in professional, technical, or managerial jobs (29%), service jobs (17%), or clerical or sales jobs (12%). Thirteen percent of the respondents were students, and 11% were retired.

Money-Saving Strategies in Pet Food Purchases

Respondents were asked how often they used the following money-saving strategies in the purchase of pet foods: (a) cents-off coupons, (b) free coupons, (c) refund offers, (d) buy product because it has a coupon on another product (coupon cross-merchandising), and (e) buy pet food on sale (see Table 1). Less than 20% of the respondents

Table 1
Use of Money-Saving Strategies in Purchase of Pet Foods

Variable	Never	Seldom	Often	Usually	Always	Missing
Use cents-off coupons	35[a] (29.7)[b]	36 (30.5)	24 (20.3)	9 (7.6)	12 (10.2)	2 (1.7)
Use free coupons	56 (47.5)	29 (24.6)	16 (13.6)	5 (4.2)	9 (7.6)	3 (2.5)
Use refund offers	71 (60.2)	29 (24.6)	7 (5.9)	6 (5.1)	2 (1.7)	3 (2.5)
Buy product because it has coupon on another product	94 (79.7)	13 (11.0)	6 (5.1)	3 (2.5)	0 (0)	2 (1.7)
Buy pet food on sale	29 (24.6)	25 (21.2)	30 (25.4)	18 (15.3)	14 (11.9)	2 (1.7)

[a]Frequency of responses.

[b]Percentage of responses.

usually or always used any of the money-saving strategies, except for buy pet food on sale. Twenty-seven percent usually or always bought pet food on sale. There was a high percentage of respondents who seldom or never used any of the following money-saving strategies: (a) cents-off coupons, 60%; (b) free coupons, 72%; and (c) coupon cross-merchandising, 91%. Forty-six percent seldom or never bought pet food on sale. These results suggest that consumers do not regularly take advantage of money-saving strategies in the pet food aisle of the grocery store. Not surprising, the respondents were much more likely to buy pet food on sale and to use cents-off coupons and free coupons than to use refunds or coupon cross-merchandising. This is consistent with findings reported by Direct Marketing (1991) about the use of coupons and cents-off promotions over money-back/cash refunds as a means of instant gratification rather than delayed savings. Buying on sale, too, gives instant gratification, while coupon cross-merchandising results in delayed savings. Further, buying pet food on sale requires little effort on the consumer's part, perhaps some planning to take advantage of sales. Coupons take not only planning but also effort in clipping and organizing coupons for later use and cost-comparisons in the store to see if the coupon lowers the product's cost over other available brands. Refunds, though, take more effort as the consumer must accumulate the required proofs of purchase and often the grocery receipt, then complete the mail-in form, add postage and mail. Coupon cross-merchandising had the highest frequency of never responses. The added effort here is to redeem the coupon later on another product. If this is a product the consumer does not regularly purchase, the perceived return will be nil.

Some respondents, though, used a combination of money-saving strategies. For analysis purposes, cents-off coupons and free coupons were collapsed into one category, use coupons. Combined strategies listed by respondents were: (a) coupon plus buy on sale, (b) coupon plus refund, (c) coupon plus coupon cross-merchandising, (d) coupon plus refund plus buy on sale, (e) coupon plus refund plus coupon cross-merchandising, and (f) coupon plus refund plus coupon cross-merchandising plus buy on sale. Slightly less than 2/3 of the respondents used no combination of money-saving strategies. By far, the most commonly used combined strategy was use coupon plus buy product on sale (20%). Only a small percentage of respondents used the other combined strategies. These results are not too surprising when considered in light of the cost/return relationship to the consumer. More effort is required to combine more strategies, but the return can be quite great; for example, if the product is on sale, a cents-off coupon is used, and the product proof of purchase is used to obtain a refund, the total savings can be sizeable, even equal to or greater than the original price. Thus, combining as many strategies as possible can lower the final cost of the product greatly. But, if the consumer does not perceive the possible savings, the combined strategies will not be used, and potential savings will be lost to the consumer. Another explanation for lack of money-saving strategy use is that the cost of using the strategies may be perceived as higher than the resulting savings; thus, total utility would not increase with money-saving strategies use.

Determinants of Money-Saving Strategies Use

At the next stage of analysis, a multiple regression equation was developed to investigate the determinants of frequency of money-saving strategies used in pet food purchases. All independent variables were entered at once because the correlation matrix of the independent variables showed no multicollinearity problems. Results are reported in Table 2.

Table 2
__Determinants of Frequency of Money-Saving Strategies Used in Pet Food Purchases__

Variable	Beta
Sex	.101
Household income	.095
Importance of price	.273**
Importance of pet's preference	.042
Importance of nutrition	-.003
Age	-.054
Importance of refund order	.176*
Total number of pets	-.059
Household size	.139
Marital status	-.010
Importance of using a coupon	.429***
Occupation	
Professional, technical, managerial	-.253*
Clerical, sales	-.093
Blue-collar	-.041
Service	-.187*
Not employed (omitted category)	

R^2*=.521; $p \le .001$

*$p \le .05$
**$p \le .01$
***$p \le .001$

The adjusted R^2 was .521 and significant at the .001 level. Thus, 52% of the variance in frequency of money-saving strategies used in pet food purchases was explained by the independent variables. Five variables had significant __beta__ coefficients. The most important determinant was importance of using a coupon ($p \le .001$) followed by importance of price ($p \le .01$); professional, technical, managerial occupations ($p \le .05$); service occupations ($p \le .05$); and importance of refund offer ($p \le .05$). The more importance respondents attached to using a coupon, price, and refund offer, the greater their use of money-saving strategies. Of these, importance of using a coupon is the major factor in determining whether pet owners use money-saving strategies. When compared to those respondents who were not employed, the two occupational groups of service and professional, technical, or managerial used money-saving strategies much less frequently. This finding is not surprising; those who are employed have less time to use money-saving strategies than those who are not employed. The results about importance of using a coupon, price, and refund offer confirm the cost/return relationship between money-saving strategies and consumers' use of them. Consumers who perceive the returns will recognize the importance of money-saving strategies and will use them.

Reasons for Pet Food Purchases

To further understand pet food shopping behavior and low use of money-saving strategies, it is helpful to examine the reasons respondents gave for buying the brand of pet food they usually do. As shown in Table 3, respondents' perception of pet's preference is by far the most frequent reason given for buying a certain brand of pet food with slightly more than 60% of the respondents identifying this as the reason they bought a certain brand.

Table 3
__Reasons Respondents Buy Certain Brand of Pet Food, n=118__

Variable	Frequency	Percentage
Pet's preference	72	61.0
On sale	3	2.5
Coupon or refund	1	0.8
Professional recommendation	10	8.5
Nutrition	6	5.1
Price; it's cheap	10	8.5
Miscellaneous reasons*	10	8.5
Missing information	6	5.1

*These included: (a) family/friend's preference, (b) sounds good, (c) good size, (d) dog is chunky, (e) easy to store, (f) lowest fish content, and (g) previously used.

A similar result was found when respondents were asked to indicate the importance of selected factors related to pet food shopping: (a) nutrition, (b) price, (c) coupon, (d) refund offer, and (e) pet's preference (Table 4).

Table 4

Importance   of   Selected   Factors   in   Pet   Food
Purchases

Variable	Not important	Important	Very important
Nutrition (n=115)	13[a] (11.3)[b]	50 (43.5)	52 (45.2)[c]
Price (n=117)	39 (33.3)	47 (40.2)	31 (26.5)
Coupon (n=118)	70 (60.9)	37 (32.2)	8 (7.0)
Refund offer (n=116)	95 (81.9)	17 (14.7)	4 (3.4)
Pet's preference (n=115)	14 (12.2)	26 (22.6)	75 (65.2)

[a]Frequency of responses.

[b]Percentage of responses.

[c]Totals may not sum to 100% due to rounding.

Slightly less than 90% of the respondents reported that pet's preference, as well as nutrition, was important or very important in their shopping. Price was important or very important to 67%, while coupons and refunds were far less important with the majority of respondents saying they were not important (61% and 82%, respectively).

The overwhelming importance of nutrition and pet's preference helps to explain the low importance attached to coupons and refunds. Price, though, still seems to be more than moderately important for many consumers. Possibly, the same respondents indicating nutrition and pet's preference as important would use coupons, refunds, or other money-saving strategies if they were assured of good nutrition and their pet would like the pet food.

Respondents were asked what changes they had made in their pet food shopping in response to the economic recession (Table 5). Respondents

Table 5

Changes in Pet Food Shopping in Response to the
Economic Recession

Variable	Made change	No change
Spending less	7[a] (5.9)[b]	111 (94.1)
Using coupons more	31 (26.3)	87 (73.7)
Using rebates/refunds more	11 (9.3)	107 (90.7)
Buying different brands than before	15 (12.7)	103 (87.3)
Made other changes[c]	6 (5.1)	112 (94.9)

[a]Frequency of responses; n=118.

[b]Percentage of responses; may not sum to 100% due to rounding.

[c]Responses given were: (a) going to larger bags, buying less often; (b) special diet; (c) shop for sales; (d) not as many treats; (e) fewer cats; and (f) buy turkey breast and cook for cat.

mostly reported no change in their use of pet food money-saving strategies, contrary to Hume's (1991) report about increased use of money-saving strategies for shopping in general during economic hard times. The largest change was in the use of coupons, but only 26% reported using them more. Some brand switching was evident but in only 13% of the sample. Thus, it can be concluded that pet food consumers are somewhat brand loyal even in economic hard times. Nine percent of the respondents said they were using rebates/refunds more, and 6% said they were spending less on pet food. Five percent indicated they had made other changes: (a) going to larger bags, buying less often, (b) special diet, (c) shop for sales, (d) not as many treats, (e) fewer cats, and (f) buy turkey breast and cook for cat. Apparently, consumers are cutting back on non-pet food expenditures rather than using money-saving strategies in the pet food aisle.

Implications

Results of this study are important in providing knowledge about pet food shopping and money-saving strategies consumers use in their shopping. Consumer use of money-saving strategies is different for pet food shopping than for food shopping in general. An important finding of this research is that consumers do not regularly use money-saving strategies in pet food shopping, even in economic hard times.

For educators, this indicates that educational materials and programs are needed in this area. Consumers need help in assessing the cost/return relationship of money-saving strategies in the pet food aisle. They need to understand how to use money-saving strategies in combination so as to obtain the greatest return. Planning and organizing are needed skills for the maximum use of purchasing sale items and using coupons, and lessons could be developed to teach these skills with direct application to pet food shopping. Further, consumers need to understand shelf life of pet food and the effect on the product's nutrition. Although stocking up on pet food on sale and buying in large quantities can maximize savings, these can be diminished if nutritional value decreases because the food is not used within its shelf life. Some costs of couponing and refunding could be decreased by enlisting all family members in these activities. Children who learn how to comparison shop and use coupons and refund offers wisely learn a lot about financial management. And, shopping for the children's pet is another aspect of pet responsibility for children to learn.

For marketing experts, these findings suggest that coupons, coupon cross-merchandising, and refunds need to be set up so consumers can more easily take advantage of them. For example, the increasing practice of requiring an original grocery receipt is frustrating for consumers who accidentally discard the receipt before reading the terms of the refund offer. Or, the consumer has two different refund offers requiring an original receipt, but both items were purchased on the same grocery receipt. Or, coupons could be used instead of refunds if increased consumer use of the money-saving strategy is desirable. Finally, marketing experts could discontinue coupons, refunds, and coupon cross-merchandising in favor of lowered product prices.

One of the most important findings of this study is that consumers are concerned about nutrition for their pets. Price is a consideration but not nearly as important as nutrition. The principal investigator's assessment of product choices available to shoppers during this survey indicates there are price breaks available in nutritionally adequate pet food. Consistent use of special offers and sale prices could result in considerable savings annually while still purchasing nutritionally adequate products. Some consumer education might be needed to help consumers to plan ahead so they can take advantage of sales, for example.

Further, investigation of consumer knowledge about pet nutrition is advised, especially in regard to price and money-saving strategies. Although respondents in this study reported that nutrition was important or very important, no questions were asked to determine whether consumers understand their pets' nutritional needs or how to determine the nutritional adequacy of pet food. This is an area for further study. If such a study finds that consumers do not understand pet nutrition, then educational materials addressing nutrition and money-saving strategies could be developed and provide a valuable service to pet food consumers.

Respondents also were aware of their pet's preference in pet food, and this is another area of consumer education. Consumers need to understand how to change pet's preference if money-saving strategies are to be maximized. It is possible to change a pet's food to another brand, even though the pet seems to prefer a particular brand. Pet nutritionists recommend this be done gradually. If not, the pet is likely to reject the new product and reinforce the concept of the preferred brand.

Consumers spend sizeable amounts of money on pet food each year, yet do not necessarily use money-saving strategies to get the most for their money. Often, people become so emotionally attached to their pets that it is possible they do not get the best buy in the pet food aisle of the grocery store. They may assume that certain kinds of food are good for their pets because of labeling and advertising claims. Still others may purchase pet food at specialized stores or from veterinarians assuming the food is better for the pet. These aspects of pet food purchasing were not covered in this study but would provide important insight into consumer pet food purchasing, especially as they relate to the use of money-saving strategies.

References

Avery, R.J. & Bautista, M.E. (1991). An examination of the psychological aspects of purchase behavior: Motivations for coupon use. In V. Haldeman (Ed.), Proceedings of the American Council on Consumer Interests, 271-276. Columbia, MO: University of Missouri.

Avery, R.J. & Haynes, G.W. (1991). Price discrimination in the grocery market? A cost benefit analysis of coupon use. In V. Haldeman (Ed.), Proceedings of the American Council on Consumer Interests, 263-270. Columbia, MO: University of Missouri.

Avery, R.J. & Haynes, G.W. (1991). Coupons: Boon or boondoggle for consumers? Human Ecology Forum, 19, 13-16.

Borgatta, E.F. & Bohrnstedt, G.W. (1980). Level of measurement: Once over again. Sociological Methods and Research, 9, 139-160.

Consumer Reports. (1991, May 15). Pet census. Consumer Reports News Digest, 10.

Crispell, D. (1991). Pet sounds. American Demographics, 13(5), 40-44, 53.

Direct Marketing. (1991, December). Coupons maintain redeeming qualities. Direct Marketing, 25-27.

Hume, S. (1991, April 29). Recession-proof industry feels pinch. Advertising Age, 31, 38.

Kerwin, A.M. (1991). Snip, clip, rip. Advertising, 124(12), 20-21, 50.

Maynes, E.S. (1991). Couponing: Lessons for consumers. In V. Haldeman (Ed.), Proceedings of the American Council on Consumer Interests, 254-255. Columbia, MO: University of Missouri.

Packaged Facts. (1991). The pet food market: November 1991. 581 Avenue of the Americas. New York: Packaged Facts.

Waldrop, J. (1988). Coupon clippers of America. American Demographics, 10(May), 60-61.

Warme, R. & Maynes, E.S. (1991). Role theory: A psychographic explanation for coupon redemption. In V. Haldeman (Ed.), Proceedings of the American Council on Consumer Interests, 256-262. Columbia, MO: University of Missouri.

Apparel Shopping Patterns and Problems Among Children's Wear Consumer

Pamela S. Norum, University of Missouri-Columbia[1]

The creation of a baby boomlet has had a tremendous impact on consumer demand, and in particular, for children's apparel. During the late 1980's, the children's wear market experienced steady growth. Nonetheless, the needs and wants of this market segment have not been fully explored. This research was undertaken in order to develop a better understanding of the product attributes important to the children's wear customer, as well as, shopping and apparel problems encountered with children's wear.

Introduction

A number of socio-economic and demographic factors have a tremendous effect on the purchasing and consumption patterns of households in the United States. These factors range from the aging of the population to the formation of non-traditional households to the bearing of children by baby boomers. Not since the 1950's and 60's has the birth rate been as high as it has been in the late 1980's and early 1990's. In 1990 there were 4.1 million births in the United States, a number that was higher than anticipated by the Census Bureau. This baby boomlet, or echo boom, has an impact on the demand for goods and services in the marketplace. Markets particularly affected by this surge in the youth population include specific food products, toys and children's apparel. In 1991, the children's apparel market grew to $20.3 billion in sales. Although this was only a .3 percent increase over 1990, children's wear outperformed many other apparel segments during this recessionary period. This growth also came on the heels of rather astounding growth during the late 1980's. Although the children's wear market provides a potential opportunity for businesses interested in satisfying the needs and wants of this market segment, it is a frequently overlooked market. Not only do apparel marketers tend to focus on their traditional mainstays (eg. women's wear), academic research has also neglected this area.

Retailers' views regarding the children's wear customer have been surveyed periodically by a major trade publication (Earnshaw's). Typically, the survey will ask a question such as "What do you perceive is your customers' greatest dissatisfaction with children's wear?" The results from the most recent survey (Earnshaw's Review, 1992) are shown in Table 1.

Table 1
Retailers View of Consumer Problems

	Dept. Store	Discount Store	Specialty Chain	Indep. Specialty
SIZING NOT UNIFORM	43	21	38	55
PRICE	24	29	38	39
QUALITY	19	21	25	--
LACK OF SERVICE	14	21	12	6
LACK OF BRANDS	--	8	--	--
LACK OF FASHION DIRECTION	--	--	--	--

(EARNSHAW'S, JUNE 1992, P. 56)

These results suggest that retailers perceive sizing and price to be the children's wear customers' greatest problems. An interesting question that arises is "Do these results reflect what consumers believe to be their greatest problems when purchasing children's wear?" Additionally, "What problems do consumers encounter after purchasing children's wear?" It was the purpose of this research to address these questions. The specific objectives were:

1. To identify product attributes that are important to customers when purchasing children's wear.

2. To determine problems customers encounter when shopping for children's wear.

3. To determine problems customers encounter after purchasing children's wear.

Apparel manufacturers have been criticized for lacking a marketing orientation-that is-failing to understand the needs and wants of their customer and satisfying them (Carideo, 1985). Insight gained through this research will be useful to both apparel manufacturers and retailers in better serving this market segment. In addition, the data collected for this study will also be useful in

---

[1]Associate Professor

addressing consumer behavior issues of interest to academic researchers.

Literature Review

Despite the fact that the children's wear market experienced substantial growth during the 1980's, much of the research on purchasing behavior for children's wear was conducted prior to 1980. These studies address evaluative criteria and store choice. Shopping and apparel problems have not been addressed by previous researchers.

Findings from a study of 100 families located in the Eastern United State (Blake, Glission and Tate, 1953) found that durability and price, respectively, were the first and second most important factors considered by homemakers when purchasing children's wear. The results indicated that homemakers seldom bought children's clothing based on brand name. Homemakers in the highest income group, and those with more formal education, had a greater tendency to buy based on brand name.

Joyce (1966), in a study of 236 families, found that quality was the most important factor to the upper income group when buying children's wear. The middle income group considered price and quality as important factors. The lower income group cited price as their first priority.

Frankenbach (1970) asked a sample of mothers to rank seven factors--easy care finish, price, care instructions, fiber content, garment brand name, fiber brand name, and fiber generic name. The two top ranked factors (easy care and price) were in reverse order depending on the mothers' employment status. Employed mothers ranked easy care finish as more important than price; their unemployed counterparts placed greater importance on price.

Blake et. al (1953) found that families with a homemaker most frequently purchased children's wear in department stores followed by mail-order purchases. Frankebach (1970) found that the department store was most frequently used by all households in her sample. Mail order was second.

Theoretical Model

The Engel, Blackwell and Miniard (EBM) model of consumer behavior was the theoretical model used to guide the development of the survey instrument used in this research (See Figure 1).
This model emphasizes the consumer decision making process and the variables influencing the decision process. Consumer decision making is viewed as consisting of five basic steps: problem recognition, search, alternative evaluation, purchase, outcomes, and postpurchase evaluation (satisfaction/dissatisfaction).

Engel et al. (1986) suggested that problem recognition occurs when an individual senses a difference between what he or she perceives to be the ideal state of affairs as compared to the actual state of affairs at any point in time. After the individual recognizes a problem, he or she continues with the decision making process.

The second step is the search process. Internal search (memory) and external search (seeking information from outside sources) occurs. This is followed by the third step-alternative evaluation.

Alternative evaluation has three components -- beliefs, attitudes and intentions. Engel et al. (1986) explained that the foundation of beliefs is evaluative criteria-the standards and specifications used by consumers to compare and evaluate different products and brands. Beliefs about alternatives form attitudes, such as "acceptable" or "unacceptable." Attitude leads to intention which is directly linked to actual purchase behavior.

The purchase is made after evaluating the alternatives identified by the consumer. Purchase occurs primarily in the retail store setting; however, non-store forms of retailing may also be used. After the purchase, the consumer compares product performance against his/her expectations.

Dissatisfaction occurs if performance is less than expected. Dissatisfaction affects one's beliefs and attitudes about the choice in an unfavorable manner, whereas, satisfaction strengthens the belief and attitude about the product and/or store in a favorable way.

Variables that are believed to influence the decision process include 1) individual characteristics, 2) social influences and 3) situational influences.

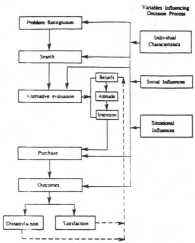

Figure 1 Engel, Blackwell and Miniard's Consumer Behavior Model

Research Approach

The focus of this research was on households with children ages 10 and under. This limitation was placed on the sample for a number of reasons. First, children of different ages have varying clothing needs. As a result, parents will look for different attributes in apparel depending on the age of the child; they will also encounter different types of problems in the purchase and use of children's apparel. Second, as children become older, they become much more involved with the decision making process regarding their clothing choices. As a result, two different points of view (the childs' and the parents') would need to be considered in understanding the pre-teen and teenage market. Third, the needs and wants of consumers with younger children have not been adequately addressed in previous research.

To carry out this research, a pilot study was conducted in June 1991. Based upon background reading, interviews with a number of mothers regarding the issues at hand, and personal knowledge, a survey instrument was developed. To pretest the questionnaire, the kindergarten enrollment list from one midwestern school district was used as the sampling frame. From the kindergarten enrollment list, 400 households were randomly selected. A questionnaire and self-addressed, stamped, return envelope were delivered to each household. One hundred and thirty-one households responded resulting in a 32% response rate. Based on the results of the pilot study, the same revisions were done to the questionnaire.

In March 1992, the full scale study was carried out using households with either a kindergartner or fourth grader present. Eleven school districts in one midwestern state provided the enrollment lists for these two grades. Two thousand households were randomly selected-1000 kindergarten families and 1000 fourth grade families. Seventy-one surveys were undeliverable. A follow-up postcard, followed by a second survey for non-respondents were sent after the initial mailing (Dillman). There were 953 surveys returned, for a response rate of 49% (based upon deliverable surveys).

The survey that was used for this study contained four sections. The various components of the consumer decision making model were considered in developing the instrument. Specifically, store patronage, evaluative criteria, shopping and apparel problems, satisfaction/dissatisfaction and complaint behavior were addressed. Section I of the questionnaire addressed issues related to the shopping experience. Respondents provided information on clothing acquisition sources; retail store patronage; evaluative criteria; satisfaction with their shopping experiences for children's clothes; and shopping problems. Section II of the survey pertained to clothing purchase practices; satisfaction with the quality of clothes they can buy for their youngest child; and apparel problems.

Section III asked information about clothing purchases in the previous year, and for those items with which they experienced dissatisfaction, their response to the problem. Section IV contained questions regarding respondent and household characteristics.

Sample

Tables 2-5 provide descriptive statistics for the sample. As can be seen in Table 2, the majority (95.4%) of the respondents are female.

Table 2
Sex, Race and Marital Status of the Respondent

CATEGORY	NUMBER	PERCENT
SEX OF RESPONDENT		
FEMALE	902	95.4
MALE	43	4.6
TOTAL	945	100.0
RACE		
CAUCASIAN	789	84.9
AFRO-AMERICAN	102	11.0
ASIAN	11	1.2
HISPANIC	6	0.6
OTHER	21	2.3
TOTAL	929	100.0
MARITAL STATUS		
MARRIED	731	77.2
DIVORCED	132	13.9
SEPARATED	29	3.1
NEVER MARRIED	45	4.8
WIDOWED	10	1.1
TOTAL	947	100.0

Almost 85% of the respondents are Caucasian and 11% are Afro-american. Seventy-seven percent of the respondents are married, while 17% are divorced. Over 90% had at least a high school education and 70% had some type of educational training beyond high school (Table 3). Slightly over 64% were employed with an average salary of $18,549. Over 50% of the households had a total household income of less than $40,000 with an average family size of 4.27 people (Table 4).

Table 3
Education, Employment Status and Salary of the Respondent

CATEGORY	NUMBER	PERCENT
EDUCATION		
LESS THAN HIGH SCHOOL	60	6.3
COMPLETED HIGH SCHOOL	222	23.4
SOME COLLEGE OR VOCATIONAL TRAINING	269	28.4
COMPLETED VOCATIONAL TRAINING	80	8.4
COMPLETED COLLEGE	163	17.2
SOME GRADUATE WORK	68	7.2
A GRADUATE DEGREE	85	9.0
TOTAL	947	100.0
EMPLOYMENT STATUS		
EMPLOYED	609	64.4
UNEMPLOYED	337	35.6
TOTAL	946	100.0

RESPONDENTS' AVERAGE SALARY: $18,549

Table 4
Income and family size of the respondents' household

CATEGORY	NUMBER	PERCENT
INCOME		
< $10,000	97	11.2
$10,000-19,999	111	12.8
$20,000-29,999	136	15.7
$30,000-39,999	150	17.4
$40,000-49,999	124	14.4
$50,000-59,999	97	11.2
$60,000-69,999	56	6.5
$70,000-79,999	24	2.8
$80,000-89,999	21	2.4
$90,000-99,999	14	1.6
OVER $100,000	34	3.9
TOTAL	864	100.0

AVERAGE FAMILY SIZE: 4.27

Besides providing information on selected household characteristics, respondents were asked to answer a series of questions using their youngest child as a point of reference. This was done for two reasons. First, responses could vary for different children (if more than one was present in the household). Second, the survey would be too long if respondents were asked to provide information in regard to each child in their household. As can been seen in Table 5, the sample was pretty evenly split between boys and girls. In terms of the age distribution of the youngest child, one-third are under the age of four, and almost half are six or older.

Results

This section presents the results, based on simple descriptive statistics, for consumer responses regarding their apparel shopping patterns and problems. The various acquisition forms used by consumers to obtain both playwear and dresswear are presented. Results for evaluative criteria consumers consider important when purchasing children's playwear, as well as, shopping and apparel problems they encounter are presented and discussed. Since responses regarding play wear and dress wear may vary, respondents were asked to provide responses in reference to playwear only.

Table 5
Sex and Age Distribution of the Youngest Child

CATEGORY	NUMBER	PERCENT
SEX DISTRIBUTION		
BOYS	481	50.7
GIRLS	468	49.3
TOTAL	949	100.0
AGE DISTRIBUTION		
0-23 MONTHS	101	10.6
24-47 MONTHS	121	12.7
48-71 MONTHS	176	18.5
72-95 MONTHS	270	28.3
96-119 MONTHS	104	10.9
120+ MONTHS	181	9.0
TOTAL	953	100.0

Table 6
Sources of Clothing Acquistion

CATEGORY	NUMBER	PERCENT
BUY NEW	915	96.6
GIFTS	654	69.1
HAND-ME-DOWNS	513	54.2
GARAGE SALES	414	42.8
CATALOGS	315	33.3
BUY USED	216	22.8
SEW	182	19.2
CHARITY	17	1.8

Respondents were asked to indicate the various sources from which they acquire children's wear, as well as, specific types of stores from which they purchase both playwear and dresswear. This is an important facet of the decision process for marketers to understand. It may come as a surprise to many children's wear retailers that a number of sources are used by consumers. In looking at Table 6, one can see that many non-traditional retail outlets provide competition for traditional retailers, particularly garage sales. Purchasing clothes at garage sales and used clothing stores are ways for consumers to truly get name brand merchandise at low prices. It is also a signal to consumers that they are purchasing clothes that have already stood the test of time. Table 7 shows the important role that discount stores play in the purchase of playwear. The results also indicate that parents will trade up when purchasing dress wear for their children.

Table 7
Retail Store Patronage

PLAYWEAR	DRESSWEAR	RETAIL STORE
(PERCENTAGES)		
91.1	62.7	DISCOUNT STORE
55.3	62.4	MASS MERCHANDISER
27.8	41.3	DEPARTMENT STORE
9.1	13.5	SPECIALTY STORE
28.2	23.8	FACTORY OUTLET
30.4	24.6	CATALOG ORDER
21.9	15.2	USED CLOTHING STORE

Based on the Engel, Blackwell and Miniard model of consumer behavior, consumers will utilize any number of evaluative criteria for products they purchase. Given the lack of recent research on the purchase process for children's wear, one goal of this research was to develop an initial understanding of the relative importance of various product attributes in the purchase of children's play wear. Respondents were asked to rate 17 different factors that consumers may consider when purchasing children's play wear. A 4-point scale was used. Table 8 shows the ranking based on mean values (with a lower mean indicating greater importance). The results suggests that parents will not buy an item that doesn't fit their child, or that appears uncomfortable (no matter how inexpensive). However, if the first two criteria are satisfied, then price becomes an important consideration. The fashion aspects of the garment appear to be secondary considerations. Brand name was found to be the least important consideration. This is in direct contrast to other apparel market segments (eg. women's wear) where research has shown brand name to be an important consideration.

Table 8
Factors Consumers Consider When Purchasing
  Playwear

MEAN VALUE	CHARACTERISTIC
PRIMARY CONSIDERATIONS	
1.20	COMFORT
1.21	FIT
1.27	PRICE
1.34	QUALITY
1.35	DURABILITY
1.39	EASY CARE
SECONDARY CONSIDERATIONS	
1.76	STYLE
1.79	FASHION
1.80	MIX & MATCH
1.85	GROWTH FEATURES
1.96	COLOR
LEAST IMPORTANT CONSIDERATIONS	
2.04	STORE REPUTATION
2.05	MADE IN AMERICA
2.10	FIBER CONTENT
2.12	STORE SERVICE
2.38	SELF-HELP FEATURES
2.94	BRAND

To understand the extent to which the needs and wants of the children's wear consumer are being met in the marketplace, it is important to identify problems that customers encounter with both the shopping experience, and apparel products themselves. Respondents were asked to rate 22 shopping problems and 19 apparel problems using a 4-point scale. The lower the score, the greater the problem. Table 9 presents the mean values for the shopping problems; it appears that high prices are the greatest problem consumers encounter when shopping for children's clothes. Sizing/fit related problems are also troublesome. To understand the sizing/fit problem better, respondents were asked the following question: If you were to buy clothes that corresponded to your youngest child's age, would the clothes usually FIT JUST RIGHT, BE TOO BIG, OR BE TOO SMALL? Almost 45% responded that the clothes would be too small. Only 26.5% said they would fit just right. Sizing/fit problems were found to encompass issues such as inconsistent sizing among brands, lack of sizes that matches the childs' age, disproportionate fit, lack of body measurement and sizing information, and lack of transitional sizes.

Table 10 presents the mean values for the apparel problems. Staining appears to be a major problem once the apparel has been purchased and worn. In addition, factors related to the durability/quality of garments appear to present problems after purchase.

Table 9
Shopping Problems

MEAN VALUE	PROBLEM
1.51	HIGH PRICES
2.18	INCONSISTENT SIZING AMONG BRANDS
2.30	NARROW AISLE SPACE
2.31	LIMITED CHOICES FOR BOYS
2.33	LACK OF BODY MEASUREMENT AND SIZING INFORMATION
2.36	TOO MANY CARTOON CHARACTERS
2.39	LACK OF AMERICAN MADE CLOTHES
2.40	DISPROPORTIONATE FIT
2.43	LACK OF STYLES I LIKE
2.47	LACK OF SIZES THAT MATCH THE CHILDS' AGE
2.54	LACK OF TRANSITIONAL SIZES
2.60	STYLES NOT APPROPRIATE FOR AGE
2.73	LIMITED COLOR CHOICES
2.72	LACK OF MIX AND MATCH ITEMS
2.87	LACK OF CHILDREN'S PLAY AREA
2.93	LACK OF SLIM/PETITE SIZES
3.24	LACK OF HUSKY/LARGE SIZES
3.33	LACK OF BRAND NAMES

Table 10
Apparel Problems

MEAN VALUE	PROBLEM
1.95	GARMENT STAINS EASILY
2.13	SOCKS LOSE ELASTICITY
2.18	SEAMS FALL APART
2.19	GROWS OUT OF GARMENT TOO FAST
2.22	GARMENT SHRINKS
2.23	GARMENT FADES
2.24	GARMENT ISN'T DURABLE
2.31	GARMENT LACKS GROWTH FEATURES
2.14	NECK HOLE GETS TOO SMALL
2.52	GARMENT NEEDS IRONING
2.56	FASTENER DOESN'T WORK
2.72	STRAPS AREN'T EASILY ADJUSTABLE
2.85	GARMENT IS UNCOMFORTABLE
2.89	GARMENT DOESN'T ALLOW CHILD TO USE POTTY
2.98	GARMENT DOESN'T ALLOW CHILD TO DRESS SELF
3.19	SOCKS CUT OFF CIRCULATION
3.46	GARMENT LACKS SNAPS FOR CHANGING DIAPERS
3.53	GARMENT LACKS ROOM FOR DIAPERS

Taking a closer look at these results, one might consider how responses vary based on the age and sex of the child. With respect to shopping problems, it appears that the greatest difference between parents of boys and girls is the limited selection of choices for boys (See Table 11).

Table 11
Shopping Problems Based on the Sex of the Youngest Child, Mean Values

BOYS		GIRLS	
HIGH PRICES	1.54	HIGH PRICES	1.47
LIMITED SELECTION	1.70	INCONSISTENT SIZING	2.17
INCONSISTENT SIZING	2.19	NARROW AISLE SPACE	2.31
LACK OF SIZE INFO.	2.32	LACK OF SIZE INFO.	2.34
LACK OF STYLES	2.32	CARTOON CHARACTERS	2.40
CARTOON CHARACTERS	2.33	LACK OF MADE IN USA	2.40
DISPROPOR- TIONATE FIT	2.37	DISPROPOR- TIONATE FIT	2.43
LACK OF USA MADE	2.37	LACK OF TRANSIT. SIZES	2.46
SIZES DON'T MATCH AGE	2.46	SIZES DON'T MATCH AGE	2.47
LACK OF TRANSIT. SIZES	2.62	INAPPROPRIATE STYLES	2.53
LIMITED COLOR CHOICES	2.65	LACK OF STYLES	2.54
INAPPROPRIATE STYLES	2.67	LIMITED SELECTION	2.70

Based on the age of the youngest child, it appears that there are a number of shopping and apparel problems that are unique to consumers with young children. The shopping problems include lack of aisle space (presumably for strollers and carts), and lack of a play area (Table 12).

Table 12
Shopping Problems Based on the Age of the Youngest Child, Mean Values

	SHOPPING PROBLEM	
AGE	NARROW AISLES	LACK OF PLAY AREA
0-23	1.99	2.47
24-47	2.13	2.52
48-71	2.28	2.65
72-95	2.37	2.87
96-119	2.57	3.30
120+	2.36	3.28

Apparel problems included neck openings that are too small (stemming from the fact that babies/toddlers heads are large relative to the rest of their body) and diaper related problems (Table 13). Diaper related problems included lack of room for diapers, as well as, a lack of snaps on garments to facilitate changing diapers. This latter one is a common problem since most manufacturers of toddler clothing (sizes 2T, 3T and 4T) do not include snaps on one piece outfits (such as overalls). However, most children are not potty trained until the age of 2, and sometimes 3. Thus, changing diapers can become quite a nuisance in garments without snaps.

Table 13
Apparel Problems Based on the Age of the Youngest Child, Mean Values

	APPAREL PROBLEM		
AGE	NECK TOO SMALL	NO SNAPS FOR DIAPERS	NO ROOM FOR DIAPERS
0-23	1.92	2.39	2.49
24-47	1.99	2.96	3.21
48-71	2.24	3.55	3.64
72-95	2.43	3.70	3.74
96-119	2.74	3.92	3.90
120+	2.92	3.69	3.70

Conclusions And Implications

The intent of this research was to provide preliminary insight into the children's wear market that can serve as a foundation for further investigation. It is apparent, based on the results presented in this paper, that the needs and wants of customers are not being fully met by apparel retailers or manufacturers.

In understanding the children's wear market, it is important to realize that the actual consumer of children's wear (which is typically not the purchaser) differs from the adult apparel consumer in a number of ways. The growth and development of children results in the need for a fairly rapidly changing inventory of clothes. Since new clothes are continuously needed as the child grows, the typical parent does not want to invest a lot of money in children's apparel, especially playwear. Consequently, parents may not buy the highest quality clothes even if they could "afford" them. Parents do, however, expect the clothes to hold up and perform well for the relatively short time period that a child wears them. If there is more than one child in the family, then they may also want other children to wear the clothes as well.

Regarding implications for apparel manufacturers and retailers, it appears that staining is a problem that it may be well to address. The economic feasibility and consumer acceptance of stain resistant finishes on children's garments is an opportunity that deserves exploration. Additionally, updating the sizing standards currently in use (and developed over 30 years age) needs to be given serious consideration. An increased emphasis on separates and growth features may help alleviate some problems related to disproportionate fit and growing out of a garment too fast. Additionally, improved designs for, and variety of, boys' wear may be an area of potential opportunity.

Within the store setting, the retailer who provides an increased selection of boys' wear (at all age levels) may find themselves at a competitive advantage in serving the needs of this market segment. It is an idea worth testing. In addition, as stores are built or redesigned, wider aisles in the infant/toddler area should be considered. This will mean a loss of selling space, but the trade-off may be that more customers will enter the area rather than bypassing it. As retailers make purchases from manufacturers, or develop their own private label merchandise, there are a number of factors worth considering. One is the need to keep the prices of play wear low. The clothes also need to be reasonably durable. A wide selection of mix and match separates may be one approach to satisfying a number of needs related to children's wear.

Although the results presented in this research are based on simple statistics, it is important to have a basic understanding of the children's wear consumer in terms of their needs and wants before proceeding with more sophisticated and indepth analyses. Future research that builds upon the work presented here will include: 1) an indepth analysis of store patronage and its determinants; 2) characteristics of respondents (and their children) who encounter various types of shopping and apparel problems; and 3) further exploration of the nature of specific problems such as fit and sizing. Clearly, there are many issues that are yet to be addressed; however, the information presented here does provide apparel marketers with some direction regarding issues they need to begin to consider in order to better serve the children's wear market.

Acknowledgement

Funding for this study was provided by Venture Stores and the Kellwood Company.

References

Blake, E., Glisson, O. & Tate, M.T. (1953). A study of the preschool child's clothing in 100 families of Radford, Virginia. Journal of Home Economics, 45(3), 179-186.

Carideo, Joseph (1985). Apparel manufacturers face extinction because of their failure to assume a marketing orientation, consultant says. Marketing News, 19(2), pp. 1,3.

Dillman, D. A. (1978). Mail and telephone surveys, the total design method. New York: John Wiley & Sons.

Earnstats: the 1992 retail survey (1992). Earnshaw's Infants', Boys' and Girls' Wear Review, June, pp. 49-57.

Engel, J.F., Blackwell, R.D. & Miniard, P.W. (1986). Consumer Behavior. New York: The Dryden Press.

Frankenback, M.F. (1970). The influence of socioeconomic factors, employment, income and residence upon clothing buying behavior of families with preschool children. Unpublished thesis, University of Missouri-Columbia

Joyce, M.C. (1966). A study of 236 families' purchase of children's clothing. Journal of Home Economics, 58(6), 445-447.

An Exploratory Analysis of Some Dynamic Effects of Advertising on Fresh Meat Demand

David B. Eastwood, The University of Tennessee[1]
Morgan D. Gray, The University of Tennessee[2]
John R. Brooker, The University of Tennessee[3]

Supermarket scan data are combined with newspaper and broadcast advertising to evaluate possible short-run and long-run effects. This is the first study to report on a dynamic analysis that uses a more appropriate time frame -- weekly data. Results indicate significant own-advertising effects for the newspaper and little electronic media impact on sales.

Although consumer economists have built an extensive literature of applied demand studies, little attention has been directed toward incorporating advertising and other merchandising strategies into the analyses. With respect to food, the economics of information, changing consumption patterns, and the effects of the generic promotions have led to some preliminary analyses of advertising impacts (e.g., Buse; Capps; Capps and Nayga; Eastwood, Gray, and Brooker; Jensen and Schroeter; and Kinnucan, Thompson, and Chang). These studies have been limited in several important ways. Cross media effects have been omitted and limited measures of advertising have been used. Until recently, most of the research has been static. However, dynamic investigations (Kinnucan, Venkateswaran, and Chang; Thompson and Eiler; Ward; Ward and Dixon) have been for time periods that may not be consistent with the consumer's time horizon for foods (e.g., months or quarters) and have not allowed for possible different media effects. This paper reports on a preliminary study that incorporated some dynamic features for weekly food purchases and distinguishes between electronic and newspaper advertising.

The outline of the paper is as follows. Initially, the data and measures are described. Descriptive statistics are then presented. Pairwise correlations that provide dynamic insights are discussed. Results of regression analyses are outlined, and the consumer implications are presented.

Data

Two related data sets were combined in the study. Scan data from five supermarkets located in a metropolitan area in the Southeast were the source of the weekly sales and price information. The other was an advertising data base that comprised the print and electronic media promotions corresponding to the scan data. Each is briefly described below.

The supermarkets were part of the same chain. Two stores were in higher income areas, two in more moderate income areas, and one was on a border between high and low income neighborhoods. Data were obtained for each store beginning Sunday and ending Saturday. Weeks ending May 14, 1988 through June 29, 1991 comprised the time period. Out of the 161 weeks, there were eight for which none of the stores reported scan data sales.

Computer software used by the chain to generate the by-store corporate-level data only recorded the number of times individual bar codes were read by the scanners, called item movement (IM). Meat managers in the stores indicated that the distributions of package sizes for the various cuts did not change very much from week to week. Given this situation, IM was used as a proxy for pounds sold. Three fresh beef groups were created. IMs for 14 bar codes of ground beef were aggregated into ground, 23 for roast, and 45 for steak.

IM was converted to a per thousand customer basis, which has been found to be appropriate for demand analyses (Capps; Capps and Nayga). This was to adjust for differences in the number of shoppers patronizing the outlets and in the number of reporting stores for a week. For each of the bar codes in the groups, the IMs for the reporting stores were added together, divided by the customer counts of these stores, multiplied by a thousand, and aggregated.

Weighted prices were generated when the stores appeared to have slightly different prices. The weights were the store's share of that week's total IM for the respective product. Demand group weighted price series were calculated. These

[1]Professor, Ag. Econ. & Rur. Soc.

[2]Computer Analyst, Ag.Econ. & Rur. Soc.

[3]Professor, Ag. Econ. & Rur. Soc.

weights were the ratios of each bar code's IM to that of the respective IM.

Electronic media advertising by product by the chain for the area was provided separately from the scan data. The measure was the gross rating points (GRP) for the individual foods and covered the seven day period corresponding to the scan data week. GRPs for fresh beef cuts were aggregated to conform with the ground, roast, and steak groups.

Newspaper advertising occurred primarily through weekly inserts, although ads appeared in the daily paper on an irregular basis. Three measures were used: size of the ad in square inches, page on which the ad appeared, and the use of a color. Usually the chain advertised more than one cut within each group, and this is reflected in the coding scheme shown in Table 1.

Table 1
Advertisement Coding System.

Media	Description
Radio and Television	Gross rating points for specific products for each type of commercial. If more than one product in a demand category was advertised, the sum was used.
Newspaper	
Page	Page on which a product appears. No ad=0; regular paper ad=1; Other supplement page=2; front, middle, or last supplement page=3; other plus front and/or middle supplement, regular paper plus supplement=4, front and middle of supplement=5.
Space	Sum of the square inches of advertised products by demand category.
Color	No ad=0, single black and white=1, single color=2, more than one black and white=3, more than one color=4, and combination of black and white and color ads=5.

Because of colinearities among these measures, an index was generated. The index's minimum value was 0, indicating no newspaper ads for any cuts within the respective aggregate for the respective week, while the maximum value of 24 indicated three or more ads with colors other than black and white were on the front and middle pages of the supplement and regular paper. The index was designed to reflect increasing visibility as well as cost of the ads. Table 2 outlines the index.

Descriptive Statistics

Ground beef had the largest weekly IM per thousand customers (Table 3). IM for steak was about 55 percent of that for ground, and roast IM

Table 2
Index of Newspaper Advertisements*

Page		Color	Code	Code	Index
Page Color					
No ad		None	0	0	0
Paper only		B&W	1	1	1
		C	1	3	2
			5	3	
Other supplement page only					
		B&W	2	1	4
			3	5	
		C	2	2	6
			4	7	
			5	8	
Front, middle, last page only of supplement					
		B&W	3	1	9
			3	10	
		C	2	11	
			4	12	
			5	13	
Front, middle, last page only plus an other supplement page					
		B&W	4	1	14
			3	15	
		C	2	16	
			4	17	
			5	18	
Front plus middle of supplement					
		B&W	5	1	19
			3	20	
		C	2	21	
			4	22	
			5	23	
Holiday		C	6	24	

*See Table 1 for an explanation of codes.

was approximately 19 percent of ground IM. The coefficients of variation showed that roast IM was relatively more volatile than either ground or steak. Average prices for the three products reflected the expected differences in price levels. Price coefficients of variation were comparable and relatively low. The average values of the advertising index showed that ground was promoted at a higher level than roast or steak. GRPs also revealed a higher level of ground advertising vis-a-vis roast and steak. For all advertising variables, it appeared that ground beef promotions were more frequent and less variable than promotions for roast and steak.

Graphs of the three IM and price series are shown in Figures 1-3. No explicit vertical scales are provided due to the proprietary nature sales. For the first six months IMs were relatively low, especially for ground beef. Inspections of the graphs suggested there was no consistent monthly pattern. However, there was a

Figure 1. Ground Item Movement and Price

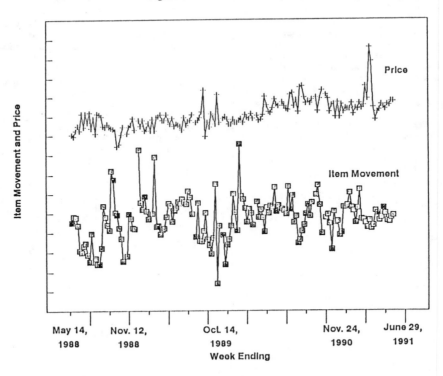

Figure 2. Roast Item Movement and Price

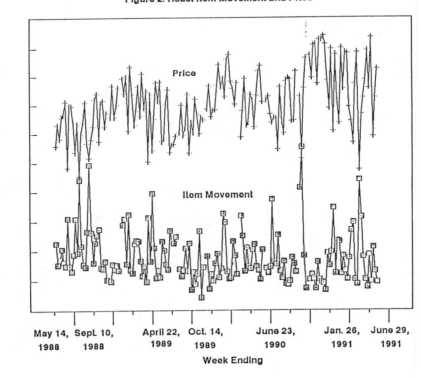

Figure 3. Steak Item Movement and Price

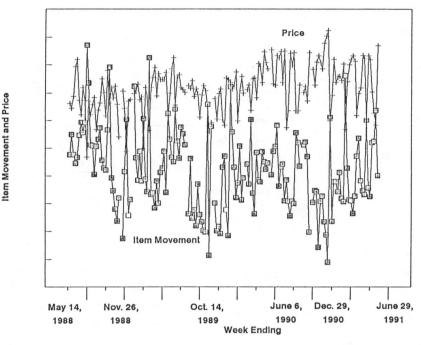

Table 3
Descriptive Statistics.

Variable	Mean	Min	Max	Std. Dev.	C. Var.
IM					
Ground	94.36	24.88	171.12	21.83	.23
Roast	18.00	4.31	55.35	8.76	.48
Steak	51.67	18.98	97.09	14.50	.28
Price					
Ground	2.07	1.69	4.19	.31	.15
Roast	2.35	1.51	3.13	.36	.15
Steak	4.09	2.84	5.12	.42	.10
ADINDEX					
Ground	10.75	0.00	24.00	5.08	.47
Roast	8.28	0.00	23.00	6.59	.80
Steak	9.18	0.00	23.00	7.52	.82
GRP					
Ground	121.12	0.00	1000.00	183.17	1.51
Roast	51.24	0.00	750.00	134.16	2.62
Steak	30.75	0.00	759.00	103.99	3.38

tendency for some months to be better or worse than others. For example, steak seemed to do relatively better in the second quarter versus the of the data. Thanksgiving was a period of low fourth. The patterns also suggested stock adjustment behavior. Ground and roast prices trended upward, whereas the aggregate steak prices had no trend. All three figures suggested negative own-price IM relationships.

Pairwise correlations are shown in Table 4. Positive IM correlations suggest there were tendencies to purchase the groups together, and these were greater for ground and steak. Own-price and IM correlations were negative, with the strongest inverse patterns for roast, followed by steak. There was little tendency for ground IM and price to move in a linear fashion. Cross-IM and price correlations were fairly low, suggesting little tradeoff.

The advertising correlations are interesting. Own ADINDEX and GRP correlations with IM suggest positive effects of the advertising, although the steak GRP-IM value is very small. Cross-group effects are also close to zero with the exception of ground ADINDEX and steak IM. Notice that the own-ADINDEX and GRP correlations with price for ground and steak are not negative, whereas those for roast are. An interpretation is that the chain advertises specific cuts and may lower these prices and at the same time raise the prices of other cuts in the same aggregate. Both the ADINDEX and GRP correlations indicate independence across the beef groups and little coordination across the two media for the same group.

Table 5 presents the simple correlations between IMs and the respective lagged GRP series. Ground has the expected pattern of positive and declining correlations as the lag increases. Roast and steak correlations are negative beyond the current period. This suggests there may be a slight tendency to purchase during the week of the broadcast and then not purchase subsequently. The

Table 4
Pairwise Correlations

IM	Item Movement			Price			Index			GRP		
	G	R	S	G	R	S	G	R	S	G	R	S
Ground	1.00											
Roast	.37	1.00										
Steak	.46	.36	1.00									
Price												
Ground	-.03	-.18	-.20	1.00								
Roast	.13	-.62	-.18	.28	1.00							
Steak	.19	-.01	.-46	.30	.29	1.00						
Index												
Ground	.15	.08	.25	.07	-.13	-.10	1.00					
Roast	-.07	.52	.00	-.06	-.54	-.11	.03	1.00				
Steak	-.09	-.05	.50	-.08	-.11	.49	.19	.00	1.00			
GRP												
Ground	.11	-.16	-.03	.22	.12	.12	.34	-.20	.02	1.00		
Roast	.02	.43	.07	-.05	-.36	-.04	.00	.22	.11	-.14	1.00	
Steak	.06	-.12	.04	.01	.13	-.04	.01	-.04	.09	-.05	-.06	1.00

Table 5
Item Movement and Lagged GPR Correlations: Ground,
Roast, and Steak.

	Item Movement		
Lagged GRPi	Ground	Roast	Steak
Current	.11	.43	.04
One Week	.13	-.04	-.14
Two Weeks	.10	-.15	-.12
Three Weeks	.03	-.02	-.14
Four Weeks	.08	-.07	.12
Five Weeks	.03	-.03	-.07

current period roast IM and GRP correlation is much higher than for the other two. This is initial evidence that the broadcast media does not have a uniform impact on sales across food categories.

A Meat Demand Model

The approach taken in this exploratory study was to follow the conventional practice of assuming that fresh beef is separable from other goods. Over the time period for which data are available, there was little change in consumer income, so this variable could be eliminated from the demand relationships. The nature of the fresh beef industry is such that there are no branded products, processor promotional campaigns, or coupons. Implicit in the use of chain level regressions is the assumption that food shoppers are store loyal. This is supported by an industry study that found nearly three-fourths of the customers do not compare prices across stores (Cox and Foster) and by Funk, Meilke, and Huff who found that competitors' meat prices were highly colinear.

Based on the framework developed by Holdren and modified by Capps and Nayga, the following analytical model was developed. The quantity demand is expressed as a linear function of a price vector and a vector of nonprice variables that affect demand, shown as equation (1).

$$IM_{i,t} = f(P_t, ADINDEX_{i,t}, GRP_{i,t}, TG, QT, IM_{i,t-j}).   (1)$$

where:

IM = item movement.
P = vector of weighted average prices.
ADINDEX = vector of newspaper advertising indices.
GRP = vector of gross rating points.
TG = dummy variable for Thanksgiving.
QT = vector of dummy variables for quarters.
i = fresh beef aggregate subscript (i=ground, roast, steak).
t = week subscript.
j = lag subscript (j=0,...,5).

Viewed from the consumer's perspective, there is quite a difference between newspaper and electronic media food advertising. The former is considered to be a high involvement way of reaching shoppers, and the supplements and regular paper ads tend to focus on price information that pertains to the respective week. The latter is a lower involvement approach that focuses more on building store image (e.g., Rotschild). These observations indicate that there is no lag structure associated with newspaper advertising, although one may be present for the broadcast media. However, Table 5 suggests that, although electronic advertising may increase customer counts, it does not affect item movement per thousand customers.

Based on the preliminary analyses of the data, a dummy variable for Thanksgiving was included to account for this holiday when fresh beef sales are typically low. Dummy variables for quarters were also included to account for seasonal factors associated with each cut. Initial regressions led to the incorporation of the third quarter in all three equations and the second quarter in the steak regression.

Several regressions were estimated that incorporated alternative lag structures and measures of electronic advertising. These alternatives focused on one to five week lags based on the patterns of weekly IMs. Another formulation included the sum of the GRPs for each week to allow for the possibility that the electronic media's store image was more important than the message for the separate groups. A dummy variable was also created to denote the presence/absence of the broadcast media. Alternative distributed lag structures were estimated with IM being lagged from one to five weeks. Autocorrelation was present in the roast regressions. The remedy was to include a binary variable for the unusually high (H) and low (L) IM weeks. There were six instances where H=1 and one where L=1. This was justified by the unique roast IM series vis-a-vis the other two groups. There were no pronounced troughs for roast comparable to those for ground and steak. In addition, the roast IM series had a much higher coefficient of variation. These observations suggested that the OLS algorithm adjusted to the six high peaks and single low week, leading to autocorrelation. Table 6 presents the estimated equations that provided the best overall fits for each fresh beef aggregate.

Given the dynamic structure, the coefficients should be interpreted as measures of short-run effects. In all three cases the overall F statistics are significant. The R^2s are reasonably high in light of the relatively high variability present in each series. Due to the presence of the lagged dependent variable, Durbin's h statistic is used, and the inference to be drawn is that autocorrelation is not present in any equation.

Each own-price coefficient is significant and has the expected sign. Only steak had a significant cross-price coefficient, and it was positive in the roast equation. This leads to the inference that as the price of steak rose, food shoppers increased their purchases of roast. An interpretation is that consumers may have had target amounts of fresh beef aggregates they

Table 6
IM per Thousand Customers Regression Results: Ground, Roast, and Steak (t values in parentheses) and [long-run coefficients in brackets].

Variable	Ground	Roast	Steak
Intercept	92.887* (3.12)	38.681* (5.13)	105.600* (5.63)
Price			
Ground	-23.076* (-1.90) [-32.283]	-2.431 (-0.77)	-11.919 (-1.64)
Roast	.573 (.09)	-11.341* (-6.96) [-12.883]	.916 (.26)
Steak	4.841 (1.01)	2.088* (1.69) [2.372]	-11.551* (-3.79) [-13.619]
AD INDEX			
Ground	.645* (1.92) [.902]	.030 (.34)	.429* (2.10) [.507]
Roast	-.392 (-1.37)	.119 (1.62)	-.216 (-1.28)
Steak	-.167 (-.64)	-.044 (-.65)	.434* (2.64) [.512]
GRP			
Ground	.006 (.62)	-.004* (-1.81) [-.005]	-.006 (-.96)
Roast	.013 (1.07)	.007* (2.21) [.008]	.004 (.53)
Steak	.004 (.29)	-.003 (-1.00)	-.004 (-.46)
TG	-20.363* (-2.52)	-5.778* (-2.84)	-11.338* (-2.33)
QT			
2			5.871* (2.56)
3	-11.192* (-2.73)	-3.519* (-3.50)	.152* (2.56)
H		17.287* (6.97)	
L		-13.793* (-2.83)	
$IM_{i,t-1}$	.285* (3.71)	.108* (1.98)	.152* (2.28)
F	5.34*	18.24*	9.22*
R^2	.33	.62	.46
Durbin's h	.25**	1.73**	1.27**

* Significant at the .10 level.
** Not significant at the .05 level.

wanted to purchase with fixed food budgets. Insignificant cross-price coefficients were consistent with the results of Capps and Nayga; Funk Meilke and Huff; Marion and Walker.

Own newspaper advertising was positive and significant for ground and steak. The larger marginal effect was for ground, followed by steak. The only significant cross-advertising effect was for ground advertising on steak where increased ground advertising led to increased steak IM. Insignificant cross effects in the other instances led to inferences that these promotions did not affect sales beyond their own groups. A similar pattern was found by Capps and Nayga.

The only significant GRP impacts were in the roast equation. Food shoppers responded positively to the roast advertising via the electronic media, but broadcast media ground advertising decreased roast IM. The result is consistent with the correlation patterns in Table 4. This supports the arguments that broadcast promotions are really directed toward presenting different information to consumers than newspaper promotions and that the effects also differ by food group.

With respect to the dummy variables, the following coefficients were significant. TG is associated with significantly lower IMs, with the largest decline for ground followed by steak and then roast. The third quarter has lower ground and roast IMs, while steak IM is considerably higher in the spring and somewhat higher in the summer. The latter is consistent with consumers purchasing more during the return of warmer weather for grilling. Lower sales of ground and roast in the third quarter could reflect a switch to other foods that require less cooking.

IM lagged one period is significant in each equation. The magnitudes of the coefficients reflect a declining geometric lag structure. Table 6 presents the long-run estimated coefficients for the significant variables in brackets. In all instances these impacts are larger than those for the short run, reflecting the additional time consumers have to make adjustments.

Elasticities were estimated for the significant price, ADINDEX and GRP short-run and long-run coefficients (Table 7). Roast was most elastic, that for steak was nearly unitary, and that for ground was inelastic. This suggests that food shopperes were most responsive to changes in the own-price of roast and least responsive to the own-price of ground. An interpretation is that ground may be considered in terms of a more staple fresh beef aggregate and that food shoppers were much more willing to change their roast purchases vis-a-vis steak then ground. The advertising elasticities are all quite small. Due to the indexing scheme, the values themselves should not be given much consideration. However, their relative values suggest that consumers were about as responsive to ground as to steak paper ads on a percentage basis. The GRP elasticities indicate that promoting fresh beef via the broadcast media does not bring about large percentage increases in IM per 1,000 customers and suggest there are tradeoffs.

Consumer Implications

This preliminary analysis provides some useful insights regarding consumer demand for fresh beef and chain level advertising. It is the first study that explicitly examines dynamic own- and cross-advertising effects for the newspaper

Table 7
Price, ADINDEX, and GRP Estimated Elasticities[a].

	Elasticity		
	Ground	Round	Steak
Price			
Ground	-.506 [-.708]		
Roast		-1.481 [-1.682]	
Steak		.474 [.539]	-.914 [-1.078]
ADINDEX			
Ground	.075 [.105]		.091 [.108]
Roast			.077 [.099]
GRP			
Ground		-.027 [-.034]	
Roast		.020 [.023]	
Steak			

[a]Evaluated at the sample means. Based on significant coefficients in Table 6.

and broadcast media. The results also are based on weekly scan data which are more consistent with consumer planning horizons and the advertising information.

Significant, positive own-newspaper advertising effects indicate that consumers have responded positively to fresh beef promotions through this medium. Insignificant cross-group paper effects imply that food shoppers are cut-loyal. That is, they use the paper ad information for decision making with respect to the groups but a paper ad for one cut does not affect the others. This suggests that the paper promotions affect the timing of purchases but not the type of fresh beef to buy. Electronic media effects are much more limited. Food shoppers do not seem to use the information contained in the electronic medium product promotions for ground and steak, but there is a small positive own impact on roasts. An interpretation is that the broadcast media are used by supermarkets to build store image and to keep the chain visible. To the extent that this is a successful strategy, more customers may result, but there is no (or little) increase in the purchases of fresh beef on a per customer basis.

An overall implication is that newspaper advertising is used by food shoppers in their decision making for specific products. To the extent that such information can be used by food shoppers prior to entering the supermarket, this form of advertising is relevant and enhances the efficiency of food retailing for at home consumption. The electronic media expenditures, on the other hand, are less useful to food shoppers, although they may impact store choice.

References

Buse, R. C.(1989). The Economics of Meat Demand. Madison, WI: The University of Wisconsin Press.

Capps, O. C., Jr. (1989). Utilizing Scanner Data to Estimate Retail Demand Functions. American Journal of Agricultural Economics. 71,750-760.

Capps, O. C., Jr., & Nayga,R., Jr. (1991). Leanness and Convenience Dimensions of Beef Products: An Exploratory Analysis Using Scanner Data. Bull. No. 1693, The Texas Agricultural Experiment Station, Texas A & M University System, College Station, TX.

Chavas, J.P.(1983). Structural Change in the Demand for Meat. Joural of Agricultural Economics. 65, 148-53.

Cox, C., & Foster, R.(1985). What's Ahead for the U. S. Food Processing Industry? Discussion. American Journal of Agricultural Economics, 67, 155-7.

Dahlgran, R.(1987). The Changing Structure of U. S. Meat Demand: Implications for Meat Price Forecasting. Proceedings of the NCR-134 Conference on Applied Commodity Price Analysis, Forecasting, and Market Risk Management, St. Louis, MO, pp. 22-3.

Eales, J., & Unnevehr,L. (1988). Demand for Beef and Chicken Products: Separability and Structural Change. American Journal of Agricultural Economics. 70, 522-32.

Eastwood, D. B., Gray,M.D., & Brooker, J.R. (1992). A Case Study of Promoting Fresh Beef Through In-store Demonstrations. Journal of Food Distrib. Res. 23(2), 23-31.

Funk,T. F., Weilke,K.D., & Huff, H.B.(1977). Effects of Retail Pricing and Advertising on Fresh Beef Sales. American Journal of Agricultural Economics. 59, 533-37.

Holdren, B. R.(1960). The Structure of a Retail Market and the Market Behavior of Retail Units. Prentice-Hall, Inc.

Hudson, M. A., & Vertin,J.P. (1985). Income Elasticities for Beef, Pork, and Poultry: Changes and Implications. Journal of Food Distrib. Res. 16(2), 25-32.

Jensen, H. H., & Schroeter, J.R.(1989). Estimating Retail Beef Demand Using Household Panel Scanner Data. Paper presented at the Annual Meeting of the American Agricultural Economics Association.

Kinnucan, H., Thompson, S., & Chang, H.S.(1992). Commodity Advertising and Promotion. Iowa State University Press.

Marion, B. W., & Walker, F.E. (1978). Short-Run Predictive Models for Retail Meat Sales. American Journal of Agricultural Economics. 60, 667-73.

Moschini, G., & Meilke,K.D. (1984). The U. S. Demand for Beef - Has There Been a Structural Change? Western Journal of Agricultural Economics. 9, 271-82.

Rotschild, M. (1987). Advertising. D. C. Heath & Co.

Thompson, S. R., & Eiler, D.A.(1975). Producer Returns from Increased Milk Advertising. American Journal of Agricultural Economics. 57, 505-8.

Venkateswaran, M., Kinnucan, H., & Chang, H.S. (1992). Performance of Shiller Lags in Modeling Advertising Carryover: Evidence for Fluid Milk. Paper presented at the Annual Meetings of the American Agricultural Economics Association.

Ward, R. W.(1992). The Beef Checkoff: Its Economic Impact and Producer Benefits. Institute of Food and Agricultural Sciences, University of Florida and the Beef Promotion and Research Board, National Cattlemen's Association.

Ward, R. W., & Dixon, B.L. (1989). Effectiveness of Milk Advertising Since the Dairy and Tobacco Adjustment Act of 1983. American Journal of Agricultural Economics. 71, 730-40.

Anaylsis of Leisure Expenditures
in the United States

Rachel Dardis, University of Maryland[1]
Horacio Soberon-Ferrer, University of Maryland[2]
Dilip Patro, University of Maryland[3]

The objective of this research was to investigate the impact of household socio-economic characteristics on three categories of leisure expenditures. Tobit analysis was applied to data from the U.S. 1988-89 Consumer Expenditure Surveys. The dependent variables were household expenditures on active leisure, passive leisure and social entertainment. The results indicated that salary of household head and non-salary income were the two major income variables while the number of adults and age, race and education of the household head were the major demographic variables.

Introduction

In the past few decades the United States has undergone significant social and economic changes. These include increased participation by married women in the labor force, greater interest in physical fitness and changes in the composition of the population. These economic and social changes have affected leisure and non-leisure aspects of life. Time use studies indicate that from 1960s to 1980s there has been an increase in time spent on leisure activities, particularly by younger people (Robinson, 1985; Hill, 1985; Juster, 1985a; Juster, 1985b; Stafford and Duncan, 1985). However, information on expenditures on leisure activities is limited.

This research was undertaken to investigate the determinants of leisure expenditures by households in the United States. Three leisure categories were investigated. They were active leisure, passive leisure and social entertainment. These three categories were chosen based on previous time use studies. Quarterly data from the 1988-89 Bureau of Labor Statistics' Consumer Expenditure Study were used and resulted in a sample size of 2,088 households. The sample was confined to households for which information was available for four consecutive quarters.

The research differs from previous leisure expenditures in several ways. First, three categories of leisure activities are examined. Second, consideration is given to the source of income in examining the impact of income on the demand for leisure. Finally, tobit analysis is used since some households have zero expenditures in a particular category. The results of this research should be of use to consumer economists and to leisure activities industries by providing information on the impact of economic and demographic conditions on the demand for three types of leisure activities.

Leisure Activity Studies

There have been only a few studies on the demand for leisure activities.

White (1975) used multiple regression analysis to analyze participation in outdoor recreation activities by 2,969 households. The dependent variable was the number of times an individual reported participating in an activity. The independent variables were occupation, income, family size, age and city size. Occupation turned out to be a weak predictor of participation in outdoor recreation activities. The main predictors were income and education.

Thompson and Tinsley (1978) used time series data from 1955 to 1975. The dependent variable was per capita recreation expenditures and included expenditures on vacations, club dues, sporting equipment and tickets to sporting events and movies. The independent variable was per capita take home pay. There were five income classes and each income group was analyzed separately using OLS analysis. Expenditures on recreation were significantly and positively related to income in all instances and income elasticities were greater than one in most instances.

Dardis, Derrick, Lehfeld and Wolfe (1981) analyzed data from the 1972-73 BLS Consumer Expenditure Surveys to determine factors influencing recreation expenditures in the United States. Separate analyses were performed for 1972 and 1973 using OLS analysis. The dependent variable was expenditures on total recreation and included expenditures on vacation homes, boats, wheel goods, lodging and transportation, television and other recreational items. The independent

---

[1]Professor

[2]Assistant Professor

[3]Graduate Student

variables were household income; age, marital status, race, occupation and education of household head; presence of children under six, location, and employment status of wife. Similar results were obtained for both years. Recreation expenditures were influenced positively by income and education and negatively influenced by age of household head.

Procedure

The first section gives the demand model while the second and third sections provide information on the dependent and independent variables. Tobit analysis and data sources are discussed in the last two sections.

Model

A single equation model is used to estimate the relationship between leisure expenditures, household income and other household characteristics.

$$E_i = \alpha + \sum_k \beta_k Y_{ik} + \sum_j \gamma_j X_{ij} + U_i \qquad (1)$$

where

E_i = expenditures on a particular type of leisure by household i

Y_{ik} = income of household i from source k, k=1,...,4

X_{ij} = other demographic characteristics of household i, and

u_i = the disturbance term

The value of the dependent variable was zero in some instances necessitating the use of tobit analysis.

Selection of Dependent Variables
The dependent variables were expenditures on active leisure, passive leisure and social entertainment. The categories were identified as major categories of leisure time use by Hill (1985), Stafford and Duncan (1985) and Juster (1985b). Each category is discussed below.

Active leisure. This includes a wide range of activities needing some physical effort. Activities range from jogging and cycling, which are primarily physical, to other activities such as fishing, and photography.

Passive leisure. This category involves recreational activities which do not demand active participation on the part of the individual. Television watching is a dominant form of passive leisure. Other forms include the use of radios, VCRs, and other sound equipment.

Social entertainment. This category includes attendance at spectator activities such as sports events as well as going to theaters and museums. It differs from active leisure in that the individual is a spectator rather than a participant.

Selection of Independent Variables
The independent variables were income, family life cycle variables, education and race of household head and household location. The family life cycle variables were age and marital status of household head, the number of adults and the number of children. Each of the variables is discussed below.

Income. There were four income variables based on income. They were income of the head of the household, income of the spouse, income of other household members, and non-salary income. It was hypothesized that income would have a positive impact on all the three types of leisure expenditures based on previous studies by Thompson and Tinsley (1978) and Dardis et al. (1981).

Age of household head. Six age categories were used. They were below 25, 25-34, 35-44, 45-54, 55-64 and above 64. Dummy variables were used for the age variable and the 35-44 age group was the omitted category. It was hypothesized that age would have a positive impact on expenditures involving passive leisure activities but a negative impact on expenditures involving active leisure and social entertainment activities. Rapoport and Rapoport (1975) cite family life cycle as a major determinant of leisure spending behavior.

Marital status of household head. There were two categories, married and not married. The later category included widowed, divorced, separated or never married individuals.

Number of children. All individuals below sixteen years of age were classified as children. It was hypothesized that the number of children would have a negative impact on leisure expenditures.

Number of adults. This variable was hypothesized to have a positive impact on all three types of leisure expenditures since it was expected to increase the demand for leisure activities.

Education of household head. Three categories were used for education. They were not a high school graduate, high school graduate, and beyond high school. The high school graduate category was the omitted category. It was hypothesized that education would have a positive impact on all the three categories of leisure expenditures based on studies by Dardis et al. (1981) and Juster (1985a).

Race and sex of household head. Three race categories were included in this study to account for possible differences in expenditures due to racial differences. The categories were white, black and others (Asian, Pacific Islander, Aleut, and Eskimos). The white category was the omitted category. It was hypothesized that white households would spend more on leisure activities than the other two groups of households. It was also hypothesized that male headed households would spend more on all the three types of leisure activities than female headed households due to the different time constraints faced by the two household heads (Becker 1981).

Location. Five regions were included in the analysis; one was rural and four were urban. Four dummy variables were used and the urban midwest was the omitted category. It was hypothesized that rural households would spend less than urban households based on the study by Dardis et al. (1981).

Data Source

Consumer Expenditure Survey (CES) data for 1988-89 were used in this study. These data were obtained from the Bureau of Labor Statistics (BLS), U. S. Department of Labor. Consumer units are interviewed once each quarter for five consecutive quarters. Expenditure information is collected in the second through fifth interviews. Every quarter one fifth of the sample is dropped and replaced by a new group in order to improve efficiency. In this study, only those households for which information was available for four consecutive quarters were selected for analysis in order to allow for purchases of durable goods such as TV sets and sports equipment.

Tobit Analysis

The proportion of households with no leisure expenditures ranged from 30 percent for active leisure to 53 percent for passive leisure. Thus, a censored sample was involved (we had complete information on the independent variables but zero observations on the dependent variables in some instances). Tobit analysis is appropriate if there are no systematic differences between participants and non-participants (Kinsey 1984). This possibility was investigated using two stage probit analysis and the results indicated that there was no selection bias, i.e. no difference between the two groups (Heckman 1976).

The general Tobit model is defined as

$$Y_i = Y_i^*, \quad \text{if } Y_i^* > 0$$
$$Y_i = 0 \quad \text{otherwise} \quad \quad (2)$$

The resulting sample $Y_1, Y_2, \ldots, Y_N$ is called a censored sample. For the observations $Y_i = 0$, all we know is that $Y_i^* \leq 0$; so the probability that $Y_i = 0$ is the probability that $Y_i^* \leq 0$. Iterative methods, using the Lindep softwear package, were used to obtain the maximum likelihood estimates of β and σ^2.

The significance of the model was tested using the following statistical test. Chi-square= -2 [log likelihood$_R$ - log likelihood$_U$] where the restricted model(R) only included the constant and the unrestricted model (U) included all variables. This statistic has a chi-square distribution with k degrees of freedom where k is equal to the number of independent variable minus the constant. The likelihood ratio statistic was computed from the log likelihood values obtained from the tobit analysis. Asymptotic t-test were used to test the significance of individual variables (Maddala 1987).

Results

Sample characteristics are described first followed by the results of the tobit analysis for the three leisure expenditure categories.

Sample Characteristics

There were a total of 2,088 households in the sample, of which 1,466 participated in active leisure activities, 982 in passive leisure activities and 1,106 in social entertainment activities. Table 1 presents the distribution of households by income source for the three leisure categories.

Table 2 presents the mean values and distributions of independent variables describing households with three types of leisure expenditures. While non-salary income is similar for the three groups there are differences with respect to the other income sources.

The distribution of the three groups of households is similar in terms of age, marital status, number of adults, number of children and sex. However, there are differences in terms of education, race and location.

Tobit Analysis

The results of the analysis for the three leisure expenditure categories are given in Table 3. The model was significant in all instances as indicated by the likelihood ratio statistics. The effects of the independent variables were similar in many instances and are discussed below.

Income. Income had a significant and positive impact in seven out of twelve instances. These results are in agreement with previous leisure demand studies by White (1975), Thompson and Tinsley (1978), and Dardis et al. (1981), and with time use studies by Stafford and Duncan (1985) and Juster (1985a). The salary of household head was significant for passive leisure and social entertainment while it was not significant for active leisure. However, it was significant in the probit analysis. In contrast, the salary of spouse and salary of other members in the household were only significant for active leisure. This implies that

Table 1. Percentage of Households Receiving Income from Different Sources[a]

Income Source	Leisure Category		
	Active Leisure (n=1,466)	Passive Leisure (n=982)	Social Entertainment (n=1,106)
Salary of Household Head	65%	66%	69%
Salary of Spouse	39%	40%	41%
Salary of Others	19%	19%	20%
Non-Salary Income	90%	88%	93%

[a]Percentages add to more than 100 due to multiple income sources.

Table 2. Mean Values and Distribution of Independent Variables Describing Households with Three Types of Leisure Expenditures.

Variable	Active (1,466)	Passive (982)	Social Entertainment (1,106)
Income			
Salary of head	$17,574.40	$18,435.29	$10,983.70
Salary of spouse	$6,745.66	$6,555.48	$4,328.41
Salary of others	$2,076.79	$2,045.00	$1,515.72
Non-salary income	$7,906.65	$7,963.57	$7,284.38
Family Life Cycle			
Age			
0-24	3.75%	3.76%	3.79%
25-34	24.48%	24.94%	24.91%
35-44	28.03%	27.69%	28.10%
45-54	17.94%	17.51%	17.75%
55-64	13.36%	14.05%	13.70%
above 64	12.41%	12.01%	11.72%
Married	66.91%	68.12%	67.84%
Not married	33.09%	31.88%	32.16%
Number of adults	2.15	2.16	2.00
Number of children	0.72	0.68	0.59
Education			
Not a high school graduate	14.18%	13.44%	33.09%
High school graduate	33.22%	34.11%	30.56%
Beyond high school	52.50%	52.44%	36.34%
Race			
White	89.90%	90.90%	84.72%
Black	6.90%	5.90%	12.65%
Others	3.00%	3.15%	2.62%
Sex			
Male	71.69%	74.23	73.44%
Female	28.31%	25.77%	26.56%
Location			
Rural	10.02%	9.98%	12.74%
Urban Northwest	20.53%	20.87%	21.51%
Urban Midwest	26.46%	27.18%	22.87%
Urban South	23.67%	23.42%	24.05%
Urban West	19.30%	18.53%	18.80%

Table 3. Results of Tobit Analysis

Variable (Reference Group in Parenthesis)	Coefficients		
	Active	Passive	Social Entertainment
Constant	19.558	-262.650**	-200.130**
Income			
Salary of head	0.185E-02	0.295E-02**	0.421E-02**
Salary of spouse	0.442E-02**	-0.105E-02	0.113E-02
Salary of others	0.760E-02**	0.368E-02	0.224E-02
Non-salary income	0.644E-02**	0.388E-02**	0.752E-02**
Family Life Cycle			
Age (35-44)			
0-24	136.760	177.070	44.613
25-34	56.152	65.217	-2.101
45-54	-116.420	-77.151	-36.694
55-64	-313.450**	-117.220	-96.349**
Above 64	-485.200**	-330.490**	-198.240**
Married (not married)	-43.221	79.630	-19.430
Number of adults	66.209**	58.171*	37.042**
Number of children	-24.877	-47.681*	-14.554
Education			
(High school graduate)			
Not a high school graduate	-296.100**	-332.050**	-178.170**
Beyond high school	121.610**	41.527	76.808**
Race (white)			
Black	-223.660**	-297.090**	-145.460**
Others	-86.296	20.880	-14.250
Sex (female)			
Male	125.940**	80.505	90.360**
Location (urban midwest)			
Rural	99.260	-166.570**	-62.121
Urban northeast	-39.990	-104.880	-35.712
Urban south	-10.814	-66.256	-48.362
Urban west	-57.517	-196.180**	-52.455
Likelihood ratio	252.74**	180.74**	344.44**

*Significant at 0.10 level.
**Significant at 0.05 level.

Table 4. Income Elasticities for Three Types of Leisure Expenditures

Income Source	Active Leisure (1466)	Passive Leisure (982)	Social Entertainment (1106)
Salary of household head	n.s.	1.11	1.71
Salary of spouse	0.26	n.s.	n.s.
Salary of others	0.14	n.s.	n.s.
Non-salary income	0.40	0.59	0.72

n.s.: Variable not significant.

income of spouse and other household members play a role in determining expenditures on active leisure activities. Non-salary income had a significant and positive impact on all three types of leisure expenditures. This result is in agreement with the household production model (Becker 1965).

Age of household head. In general, older households spent less than younger households. This is in agreement with studies by Dardis et al. (1981) and Hill (1985). The study by Hill reported that the time spent on active leisure and social entertainment declined after the age of 44. There are several reasons for this result. First, older households are less likely to participate in active or social entertainment activities than other households. Second, older households are more likely to have inventories of durable goods such as sports equipment and TV sets which are included in active and passive leisure expenditures. Thus, they are less likely to purchase such items. Finally, older households may pay lower prices due to discounts for senior citizens.

Family size. The number of adults in the household had a significant and positive impact in all three instances. This reflects the fact that we are analyzing household expenditures rather than per capita expenditures. Thus, the number of adults should increase the demand for household leisure activities and hence expenditures. In contrast, the number of children was only significant for passive leisure where its impact was negative. A similar result was obtained by Juster (1985a) for children under five.

Education of household head. This variable had a significant and positive impact in all instances and is in agreement with previous research by White (1975), Dardis et al. (1981), and Juster (1985a). On explanation for the positive effect of education is that the knowledge and skills acquired in the process of education are likely to increase the range of potential leisure activities in all areas. Justin (1985a) also argued that leisure activities might be considered as a type of investment. More educated individuals tend to have a longer time horizon and be more aware of future needs. Investments in active leisure are linked to improvements in the state of one's physical health while investments in passive leisure are linked to the acquisition of knowledge and the development of skills that will yield future benefits.

Race and sex of household head. Households with a black head spent less than other households in all instances. This result is also in agreement with that of Dardis et al. (1981) and may reflect cultural differences and/or racial barriers. Households with a male head spent more on active leisure and social entertainment than households with a female head. In addition, households with a male head were more likely to participate in all three types of leisure activities (probit analysis). This may be due to several factors

including the different time constraints faced by the two households. A female head is likely to have both work and household responsibilities and hence less time for leisure activities (Becker 1981).

Location. Location was significant in only two instances where rural and western households spent less than other households for passive leisure. Similar results were obtained by Dardis et al. (1981).

Income Elasticities

Income elasticities were calculated for all sources of income whose coefficients were significant. The results are presented in Table 4. The elasticities range from 0.14 to 1.71. The highest elasticity values were obtained for salary of household head. They were 1.11 and 1.71 for passive leisure and social entertainment respectively.

In contrast, the elasticities with respect to salary of spouse and salary of others were either low (0.26 and 0.14) or insignificant. Thus, expenditures on the three leisure categories are not very responsive to changes in these income sources. The elasticities with respect to non-salary income ranged from 0.40 to 0.72.

Summary

Tobit analysis was used to examine the impact of income and household characteristics on expenditures on three leisure categories - active leisure, passive leisure and social entertainment. There were some differences in the impact of the independent variables on the three leisure categories suggesting that it was appropriate to examine each category separately. In particular, the effects of three income sources (salary of household head, salary of spouse and salary of others) varied according to leisure expenditure category. In general, the results for the four income variables indicated that leisure expenditures are sensitive to economic conditions. The salary of household head and non-salary income were the two major income variables based on the proportion of households with income from this source and average income by source. These two income variables also had the greatest impact on expenditures as measured by the income elasticities.

Age was another major variable and older households spent less on leisure activities than younger households, particularly for active leisure and social entertainment. Female headed households also spent less than male headed households. Thus, an increase in the proportion of older households or in the proportion of female headed households will reduce the demand for leisure activities. These two negative effects might be offset by rising levels of education since education had a positive impact in all instances.

The results of this study should be of interest to organizers of various sports activities, owners of movie theaters and other leisure facilities and manufacturers of recreation equipment and home entertainment equipment. Further research in this area might examine the demand for more specific leisure categories and/or demand by different population groups. The percentage of older people in the U.S. population is increasing and this is likely to have long term consequences on the demand for leisure. Therefore, it might be interesting to examine the demand for different leisure activities by older households.

References

Becker, G. (1965). A Theory of the Allocation of Time. The Economic Journal. 75, 493-517.

Becker, G. (1981). Division of Labor in House holds and Families. In G. Becker, A Treatise on the Family. Cambridge, MA: Harvard University Press, 14-37.

Dardis, R., Derrick, F., Lehfeld, A. & Wolfe, E. K. (1981). Cross-Section Studies of Recreation Expenditures in the United States. Journal of Leisure Research. 13 (3), 181-194.

Heckman, J. (1976). The Common Structure of Statistical Models of Truncation, Sample Selection and Limited Dependent Variables and a Simple Estimator for Such Models. Annals of Economic and Social Measurement. 5(4), 474-492.

Hill, M. S. (1985). Patterns of Time Use. In F. T. Juster & F. P. Stafford (Eds.), Time, Goods and Well-Being. Ann Arbor, MI: Institute for Social Research, 133-166.

Juster, F. T. (1985a). Investments of Time by Men and Women. In F. T. Juster & F. P. Stafford (Eds.), Time, Goods, and Well-Being. Ann Arbor, MI: Institute for Social Research, 177-202.

Juster, F. T. (1985b). A Note on Recent Changes in Time Use. In F. T. Juster, & F. P. Stafford (Eds.), Time, Goods, and Well-Being. Ann Arbot, MI: Institute for Social Research, 313-332.

Kinsey, J. (1984). Probit and Tobit Analysis in Consumer Research. The Proceedings of the American Council on Consumer Interests, 30th Annual Conference, 155-161.

Maddala, G. S. (1987). Limited-Dependent and Qualitative Variables in Economics. New York: Cambridge University Press.

Rapoport, R. & Rapoport, R. N. (1975). Leisure and the Family Life Cycle. Boston, MA: Routledge and Kegen Paul.

Robinson, J. P. (1985). Changes in Time Use: An Historical Overview. In F. T. Juster & F. P. Stafford (Eds.), Time, Goods, and Well-Being. Ann Arbor, MI: Institute for Social Research, 289-306.

Stafford, F. P. & Duncan, G. J. (1985). The Use of Time and Technology by Households in the United States. In F. T. Juster & F. P. Stafford (Eds.), Time Goods, and Well-Being. Ann Arbor, MI: Institute for Social Research, 245-282.

Thompson, C. S. & Tinsley, A. W. (1978). Income Expenditure Elasticities for Recreation: Their Estimation and Relation to Demand for Recreation. Journal of Leisure Research. 10(4), 265-270.

White, T. H. (1975). The Relative Importance of Education and Income as Predictors in Outdoor Recreation Participation. Journal of Leisure Research. 7(3), 191-199.

Tobacco Consumption Patterns: Implications For Consumer Education

Mi Kyeong Bae, The University of Texas-Austin[1]
Sherman Hanna, The Ohio State University[2]
Chandrika Jayathirtha, The Ohio State University[3]

Tobacco spending was investigated, using the 1990 BLS Consumer Expenditure Interview data. The mean tobacco budget share was 1.2%, but only 43% had tobacco spending. For those, mean budget share was 2.8%. Based on tobit there was a positive relationship between tobacco expenditures and total expenditures for over age 40, but a negative relationship for those under 40. Tobacco expenditure was negatively related to education. Higher taxes may be more effective than consumer education in reducing tobacco consumption.

Tobacco use is an obvious example of a dangerous health practice that has been the subject of substantial public education and labeling warnings. Over 23 years ago in the Journal of Consumer Affairs, Gellhorn stated:

> "Cigarette smoking is dangerous to one's health. The label on each cigarette pack constantly reminds us of this, yet almost half the adult population in the United States continues to smoke. How to discourage a habit which contributes to over 75,000 deaths each year -- twice the total Vietnam toll -- continues to perplex a nation which has landed men on the moon." (Gellhorn, 1969, 145).

Since that time, there has been much success in reducing tobacco use in many segments of the U.S. population, but this success has been uneven. The patterns of use of tobacco may provide insights into challenges of other health and safety education issues. This paper analyzes spending on tobacco products. Expenditure patterns provide additional evidence on tobacco use to supplement self-reported usage. Evidence on tobacco spending is important because one important anti-smoking strategy is to increase the price of tobacco products. Taxes on tobacco are very regressive, but may be very effective in reducing the number of teenagers who become addicted to tobacco (Wartzman, 1993). The combined evidence from self-reported usage and from spending can be used to design better education programs on health risks such as tobacco use. Understanding of tobacco consumption patterns may also help in consideration of

regulatory efforts to deal with marketing efforts targeted at special groups such as Blacks or teenagers (Mintz, 1991).

Understanding of tobacco consumption patterns in the United States may also be helpful in addressing concerns about the rapid increase in tobacco consumption in some developing nations such as the People's Republic of China (Yu, et al., 1990).

Literature

The consumption of cigarettes in the United States reached a maximum in 1981, at 640 billion cigarettes, then declined to 510 billion by 1991 (Grise, 1992, p. 35). The number of cigarettes consumed per U.S. adult has fallen from 4,287 in 1966 to about 3,200 in 1987 (USHHS, 1989, p. 268). The effects of past and present smoking will be with the United States for years to come. The U.S. Surgeon General's report attributed 390,000 deaths in 1985 to smoking (USHHS, 1989, p.22).

Other forms of tobacco also cause health problems, but cigarette expenditures amounted to 95 percent of tobacco expenditures in 1990. (Grise, 1992, p. 36). Therefore, the primary focus of this literature review is on research related to cigarette consumption.

Estimates of smoking from self-reported data may only account for about 70% of actual cigarette smoking, but trends from self-reported data follow trends from aggregate estimates very closely (USHHS, 1989, p. 266). The percentage of adults with post-BS education who smoked was less than half the rate among adults who were not high school graduates (USHHS, 1988, p. 571). The prevalence of smoking among Blacks in 1987 was 34 percent, compared to 29 percent among Whites (USHHS, 1989, p. 269). A multivariate analysis of smoking found that, controlling for age, education, marital status, employment status and poverty status, blacks were no more likely to smoke than whites (USHHS, 1988, p. 572). "Although black smokers smoke fewer cigarettes per day than white smokers, they smoke brands with higher tar/nicotine yields.." (USHHS, 1988, p. 510)

Lee and Kidane (1988) used the 1973 U.S.

---

[1]Visiting Scholar, Human Ecology Department

[2]Professor and Chair, Family Resource Management

[3]Ph.D. Student, Family Resource Management

Consumer Expenditure Interview Survey involving 10,105 consumer units to analyze tobacco spending. About half of the consumer units had tobacco expenditures. Multiple regression analysis using tobacco consumption expenditure as the dependent variable and about 60 other economic and demographic attributes as independent variables. Except for the dependent variable, income, and family size, the rest of the variables are treated as dummy variables for specific groups of interest. The results show that several socioeconomic factors affect significantly consumption of tobacco products. Other things being equal heads of a consumer unit with college education, Blacks, and married couples spend less on tobacco consumption.

Browning (1987), in an analysis of United Kingdom data, found that tobacco expenditures increased until age 50, then decreased. The presence of children did not significantly affect tobacco spending.

Sharp increases in taxes may be effective in decreasing smoking. Canada instituted tax increases that changed the average price of a pack of cigarettes from $1.74(U.S.) to $4.43 during the past decade, and now Canadians smoke 40% fewer cigarettes (Wartzman, 1993).

Methods

This paper uses the U.S. Bureau of Labor Statistics Survey of Consumer Expenditures for its analysis of tobacco expenditures. Tobacco expenditure includes chewing tobacco, smoking related products, and accessories. The 1990 BLS public use tape, EXPN, was used to construct a sample of consumer units with four quarters of 1990 interviews for some simple statistics, and a multivariate tobit analysis of tobacco spending. Details of the methods and assumptions used are in Bae (1992). The number of consuming units (hereafter referred to as households) in the four quarter sample was 1,109. For comparison, overall means for tobacco spending and tobacco budget shares were obtained from spreadsheet files available from the Bureau of Labor Statistics. These files have integrated estimates of consumer unit characteristics and expenditures from the 1990 Quarterly Interview Survey and the Diary Survey.

In the Consumer Expenditure Survey spreadsheet files, mean tobacco expenditures equal 1.0% of personal expenditures. In the U.S. Department of Commerce National Income Accounts, based on aggregate data sources, tobacco expenditures amount to 1.2% of personal consumption expenditures. It is probable that the results presented in this paper underestimate expenditures by approximately 20%. In this study, a sample of consumer units with four quarters of interviews was used in order to obtain a good estimate of total spending during the year. By having a good estimate of total spending during the year, a more accurate estimate of the tobacco budget share may be obtained. Total spending during the year may

also give the most complete single measure of the resources (past and present) available to a household. This is particularly evident based on the finding that 39% of the households spent more than their income after taxes and Social Security and pension contributions. This study adjusts the BLS definition of total spending in two ways: Social Security and pension contributions are subtracted; and net vehicle purchases are replaced by vehicle loan payments to make the total spending estimate correspond to actual spending.

The mean tobacco spending in the four quarter sample is $262, which is slightly lower than the mean of $274 in the Integrated Spreadsheet sample.

Results

Distribution of Tobacco Spending

In the four quarter sample, the maximum tobacco budget share was 18%. Only 43% of the consumer units reported spending on tobacco during the year. Of those who spent some money on tobacco during the year, the mean expenditure was about $614, and 10% spent $1209 or more during the year. The median percent of income after taxes and pension deductions devoted to tobacco among those who spent some money on tobacco was 2.6%, although 10% of that group spent 15% or more of income on tobacco. The mean budget share of those who spent money on tobacco was 2.8% and the median budget share was 2.0%, but 10% devoted 6.2% or more of their spending to tobacco. Table 1 shows other aspects of the distribution of tobacco spending and budget shares.

Table 1

Distribution of Tobacco Spending and Budget Share, for Households with Some Spending on Tobacco, 1990 BLS EXPN, Households in Survey Four Quarters of 1990. (n=373)

	Spending	Budget Share
Maximum	$3,939	18.1%
95th percentile	$1,482	8.2%
90th percentile	$1,235	6.2%
75th percentile	$845	3.6%
Median	$572	2.0%
25th percentile	$312	1.1%
10th percentile	$130	0.4%
5th percentile	$52	0.2%

Tobit Analysis

Tobit was used for a multivariate analysis, because tobacco spending is a limited dependent variable. The independent variables used included a set of household characteristics: total expenditure as a proxy for permanent income, household size, age and race of reference person, race of reference person, education, occupation, family type, region, and city size. The set of independent variables explained 14.4 percent of the variation of tobacco expenditure.

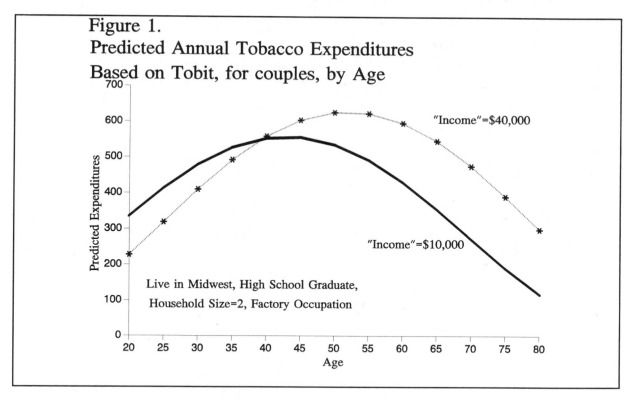

Figure 1.
Predicted Annual Tobacco Expenditures
Based on Tobit, for couples, by Age

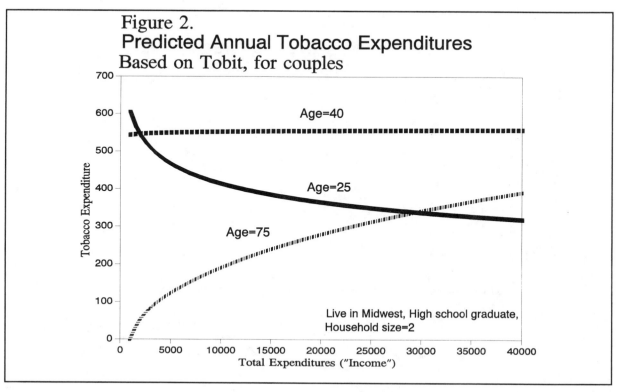

Figure 2.
Predicted Annual Tobacco Expenditures
Based on Tobit, for couples

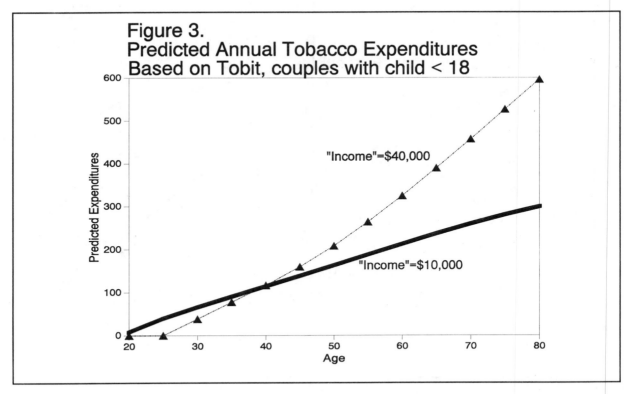

Figure 3.
Predicted Annual Tobacco Expenditures
Based on Tobit, couples with child < 18

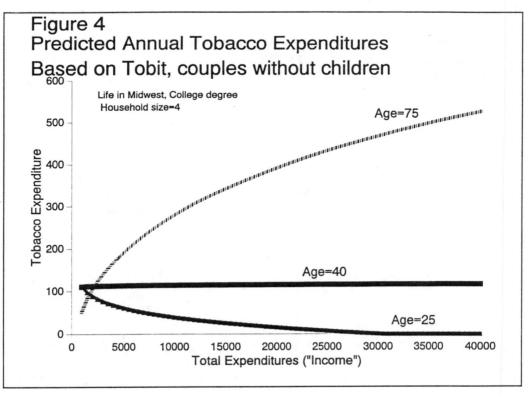

Figure 4
Predicted Annual Tobacco Expenditures
Based on Tobit, couples without children

Table 2
Tobacco Tobit Estimates. Consuming Units with 4
quarters of interviews in 1990 BLS EXPN tape.
(n=872)

Variables	Normalized Coef
Ln(Total Spending)	-0.44434*
Number of earners	-0.11556
Household size	0.77290
Age of reference person	-0.41989E-01
Age squared	-0.15082E-02**
Black (0=non-Black)	-0.67077E-01
Hispanic	-0.44150**
Homeowner with mortgage	-0.29815**
Homeowner without mortgage	-0.41114**
Less than high school degree	0.71347**
Highest ed. H.S. degree	0.59828**
Some college but not degree	0.63426**
Married couple w/o children	0.66444
Married couple, child<18	-0.55432
Other married couple	1.3307
Single parent unit	-2.0785
Factory,Service & Misc. Occ.	0.10244
Self-employed	-0.24314
Retired	-0.11316
Not working	0.55597E-01
City size > = 4 million	0.37775E-01
City size 1.3-3.9 million	-0.14052
City size .33-1.29 million	0.76654E-01
City size 75,000-330,000	0.70000E-02
City size missing(West)	0.59571E-01
Region Northeast	-0.11648
Region Midwest	0.60014E-01
Region West	-0.36737**
Age*couple without children	-0.11041E-01
Age*couple with child<18	0.94677E-02
Age*Other married couple	-0.37771E-01
Age*Single parent unit	0.59362E-01
Age^2*Married couple w/o children	0.59121E-04
Age^2*Married couple with child<18	0.19714E-03
Age^2*Other married couple	0.42739E-03
Age^2*Single parent unit	-0.33179E-03
Age*Household Size	-0.29505E-01
Age^2*Household Size	0.28388E-03
Ln(Total Spending)*Age	0.11292E-01**
Intercept	0.39043
Tobin's a	0.13382E-02
R^2 = .145	

Note. * Significant at the .10 level
** Significant at the .05 level (2-tail test)

Predicted Effects of Age and Total Spending.
Table 2 shows the results of the tobit analysis. At mean values of the independent variables, the combined effect of the log of total spending and the interaction term between age and the log of total spending results in an "income" elasticity (elasticity of total spending with respect to tobacco spending) of only 0.13. At age 25, the "income" elasticity is -0.27. At age 75, the "income" elasticity is 0.35.

The interaction terms in the tobit make interpretation difficult. Figures 1 and 2 illustrate the relationship between the tobacco expenditure, total spending and the age of reference person based on the tobit results in Table 2. The example is a household with the following characteristics: a married couple with no children living in a mid-size city in the Midwest; with one wage earner. They own a house which is mortgaged. The reference person is a high school graduate and has a factory job. In the example illustrated in Figure 1, the predicted levels of tobacco expenditure for six levels of total spending are presented. Below age 40, households with lower total spending levels spend more on tobacco than do households with higher total spending levels. The pattern is reversed for households older than 40.

In Figure 2, the relationship between tobacco expenditures and total spending is negative for households with 25 year old heads and positive for consumers older than 40. Consumers aged 40 had predicted tobacco spending that was virtually constant with total expenditure. The predicted levels of tobacco spending amounted to over 10 percent of total spending for young consumers with low total spending.

Figures 3 and 4 show another example based on predictions from the tobit results in Table 2. The household has the following characteristics: married couple with two children under 18, living in a mid-sized city in the West, with one wage earner. The reference person is a college graduate in a managerial or professional occupation. In Figure 3, such households with total spending ("income") of $40,000 would spend nothing on tobacco if the reference person were age 25 or under. Tobacco spending would be somewhat higher for households with lower "incomes" up to age 40. Predicted tobacco spending would increase with age for both low and high "income" households. In Figure 4, the relationship between tobacco spending and "income" is negative for those age 25, with zero predicted levels of tobacco spending above $15,000 per year. The relationship between tobacco spending and "income" is positive for those older than 40, as with the example for age 75.

Predicted Effects of Other Variables.
Households headed by a college graduate had predicted tobacco spending at less than half the amount of otherwise similar households with less than a college degree. High school dropouts had predicted tobacco spending 2.4 times as high as college graduates. Homeowners with mortgages had predicted tobacco spending 28 percent less than otherwise similar renters, and homeowners without mortgages had predicted tobacco spending 38 percent less than otherwise similar renters. Households in the West had predicted tobacco spending 41 percent less than otherwise similar households in the Midwest. At the mean values of the other variables, predicted tobacco spending by Hispanic households was 19 percent less than non-Hispanics.

Conclusions

Most of the results presented in this paper are consistent with patterns previously reported in the literature. The most interesting result was obtained by including interaction terms for age and other variables, especially total spending. It has long been known that tobacco taxes were regressive, but the results presented in this paper suggest that they may be extremely regressive for young consumers. Given the possibility that many young smoker households are less educated, they may not be very responsive to traditional consumer education efforts. Further large increases in taxes on tobacco may be unfair in the traditional evaluation of tax fairness, but they may have significant impacts on smoking habits of young consumers, as the budgets of some of these households may stretched very tightly. The results also suggest that the impact of tobacco taxes on older, more addicted smokers is likely to be less than on the younger consumers, as the more affluent consumers are more likely to spend more on tobacco, at any particular level of education. Consumer education efforts should be targeted on the groups more likely to smoke, but a policy of drastic increases in tobacco taxes may provide the most behavior change for young consumers.

References

Bae, M.K. (1992). Analysis of Household Spending Patterns. Ph.D. dissertation, The Ohio State University.

Browning, M. (1987). Drinking, smoking, and testing the lifecycle hypothesis. Quarterly Journal of Economics, 102, 329-346.

Gellhorn, E. (1969). Braking the cigarette habit. Journal of Consumer Affairs, 3(2), 145-151.

Grise, V.N. (1992). The changing tobacco user's dollars. Tobacco Situation and Outlook Report, 35-38.

Lee, J.W & Kidane, A. (1988). Tobacco consumption pattern: A demographic analysis. Atlantic Economic Journal 16, 92.

Mintz, M. (1991). The tobacco pushers' marketing smokescreen. Business and Society Review, 79, 49-54.

U.S. Department of Health and Human Services (USHHS). (1988). The Health Consequences of Smoking: Nicotine Addiction: a report of the Surgeon General.

U.S. Department of Health and Human Services (USHHS). (1989). Reducing the Health Consequences of Smoking: 25 Years of Progress: a report of the Surgeon General.

Wartzman, R. (1993). "Clinton's proposal for 'sin taxes' may stumble by turning too many Americans into saints," The Wall Street Journal, LXXIV(127), (April 14), A16.

Yu, J.J., Mattson, M.E, Boyd, G.M., Mueller, M.M., Shopland, D.R., Pechacek, T.F. & Cullen, J.W. (1990). A comparison of smoking patterns in the People's Republic of China with the United States: An impending health catastrophe in the Middle Kingdom. Journal of the American Medical Association, 264(12), 1575-1579.

A Hierarchy of Financial Needs Reflected by Household Paper Assets

Jing-jian Xiao, University of Rhode Island[1]
Joan Gray Anderson, University of Rhode Island[2]

Through preliminary examinations and tobit results, with data from the 1983 and 1986 Surveys of Consumer Finances, shares of household paper assets among income groups indicated distinctive patterns that suggested a hierarchy of family financial needs. Based on the findings, a cosine function that describes family saving patterns, and a model indicating associations between family financial needs and financial instruments are proposed.

Numerous personal finance books and articles discuss family financial needs which motivate savings and appropriate financial instruments, and give insightful recommendations for setting family financial plans (for examples, see Garman and Forgue, 1991; Kapoor, Dlabay, and Hughes, 1991). However, few empirical research is found to address relationships between family financial needs and financial instruments.

This study attempts to fill the research gap. The research purpose is to investigate associations among family financial needs, saving motives, and family possessed financial assets. Specifically, this study is to identify family saving patterns and explore the match of financial needs and instruments, using data from surveys of consumer finances.

Literature Review

Saving Motives

In economic literature, saving motives are implied by several saving models. Retirement as a saving motive is suggested by the life-cycle hypothesis (Ando and Modigliani, 1963; Modigliani and Brumberg, 1954). This model states that saving is mainly done for retirement. Another saving motive, intergenerational transfer, is implied in Barro's (1974) model. Barro views individuals as caring not only about their own welfare but also about their offsprings, and their major savings are for their children (Kotlikoff, 1989, p.5). The third saving motive proposed by economists is for precautionary saving. Two forms of precautional saving, for uncertain life span and for uncertain health expenditure are examined (Kotlikoff, 1989, pp.109-162). This saving motive could be labeled as "for emergency".

In the view of personal finance researchers, the above models have several limitations. First, each model always considers only one saving motive when examining consumer saving behavior. Second, these models treat different components of savings as interchangeable. To improve this fungibility (interchageability) assumption, Shefrin and Thaler (1988) have proposed a behavioral life-cycle hypothesis, which suggests that consumers' marginal propensities to consume from different accounts are different, which infers varying saving motives. This model implies that consumers treat their different saving components in a dissimilar way. However, this model fails to tell why consumers behave like this.

Needs Theories

While a well-known economist Marshall proposed six levels of wants (see Haines, 1990), the most influential needs theory was developed by Maslow (1954). Maslow's theory is widely applied in the organizational behavior field. The outstanding development and elaboration of Maslow's theory in the organizational setting were provided by Alderfer (1972; 1989).

Research on the relationship between the human needs and family financial decisions is rare. One relevant study is Tang (1992). Based on Maslow's theory and other needs theories, He has developed an instrument to explore the meaning of money and found that money is related to the perception of achievement, respect, and freedom.

Family Financial Needs

Personal/family financial needs are addressed in numerous personal finance textbooks (Boon and Kurtz, 1989; Garman and Forgue, 1991; Gitman and Joehnk, 1987; Kapoor, Dlabay, and Hughes, 1991; Winger and Frasca, 1989). While textbooks and practitioners give consumers advice and recommendations regarding how to achieve financial goals with alternative financial instruments, empirical studies on this topic are scarce.

There are two exceptions: Weagley and Gannon's (1991) investigation of investor portfolio allocation and Xiao and Olson (1992)'s study of household asset portfolios. However, both studies only address the relationship between financial needs and financial assets in an indirect way.

Based on the literature review, it can be

[1]Assistant Professor, Consumer Affairs

[2]Associate Professor, Consumer Affairs

concluded that few studies directly explore the associations among family saving motives, financial needs, and matched financial instruments. This study attempts to explore this issue.

Conceptual Framework

The conceptual framework will be based on the needs theory. According to this theory, human needs: (1) are hierarchical (Maslow,1954); (2) move up to a higher-level need after the lower-level need has been met (Maslow, 1954); (3) have following features. Within the deficiency range, the more people get, the less they want; beyond a certain degree of satisfaction, the more people get, the more they want (Alderfer, 1989).

According to above notions, a chart could be drawn, the horizontal axis is motivator, and the vertical axis is indicator of needs. Along with the increase of the motivator, the indicator's lotus will show three possible shapes: (1) a mirror-image-J-shape; (2) an inverted-U-shape; and (3) a J-shape.

In this study, several assumptions are proposed. Motivations for current and future consumption are defined as financial needs. Family financial needs are the reflection of human needs, then having the same characteristics mentioned above. These family needs are expressed by family financial behavior, such as consumption activities and savings. If these assumptions are held, consumer expenditures and savings in different categories will show hierarchies as the same as in human needs.

In economics textbooks, hierarchies indicated by consumer expenditures are obvious. For example, goods are classified as inferior or normal goods, when the relationship between the demand and income is observed (Varian, 1990, p.96). Another example is the classification of luxury good and necessary good when the demand for a good increases more or less rapidly than income increases (Varian, 1990, p.101). In these two examples, income serves as the motivator, and the demand for goods is the indicator of financial needs.

Hierarchies of savings are not explored by economists, because dominant saving models hold the fungibility assumption. Based on the assumptions of this study, hierarchies in saving components should be observed if variables are appropriately chosen. Savings include paper assets, real assets, durable goods, and other assets (such as pensions, annuities). To simplify the analysis, only paper assets are considered here. Two candidates for the indicators are amounts and shares of different paper assets. Preliminary examinations show that shares of assets are a better indicator, then, used in this study.

Motivator can be income, net worth, wealth, life cycle, etc. Since paper assets are considered as the indicator in this study, and these assets accounted for a certain proportion in the total savings, net worth and wealth variables are not appropriate to be used as motivator. The family life cycle variables were used to effectively explain family expenditure behavior (Lansing and Kish, 1957). Empirical findings showed that the life cycle variable was significant in explaining family expenditure behavior, but much weaker than the explanatory power of family income (Wagner and Hanna, 1983). Consequently, income is used as motivator.

In sum, household paper assets are assumed to reflect hierarchical family financial needs, as predicted by the framework. However, what are these financial needs, and what financial instruments are for what needs? The work in the following sections tries to answer these questions.

Methodology

Data

Panel data from the 1983 and 1986 Surveys of Consumer Finances were used. In the sample, household heads who did not change spouse, or did not change single status between 1983 and 1986 were chosen. All were homeowners. In the following investigation, both unweighted and weighted samples were used, while the results from the weighted sample are usually reported. Thus, the results from the weighted sample are nationally representative of homeowners who had no marital status changes between 1983 and 1986. The unweighted sample size was 1,954 and the weighted was 57,264,470.

Variables

The dependent variables were eight paper assets, CHCK(saving and checking accounts), CD(certificates of deposit and money market accounts), LIFE(cash value of life insurances), IRA(individual retirement and Keogh accounts), THRFT(profit sharing, thrift and other saving plans), OASST(other assets), BOND(bonds), and STCK(stocks). Definitions of these variables are the same as Avery and Elliehausen (1988). The share of CHCK in the sum of paper assets (SUM) was figured out as follows:

$$\text{Share of CHCK} = \frac{CHCK_{83}/SUM_{83}+CHCK_{86}/SUM_{86}}{2}$$

Where the subscripts 83 and 86 mean the values in 1983 and 1986, respectively. Shares of other assets were calculated in the same way. Using average shares was believed to give a relative "steady" picture of family financial needs.

Family income was used as a major influential factor (motivator) in the change of family financial needs. To capture the behavior of families with a relatively stable income flow in a period of time (three years in this study), average annual income (INCOME) based on 1983, 1984, and 1985 data was used.

To investigate the matches between family financial needs and paper assets, some life-cycle related variables were chosen. Age and marital status of the household head were used to examine relationships between life cycle and life arrangement, and corresponding financial assets. Number of children (who lived in and outside the household) was used to investigate financial instruments saved for children's sake.

Saving reasons were variables that would show associations between different financial needs and varieties of paper assets. The data used to form this variable were from answers of respondents to an open-ended question "What were the household's most important reason for saving?" The respondents might give several reasons. In this study, respondents' first stated reason was used. Then this variable showed the most important saving reason perceived by the respondents. Based on the 35 categories of answers coded by previous researchers (Avery and Elliehausen, 1988), the authors of this study recoded these reasons as follows: (1) for daily expenses; (2) for emergency; (3) for purchase plans, such as for self-education, travel, wedding, second house, home improvement, and so forth; (4) for retirement; (5) for children or grandchildren; (6) for better life, advancing standard of living, or other abstract reasons. This reason was labeled "growth" in this study; (7) no savings, don't know, or not applicable.

Procedures
Two steps were used in this study. First, INCOME was broken into ten levels, and average shares of paper assets by income levels were calculated. INCOME was divided almost evenly among the unweighted sample, then weights of 1986 were employed to produce results. The reason for doing the former was to take full advantage of this data set since it oversampled high-income families. Doing the latter was to get results representative of the national population. Through this step, the behavioral patterns of consumers in regard their shares of paper assets were shown distinctively.

Secondly, shares of paper assets were regressed with several independent variables, including average income, age and marital status of the household head, number of children, and saving reasons, using tobit models. The reason for using tobit models was that some families had no certain types of paper assets, then tobit models can generate unbiased estimates when these censored samples were included (Mandala, 1983).

Results and Discussions

Average Shares of Paper Assets by Income Levels
ANOVA were conducted between asset shares by income levels and results were significant (p≤.0001). These findings are available from the authors. To illustrate the findings more straightforwardly, trimmed curves showing the relationship between asset shares and income levels, based on the findings, were drawn in

Figures 1 to 3. Three patterns were shown. In Figure 1, the share of CHCK decreases when the income level goes up. At income level 1 (≤$7,334), the value of CHCK accounts for more than 52% of the total value of paper assets. However, for families at income level 10 (≥180,001), the value of CHCK accounts for only less than eight percent of the total value of paper assets. It implies, CHCK is a financial instrument that consumers need relatively less as they become more affluent.

Figure 1
Shares of Paper Assets by Income (I)

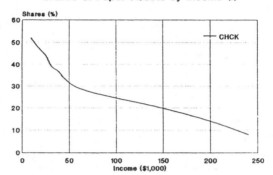

In Figure 2, CD, LIFE, IRA, and THRFT showed similar patterns. First look at LIFE, IRA, and THRFT. Three of these assets showed an inverted-U-shape pattern. It suggests that at first as consumers' incomes grow, they get more and need more. But beyond a certain point of income level, they get more and need less. The CD's curve showed two peaks. According to the same line of reasoning, the curve for CD could be viewed as a combination of two inverted-U-shape pattern.

Figure 2
Shares of Paper Assets by Income (II)

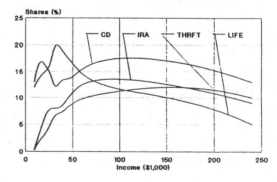

209

OASST, BOND, and STCK demonstrated a third pattern in Figure 3, a J-shape curve. It seems that, relatively, when consumers get more OASST, BOND, and STCK, they need more.

Figure 3
Shares of Paper Assets by Income (III)

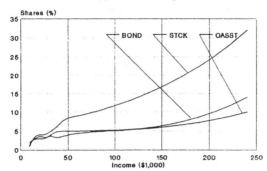

The above findings showed three distinctive patterns of paper asset shares along with the growth of income. Based on the assumptions in the framework section, these patterns could be explained as a hierarchy of financial needs. The first pattern, a mirror-image-J-shape curve represents the most basic financial need. It may be labeled as "survival need". This explanation seems reasonable because (1) almost all families have CHCK (checking and saving accounts); (2) checking accounts are always used as an instrument to receive family regular incomes (through automatic deposit services), and to deal with daily expenses (make mortgage, credit card, or other routine payments); (3) CHCKs are critical even to some families without stable income sources. That is why lifeline bank service has been selected as an important consumer issue (Garman, 1991).

The inverted-U-shape curve could be explained as representing "security need". IRA and THRFT are obviously related to retirement, the future financial security. LIFE concerns the financial security of the family in case of the death of family's breadearner(s). These needs are specific and can be saturated. Then, when the savings for these needs are achieved to a certain amount, consumers will generate another higher level of needs, and start or accelerate accumulating other accounts. This process will be shown an inverted-U-shape in a plane of asset shares and income levels. CD showed two peaks in Figure 2. It could have two explanations. First, CD may serve to meet two different needs. Since CD is a combination of certificates of deposits and money market accounts, these two peaks may imply these two components meet two different financial needs. Another possible explanation is that CD may be used to serve one need, and when the income increases further, CD once again serves another higher level of need. Both needs are achievable and can be saturated.

According to the relative location of these four curves, CD, LIFE, IRA, and THRFT could be distinguished as finer layers within this level of need. If a peak implies the saturation of a need, then the faster a peak has been achieved, the lower the need level. According to this rule, CD represents the lowest need and THRFT the highest within the second level of need, the "security need".

A J-shape pattern represents an unsaturated need. Relatively, consumers get more and want more. This level of need could be labeled as "growth need". This need represents achievement and self-actualization. According to the relative locations of OASST, BOND, and STCK, they could also be divided as hierarchical within this level. The OASST represents the lowest need and the STCK the highest.

A cosine function can be used to describe the relationships between asset shares and income levels. This cosine function combines three patterns into one chart and is convenient for the purpose of exposition. In Figure 4, a locus of a cosine function is shown. It is divided into three part, part I to III, which correspond to three types of saving patterns discussed above. The X-axis represents the growth of income, where A<A', B<B', and C<C'. The Y-axis represents the relative magnitudes of asset shares.

Figure 4
Saving Patterns

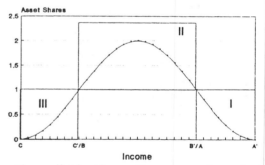

Three distinctive patterns are shown in the plane of asset shares and income levels, and they are labeled as survival, security, and growth need, respectively. These financial needs are hierarchical. Recall the saving reasons discussed above, there are not many clues to relate different saving reasons with varieties of paper assets. To explore the match of financial needs and financial instruments, the results of tobit models should be examined.

Results of Tobit Estimates

Shares of CHCK, CD, LIFE, IRA, THRFT, OASST, BOND, and STCK were regressed with average annual income, age and marital status of the household head, number of children, and saving reasons, with tobit models. All independent variables but income were dummies. Income variables were constructed in several ways when different assets were treated. These different treatments were inspired by different behavior patterns shown in Figures 1-3. Specifically, several income variables entered tobit models after some transformations were done:

$$INC0 = 1/INC$$
$$INC1 = INC$$
$$INC2 = (INC)^2$$
$$INC3 = (INC)^3$$
$$INC4 = (INC)^4$$
$$INC5 = e^{INC}$$

where INC is an average of 1983, 1984, and 1985 annual household incomes, dividing by 100,000. For example, if the three-year average annual income is $40,000, INC=.4.

Both unweighted and weighted samples were used to estimate parameters of tobit models. Estimates of those weighted samples were all statistically significant ($p \leq .0001$) and presented in Table 1.

In order to explore the match between financial needs and paper assets, attention was paid to parameter estimates of life-cycle variables and the saving reason variable. In the case of share of CHCK, compared to consumers who claimed no savings, consumers stated that savings for daily expenses tended to have a larger share of CHCK among the total value of paper assets, and those stated that savings for other reasons tended to have smaller shares of CHCK, given other conditions. This is consistent with the discussion last section. It gives support to the argument that CHCK was used for survival need.

IRA and THRFT were considered to be related to consumers' retirement needs. This argument was supported by the estimates of number of children. Presence of children decreased the shares of these two assets. Another piece of evidence was from age of household head. Compared to consumers at retirement age or older, consumers before retirement tended to have larger shares of these two assets. There was a minor difference between these two assets. For IRA, when consumers grew older toward retirement, their shares of IRA tended to be larger, compared to the retirement group. For THRFT, this tendency was a reverse one. Estimates of saving reasons showed that consumers stated retirement reasons as the most important reason tended to have largest share of IRA and THRFT.

Estimates of LIFE implied that consumers bought life insurance mainly for retirement and children. Consumers stated that savings for children and retirement tended to have a larger share of LIFE, compared to those had no savings. Compared to consumers at retirement age, younger consumers, especially the age group of 41-55, tended to have larger shares of LIFE. Estimates of number of children were interesting. Compared to consumers with no children, consumers having one to

three children tended to have a larger share of LIFE, which was consistent with the statement that purchasing life insurance for children's sake. However, consumers with four or more children tended to have a smaller share of LIFE. It implied that there was a trade off between quantity and quality of children. Married consumers tended to have a larger share of LIFE than single consumers, which was consistent with the argument that LIFE was related with the financial security of the family. One point should be noted here was the distinction between savings for children and savings for family financial security. The former represents an intergenerational transfer, an indicator of self-actualization and a form of growth need. And the later suggests a lower level of need in case of the sudden death of family breadearners. Further explorations are needed to distinguish these two different levels of needs and corresponding financial instruments.

CD once again showed its complexity. Looking at estimates of saving reasons, CD could be used for any of those financial needs, especially for children, retirement, growth, purchase plans, or emergency. Estimates of number of children implied that consumers having no children tended to have a larger share of CD. This finding was consistent with the estimate of marital status of the household head. Estimates of age of the household head suggested that consumers at retirement age tended to have a larger share of CD. It seems that CD is a favorite financial instrument for single, retired consumers without children. To consider all these findings together, it is safe to say that CD is at least saved for retirement, growth, purchase plans.

Estimates of OASST suggested its multiple functions for meeting family financial needs. Estimates of saving reasons implied that it could be used for growth, emergency, retirement, or purchase plans. Consumers at retirement age or married consumers tended to have a larger share of OASST. Consumers with four or more children tended to have a larger share of OASST, which was a reverse case compared to LIFE. Not many consumers have OASST (14.3% in weighted sample, and 21.6% in unweighted sample). Consumers with OASST may be at higher income levels. Then the behavioral patterns shown here may indicate the behavioral difference between upper-income families and low- and middle-income families.

Table 1: Estimates of Tobit Models (Weighted Sample)

Variable	Estimate	Estimate	Estimate	Estimate
Y=SHARE OF	CHCK	LIFE	THRFT	BOND
INTERCPT	0.376*	-0.307*	-0.904*	-0.208*
INC0	44.49*			
INC1		-0.016*	0.232*	
INC2		4.7E-9*	-1E-7*	
INC5				2E-18*
AGE OF HOUSEHOLD HEAD				
≤40	0.124*	0.071*	0.473*	-0.007*
41-55	0.043*	0.906*	0.429*	0.019*
56-65	-0.036*	0.067*	0.339*	0.030*
≥66	-	-	-	-
SAVING REASONS				
daily	0.077*	-0.077*	-0.032*	0.059*
emergency	-0.002*	-0.001*	0.056*	0.089*
purchase	-0.079*	-0.028*	0.117*	0.104*
retirement	-0.100*	0.023*	0.170*	0.115*
children	-0.046*	0.034*	0.053*	0.131*
growth	-0.048*	-0.065*	0.124*	0.117*
no savings	-	-	-	-
NUMBER OF CHILDREN				
1-3	0.018*	0.013*	-0.020*	0.013*
4-17	0.052*	-0.025*	-0.015*	-0.035*
no kids	-	-	-	-
MARITAL STATUS				
married	-0.054*	0.225*	0.122*	0.039*
single	-	-	-	-
Y=SHARE OF	CD	IRA	OASST	STCK
INTERCPT	-0.070*	-0.475*	-0.712*	-0.286*
INC1	0.305*	0.098*		
INC2	-6.3E-7*	-3E-8*		
INC3	3.6E-13*			
INC4	-5.5E-20*			
INC5			2E-18*	1E-18*
AGE OF HOUSEHOLD HEAD				
≤40	-0.363*	0.054*	-0.197*	-0.080*
41-55	-0.293*	0.136*	-0.107*	0.032*
56-65	-0.135*	0.195*	-0.017*	0.048*
≥66	-	-	-	-
SAVING REASONS				
daily	0.237*	0.176*	0.154*	0.134*
emergency	0.296*	0.258*	0.304*	0.091*
purchase	0.313*	0.223*	0.240*	0.134*
retirement	0.356*	0.341*	0.257*	0.183*
children	0.375*	0.263*	0.154*	0.106*
growth	0.314*	0.215*	0.311*	0.192*
no savings	-	-	-	-
NUMBER OF CHILDREN				
1-3	-0.061*	-0.084*	-0.010*	-0.048*
4-17	-0.176*	-0.159*	0.068*	-0.131*
no kids	-	-	-	-
MARITAL STATUS				
married	-0.069*	0.114*	0.052*	0.099*
single	-	-	-	-

Note: - reference category, * p<.0001

Saving reasons in BOND were for children, growth, retirement, and purchase plans, according to the findings. Married consumers and consumers with one to three children tended to have a larger share of BOND, which was consistent with the case of LIFE, and confirmed once again savings in BOND were for children. Consumers at age 41-65 tended to have a larger share of BOND. This relationship between age of consumers and share of BOND may imply the relationship between income and share of BOND, since age group of 41-65 covers the earning peak of consumers.

Estimates of STCK were very similar to the behavior of BOND in terms of age of the household head. Consumers aged 41-65 tended to have a larger share of STCK. Differences were shown in saving reasons. Estimates showed that savings in STCK were for growth, retirement, and purchase plans. Another difference between share of STCK and BOND was shown in number of children. Consumers without children tended to have a larger share of STCK, which suggested that STCK was not mainly for children.

Estimates of tobit models gave some clues about the match between family financial needs and household assets, though it was far from enough. Discussion of tobit estimates showed that sometimes certain assets can serve several financial needs, even needs at different levels. Another point that suggested in the previous discussion is that certain paper assets may meet different financial needs under different family contexts.

The topic explored in this study is logitudinal in nature, but findings and discussions are based on a virtually cross-section sample. This limitation should be noted befor the findings are summarized. Findings in this study suggest the associations between financial needs and paper assets. Along with the growth of family income, family financial needs go up to a higher level. Varieties of financial instruments can be used to meet these diverse needs. These findings are incorporated as a model shown in Figure 5.

Figure 5: A Model of Relationships between Family Financial Needs and Household Paper Assets

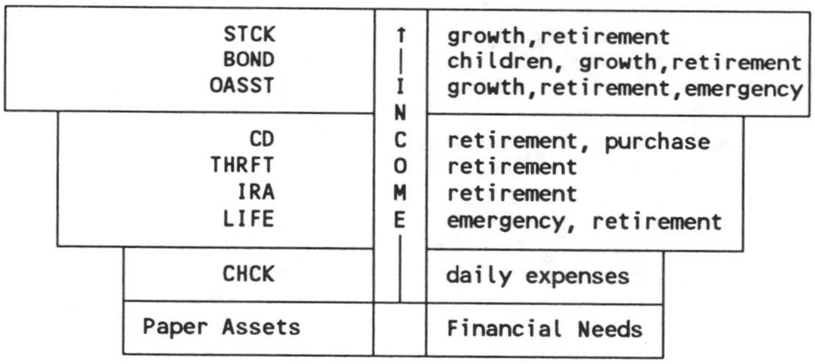

Paper Assets	INCOME	Financial Needs
STCK	↑	growth, retirement
BOND		children, growth, retirement
OASST		growth, retirement, emergency
CD		retirement, purchase
THRFT		retirement
IRA		retirement
LIFE		emergency, retirement
CHCK		daily expenses

Acknowledgement

Helpful comments by three anonymous reviewers are highly appreciated.

References

Alderfer, C. P. (1972). Existence, relatedness, and growth: Human needs in organizational settings. New York: Free Press.

Alderfer, C. P. (1989). Theories reflecting my personal experience and life development. The Journal of Applied Behavioral Science, 25(4), 351-65.

Avery, R. B., & Elliehausen, G. E. (1988). Survey of consumer finances technical manual and codebook, 1983 (Revised 1988). Washington, DC: Board of Governors of the Federal Reserve System.

Boon, L. E., & Kurtz, D. L. (1989). Personal financial management. Boston, MA: BPI and IRWIN.

Garman, E. T. (1991). Consumer economic issues in America. Boston, MA: Houghton Mifflin.

Garman, E. T., & Forgue, R. E. (1991). Personal Finance. (3rd ed.). Boston, MA: Houghton Mifflin.

Gitman, L. J., & Joehnk, M. D. (1987). Personal financial planning. (4th ed.). Chicago, IL: The Dryden Press.

Haines, W. W. (1990). Wants and metawants: Marshall's concern for higher values. International Journal of Social Economics. 17(9), 17-24.

Kapoor, J., Dlabay, L. R., & Hughes, R. J. (1991). Personal Finance. (2nd ed.). Homewood, IL: Irwin.

Kotlikoff, L. J. (1989). What determines savings?. Cambridge, MA: The MIT Press.

Lansing, J. B. & Kish, L. (1957). Family life cycle as an independent variables. American Sociological Review. 22, 512-19.

Maddala, G. S. (1983). Limited-dependent and qualitative variables in econometrics. Cambridge: Cambridge University Press.

Maslow, A. H. (1954). Motivation and personality. New York: Harper and Brothers.

Shefrin, H. M., & Thaler, R. H. (1988). The behavioral life-cycle hypothesis. Economic Inquiry. 26, 609-43.

Tang, T. L. (1992). The meaning of money revisited. Journal of Organizational Behavior, 13, 197-202.

Varian, H. R. (1990). Intermediate microeconomics: A modern approach. (2nd ed.). New York: W. W. Norton & Company.

Wagner, J., & Hanna, S. (1983). The effectiveness of family life cycle variables in consumer expenditure research. Journal of Consumer Research. 10, 281-91.

Weagley, R. O., & Gannon, C. F. (1991). Investor portfolio allocation. Financial counseling and planning. 2, 131-54.

Winger, B. J., & Frasca, R. R. (1989). Personal finance: An integrated planning approach. Columbus: Charles E. Merrill.

Xiao, J, & Olson, G. I. (1992). Mental accounting and saving behavior. In V. Haldman (ed.). The proceedings of American Council on Consumer Interests 38th annual conference.

Emergency Fund Levels of Households: Is Household Behavior Rational?

Sherman Hanna, The Ohio State University[1]
Yu-Chun Regina Chang, The Ohio State University[2]
Xiaojing Jessie Fan, The Ohio State University[3]
Mi Kyeong Bae, The University of Texas-Austin[4]

Empirical studies have found that most households do not have recommended levels of liquid savings. An analysis of the 1990 Survey of Consumer Expenditures confirms previous findings. A three period model of optimal consumption is presented. The results suggest that many consumers who do not have the recommended levels of liquid assets may be acting rationally. The results may be useful for financial counselors and educators, as well as for insight into empirical patterns of savings.

Introduction

"To be prepared for the unexpected, people should have a reserve fund - equal to at least three to six months' living expenses - invested in a combination of low-risk money funds and CDs, plus smaller amounts of riskier but higher-yielding investments, such as short- and medium-term bond funds." (Asinof, 1992).

Emergency funds are usually identified as liquid assets because they are easily and quickly converted to cash for the needs of unexpected expenses (Johnson and Widdows, 1985; Prather, 1990). However, when deciding on a level for adequate saving fund to meet emergencies, family economists and financial counselors vary somewhat -- with recommendations varying from 2 to 6 months of expenses in liquid form (Johnson and Widdows, 1985; Prather, 1990). Garman and Forgue (1991) cite this recommendation, but add that the appropriate amount for a particular family depends on the family situation and job. "A smaller amount may be sufficient if you have adequate loss of income protection through an employee fringe benefit program or a union, are employed in a job that is definitely not subject to layoffs, have an employed spouse, or have a ready source of ample credit." (Garman and Forgue, 1991).

Previous empirical studies have found that most U.S. households do not meet the recommended standards. This paper develops an original three period model of consumption for determining optimal saving in order provide insight into rational levels of emergency savings. A new empirical estimate of the proportion of U.S. households meeting the recommended standards is presented. Implications for consumer education and for further research are discussed.

The Literature

Empirical Studies

Johnson and Widdows (1985) definition of emergency funds included three types of liquidity assets. Smythe (1968) approached the question of emergency funds levels indirectly through the analysis of safe levels for family credit commitments. Smythe presented data on families' emergency saving at four stages in the life cycle, and related these to the average time a family at that life cycle stage could expect to be out of work if unemployment occurred. Average amount of income, expenditures as well as liquid and investment assets were provided for each family type. The study concluded that families at each life cycle stage could have supported their current life style during the average unemployment period.

While Smythe's study laid out a framework for analyzing emergency fund levels, more recent research tried to find adequate levels of emergency fund saving and to explore factors affecting levels of this saving. Lindqvist (1981), in a study of determinants of household savings in 429 Swedish families, found that income, family size and stage of life cycle were not significantly related to stocks of liquid assets, but that variables reflecting socio-psychological attributes of households, such as expectations and economic satisfaction, were significant.

Johnson and Widdows (1985) used three different measure of assets indicating different levels of emergency fund saving (quick emergency fund, intermediate emergency fund, and comprehensive emergency fund) for data of 1977 and 1983 Survey of Consumer Finance. The analysis

[1]Professor and Chair, Family Resource Management

[2]Ph.D Student, Family Resource Management

[3]Ph.D Student, Family Resource Management

[4]Visiting Scholar, Human Ecology Department

revealed that the majority of families had insufficient funds to cover normal total household income for the average time a household could expect to be out of work, should that event occur. In 1983, using the broadest measure of emergency funds, only 19% of households had liquid savings sufficient to cover six months of pretax income. The median level of liquid savings using the broad measure was seven percent of pretax income. In 1982-83, the mean level of consumer spending in U.S. households was 83% of the mean level of pretax income (USBLS, 1986), so the median level as a percent of annual spending was probably somewhat higher than seven percent.   Johnson and Widdows(1985) also showed that families, on the average, to be less prepared for financial emergencies in 1983 than in 1977 indicating a macroeconomic effect on emergency fund saving. Moreover, the empirical results suggest a strong and positive relationship between income and emergency fund holdings. In a cross-tabulation of emergency fund levels by stages of the life cycle, the findings showed that in each case of emergency fund measure, families in the young family stage of the life cycle showed greatest concentration of emergency funds in the "less than two months' reserve" category.   The concentration of families moves from the lower levels of emergency funds reserve to higher levels as families move through the life cycle (Johnson and Widdows, 1985).   One limitation of the Johnson and Widdows study is that income rather than spending was used to evaluate the adequacy of liquid savings. This limitation is inherent in the U.S. datasets available, as the Survey of Consumer Finances contains the best balance sheet information but little information about spending, while the Survey of Consumer Expenditures contains the best expenditure information, but only limited information about household balance sheets.

Griffith (1985) proposed 16 ratios with various components of net worth to analyze a family's financial situation. Nine ratios involve with liquid assets and provide insights into the adequacy of emergency fund holdings to cover expenses of unexpected financial crises. Using the ratios recommended by Griffith (1985), Prather (1990) analyzed 1983 Survey of Consumer Finance data and found that only 29% of households had liquid and other financial assets sufficient to cover six months of estimated spending. Prather found that income and age were significantly related to ratios of liquid assets to monthly expenses, to total debt, to non-mortgage debt, to net worth, and to one year's debt payment. These results are consistent with Johnson and Widdows' findings (1985).   Prather used an estimate of each household's annual expenditures based on a regression estimate from Survey of Consumer Expenditures data. This is a limitation of her analysis, as the estimate of spending for a particular household might have been much higher or lower than that household's actual spending.

Theoretical Literature

There has been extensive discussion in the literature of theoretical models of optimal saving and consumption behavior under uncertainty either in the context of infinite time horizon or in two-period or multiperiod intertemporal models (e.g., Leland, 1968; Levhari and Srinivasan, 1969; Sandmo, 1970; Mirman, 1971; Dreze and Modigliani, 1972; Hey, 1979; Sibley, 1975; Salyer, 1988).   In general, the authors analyzed one or two variables at a time, assuming a value for each of the other parameters. For example, in two-period models the effects of income and interest rate uncertainty on saving decisions are analyzed, given an assumption of a certain lifetime.   Infinite horizon or finite horizon models explore effects of the discount factor (lifetime uncertainty) on borrowing (saving) behavior while assuming absence of income and interest rate uncertainty.

In the discussion of income uncertainty and saving behavior, it is assumed that the consumer's beliefs about the value of future income can be summarized in a subjective probability density function; on the basis of this the consumer maximizes expected utility of consumption. Leland (1968) used a two-period model of consumption to demonstrate the effect of uncertainty on saving and concludes that with an additive utility function and the assumption of decreasing absolute risk aversion, the precautionary demand for saving is a positive function of uncertainty. Sandmo (1970) discussed the effects of increased riskiness of future income on present consumption in a two-period model and proves that increased uncertainty about future income decreases consumption (increases saving). Sibley (1975) extended a two-period result of the effects on optimal savings of increased riskiness in the future income due to Leland (1968) to the multiperiod case.   He suggested that increased wage uncertainty raises or lowers saving according to whether the third derivative of the utility function is positive or negative. Since the plausible requirement that the consumer's utility function display decreasing absolute risk aversion implies a positive third derivative, this establishes a presumption that optimal saving increases with wage uncertainty (Sibley, 1975). For the case of a constant (but negative) elasticity utility function, Levhari and Srinivasan (1969) showed that optimal savings can increase with increasing uncertainty. However, these authors emphasized the effects of subjective probability density function as a projection of uncertain future income on saving behavior. No study has been done in incorporating possible factors such as level of risk aversion, interest rate, income, and income growth rate into the model to demonstrate the effects of these uncertainties on optimal saving behavior.

The present study includes factors which influence optimal saving decisions in a three period model of consumption. Kinsey and Lane (1978) point out when consumption is accompanied by the use of consumer credit, utility maximization may be viewed in the global sense, thus a life cycle approach to the allocation of income, consumption, and saving (borrowing) is appropriate. While a multi-period model is very complicated and not feasible for this analysis, a three-period models can simulate the life cycle situation better than a two period model by appropriate interpretation. With additional assumptions on certain risk properties of utility functions, a three-period model with uncertainty for determining optimal saving facing consumers is presented and illustrated with numerical analysis. Implications for a life cycle model are then discussed.

Factors affecting optimal saving include the expected growth rate of real income, the variance of future income, the consumer's utility function (e.g., the parameter of risk aversion), the real interest rate and the consumer's personal discount rate. For an exposition of a two period model, see Chang, Fan and Hanna (1992).

A Three-Period Model of Consumption

To begin, consider the following model: assume that the consumer attempts to maximize the expected value of utility (T) for the three periods. Utility from consumption in each period i is denoted as $U(C_i)$. He/she will make his/her saving decision in conjunction with his/her known first period income. The second and third period consumption will, of course, be random variables, dependent on the actual value of second and third period income which is assumed to be affected by income growth rate (or decrease rate) and the probability of that income growth occurs, and also dependent on the interest rate of saving (or borrowing). It is assumed that there are two states of the world in the second period -- real income either decreases or stays constant, and in the third period, income will keep the level of the second period, no matter whatever happened in the second period. (The analysis could allow for other scenarios, but the discussion is limited to this scenario because it is the most plausible scenario for saving to be rational). There are other motivations for holding liquid assets than to allow for income decreases, such as preparing for accidents or illnesses, or saving to purchase durable goods. Insurance can provide for accidents, although some types of insurance may be very expensive relative to expected benefits (Hanna, 1989). Credit is often available for purchase of durable goods. However, this paper will concentrate on income decreases as a motivation for holding liquid assets. Holding liquid assets is costly, as the real rate of return is typically zero or negative.

Mathematically, the problem can be formulated

$$T = U(C_1) + \frac{P U(C_2) + (1-P) U(C_{2a})}{(1+\rho)} + \frac{P U(C_3) + (1-P) U(C_{3a})}{(1+\rho)^2} \quad (1)$$

The constraints are:

$$C_1 = I - S_1 \quad (2)$$
$$C_2 = (1+g)*I + (1+r)*S_1 - S_2 \quad (3)$$
$$C_{2a} = I + (1+r)*S_1 - S_2 \quad (4)$$
$$C_3 = (1+g)*I + (1+r)*S_2 \quad (5)$$
$$C_{3a} = I + (1+r)*S_2 \quad (6)$$

Variables:

T = Total three period utility
I = Year 1 income
I_2 = (1+g)*I (if income increases in that year), otherwise, Year 2 income = Year 1 income
C_1 = Consumption in year 1
S_1 = The amount of savings in year 1
C_2 = Consumption in year 2 if real income in year 2 increases
C_{2a} = Consumption in year 2 if real income in year 2 does not increase
S_2 = The amount of savings in year 2
C_3 = Consumption in year 3 if real income in year 2 increases
C_{3a} = Consumption in year 3 if real income in year 2 does not increase
g = Growth rate in real income (negative number means decrease rate in real income)
r = Real interest rate (Note that r may be higher for S<0, i.e., borrowing, than for S>0)
P = Probability that real income decreases
ρ = personal discount factor. (This might vary.)

A consumer may discount utility from future consumption because of the possibility that he/she may not be alive then, or because of other possible changes in capacity to derive utility from consumption. Young adults have very low risks of death, so this source of discounting should not be important for them. For analysis of savings/credit, the approximate effect of a nonzero personal discount rate is to reduce the real interest rate in the optimal solutions shown below, so that instead of an interest rate of r, the consumer in effect faces an interest rate of $r-\rho$. For the remainder of this paper, ρ is assumed to equal zero. If ρ is positive rather than zero, a consumer would save less or borrow more for any given set of values of other parameters.

Most studies of intertemporal consumption have used a constant elasticity utility function (Hurd 1989) which is time separable additively:

$$U = C^{1-x} / (1-x) \quad (7)$$

The elasticity of marginal utility with respect to consumption is -x. The elasticity of intertemporal substitution in consumption is equal to 1/x. When this type of utility function is used for analysis of risk, the parameter x is relative risk aversion. C is consumption per time period.

Estimates of Relative Risk Aversion

Grossman and Shiller (1981) have given x an interpretation as "... a measure of the concavity of the utility function or the disutility of consumption fluctuations." The higher the value of x, the more risk averse is the consumer, and the more rapidly marginal utility decreases as consumption or wealth increases. The analysis of economic behavior under uncertainty uses relative risk aversion extensively. For intertemporal consumption, empirical estimates of x range from just under 2 (Skinner, 1985) to 15 (Hall, 1988). Other estimates were between these two values.

By combining intertemporal consumption analysis with risk aversion, we can obtain the optimal amount of saving in terms of year 1 income, interest rate, income growth rate, and probability of that income increases. To give some intuitive insight into optimal savings levels, optimal savings with perfect certainty will be examined first, then uncertainty will be introduced.

Optimal Savings With Perfect Certainty

Zero Real Interest Rate
If a consumer is certain that real income will decrease with a negative growth rate g, and the consumer faces a real interest rate of zero (not unrealistic for taxable liquid savings), the consumer will plan to have equal consumption over the three periods. The amount of savings set aside in period one to allow for the income decreases in periods two and three will amount to:

$$\frac{S}{I} = \frac{-2g}{3} \qquad (8)$$

At the end of period one, the liquid savings accumulated as a proportion of period one income would equal the amount shown in Equation 8. For instance, if a consumer is certain that real income will decrease by 50% between period one and period two, then remain at that level, the optimal amount to save out of period one income is 33.3%. If the time period is years, at the end of year one, liquid savings will equal four months income. To express the proportion in the same terms as the usual prescription, it should be converted to a proportion of spending. Year one spending equals two thirds of income, so liquid savings as a proportion of spending equals six months income, which is equal to the typical prescription. The optimal savings as a percent of year one income and consumption is shown in Figure 1, for levels of income decreases ranging from 60% to zero. The real interest rate assumed is zero, so the utility function does not make any difference in the analysis, if the personal discount rate is zero. Only households who were certain that real income would drop 50% between year one and two, then remain at that level, would accumulate savings by the end of year one at the prescribed level to cover six months worth of spending.

Non-Zero Real Interest Rates
The optimal year one savings as a proportion of year one income can be derived by calculus, and is shown in Equation 9.

$$\frac{S}{I} = \frac{1 + (1+r)^{\frac{(x-1)}{x}} - (1+g)(1+r)^{\frac{(x-2)}{x}} - (1+g)(1+r)^{-\frac{2}{x}}}{1 + (1+r)^{\frac{(x-1)}{x}} + (1+r)^{\frac{2(x-1)}{x}}} \quad (9)$$

Given that the real interest rate on liquid assets is usually close to zero, the optimal savings/income ratios obtained from Equation 9 will be very close to those obtained from Equation 8. The results for other plausible real interest rates on liquid savings, ranging from -1% to 4%, are virtually identical to the results shown in Figure 1 for a range of levels of relative risk aversion.

Equations (1) through (7) were used with simulations to find the value of S that maximized expected lifetime utility for particular values of the parameters.

In this section, we discuss and illustrate the impact of the growth rate on optimal savings levels. The value assumed for relative risk aversion is six (Chang, Fan and Hanna, 1992), but results are similar for other plausible values. A graph is produced to help illustrate effects of these parameters by using a numerical simulation technique. In order to focus on scenarios with saving, it was assumed that the consumer faced either constant real income or a negative real income growth rate g with a probability p. The simulations were based on the following assumptions:

- The real interest rate on savings = 1% (e.g., nominal interest rate of 8.4%, subject to 28% tax rate and 5% inflation.)
- The real interest rate on loan = 14.095% (e.g., nominal rate of 19.8% with 5% inflation.)
- Expected utility from all possible borrowing levels (at 14.095%) is compared to expected utility from all possible saving levels (at 1%) and optimal saving/borrowing is that which produces highest expected utility.

Figure 2 shows the result of the simulations based on a range of probabilities that real income drops by 50% between year one and two, then remains at the new level during year 3. For a probability of 100% that real income drops by 50%, the results are virtually identical to the analysis illustrated in Figure 1. As the probability decreases, the optimal amount of savings drops rapidly. If the probability of real income dropping by 50% is 15%, then the household's savings should amount to 25% of annual spending. In a recession, this is possible for some occupational groups, but for many households, the probability of such a drastic decrease in real income is lower than 15%.

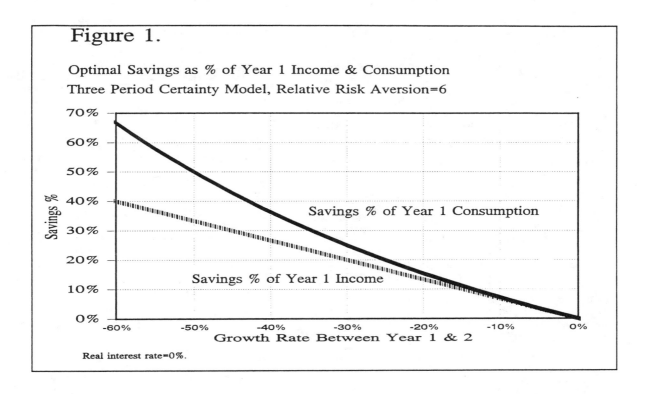

Figure 1.

Optimal Savings as % of Year 1 Income & Consumption
Three Period Certainty Model, Relative Risk Aversion=6

Real interest rate=0%.

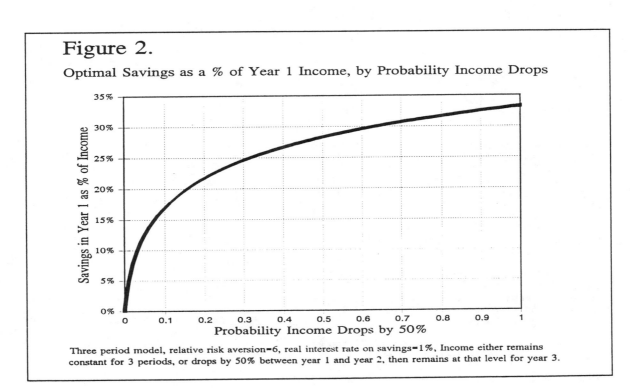

Figure 2.

Optimal Savings as a % of Year 1 Income, by Probability Income Drops

Three period model, relative risk aversion=6, real interest rate on savings=1%, Income either remains constant for 3 periods, or drops by 50% between year 1 and year 2, then remains at that level for year 3.

Empirical Analysis

A dataset was created with households who had interviews in all four quarters of 1990 in the BLS Survey of Consumer Expenditures tape (for details of the process, see Bae, 1992). With various exclusions, the sample size was 872 consumer units. Incomplete income information was supplied by 11% of the households. There were 774 consumer units with complete reporting of income. The mean income after taxes and Social Security & pension contributions ("takehome" income), was $29,849, and the median level was $24,653 (Table 1). One percent of the households with complete income reporting had takehome income less than zero. The BLS definition of expenditures included Social Security and pension contributions, so the variable "spending" was created by subtracting Social Security and pension contributions. The spending variable was also adjusted for the transportation category, as the BLS includes net vehicle purchases, regardless of how a vehicle was purchased. Net vehicle purchases were subtracted, and annual vehicle loan payments were added, to obtain the spending variable. The mean level of total expenditures was $28,863 and the median level was $24,291. Seven consumer units had takehome income less than zero, and 50% had annual spending greater than takehome income.

A measure of liquid assets was constructed using the following variables on the BLS expenditure tape:
CKBKACTX: Amount in checking accounts, brokerage accounts, etc.
SAVACCTX: Amount in savings account of banks, savings & loans, credit unions, etc.
SECESTX Amount in stocks, bonds, mutual funds etc.
USBNDX Amount in US savings bonds

Table 1 shows the distribution of income, spending and liquid assets. The mean level of liquid assets for all households was $12,893, and the median level was $1,000. Seventy five percent of the households had less than $9,056 in liquid assets. The percent meeting the six months criterion was approximately the same for pretax income, takehome income and spending. The percent of complete income reporters having sufficient liquid assets to cover six months of pretax income was 19%, the same result reported by Johnson and Widdows (1985) using a similar measure.

A dummy variable, MON6, was created for adequate liquid savings, equal to 1 if the household had liquid assets to cover six months spending, and equal to 0 otherwise. Spearman correlations between MON6 and selected demographic variables are shown in Table 2. There was a positive relationship between MON6 and age, income and education, and a negative relationship between MON6 and household size.

Only 6% of consumer units under age 25 had at least six months worth of liquid assets, while 39% of those age 65 and older did. The proportion meeting the recommended level increased with education, from 14% for those with less than a ninth grade education, to 41% for those with post-BS education. The proportion meeting the recommended level increased with pretax income, although not monotonically. Three percent of those with incomes under $5,000 met the level and 30% of those with incomes over $50,000 met the level.

There was a significant relationship between having at least six months worth of liquid assets and tenure status. Only 9% of renters and 20% of homeowners with mortgages had the recommended levels, compared to 38% of homeowners without mortgages. Consumer units with a white reference person had 23% meeting the six month standard compared to 1% for Blacks.

Table 1.
Distribution of Income, Spending, and Liquid Assets, and Percent Meeting Guidelines, for All Households and Complete Income Reporters, 1990 BLS Interview Survey, Households with 4 Quarters of Interviews.

	All Households	Complete Income Reporters
n	872	774
Takehome Income		
Mean	$26,925	$29,849
90th %tile	$56,185	$59,476
75th %tile	$37,898	$40,943
median	$21,938	$24,653
25th %tile	$10,742	$13,760
10th %tile	$2,496	$6,824
% <=0	6%	1%
Spending		
Mean	$29,005	$28,863
90th %tile	$55,712	$55,816
75th %tile	$38,650	$38,243
median	$24,468	$24,192
25th %tile	$14,818	$14,686
10th %tile	$9,061	$9,154
Liquid Assets		
Mean	$12,893	$13,938
90th %tile	$40,000	$42,450
75th %tile	$9,056	$11,050
median	$1,000	$1,500
25th %tile	$0	$20
10th %tile	$0	$0
% > 0	70%	76%
Liquid assets cover 3 months pretax income		
% meet	26%	28%
Liquid assets cover 3 months takehome income		
% meet	29%	31%
Liquid assets cover 3 months spending		
% meet	27%	29%
Liquid assets cover 6 months pretax income		
% meet	18%	19%
Liquid assets cover 6 months takehome income		
% meet	21%	22%
Liquid assets cover 6 months spending		
% meet	19%	21%

Table 2

Spearman Correlations between Dummy Variables for Adequate Liquid Savings and Age, Family Size and Income Category. Income and education are in categories.(n=872, except for income, n=774.) All correlations significant at the 0.01 level or better.

	Age	Size	Pretax Income	Education
MON6 (=1 if liquid savings >= 6 months spending)	0.26	-.12	0.13	0.18

Among occupational groups, the retired had the highest proportion meeting the six month standard, with 40%. Self-employed households had 37% meeting the standard, managers/professionals had 25%, and operatives/laborers had 10%. Those in the category "precision production, craft, repair" had only 8% meeting the standard. Amount household types, married couples with no children had the highest proportion meeting the standard, with 33%, one person households had 24% meeting the standard, and single mothers with children under 18 at home had only 2% meeting the standard.

The empirical patterns seem related mostly to the availability of resources and the accumulation of resources over the life cycle. There definitely does not seem to be a relationship between popular notions of the "need" for liquid savings and the likelihood of holding adequate levels of liquid savings.

Conclusions

The implicit assumption of previous empirical research on emergency fund holdings of households was that the typical prescription of having liquid assets equal to three to six months worth of spending was valid for most households. One might then conclude that most U.S. households were mistakenly not holding adequate levels of liquid assets. The empirical analysis presented in this paper shows that 81% of U.S. households did not have enough liquid assets to cover six months of spending. However, the original theoretical analysis presented in this paper suggests that only those who are certain that household income will drop by at least 50% should hold that level of liquid assets. The empirical patterns of households meeting the six month standard suggest that holding liquid assets is related to household resources rather than need. This paper ignores other motives for holding liquid assets, so the results should be interpreted cautiously. A multivariate analysis would provide more insight into the patterns.

Consumer education related to holding emergency funds should focus on specific motivations for holding liquid savings. Garman & Forgue (1991) provide a good approach to this issue, but the analysis should be taken further. The fact that 80% of households do not follow a common prescription might suggest vigorous efforts at education, but further research to refine that prescription and tailor it to the situation of a specific household would be useful. In the future, perhaps computer expert systems could help individual consumers decide on optimal levels of emergency funds.

References

Asinof, L. (1992). Paying down your debt can boost your returns. The Wall Street Journal. V. LXXIII(254), C1 (October 9).

Bae, M.K. (1992). Analysis of Household Spending Patterns, Ph.D. dissertation, The Ohio State University.

Chang, Y., Fan, J. & Hanna, S. (1992). Relative risk aversion and optimal credit use with uncertain income, The Proceedings of the American Council on Consumer Interests, 14-22.

Dreze, J. & Modigliani, F. (1972). Consumption decision under uncertainty. Journal of Economic Theory, 5(3), 308-335.

Garman, E. & Forgue, R. (1991). Personal Finance. Boston, Mass: Houghton Mifflin Company.

Griffith, R. (1985). Personal financial statement analysis: a modest beginning. In G. Langrehr (Ed.), The Proceedings of the Third Annual Conference of the Association for Financial Counseling and Planning Education, 123-131.

Grossman, S. & Shiller, R. (1981). The determinants of the variability of stock market prices. American Economic Review: Papers and Proceedings, 71(2), 222-227.

Hall, R. (1988). Intertemporal substitution in consumption. Journal of Political Economy, 96(2), 339-357.

Hanna, S. (1989). "Risk Aversion and Optimal Insurance Deductibles," American Council on Consumer Interests Proceedings.

Hey, J. (1979). Uncertainty in microeconomics. New York: New York University Press.

Hurd, M. (1989). Mortality risk and bequests. Econometrica, 57(4), 779-813.

Johnson, D. & Widdows, R. (1985). Emergency fund levels of households. In K. Schnittgrund (Ed.), The Proceedings of the American Council on Consumer Interests 31th Annual Conference, 235-241.

Kinsey, J. & Lane, S. (1978). The effect of debt on perceived household welfare. The Journal of Consumer Affairs, 12(1), 48-62.

Leland, H. (1968). Saving and uncertainty: the precautionary demand for saving. Quarterly Journal of Economics, LXXXII(3), 465-473.

Levhari, D. & Srinivasan, T. (1969). Optimal savings under uncertainty. Review of Economic Studies, 36(106), 153-163.

Lindqvist, A. (1981). A note on the determinants of household saving behavior. Journal of Economic Psychology, Vol. 1, 39-57.

Mirman, L. (1971). Uncertainty and optimal consumption decisions. Econometrica, 39(1), 179-185.

Prather, C. (1990). The ratio analysis technique applied to personal financial statements: development of household norms. Financial Counseling and Planning, (Vol. 1), 53-69.

Sandmo, A. (1970). The effect of uncertainty on saving decisions. Review of Economic Studies, 37(111), 353-360.

Salyer, K. (1988). The characterization of savings under uncertainty: the case of serially correlated returns. Economic Letters, 26(1), 21-27.

Sibley, D. (1975). Permanent and transitory income effects in a model of optimal consumption with wage income uncertainty. Journal of Economic Theory, 11(1), 68-82.

Skinner, J. (1985). Variable lifespan and the intertemporal elasticity of consumption. Review of Economics and Statistics, 67, 616-623.

Smythe, K. (1968). An approach to determine "safe" levels for family credit commitments. Journal of Consumer Affairs, 2(2), 167-181.

U.S. Bureau of Labor Statistics [USBLS] (1986). Consumer Expenditure Survey: Interview Survey, 1982-83. Bulletin 2246.

Determinants of Holdings of Types of Savings

Ann M. Davis, Purdue University[1]

The determinants of holdings of IRAs and Keoghs, CDs, bonds, MMMFs, MMDAs, and stocks were investigated. Logistic procedures were run on data from the 1983 Survey of Consumer Finances. Savings were found not to be homogeneous products. Bonds were more likely to be held by households with children. Publicly traded stocks were found to be held by those with smaller households. Race, income squared and education were significant determinants for all types of savings.

The deregulation of banking as well as changes in federal tax laws has resulted in an increase in the offerings of financial assets. The financial market has expanded into individual retirement accounts and Keoghs, money market mutual funds, and money market deposit accounts. These changes have affected the entire market for savings, as well as credit. Avery, Elliehausen, and Canner (1984) noted from the 1983 Survey of Consumer Finances that the amount of holdings in saving and checking accounts decreased between 1977 and 1983. This decrease may reflect a shift from conventional checking and savings accounts into the more recent offerings of banks and other financial companies.

Although each type of saving instrument accounts for a small proportion of total savings, the dollar amount invested is into the billions. Mutual funds account for 4% of all assets or $226 billion dollars. Money market accounts make up 3.6 percent of all the savings in 1990; this was equivalent to $196 billion (Courtless, 1991). Courtless (1991) states that in the "last 40 years stocks have been a major share of financial assets of individuals" (p. 16). Savings bonds accounted for $57 billion of savings (Courtless, 1991).

Holdings of savings are affected by characteristics of households and also economic variables. Courtless (1990) suggests that the economic variables that affect savings are inflation, interest rates, the 1986 tax reform, social security, and availability of individual retirement accounts. Savings are decreased by a higher inflation rate (Courtless, 1991). The effect of the tax reform of 1986 on savings is unclear as is the relationship between savings and social security (Courtless, 1991). Venti and Wise (1990) found that savings created through individual retirement accounts was new savings and was not followed by a decrease in other types of savings.

Hefferan (1982) suggests that there are three aspects of the choice to save. These are the deferment of spending, saving a specific dollar amount, and the choice of instrument used. Her study analyzed the factors related to the decision to save and the amount saved. She describes what types of households used different types of saving instruments.

This study will deal with the last choice that consumers make; it will examine the determinants of the holdings of various types of saving. The purpose of the study is to further understand the factors determining ownership of each type of savings instrument.

Related Literature

The life cycle hypothesis of saving (Ando & Modigliani, 1963) has been used extensively to account for changes in savings over the life cycle. This theory is similar to Thurow's (1969) life cycle theory of consumption; the foundation of both of the theories is the same although they deal with converse issues. The basis of both theories is the utility function which says that consumers will optimize their saving over the lifetime.

There are three assumptions of the life cycle hypothesis of saving: 1) consumers think about the future 2) desire to borrow against the future and 3) preference for greater consumption (Wilcox, 1991). At any given period during their life, consumers could be saving or dissaving; however, the desired result is maximum utility over the lifetime. Because the types of savings have distinct qualities and risks associated with them, there will be a varied number of optimal uses of those types of savings. Thus, at different points in the life cycle, individuals will use the types of savings that best suit their consumption and savings patterns at that time.

Although Wilcox (1991) states that the life cycle theory of saving does not seem to hold up very strongly for aggregate data he concedes that there are some "valuable reference points" (p. 12) that remain from the theory. Juster (1986) also believes that the life cycle theory provides an important basis on which to study.

Previous research has suggested that the various types of saving should be studied separately (Lindqvist, 1980). Lindqvist's research begins to indicate that the determinants may be different for the holding of types of savings. He found that income and education are strong

---

[1]Graduate Student,
Consumer Sciences and Retailing

predictors of the change in total saving. Also, life cycle and type of residence were important factors. These variables all had a positive impact on the change in total saving of households.

Davis and Schumm, (1984) in their study comparing high and low income groups' saving, found that family income had no effect on saving in lower income households; however, it was a strong predictor of saving for higher income households. They found that there seemed to be a threshold level of income at which saving occurred.

Avery, Elliehausen and Canner (1984) have noted from the 1983 Survey of Consumer Finance that liquid assets increased with income. Through univariate analysis the researchers found that age, stage of the life cycle, education, home ownership, marital status, and race are also related to income. In the 1983 Survey of Consumer Finances, holdings of money market accounts, certificates of deposit, individual retirement accounts, Keoghs and savings bonds increase with income.   Stocks, however, are lower for incomes between $20,00 and $29,000.   These figures indicate that the market for financial assets may not be homogeneous.

In Avery, Elliehausen and Canner's (1984) second report on the 1983 Survey of Consumer Finances, they found that younger and higher income households hold brokered money market mutual funds more often than money market deposit accounts. This reflects the fact that higher incomes can accept the higher risk that is associated with money market mutual funds. Stockholders also have similar characteristics to money market mutual fund holders, although holders of stock have greater assets.

It has also been found that female headed households had lower holdings of savings overall when controlling for several variables (Hefferan, 1982). Hefferan controlled for income, number of workers in the household, contribution of the second worker, total assets, housing status, education, social class, and family life cycle. The assets
held by female headed households were one-third that of two earner families.   The greatest disparity between female and two earner families was the dollar amount of holdings of securities and bonds.

Hypotheses

Only general predictions can be made from the literature in terms of the specific effects of variables on the various types of saving; there has not been sufficient research in this area to make predictions about every individual type of savings. Following the life cycle hypothesis, the holding of various saving instruments are expected to be related to factors associated with the households' life cycle stage. The period of greatest saving is during middle age when households are preparing for a decrease in income during retirement.   The

variables used in this study to operationalize the period of the life cycle are the age of the head of household, the number of persons under 18 in the household, the total number of persons in the household and the marital status of the head of the household. As the age of the head of household increases, it is expected that the holdings of those households will increase. A greater number of persons under 18 as well as a larger number of persons in the household are expected to decrease the holdings of the types of savings in those households. Heads of households that are married are expected to have holdings in a greater number of savings than those who are not married.

Income is hypothesized to have a positive relationship with the holdings of savings. This will be particularly strong for brokered money market mutual funds and stocks because higher income households will be better able to accept greater risk with their investments.   Income squared was used to reflect the expected decline in the impact of income to affect ownership of types of savings instruments.

Consistent with findings of Hefferan (1982), it is hypothesized that female headed households will hold fewer types of savings instruments than male headed households.

The variables used to operationalize wealth are net worth, total amount of liquid assets and total amount of non-liquid assets. These variables are expected to have a positive relationship with holdings of all types of savings.   This would be the case particularly with stocks and money market mutual funds due to the greater risk associated with these types of savings.

Various demographic variables were included to account for the effects of other variables on holdings of types of saving. Race was expected to have an effect such that nonwhites would have lower probabilities of holding than would whites, controlling for other variables in the model. This would be due to differing experiences and culture of different racial groups. Rural households were expected to have fewer holdings than were urban households.   This may be simply because of the difficulty they may have of reaching financial institutions or differences in investment strategies.   Occupation was expected to have a positive effect for white collar workers due to the fact that they have greater security in their jobs. Education was expected to have an effect similar to income.   As the educational level increases the probability of holding all savings types will increase also.

Methodology

The 1983 Survey of Consumer Finance data collected by the Survey Research Center was used for this study.   The original sample was 4,103 households.   Those in the high income sample as well as those reporting negative incomes were not used in this study. Those with negative net worth were left in the analysis. The remaining sample used in the analysis was 3663 households.

The dependent variables were converted to binary variables to run a logistic regression. If the survey indicated a dollar amount greater than zero for each of the savings, the household was assumed to hold that type of savings instrument. Logistic models were obtained for seven dependent variables: the ownership of individual retirement accounts and Keoghs, certificates of deposit, government savings bonds, money market mutual funds (brokered and non-brokered), money market deposit accounts, and stocks.   Stocks were divided into publicly traded stocks and those given as benefits to employees (company stocks).

The independent variables are listed in Table 1.

Table 1
Independent Variables and their coding.

Life Cycle Variables:		
age	continuous	
persons in the HH under age 18	1=yes	2=no
number of persons in the HH	continuous	
marital status	1=married 2=not	
Demographic Variables:		
race	1=white	1=non-white
gender	1=female 2=male	
rural or urban HH	1=urban 2=rural	
Financial Variables:		
rent or own their home	1=own	2=rent
income	continuous	
total amount of:		
liquid assets	continuous	
financial assets	continuous	
net worth	continuous	

The variable for the presence of persons under the age of 18 was an operationalization of part of the life cycle. It was assumed that this, in combination with age, number of persons in the household, and marital status, would indicate the family's placement in the life cycle. The variable for renting versus ownership of a home was a recode of a variable from the 1983 data for the value of the home. If the value of the home was zero it was assumed that the household was renting their residence.

A test for multicollinearity was done on the independent variables. The highest correlation between the variables was found between marital status and sex. The Pearson Correlation was .75 which was not assumed to be too great given the large sample size.

Results

Table 2 shows the results of the logistic analysis. Race, education, and income squared were significant for all of the types of savings. Race is positive, indicating that whites have a greater probability of holding all of these types of saving when controlling for other variables in the model. The greater amount of educational attainment of heads of households, the greater the probability of holding these types of savings. Income squared is negatively related to savings which indicates that as higher income levels are attained the probability of ownership decreases. This would indicate that the relationship between income and ownership of savings produces a bell-shaped curve.

Age is a significant variable for determining holdings of certificates of deposit, money market deposit accounts and publicly traded stocks. The relationship is negative for government savings bonds which indicates that holdings of bonds are less likely as age increases, controlling for all other variables in the model.

The existence of children under 18 in the household is only significant for government savings bonds. This may be due to the purchase of bonds by parents in the child's name.

Contrary to what was hypothesized and also found by Hefferan (1982), sex was not significant in determining ownership of any of the types of savings.

The number of persons in the household was significant and negative for publicly traded stocks.   This may be due to the fact that as household size decreases, discretionary income increases, allowing saving because they lack the financial burden of children.

Marital status was significant for IRA's and Keoghs and government savings bonds. Those who are married may place a higher priority on planning ahead for their retirement years than unmarried households.   Government savings bonds may be purchased more for children by those who are married, as mentioned above.

The concordance for each model is listed in Table 2.   The values ranged from 70.6% for government savings bonds to 87.6% for certificates of deposit.

Pseudo R-squares were calculated for each model as well and are shown in Table 2. Pseudo R-squares are created in logistic procedures to produce greater interpritability of the data; and, they can be interpreted in the same manner as R-squares produced in regression analysis.   These values range from 7% for money market deposit accounts to 22.9 percent for certificates of deposit.

Table 2
Beta Values of Determinants of Types of Savings.

	IRAs/Keoghs	CDs	Bonds	MMMF	MMMD	Company Stocks	Public Stocks
intercept	-6.015 **	-5.189**	-3.889**	-9.264**	-5.885**	-7.0978**	-5.626**
age	0.006	.021**	-.0069	.0018	.0139**	.0156**	.0046
under 18	-.013	.0445	.3719**	-.1750	-.3144	.0287	-.1071
sex	.221	-.2958	.00119	-.2951	.0753	-.1296	-.0894
race	.881 **	1.111**	.7060**	1.11**	.8403**	.9654**	.8778**
# in HH	-.106	-.0773	-.0439	-.0999	-.1040	-.1881*	-.0978
own/rent	.549 **	.6213**	.5477**	.1411	.4892**	.5343**	.5265**
education	.092 **	.0732**	.0781**	.3105**	.0813**	.1855**	.1341**
net worth	-2.39E-7	-4.94E-9	-1.63E-7	-3.685E-8-	.226E-8	2.413E-7	4.293E-8
liquid	.00001 **	.000065**	5.688E-6**	7.72E-6**	9.28E-6**	-3.92E-6	-.00002**
financial	-1.11E-6	-2.33E-6*	1.184E-7	-4.956E-7	1.377E-6	.00001**	.000022**
marital	.397 *	.2369	.3744*	.3395	.1892	.3848	.3056
urban/rural	.403 **	-0.0147	.2178*	.8400**	.3663*	.6262**	.5846**
income	.00004 **	-1.68E-6	.000015**	.00002**	.000016**	.00001**	.000019**
income^2	-96.7E-12 **	-41.5E-12*	-53.5E-12 **	-3.8E-11**	-.539E-10**	-.343E-10**	-.615E-10**
pseudo R^2	.165	.229	.081	.087	.07	.124	.15
concordance	82.7%	87.6%	70.6%	83.8%	78.8%	81.6%	81.4%

** denotes significance level of .01
* denotes significance level of .05

Conclusions

There are differences between the types of savings. The findings indicate that government savings bonds are an important method of saving for those with families. Stocks and money market mutual funds may be useful to those with higher incomes who could accept the risk of these types of accounts. These findings may be important to financial planners to better understand the users of thevarious types of savings. Through these findings the financial planner would be knowledgeable about the types of households that would be most apt to use the individual types of savings.

It was an intention of this study to analyze money market mutual funds that are brokered and those that are not brokered separately. The sample of households holding these types of accounts was not large enough to do this, however. It is assumed that these accounts would not be held by the same groups of people. A study to analyze these individually would be useful.

Acknowledgement

The data were obtained through the Federal Reserve. I would like to thank Dr. Dixie Porter Johnson for her assistance with this project and in the preparation of the manuscript.

References

Ando, A. & Modigliani, F. (1963). The "life cycle" hypothesis of saving: Aggregate implications and tests. American Economic Review, 53, 55-84.

Avery, R. B., Elliehausen, G. E. & Canner, G. B. (1984). Survey of Consumer Finances, 1983. Federal Reserve Bulletin. pp. 679-682.

Avery, R. B., Elliehausen, G. E. & Canner, G. B. (1984). Survey of Consumer Finances, 1983: A second report. Federal Reserve Bulletin. pp. 857-868.

Courtless, J. C. (1991). Trends in savings. Family Economics Review, 4(4), 15-21.

Davis, E. P. & Schumm, W. R. (1987). Saving behavior and satisfaction with savings: A comparison of low and high income groups. Home Economics Research Journal, 15(4), 247-256.

Hefferan, C. (1982). Determinants and patterns of family saving. Home Economics Research Journal, 11(1), 47-55.

Juster, F. T. (1986). What do we know about saving behavior? Economic Outlook USA, 13(4), 17-23.

Lindqvist, A. (1981). A note on determinants of household saving behavior. Journal of Economic Psychology, 1, 39-57.

1983 Survey of Consumer Finances. Survey Research Center, Institute for Social Research, University of Michigan, Ann Arbor.

Thurow, L. (1969). The optimum lifetime distribution of consumption expenditures. American Economic Review, 59(2), 324-330.

Venti, S. F. & Wise. D. A. (1990). Have IRA's increased U.S. saving?: Evidence from consumer expenditure surveys. <u>Quarterly Journal of Economics</u>, <u>105</u>, 661-698.

Wilcox, D. W. (1991). Household spending and saving: Measurement, trends, and analysis. <u>Federal Reserve Bulletin</u>, <u>77</u>, 1-17.

Materialism and Other Consumption Orientations

Monroe Friedman, Eastern Michigan University[1]

Materialism is a subject which is enjoying a rebirth of interest on the part of scholars as well as practitioners. This paper briefly reviews some of the problems and approaches associated with efforts to conceptualize materialism.

This paper presents observations stimulated by the author's participation in the recently held Research Workshop on Materialism and Other Consumption Orientations. The workshop which was held in June 1992 in Kingston, Ontario, was sponsored by the School of Business of Queen's University and the Association for Consumer Research. The workshop was not only multi-disciplinary in character (with representation from such fields as advertising, anthropology, psychology, philosophy, sociology, marketing, and law, but international as well (with participants from Canada, Britain, New Zealand, Poland, and the United States). That this workshop was the first of its kind to be held reflects the fact that the cross disciplinary study of materialism as a consumption orientation is in its very early stages. The workshop focused on some of the principal approaches and problems of this young field.

In light of limitations of time and space, this paper will restrict its focus to a discussion of problems and approaches associated with conceptualizing materialism.

Conceptualizing Materialism

As Richins and Dawson (1992) have noted recently, scholars differ considerably in their views of materialism. One of the research pioneers in the area (Belk, 1984, p. 291) defines it as "the importance a consumer attaches to worldly possessions." Two others (Rassuli and Hollander, 1986, p. 10) see materialism as "a mindset...an interest in getting and spending." Murkerji (1983, p. 8), on the other hand, views materialism as "a cultural system in which material interests are not made subservient to other social goals."

While this brief sampling of definitions of materialism does not begin to exhaust the field, it does illustrate the possibilities and the problems in conceptualizing materialism. Some of the dilemmas confronted are as follows:

1. Is materialism a psychological or a sociological concept?

[1]Professor of Psychology

Does materialism describe an individual or a society? As we have just seen, both uses have been evident in the scholarly literature, with both individuals and societies being referred to as "materialistic."

2. Does the concept focus on material in general, or on material wealth in particular?

While a focus on the material world as compared to the spiritual world would seem to define the materialist, many scholars and practitioners find this domain too broad; agreeing with Madonna's "Material Girl" they opt for a conceptualization which concentrates on material wealth. Yet one wonders if this definition is too confining, eliminating as it does from consideration, such interesting phenomena as the voluntary simplicity movement with its emphasis on the beauty and value of simple tools and devices to help one live a more self-sufficient life.

3. Does the concept focus on acquisition or possession?

Acquiring material things would appear to be a major concern and source of satisfaction for materialists but most scholars also stress the importance of possession. In practice it is difficult to separate these two entities in that most of our possessions don't just land on our doorsteps but become ours through an acquisition process. So the joy of owning may in part derive from the joy of acquiring, especially if it entailed something memorable like a gift from a loved one. Yet the two entities are sometimes separated in the real world and such occasions may present research opportunities for social scientists. For example, the professional shopper buys goods for others, and is thus an example of one who may acquire without the objective of ownership. Conversely, the "old money crowd" is said to consist of individuals who are born to wealth and comfortable circumstances, and yet show little inclination to acquire more material goods, especially those associated with affluence.

4. Does the concept focus on instrumental materialism or terminal materialism?

Rochberg-Halton (1986) and Csikszentmihalyi and Rochberg-Halton (1978, 1981) have proposed two types of materialism based on the intended purposes of consumption. When objects act "as essential means for discovering and furthering personal values and goals of life," the materialism is referred to as "instrumental" (Csikszentmihalyi and Rochberg-Halton 1978, p. 8). When, on the other hand, consumption satisfies no objective other than possession, materialism is regarded as "terminal." Needless to say, these terms are hardly neutral, with terminal materialism, like its cancer counterpart, being viewed as an unhealthy human condition. Also of interest are the difficulties in operationalizing the concepts. As Richins and Dawson (1992) have noted, it is not always clear which relationships with objects are instrumental and which are terminal. Also not clear is whether materialistic relationships exist which are neither instrumental nor terminal.

5. Does the concept focus on commercial or non-commercial materialism?

Although claims of increasing interest in materialism in American society have long been made by humanists, supporting empirical evidence has been in short supply. Recently this changed with documentation of dramatic increases in the use of brand names (but not generic names) in popular American novels, plays and music of the post World War II era (Friedman 1991). This finding, along with others, prompted Friedman to propose that the brand-name phenomenon be called "commercial materialism" to distinguish it from its generic name counterpart of "non-commercial materialism." By proposing this distinction Friedman is suggesting that the two types of materialism may not only behave differently empirically but that they may also relate theoretically to different explanatory systems.

The foregoing brief discussion illustrates some of the complexities encountered in attempting to conceptualize materialism. Additional problems arise when one realizes that many of the either-or dichotomies set forth are false in that some scholars have viewed materialism as embracing both categories (e.g., acquisition and possession). Also not considered are the cultural and sub-cultural contexts in which materialism manifests itself. Thus an act viewed as an example of instrumental materialism in one context may be viewed as an example of terminal materialism in another.

References

Belk, R. W. (1984). Three Scales to Measure Constructs Related to Materialism: Reliability, Validity, and Relationships to Measures of Happiness. In T. Kinnear (Ed.), Advances in Consumer Research Vol 11 (pp. 291-297). Provo, UT: Association for Consumer Research.

Csikszentmihalyi, M., & Rochberg-Halton, E. (1978) Reflections on Materialism. University of Chicago Magazine, 70 (3), 6-15.

Csikszentmihalyi, M., & Rochberg-Halton, E. (1981). The Meaning of Things: Domestic Symbols and the Self. Cambridge: Cambridge University Press.

Friedman, M. (1991). A "Brand" New Language. Westport, CT: Greenwood.

Mukerji, C. (1983). From Graven Images: Patterns of Modern Materialism, New York: Columbia University.

Rassuli, K. M., & Hollander, S.C. (1986). Desire - Induced, Innate, Insatiable? Journal of Macromarketing, 6 (Fall), 4-24.

Richins, M. L., & Dawson, S. (1992). A Consumer Values Orientation for Materialism and Its Measurement. Journal of Consumer Research, 19 (December), 303-316.

Rochberg-Halton, E. (1986). Meaning and Modernity: Social Theory in the Pragmatic Attitude. Chicago: University of Chicago Press.

Rudmin, F., & Richins, M.L. (Eds.) (1992). Meaning, Measure, and Morality of Materialism. Provo, UT: Association for Consumer Research.

The Coming Resurgence of the Consumer Movement: Prospects and Potential

Roger Swagler, The University of Georgia[1]

Discussions of the future of the consumer movement should not neglect consideration of its past. The consumer activism of the 1960's and 1970's represents the third such period this century. Periods of reform, which occur at fairly regular 30-year intervals, seem to be linked to intergenerational change. A new period of consumer reform may, therefore, be near. Because of changes in the economy, this new period will have its distinctive features and challenges.

Introduction

"Does Consumerism Have a Future?" Herrmann asked that question at this conference over a dozen years ago. While he labored to answer in the affirmative, he made it clear that the consumer movement was in a period of "fragmentation and demise" (Herrmann and Warland 1980, 13). Since then, his judgment has been confirmed. It is now conventional to date the decline of the consumer movement from the mid-1970's (Garman 1991).

However, before one becomes too nostalgic about what Herrmann later called "the halcyon days of the 1970's" (Herrmann, Walsh and Warland 1988, 474), it is necessary to probe more deeply. First of all, it is not at all surprising that the burst of activity which characterized the consumer movement from the mid-1960's should have played out. That is the typical pattern for all social movements. Early initiatives develop momentum and generate activity: however, the process eventually wanes as enthusiasm, and then interest, decline (Herrmann and Warland 1980).

Indeed, it had all happened before, not once, but twice. The consumer movement of the 1960's and 1970's represented the third wave of activity this century. The first came during the Progressive Era prior to World War I; the second wave was during the decade of the Great Depression (Dameron, 1939; Herrmann 1974). Rather than lamenting the passage of the last wave, then, we might want to reflect on if, or when, the next one is due.

The if? question is easily answered: yes. Consumer issues are so fundamental to everyone's well being that they will surely reemerge near the top of the public's agenda. That is clear, but not very helpful, since the same could be said of almost any other major issue. The answer to the when? question is at once more important and less evident. However, there is reason to believe that the next wave may be approaching even now. The next great period of consumer activism may be at hand.

Intergenerational Cycles

The most obvious basis for that contention lies in simple arithmetic: the three periods of reform noted above occurred roughly at 30 year intervals. The Pure Food and Drug Act of 1906 was revised and extended 32 years later, to be followed in another 30 years by the Consumer Credit Protection Act ("Truth in Lending,") (Gaedeke and Etcheson 1972).[1] Given that pattern, the next period of reform should begin before the end of this decade.

Chronological patterns, however, are, at best, a crude basis for establishing a cycle. The chronology is subject to the post hoc, ergo hoc fallacy; that is, the 30-year interval may be chance. Lacking logical content, the formulation is essentially artificial, with no basis for arguing that events will develop in a particular way simply because they did so in the past.

The historian Arthur M. Schlesinger, Jr. and his father are among the numerous scholars who have grappled with the question of cycles. The elder Schlesinger identified a pattern of cycles extending back to the founding of the Republic with hardly an interruption (Schlesinger 1949).[2] In an extension of his father's work, Arthur Schlesinger, Jr. (Schlesinger 1986, 27) defined the cycle "as a continuing shift in national involvement between public purpose and private interest" (emphasis added). For the "genuine cycle," he continued:

> the explanation must be primarily internal. Each new phase must flow out of the conditions -- and contradictions -- of the phase before and then itself prepare the way for the next recurrence. A true cycle, in other words, is self-generating (27).

The power for Schlesinger's cycles is provided by "the generational experience." He noted (1986):

> a generation's political life lasts about thirty years. Each generation spends is first fifteen years after coming of political age in challenging the generation already entrenched in power. Then the new generation comes to power itself for another fifteen years, after which its policies pall and the generation coming up behind claims the

---

[1] Housing and Consumer Economics

succession (30).

From this perspective, recent national leadership in the United States reflected the attitudes learned during the Eisenhower years, to be replaced by those who came of age during the Kennedy-Johnson administrations. According to Schlesinger (1986, 30), the latter will tend "to repudiate the work of the generation it has displaced and to reenact the ideals of its own formative days thirty years before."

Schlesinger (1986, 30) stressed that the generational sequences feature neither "arithmetical inevitability" nor swings which are "grandiose and immutable." Rather, the cycles result from an all-too-human tendency for people to tire of existing patterns. The continual change associated with the reforms of the public periods eventually turns people's thoughts inward; conversely, during years of preoccupation with private matters, problems accumulate which finally require concerted action.

The years when the consumer movement flourished correspond to Schlesinger's periods of "public purpose."[3] Those years followed, as Garman (1991, 39) noted, "periods when the good of the corporation was equated with the good of the nation." During such intervals of "private interest," -- which surely include the 1980's and the early 1990's -- the movement has languished. If the pattern suggested by this formulation holds, the consumer movement will be carried upward again as the tide of public purpose rises later this decade.[4]

The Changed Environment

The revived consumer movement, however, will not pick up where things left off in 1975. Schlesinger correctly rejected the analogy of a pendulum which swings between two fixed points and returns to where it began. A change in cycles does not mean a return to the status quo ante. Instead, he suggested a "spiral, in which the alternation proceeded at successively higher levels" and change accumulated (Schlesinger 1986, 24).

Thus, despite a certain laxness in enforcement, the reforms of the 1960's and 1970's remain in place. So, too, however, will the changes in the economic environment which have taken place during these most recent years of private interest. Indeed, those changes help explain why the new generation seeks to displace the old. The reforms of the 1960's and 1970's did not -- could not -- address the realities of the 1990's. The accumulation of change has resulted in unmet needs which, when they become sufficiently acute, will usher in a new era of public purpose.

It is difficult to summarize all the changes which have taken place in the economy over the past two decades. However, the most fundamental developments surely include the following.

1. The **globalization of the economy** has raised the cost of information and made it even more difficult to ensure corporate accountability.

2. The dawn of the **information age** has increased both the amount of, and need for, information. Access, however, is not ensured and large numbers of consumers may be marginalized because they are cut off from necessary information.

3. **Technological change** has meant significant restructuring in areas such as communications and the media. In the case of biotechnology, whole new categories of products are being created which may raise problems for consumers.

4. **Deregulation** has raised information costs for all consumers and, in instances such as the savings and loan crisis, has imposed a public burden. In most cases of deregulation, it is possible to identify a group of consumers who have suffered.

5. **Environmental concerns** have focused attention on the relationship between high levels of consumption and environmental deterioration, while highlighting the need to consider the environmental impact of any initiative from the private or public sectors.

The cumulative impact of these various elements is a new set of economic imperatives which help frame the agenda for the consumer movement.

That agenda, however, will have to be crafted carefully. The elements noted here are not simply new, they are part of a much more complex economic environment. That complexity, in turn, requires a more flexible set of responses. There are two reasons for making that contention.

First, the elements listed above have created problems, but do not represent evils in and of themselves. Consider that:

1. globalization of the economy has benefitted American consumers through lowering production costs, increasing choice and promoting competition in key sectors (such as automobiles);

2. increased access to information provides consumers with added leverage and has facilitated the exchange of information;

3. some consumers have suffered because of deregulation in areas such as banking and long-distance telephone services, but others have gained;

4.   there is a need for prudence, but biotechnology holds promise for the development of useful, potentially life-saving, products.

5.   the environment is consumed at so many levels -- directly in the form of clean air or wilderness, indirectly through new con-struction and waste disposal -- that one can link a "consumer interest" to any environmental position.

There are more examples, but the point should be clear: generalized positions will be more difficult to maintain because the particulars of each issue will have to be evaluated. Otherwise, consumer groups cannot claim to be speaking in the consumer interest because significant numbers -- in some cases, the majority -- of everyday consumers will oppose them. Trade offs among various groups of consumers will make it more difficult to project a clear image to the public and build a consensus,[5] but the common ground must be found if action is to be effective.

The second consideration has to do with the heightened distrust of big government. Disenchantment with perceived failures of past government programs may fade as the cycle changes, but to the extent that the response is fundamentally anti-bureaucratic, it is unlikely to go away. Thus, calling for new regulations or government programs as a routine response to problems is likely to remain unpopular.

These developments present new challenges, but do not represent impossible obstacles. Indeed, they will have a positive impact if they result in programs which are better thought out or encourage the emergence of creative solutions. Maximizing efficiency and minimizing unintended consequences are surely beneficial. Nontraditional, market-oriented responses may offer a range of possibilities.

Whatever new approaches do emerge will merely represent the continued evolution of consumer policy responses. During the first two periods of consumer reform, legislation focused on classic regulation, as illustrated by the Pure Food and Drug Act of 1906 and its extension in 1938. That option also played a role in the 1960's and 1970's, but information-based policies -- such as Truth in Lending -- came to be relied upon with increasing frequency. One would expect that trend to continue, with increased emphasis on empowering individuals and making it easier for consumers to protect their own interests in the market.

Final Observations and Conclusions

Three final points should be made. The first has to do with political considerations which have been ignored thus far. That may seem strange following a presidential election, because public purpose cycles tend to be associated with the Democrats and private interest with the Republicans. The fit, however, is not perfect. When this paper was first written, the outcome of the presidential election was unclear; since then, a Democratic president has been elected, but that does not guarantee the resurgence of the consumer movement any more than the election of a Democrat in 1976 arrested the movement's decline (Richardson 1986).

During the campaign, the Democratic ticket distanced itself from both the term liberal and the concept of large-scale government programs. Whether that Clinton presidency continues that course remains to be seen. Recall, however, that despite the promise of President Kennedy's "Consumer Bill of Rights" in 1962 (Lampman 1988), the real acceleration in the pace of reform came two years later. Thus, if 1993 does not turn out to be the watershed year, chances are improved that the change in cycles will follow soon thereafter.[6]

Schlesinger, for one, believes that the change is underway. Writing in the Wall Street Journal soon after the election (1992: A15), he noted that President Clinton took over in a "comparably ragged time from the conservative to the liberal phase of the cycle." Comparing 1992 to 1960, Schlesinger continued:

> Like President Kennedy in 1961, Mr. Clinton will confront a mixture of contradictory political pressures, some urging him forward toward activism, some pulling him back toward conservatism. But soon, if the usual rhythm holds, the liberal tide, in the 1990s as in the 1960s, will run in full flood (emphasis added).

The second point has to do with emphasis. The continued references to the "resurgence" of the consumer movement are not meant to suggest that the movement is currently ineffectual. The emphasis here is on relative strength. The possi-bility of greater influence in the future does not imply a lack of influence now.[7] Indeed, the impact of sustained pressure over time is probably undervalued. Remember that when consumer groups began raising safety questions about automobiles 30 years ago, the industry claimed that "safety won't sell." Now manufactures emphasize the added safety of "crumble zones," air bags and anti-lock breaking systems. Without the on-going influence of the consumer movement, the outcome might well have been different.

Finally, it should be emphasized that no discussion of the future can deal in absolutes. There is a compelling logic to the idea of cycles, but the pattern is by no means assured. Schlesinger (1986) himself emphasized:

> As the cycle is not automatic, neither is it self-enforcing. It takes people to make the cycle work. Those

who believe in public purpose must interpret events, press issues and devise remedies. They must rise above those worthy special interests . . . that have become their electoral refuge and regain a commanding national vision. . . (45-6).

In short, the system is not deterministic. It takes individuals with courage, vision and ideas to seize the moment.

With respect to ideas, the future holds promise. Indeed, if one can be certain about anything concerning the future, it is that in its next up-cycle, the consumer movement will have the benefit of a much sounder research base. Thirty years ago, this organization was still young; there was no Journal of Consumer Affairs, and if anyone had thought (or could have afforded) to compile The Frontier of Research in the Consumer Interest, it would have been a much slimmer volume than the one with which we are familiar.

This is not meant to deprecate those who were working in the field at the time; rather, it emphasizes the solid nature of the structure which has been built on the foundations they laid. It follows that broadening and deepening the research base is the greatest contribution consumer researchers can make to the revival of the consumer movement. The carefully crafted agenda discussed above cannot be developed without a body of research to draw upon. If, however, as much can be achieved in the next generation as was accomplished in the last one, the future is secure.

References

Brobek, S. (1990). The Consumer Movement: References and Resources, Boston: G.K. Hill.

Dameron, K. (1939). The Consumer Movement, Harvard Business Review, 18(January), 271-89

Gaedeke, R., & Etcheson, W. (1972). Consumerism. San Franscisco: Canfield.

Herrmann, R. (1974). The Consumer Movement in Historical Perspective. In D. Aaker & G. Day (Eds.), Consumerism: Search for the Consumer Interest (2nd ed.) (pp. 10-18). New York: The Free Press.

Herrmann, R., Walsh, E., & Warland, R. (1988). The Organization of the Consumer Movement: A Comparative Perspective. In E.S. Maynes (Ed.), The Frontier of Research in the Consumer Interest. Columbia, MO: American Council on Consumer Interests, 469-494.

Herrman, R., & Warland, R. (1980). Does Consumerism Have a Future? In Proceedings, 26th Annual Conference of the American Council on Consumer Interests. Columbia, MO. 12-17.

Hirschman, A. O.(1982), Shifting Involvements: Private Interest and Public Action. Princeton, NJ: Princeton University Press.

Garman, E. T. (1991). Consumer Economic Issues in America. Boston: Houghton Mifflin.

Lampman, R. J. (1988). JFK's Four Consumer Rights: A Retrospective View. In E.S. Maynes (Ed.), The Frontier of Research in the Consumer Interest. Columbia, MO: American Council on Consumer Interests, 19-36.

Richardson, S. L. (1986). The Evolving Consumer Movement: Predictions for the 1990s. In P. Bloom & R. Smith (Eds)., The Future of Consumerism. Lexington, MA: Lexington.

Schlesinger, A. M. (1949). Paths to the Present, New York: Macmillan.

Schlesinger, A. M., Jr. (1992). Thoughts for the Interrednum, The Wall Street Journal, 96 (CCXX) (November 12), A15.

Schlesinger, A. M., Jr. (1986). The Cycles of American History. Boston: Haughton Mifflin

Endnotes

1. Although the Sherman Antitrust Act was passed in 1890, enforcement lagged. Reform was at its heighth between 1906 (Pure Food and Drug Act) and 1914 (Federal Trade Commission Act). Reform in 1930's came later in the decade, around the date given. The most recent period was foreshadowed by President's Kennedy's "Consumer Bill of Rights" in 1962, but the bulk of substantive reform come later in the decade.

2. The major exception is the Civil War-Reconstruction period. Changes during that time were so monumental that it may have taken longer to accomodate them (Schlesinger 1986).

3. In an extension of consumption theory to the political sphere, Hirschman developed a similar theory of cycles which alternate between "private interest" and "public action" (Hirschman 1982).

4. Richardson mentioned cycles and the consumer movement in the 1986 article dealing with "Predictions for the 1990s." His focus, however, was on organizational elements, and he did not deal with the pattern of periodic revival.

5. That is, is easier for a group to explain itself (and to get attention) by saying: "We oppose all deregulation," than by saying: "We favor deregulation in Case A, but oppose it in B."

6. In retrospect, it may be significant that the only Congressional override of a presidential

veto during the Bush presidency came on a
consumer bill (legislation to reregulate the
cable television industry).

7.   See (Brobek, 1990).

Nutrition Claims in Advertising and Food Production Trends

Pauline M. Ippolito, Federal Trade Commission[1]
Alan D. Mathios, Cornell University[2]

This paper analyzes trends in the production of foods that vary by fat content to determine whether information linking fat consumption to disease may have affected consumers' food choices. It also examines whether the change in regulatory policy in 1984, which allowed producers to link diet and disease in advertising and labeling is correlated with improvements in food choices, or as many critics of the regulatory change feared, to confusion sufficient to slow improvements in diet.

Introduction

Diet is believed to be linked substantially to five of the top ten causes of death in the U.S. (U.S. Surgeon General (1988)). The question of how best to get developing information about diet and health to consumers has been much debated in policy circles, especially as it relates to producers' role in disseminating this type of information. This debate has culminated in the recent passage of the Nutrition Labeling Education Act, which will result in sweeping changes in the regulations governing the types of claims producers are permitted to use in food labeling.

This paper focuses on trends in the production of foods that vary in fat and cholesterol content to determine whether information linking fat and cholesterol consumption to heart disease and cancer may have affected consumers' food choices. This study also attempts to determine if the change in the policy governing producer claims in late 1984, which allowed producers to play a role in spreading information linking diet to disease risks, appears to have led to improvements in food choices, or as many critics have feared, to confusion sufficient to slow improvements in diet that would have otherwise occurred.

Critics of producer health claims contend that the rapid increase in the number of health claims has been detrimental to the American public. For example, a consumer advocacy group stated in a recent submission to FDA, "It is widely acknowledged, however, from this chaotic, deregulatory period, that bombarding consumers with a plethora of claims is not the best method of educating the public about the relationship between diet and health. The marketplace free-for-all that resulted prompted Congress to pass the NLEA in order to limit claims to those the FDA believes are appropriate." (CSPI (1992))

Similarly, the Secretary of Health and Human Services has characterized this period as one of "mayhem" where "the grocery store has become a Tower of Babel, and consumers need to be linguists, scientists and mind readers to understand the many labels they see." (HHS News (1990).

Yet despite the widespread skepticism of producer-provided information, almost no empirical work has been undertaken examining the relationship between producer claims and dietary choices of consumers. In a study of the ready-to-eat cereal market Ippolito and Mathios (1989, 1990), found that producer health claims had an important information effect, leading to significant increases in the consumption of fiber cereals and in the development of new types of fiber cereals. This paper extends the examination of information dissemination by focusing on issues related to fat and cholesterol consumption.

Developments in the Market for Fats and Cholesterol

In a study that examines how information spreads in markets, it is important to review when the information under study was available for dissemination and the regulations governing its dissemination.

Scientific Developments Related to Disease

During the 1930s and 1940s research linking serum cholesterol levels and heart disease emerged. A number of studies found that those

[1]Economist: This article does not necessarily represent the views of the Federal Trade Commission or any of its members.

[2]Associate Professor - Consumer Economics and Housing

affected with heart disease had higher levels of serum cholesterol than control groups. More evidence relating diet to heart disease through its effect on serum cholesterol developed in the 1950s and 1960s. Since then there has been continuous flow of scientific research supporting these results.

Studies also provide strong support for a relationship between fat intake and the incidence of some types of cancer. In the 1970s substantial evidence developed supporting the relationship between fat intake and breast, prostrate and colon cancer.

Information Dissemination to Consumers

Government and General Sources of Diet Information. By the early 1960s, articles were appearing in the popular press discussing the relationship between saturated and polyunsaturated fat consumption, serum cholesterol levels, and heart disease. Articles in the popular press on the relationship between fat and cancer began in the later 1970s.

Government also played a role in disseminating this information. The January 1977 report Dietary Goals for the United States recommended quantitative targets for fat and cholesterol. Similar advice was given to the public in 1980, and revised in 1985, in Dietary Guidelines for Americans, in 1988 in The Surgeon General's Report on Nutrition and Health and in 1989 in Diet and Health: Implications for Reducing Chronic Disease Risk.

Regulatory Constraints on Producers. Some forms of information dissemination were prohibited, however. Manufacturers' use of information linking a dietary component to disease risks was prohibited throughout the 1970s and early 1980s. The ban on health claims by producers was effectively lifted in late 1984, when the Kellogg Co. began a highly publicized advertising and labeling campaign explicitly using the National Cancer Institute's statements on the potential relationship between fiber and cancer to promote its high fiber cereals. This campaign led to a relaxation of the policy towards the use of health claims by producers. After 1984, a number of food manufacturers began to explicitly advertise the relationship between fats and cholesterol consumption and heart disease.

Methodology and Data

Methodology

This study uses two approaches to examine how information affected dietary choices during the period prior to producer health claims and the post-advertising period. First, trends in broad food categories that comprise a sizable portion of the diet are examined to determine if consumption shifted away from higher-fat and cholesterol food categories towards lower-fat and cholesterol categories during the periods under analysis.

The second approach uses more refined tests by focusing on particular food substitutions for which other factors that could affect food choices are not likely to play an important role and where advertising and labeling may have played a more central role. In particular, pairs of foods are chosen that first satisfy the condition there be clear a priori predictions on how the relative trends of the two foods should move in response to the dissemination of the diet-health information, and second, the foods are required to be similar enough (very close substitutes) that potential confounding factors are common to both products, thereby eliminating the importance of controlling for these factors.

Given the aggregated level of USDA production data, the requirement that foods be close substitutes sharply limits the number of products that can be analyzed with this second approach.

Data and Empirical Specification

Annual per capita production data for red meat, poultry, fish, eggs, milk and cream products, cheese, fats and oils, flour and cereal products, vegetables and fruit, butter and margarine, ice cream, ice milk and other frozen dairy products (which includes frozen yogurt) were obtained from the USDA's Food Consumption, Prices, and Expenditures, 1970-90. Data for cottage cheese, by type, and for the fat content of frozen dairy products were obtained from Dairy Products Annual Summary for the years 1977 through 1990.

For each food group the changes in production were analyzed between the years 1977-1985 (the pre-health-claim period) and 1985-1990 (the post-health-claim period). Simple regression analyses are used to determine whether statistically significant changes occurred between the two periods. The regression model is given by:

$$\text{Prod}_{it} = a_{0i} + a_{1i}\text{YEAR}_t + a_{2i}\text{D8590} + a_{3i}\text{YEAR}_t*\text{D8590} + e_{it},$$

where

Prod_{it} = Per capita production of food i in year t,

YEAR_t = the year t, for t=77,...,90,

D8590 = 1 during the health claims period, = 0 otherwise, $a_{0i},...,a_{3i}$ = coefficients to be estimated for each food i,

e_{it} = normally distributed error term for food i in year t.   (1)

The evidence is consistent with the hypothesis that government and general sources of information had an ongoing effect in informing consumers if high-fat foods exhibit a downward trend across the various foods analyzed, that is, the coefficient a$_i$ is significantly negative. The evidence is consistent with the hypothesis that the addition of health claims advertising and labeling added to the dissemination of information if the decline in high fat foods accelerated during the period, that is, if the coefficient on a$_3$ is significantly negative.

Results

Trends in Production for Major Food Categories
Meat, Poultry, Fish and Egg Products. Per capita production for red meat, poultry, fish and eggs is given in Table 1 for the years 1977-1990. The regression results in Table 1 indicate a significant decline in per capita red meat production during the government period and a significant acceleration of the decline during the health claims period.

The results also reveal a significant positive trend in per capita poultry production during the government period and a significant increase in this production trend during the health claims period.

Per capita fish production showed some tendency to increase during the 1977-1985 period, and mixed movements in the health claims period. Regression analysis shows no significant trend toward higher fish production during the 1977-1985 period or during the health claims period.

Finally, the regression results for per capita egg consumption show a significant reduction during the years 1977-1985 and a significant incremental reduction during the health claims period.

Milk and Cream Products. Table 2 shows that per capita milk production declined during the period under analysis. However, the decline masks dramatic trends in the production of whole, lowfat and skim milk.

The regression results indicate that during the government period the downward trend in whole milk production was statistically significant, as

Table 1
Per Capita Production of Red Meat, Poultry, Fish and Eggs (Pounds per Year)

Year	Red Meat	Poultry	Fish	Eggs
1977	132.2	35.9	12.6	33.9
1978	127.5	37.3	13.4	34.5
1979	124.4	40.0	13.0	35.1
1980	126.4	40.6	12.4	34.4
1981	125.1	41.9	12.6	33.6
1982	119.8	42.0	12.4	33.5
1983	123.9	42.6	13.3	33.0
1984	123.7	43.7	14.1	33.0
1985	124.9	45.2	15.0	32.4
1986	122.2	47.1	15.4	32.2
1987	117.4	50.7	16.1	32.2
1988	119.5	51.7	15.1	31.2
1989	115.9	53.6	15.6	29.9
1990	112.4	55.4	15.0	29.6
Intercept	214.80 (7.77)*	-44.22 (-4.74)*	4.93 (0.72	52.47 8.45)*
YEAR	-1.11 (-3.24	1.05 (9.08)*	0.10 (1.18)	-0.23 (-3.00)
D8590	102.17 (1.89)*	-83.92 (-4.59)*	11.44 (0.86	33.53 2.76)*
YEAR*D8590	-1.16 (-1.82	0.99 (4.64)*	-0.11 (-0.71	-0.39 (-2.78)*
Adj. R-square	.81	.98	.83	.91

DATA. Food Consumption, Prices and Expenditures, 1970-1990, USDA Statistical Bulletin No. 840, p. 28. Boneless, trimmed equivalent production for meat and retail weight for eggs. *indicates significance at the 5 percent level.

Table 2
Per Capita Production of Milk and Cream Products (Pounds per Year)

Year	All Milk	Whole Milk	Lowfat Milk	Skim Milk	Cream Products
1977	249.7	167.3	70.5	11.9	5.0
1978	246.0	161.0	73.5	11.5	5.0
1979	242.6	154.8	76.2	11.6	5.1
1980	237.4	146.4	79.4	11.6	5.2
1981	233.5	140.0	82.2	11.3	5.3
1982	227.2	133.4	83.2	10.6	5.4
1983	226.5	130.3	85.6	10.6	5.7
1984	227.2	126.8	88.8	11.6	6.2
1985	229.6	123.3	93.7	12.6	6.7
1986	228.6	116.5	98.6	13.5	7.0
1987	226.5	111.9	100.6	14.0	7.1
1988	222.3	105.7	100.5	16.1	7.1
1989	224.3	97.6	106.5	20.2	7.3
1990	221.5	90.3	108.3	22.9	7.1
Intercept	528.7 (21.9)*	631.5 (29.5)*	-123.6 (-9.3)*	20.8 (1.8)*	-7.0 (-3.5)*
YEAR	-3.6 (-12.13)*	-6.0 (-22.8)*	2.5 (15.3)*	-0.1 (-0.8)	0.2 (6.1)*
D8590	-159.2 (-3.4)	45.9 (1.1)	-16.5 (-0.6)	-188.5 (-8.3)	6.8 (1.7)*
YEAR*D8590	2.0 (3.6)*	-0.5 (-1.0)	0.2 (0.8)	2.2 (8.4)*	-0.1 (-1.5)
Adj. R-square	.95	.99	.99	.94	.97

DATA. Food Consumption, Prices and Expenditures, 1970-1990. USDA Statistical Bulletin No. 840, Table 13, p. 40.
* indicates significance at 10 percent level

was the upward trend in lowfat milk. Skim milk production showed no trend during the government period. The downward trend in whole milk production and the upward trend in lowfat milk production continued at essentially the same pace during the advertising period, while the increase in skim milk production showed a marked acceleration.

The evidence on cream products shows a somewhat different pattern. Regression results shown in Table 2 indicate that, contrary to expectations there was a significant rate of increase during the government period. This rate of increase fell during the health claims period, though this improvement is not quite significant at conventional level.

Cheese Production.   Table 3 gives per capita cheese production for Italian cheeses and all other cheeses. The regression results indicate that the growth in per capita Italian cheese production was statistically significant during the government period, as was the increase in the rate of growth during the advertising period. For non-Italian cheese, the regression results indicate a statistically significant growth in

production during the government period and a highly significant decline in the rate of growth during the advertising period.

In interpreting these results, a note of caution is warranted. During the period under analysis, non-Italian cheese products were donated to consumers under USDA food programs. As one simple test of the potential confounding effect of these stabilization programs, Table 3 also reports the trend model for all other cheeses with a control for the USDA cheese donations. Though magnitudes have changed somewhat, the signs on the coefficients remain the same.

Fats and Oils.   The regression results in Table 4 indicate that both vegetable- and animal-based fats exhibit a statistically significant positive trend during the government period and a statistically significant decline in the trend during the advertising period. The results also show that the decline in animal-based fats during the advertising period is a more significant decline than for vegetable-based fats. Thus, in addition to the significant shifting from animal-to vegetable-based fats, the evidence shows that total fat consumption began to fall significantly once the policy on health claims was changed, reversing a positive trend in the data during the government information period.

Table 3
Per Capita Production of Cheese (Pounds per Year)

	Italian Cheese	All Other Cheese	All Other\ USDA Donations
1977	3.73	12.3	.53
1978	4.07	12.8	.31
1979	4.24	12.9	.19
1980	4.44	13.1	.79
1981	4.45	13.7	.86
1982	4.84	15.1	2.04
1983	5.29	15.3	2.75
1984	5.77	15.7	2.37
1985	6.46	16.1	2.67
1986	6.99	16.1	2.33
1987	7.63	16.5	2.50
1988	8.13	15.6	1.05
1989	8.50	15.3	.27
1990	9.10	15.6	.08
Intercept	16.66 (-9.28)*	-28.01 (-6.53)	-10.85 (-2.26)
YEAR	0.26 (11.84)	0.52 (9.76)*	0.30 (4.85)*
D8590	-21.11 (-6.00)*	58.81 (7.00)*	9.45 (0.75)
YEAR*D8590	0.26 (6.24)*	-0.69 (-7.03)	-0.11 (0.75)
USDA-CHES	--	--	0.61 (4.26)*
Adj.R-squ	.99	.94	.98

DATA. Food Consumption, Prices and Expenditures, 1970-1990. USDA Statistical Bulletin No, 840, pp. 41 & 83. * indicates significance at 5 percent level.

Table 4
Per Capita Production Fats & Oils (Pounds per Year)

Year	Animal Fat	Vegetable Fat	Total Fat
1977	10.6	42.7	53.3
1978	10.6	44.1	54.9
1979	11.5	44.9	56.4
1980	12.3	44.8	57.1
1981	11.7	45.7	57.4
1982	11.4	46.8	58.2
1983	12.1	47.9	60.0
1984	12.4	46.4	58.8
1985	13.3	50.9	64.2
1986	12.6	51.7	64.3
1987	11.1	51.8	62.9
1988	10.8	52.2	63.0
1989	10.6	50.5	61.1
1990	10.2	52.5	62.7
Intercept	-5.84 (-1.08)	-3.94 (-0.42)	-9.78 (-1.01)
YEAR	0.22 (3.23)*	0.61 (5.27)*	0.83 (6.89)*
D8590	71.78 (6.78)*	43.54 (2.37)*	115.32 (6.07)*
YEAR*D8590	-0.84 (-6.78)*	-0.48 (-2.22)*	-1.32 (5.92)*
Adj. R-square	.77	.95	.95

DATA. Food Consumption, Prices and Expenditures, 1970-1990. USDA Statistical Bulletin No. 840, p. 42. * indicates significance at 5 percent level.

Flour and Cereal Products. Table 5 displays per capita production of flour and cereal products (which are both recommended for increased consumption as a replacement for fats). The regressions show that per capita production increased significanlty during both periods under analysis and that the growth in the post-1985 period accelerated significantly.

Table 5

Per Capita Production of Flour & Cereal, Select Vegetables & Fruit (Pounds per Year)

Year	Flour & Cereal	Vege-tables[1]	Fruit[1]
1977	141.2	192.2	97.0
1978	139.6	184.5	99.5
1979	145.9	191.2	98.5
1980	145.8	190.3	105.0
1981	146.7	183.6	99.6
1982	149.2	186.9	101.4
1983	149.1	185.7	105.6
1984	150.4	202.0	103.7
1985	157.5	197.4	102.1
1986	163.7	195.0	109.0
1987	172.5	201.5	115.0
1988	174.3	202.6	112.6
1989	174.9	212.3	113.4
1990	183.0	213.8	106.7
Intercept	28.40	143.43	24.13
	(1.10)	(2.32)*	(0.53)
YEAR	1.46	0.57	0.96
	(4.57)*	(0.75)	(1.71)*
D8590	-264.67	-277.16	1.28
	(-5.25)*	(-2.29)*	(0.01)
YEAR*D8590	3.19	3.29	0.01
	(5.42)*	(2.32)*	(0.01)
Adj.R-square	.98	.74	.60

DATA. Food Consumption, Prices and Expenditures, 1970-1990. USDA Statistical Bulletin No, 840. pp. 28, 43-44, 46 and 53-54. *indicates significance at 10 percent level; [1] Includes select fresh, canned/chilled and frozen fruit and fresh and processed vegetables currently reported by USDA.

Fruits and Vegetables. Table 5 gives per capita production of fruits and vegetables, also foods recommended for increased consumption in place of fats. Regression results indicate positive trends during the government period for both vegetables and fruit, though the trend was statistically significant only for fruit. These trends both increased during the advertising period, though the increment to the trend is significant only for vegetables.

Summary of Trends in Major Food Categories. Examination of per capita production data for major food categories of interest during the years 1977-1985, when health claims were prohibited, provides some substantial evidence that information about fat, cholesterol and disease was spreading to consumers, leading to improvements in some important aspects of diet. The evidence for this period is not entirely consistent, however. Per capita production of some higher-fat dairy products (cheese and cream products) and fats and oils also increased during the government period, contrary to expectations based on information effects alone.

The production evidence for major food groups provides a more consistent picture during the 1985-1990 period of analysis, when the policy was changed to allow producers to use health claims. During this period, per capita production from food categories with the highest fat levels either stayed on the trend that existed during the government period or experienced a decline in the trend relative to the earlier period. None of the increments to the trends was contrary to expectations under our information hypotheses, and thus, the production data for broad food categories provide no evidence consistent with the view that the addition of health claim advertising had adverse effects on dietary patterns. In fact, during the advertising period movements away from the high-fat food categories increased for all categories, except Italian cheese. Similarly, the production data show a consistent pattern during the advertising period of additional movements towards lower-fat food categories.

Changes in Production for Selected Food Substitutions

This section analyzes three pairs of specific food substitutes for which data are available and for which costs and other noninformation issues are likely to affect the products relatively equally.

Butter and Margarine. Table 6 gives per capita production of butter and margarine products for the periods under analysis. The per capita amount of fat used in the production of margarine products is also given, which reflects changes in the average type of margarine product over time. Finally, Table 6 also lists USDA annual donations of butter on a per capita basis.

Table 6

Per Capita Production of Butter & Margarine Products (Pounds per Year)

Year	USDA Butter Donations	Butter	Margarine	Fat in Margarine
1977	.4	4.3	11.4	9.2
1978	.3	4.4	11.3	9.0
1979	.4	4.5	11.2	9.0
1980	.5	4.5	11.3	9.0
1981	.5	4.2	11.1	8.8
1982	.6	4.3	11.0	8.6
1983	1.1	4.9	10.4	7.9
1984	1.1	4.9	10.4	7.8
1985	1.0	4.9	10.8	8.2

Table 6 con't.

1986	.8	4.6	11.4	8.5
1987	1.0	4.7	10.5	8.0
1988	.8	4.5	10.3	7.7
1989	.9	4.4	10.2	7.6
1990	.7	4.4	10.9	8.6

Intercept	-1.1	7.8	22.8	12.3	24.5	13.3
	(-0.5)	(3.5)*	(5.7)*	(2.0)*	(5.8)*	(2.0)*
YEAR	0.1	-0.1	-0.1	-0.0	-0.2	-0.0
	(2.5)*	(-1.7)*	(-2.9)*	(-0.1)	(-3.7)*	(-0.6)
D8590	13.9	-0.1	-3.9	12.7	-15.1	2.4
	(3.1)*	(-0.0)	(-0.5)	(1.2)	(-1.8)*	(0.2)
YEAR*D8590	-0.2	0.0	0.1	-0.1	0.2	-0.0
	(-3.1)*	(0.1)	(0.6)	(-1.2)	(1.9)*	(-0.2)
USDA-Butter	--	1.0		1.2	---	1.3
		(4.8)*		(-2.1)*		(2.1)*
Adj. R-square	.39	.81	.45	.59	.61	.7

DATA. Food Consumption, Prices and Expenditures, 1970-1990. USDA Statistical Bulletin No. 840, p. 42; and Fats and Oils. U.S. Dept of Commerce. Annual. Table 3A * indicates significance at 5 percent level. Most margarine products are 40-80 percent fat.

Surprisingly, per capita butter production increased during the government/general information period. USDA donations of butter also rose substantially during this period, however. Controlling for USDA donations, the butter regression indicates that the underlying trend in butter consumption was negative and significant during the pre-advertising period, as expected.

By 1990, per capita butter production was almost back down to its 1977 level. In part, this reduction again reflects lower government donations. As shown in the regression controlling for USDA butter donations, the underlying trend towards lower butter consumption continues unchanged during the advertising period.

Per capita production of margarine products declined during both periods of analysis. The per capita fat content of margarine products declined even more as the fat content of margarine shifted to lower-fat products, from 9.2 pounds in 1977, to 8.2 pounds in 1985, to 7.6 pounds in 1989, though the 1990 data shows a substantial increase.

For both margarine products and for the fat in margarine products, the regression results indicate a negative (but quite insignificant) trend in per capita production during the government/general information period, controlling for USDA donations. These results also indicate no significant change in the negative trend for both during the advertising period.

Taken together, these results are consistent with the hypothesis that, controlling for government butter donations, government and general information had some effect in lowering butter and margarine sales, other things equal, though these results are statistically insignificant for margarine. The results are also consistent with the hypothesis that margarine consumption did not change significantly once the ban on producer claims was removed. Finally, controlling for government butter donations, these results do not support the hypothesis that the dissemination of information about the health benefits of the lower saturated fat content of high-fat margarine products lead to an increase in the total demand for margarine products.

Ice Cream and Ice Milk. Table 7 gives per capita production of ice cream and ice milk. The regression results indicate that during the government period the trend in ice cream production was positive but insignificant, and this trend showed a significant reversal during the health claims period. Similarly, the results for ice milk show a significant negative trend in ice milk production during the government period and a significant reversal of this trend during the advertising period.

Table 7
Per Capita Production of Ice Cream, Ice Milk & Cottage Cheese (Pounds per Year)

Year	Ice Cream	Ice Milk	Creamed Cottage Cheese	Lowfat Cottage Cheese
1977	17.6	7.7	3.99	0.63
1978	17.6	7.7	3.82	0.69
1979	17.3	7.3	3.73	0.70
1980	17.5	7.1	3.62	0.79
1981	17.4	7.0	3.36	0.91
1982	17.6	6.6	3.23	0.94
1983	18.1	6.9	3.17	0.92
1984	18.2	7.0	3.11	0.97
1985	18.1	6.9	3.00	1.02
1986	18.4	7.2	2.93	1.10
1987	18.3	7.4	2.78	1.11
1988	17.3	8.0	2.64	1.19
1989	16.1	8.4	2.31	1.22
1990	15.7	7.7	2.12	1.21

Intercept	10.48	17.80	-14.18	-3.36
	(2.12)*	(4.93)*	(16.58)*	(-8.09)*
YEAR	0.09	-0.13	-0.13	0.05
	(1.46)	(-2.95)*	(-12.49)*	(10.06)
D8590	56.59	-30.70	4.37	1.17
	(5.86)*	(-4.34)*	(2.61)*	(1.44)*
YEAR*D8590	-0.66	0.37	0.05	-0.01
	(-5.83)*	(4.43)*	(-2.52)*	(-1.46)*
Adj. R-square	.74	.66	.98	.97

DATA. Food Consumption, Prices and Expenditures, 1970-1990. USDA Statistical Bulletin. No. 840. p. 39; Dairy Products Annual Summary. Table 47. *indicates significance at 5 percent level.

Creamed and Lowfat Cottage Cheese. Creamed cottage cheese has at least 4.0 percent milkfat, while lowfat cottage cheese has less, usually .5 percent or 2.0 percent milkfat. The regression results in Table 7 indicate that the production of creamed cottage cheese declined significantly during the government period and declined significantly further during the advertising period. The results for lowfat cottage cheese show a significant increase in production during the government period, with a negative but insignificant change in the trend during the advertising period.

Thus, the evidence on cottage cheese production again indicates a shift from the higher-fat product to the lower-fat product, and a reduction in the total fat consumed in cottage cheese products, which began prior to the health claims period and was significantly increased during the health claims period.

Summary and Conclusion

Examination of specific food substitutions supports the hypothesis that during the health claims period movements towards lower-fat substitutions accelerated compared to the movements during the government period. These results, combined with the evidence from the examination of broad food categories, provide no evidence that the use of health claims in advertising and labeling had adverse effects on diet. On the contrary, most of the evidence suggests that the use of producer health claims may have been an added source of information and led to improvements in the diet.

The motivation for this study was to provide some evidence on fat and cholesterol in the diet before and after the controversial period following the relaxation of the ban on health claims. Evidence on this matter is important because many provisions of the NLEA are based on the assumption that the use of producer health claims had detrimental effects on the marketplace. Yet in the over 500 pages of proposed regulations, there is almost no evaluation of the effect of previous or current labeling policies on diet.

The presumption that the marketplace has become a "Tower of Babel" has led to some provisions in the NLEA that closely resemble the labeling policies of the 1970s. For example, in the proposed regulations, it will be illegal for manufacturers to make claims regarding developing nutrient-disease relationships. Moreover, even for allowed claims, the number of food products that will be permitted to make claims is very limited, so limited that many fat-free bread and cereal products will not be permitted to make claims linking low fat diets to heart disease or cancer. The evidence presented in this paper provides some evaluation of advertising and labeling policy and suggests caution in the adoption of many of the proposals outlined in FDA's implementation of the NLEA. In other work, we address the specific provisions of the NLEA and assess its potential to help or hinder consumer understanding of the impact of diet on health.

References

Calfee, J. & Pappalardo, J., (1989). The regulation of health claims for foods. Staff Report, Federal Trade Commission, Washington D.C. September.

Center for Science in the Public Interest. (CSPI) (1992). Response to the comments of the Federal Trade Commission on nutrition labeling. August.

Hutt, P.B. Government regulation of health claims in food labeling and advertising. (1986). Food, Drug and Cosmetic Law Journal, 41, 3-73.

Ippolito, P. & Mathios, A. (1989). Health claims in advertising and labeling: A study of the cereal market. Federal Trade Commission Staff Report. August.

Ippolito, P. & Mathios, A. (1990). Information, advertising, and health choices: A study of the cereal market. RAND Journal of Economics. 21, (Autumn).

National Academy of Sciences. (1989). Diet and health: Implications for reducing chronic disease risk.

U.S. Surgeon General. (1988). The Surgeon General's Report on Nutrition and Health. U.S. Department of Health and Human Services, Public Health Service. Washington, D.C.: U.S. Government Printing Office.

U.S. Department of Agriculture. National Agricultural Statistics Board, Dairy Products, Food Consumption, 1970-1990.

U.S. Department of Commerce. Current Industrial Reports, Fats and Oils, Production, Consumption and Stocks, M20K-13, Bureau of the Census.

U.S. Department of Health and Human Services. (1990). HHS News. March 7.

RECIPIENT OF THE ACCI DISSERTATION AWARD

Relative Bargaining Power of Spouses: Empirical Results Using An Economic Model of Cooperative Bargaining

Catherine Phillips Montalto, The Ohio State University[1]

A cooperative Nash bargaining model is used to explore relative bargaining power of spouses with respect to allocation of household expenditure between food and other consumption. The theoretical bargaining model generates an explicit expression for relative bargaining power which is empirically operationalized. Household specific estimates of relative bargaining power are derived and the empirical data are assessed for consistency with bargaining behavior. Association between characteristics of spouses and relative bargaining power is examined.

This research focuses on household decision making behavior, specifically bargaining behavior over the allocation of household expenditure. Decisions made by households regarding allocation of household resources are critically related to the quality of life of individual household members. Though household members share the same physical environment, the quality of life experienced by individuals may vary across members of the same household. The ways in which households allocate resources among members affect household behavior and have implications for policy.

For example, allocation of resources affects the behavior of and interaction among individuals within the household. These resource allocation decisions determine the nature of investments in children including the type, quality and quantity of goods consumed by each child as well as the quality of the environment in which each child is nurtured. Such allocations influence, in very important ways, the human capital of future generations.

Resource allocation decisions influence and in turn are influenced by the roles assumed by men and women within the family. Time of household members must be allocated to market work, to care of dependent household members, to household production activities, as well as to personal care. Individual characteristics of household members influence how their time is allocated, and allocation of time in turn influences human capital formation.

Resource allocation decisions influence cohesiveness of the family unit. Level of satisfaction with the process and outcome of intrahousehold resource allocation influence an individual's commitment to the family. Interpersonal relationships will be affected by perceived fairnessor equity of resource allocations.

Finally, the effectiveness of policies or programs which transfer resources to households rather than directly to individuals will be influenced by intrahousehold resource allocation processes. If resources controlled by mothers are used differently than resources controlled by fathers, programs which transfer resources to mothers will have different effects on family well being than programs which transfer resources to fathers. In these situations it matters who receives the medical care supplement, the financial aid check, or the child care allowance.

Research Framework

The notion that household members bargain to determine household resource allocation is intuitively appealing. Preferences of individual household members need not be identical and the extent to which these preferences count in the household decision making process is likely to be a function of bargaining power relative to other household members. Various theories in family resource management and family sociology suggest that a spouse's influence in household decision making increases with his or her relative resource contribution to the household. A resource which has received considerable attention in the literature is relative earnings or wealth (Bloode & Wolfe, 1980; Blumberg, 1988; Pahl, 1980; Thomas, 1990, 1992).

The increase in female labor force participation in the United States over the past four decades and the resultant increase in dual-earner families as a proportion of all families contribute to the relevance of this topic. Of particular interest is the suggestion that changes in labor force behavior of wives, and therefore their earnings, translate into changes in behavior within households. Specifically, it has been suggested that increases in labor force participation by wives are associated with increases in their decision making power within households (Bloode & Wolfe, 1960).

---

[1]Lecturer, Department of Family Resource Management

While much has been hypothesized about the relationship between characteristics of spouses and their decision making power, empirical research into this topic is hampered by issues of how to measure "power" and how this "power" operates to influence household decisions (Gray-Little & Burks, 1980; McDonald, 1980; Safilios-Rothschild, 1970). Additionally, economic models of household behavior have typically ignored the process by which spouses with conflicting interests reach observed household decisions (Brown & Deaton, 1972; Deaton & Muellbauer, 1980).

In this research, a theoretical bargaining model is used to generate an expression for relative bargaining power within the household which can in turn be estimated with data. The empirical estimates of relative bargaining power are then used to explore association between household relative bargaining power and characteristics of spouses.

The resource allocation decision of interest in this research is the allocation of consumption expenditure between food at home and all other consumption. Food consumption was selected for several reasons. First, food is an important component of the household consumption bundle, accounting for 10-15 percent of disposable personal income (Blaylock & Elitzak, 1990). Second, even though low income households devote a large proportion of income to food expenditure, the available household food supply is often inadequate, and as a result these limited food resources must somehow be allocated across household members. Previous research focusing on households in poverty has shown that allocation of these limited resources is influenced by the roles mothers and fathers have in the decision making process (Blumberg, 1988; Pahl, 1988). Finally, the Nationwide Food Consumption Survey which is used in this research contains detailed information on household food consumption. The data are a sample of observations from USDA's 1977-78 Nationwide Food Consumption Survey. This data set offers detailed information about expenditures on food as well as household and individual demographic and economic data.

The theoretical model of household behavior used in this research is a cooperative Nash bargaining model. The cooperative Nash model has more often been applied to the study of household behavior than other bargaining models due to the properties of the model as well as its ability to generate a unique solution. Manser and Brown (1980) and McElroy and Horney (1981) separately applied the cooperative Nash bargaining model to household behavior. Manser and Brown (1980) focus on marriage behavior: marriage occurs when utility gains to the marriage exceed utility in the best alternative state for each individual. McElroy and Horney (1981) focus on Nash bargained outcomes of the joint allocation of money and time within a married couple household.

The cooperative Nash bargaining model as developed by McElroy and Horney (1981) and employed in this research is a model of bargaining behavior conditional on marriage. In this context a married couple bargains to determine how household expenditure will be allocated across consumption categories. Specifically, spouses cooperate to maximize the weighted product of their individual gains from the bargain, where the objective function is represented by:

$$N = \left[U^f(X) - V_o^f \right]^{\theta_f} \left[U^m(X) - V_o^m \right]^{\theta_m} \qquad (1)$$

U^f is the individual utility function of the wife. $U^f(X)$ is the utility the wife receives from the bargained contract which yields the solution X. V_o^f is the wife's threat point expressed in the form of the indirect utility function. U^m, $U^m(X)$ and V_o^m are similarly defined for the husband. The bargaining power of the wife and the husband are represented by θ_f and θ_m respectively.

The value of the cooperative Nash bargaining model in this research is that it allows individual preferences of spouses to differ and generates an explicit expression for the relative bargaining power of spouses. In this model, the total gain to the bargain within the marriage is distributed between the two spouses in proportion to their relative bargaining power, such that the spouse with relatively more bargaining power receives a larger proportion of the total gain to the bargain. More intuitively, as one's bargaining power increases, the observed household consumption behavior more closely resembles one's individual preferences.

The two-person household maximizes the objective function in equation (1) subject to the relevant constraints. Ideally, one would want to derive explicit expressions for the Nash bargained demand equations, and then estimate all parameters of the demand equations including the bargaining power of each spouse. However, the Nash objective function is a multiplicative function of the individual utility functions. As a result, the first order conditions of the constrained optimization problem are highly nonlinear functions. Solving the first order conditions for explicit expressions of the demand equations is extremely complicated. Therefore, in this research the first order conditions are used to derive an explicit expression for bargaining power which can be operationalized with empirical data.

From the first order conditions, the following expression can be derived:

$$\frac{\theta_l}{\theta_m} = \frac{\dfrac{U' - V'_o}{P_2 \dfrac{\partial U'}{\partial X_1} - P_1 \dfrac{\partial U'}{\partial X_2}}}{\dfrac{U^m - V^m_o}{P_1 \dfrac{\partial U^m}{\partial X_2} - P_2 \dfrac{\partial U^m}{\partial X_1}}} \qquad (2)$$

This expression is a weighted ratio of the individual gains to the bargain. The gain to the bargain for an individual spouse is the difference between the utility derived from the bargained contract and the individual's threat point. The weights capture the effect of reallocation of expenditure between food and composite consumption at the observed household consumption bundle for the wife and the husband. The magnitude of this reallocation effect is inversely related to relative bargaining power ceteris paribus. In other words, the greater one's relative bargaining power, the lower one's relative gain from further reallocation. Since θ_l is the bargaining power of the wife and θ_m is the bargaining power of the husband, this expression can be used to derive an expression for the relative bargaining power. This expression is a function of individual threat points, individual preferences, and observed consumption in the married household for each spouse. The first step is to obtain empirical estimates for each argument on the right hand side of the expression in equation (2).

Assuming individual utility functions of the Stone-Geary type, each argument can be expressed in explicit form. Utility in the current married state, specified as the direct utility function, is a function of individual preferences and observed consumption in the married household. The individual threat point, specified as the indirect utility function, is defined as withdrawal from the household to the best alternative state, and is a function of prices and income. Individual are assumed to face the same prices in either the married or the alternative state; income in the alternative state is predicted for each wife and husband in the sample. Information on observed consumption in the married household is available in the data.

In order to derive empirical estimates of relative bargaining power, information is needed on individual preferences of spouses. It is assumed that individual preferences are independent of marital status, and that non-married households do not bargain. These assumptions enable use of non-married households to identify individual preferences of women and men.

First, demand equations are estimated separately for households headed by non-married women (N=2,551) and households headed by non-married men (N=931). The parameters of the individual demand equations uniquely identify the parameters of the individual utility functions for women and for men, or the individual preferences. With estimates of the individual utility function parameters, it is possible to generate empirical estimates of household relative bargaining power in the sample of married couple households (N=5,535). However, before proceeding it is worthwhile to assess what has been learned from the empirical data so far. Specifically, consideration is given to what can be learned about individual preferences and about household bargaining behavior.

Evidence from the Data Regarding Individual Preferences and Household Bargaining Behavior

Household bargaining, or more generally how preferences of individual household members are combined in the household decision making process, is more interesting when individual preferences of household members differ. The most interesting empirical evidence comes from comparison of individual marginal rates of substitution of wives and husbands.

The marginal rate of substitution (MRS) measures the rate at which an individual is just willing to substitute one good for another. To the extent that spouses have similar or different marginal rates of substitution at a defined consumption point, it may be possible to infer similarity or divergence in preferences.

With estimates of the individual utility function parameters, the marginal rate of substitution between food and the composite consumption good can be calculated at the observed household consumption bundle (X^{*H}) separately for the wife and the husband for each household in the sample. When the wife's MRS at the observed household consumption bundle is less than the husband's MRS at that point, the wife is willing to give up less of the composite consumption good to obtain more food relative to the husband. In this instance the wife exhibits a stronger relative preference for the composite consumption good.

The empirical results suggest that preferences differ between wives and husbands, and that in general, husbands exhibit a stronger relative preference for food. (In 88% of the households the wife's MRS is less than the husband's MRS). Additionally, there is evidence in the data of variation in individual marginal rates of substitution between wives and husbands. The individual MRSs are within 20% of each other in 50% of the households, which may suggest some degree of similarity. However, in 50% of the households the individual MRSs differ by more than 20%, suggesting greater divergence. To the extent that household members have different preferences, the household bargaining process becomes more interesting.

In addition to assessing the extent of similarity of preferences between wives and husband, the estimates of the individual utility function parameters can also be used to determine the extent to which the empirical data is consistent with a general bargaining framework. Given information on individual preferences, household allocation which would result from decisions made independently by each spouse can be derived and compared to the actual allocation in the married couple household. These three consumption points can be plotted in two-good space (Figure 1).

Figure 1.
Household Bargaining Behavior

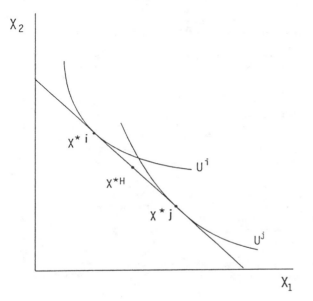

For behavior consistent with bargaining, the observed household consumption bundle, X^{*H}, should lie somewhere on the household budget constraint between the consumption bundle which would result from decisions made independently by each spouse, designated as X^{*i} and X^{*j}. If the observed household consumption bundle lies on the same side of the two dictator bundles, both spouses prefer reallocation away from the same good toward the other good in the two-good model. However, something precludes the reallocation and the household is observed to consume a non-optimal and inconsistent bundle. A general bargaining model cannot explain this behavior, nor can it provide guidance to interpretation of relative bargaining power within this context.

Accordingly, a statistical test is used to determine the probability of consistent behavior for each married couple. In the sample, approximately 38% of the married couple households reject the null hypothesis of consistent behavior at the 95% confidence level. Thus, the data suggest that many households exhibit behavior

inconsistent with a general cooperative bargaining framework.

It is important to understand why the empirical data could be inconsistent with a bargaining framework. If the estimates of the individual utility function parameters are biased, this bias will introduce measurement error into the empirical measure of the consumption bundle chosen independently by each spouse (i.e. the dictator consumption bundles). This could result in the type of inconsistency observed in the empirical data.

There are two reasons to suspect that the individual utility function parameter estimates might be biased. In order to obtain information about parameters of the individual utility functions of the wife and the husband, it was assumed that bargaining does not take place in non-married households and that individual preferences are independent of marital status. The first assumption rules out negotiation or bargaining behavior among adults or between adults and children in non-married households. The second assumption rules out changes in individual preferences due to changes in marital status as well as systematic differences between non-married individuals and married individuals.

If these behaviors are empirically important, the estimates of individual preferences derived in this research will be biased: the behavior of non-married households will not reflect the individual preferences of the household head, and estimated individual preferences of non-married individual will not accurately represent the individual preferences of married individuals. With respect to the graph, the empirical estimates of the consumption bundles which would be chosen independently by each spouse will be estimated with error.

Another possible explanation for the inconsistency of the data with a bargaining framework is that the arguments of the individual utility function have been mis-specified. There may exist a third argument in the individual utility function in addition to food and composite consumption, such that observed behavior which is inconsistent in the two-good model, would be consistent in a three-good model.

Association Between Household Relative Bargaining Power and Characteristics of Spouses

Since the measure of relative bargaining power is derived from a bargaining model, it is only appropriate to infer relative bargaining power in households which fail to reject the null hypothesis of consistent behavior. Only these households are retained for the remaining analysis (N=3,440). Empirical estimates of relative bargaining power are derived for each married couple household. The estimates indicate that relative bargaining power varies across households. In general, wives have more bargaining power relative to husbands in the allocation of expenditure between food and other consumption.

One explanation for why the empirical measure of relative bargaining power is so skewed in favor of wives may rest in the decision making area which generates this measure. It could be that decisions regarding household food expenditure are, in fact, made predominately by wives. Wives may determine the food budget quite independently because food decisions are part of the wife's role, or because husbands want their wives to make these decisions.

Another explanation rests in the model which generates this empirical measure. In the model used in this research individual utility is independent of the intrahousehold allocation of goods. As a result, the effect of private good transfers on the bargaining outcome is ignored, and this introduces potential error into the empirical measure of relative bargaining power.

Given empirical estimates of household relative bargaining power, regression analysis was used to explore association between household relative bargaining power and characteristics of spouses. The conceptual model which motivates this research suggests that relative characteristics of spouses should be associated with relative bargaining power. Characteristics explored in this research included age, education, occupation, earned income, non-labor income, total income, labor force participation, and measures of wage rates of the wife and the husband.

In general, the regression equations explained only a small part of the variation in relative bargaining power. While characteristics of spouses (i.e. labor force participation, income and earning power) were associated with variation in household relative bargaining power, household demographic variables had the most explanatory power. This finding is consistent with previous empirical work which has found that characteristics of household members influence household behavior (Lazear and Michael, 1988).

The presence of children in the household was positively associated with the wife's relative bargaining power, with older children having a stronger effect than younger children. Presence of children in the household may reinforce the wife's role as household manager including responsibility for food expenditure. Alternatively, when the household includes children, husbands may feel that food expenditure decisions are better made by the wife who is generally viewed as the primary care giver.

It is interesting that the effect is larger for older children. This effect remains even after controlling for labor force participation of the wife and wife's income. One explanation for this effect could be that as children get older they become more goods-intensive and less time-

intensive. If husbands have the comparative advantage in the labor market, they may increase hours of market work in response to increasing expenditure for children. In turn wives may assume more of the responsibility for household work, thus reflecting an increase in her relative bargaining power with respect to food expenditure decisions.

The regression analysis provided some evidence that variation in income and wage rates of spouses were associated with variation in relative bargaining power. The total income of the wife and the total income of the husband had more explanatory power than separate measures of earned income and non-labor income of the wife and the husband. Variation in relative wage rates of the wife and the husband was also associated with variation in relative bargaining power.

The results suggest that a wife's total income and earning power are positively associated with her bargaining power. An increase in the wife's income relative to her husband's income, controlling for her employment status and for relative wages, increases her relative bargaining power. Similarly, an increase in the wife's relative earning power, controlling for her employment status and for relative income, increases her relative bargaining power.

However, controlling for relative income and relative wage rates, employed wives have less relative bargaining power than non-employed wives. This suggests that earned income and non-labor income affect bargaining power differently: holding relative income and wages of the wife and husband constant, wives with high proportions of their own income from non-labor sources have more relative bargaining power than wives with high proportions of their own income from earnings.

One explanation for this result is that in households in which both spouses participate in the labor market both spouses may be more likely to jointly participate in household decision making including the allocation of expenditure between food and other consumption, while in single earner households, some domains of household decision making may be dominated by one spouse and other areas by the other spouse. The regression results did not suggest that one has to exercise earning power in order for it to translate into bargaining power.

In general, the cooperative bargaining model as implemented in this research is not strongly supported by the empirical evidence. While it is highly likely that households engage in bargaining, the empirical specification used in this research is unable to accurately capture this behavior. As previously discussed, potential bias in the estimates of the individual utility function parameters likely contributed to this result. However, for those households exhibiting consistent behavior, evidence suggests that household composition is more strongly associated with variation in relative bargaining power than the relative socioeconomic characteristics of the spouses examined in this research.

Future research should investigate alternative models of household decision making behavior in an attempt to find models which capture the complexity of household behavior and are compatible with empirical data. Empirical research which continues to focus on intrahousehold resource allocation will improve understanding of the inner workings of the household. Intrahousehold resource allocation affects the quality of family life, the interrelationships of household members, and cohesiveness of the household unit. Additionally, the impact of policies and programs targeted to improve well being of household members will be affected by how resources are allocated within the household.

References

Blaylock, J. & Elitzak, H. (1990). Food expenditures. National Food Review, July-September, 17-25.

Blood, R.O. Jr. & Wolfe, D.M. (1960). Husbands and wives: The dynamics of married living. New York: The Free Press.

Blumberg, R. (1988). Income under female and male control: Hypothesis from a theory of gender stratification and data from the Third World. Journal of Family Issues, 9(1), 51-84

Brown, J. & Deaton, A. (1972). Models of consumer behavior: A survey. Economic Journal, 82(823), 1145-1236.

Deaton, A. & Muellbauer, J. (1980). Economics and Consumer Behavior. Cambridge: Cambridge University Press.

Gray-Little, B. & Burks, N. (1983). Power and satisfaction in marriage: A review and critique. Psychological Bulletin, 93(3), 513-538.

Lazear, E.P. & Michael, R.T. (1988). Allocation of income within the household. Chicago: University of Chicago Press.

Manser, M. & Brown, M. (1980). Marriage and household decision-making: A bargaining analysis. International Economic Review, 21(1), 31-44.

McDonald, G.W. (1980). Family power: The assessment of a decade of theory and research: 1970-1979. Journal of Marriage and the Family, 42(4), 111-124.

McElroy, M.B. & Horney, M.J. (1981). Nash-bargained household decisions: Toward a generalization of the theory of demand. International Economic Review, 22(2), 333-349.

Pahl, J. (1988). Earning, sharing, spending: Married couples and their money. In Walker, R. & Parker, G., eds. Money matters: Income, wealth and financial welfare. London: Sage Publications.

Pahl, J. (1980). Patterns of money management within marriage. Journal of Social Policy, 9(3), 313-335.

Safilios-Rothschild, C. (1970). The study of family power structure: A review 1960-1969. Journal of Marriage and the Family, 32(4), 539-552.

Thomas, D. (1990). Intra-household resource allocation: An inferential approach. Journal of Human Resources, 25(4), 635-664.

Thomas, D. (1992). The distribution of income and expenditure within the household. Working paper. Yale University.

The Simple Analytics of Health Fringes and Job Lock

John E. Kushman, University of Delaware[1]

This presentation gives a symbolic representation of a job locked consumer/worker. A job locked consumer worker stays in their current job only because health fringe benefits offered on that job make it a better than the best alternative. Job locking by health fringes is common in the U.S. Some proposed national health reforms would tend to equalize health fringe benefits across jobs, perhaps unlocking workers from their jobs. More generally, this is a topical instance of important notches in consumer budget constraints produced by public policy and private business decisions.

Health, medical care insurance and medical care are financially and politically salient issues. This presentation shows, symbolically, the "job lock" situation faced by many consumers. Leading medical sociologist Paul Starr recently spoke of job lock at a symposium on health care. He noted consumers living "constricted lives-- people who can't change their lives because of the necessity to provide health care coverage." (Starr, 1992). According to Starr, three of four people say someone in their family is stuck in a job because of health benefits that are essential to the family. David Mechanic, also a prominent health care researcher, noted "more and more employees are unable or unwilling to change jobs because of potential loss of health coverage." (Mechanic, 1992). Gardiner reports that 30 percent of employees are afraid to change jobs for fear of losing health coverage (Gardiner, 1992, p. 222). Braus reports on a Gallup poll in 1991 in which "Good health insurance and other benefits" was named by a higher proportion of American workers as important in a job than any other job characteristic (Braus, August 1992, p. 34). Currently, employment and health care insurance are closely linked. Health care insurance "locks" many employees in jobs they would otherwise leave.

A variation of traditional indifference maps and budget constraints shows a consumer who is job locked. The consumer's current job, with its relatively generous health care insurance fringes, gives a budget constraint notched by deductibles, coinsurance and other insurance parameters. The budget line between all other goods and health care has a relatively shallow slope, reflecting a low copayment rate. A small premium and low copayment rate make a relatively generous health plan in the current job. The consumer maximizes welfare on an indifference curve designated U_0.

An alternative job exists which offers advantages. The alternative job may have better ambience, more agreeable coworkers, or more agreeable tasks. The figure's two axes do not capture these advantages that are beyond "All Other Goods" and health care. I assume the alternative job is better than the current job in terms of these advantages. It's superiority is symbolized by an indifference map that shows the level of welfare corresponding to U_0 lying closer to the origin in Other Goods and health care. The better amenities of the alternative job make up for the lower levels of Other Goods and health care in the new job.

The alternative job has a less generous health care fringe package. The premium may be higher, the coinsurance rate higher or the deductible higher. In the alternative job the consumer cannot reach welfare level U_0 but has to settle for a lower welfare level U_L. Indifference curve U_L is in the alternative job indifference map. The consumer remains in the current job, because the current welfare is not available in the alternative, despite the alternative's amenity advantage.

This consumer is "job locked." From a positive perspective, they have a job with relatively generous fringe benefits for health care. From a negative perspective, if the alternative job had the same benefit package, the consumer could reach a level of welfare higher than U_0 by moving to the alternative job. The best indifference curve would belong to the alternative job indifference map and be tangent to the budget constraint for the current job.

Some proposed national health coverage plans would equalize health insurance fringes among jobs. This seems to move budget constraints for different jobs closer together and seems to reduce job lock. Whether it would result in more people changing jobs would depend on related, but perhaps unforeseen, effects on wages and other amenities. There is a tradeoff for employers between wages and fringe benefits and tradeoffs among fringes. The net effect of changing health fringes and related tax laws is likely to be complex. The market is clever at evading or diverting the expected effects of public policies.

The diagram that shows job lock can be more or less complicated, depending on deductibles, coinsurance rates, premiums and catastrophic expenditure limits. Like simpler cases, these plans introduce "notches" into consumer budget

[1]Professor, Textiles, Design and Consumer Economics

constraints. It is important to introduce consumer policy students to notches. As Blinder and Rosen note in their important article (Binder and Rosen, 1985), notched budget constraints are common in public policy, and they may be more efficient than more traditional per-unit subsidies or taxes for many policy purposes.

This is one example of an important role for notches in the consumer budget constraint. Transitivity of preferences also play a key role in this illustration. Using two families of indifference curves on the same diagram requires a transitive relationship between indifference curves across maps.

References

Blinder, A. S., & Rosen, H.S. (1985). Notches. American Economic Review. 75(4), 736-747.

Braus, P. (1992). What Workers Want. American Demographics. 14(8), 30-35.

Jones, M. G. (1992). Consumer Access to Health Care: Basic Right 21st Century Challenge. Journal of Consumer Affairs. 26(2), 221-242.

Mechanic, D. (September 12, 1992). Remarks to Symposium on "Health Care: Right or Privilege? Searching for Solutions." Wilmington, Delaware.

Starr, P. (September 12, 1992). Remarks to Symposium on "Health Care: Right or Privilege? Searching for Solutions." Wilmington, Delaware.

Quality of Nursing Home Care: Family Members as Extended Consumers

Marlene Stum, University of Minnesota[1]
Kathleen Schmitz, University of Minnesota[2]
Janet Sarver, University of Minnesota[3]

This qualitative study involved interviewing family members of 25 nursing home residents to gain an understanding of how family members as extended consumers perceive their roles and describe quality expectations and perceptions of nursing home quality life and care. Emerging themes provide insight into needed training for nursing home administrators and staff and suggest a need for quality assurance policy evaluation.

Improving the quality of life and care in nursing homes is a continuing challenge in this country where nursing homes remain the dominant form of publicly financed long term care. Much of the focus on improving quality of care in nursing homes has been on physical settings, staff credentials and ratios, types of facilities, policies and procedures and funding mechanisms. While all of these factors are important components of a quality of care system, "family" as an extended consumer has typically received less attention. Few studies have explored the roles that family members of residents might play to improve the quality of life and care in nursing home settings (Bowers, 1988). While a majority of studies have analyzed quality from a nursing home administrative/staff perspective, or residents' respective, analyzing quality from a family perspective also seems essential.

The purpose of this qualitative pilot study was to gain an understanding of the roles that family members assume and family perceptions of quality of life and care to provide insights into improving nursing home quality of life and care. Brubaker's Triadic Relationship (1987) model provided the conceptual framework for this study and suggests that family and nursing homes as institutions interact to affect a dependent older family member's well-being along several dimensions. The overall research questions for this study included: 1) How do families as caregivers of the institutionalized elderly interact to impact the quality of life and care for a resident?; and 2) What major themes do families emphasize as they talk about quality of life and care?

Methodology

Three metropolitan nursing homes agreed to participate by allowing access to family members. Nursing home settings ranged in size from 125 to 500 residents and represented private pay, Medicaid and Medicare beds. Invitations to participate in the study were mailed to 90 family members listed as "first contact" in resident's records. Family members representing 25 nursing home residents participated in 1-2 hour semi-structured interviews.

Family members were asked to describe: 1) nursing home placement decision process and context; 2) roles and involvement in resident's life; 3) expectations and perceptions of quality of life and care. Interviews were audiotaped and thematic analysis was conducted by two independent coders to identify emerging themes.

From 1-5 family members identified themselves as caregivers of a resident and volunteered to participate in each family interview. Primary caregivers were mostly daughters (15), followed by sons (8), daughter-in-laws (4), nieces (3) and spouses (3). Secondary caregivers included grandchildren (11), daughter-in-laws (7), and sons (8). Caregivers ranged from 31 to 81 years of age. Family visits varied from less than once a week to 2 times per day. Residents of the nursing homes ranged in age from 64-97, were mostly mothers of primary caregivers, and had been a resident of the current nursing home from 2 months to 8 years.

Findings

Family Involvement in Quality of Care

Family members engaged in two major types of involvement to ensure quality of care: 1) preservative, and 2) technical care. The major purpose of preservative care was to assist in meeting the social, emotional, and economic needs of family members. Family members consistently talked about five major reasons they are involved in preservative care: 1) to maintain family connectedness; 2) to maintain the resident's dignity; 3) to help the resident maintain control over the environment, 4) to manage the resident's financial affairs for financial independence; and

[1]Assistant Professor, Family Social Science

[2]Graduate Student, Family Social Science

[3]Graduate Student, Family Social Science

5) to serve as an advocate for the family member and other residents. Technical care involvement focused on meeting the physical needs of the resident with the purpose of maintaining and improving the resident's health and well-being.

Family Perceptions of Quality of Care

A majority of families indicated overall satisfaction with the quality of life and care the resident was receiving. Only 20% of the families were searching for other care or were very frustrated with the current quality. Even though families expressed overall satisfaction with the care, they also identified quality concerns which often frustrated and angered them. Staff and administrative problems such as short staffing, inconsistency in staff, poor attitudes, and work overload resulting in poor technical and preservative care were consistently mentioned as the most frequent quality concerns by all families. Additional concerns focused on a lack of communication among staff, the resident, and family members; a lack of trust regarding care the residents might receive and a felt need to monitor the care; failure of staff to maintain resident's dignity and control over the environment; and discouraging or preventing families to maintain connectedness.

Family caregivers consistently emphasized that quality of care could be strengthened through changes in policies and procedures as well as attitudes and practices of individuals. Specifically: 1) have staff provide both technical and preservative care; 2) make available activities for both the resident and family members; 3) improve staff, family and resident communication; 4) provide personal home-like environments; and 5) raise expectations and encourage family and volunteer involvement.

Conclusions and Implications

Family members feel that they play an integral and critical role in improving a resident's quality of life and care. Most families were convinced that residents who did not have involved family members had a lower quality of life and care. While other studies have found family members to focus on meeting social and emotional needs of residents, few have suggested the major role that family members play in assisting in economic needs or in the overall role of advocacy and monitoring quality of care. Overall, family members were pleasantly surprised at the quality of care experienced given their expectations. Family expectations for quality of care were not always met and concerns focused on gaps in technical and preservative care. Family members learned to negotiate and balance roles and involvement in an unfamiliar bureaucracy where expectations were not often verbalized.

The results have implications for: a) nursing home administration and staff training and education, b) nursing home regulation and policy, and c) future research on perceptions of quality care and family involvement. Nursing home administrators and staff should be knowledgeable about how to develop policies and programs to orient, support, and develop family members as an important resource in collaboratively providing quality technical and preservative care.

References

Bowers, B. (1988). Family perceptions of care in a nursing home. The Gerontologist, 28(3), 361-368.

Brubaker, T. (1987). The long-term care triad: The elderly, their families, and bureaucracies. In Brubaker, T. (Ed.), Aging, Health and Family Long Term Care (pp. 12-22). Newbury Park, CA: Sage.

A Parsimonious Model of Dining Out Behavior

Terrence V. O'Brien, Northern Illinois University[1]
Mary E. Pritchard, Northern Illinois University[2]
Christine L. Scheck, Northern Illinois University[3]

The paper presents a continuation of work on explaining the decision to dine out (versus in the home). Determinants of such food purchases were previously found to be time pressure, family composition, resources, social class, region, and urbanity. The present research improves on the explanation by evaluating these determinants to see which ones may be dropped or merged without reducing the significance of the level of explanation; the result is a more parsimonious model.

Recent work in explaining dining out behavior of households has used structural equation modeling techniques and confirmatory factor analysis, so-called 'causal methodology.' The purpose is to represent the phenomenon using manifest indicator variables and inferred latent variables (O'Brien and Pritchard, 1989). For example, a study of twenty BLS interview items yielded seven latent factors from principal components analysis and application of the EQS computational procedure (U. S. Labor Department, 1986; O'Brien, Pritchard, and Scheck, 1992; Bentler, 1985). But do such techniques produce the most efficient explanation of behavior? That is, how can we be sure we have a parsimonious model, one with the fewest underlying constructs (latent variables) at a given level of explanation? This paper presents an application of a procedure to answer this question.

Method

A previous study related the determination of a seven latent factor model of dining out behavior, where food purchase is a result of time pressure, urbanity or region, and family composition and resources. Additionally, time pressure is caused by family composition and social class, and resources is the result of family composition and time pressure (O'Brien, Pritchard, and Scheck, 1992). However, examining the covariances between latent factors revealed several that were rather high (.5 to .9): resources with family composition, social class, and time pressure, and social class with time pressure. A seven factor model was first fitted on our proposed measurement model. Then this model was contrasted to several nested measurement models, each presuming that two latent variables were alike. The sequential chi-square differential test was used to interpret whether equating two variables materially reduced the fit (James, Muliak, and Brett, 1982).

Results

Table 1 shows the five models, fit indices, and chi-square computations. The last column is the difference between the original chi-square and that of the nested model, while the parsimonious fit index is the comparative fit index times the ratio of degrees of freedom for the two models (Anderson and Gerbing, 1988). Note that one nested model, number 2, is not significantly different from the original. The conclusion, then, is that this collapsed version is equal to the original in explanatory power.

Conclusion

We have found that two previous latent factors in determining dining out behavior, resources and social class, do not appear to be separable in their effects. From a philosophy of science perspective, we have determined a more parsimonious explanation and should adopt it. Other researchers have reached a comparable conclusion. For example, ". . . we always have to use other variables. . . to understand why income has sometimes operated quite well as a predictor and other times rather poorly. As often as not, the reason will be found in social class, which may be acting all by itself or possible in concert with one or more other social-psychological or demographic variables." (Coleman 1983, p. 275). Note that a major indicator for our resources variable was income. Coleman's recommendation is to use a composite measure of status that consists of such elements as education, occupation, neighborhood, and income. We intend to explore ways to do this in further research.

---

[1]Professor of Marketing

[2]Associate Professor and Chair,
    Human and Family Resources

[3]Associate Professor of Management

Table 1
Fit Indices for Nested Measurement Models.

Model	Degrees of Freedom	Chi-Square	Comparative Fit Index	Parsimonious Fit Index	Sequential Chi-Square Differential Test
1. Seven factor measurement	153	1643.379**	.593	.462	
2. Resources = social class	159	1646.110**	.590	.476	2.731
3. Resources = family status	159	1843.148**	.536	.432	199.769*
4. Social class = time pressure	159	1507.727**	.628	.506	135.652*
5. Resources = time pressure	159	1580.935**	.608	.490	62.444*

*p <.05
**p <.01

References

Anderson, J. G., & Gerbing, D. W. (1988). Structural equation modeling in practice: A review and recommended two-step approach. Psychological Bulletin, 103, 411-423.

Bentler, P. M. (1990). Comparative fit indexes in structural models. Psychological Bulletin, 107, 238-246.

Bentler, P. M. (1985). Theory and implementation of EQS: A structural equations program, Los Angeles, CA: BMOP Statistical Software.

Bentler, P. M., & Bonett, D. G. (1980). Significance tests and goodness of fit in the analysis of covariance structures. Psychological Bulletin, 88, 588-606.

Coleman, R. B. (1983). The continuing significance of social class to marketing. Journal of Consumer Research, 10(4), December, 265-289.

James, S., Muliak, S., & Brett, J. (1982). Causal analysis: Assumptions, models, and data. Beverly Hills, CA: Sage Publication.

Lippert, A., & Love, D. (1986). Family expenditures for food away from home and prepared foods. Family Economics Review, 3, 9-14.

Marsh, H. W., Balla, J. R., & McDonald, R. P. (1988). Goodness of fit indexes in confirmatory factor analysis. Psychological Bulletin, 103, 391-410.

Muliak, S. A., James, L. R., Van Alstine, J., Bennett, N., Lind, S., & Stillwell, C. D. (1989). Evaluation of goodness of fit indices for structural equation models. Psychological Bulletin, 105, 430-445.

O'Brien, T.V., & Pritchard, M.E.(1989). Development of a causal model of family expenditures for food consumed outside the home. Proceedings of the American Council on Consumer Interests, April.

O'Brien, T. V., Pritchard, M. E., & Scheck, C. L. (1992). Dining out behavior: A structural equation modeling assessment. Working paper, Northern Illinois University.

Prochaska, F. J., & Schrimper, R. A. (1973). Opportunity cost of time and other socioeconomic effects on away from home food consumption. American Journal of Agricultural Economics, November, 595-603.

Smallwood, D. M., Blisard, N., & Blaylock, J. R. (1991). Food spending in American households 1980-88. U.S. Department of Agriculture Statistical Bulletin No. 8243.

United States Department of Labor. (1986). Consumer expenditure survey: Interview survey 1982-83 Bulletin 2246. Washington, D.C.: Government Printing Office.

Practices and Beliefs of Consumers Who Shopped in Health and Natural Food Stores

Mary Ellen Cunningham, University of Maine[1]
Peggy K. Schomaker, University of Maine[2]

This study examined the practices and beliefs of consumers who shopped in health and natural food stores. Factors such as age, education, marital status, income, and gender of the consumers were studied to determine their influence on these practices and beliefs.

Introduction

The publication of the "Dietary Goals for the United States" by the U.S. Senate Select Committee on Nutrition and Human Needs in the late seventies generated interest in the relationship between nutrition and health- the risk of heart disease, cancer, and obesity. This interest by consumers has contributed to a growth in health and natural food stores. Yet, little is known about the consumers who shop in these stores.

Purpose and Method

There were two objectives for this study. The first objective was to examine the practices and beliefs of consumers who shop in health and natural food stores. The second objective was to determine the influence that factors such as age, education, income, marital status, and gender of the consumer have on these practices and beliefs.

Data for this study were obtained from questionnaires distributed to consumers shopping in health and natural food stores during summer of 1991. The communities in which the health and natural food stores were located were selected at random from all such communities in the state. The number of questionnaires distributed in each community was dependent on population size. Data analysis involved descriptive statistics (Excel 3.0), Chi-Square (MYSTAT), and Fisher's Exact Test (SYSTAT).

Results and Implications

A total of 185 usable questionnaires were obtained from consumers shopping in 3 communities in the state in which health and natural food stores were located.

Findings showed that 55 percent of the consumers who shopped at health and natural food stores were over the age of 35, 61 percent were college graduates, 68 percent had incomes of $15,000 and over, 43 percent were single and 68 percent were female.

The consumers surveyed spent an average of $88 per month in health and natural food stores. Major reasons for shopping at these stores were that some of the products were not available at the supermarkets, the store was conveniently located, and the product quality was reliable. A larger percentage of consumers who were female than those who were male mentioned these reasons. Items most frequently purchased were bulk foods, produce, herbs, and specialty foods.

Nearly three-quarters of consumers shopping in health and natural food stores were meat eaters; one-quarter were vegetarians. Seventy-five percent of the respondents had made changes in the diet. The major reasons for the changes were that they had read a lot about health and nutrition, they were concerned about food additives and preservatives, and they were concerned about pesticides in foods. Of consumers making changes for these reasons, a larger percentage were female than male. Sixty-eight percent said they were very concerned with environmental issues. As income increased, the percentage of consumers who were "very concerned" decreased.

In examining the health concerns of consumers shopping in health and natural food stores, the largest percentage were concerned about their weight. This was followed with concern about cholesterol, and concern about cancer. A larger percentage of those who were married than those who were single, separated or divorced had these concerns.

The two major sources of nutrition information for the respondents were food labels and magazine articles. Consumers with the least education were those least apt to use food labels and magazine articles as a source of information. The consumers were also asked if they took vitamin and mineral supplements and why. Sixty-two percent of the respondents reported taking supplements. The major

---

[1]Graduate student, Consumer Economics and Management

[2]Associate Professor, Consumer Economics and Management

reasons given were to prevent and cure colds, help cope with stress, and improve physical performance. A larger percentage of those who were over 35 years of age than those under 35 took supplements for these reasons.

This study has implications for educators. Nutrition education should focus on the major concerns of consumers- weight control, management of cholesterol levels, and foods that reduce the risk of cancer and heart disease. The use of food labels is important for all consumers. Since this study showed that lower income individuals were not as apt to use food labels, education should target this consumer group. Education about vitamin and mineral supplements is recommended especially for older persons who were the major consumers of these products.

References

McArthur, L. H., Grivetti, L.E., & Schutz, H.G.(1990). Practices, Beliefs and Knowledge of International and U.S. Students Regarding Food Supplements and Health Foods. Ecology of Food and Nutrition, 24, 233-249.

National Research Council. Committee on Diet and Health.(1990). Diet and Health: Implications for Reducing Chronic Disease Risk. Washington, D.C.: National Academy Press, 509-525.

U.S. Congress. Senate. Select Committee on Nutrition and Human Needs.(1985). Dietary Goals for the United States.

Child Custody and Divorce Settlements

Wendy L. Reiboldt, California State University, Long Beach[1]
Sharon B. Seiling, The Ohio State University[2]

Child custody arrangements following divorce are important in determining the welfare of divorcing parties and their children. Previous research has established that there are differences in settlement awards among various custody types. This study investigates three types of custody, sole-maternal, sole-paternal, and joint custody. Results reveal that characteristics of the settlement are in fact different among the three custody arrangements.

Introduction and Literature Review

Child custody arrangements following divorce play an important part in determining negotiated settlements in the divorce process. Previous research has established that there are differences in legal, socio-economic, and personal characteristics among the various custody types.

Judicial decisions increasingly involve paternal and joint custody arrangements, not just maternal arrangements which has been the trend in the past. Furthermore, the divorce negotiation process has become more equitable through the removal of the maternal preference clause, use of a no fault procedure, and ability to receive joint custody at one parent's request. Despite these changes, however, awards of child support, assets, and liabilities are not distributed equally between mothers and fathers. Joint custody cases often require one parent to pay support to the other despite the presumption that care, custody and control are assumed jointly. This study compares sole-maternal custody with both sole-paternal and joint custody and investigates the distribution of property, the legal environment, and the socio-economic characteristics of the divorcing parties.

Methodology

This study looks at three types of custody: sole-maternal, sole-paternal, and joint custody (sometimes called shared parenting), using data from 453 court records from one urban Ohio county in 1991. The variables investigated include custody variables, legal process variables (use of attorney, procedure used), characteristics of the divorcing party (employment status, income, length of marriage), characteristics of the children (age, gender), and settlement variables (amount of child support, amount of property, home ownership).

Multiple comparisons procedures (Bonferroni for the continuous variables and Chi-square tests for the categorical variables) were used to analyze differences which occurred between the independent variables and custody type. The Bonferroni procedure compares the population means of continuous variables among the three custody groups to see which groupings of two differ. The Chi-square procedure tests for independence between two categorical variables. That is, whether custody type and other dichotomous variable are independent of each other.

Results

Results of the multiple comparisons procedures indicate that there are differences in characteristics of the divorcing parties' settlement awards by custody type. Results of the comparisons revealed the following differences in characteristics of the divorcing parties: father's employment status, mother's employment status, father's total income, mother's total income, marriage length, and number of children.

Neither father's nor mother's employment status was independent of custody type; a relationship exists. Father's total income among joint custody cases was significantly higher that father's income in both sole-maternal and sole-paternal cases. Similarly, among joint cases, mother's total income was higher than among sole-maternal and sole-paternal custody cases. Marriage length among couples awarded joint custody was significantly higher that sole-maternal custody cases. Finally, among sole-paternal cases, number of children was significantly higher that among joint custody cases.

Divorce settlement differences among the custody types included: father's net asset, award of child support, amount of child support awarded, award of home to father, and award of home to mother. Net assets awarded to the father were significantly lower among sole-maternal custody cases that either sole-paternal or joint custody cases. Award of child support was found to be not independent, and therefore related to custody arrangement. The amount of child support was significantly different among the three custody types. The amount of support awarded in the sole-paternal custody group was significantly lower that the joint custody group. Child support awarded to custodial parents in joint custody cases was higher

---

[1]Assistant Professor, Consumer Affairs

[2]Associate Professor, Family Resource Management

than among sole-maternal cases. Award of the home was found to be not independent of custody arrangement. Therefore, a relationship exists between the two.

Conclusions

Research on custody following divorce has been an important issue of concern to researchers, legislators, judges, and attorneys. Custody and child support decisions following divorce affect the lives of everyone involved. It is important to understand the factors that impact custody decisions and issues related to divorce settlements.

Results of these analyses indicate that while equities in the negotiating process have improved, this study supports the notion that circumstances surrounding the custody issue are not the same for the various custody groups. Important differences in legal, socio-economic, and personal characteristics among the various custody groups exist. Research on the effects of these differences are to be fully understood.

An Approach to Health Care for Family Caregivers
- as partners in their own health care
- as managers of the care of older family members

Janice Holm Lloyd, North Carolina State University [1]
Louise Mallet, Campbell University School of Pharmacy [2]
Thomas Lloyd, Communications/Media Consultant, Raleigh NC [3]

This multi-media program was developed in 1991-92 as an additional resource for use in Extension-sponsored training programs for unpaid family caregivers of the dependent elderly. The basic objective of the new resource is to increase the competency and effectiveness of the family caregiver of a dependent older adult in his/her own health care, and in the health care of the care receiver. This program proposes to reach its objective by helping these special health care consumers develop a better understanding of the personal health care process and their role and responsibilities as partners in that process. Consistent with that understanding, the program proposes to teach certain management, interpersonal and information-gathering skills that can help them become more effective health care partners.

Research Findings

Research included three original field studies of family caregivers as well as extensive literature review. The findings indicate multiple, extremely serious problems among older adults in regard to many aspects of older health care consumer decision making, especially in terms of medication management. These problems include inappropriate use of over-the-counter drugs (OTCs); polypharmacy; adverse drug reactions; non-compliance with medical advice (for a variety of reasons); and poor communication between health professionals and elderly patients.

"Lack of effective communication between older people and their health care provider was a major contributor to medicine misuse".....efforts must be undertaken to encourage consumers to work with their health care professionals and "to see themselves as partners in improving their health" (NCPIE Report 1987).

The average home of older adults has 17 OTCs (Coons 1988), yet only 12.3% had talked with a pharmacist about their use of OTCs in the past six months (Smith and Sharpe 1984). The magnitude of OTC selection -- and the potential for misuse -- is

overwhelming, with over 300,000 OTC products on the market representing various combinations of 725 approved active ingredients. It is estimated that more than 200 of today's OTC products were unavailable except by prescription in 1976 (Coons 1988).

The incidence of multiple prescription and non-prescription drug use (polypharmacy) is greatest among older adults. Over 60% of all visits to a doctor by older adults include a prescription for medicine (Beers and Ouslander 1989). Polypharmacy is demonstrably a major factor in the large number of adverse drug reactions (ADRs) among older adults. In 1989, 243,000 persons required hospitalization for treatment of ADRs (Kusserow 1989). "The estimated annual costs of drug-related hospital admissions of the elderly, along with their subsequent treatment, was $4.5 billion in 1983" (Lipton and Lee 1988). Also linked to ADRs is the consumer's use of more than one pharmacy (Fincham 1988) and inadequate communication between doctors and older patients (Klein 1985).

Older consumers were found to have low levels of reliable health care knowledge, coupled with a generational unwillingness to ask questions of health professionals. In testimony before the Inspector General of U.S. Department of Health and Human Services, it was reported that only 2% of older adults asked ANY questions of their doctors -- about diagnosis, recommended tests, or prescribed medication and other forms of treatment (Kusserow 1989).

A comparison study of patients discharged from a Boston hospital -- with and without lengthy explanations by their doctors of the regimen prescribed -- found no difference in medication knowledge one month later (Klein 1985), a communications challenge for both professionals and consumers. For U.S. adults over age 16, one study indicated that 20% could not follow written instructions that stated, "Take two pills twice a day" (Mallet and Spruill 1988). Older adults may

---

[1]Extension Specialist, in Family
    Resource Management

[2]Pharm.D., in Geriatric Pharmacy and
    Clinical Pharmacist in Geriatrics

[3]Instructional Materials Designer

have both reading and comprehension problems, compounded typically by loss of visual acuity.

The problems involved in the relationship between health care consumers and health care professionals are complex (Vickery 1990). Clearly, these problems can not be significantly improved without simultaneous address by consumer and health educators AND the persons involved in continuing education programs for health care professionals. After further field testing of the program materials with older health care consumers, recommendations to appropriate professional associations will be made in mid-1993.

Program Design

A flow chart was created by the Instructional Materials Designer to help family caregivers visualize five specific "tasks" for the health care consumer to carry out as partner in his/her own health care.

Tasks in your own health care...

The five-task concept is then applied to the caregiver's role as manager of the health care of dependent older family members.

Program components include: 1) an hour-long video for use during the ongoing family caregiver training program; 2) a complementary folder of original print materials for distribution to family caregivers (diagrams, checklists, worksheets and fact sheets); and 3) a packet of print materials for program coordinators (training leader's guide, videoscript, bibliography and evaluation instruments).

The program materials were introduced and tested in a single county in May 1992. Revised materials were sent in September 1992 to Extension

Agents in the 37 counties already trained to conduct local caregiver training programs, with guidelines for expanding the training and reporting on program impact. An Extension Home Economics Agent and two representatives of her local aging network from 30 additional counties took part in team training in January-February 1993, and received direct training in the use of the new materials. Evaluation instruments include pre- and post- training surveys and a two-months later follow-up measurement.

Data collection as of June 1993 will be reported to the funding source in July 1993, and will be made available to anyone requesting a copy of that report.

Short-term benefits of the program are being measured in terms of improved knowledge and decision-making skill, and in reduced stress among family caregivers as health care consumers. Additional benefits are expected to include the improved health care of both caregivers and care receivers. A long-term, anticipated benefit of the program is the more appropriate, efficient use of the health care system by more knowledgeable, responsible consumers -- and a reduction of inappropriate demand on the health care system.

Review of program materials by representatives of other organizations in the health and aging networks resulted in a unanimous recommendation to adapt the materials for use with a variety of audiences in more flexible settings. A proposal to fund such a project, plus a new segment on health care costs, has been submitted to an appropriate foundation.

Implications for Consumer Educators

Some of the generalized lessons of consumer education require qualification when applied to the problems of older health care consumers. For example, grave limitations in the availability, accessibility and affordability of local health care may make the idea of investigating one's options or asserting one's rights a moot question. And advising consumers to shop for the best price for medications may lead to medication problems if there is no single doctor or pharmacist who reviews all the medications being taken.

If educational materials for older health care consumers are to be effective, they must incorporate the research findings from multiple disciplines which have addressed individual problem areas: communication between consumers and health care professionals; older adult usage of prescription medicines, non-prescription products and nutritional supplements; the factors involved in polypharmacy; the causes and costs of adverse drug reactions; the multiple reasons for non-compliance; and proven instructional techniques for older audiences.

Audiences of older adults will benefit from

special attention in the design and delivery of instructional materials. Research suggests the employment of such techniques as: providing as much structure as possible...using slow pacing of material... discussing one subject or task at a time...matching A-V message to verbal, point by point...avoiding bright colors, excessive contrast and glossy surfaces (Jinks and Baker 1987).

Selected References

Beers, M.H. and J.G. Ouslander. (1989). Risk factors in geriatric drug prescribing. Practical Therapeutics, Drugs 37, 105-112.

Coons, S.J. (1988). The pharmacist's role in the expanding OTC marketplace. The Kentucky Pharmacist, 223-242.

Fincham, J.E. (1988) Patient compliance in the ambulatory elderly: a review of the literature. Journal of Geriatric Drug Therapy, 2(4), 31-52.

Jinks, M.J. & D.E. Baker. (1987). Addressing audiences of older adults. Journal of Geriatric Drug Therapy, 1(3), 89-99.

Klein, L.E. (1985). Adverse drug reactions in the elderly. Drug Information Journal, 19, 469-473.

Kusserow, R. 1989. Medicare drug utilization review. Report OA1-01-88-00980.

Lipton, H.L. & P.R. Lee. 1988. Drugs and the elderly: clinical, social and policy perspectives. Stanford University Press, Palo Alto CA.

Mallet, L. & W.J. Spruill. 1988. Readability evaluation of nine patient drug education sources. American Pharmacy, NS28(11) 33-36.

Priorities and approaches for improving prescription medicine use by older americans. 1987. A Report of the National Council on Patient Information and Education, Washington DC.

Smith, M.C. & T.R. Sharpe. 1984. A study of pharmacists' involvement in drug use by the elderly. Drug Intelligence and Clinical Pharmacy, 18, 525-529.

Vickery, D.M. & J.F. Fries. 1990. Take care of yourself: the consumer's guide to medical care. Addison Wesley Publishing Co., Reading MA.

Consumer Knowledge: Does Practical Experience Make a Difference?

Karen Fox Folk, University of Illinois at Urbana-Champaign[1]
Kim Durum, University of Illinois at Urbana-Champaign[2]

This study examined the relationship between college students' scores on a national test of consumer knowledge and their actual life experience in areas tested. Currently renting, bearing responsibility for credit card payments and being male were positively related to overall test scores. Experiences with housing and credit were positively related to knowledge of housing and credit while experience with auto purchasing was not related to greater knowledge of automobile purchasing or insurance. Implications for consumer educators are discussed.

The purpose of this study was to investigate the relationship between life experience and consumer knowledge, using a convenience sample of college students with varying degrees of consumer experience. College students gain consumer experience by establishing checking accounts, obtaining credit cards, renting an apartment, and possibly purchasing a car. As beginning consumers they have varying degrees of experience with the above activities.

In 1991, a nationally representative sample of high school seniors taking a test of consumer knowledge scored much lower (mean of 42% correct) than a sample of adult Americans (mean of 62% correct) (Brobeck, 1992). Adults' higher scores could be due to more education, but also to their greater life experience in the areas tested. This study of high school seniors concluded that those with greater consumer experience (measured by monthly spending) had significantly higher test scores. Garman (1979, p. 60) also found that college seniors performed better on the Test of Consumer Competencies in areas in which they were more likely to have had "relevant life experiences."

The American Express and Consumer Federation of America test described above was taken by 110 students during the second class period of consumer economics classes at the University of Illinois spring and fall semesters 1992. To measure life experience, 14 questions were added which measured use of a checking account and credit cards, involvement in car and auto insurance purchase, experience with housing rental and food shopping,

as well as class, major, age, and sex. These college students averaged 68% correct overall with students scoring above average on sections testing knowledge of housing (86%) and car purchase (78%) and below average on credit (57%) and insurance (60%).

The classes tested contained 15% freshmen, 15% sophomores, 28% juniors, and 42% seniors. Half of the students lived in group housing, 45% rented, and 4% lived with parents. Most students had a checking account (93%). Three-fourths had a credit card and 62% made their own payments. Fewer students (61%) had a car and of those with a car, 43% had been moderately or very involved in the car purchase. However, 80% had not been involved in the auto insurance purchase decision.

Scores on test items measuring life experience as well as demographic variables were used to estimate overall test score and test section scores using multiple regression analysis. Currently renting, having a credit card on which the student made payments, and being male significantly increased total score, explaining 32% of the variance. Variables with no significant effect included: business-related or consumer economics major, year in school, having a checking account, balancing the bank statement, having a car, and regularly food shopping.

Analyses of individual test sections found that credit and housing knowledge was significantly related to experiences in those areas. Being male, a business or consumer economics major, and number of years in college were positively associated with scores on car purchasing, but student's extent of involvement in previous car purchase was not significantly related to car purchase test score. Test scores for banking and food shopping were not significantly related to the independent variables and auto insurance scores were related only to being male.

These findings support the hypothesis that students gain some consumer knowledge from life experiences, particularly in the areas of credit and housing. The lack of effect of experience on car purchase and insurance knowledge may be related to the fact that most students have at most one car purchase experience and that parents may oversee

---

[1]Assistant Professor, Division of Consumer Sciences

[2]Graduate Student, Division of Consumer Sciences

the purchase and arrange for auto insurance. A study of Canadian high school students also found that males scored higher than females (Smith, 1987). This may indicate that female students have less exposure to life experiences which increase consumer knowledge.

The relationship of life experience to consumer knowledge suggests that consumer educators should design programs which use experiential techniques or target consumers close to the point of purchase. This will be more difficult for items less frequently purchased such as autos and auto insurance, but these are also the areas in which life experience does not appear to assist consumers. Creative approaches might include videos made available through credit unions and banks for auto loan applicants or consumer education briefs enclosed with yearly auto registration renewals.

References

Brobeck, S.J. (1992). Student consumer knowledge: The results of a nationwide test. Unpublished report.   Washington,   D.C.:   Consumer Federation of America.

Garman, E.T.   (1979).   The cognitive consumer education knowledge of prospective teachers: A national assessment. Journal of Consumer Affairs, 13, 54-63.

Smith, B.S. (1987). An investigation of consumer knowledge, attitudes and behaviour of Quebec english public CEGEP students as a basis for consumer education curriculum development. Unpublished Ph.D. dissertation.   Montreal: McGill University.

Is There Expert Consensus on Quality in a Regulated Profession?

John E. Kushman, University of Delaware[1]
James R. Freed, UCLA[2]
Ronald W. Phelon, Federal Trade Commission[3]

Self regulation of professions rests on a consumer protection effect. It also requires a consensus among leading practitioners on what constitutes quality care. Evidence from a Federal Trade Commission study suggests there is little consensus among leading dental practitioners on what constitutes quality care. This brings into question self regulation in dentistry. The analysis uses three measures of consensus on quality among five leading practitioners. The best measure of agreement among practitioners is the Kappa statistic.

In 1979-1982 the Federal Trade Commission conducted a study of quality of care and commercial characteristics of dental practices. As a part of this larger effort, there was a smaller study of reliability of quality judgments among five leading dental practitioners.

The five leading practitioners evaluated appropriateness of services through treatment plans and their supporting radiographs as submitted to a third party administrator. The reliability study used a sample of 170 claims, including 190 radiographs and 1463 other services. Each service on each claim was reviewed independently by each practitioner, based on their expertise and widely accepted, written guidelines. Each reviewer classified a service as acceptable, no determination or unacceptable. The analysis reported here looked at the extent to which the practitioners' judgments agreed.

Self regulation of a profession is only possible when at least the leading practitioners agree to a large extent on what is acceptable practice. It is shared professional judgment that enables the profession to provide any consumer protection. Lack of reliability in professional judgments undermines a claim to self regulation.

The analysis includes three measures of agreement between pairs of reviewers:

1. **Agreement Rate** - proportion of services for which the reviewers gave the same evaluation. This measure is simple, but it has no probabilistic standard.

2. **Confidence for Binomial Test** - If the first reviewer chooses one of the outcomes (A,N or U) for each service, the null hypothesis is that the second reviewer has equal likelihood of choosing each of the three outcomes. That is, for the second reviewer, $P(A)=1/3$, $P(N)=1/3$ and $P(U)=1/3$. The sequence of services is a Bernoulli process with $P(agreement)=1/3$. Agreement is a binomial variable with a null hypothesis $P(Agreement=1)=1/3$. At what confidence level would the observed agreement reject this null hypothesis? The higher this confidence level, the greater the evidence against agreement being by chance. This approach gives agreement a probabilistic context and standard. It assumes, however, equal likelihood of the outcomes for the second reviewer. Observed evaluations show outcomes are not equally likely for any reviewer. This interpretation of "chance" is artificial.

There was only one "no determination" outcome for all radiographs. The study excluded this service, so the null hypothesis for radiographs is $P(agreement)=.5$.

3. **Kappa Statistic** - Kappa compares observed agreement to the agreement expected by chance, given the outcome proportions observed for the reviewers. It also compares observed agreement to perfect agreement. Kappa is widely used in biomedical research and epidemiology to evaluate interrater reliability (Fleiss, 1981, pp. 212-236; Elwood, 1988, pp. 67-69). Benchmark values are:

> Kappa=1 =>maximum possible agreement,
> Kappa=0 =>no agreement beyond that expected by chance and
> Kappa<0 =>agreement less than that expected by chance.

The reliability study includes each measure of agreement for each possible pair from the five reviewers. The analysis is separate for

---

[1]Professor, Textiles, Design and Consumer Economics

[2] Clinical Professor, Public Health Dentistry

[3] Economist, San Francisco Regional Office

radiographs, restorative services, prosthodontic services, endodontic services, periodontic services and surgical services.

The raw agreement rates look promising for prosthodontic, endodontic and surgical services, with nearly all pairs at .67 or greater. The agreement rates do not show evidence for a consensus in radiographs, restorative services or periodontic services. The binomial null hypothesis of P(agreement)=1/3 is rejected at confidence levels near 1.00 for nearly all pairs and types of services. This is strong evidence statistically, but the null hypothesis is somewhat artificial.

The Kappa statistics show little or no improvement in agreement over what would be expected by chance for any category of services. This best measure gives no evidence for reliability or a consensus of quality judgments. Some Kappa statistics are negative (agreement less than expected by chance) for pairs with agreement rates over .67 and confidence levels around 1.00.

The best evidence is that consensus required for self regulation is not present among leading dental practitioners. This study is preliminary, but it calls into question self regulation in dentistry. Even using the same written guidelines to supplement their intuitive judgment, leading practitioners do not agree on appropriateness of many more services than they would by chance.

References

Fleiss, J. L. (1981) Statistical methods for rates and proportions, second edition. New York: John Wiley and Sons.

Elwood, J. M. (1988) Causal relationships in medicine: a practical system for critical appraisal. New York: Oxford University Press.

Information Use and Demographic Characteristics: Differences Among Consumers With and Without Purchase Problems

Joan Koonce Lewis, University of Georgia[1]
Teresa Mauldin, University of Georgia[2]

The relationship between various demographic characteristics of consumers with and without purchase problems and use of information sources in the search process were examined. Responses of 358 consumers who had not encountered a problem with a product purchase and 520 consumers who had encountered a problem with a product purchase were analyzed using t-test procedures. Differences among consumers who had a product purchase problem and than those who did not were found.

Consumer researchers, consumer educators, and government agencies are concerned with consumers' ability to make better purchase decisions. This concern is warranted given the fact that there is a growing number of complicated consumer products and innovations in the marketplace. In addition, acquiring and processing consumer information about products are complex (Fast, Vosburgh & Frisbee, 1989). If consumers are better educated and informed, they may be able to deal with problems encountered in the marketplace more effectively, and third party regulation may be reduced (Udell, 1974; Uhl, 1970). However, few studies have systematically examined the benefits of investing in consumer information and education.

This paper examined the relationship between age, education, income, employment status, marital status, sex, confidence in ability to make a purchase, degree of social involvement, consumer knowledge, the use of a sales person's advice and articles or books about a product or service before making a purchase, and product purchase problems of consumers. More specifically, it determined whether or not those who had encountered a purchase problem differ from those who had not.

The sample was taken from a 1989 nationwide telephone survey of consumer behavior conducted by Market Facts for the American Association of Retired Persons (AARP) (Market Facts, 1990). Questions asked in the survey included information about knowledge of consumer rights, perceptions of the marketplace, bad buying experiences, purchasing behavior, social integration, and demographic characteristics. A total of 1,305 respondents age 25 and older were included in the study, with a disproportionately large number of older persons. Because of missing data, responses of 868 consumers were utilized in this study; 348 who had not encountered a problem with a product purchase and 520 who had.

T-tests were used to analyze the data. A p-value of .05 was used to determine significance. There were significant differences in respondents who had encountered a problem with a product purchase and those who had not.

Sixty seven percent of those who had encountered a problem were under 65 compared to 32.8 percent of those who had not. The mean level of education and income of those who had encountered a problem was 13.4 years and $30,415 compared to 12.8 years and $22,851 for those who had not. Among those who had encountered a problem, 67.9 percent were married, 52.3 percent were employed, and 52.3 percent were male. These percentages were 54 percent, 27.3 percent, and 44.0 percent, respectively for those who had not. Well over half of those who had encountered a problem (56.5 percent) had confidence in their ability to make a purchase decision compared to 64.1 percent of those who had not.

A consumer knowledge score was obtained by summing responses to 12 questions that dealt with legal and illegal business practices and consumer laws. A high score indicated a high degree of consumer knowledge; the highest score was 12. Surprisingly, the consumer knowledge score was slightly higher for those who had encountered a problem than those who had not (5.6 and 5, respectively).

A degree of social contact variable was examined because a high degree of social involvement may increase a consumer's knowledge. The variable was obtained by summing responses to five questions that dealt with attendance at meetings and religious services, volunteer work, classes taken, and how often a newspaper was read. A high number indicated a high degree of social

---

[1] Assistant Professor, Housing and Consumer Economics

[2] Associate Professor, Housing and Consumer Economics

involvement; the highest number was 5. The number of social contacts was slightly higher for those who had encountered a problem than those who had not (2.6 and 2.2, respectively).

Among those who had encountered a problem, 99.6 percent used a sales person's advice when making a major purchase decision compared to 97.7 percent who had not. Approximately 95 percent of those who had encountered a problem used articles or books before making a major purchase decision compared to 97.4 percent of those had not.

This research serves as a base for researchers interested in further exploring this population and helps consumer educators determine where educational efforts should be focused. Understanding the relationship between demographic characteristics, the use of consumer information and education, and product purchase problems of consumers is important in developing effective consumer information and education programs.

References

Market Facts, Inc. (1990). A report on the survey of older consumer behavior. Washington, DC: Consumer Affairs, American Association of Retired Persons.

Fast, J., & Vosburgh, R. E. (1989). The effects of consumer education on consumer search. Journal of Consumer Affairs, 23(1), 65-90.

Udell, G. G. (1974). The consumer's right to consumer education: A rejoinder. Journal of Consumer Affairs, 8, 86-92.

Uhl, J. H. (1970). The Purdue consumer education study: Some findings and implications. Journal of Consumer Affairs, 4, 124-134.

Gender and Religion: Their Relationship to
"The Money in the Past and Future Scale"

William C. Bailey, Ph.D., University of Arkansas[1]
Jean M. Lown, Ph.D., Utah State University[2]

Previous research has examined both religion and gender as important variables that influence the development of attitudes toward money. This study examined the relationship of religious affiliation and gender on responses to "The Money in the Past and Future Scale" (Furnham, 1984). It found that in this sample from the Western U.S. that religious affiliation had more of an impact than gender.

Introduction

Money has many roles in the lives of Americans besides being a medium of exchange and a unit of accounting. Recently, Belk and Wallendorf (1990) have suggested that money has taken on a sacred meaning in the context of an increasingly secularized society. Money has become surrounded with a aura of mystery, treated with deep respect, worshipped by some, and revered. Some even contend that money had it origins in the context of religion (Hodges, 1988).

Money was extensively written about in both the Old and New Testaments of the Bible. Many Judeo-Christian writings since have focused on the relationship between the believer, money, and God. The so-called "Protestant ethic" upon which this nation was founded suggests that a sign of God's blessing upon the hard working faithful is wealth. Religion remains an integral part of American culture and may have an important role in developing individual attitudes and behaviors toward money. However, few empirical studies have examined the relationship between religious affiliation and money.

Gender also has a major role in the development of attitudes toward money. Both popular books (Lieberman and Lindner, 1987) and empirical studies (Bailey and Lown, 1992) have focused on gender differences in developing attitudes toward money. However, there are few empirical studies that have examined the relationship between religion and gender in the development of attitudes toward money.

Methodology

Data were collected in 1988 from a convenience sample of 627 adults from three Western states. One group of subjects was recruited from a state-wide meeting of the Cooperative Extension Adult Leader's school. In addition, university students in personal finance classes collected data from adults who were not students. The instrument was self-administered. There were 343 males and 284 females in the sample.

Religious affiliation was determined by a single items that stated "what is your religious preference?" The religious affiliation was reported as follows: 171 Protestants, 247 LDS or Mormons, 112 Catholics, and 97 reported no or other religious preference. Judism was not a choice since very few live in the rural areas of Colorado, Wyoming, and Utah.

Results

A series of ANOVAs was computed in order to determine how the two socio-demographic variables, religious affiliation and gender, were related to the items on the MPFS. Contrary to expectations and previously reported results, gender was not as significant as religion in relationship to the variables on the MPFS. In addition, there were no significant interactions between gender and religion on any item. The following table indicates that gender was significant on only two items while religion was significant on fourteen items.

An examination of the means scores indicate few patterns in the results. However, one was in the "worry" questions. Members of the LSD church are less worried about these issues than members of other religions.

Implications

These results suggest that religion may have more significance in determining the development of individual's attitudes and behavior toward money. These findings are contradictory to previous research. They also

[1]Assistant Professor, Department of
    Home Economics

[2]Associate Professor, Home Economics and
    Consumer Education

suggest to researchers that they should examine in depth what American religious communities are teaching about money and probe the impact of these teaching in future research. For those involved in financial counseling or financial planning they should be aware of the religious affiliation of their clients and discuss with their clients their level of religious commitment as it may impact their behavior toward money. This research indicates that association between religion and money much stronger previously suspected. This association must be further evaluated.

Abbreviated Question	F-Ratio Gender	F-Ratio Religion
Family's financial position as child	.01	6.71[c]
Change in financial position	4.95[a]	0.02
Parent's discussion of financial matters	5.76[a]	59.10[c]
Mother's concern about money	0.18	7.57[c]
Father's concern about money	2.43	23.77[c]
Siblings' concern about money	0.47	15.48[c]
Respondent's concern about money	0.26	27.13[c]
Expect change in personal finances	0.12	35.25[c]
Expect change in nation's finances	0.42	4.68[c]
Worry about losing job	0.26	11.02[c]
Worry about having to sell house/car	0.93	27.19[c]
Worry about losing all savings	1.20	1.38
Worry about maintaining living standard	0.74	56.77[c]
Worry about making ends meet	0.67	20.32[c]
Worry about saving for old age	0.58	36.84[c]
Worry about not giving family all	3.49	30.70[c]

[a] $p < 0.05$;   [b] $p < 0.01$; [c] $p < 0.001$

References

Bailey, W.C. & Lown, J.M. (1992). A cross cultural examination of the etiology of attitudes toward money. Proceeding of the 1992 Conference of the Southern Regional Association of Family Economics/Home Management. Columbus, Ohio, 66-74.

Belk, R.W. & Wallendorf, M. (1990). The sacred meaning of money. Journal of Economic Psychology, 11, 35-67.

Furnham, A. (1984) Many sides of the coin: The psychology of money usage. Personality and Individual Differences, 5, 95-103.

Hodges, R. (1988). Primitive and peasant markets. Oxford: Basil Blackwell.

Lieberman, A. & Lindner, V. (1987). Unbalanced accounts: Why women are still afraid of money. New York: Atlantic Monthly Press.

"Needs Assessment:
How Do We Know What To Teach?"

Susan J. Jenkins, Idaho State University[1]

Needs assessment is a fundamental component of curriculum design. Understanding the knowledge base, as well as the perceptions and desires, of the delivery audience is critical to the success of educational programming. Needs assessment must therefore be designed as a comprehensive, integrated and unbiased process.

Because of the dynamic and expanding nature of consumer issues, decisions and information, many critical challenges face professionals within the discipline. A key element and one which continues to be fundamental to the success of consumer education programming is the question, "how do we know what to teach?" The answer hinges on comprehensive, integrated and unbiased needs assessment of the audience in question.

A "need" can be defined as the discrepancy between "what is" and "what ought to be" (Isaac and Michael, 1981). "Assessment" describes the status of phenomena at a particular point in time (Best, 1981). "It may deal with prevailing opinion, knowledge, practices or conditions," (Best, p. 93). Importantly, assessment merely describes a situation without value judgement or underlying rationale. Therefore, "needs assessment" is fundamentally a process which determines the concerns or needs of a reference group. Once identified, these concerns are then prioritized (often by the reference group and/or a consultant or outside agency) and ultimately they become the basis for defining program goals (Isaac and Michael) and developing curriculum.

Purpose

"The process begins inside a system with a felt need. If no need is perceived, then the rest of the change process does not occur" (Rushing as cited in Walstad and Soper, 1991, p. 295). Therefore, the purpose of this study was twofold: (1) consider the challenge of "needs assessment:" and (2) assess the needs of Idaho teachers for consumer and economic education programming.

Procedures

A survey instrument was developed by the Idaho Council on Economic Education (ICEE) network; reviewed by a panel of experts; and pilot tested to insure content validity and reliability. The project was endorsed by the Idaho State Department of Education and data were collected from a selected sample of schools within the fourteen (14) DEEP (Developmental Economic Education Programming) districts currently serviced by the ISU Center for Economic Education.

Sample

The sample included a total of 1,230 teachers (kindergarten through grade twelve, from all curricula) in twenty-two (22) schools. Return rate from the mailed questionnaire was 50% with a usable sample of 49% (n = 598). Data were treated and analyzed using the Statistical Package for the Social Sciences - x. All recorded percentages were the valid percentage for the teachers who responded to that particular item.

Results

Preliminary findings indicated that the teachers who participated in this project had the following demographic characteristics:

*Educational Background
   - only 19% had completed a degree beyond the bachelor's
   - average year of graduation was 1976 (sd 9.44)
   - only 20% had completed their degree within the last five years
   - 40% had NO college course work in consumer/economics
   - mean credits earned in consumer/economics was 3.44 (sd 3.67)
   - 29% completed their MOST RECENT course in consumer/economics prior to 1970
   - 61% had completed any related course work prior to 1980

*Current Teaching Assignment
   - 47% were elementary teachers
   - 53% taught at the secondary level
   - only 15% taught social studies/government or business

*Economic Education Involvement/Perceptions
   - 22% felt unqualified to teach consumer/economics OR that it was too difficult for students to learn
   - 14% indicated lack of time and/or resources to teach the subject
   - 64% believed that economics was "not formally included in required curriculum"

---

[1]Associate Professor and Director, Center for Economic Education

Conclusions

As it related to the research sample, <u>initial</u> training in basic consumer/economics is needed. <u>Additional</u> training is necessary to update teacher training. Inservice, preservice, adult and community education must be utilized to reverse the current "involvement" with consumer/economics. Sixty-four percent indicated that they thought consumer/economics was "not formally included in required content." Idaho does in fact have a state mandate that requires a minimum of one semester in "consumer economics" for high school graduation. It is also a required component in the elementary curriculum for the state of Idaho.

The importance of needs assessment as a fundamental foundation in successful consumer/economic education programming must be reemphasized. To be valuable, it should be designed as a cooperative, integrated effort. Adequate orientation must precede the process and a variety of information should be collected---both issues to counteract the problem of confounding "needs" with preferences.

Implications

Although regional, state and local needs for consumer/economics programming may vary widely, a basic framework for needs assessment throughout the economic education network would be beneficial. Such a model could not only serve as a springboard for more unique and individualized assessment techniques, but would also allow at least minimal standardization and therefore comparison of DEEP district needs between school districts, throughout a Center service area, statewide or even nationally.

Possibilities for future research include: (1) replication of this study throughout Idaho; (2) regional or multi-state comparative studies; and (3) development of a standard data set to be assessed on an annual basis and utilized to evaluate and improve curriculum and programming in consumer/economics. University, Cooperative Extension and other applications should also be considered.

References

Best, J.W. (1981). <u>Research in education</u> (4th ed.). Englewood Cliffs, NJ: Prentice Hall.

Isaac, S. & Michael, W. B. (1981). <u>Handbook in research and evaluation</u> (2nd ed.). San Diego: EdiTS.

Walstad, W. G. & Soper, J. C. (Eds.). (1991). <u>Effective economic education in the schools</u>. Washington, D.C.: National Education Association.

Older Consumers' Knowledge of Health Insurance: An Exploratory Study

Kathleen Prochaska-Cue, University of Nebraska-Lincoln[1]
Rebecca Cunningham, University of Nebraska-Lincoln[2]

Health insurance, whether obtained from a private insurance company or through a government program such as Medicare or Medicaid, is a complex consumer product. To attain satisfaction in the health insurance marketplace, consumers need to be knowledgeable about their insurance coverage. The purposes of the study reported here were to (1) measure insurance knowledge levels, experience, and attitudes, and (2) define topics and audiences for future insurance educational programs.

Health insurance consumers 65 and older living an SMSA and a nonSMSA Nebraska county were the population for this exploratory study of 150 interviews. Individuals who participated were recruited while attending a service club or senior center event. One-way analysis of variance using the General Linear Model procedures of the Statistical Analysis System computer program was used for data analysis. Mean comparisons were performed using the Bonfenoi t test. An alpha of .01 was established a priori to indicate significance.

Retired persons with greater general knowledge of health insurance tended to be male, 65-74 years of age, married, living with a relative, and with education beyond high school and/or annual incomes of $30,000 or more. Age and education made no significant difference in knowledge of Medicare and supplemental insurance including long-term care insurance. In addition, marital status and income made no significant difference in knowledge of long-term care insurance.

On a scale of 1 (extremely negative) to 6 (extremely positive), the mean score for how those interviewed felt about health insurance coverage was M = 4.700. The mean scores for health insurance providers were: Medicare, M = 4.097; supplemental insurance, M = 5.371; and long term care insurance, M = 4.476.

When a spouse was identified as head of household, individuals had a significantly higher mean score (M = 5.105) reflecting their attitude towards health insurance in general than did those who identified themselves as head of household (M = 4.523). Overall attitudes about health insurance of individuals who live independently had a significantly lower mean score (M = 4.569) than those that lived with a relative, including a spouse (M = 4.870).

Individuals with incomes of more than $30,000 scored significantly higher (M = 5.071) than those with incomes of less than $10,000 (M = 4.578). People with incomes of more than $30,000 also had a more positive attitude about their health insurance providers (M = 4.955) than those with incomes under $10,000 (M = 4.473).

Overall, the more satisfied individuals are with health insurance in general and/or with their supplemental insurance, the more satisfied they were with Medicare.

Consumer experience with health insurance appeals was reported to be minimal indicating the insurance appeals process as an area for future health insurance education. Study results also indicated other targeted educational efforts be directed to women, older retirees or their caregivers, single people, those with less education and/or income, and those who live alone.

---

[1]Associate Professor, Cooperative Extension

[2]Former Graduate Student

A New State Comparative Price Advertising Statute

Irene E. Leech
Virginia Polytechnic Institute and State University[1]

In 1990 retail merchants requested that the General Assembly study Virginia's comparative price advertising law. They felt that it was too restrictive and noted that the marketplace had changed substantially since the General Assembly last amended the statute in 1974. A study was requested because this is typically required before changes are made. The General Assembly responded by approving a joint House and Senate subcommittee to study the necessity and desirability of revising the statute.

Public hearings were held across the state and the subcommittee concluded that changes were necessary. Consumer advocates did not share the view of business concerning the type of change needed, but called for changes to make the law more restrictive. They noted that in recent years other states, such as Maryland and Pennsylvania, had taken action concerning advertising against businesses which also do business in Virginia. However, under the existing law, those businesses could not be prosecuted in Virginia.

Some retailers requested a more stringent law. They found it difficult to compete in a marketplace where consumers could not understand comparative prices or trust that the prices meant what advertisers said they meant. The retailers were convinced that they were losing business to competitors who used unfair comparisons.

At the request of the State Division of Consumer Affairs, a study was designed to describe in a comprehensive way citizens attitudes about retail store advertising. General questions which identified no particular industry or merchant were designed by the researcher and the Division. The questionnaire was pilot tested and refined.

The statistically valid stratified telephone survey collected data from 415 residents in four localities across the state. The sample was systematically drawn from the latest telephone book published for each locality. Data were collected in January 1992 by trained interviewers.

Respondents were highly educated; nearly half had taken at least some college courses. Sixty percent lived in one or two person households and 70% had no children living with them. Half of the sample was under age 40 and 46% had annual household incomes below $40,000.

Citizens said that they did not trust comparative price advertising. In fact, 37% reported almost never believing that markdowns were real. However, 81% also said that they usually bought things at sale prices.

Almost three-quarters of these consumers said that they wanted stores to compare their prices to actual prices in other stores, and two-thirds wanted to have prices compared to the average price in the area.

Consumers wanted this information, but apparently were not willing to work very hard to comparison shop. Almost half said that they did not check prices in several stores before buying.

Since disclaimers were proposed as a way to make comparisons fair, interviewers asked respondents if they read disclaimers. Nearly a third said they rarely read disclaimers and 46% almost always read them. While 46.5% of respondents believed that disclaimers make advertisements more clear, 21% said disclaimers make advertisements less clear, and 33% said disclaimers make no difference.

Another issue was whether stores should be required to actually offer an item at one price before advertising a sale price compared to the original price. Respondents (67%) agreed that stores should offer items at a regular price before advertising a sale price compared to that regular price. Only 11% of respondents felt that it was not necessary for stores to first offer items at a regular price.

Some respondents told interviewers that they did not know the difference between terms like manufacturer's suggested retail price and market value. Others informed interviewers that they knew of merchants in their area who used artificial comparison prices to lure consumers into their stores.

Since respondents report buying items on sale, merchants have tremendous incentive to make consumers think they are on sale. It is clear that while consumers say they want to comparison shop, they often do not do so. They want a simple, clear, comparison.

These results were reported to legislators working on a new comparative price advertising

[1] Assistant Professor, Housing, Interior Design and Resource Management

statute.   While the law was changed, making it
easier for the Division of Consumer Affairs to
enforce, it is still possible for advertisements to
confuse consumers.

Disclaimers were not required.   Although
business lobbied against it, the law requires that
items be offered at a regular price before a sale
price can be advertised.   It also requires
businesses to keep records to prove previous prices
when comparisons are made. The statute was removed
from the criminal code and placed in the Consumer
Protection Act for easier enforcement.

In the end this legislation, like all
legislation, was a compromise. Neither business
nor consumer advocates achieved all their goals.
However, the statute is clearer and more
enforceable, so it is an improvement for consumers
and businesses.

Consumer Behavior of Low-Income Persons:
A Pilot Study

Joan Koonce Lewis, University of Georgia[1]

A pilot test of an interview schedule to examine consumer behavior of low-income persons was conducted in two low-income housing projects in Georgia. Behaviors explored included use of different type of product information, assistance with major purchase decisions, and how major purchase problems were handled.

Low-income consumers have inadequate financial resources and difficulty making ends meet. Understanding how they function in today's complex marketplace is important. Their potential problems in the marketplace are reasons they should be studied.

In addition, the increasing number of low-income consumers demands greater attention to this population. According to the U.S. Census Bureau, the number of persons below the official Government poverty level was 25.9 million in 1977, representing 12.6 percent of the American population. Approximately 33.6 million persons presently live in poverty, representing 13.5 percent of the United States population (U.S. Department of Commerce, 1990, 1991). As the low-income population continues to increase, the importance of helping them make good purchase decisions also increases. To ignore factors that interfere with their ability to function effectively in the marketplace increases the demands by low-income consumers on public financial resources.

However, knowledge about individuals' consumer behavior is scarce and particularly so for low-income persons. Low-income consumer behavior was studied extensively in the late 60s and early 70s; however, recent research in this area is limited.

In an attempt to investigate the consumer behavior of the low-income population, the investigator submitted a planning grant to the National Science Foundation (NSF). The NSF funded the grant which enabled the investigator to develop a research proposal to conduct research in this area. The proposed research project will examine consumer behavior of low-income persons.

As part of the research proposal, an interview schedule was developed and pilot tested in two low-income housing projects in Athens, Georgia. Twenty one low-income persons were interviewed. This paper will report some of the results of the pilot test.

Demographic Characteristics

The majority of the respondents were black (85.7%), female (95.2%), unmarried (85.7%), unemployed (76.1%), and less than 50 years old (71.4%). Approximately 62 percent had less than a high school education, and 80.9 percent had a total household income less than $7,500. A large number received food stamps (76.1%), medicaid (76.1%), AFDC (57.1%), and WIC coupons (42.8%). Thirty eight percent had problems meeting their basic needs. Eighty one percent had no training in consumer education, and 47.6 percent were not exposed to any consumer education when growing up in the home with their parents. A large number (71.4%) discussed their purchase decisions with their spouse, friends, neighbors, and/or family members.

Consumer Behavior

Approximately 71 percent of the sample rarely or never used a sales person's advice when making a purchase decision. Some rarely or never used the Better Business Bureau or a consumer protection agency (66.6%), product ratings from consumer magazines (61.9%), articles or books about a product or service (42.8%), advertising (33.3%), family or friends (28.7%), point-of-purchase information (23.8%), and past buying experience (4.7%).

The majority of the respondents (80.9%) made major purchase decisions by themselves; only 4.7 percent made purchase decisions with their spouse. Fourteen percent made these decisions with their children. Only 33.3 percent made major purchases when they just wanted a new or different type of product. Nineteen percent would make a major purchase via the rent-to-own industry, and 42.8 percent would use some form of credit.

Only 28.5 percent of the sample previously had a problem with a major purchase, and 33.3 percent of the ones who had a problem did nothing to correct it. Reasons given for doing nothing included did not think it was worth the time, not sure of consumer rights, and thought it would be embarrassing.

This research serves as a base for researchers

---

[1]Assistant Professor, Housing and Consumer Economics

interested in further exploring this population and helps consumer educators determine where educational efforts should be focused.

References

U.S. Department of Commerce, Bureau of the Census. (1990). Poverty in the United States: 1990. Current Population Reports, Series P-60, No. 175.

U.S. Department of Commerce, Bureau of the Census. (1991). Poverty in the United States: 1988 and 1989. Current Population Reports, Series P-60, No. 171.

California Consumers: Choices and Decisions
A Community Outreach Program

Wendy L. Reiboldt, California State University, Long Beach[1]
Carol E. Kellett, California State University, Long Beach[2]
M. Elizabeth Hyland, California State University, Long Beach[3]

This outreach program is a collaborative effort between California State University, Long Beach, Wells Fargo Bank, and several community agencies. The program reaches out to minority communities in an effort to provide information to them about budgeting, banking and credit. The pilot test found the results to be promising. Participants were interested in the information they received, and gave further suggestions for future workshops.

Introduction

The civil unrest that shook Los Angeles County following the Rodney King verdict in 1992 have provided a unique opportunity for researchers and academicians in the Southern California area. This ongoing study seeks to increase consumer awareness, knowledge and skills of low-income immigrant urban families in Los Angeles and Orange Counties. Solutions to consumer issues will strengthen and support families and neighborhoods for future generations. The first pilot tests of this program have been encouraging.

Past studies have found that lower income families rarely have a monthly budget. Furthermore, they seldom balance their checkbook if they have a checking account at all. For immigrant families, language barriers pose complications, making them vulnerable to fraud. The Project helps enable low income and immigrant consumers to improve their resource management skills by providing information regarding budgeting, use of banking services, expenditures and savings.

Planning

The Project fosters a collaborative relationship between existing programs and services, linking education, private and public sectors. An Advisory Board which establishes partnerships with exiting programs and services was convened. The Board discussed past experiences with similar programs, and made suggestions for the successful implementation of the current program.

Two neighborhoods were selected for implementation of the project, one in Los Angeles County and one in Orange County. Spanish speaking students were hired and trained to serve as translators and facilitators of presentation materials and to conduct interviews in the community outreach effort.

Project directors and students attended (and continue to attend) ongoing community and neighborhood group meetings in the two target communities. Community members were surveyed to see what type of consumer information they desired to assist them in the decision making process. Based on the survey, 40 of the 62 respondents desired knowledge on how to set up a monthly family budget. Appropriate educational materials were adapted, translated, and organized into a lesson plan.

Implementation

The first pilot program focused on planning a family budget. The presentation was given in both Spanish and English. Information tables were set up for attendees. Representatives from several corporations and agencies (with both Spanish and English speaking personnel) were present, including a local mortgage company, Souther California Edison, Southern California Gas Company, Consumer Credit Counselors of Orange County, and Community Development Council.

A pre- and post-test was administered to determine if attendees currently had a budget, bank account, and credit cards. Furthermore, the tests asked if the respondents would be willing to participate in future programs. The post-test asked for suggestions on future programs they would be interested in.

Results

The results of the pre- and post-test are as follows. While the attendance was low (6 attendees), survey information collected was complete. The pre-test revealed that the majority of respondents did not have a budget or bank account, and only one respondent had a credit card.

---

[1]Assistant Professor, Consumer Affairs

[2]Professor, Home Economics Communication

[3]Lecturer, Consumer Affairs

The post-test results found that respondents were interested in the topic and that they learned about monthly budgets, how to plan for purchases, and how to cut down on expenses. Respondents also reported that they would welcome future programs, and made suggestions as to the format they would desire. The majority of respondents stated they would like to have information in a brochure or booklet.

Future Implications

A need has been identified in the minority community. Preliminary surveys found that members were interested in learning about budgeting, banking, and credit. An increase in awareness of these issues would serve to help minority communities better manage their resources.

Future directions for the study are being discussed. Participation of project members continue in the targeted communities. Following from the pilot study and post-test results, several possible directions have been identified.

Possible future directions include: providing information tables at an existing meeting, opening a program to the general public and announce it through the utility companies' mailings, and having a program on fraud and scams which are prevalent in the communities. Further proposals will be developed to request additional funding to address these areas.

Credit Use of Three Cohorts of Rural Women

Constance Young Kratzer, Virginia Polytechnic Institute & State University[1]
Dennis Keefe, Michigan State University[2]

Consumer credit can be considered as one of several money management tools available to the family. The purpose of this study is to look at some credit practices, and the relationship of debt/income ratios to perceived economic well-being of three cohorts of rural women.

Access to credit has played a role in economic well-being by adding to the level of money income at a given point in time while committing future income for repayment. Jensen and Reynolds (1986) found credit users were generally better educated, younger, and more often had children. Credit use by older persons was more likely to be for convenience and less likely to be for installment purchases. Debt/income ratios are a measure of the amount of credit used in relation to income and have been used as one predictor of economic well-being. Kinsey and Lane (1978) found higher debt-asset ratios were generally non-significant, but smaller family size, income and rurality were related to the probability of feeling better off.

Methods

This study utilized data from the NC-182 regional project funded by the Agricultural Experiment Stations in eight states. The sample was selected from two rural counties in each of the participating states. A county was defined as rural if at least 20% or more of the employed persons were engaged in the occupations of agriculture, livestock, forestry, mining and/or fishing. The sample in each county was randomly selected from a commercial directory service list. Data were collected from rural households by means of mailed questionnaires using a modified Dillman method. For this study, questionnaires completed by female financial managers in three specific cohorts were used.

Sample

The Cohorts were selected based on an historical event occurring at the time the women reached age 18.

Cohort 1: turned 18 during the depression years 1929 to 1934 and were 72-77 at the time of the study.

Cohort 2: turned 18 between 1950 and 1955 when the economy was booming and were 51 to 56 at the time of the study.

Cohort 3: were among the first of the Baby Boomers to turn 18 between 1964 and 1969 and were 37 to 42 at the time of the study.

Questions

Respondents were asked:

Whether or not they used credit (Number of credit sources - Range 1 to 7)

To indicate on a 5 point scale, never to most of the time how often they
1) paid interest on charge accounts
2) made only minimum payments on charge accounts

Findings

Mean number of Credit Sources

Cohort 1   1.4
Cohort 2   1.9
Cohort 3   2.1

Percent who did not use Credit

Cohort 1   55%
Cohort 2   10%
Cohort 3   8%

Debt/income ratio

Cohort 1   .237
Cohort 2   .726
Cohort 3   .731

Percent of Perceived Economic Well-being explained by debt/income ratio

Cohort 1   22.0%
Cohort 2   13.5%
Cohort 3   0.5%

[1]Assistant Professor, Housing, Interior Design and Resource Management

[2]Assistant Professor, Family and Child Ecology

Discussion

Overall, the younger the woman, the more credit used. This finding may reflect the need for more credit by younger women, or reluctance on the part of the older women to use credit. Cohort 2 and Cohort 3 were more likely to pay interest on charge accounts than was Cohort 1. They also more frequently reported making the minimum payment on charge accounts.

Debt/income ratio was significantly related to perceived economic well-being for Cohort 1 and Cohort 2 but not for Cohort 3. Younger families may more readily accept consumer credit as a normal part of doing business as a household than do their older counterparts.

The women in this study lived in a rural area but findings did not support that they differed from nonrural women. The data supports less credit use by older cohorts than younger ones. Also higher debt/income ratios had a more negative effect on the perceived economic well-being of the older cohorts. Additional research is needed to explore whether or not there are differences in attitude about credit use among the cohorts.

References

Jensen, H. H. & Reynolds, S. W. (1986). Consumer credit use and age: An analysis of the effects of preretirment. In V. Hempler (Ed.) Proceedings of American Council on Consumer Interests. (pp.261-264) Comumbia, MO: ACCI.

Kinsey, J. & Lane, S. (1978). The effect of debt on perceived houshold welfare. Journal of Consumer Affairs, 12(1), 48-61.

Utility Function & Decision Rule: The Missing Link

Jinkook Lee, University of Tennessee[1]

To help individual consumer make better decisions individual consumer's utility function rather than a universal utility function needs to be identified and applied to consumer decision making aids. By linking individual consumer's utility function to a behavioral decision rule, the optimal decision rule for individual consumer can be assessed.

Neoclassical economists assume consumer buying decisions are always utility maximizing. That is, consumers not only are able to but also try to make optimal (utility maximizing) buying decisions. Both the ability and willingness of consumers to make an optimal decision have been challenged, however. Inability to make an optimal decision comes from information failure. While the economic theory underlying consumer choice assumes full information which guarantees the optimizing decision, it is unusual for consumers to have full information about the products or services purchased. On the other hand, since information is not free consumers do not always try to make an optimal decision. A consumer who does not gather information may be perfectly rational since the costs of searching for information may exceed its benefits.

The purpose of this study is to enhance effectiveness of consumer decision making. The need for aids to improve effectiveness of consumer decision making is recognized. One of the most promising consumer decision making aids is the computer (Geistfeld, 1990; Russo, 1988). A Computer Assisted Decision Making Aid (CADMA) reduces information processing costs. Russo et al. (1986) identified three types of information processing costs: collection, comprehension and computation. Collection cost refers to the time and effort spent in acquiring relevant information. Comprehension cost refers to the time and effort needed to understand the information. Computation cost refers to the time and effort needed to combine the information and draw an inference.

CADMA reduces information collection costs to the extent that it is a source of information. CADMA also reduces comprehension costs by presenting information in a more easily understood manner and by providing explanations to compensate for a consumer's lack of knowledge. CADMA can also reduce information computation costs because it can draw inferences. It is important that CADMA imitates a consumer's utility function in order to

give an optimal choice. Utility function is a relationship that identifies the amount of utility the consumer derives from an alternative.

Neoclassical economists treat goods (alternatives) as the direct source of utility. However, Lancaster (1971) proposed a characteristic model that each good embodies various characteristics that ultimately yield utility. That is, utility comes from characteristics rather than the goods themselves. Therefore, a utility function is how individual consumers assess the utility of an alternative when each alternative can be evaluated in terms of a set of multidimensional attributes (characteristics).

Typically, it has been assumed that the utility of an alternative is a linear combination of the utilities of the various attributes making up that alternative (Einhorn, 1970). The linear form of utility function implies a consumer decision making process that considers all attributes of a given alternative in such a way, that a desirable attribute may offset or compensate for an undesirable attribute. However, in consumer behavior literature, when choosing an alternative from a choice set, consumer decision making behavior varies. Other nonlinear, noncompensatory models of decision rules have been found. These models, such as conjunctive, disjunctive, and so on, are approximated by nonlinear functions of utility.

Researchers have explained the departure from the linear utility function by the cost of information processing. Since information processing is costly (it involves time and effort), and consumers have limited time and energy, consumers may use a simpler model of decision rules rather than a linear compensatory decision rule. The argument is that consumers use simpler decision rules in order to reduce information processing demands when they face a complex decision making situation. A series of experiments support this argument. However, on the other hand, there is evidence of the use of noncompensatory decision rules such as conjunctive, disjunctive and lexicographic rules even in a non-complex decision making situation.

To help make consumer decision making become more effective, individual consumers' utility functions need to be identified. If a linear utility function is all consumers' universal utility function, a universal form of utility

[1]Assistant Professor, Retail and Consumer Science

function implies that all consumers have identical preferences.   Therefore, the first research question is to identify the form of the utility function.   Whether different consumers have an identical utility function is then investigated. The second research question is to relate the utility functions to decision rules. A decision rule refers to how consumers actually combine information to identify the best alternative. To bridge the gap between preference structure and choice behavior, this study will investigate which models of decision rules consumers use with which models of utility functions.

The findings of these research questions can be used to develop CADMA's inference process, which will help consumers make better decisions by reducing information computation costs.   By employing each consumer's utility functions rather than a universal utility function, CADMA can individualize decision making. That is, a consumer will get what is best for him/her rather than what is best for all consumers.   Examination of the relationship between utility functions and decision rules will clarify the connection between the normative and descriptive approaches to consumer decision making.

References

Einhorn,   H.   J.   (1970).   The   use   of nonlinear,noncompensatory models in decision making. Psychological Bulletin, 73 (3), 221-30.

Geistfeld, L. V. (1990). Enhancing consumer choice through decision-making aids. In R. N. Mayer (ed.), Enhancing Consumer Choice: Proceedings of the Second International Conference on Research in the Consumer Interest. Columbia, Missouri; American Council on Consumer Interests, 477-84.

Lancaster, K.(1971). Consumer Demand: A New Approach, New York & London; Columbia University Press.

Russo, E. J. (1988). Information processing from the consumer's perspective. In E. Scott Maynes & The ACCI Research Committee (Eds.), The Frontier of Research in The Consumer Interest: Proceedings of the International Conference on Research in the Consumer Interest.   Columbia, Missouri; American Council on Consumer Interests, 185-218.

Russo, E. J., Staelin, R.,Nolan, C.A., Russell, G., & Metcalf, B.L. (1986). Nutrition information in the supermarket. Journal of Consumer   Research,   13,   48-70.

Characteristics of Parents Who Pay for Child Care

Sharon A. DeVaney, The Ohio State University[1]

Decisions about child care focus on three major areas: accessibility, affordability, and quality. Affordability may be a problem because families are unwilling or unable to pay the market cost for the level of quality of child care that they demand. Parents choose lower quality care because it costs less, not because they are ignorant (Connelly, 1991). The purpose of this study was to explore the characteristics of parents who pay for child care.

Importance of the Problem

Hofferth and Phillips (1987) project that by 1995 over three-fourths of school-age children and two-thirds of preschool children will have employed mothers. Although nearly half of employed parents with children needing care manage to arrange for low or no-cost care by spouse or relatives, expenditure for child care is substantial for many families. Kahn and Kamerman (1987) found that child care is the 4th largest expenditure category for families with children; housing, food and taxes are the top three expenditures. The purpose of this paper is to explore the characteristics of parents who pay for child care.

Methodology

Data for the study were drawn from the National Longitudinal Study of Youth. The sample (n = 1495) consisted of those respondents whose youngest child was 5 years of age or younger and who indicated that they were working, in school, or in training. The dependent variable indicated whether paid child care was used. It has codes of 1 or 0. Independent variables were family size, urban residence, net income, poverty status, number of weeks worked, if a single female was family head, region of the country, and education degree points. Logistic regression was used for the analysis. It yields estimates of probabilities between zero and one. The logit coefficient is the percentage change in the logarithm of the odds ratio of probabilities, ln(P/1-P), given a small change in the value of the independent variable and holding all other variables constant.

Findings

Sixty-one percent of the sample (909 respondents) were white, 22% (332) were black, and 17% (254) were Hispanic. The mean age was 24 years. Of the proportion (24%) who were single parent families, only 5% were male headed. Forty-three (43) percent of black families were female headed. Among white and Hispanic families, 13% were female headed. One-fifth of the sample had less than a high school diploma. Only 7% had college degrees. More than three-fourths (77%) of the sample lived in urban areas. The mean income in 1985 was $24,272 while the median income was $21,013.

For respondents in the total sample and white respondents, an increase in family size was associated with lower odds of using paid child care (Figure 1). Support was found for the hypotheses regarding increased use of child care by respondents who were single female family heads; such respondents in the total group and white and black subsamples showed increased odds of using paid care (Figure 2). As net income increased, respondents in the total sample and white respondents were more likely to use paid child care. Support was found for the lower odds of using child care for respondents who were below the poverty level. The finding that those who live in the South have higher odds of paying for child care was consistent with previous studies.

Implications

Previous research suggests that low income families spend a disproportionate amount of income on child care. This study indicates that female-headed families are likely to be significant users of paid care. Such families often have lower incomes and poorer prospects for improving their status. For families at the lower end of the income scale and for many middle-income families, the costs of child care may represent a burden. Other pertinent questions which could not be addressed in this study are the quality of care and level of satisfaction of parents with purchased care.

References

Connelly, R. (1991). The importance of child care costs to women's decision making. In D. M. Blau (Ed.), The economics of child care(pp. 87-118). New York: Russell Sage Foundation.

Hofferth, S. L. & Phillips, D. A. (1987). Child care in the United States, 1970-1995. Journal of Marriage and the Family, 47, 559-571.

Kahn, A. J. & Kamerman, S. B. (1987). Child care:

---

[1]Graduate student

Facing the hard choices.   Dover, MA: Auburn
Publishing Co.

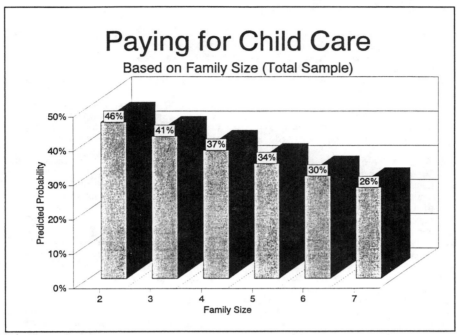

Figure 1

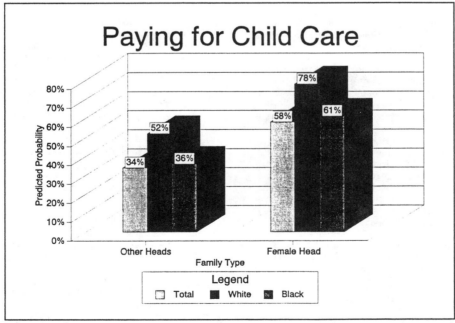

Figure 2

Spending as a Function of Income and Other Variables

Mi Kyeong Bae, The University of Texas-Austin[1]
Sherman Hanna, The Ohio State University[2]

The consumption function has long been of interest in macroeconomics, and the permanent income and related theories have been studied by examination of aggregate and household cross-sectional patterns of consumption versus current income. The focus of this poster is somewhat similar to consumption function studies, but emphasizes the budget implications of the relationship between spending and current income, as well as other demographic variables. Why do some households spend more than their current income and others spend less? The life cycle model suggests some plausible patterns, but little research has been done that focuses on the household "spending function." The 1990 Consumer Expenditure Survey was the data source for this analysis, and the study includes only households interviewed in all four quarters. With various exclusions, the sample size was 872 consumer units. The BLS definition of expenditures included Social Security and pension contributions, so the variable "spending" was created by subtracting Social Security and pension contributions. The spending variable was also adjusted for the transportation category, as the BLS includes net vehicle purchases, regardless of how a vehicle was purchased. Net vehicle purchases were subtracted, and annual vehicle loan payments were added, to obtain the spending variable. The mean level of total expenditures was $28,863 and the median level was $24,291. Seven consumer units had takehome income less than zero, and 50% had annual spending greater than takehome income.

A regression of annual spending on takehome income and other variables was estimated. In addition to income terms through income cubed, similar income terms were created for units with negative incomes and for households with income reported but who were listed as incomplete income reporters. Stepwise regression was used, in order to test the potential effects of a large number of variables in an equation, including interaction terms, to obtain a better prediction for the total expenditure, while at the same time keeping the number of parameters to interpret and use in predictions manageable. Other independent variables included net financial assets, home equity, the number of earners, household size and size squared, age and age squared, dummy variables for Black, Hispanic, tenure, education, family type, occupation, city size and region, and interaction terms. This consumption function equation had an R^2 of 0.58. Twenty variables entered the regression, all significant at the 0.10 level or better. Variables involving age, income, negative income, and incomplete income entered the regression. Controlling for other variables (including income), spending was positively related to home equity, education, having a mortgage, , living in a city with over four million population, and the number of earners. Spending was negatively related to living in the Northeast and Hispanic reference person. Couples without children at home, couples with at least one child over 17 at home and couples with children under 18 all spent more than single consumers and single parent households. (The complete regression table is available from Hanna.)

The overall relationship between total annual spending and income ranging from the most negative income reported to the highest income reported was roughly "V" shaped, with predicted spending increasing as income became more negative or more positive.

Figure 1 shows an example of the pattern for non-Black, non-Hispanic households with the reference person aged 40, and homeowners with mortgages, for two types of households:

1. Married couples without children with a reference person with highest education being high school graduate, not living in the Northeast or in a city of over four million population.

2. Married couples with two children under 18, college degree, not living in the Northeast or in a city of over four million population.

For the first example (high school graduate, etc.), predicted spending exceeded takehome income for incomes below $25,000 per year. For the second example (college graduate, etc.), predicted spending exceeded takehome income for incomes below $42,000.

Figure 2 shows the relationship between spending and income for the type of household in the second example above, for households who were complete income reporters and for households who were incomplete income reporters. The increasing

---

[1]Visiting Scholar, Human Ecology Department

[2]Professor and Chair, Family Resource Management

gap between predicted spending amounts suggest the
amount of under-reporting of income by incomplete
income reporters.

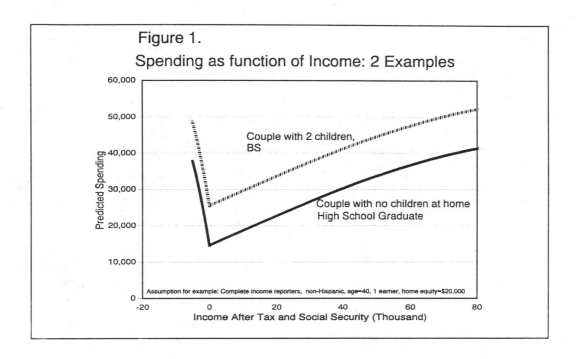

Figure 1.
Spending as function of Income: 2 Examples

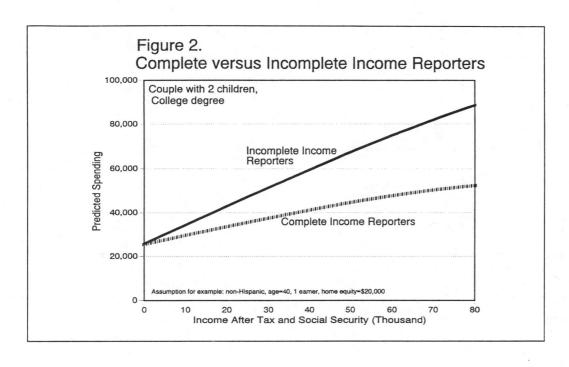

Figure 2.
Complete versus Incomplete Income Reporters

Demand Side Management: What, Why, and How?

Marsha P. Ryan, American Electric Power[1]
Barbara M. Collins, Barbara Collins & Associates[2]

Demand Side Management is a new concept based on the notion that the best use of electricity is the most efficient use. It is defined as influencing customer load characteristics and changes that customers can make which affect their usage of electricity. Successful DSM programs will require changes in consumer behavior. Because DSM programs are designed to affect the usage pattern of large groups of customers with diverse needs, extensive customer education will be necessary.

Over the past decade, a new relationship between electric utility companies and their customers has begun to emerge in virtually all parts of the country. This new relationship is based on the notion that the best use of electricity is the most efficient use. In many areas, utilities are offering incentives and special programs and are engaging in extensive education efforts to encourage their customers to use electricity efficiently.

What is DSM

The term "demand side management" is used to describe the many programs, projects, and initiatives which form the backbone of this new relationship. Demand Side Management, or DSM, can be defined in two ways:

1. Influencing customer load characteristics (where the "load" is described as the amount of electricity consumed, or the time of day when it is consumed, or how much is consumed at any one time on the system); and

2. Changes on the customer's side of the meter which affect usage of electricity.

There are four generally recognized categories of DSM, and utilities have designed and are offering programs to customers which fall within those categories:

1. Conservation -- saving kilowatt hours by reducing usage. Programs such as weatherization, wrapping water heaters, and trading inefficient older appliances for newer more efficient models fall into this category.

2. Peak Clipping -- reducing use at critical times when the demand for electricity is highest from many customers. A typical example of this is a "direct control" program, in which the electric utility shuts off selected customers' air conditioners for 15 minutes every hour during the peak air conditioning season.

3. Load Shifting -- pushing electric usage to off-peak periods. Typically, this would involve something like installing specially-constructed storage water heaters which heat water only at night.

4. Valley-filling/load building -- encouraging the use of electricity during off-peak times, or when plants are not running at full capacity to make better use of generating facilities.

Why DSM, and Why Now?

Power plants and facilities are expensive to construct, and difficult to site because few people want to live in close proximity to them. Further, emissions from power plants are considered to be sources of pollution in the environment. Thus, there are incentives for both customers and utilities to use power in the most efficient ways possible. The movement towards greater electric efficiency is seen to be a "win-win" situation for both customers and utilities in the long run, although rates may rise to cover the costs of the DSM programs in the short term.

There are five primary benefits which can be ascribed to effective DSM programs:

1. DSM should be less expensive than new supply-side resources. The cost-effectiveness of all programs is rigorously tested to determine if the program is worthwhile and will cost less than constructing new electric facilities.

2. DSM programs should reduce customer bills (although not necessarily their rates) if they participate.

3. Environmental impacts of electricity generation can be reduced.

4. More efficient use of electricity can strengthen the competitiveness of commercial and industrial customers, when more units can be produced using less energy per unit.

---

[1]Manager, Demand Side Programs

[2]Consumer Affairs Consultant

5. DSM programs can create business opportunities for others, such as companies which provide conservation services, thus contributing to economic development.

Clearly, from technical perspective, there is a great deal at stake in DSM. Utility companies are beginning to bank on the fact that DSM will deliver 45,000 MW in demand reductions by the year 2000 (Electric Power Research Institute estimate). Investments of as much as $30 - 50 billion in DSM programs will be made to achieve this.

How?
Managing the demand side in a way that makes it a predictable and reliable resource is a very serious business. Electric companies are used to building power plants, managing transmission and distribution -- and most do that with extraordinary efficiency in this country. But, companies are less comfortable with learning to manage that unpredictable factor -- human behavior in energy use -- on which many of the savings associated with demand side programs depend.

From the utility's perspective, DSM programs are planning tools which must deliver predictable and quantifiable results if they are to be of use in delaying construction of power plants. The utility must be able to measure -- and measure accurately -- both the penetration (percentage or actual number of people who will participate in a particular program) and the persistence of the technology or measure put in place (i.e., how long the water heater will remain "wrapped," or how long the low flow showerhead will remain installed).

Thus, the role of consumer behavior -- and how to influence it through consumer education -- cannot be underestimated in the effort to successfully "manage the demand-side."

Consumer Education Strategies

An Overview
Consumer education is often thought of in terms of a classroom setting where students learn the principles of being wise shoppers in the marketplace. However, another aspect of it occurs outside the classroom where businesses educate existing or potential customers on how to, for example, use a product or service. For example, customers didn't instinctively know how to use products such as microwave ovens, ATM's or instant cameras -- they were taught.

In programs such as DSM, educating the customer is particularly important and somewhat complicated. Traditionally, a marketing strategy is relatively straight forward; the company identifies a particular market segment and then matches the message to that market. In this manner a message is targeted at a specific audience and other customers, to the extent possible, are screened out. DSM programs present a different challenge. They are designed to affect the energy usage of large groups of customers, often numbering in the thousands, with vastly different needs. As a result, market segmentation and targeted messages are still necessary, but selective screening is more difficult, if not altogether impossible. It is inevitable that information "spill over" will occur where a customer receives a message, intended for a different market segment, that is inappropriate for them. When this situation arises, companies will need to have well-educated customers who are able to differentiate and screen messages for themselves.

Program Components

The goal of a consumer education program is to help consumers become more rational and skilled decision makers in the marketplace. The materials must be organized so that consumers will:

1. Receive and understand the message,
2. Agree with the message, and
3. Act in accordance with the message.

To accomplish this multi-step goal, the following program components should be considered.

Consistency of Message
Critical to the success of any education program is the clarity, consistency and reliability of the message to the customer. A core of basic principles or data should be developed and used as the source of all DSM information. The information should be organized as a quick reference and include topics such as residential electric usage charts and demand side management principles. For example, equipment in the home could be divided into groups according to usage, such as: heating and cooling, electronics, motor-driven and lighting. Each could be ranked so that consumers would know that efficiencies in heating and cooling equipment have a greater impact on usage than other equipment in their home. Presented in this way, customers can make informed decisions that will have maximum impact on their energy bill.

A consistent message also helps in correcting misconceptions about DSM. A limited amount of new information or research on energy has emerged in the popular press since the early 1980's. Therefore, some DSM information in use today is little more than recycled energy conservation tips from the mid-70's. It does not reflect any changes in usage patterns, increases in appliance efficiencies, emergence of new technologies, or changes in demographics that have occurred in the past 20 years. Further, people who recall that era of energy shortages, may not have such fond memories of it; conservation to them may mean deprivation.

Specific materials should be developed that reinforce the DSM message. Materials with consistent information, concepts, logos etc. increase the likelihood that consumers will receive the desired message. Recycling dated materials could be inconsistent with the desired DSM message or worse, seem to be "the same old thing" to customers.

A final point on consistency of the message is that it helps customers sort through what appears to be conflicting information about demand side management. As public awareness of DSM programs increases, customers could have difficulty determining what is - and isn't - applicable to them. Part of the confusion will arise because DSM strategies vary according to customer usage, customer class, corporate goals or region of the country. Here are a few examples.

If a goal of a business is to reduce energy usage 15% through the replacement of lighting fixtures, an employee of that business may expect to replicate those results, through light replacement in his/her home.

If a person hears in a news story that lighting accounts for 20% of the electricity used throughout the United States, he/she could easily assume that lighting accounts for 20% of the home electric bill.

Two companies with contiguous service areas could offer different programs. Stories about the programs may be completely accurate, but give consumers information that is not applicable to them.

Training of customer service (public contact) personnel must be an integral part of the program. The company must never be a source of confusing or inconsistent information to the customer. Even employees with minimal (or no) contact with customers must be aware of the program. Word-of-mouth is a powerful communications tool and company employees are seen by customers to be credible sources.

Market Segmentation
The various "publics" should be defined and segmented and communications strategies developed for each. Examples of various "publics" are as follows:

Residential customers
    low-income
    elderly/aging
    illiterate
    non-English speaking
    subdivided by usage

Commercial/Industrial
    subdivided by usage pattern, size, kwh sales

Interested third-parties
    governmental groups
    environmental/special interest groups
    educators
    community groups

Business and Trade Allies
    builders
    realtors
    crafts & trades i.e. plumbers, HVAC contractors

Internal audiences
    customer service personnel
    marketing personnel
    other public contact personnel
    all employees

Once the various markets are identified, materials should be targeted to the audience. For example, providing energy efficient appliance information to a low-income home owner whose house is not weatherized would send the wrong message. However, it would be very appropriate for a low-income home owner whose house is weatherized. The customer's needs, values, attitudes and abilities should all be considered.

Dissemination of Information
The method by which information is provided to customers is extremely important because it must be on their terms. Therefore, a mix of communication methods should be considered. Methods that utilize one-to-one communications, such as an energy efficiency hotline, are especially desirable. Companies have found 800-lines to be effective in reaching consumers who are not reached by other methods. People who will not write a letter or ask a question in person will pick up a phone, particularly if it is convenient when a question occurs to them, such as at point-of-sale locations. An 800-line can ensure the consistency and accuracy of information flowing from the company. Plus, it can serve as a quick response mechanism to changing externalities.

Visual and interactive technologies are an increasingly attractive alternative because they are the preferred method of communication for many people. There are significant numbers of customers who can not read or don't read well enough to understand the message, but there are probably even more who simply choose not to. Video and computer-based formats offer an entertaining and memorable way of communicating with customers. They allow for instantaneous updating and retrieval of accurate information. And perhaps most importantly, they offer a customer choice. Customers decide what they want to know, when they want to know it and can replay the message as often as needed. Finally, these technologies offer a flexibility ideally suited to community outreach. The message can go where the people are: recreation centers, churches, shopping malls, classrooms, meetings or even into the customer's own living room. The list is endless. Brochures and other written materials should still be utilized as a leave-behind piece or as reinforcement of the message. However, used alone they will be totally lost on some market segments and will be ineffective on others.

Use of Outside Experts

Program development & customer acceptance of DSM programs can be enhanced by the use of outside experts. These include educators, community leaders, advocates, service providers etc. who can serve as "credible third-parties" for the company's message. Since a critical factor in educating customers is to make the information easy to access and understand, this group is invaluable. They have high credibility and in addition, educators have expertise in the area of adult learning and literacy. If properly utilized, outside experts can be a relatively inexpensive source of expertise and provide an important vehicle to disseminate the information.

One source of outside expertise that is presently enjoying a resurgence in popularity are collaboratives or customer advisory panels. Such groups were common in the industry during the 70's and 80's due to customer dissatisfaction, or ratepayer revolts. Today's version often includes parties to regulatory proceedings; professional engineers, environmentalists or architects; business and community leaders; or attorneys. These groups, acting in a consulting capacity, assist companies in the design, implementation and evaluation of DSM programs. They serve as a "sounding board" for the company, a communications link with the community and a credible third party adding credibility to DSM programs. Energy companies clearly know how to design programs that will achieve the DSM goals of increased efficiency and manage future growth. However, once those programs are designed, external resources are extremely useful in the design and implementation of outreach programs such as communication, education and marketing.

In summary, if consumer education programs designed to change consumer behavior are to be successful they need to be sensitive to the following points:

1. Informational programs should be structured so they:
   o Clearly address defined consumer needs
   o Are easily understood and well organized
      o Emphasize benefits.

2. Customers should be given sufficient information to make their own choices.

3. Clarify conflicting information that would lead to consumer confusion and potential dissatisfaction with DSM.

4. Reflect demographic changes within the population.

Information Strategies

1. Develop a core of basic DSM information that includes program information, goals, usage information (any area of potential confusion) and make it available externally.

2. Establish the company as the authoritative source of consistent and accurate information. Employee training and toll-free hotlines can help assure the quality of information going to consumers.

3. Identify sources of misinformation -- media, third parties, trade allies etc. -- and work directly with them to assure that consistent, accurate information is going to the public from sources external to the company.

4. Develop DSM-specific materials that will reinforce the message. Utilize technologies such as videotapes, demonstrations and interactive technologies that are effective educational tools which allow for easy access and have wide consumer acceptance. Written materials such as brochures or bill inserts should be utilized, but only in conjunction with other educational approaches.

5. Segment the residential market to target appropriate messages to various customer groups.

6. Utilize outside experts -- educators, community groups, social service agencies -- to develop the content and the delivery of DSM messages to various groups and their constituencies.

Demand Side Management: Changing Consumer Behavior

Loren V. Geistfeld, The Ohio State University[1]

A benefit/cost approach is used to assess why certain types of programs designed to affect energy consumption are more effective than others. The conclusion is that consumers are responsive to the perceived benefits and costs associated with a behavior change and if policy makers wish to effect behavior change, attention needs to be paid to perceived benefits and costs.

Energy conservation and demand reduction activities are focused on technological and/or behavioral changes. Technological changes such as the development of energy efficient appliances, while often being necessary, are not sufficient for energy conservation. The underlying rationale is that the most technologically perfect conservation measure will produce no savings if consumers refuse to adopt it. The critical point is that when trying to reduce energy consumption, consumer behavior must not be overlooked.

The Benefit-Cost Perspective

Consumer willingness (or lack thereof) to change behavior can be explained with a benefit-cost model. This view of behavior change says that consumers will change behavior as long as the benefits at least equal the costs associated with the change. This perspective has been employed by Russo and Leclerc (1991) to determine characteristics of successful product information programs and by Russo, Staelin, Nolan, Russell and Metcalf (1986) when studying consumer use of nutrition information.

Benefit-cost analysis applied to consumer decision-making is based on consumer perceptions of benefits and costs. A consumer decision to change or not change behavior is based on perceptions or beliefs as to the existence and magnitude of benefits and costs. Perceptions and beliefs may not always agree with an objective view of the world.

For consumers to be willing to consider any change in their behavior, non-negligible benefits must be perceived. Benefits may be financial or non-financial in nature. For example, a financial benefit of energy conservation is a reduced expenditure on energy, while a non-financial benefit is a sense of satisfaction from improving the quality of the environment. Non-financial benefits often fall into the "warm fuzzy" category. While consumers do respond to "warm fuzzies," these types of non-financial benefits are often dominated by the more tangible financial benefits associated with change.

Benefits realized soon after making a behavior change will more likely be associated with a perception of non-trivial benefits. Benefits which are primarily long term will tend to be ignored since, even if consumers value them, these benefits occur far into the future resulting in a small present value.

The cost side of the equation reflects the financial and non-financial resources the consumer must use to realize the potential benefits. While information acquisition and utilization is not the only cost factor consumers consider when making a behavior change, it is likely to be among the most significant. Russo et al. (1986) argue that major costs are associated with the collection, comprehension and computation of the information needed to decide whether or not to make a behavior change. Collection costs are those that relate to the acquisition of information relevant to the decision. Computation costs are those incurred when trying to combine the information into an overall evaluation of the outcome(s). Comprehension costs reflect the costs associated with the actual understanding of the information and is affected by the level of knowledge a consumer possesses. Time and cognitive effort can be significant non-financial costs associated with behavior changes. Even if a consumer does not use financial resources to make a behavior change, there may still be a significant use of time to collect, compute and process information.

In summary, the benefit-cost approach reflects the likelihood of a change in consumer behavior. For a consumer to consider a change in behavior the perceived benefits of the change must exceed the perceived costs of the change. However, for the consumer to even consider the possibility of making a behavior change, the benefits of the change must be perceived to nontrivial. The next step is to use benefit-cost analysis to analyze programs designed to influence consumer behavior.

Energy Consumption Modification

Efforts to modify consumer behavior have been classified according to the strategy used: antecedent strategies and consequence strategies (Winett and Kagel, 1984; Ester, 1985). Both types of strategies are intended to affect the probability of a consumer choosing whether or not to engage in an activity. Antecedent strategies increase or reduce the probability that a consumer

---

[1]Professor, Family Resource Management

will engage in an activity by providing a stimulus to which a consumer is exposed without having to actually engage in the activity. Three antecedent strategies are considered: information, prompts, and modeling. Consequence strategies affect behavior by modifying the outcome associated with a particular behavior. To realize the effect of this stimulus a consumer must engage in an activity. Two types of consequence strategies are considered: feedback strategies and incentives.

Antecedent Strategies

Information Strategies. The purpose of information strategies is to inform consumers about the consequences of particular behaviors and to educate them as to ways that they can change their behaviors. For example, a consequence of reduced energy consumption may be lower heating bills. Consumers can address this issue by adjusting house temperatures so that less energy is consumed. These strategies are intended to increase consumer awareness and sensitivity to a problem thereby increasing the probability that they will engage in a particular behavior. This is the most commonly used strategy due to its relatively low cost to the information provider. Examples of this procedure are brochures, bill inserts, booklets, leaflets, television spots, and newspaper advertisements.

In a review of studies using information strategies, Ester (1985:50ff) noted that in one study "none of the experimental conditions turned out to have any effect on electricity use....the energy crises [the 1973 oil boycott] and the large-scale conservation campaigns appeared to have no direct effect on conservation behavior." Ester concluded, based on all of the studies he reviewed, that "communicating energy information alone [emphasis added] is not a very powerful instrument in promoting consumer energy conservation." This view was supported by Winett and Kagel (1984:657) who noted that "this type of strategy [an information strategy] has no effect on consumers' target behaviors."

The effectiveness of an information program is dependent upon the context in which the program is set. Ester (1985) noted that the effectiveness of information strategies depends on consumer perception of the credibility of the information and its source, the extent to which the consumer is actively involved with the behavior being addressed, and how well the information meets a consumer's particular needs. Winett and Kagel (1984:657) warn that "the focus...on behavioral outcomes measures alone (e.g. electricity consumption) has somewhat obscured the reasons for the noneffectiveness of brochures and booklets. It is not clear, for example, whether most consumers simply do not read this material, or whether they read it but do not understand suggested applications. When consumers do read brochures and booklets, it is also not clear how much information is gained or how resource-related attitudes have been affected."

In summary, information strategies are desirable from the information provider's perspective since they provide an inexpensive way to reach large numbers of consumers. These strategies, however, do not generally result in behavior change. A likely cause is that the costs of understanding and applying the information may be too high as implied by Winett and Kagel. In addition, the benefits of the behavioral change are likely to be too abstract for consumers to perceive the benefits as nontrivial. Information strategies should be structured such that they address clearly defined consumer needs, are easy to understand, and highlight the benefits to be realized in a way that will motivate consumer behavior--in other words make sure the perceived costs of a behavior change are not so large as to work against change and make sure consumers perceive benefits from the change. It should be noted, however, that information strategies tend to be more effective when combined with other strategies.

Prompts. Prompts are techniques used to encourage a behavior before a consumer engages in a behavior. They can be a message or some type of signal. For example, a sign by a light switch requesting that the lights be turned off when leaving a room is a prompt. The purpose of the sign is to encourage consumers to engage in a particular behavior--turn the light off. Ester (1985:54) noted "that prompting proenvironmental behavior does produce behavior change under certain conditions. The conditions appear to be that effectiveness of prompting is related among other things to its specificity and non-demanding character, as well as to the psychological convenience of the requested behavior." Winett and Kagel (1984) expanded this by noting that the likelihood of prompts being successful is increased when the prompt is highly specific; it employs language that is nondemanding and nonthreatening; it is relevant to the context in which it is given; it is convenient and close to the requested behavior; and it is repeated. To illustrate the significance of these points in determining the effectiveness prompts, Winett and Kagel reported an experiment in which the small stickers placed by light switches requesting lights be turned off were found to be ineffective; however, when the same request was made using bold letters on large signs, lights were turned off.

For a prompt to be effective, consumers need to perceive a benefit from the behavior change--large signs were more effective than small signs. This is conditioned by consumer perception of psychological and cognitive costs associated with the change--nondemanding and specific.

Modeling. This antecedent strategy focuses on observational learning. The underlying principal is that a consumer observes a desirable behavior in others and then seeks to emulate the behavior. The medium for modeling strategies is often videotape; however, it can be done through direct demonstrations also. While direct participant modeling may be more effective, it is more costly to implement than an indirect approach using videotape. Winett and Kagel (1984:658) noted that "the effectiveness of modeling is enhanced by (1) attention to such factors as the status of the model and the use of setting and model characteristics that viewers can identify with; (2) the use of coping models who gradually demonstrate mastery over a problem; (3) multiple demonstrations of a behavior; (4) showing models being rewarded for changing their behavior; and (5) giving rules and chains of behavior to follow to guide behavior change." These authors concluded based on a review of the studies using modeling that the mode through which information is presented is important as well as demonstrations of procedures in "real-life" settings.

Videotape "messages" were in important component of a study to reduce energy consumption in all-electric homes (Winett et al. 1982). Two 20-minute video tapes were prepared. One videotape was a discussion tape and consisted of a male and female being interviewed on energy issues such as the importance of the energy problem, alternative energy sources, and the need for conservation. The second videotape utilized modeling to convey its message. This tape presented a series of vignettes using the same actors as the discussion tape. The vignettes demonstrated ways to save energy such an adjusting the thermostat setting, wearing different clothes, etc. The vignettes emphasized the benefits of reduced energy consumption. While the discussion tape was found to be ineffective, the modeling tape was associated with reduced energy consumption. In a review of this study it was noted that "specifically produced, brief (20-minute) videotaped programs, seen by small groups of viewers, that portrayed specific conservation strategies within a story line were found to affect viewers' home energy consumption for at least six months....in effective programs characters acted out the conservation strategies and were shown being rewarded socially and monetarily (through reduced bills) for their efforts." (Winett, Hatcher, Fort, Leckliter, Love, Riley and Fishback, 1984:38)

The videotape modeling idea was extended to cable television to determine if a single television program could affect energy consumption (Winett et al., 1984). The focus of this study was reduced electric energy consumption with the primary tool being a 20-minute television program titled "Summer Breeze." The program began by providing reasons why it may be to a consumer's advantage to reduce energy consumption even in an era of relatively stable prices. A dramatized story was the vehicle to convey energy saving techniques. In this story a young couple interacted with an older couple who demonstrated different conservation strategies. This resulted in a program emphasizing the benefits of energy conservation practices and demonstrating how to achieve such benefits. Participants in the study were asked to watch the program on cable television

at one of four showings. In addition, participants received a 10-page booklet that illustrated in cartoon form the strategies demonstrated in the program. The study revealed that while the control groups increased energy consumption, the media groups reduced consumption. This behavior was found to continue after the intervention phase of the study ended. The authors of the study noted that the strategies used to reduced energy consumption were typically simple and no-cost such as closing drapes during the day and turning off the air conditioner when gone. In addition, it was noted that the behavior change was accomplished during a period of time when the economic and political environments were not conducive to energy conservation--1982.

From a benefit-cost perspective, modeling appears to have been successful for two reasons. First, the benefits of change have been vividly illustrated. Second, ways to achieve the benefits are demonstrated thereby reducing the costs associated with determining how to implement change.

Consequence Strategies
    Feedback Strategies. Feedback is intended to provide consumers with frequent information such that the consequences of a particular behavior are immediately obvious and relevant to a situation. An example of feedback is when companies install equipment signalling the amount of time one has spent on a long distance telephone call. The information is immediate since it occurs while one is on the telephone and it is relevant since it relates to the need to control telephone expenses while on the telephone. If the cost information associated with a particular telephone call is not received until six weeks after the call was made, the information is too distant from the behavior to have a significant effect.

Energy consumption feed back is predicated on the notion that monthly energy billing is not sufficiently frequent to affect consumer behavior. Three common techniques have been developed to provide feedback. First, someone reads a consumer's meter and provides a daily or weekly energy consumption and cost report. Second, an electronic device is installed in a home to provide instantaneous energy consumption and cost information. A variant on this approach is to compare actual consumption to a goal consumption level. Third, consumers monitor their own energy consumption. This approach demands the most effort on the part of the consumer since the consumer records energy consumption on a special form.

Based on his review of numerous feedback studies, Ester (1985) concluded that feedback is a viable way to reduce energy consumption. Winett and Kagel (1984:659) noted that feedback can have a significant effect on residential energy consumption, that more frequent feedback and feedback tied to specific goals tend to be more effective, and that large savings relative to family budget increase feedback effectiveness. van Houwelingen and van Raaij (1989) reported that electronic devices relating actual consumption to a predetermined consumption goal were more effective feedback mechanisms than external feedback and self-monitoring. Sexton, Johnson and Konakayama (1987) noted that an electronic device providing consumption cost information resulted in increased energy consumption and a shift from relatively expensive peak energy to less expensive off-peak energy.

In the context of the benefit-cost approach, feedback strategies focus on the benefit side of the equation. The consumer is given information suggesting that a certain behavior will reduce energy costs. However, when the process of computing the savings is complex, such as self-monitoring, the effect is reduced since the costs of realizing the benefit have increased.

Incentives. Incentives are rewards or counter-rewards associated with behaviors. Positive and negative reinforcements are incentives. Common energy related incentives are tax breaks for making one's home more energy efficient, peak/off-peak pricing, etc.

In a review of studies in which cash payments were made to consumers when attaining a given conservation goal, Ester (1985:65) noted that "one may conclude that monetary incentives are effective in reducing residential energy consumption...however, ...the rebate schedules used often amount to price changes of several hundred percent!" Another argument for the efficacy of incentives is the study by Sexton, et al. (1987) reported above in which it was found that consumers responded to off-peak pricing; however, it is likely that the pricing differential would not have been as effective had feedback not been provided.

In a pilot implementation of a residential energy conservation program in six Michigan communities (Michigan Energy Fitness Program), two person energy audit teams canvassed door-to-door offering consumers energy conservation information and devices. One team member provided information on opportunities for saving energy. The second team member installed up to six inexpensive energy conservation devices (Kushler, Witte and Ehlke, 1992). While the authors indicated the participation rate was high, they did not postulate reasons for the high participation rate. In the context of this paper, it is likely that immediate installation of the devices had an important impact on participation. The effectiveness of device installation as a stimulant to participation likely arose for two reasons. First, the consumers realized an immediate potential benefit from participation. Second, the time and effort required of consumers was minimal since the entire conservation activity took place in a single visit.

As with feedback, incentives affect the benefits consumers perceive from a behavioral

change. A strength of consequence strategies is that they make the benefits of a behavior change obvious to consumers.

Effective Consumer Information Programs

The importance of considering the perceived benefits and costs associated with a consumer behavior change was a recurring theme throughout the discussion of the preceding section. The significance of this point is reinforced by Fowler (1992:78-9) who noted that:

"Both products [setback clock thermostats and whole-house fans] require customer education as part of the marketing effort. In both cases, the marketing campaigns emphasized customer comfort, savings on energy bills, and, most importantly, a simple customer request procedure...surveys found that the lack of effort on customer's part was significant. The fact that the seller--in this case, the utility--was taking responsibility for planning, scheduling, installation, trouble-shooting, and any necessary follow-up was definitely worth something to the customer. Customers wanted the utility to absorb as much inconvenience and uncertainty as reasonable possible. That is, they wanted both a turnkey (completely installed and immediately operable) installation, and clearly identified accountability."

From a benefit-cost perspective, paying attention to the following criteria could increase the effectiveness of a program to change consumer behavior. (1) Address a clearly defined consumer need. (2) Make sure the benefits of change are obvious to consumers. Short-term benefits tend to be visible while long-term benefits are more distant and remote; however, do not overlook "social benefits" since many consumers will respond to them at the margin. (3) Identify and minimize costs associated with behavior changes. These costs include information acquisition and utilization costs, expenditures needed to purchase equipment and to make modifications to facilitate a change, and the risk associated with change.

If a conscientious effort is made to identify the benefits and costs consumers associate with a behavior change, there is a greater likelihood of developing and implementing a successful program. Clear identification of benefits and attempts to reduce the costs associated with a desired behavior change should encourage program participation by consumers.

References

Ester, P. (1985). Consumer behavior and energy conservation. Dordrecht: Martinus Nijhoff Publishers.

Fowler, H. (1992). Marketing energy conservation

in an environment of abundance. Policy Studies Journal, 20(1), 76-86.

Kushler, M., Witte, P. & Ehlke, S. (1992). Are high-participation residential conservation programs still feasible? Policy Studies Journal, 20(1), 57-67.

Russo, J. E., Staelin, R., Nolan, C. A., Russell, G. J. & Metcalf, B. L. (1986). Nutrition information in the supermarket. Journal of Consumer Research, 13(1), 48-70.

Russo, J. E. & Leclerc, F. (1991). Characteristics of successful product information programs. Journal of Social Issues, 47(1), 73-92.

Sexton, R. J., Johnson, N. B. & Konakayama, A. (1987). Consumer response to continuous-display electricity-use monitors in a time-of-use pricing experiment. Journal of Consumer Research, 14(1), 55-62.

van Houwelingen, J. H. & van Raaij, W. F. (1989). The effect of goal-setting and daily electronic feedback on in-home energy use. Journal of Consumer Research, 16(1), 98-105.

Winett, R. A., Hatcher, J. W., Fort, T. R., Leckliter, I. N., Love, S. Q., Riley, A. W. & Fishback, J. F. (1982). The effects of videotape modeling and daily feedback on residential electricity conservation, home temperature and humidity, perceived comfort, and clothing worn: winter and summer. Journal of Applied Behavior Analysis, 15(3), 381-402.

Winett, R. A. & Kagel, J. H. (1984). Effects of information presentation format on resource use in field settings. Journal of Consumer Research, 11(2), 655-667.

Winett, R. A., Leckliter, I. N., Chinn, D. E. & Stahl, B. (1984). Reducing energy consumption: the long-term effects of a single TV program. Journal of Communications, 34(3), 37-51.

Parents As Consumers of Child Care: A Decision-Making Model

Brenda J. Cude, University of Illinois at Urbana-Champaign[1]
Brent McBride, University of Illinois at Urbana-Champaign[2]
Chris Todd, University of Illinois at Urbana-Champaign[3]

This paper presents a model applying consumer information search and decision-making theory to the child care decision. The model hypothesizes that a parent's decision not to search for information before making a child care choice may be a rational one. The paper outlines components of a model of child care choice and describes a research project designed to test the model.

In the United States, government, parents, and other private organizations collectively spend $15 to $17 billion each year on child care (Hayes, Palmer & Zaslow, 1990). Approximately 28 million children are in care part- or full-time (U.S. Bureau of the Census, 1990). Therefore, child care is an important consumer decision that impacts a substantial portion of our population as well as our economy. Yet how parents select child care has received relatively little attention from consumer economists.

This paper merges several existing search models to create a model of child care choice. The paper consists of five sections. The first section explores the significance of the child care decision for families and briefly reviews the available literature on parents as consumers of child care. The second section presents a model of child care as a consumer choice. The third and fourth sections describe the methodology being used in a research project designed to test the model and report some preliminary findings. The final section outlines research objectives for the future.

Parents As Consumers of Child Care

The child care decision is an important consumer decision from a number of perspectives. The availability of quality child care is important to the well-being of children as well as their parents (Mason & Duberstein, 1990). Unavailable and/or unaffordable child care can be a constraint to employment, especially for low-income women (Blau & Robins, 1986). Child care can also take a significant portion of the family budget, especially in low-income families. Overall, the poor pay an average of 23% of their incomes for child care; the nonpoor pay only 9% (Hayes, et al., 1990).

Although child care is clearly an important component of the lives of many parents, researchers have generally been critical of the behaviors that parents report they use to choose child care. Child care researchers (Bradbard, Endsley & Readdick, 1983; Fuqua & Labensohn, 1986; Hayes, et al., 1990; Kisker, Gordon & Shain, 1989; Waite, Leibowitz & Witsberger, 1988; Widdows & Powell, 1990) appear to have defined "good" consumer behavior in child care choices as consisting of visits to multiple child care arrangements to make first-hand comparisons, actively checking a variety of factors during the visits, consulting multiple sources of information (primarily resource and referral centers and child care providers), and giving greatest consideration to the factors research has identified as related to quality care. However, previous research has generally not provided evidence that parents' behaviors are consistent with those recommended. Hayes, et al. (1990) echoed the sentiments of various researchers when they concluded that "Many parents are not well informed about how to identify high-quality child care and what to look for when visiting programs."

A Model of the Child Care Decision Process

This section describes a model of the child care decision process. First, the demand for child care is modeled. A second component of the model describes how parents acquire information prior to making a child care decision and identifies the influences on parents' decision-making. Finally, the model suggests how parents may evaluate information.

The Demand for Child Care

The basic elements of the model described in this paper are those initially developed by Widdows and Powell (1990) to explain parental choice of after-school child care. The model follows

[1]Associate Professor, Division of Consumer Sciences

[2]Assistant Professor, Division of Human Development and Family Studies

[3]Associate Professor, Division of Human Development and Family Studies

Becker's (1981) theory and hypothesizes that parents choose the cost-quality combination of child care that maximizes the following utility function:

$$U = u(C, q, Z_1, \ldots Z_m)^1 \qquad (1)$$

where U = utility, C = the amount of child care consumed, q = the quality of child care, and $Z_1 \ldots Z_m$ = quantities of other commodities consumed. If pcq is the cost of a unit of child care of quality level q, the budget constraint is written as:

$$Y = pcqC + pz_1Z_1 + \ldots + pz_mZ_m \qquad (2)$$

where Y = family resources, and p = price.

The demand function in terms of market prices of the general form is:

$$D = d(pcq, pz, Y).$$

Situations Prompting Changes in Child Care

This section models approaches parents may use to determine how much, if any, information about price and quality to acquire prior to making a child care decision.

The model (see Figure 1) identifies five influences likely to prompt parents to recognize a need for change in their current child care situation. Changes in work, such as a parent returning to work or taking a new job, may prompt a change in child care. Parents are likely to look for a new situation when a provider changes his/her hours or cost of care or stops caring for children. Significant life events, such as a divorce, marriage, or birth of another child, may prompt a change in child care. Parents may also recognize the need for a new situation if their expectations for child care change or their quality assessments of the current or alternative arrangements change. A new situation may also seem important if the child becomes unhappy with his/her current situation or seems ready for a new environment as s/he grows older.

Assessing Information About Cost-Quality Options

Widdows and Powell (1990) suggested that parents have an existing body of knowledge to consult when a child care decision is needed. By implication, parents engage in what Bloch, Sherrell and Ridgway (1986) called "ongoing" search--search activities that are independent of specific purchase needs or decisions. If parents with children who are or will soon be in child care engage in ongoing search, they continually acquire information either actively or passively for use in future child care decisions.

When parents recognize the need for a child care decision, they will search their existing knowledge on the cost and quality of available child care options. If they find that knowledge

Figure 1.
Child Care Choice Model.

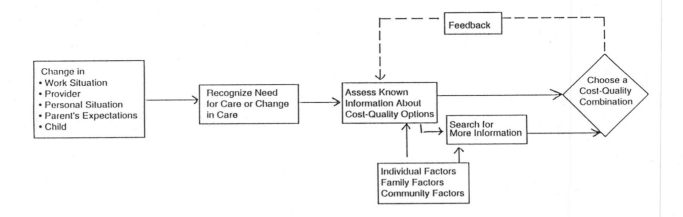

lacking, parents will search for information until the costs of additional search exceed the benefits. Widdows and Powell (1990) represented the search function in reduced form as:

$$S = [E(pc_1/pc_0), E(q_1/q_0), SC] \qquad (3)$$

where S = the amount of price and quality search; $E(pc_1/pc_0)$ = the expected return to price search, i.e., a lower price found in search 1 than in the previous search (p_0); $E(q_1/q_0)$ = the expected return to search for quality, i.e., a higher quality found in search 1 than in the previous search (q_0); and SC = search costs.
Thus, parents will search for information only if the perceived benefits of search are expected to exceed the perceived costs.

Child care and experience. This paper adds to Widdows and Powell's model by postulating that parents may substitute experience for search to acquire information about price and quality. Parents may believe that some aspects of child care can be assessed only by placing the child in care and observing the results. Nelson (1970) called this "experience."

Nelson hypothesized that, just as in the case of search, consumers will use experience to acquire information until the marginal cost of additional information becomes greater than the marginal return. Unlike search, however, information is acquired through experience only by sampling the desired good or service. Thus, the marginal costs of search and experience differ. The marginal cost of one additional search effort is likely to consist largely of time spent to acquire information and, in some cases, a money expenditure as well. In contrast, the marginal cost of experience is the loss of utility from consuming the sampled choice rather than the best choice that one has already discovered.

The experience function can be represented in reduced form as:

$$E = [E(pc_1/pc_0), E(q_1/q_0), EC] \qquad (4)$$

where E = the number of options sampled; $E(pc_1/pc_0)$ = the expected return to experience in terms of price, i.e., a lower price found by sampling p_1 than in the previous option experienced (p_0); $E(q_1/q_0)$ = the expected return to experience in terms of quality, i.e., a higher quality found in q_1 than in the previous option experienced (q_0); and EC = experience costs.

For example, to use experience to discover a better quality long-distance phone service, you would sign up with one or more services and use them. The cost of experience is the possibility that the service(s) you choose to sample is a poorer choice than the best long-distance phone service you have yet discovered.

Similarly, parents may choose experience rather than search as a way to learn about child care, especially the quality dimensions. Some parents may find information about how other parents and children respond to a child care situation inadequate. If parents believe their child to be unique, they would not expect information about how well an arrangement suits another child to be very useful. There are few sources of objective evaluation of child care options, and parents may be unaware of those that do exist. Since even formal advertising may be used infrequently, information flows tend to be local and informal (Walker, 1992). While parents could "sample" a child care option by visiting the site with their child, parents may not believe that information to be useful if they think the child and/or the provider will behave differently in the absence of the parent. Many parents also may not feel prepared to evaluate the quality of child care, not knowing what questions to ask or which activities to observe (Fuqua & Labensohn, 1986).

A parent may also believe that experience is the most cost-effective way to learn about the price of a child care arrangement. Asking questions about costs would not seem worthwhile to the parent who believed there were likely to be frequent costs (such as for craft supplies, field trips, or food) or variations in the basic fee that the parent didn't think s/he could anticipate.

If a parent does choose to learn about a child care option by placing a child in care and observing the outcomes, the costs will largely be subjective. For example, one cost might be short- and/or long-term harm to a child placed in a poor quality situation. Another cost might be a missed opportunity to place a child in a better quality and/or lower cost option. Since demand exceeds supply in some child care markets, parents who take their time to make a child care decision may find that some choices available initially are no longer options.

Therefore, the model suggests that in some situations parents may rationally choose not to search for information prior to making a child care decision or to engage in only very limited search. Parents may not search because the knowledge they acquired through previous ongoing search seemed sufficient to make a choice. Or, it may be that some or all of the information that parents considered important to their decision could be most efficiently acquired through experience.

Individual, family, and community factors. The model describes three categories of influence on child care decisions: individual, family, and community factors. Individual factors, such as a parent's views on child care, will influence how much and what types of information about options that a parent will seek. For example, a parent who does not think children should be cared for in for-profit centers is unlikely to seek out any information on that option. Family factors, including income, education, and previous child care experiences, will also influence the child care decision process. And, underlined: community factors will influence the availability of information and the cost to parents of search.

Evaluation of Child Care Options

The model hypothesizes that parents approach the child care decision as a two-stage decision. In the first stage, parents consider the factors that determine which child care options are available or accessible to them. Options may be out of reach financially or geographically or because the hours of care or ages of children accepted don't match the parents' needs (Morgan, n.d.). Parents may also consider some forms of care to be unacceptable to them (center care or family day care, for example). Thus, in the first stage of evaluation, parents eliminate options using various criteria that determine accessibility.

In the second stage, parents evaluate the remaining options using selection criteria. For example, when parents encounter two situations with the same or similar costs (i.e., both are accessible), they will base their decision entirely on factors other than cost.

While it seems likely that accessibility criteria may be different from selection criteria, there is little evidence from research to suggest what those differences might be. Morgan (n.d.) has suggested five factors that may be accessibility factors: location, costs, hours care is available, stability and reliability of the arrangement, and whether the parent likes the provider.

Accessibility and selection criteria. The model proposes four types of cost factors and four quality dimensions that parents may evaluate to make a child care choice.[2] The four categories of costs and examples in each category are:

Direct money costs (fees for care, transportation, special materials)

Indirect money costs (lost wages if unreliable child care causes a parent to miss work)

Psychological costs (concern that a child is not in a good environment)

Time costs (time to transport the child to and from child care, to attend special functions)

The model also proposes four dimensions of perceived child care quality. Quality is defined as the extent to which the child care arrangement provides the characteristics the parent desires. The categories and examples in each category are:

Program: Educational approach, atmosphere, stability, and reliability

Environment: Characteristics of the building,

outside areas, and neighborhood

Human: Staff/caregiver's training, qualifications, style, philosophy; characteristics of the other children

Child: Child's own preferences and characteristics

Unlike much of the research in the child care literature, the model is based on parents' perceptions of quality rather than the perceptions of child care professionals. For example, Hofferth and Wissoker's (1992) only measure of quality in one research study was the ratio of children to staff members. Yet, parents did not mention the child-provider ratio as a quality factor in either of two studies which asked parents to volunteer criteria that matter to them in choosing child care (Widdows & Powell, 1990; Bradbard, et al., 1983). Therefore, parents may define quality very differently from professionals.

Methods

To test the model, a research study was designed that involved personal, telephone, and mail interviews with parents in a panel study over a 10-week period. The primary objectives in designing the protocol were to capture ongoing search activities and to learn more about parents' criteria for choosing child care, particularly the stability of those criteria.

Researchers phoned parents of children ages 2 1/2 to 4 years old (identified through birth announcements published in the newspaper of a large midwestern city) and asked them to participate in the study. Parents selected were those whose child was cared for by someone other than the parent on a regular basis for at least 10 hours a week. Only families with a child who lived in the home with two parents (biological or adoptive) were included in the study. The 43 sets of parents who agreed to participate in the research project were offered $10 to complete the study.

Parents received a letter confirming their participation along with questionnaires about demographic characteristics, previous and current child care situations, and mothers' and fathers' participation in child care situations and decisions. Participants were next interviewed in the home by trained interviewers; interviews were audio recorded. The interviewers asked parents for more detailed information about how they chose previous child care options as well as satisfaction with previous arrangements and reasons for change.

The final portion of the in-home interviews focused on the criteria parents use to evaluate care options. Parents first named the factors most important to them in choosing care. Interviewers then asked parents about 14 categories of factors that some parents might consider in choosing care. For each category, parents were asked if there were factors important to them in choosing child care that the parent had not already mentioned. The purpose was to insure that parents had not omitted factors that they assumed would be present in any acceptable child care arrange- ment. Three of the 14 categories were cost factors--hours care is available, location, and the direct money costs of care. The remaining 11 categories were quality factors: type of care, activities, building characteristics, whether the provider or facility is licensed, meals or snacks, equipment at the facility, the neighborhood, and the caregiver or staff's education and training, years of experience caring for children, and style and philosophy in caring for children and communicating with parents.

Following the in-home interviews, parents were interviewed by phone five times at two-week intervals. Prior to the first and last interviews, parents received a set of index cards listing each factor the parent had mentioned as important in choosing child care; all factors, whether identified by the parent independently or as a result of the interviewer prompts, were included. The accompanying letter asked parents to sort the cards into three groups:[3] very important ("things the day care arrangement has to have or you would not choose it"), somewhat important ("sometimes important and sometimes not"), and least important ("things that aren't important"). Parents next rank ordered the cards within each group. They then reported the results at the beginning of the first and fifth telephone interviews. For each factor in the "Very Important" category, interviewers asked parents to assess how easy or difficult it would be to find a child care option that offered the desired characteristic if they had to find a new arrangement for their child. In all five telephone interviews, parents were also asked several questions, including ones about changes in their current child care arrangement and whether they had learned anything about other child care options in the community since the last interview.

Results

A total of 40 parents completed all of the interviews. Of the 149 parents originally contacted, 49 did not qualify, 57 refused to participate, and 3 did not complete the telephone interviews. Therefore, 40% of the qualified parents who were contacted completed all of the interviews.

The 40 children in the final sample ranged in ages from 28 to 50 months; the median age was 44 months. Eighteen of the children were male and 22 were female. Seventy-two percent of the children had one or more siblings.

The median ages of both mothers and fathers were 31 to 40 years old; the parents were well educated with an average of 15 years of education. The sample was predominately white. Median family income was $45,000 to $59,999. Eighty-four percent of the mothers and 88% of the fathers were employed

20 hours or more per week.

Most of the children (30) were currently in only one child care situation. However, seven were cared for in two settings each week and three children were in three different child care situations. Most children were in either a family day care home (23 children) or a day care center (24 children); only six children received care in their own home.

Unfortunately, only a few preliminary results were available for this paper; coding and data analysis are in progress. Across the sample, parents had placed their children in care situations a total of 125 different times. The median per child was three different situations and the median length of time a child had been in all care situations was 37 months.

Parents identified a total of 199 sources of information for the 125 child care decisions they had made. Friends and neighbors were named most frequently as a source (in 59 situations) followed by relatives (27), people at work (24), and child care resource and referral agencies (24). When asked to name the most important source of information, friends/neighbors still led the list (mentioned in 35 decisions), followed by relatives (16), ads (16), and child care resource and referral agencies (13).

Preliminary analyses of the data provided some tentative support for the hypothesis that parents engage in ongoing search for child care. Eight parents actually changed their child's care situation during the research study. Six of the eight reported in at least one of the phone interviews that they had learned something about child care or contacted a center/provider during the previous two weeks. Three other parents indicated they were very likely to change their child's care. However, only one of the three reported in any of the phone interviews that she had learned anything about child care or contacted a center/provider.

Sixteen parents who reported learning about care or contacting a center/provider in at least one of the phone interviews neither changed their child's care nor reported that a change was likely. These parents reported they learned something or made a contact in one-third (30) of the 90 reporting periods (16 parents in five phone interviews).

A third group, consisting of 13 parents, made no changes in their child's care and were unlikely to. They also reported in each of the five interviews that they hadn't learned anything about care or contacted any centers/providers.

In summary, during the research study, 11 parents either changed their child's care or indicated they were very likely to; 7 of the 11 learned something about child care during the period. Another 16 parents who didn't change and were unlikely to did learn something about child care. A final group of 13 didn't change, were unlikely to, and didn't learn anything about child care during the research study. Future analyses will attempt to identify other differences among the three groups.

Future Research Objectives

The research project has produced a wealth of data that the investigators hope to use to explore several important research questions:

- Do parents engage in ongoing search?

- Do parents substitute experience for search in child care decisions?

- What criteria do parents use to select child care and how stable are their preferences?

- Do parents use certain criteria to eliminate some options as unaccessible and other criteria to select care?

- Are parents' information-seeking/ decision-making patterns for child care similar to those for other consumer decisions?

- Do parents approach the child care decision differently depending on whether the reason for the change is external to the family (provider quits) or internal (child needs a new environment)?

The data will be more useful in answering some research questions than others. However, the project will provide the first in-depth examination of parents as consumers of child care.

References

Blau, D.M. & Robins, P.K. (1986). Fertility, employment, and child care costs: A dynamic analysis. Paper presented at the annual meeting of the Population Association of America, San Francisco.

Becker, G.S. (1981). A treatise on the family. Cambridge, Mass.: Harvard University Press.

Bloch, P.H., Sherrell, D.L. & Ridgway, N.M. (1986). Consumer search: An extended framework. Journal of Consumer Research, 13(1), 119-126.

Bradbard, M.R., Endsley, R.C. & Readdick, C.A. (1983). How and why parents select profit-making day care programs: A study of two southeastern college communities. Child Care Quarterly, 12(2), 160-169.

Fuqua, R.W. & Labensohn, D. (1986). Parents as consumers of child care. Family Relations, 35(2), 295-303.

Hayes, C.D., Palmer, J.L. & Zaslow, M.J. (Eds.). (1990). Who cares for America's children? Washington, D.C.: National Academy Press.

Hofferth, S.L. & Wissoker, D.A. (1992). Price, quality, and income in child care choices. The Journal of Human Resources, 27(1), 70-111.

Kisker, E.E., Gordon, A. & Shain, M. (1989). The child care challenge: What parents need and what is available in three metropolitan areas. Princeton, N.J.: Mathematica Policy Research.

Mason, K.O. & Duberstein, L. (1990). Consequences of child care for parents' well-being. In A. Booth, (Ed.), Child care in the 1990s: Trends and consequences. Hillsdale, N.J.: Lawrence Erlbaum Associates.

Morgan, G.C. (n.d.). Supply and demand for child day care: The need for data. Unpublished manuscript.

Nelson, P. (1970). Information and consumer behavior. Journal of Political Economy, 78(2), 311-329.

U.S. Bureau of the Census. (1990). Who's minding the kids? Child care arrangements: 1986-87. Current Population Reports, Series P-70, No. 20. Washington, D.C.: U.S. Government Printing Office.

Waite, L.J., Leibowitz, A. & Witsberger, C. (1991). What parents pay for: Child care characteristics, quality, and costs. Journal of Social Issues, 47(2), 33-48.

Walker, J.R. (1992). New evidence on the supply of child care: A statistical portrait of family providers and an analysis of their fees. The Journal of Human Resources, 27(1), 40-69.

Widdows, R. & Powell, D.R. (1990). Cost and quality factors in parents' choice of after-school child care. Journal of Consumer Affairs, 24(2), 381-391.

Endnotes

1. See Widdows and Powell (1990) for the derivation of the function.

2. Widdows and Powell (1990) suggested three cost and four quality categories.

3. Participants were instructed about the card sort procedure during the in-home interview and practiced the procedure by sorting factors important to them in planning a vacation.

Working Parents and Child Care: A Descriptive Analysis of How the Child Care Market has Responded to the Non-traditional Time Demands of Working Parents

Holly Jo Hair Hunts, Cornell University[1]

The majority of American workers do not work the traditional 40 hour week from 8am to 5pm. This paper discusses the availability of child care for workers who engage in non-traditional work hours.

Today there are 55 million women of childbearing age in the United States (U.S.) and 39.4 million of them are in the work force (Grieves, 1988). The percentage of the work force represented by women has grown from 40.5% in 1975 to 45.0% in 1988 and is projected to increase to 47.3% by the turn of the century (Hyland, 1990). A variety of social changes have had an influence on women joining and remaining in the labor force. These social changes include delays in marriage, delays in childbearing and increased educational levels of women; all of which have resulted in firmer attachments to the labor force by women (Moen, 1992).

Most ever married women in the U.S. (well over 90%) will become mothers (Maxwell, 1987). These women will likely continue to work after they become mothers, because their paycheck is often all that stands between their family and poverty (Children's Defense Fund, 1990). In 1970, 29% of children younger than 6 years of age had mothers in the work force, today this figure is over 50% (Hofferth, 1989).

With more mothers working, the care of children while mothers are on the job has become a major issue for U.S. families. This paper gives a descriptive overview of the very complex relationship between working parents, their work places and work schedules and the arrangements parents make for their children's care. The focus will be on how women and men can and do adapt their work schedules to their child care needs and conversely how women and men find child care in the market that meet their work schedules demands. The overview will begin with a brief look at how men and women can adapt their work life to accommodate the care of their children. The discussion will then move onto some of the macro changes in the U.S. economy, especially the movement towards a service economy and continuous production. The implications of these changes, including trends in occupations and work schedules and the effect of work schedules on parent's child care choices will be reviewed. A final section of this paper will present some descriptive results from several recent surveys with respect to the work schedules and market child care arrangements of American workers.

To find solutions for balancing work and family, Moen (1992) notes that women have traditionally chosen among four options for resolving the conflict between work and family obligations. These four alternatives include: 1) scheduling work and family roles sequentially; 2) reducing the number of hours worked (i.e., from full time to part-time); 3) choosing shift work to allow parents to jointly coordinate child care; and, 4) choosing less involving occupations. Each of these alternatives will be briefly discussed.

Scheduling work sequentially:

Sequential work means being in the work force before and after (but not during) the most intense child caring years. While this may seem to be idyllic, fewer women today are able to chose to balance their work and family sequentially. This is because women need the income now to support their families. Furthermore, choosing to leave the work force, even briefly, may have long term consequences for women in terms of obtaining promotions, benefits, pensions, etc.

Full-time versus part-time:

The majority of mothers in dual-earner families prefer to work fewer hours in order to have more time with their families according to Moen & Dempster-McClain (1987). Part-time work may, however, be related to lower wages and/or reduced benefits. This is because finding part-time professional work is less likely than finding part-time service or manufacturing work. Therefore, while many mothers may prefer working less hours in order to have more time with their families (reducing child care time and presumably child care cost) part-time work may come at a significant monetary cost to the family. These costs include decreased income through a lower number of hours worked, lower wages and reduced in-kind income in the form of benefits.

Shift work and joint child care:

The concept of shift work and joint child care refers to two parents working opposing shifts in order to circumvent the need for market child care. Presser (1989) found that about one is six dual-earner couples with children under the age of 6 had no overlap in the hours in which the spouses worked, making them eligible for joint child care. Women as opposed to men are the most likely to choose to work the non-traditional shifts in order

[1]Graduate Student,
Consumer Economics and Housing

Less involving occupations:

By choosing to work in less involving occupations mothers may be able to reduce their business travel time, attend fewer evening and weekend meetings and more easily take time off to transport their children and/or participate in their children's activities. Again, however, these less involved occupations may offer correspondingly lower monetary compensations.

Summary of work alternatives:

Each of these four solutions depend on the availability of jobs with the desired schedule characteristics in the market. This is because employees (for the most part) are unable to choose their own work schedule for a given job, instead they must choose a job with a given work schedule. The next section discusses changes in the U.S. economy and their impact on the availability of various schedule characteristics in the market.

Changes In The Economy

In order to compete with the changing global economic system the U.S. economy has been forced to make changes (McEnroe, 1991). One of these changes is the move from limited hours of operations (typically 9 a.m. to 5 p.m.), to continuous or "round-the-clock" operations both in production and in the provision of services (Czeisler, Moore-Ede & Coleman, 1982). Examples of continuous production lines include automobile producers and clothing manufacturers. Service oriented examples would include 24-hour grocery stores, restaurants, and round-the-clock financial services.

Corporations have several motivations for moving into continuous operation. One motivation is that 24 hour usage of equipment and facilities allows better utilization of capital stock and maximization of production capacity (Mikalauskas, 1989). Another inducement, and perhaps the most significant, is the fact that many firms' competitors have already made the switch to continuous operations. Recent studies have reported that 26.8% of the U.S. work force is employed by firms which operate on a continuous basis (Czeisler et al., 1982; Presser, 1988). In fact, the majority of workers employed outside of the agricultural industry do not work the traditional American shift of 8 a.m. to 5 p.m., weekdays. A recent study shows that only 46% of women and 42% of men in nonagricultural occupations work this traditional schedule (Presser, 1989).

Other major changes are occurring as the service sector replaces the goods-producing sector as the dominant force in the U.S. economy (Collier, 1983). In 1983, 70% of available jobs and 66% of the Gross National Product were accounted for by the service industry (Collier, 1983). Projections for job growth for the period of 1986-2000, estimate that the largest increases will be for service sector occupations and other occupations likely to require employment during non-traditional hours (Presser, 1989).

It should be noted that women comprise a disproportionate percentage of the employees in the service industry (Presser, 1989). In 1987, women comprised 28% of payroll employees in private goods-producing establishments, compared to 53% of all payroll employees in private service-producing establishments (Hayghe, 1988).

Scheduling

As service businesses are the fastest-growing employers in the U.S. economy and since they are the most likely businesses to operate continuously (Presser, 1989; McEnroe, 1991) new work schedules for service employees have evolved. Service industries have the highest percent of employed persons working non-day schedules and the highest percent working weekends (Presser, 1989).

Several schedules are possible, including fixed schedules, rotating schedules and non-static schedules. The term non-static implies a schedule which varies irregularly across time. Whereas a rotating shift will change from a fixed day schedule to a fixed evening schedule to a fixed night schedule across specified time intervals, a non-static schedule can change from day to evening to night several times within a week and is virtually defined by its erratic nature. How various work schedule alternatives effect child care choices is the topic of the next section.

Work Schedules And Child Care

Part-time work and child care:

In examining the level (part-time versus full-time) of work mothers choose, Folk & Bellar (1993) find a connection between child care type (in the broad categories of market versus non-market care) and level of employment using a nationally representative sample. They find that white, married women are the most likely to choose part-time work and non-market care (thus using a combination of the part-time work and joint child care solutions). However, other recent empirical work has found that among non-black, employed fathers neither the mother's or the father's number of hours was related to work interfering with home life, including child care when the shift times were controlled for in the equation (Riley, 1990). The father's shift was found to be significantly related to interfering with home life in the same study (Riley, 1990). From Riley's (1990) study one might question if some of the results regarding child care choice that were previously attributed to part-time work may in instead be at least partially caused by shift work.

Shift work and joint child care:

Presser (1989) found that of those fathers available to care for their children while their wives were at work, nearly all fathers did in fact provide child care. In the 1985 Current Population Survey, fathers provided about 19% of all primary care for children under the age of 5 when married mothers were employed (Presser, 1989). Presser speculates however, that for families in which one or more parent works a rotating or non-static shift it may be nearly impossible to coordinate work schedules to allow for joint child care arrangements (Presser, 1989).

Less involving work:
There may be long term costs to women (and men) by having one or both parents choose less involving work. Less involving work likely entails little chance for promotion, seniority and pay progressions and often involves minimal or no additional work benefits such as health insurance, sick leave, vacation days etc. (Moen, 1992). The hope, of course, is that at the family level these costs will be off-set by the parent's increased flexibility to cope with family strains, particularly child care constraints. The choice of less involving work may be a particularly risky career strategy for a spouse to take given that over 50% of all marriages end in divorce (Levitan, S. A., Belous, R. A. & Gallo, F., 1988) and he/she will have invested his/her time in a low wage - low opportunity career path with no provisions for pensions etc.

Non-static work schedules and child care:
Because the literature lacks descriptive work of what times of the day different types of child care are available, little is known about the choices that parentswho work non-static hours face. It seems reasonable to assume however, that not all types of child care are open 24 hours a day, 7 days a week, 365 days a year. This assumption would support the empirical work that shows that workers engaged in non-static work schedules are more likely to use multiple forms of child care to cover the hours they need for employment purposes (Folk, 1991).

Market Availability

While the academic literature has given attention to work schedules and child care from a demand perspective little attention has been given to the actual supply of child care available. Previous research approached the issue of work schedules and child care as if all types of child care were available at all times, and variation lay only among quality and cost issues. This paper gives a very preliminary look at the descriptive statistics of the work schedules American's engage in and the times market child care choices are available. Regarding the work schedules American's engage in, the May 1991 Current Population Survey provides some general descriptives. The Profile of Child Care Settings Study, both the Center Based Care Survey (Kisker & Piper, 1992a) and the Home Based Care Survey (Kisker & Piper, 1992b) are used to describe the times market child care choices are available. Both surveys concentrate on the hours of operation, fees charged and services provided by child care providers. The Center Based Care Survey includes information on both non-profit and for-profit child care centers while the Home Based Care Survey includes information on regulated Family Day Care (FDC) providers.

Work schedules in America
Table 1 notes the variety of work schedules undertaken by different occupations. Of particular interest in Table 1 is the evidence that service occupations are the least likely to

Table 1
Shift Work in the United States

Occupation	Regular	Evening	Night	Rotating	Split-shift	Non-static	Other
Managerial and professional speciality	89.6%	1.6%	1.4%	1.8%	.5%	2.8%	1.8%
Technical sales and administrative support	85.6%	3.5%	2.4%	2.7%	.4%	3.6%	1.3%
Service occupations	57.1%	14.7%	8.7%	7.9%	2.1%	6.6%	2.5%
Precision production, craft and repair	85.3%	4.3%	3.7%	3.4%	.1%	2.5%	.4%
Operators, fabricators and laborers	73.4%	8.6%	6.8%	4.8%	.7%	4.2%	.9%
Farming, forestry and fishing	89.2%	1.1%	1.2%	.7%	1.0%	4.4%	2.0%

Source: United States Department of Labor (1992b). News. (Report No. 92-491). Washington, DC: Bureau of Labor

provide day time hours and the most likely to provide evening, night, rotating shift, split-shift, non-static and other schedules. As discussed earlier, women are the predominant workers in
the service occupation industry. However, Table 2 shows that women are more likely to work regular day time shifts than are their male counterparts. The finding in Table 2 is contrary to the statement by Moen (1992) that women are more likely to choose non-traditional shifts. Table 3 shows the beginning hours for wage and salary workers, full-time and part-time. What should be the most evident in Table 3, is the wide variety of starting times American's engage in, clearly supporting Presser's (1989) notion that American's do not simply work from 8am to 5pm. In Table 3, women appear to begin their work at more traditional times of the day than do their male counterparts, consistent with the findings in Table 2.

Market child care availability in America
Given the demand for child care services outside of the traditional time, it is interesting to look at the times that market child care is provided in the United States. There are two major components of market care, center based care and family day care (FDC).

Center based care
Center based care includes all child care which occurs in buildings other than a residential home and for this paper includes both for-profit centers (national chains, local chains and, independent centers) and non-profit centers (university centers, church/synagogue centers, HeadStart, government/community centers). The survey used to examine center based care is the Profile of Child Care Settings, Center based care (Kisker & Piper, 1992a).

Family day care
Family Day Care (FDC) is child care which occurs in a residential home other than the

child's. FDC can be divided into two major categories; licensed FDC and unlicensed FDC. While regulations in nearly all of the States in the United States require licensure only approximately 6% of FDC homes are licensed (U.S. Department of Labor, 1990). Many of the unlicensed FDC providers may choose not to be licensed because of the cost involved in being licensed (costs in terms of both upgrading facilities to meet licensure requirements, and costs in terms of providing revenue information to the government). This paper will only examine the licensed FDCs because that is the information available from the Profile of Child Care Settings, Home based care (Kisker & Piper, 1992b).

Availability of child care
The center based study reveals that 95.9% (n=1879) of centers in the U.S. are open five days a week. Only 4.1% (n=81) are open on either Saturday or Sunday. This confirming the notion that the majority of centers are open during traditional days.

Centers report having drop-off times as early as 4:30 am, but only a very small percentage (1.5%, n=29) reported opening before 6:00 am. The latest drop-off time was reported as 4:00 pm, but 96.7% (n=1895) reported a drop-off time of 10:00 am or earlier. Again, this confirms the notion of the majority of centers only offering traditional beginning hours, despite the wide range of beginning hours reported for workers in Table 3.

The latest pick-up time for centers had a wide range of values reported. The most unusual time reported was 3:00 am, however, less than 1% (0.9%, n=18) reported a closing time after 7:00 pm.

FDCs reported similar traditional hours of operation. In the home based study, only 5.3% of FDC homes were open on either Saturday or Sunday. This is slightly above the percentage of centers

Table 2
Shift Work in the United States, for married full-time workers

Sex, presence of children and age of youngest child	Regular	Evening	Night	Rotating	Split-shift	Non-static	Other
Men, total: n=30,416	81.5%	4.6%	4.0%	3.9%	.5%	4.0%	1.7%
Men with own children under 6 n=9,205	79.6%	5.6%	4.4%	4.3%	.3%	3.9%	1.7%
Women, total: n=18,537	88.4%	3.5%	2.3%	2.0%	.5%	2.2%	.8%
Women with children under 6 n=3,928	86.4%	5.6%	3.3%	2.1%	.6%	2.0%	.7%

Source: Shift work: Data from the May 1991 Current Population Survey. U.S. Department of Labor (1992a)

Table 3
Beginning Hours for Full & Part Time Workers

Beginning Hour	All Workers n=96,208	Men n=50,732	Women n=45,476
1am	85	49	36
2am	101	75	26
3am	197	156	41
4am	375	276	99
5am	1287	898	390
6am	5559	3856	1704
7am	22146	14478	7668
8am	32188	16029	16158
9am	13633	4898	8735
10am	3359	1196	2163
11am	1349	466	884
12pm	1253	527	726
1pm	903	369	533
2pm	1238	527	726
3pm	3206	1689	1516
4pm	2899	1594	1306
5pm	1880	897	983
6pm	989	523	465
7pm	571	270	301
8pm	346	196	149
9pm	256	153	102
10pm	460	301	159
11pm	1324	777	547
12pm	605	443	162

Source: U.S. Department of Labor (1992c)

reported being open, but clearly supports the notion that the majority of FDCs are closed during non-traditional days.

The earliest starting time reported for FDCs was 4:00 am. While only 1.5% of centers opened before 6:00 am, 9.0% (n=24) of FDCs were open before 6:00 am. Similar to center based care, 99.5% of all FDCs reported drop-off times before 10:00 am.

Pick-up times for FDCs ranged from 1:00 pm to 1:00 am, but most 91% (n=514) lied within the range of 1:00 pm to 7:00 pm. Again, confirming the traditional notion that child care is available during daylight hours, Monday through Friday.

Conclusions and Implications for Future Work:
From this very preliminary study, it appears that market child care has not adjusted to the hours that Americans are working. Several reasons may lie behind market child care provider's decisions not to be open during those hours. One reason may be that parents simply do not demand market child care for non-traditional hours. Parents engaged in non-traditional work schedules may be choosing relative care or joint child care arrangements for their children during their work hours. Another reason may be that suppliers do not have sufficient volumes of children at all hours of the day to warrant 24 hour service therefore they only offer services during the times for which there is sufficient volume which

apparently is during the traditional hours. A third reason may stem from an ethical dilemma, which is how children should be cared for during non-traditional hours. Should, for example, children be kept awake and busy during the hours of midnight and 8:00am so that when their parents pick them up at 8:00am they will be ready to sleep just as their parents are, or should children be allowed to sleep from midnight to 8:00am as their circadian system expects. These reasons can and should be explored in future research.

Several suggestions can be made for future research. Firstly, a major improvement of the investigation into market child care would involve access to a nationally representative data set that includes not only child care centers and regulated FDC homes but also unregulated FDC homes. This would provide a much more accurate depiction of the market since the large majority of FDC providers are unlicensed.

Secondly, a study which examined the child care choices of parents who work non-traditional schedules that included all child care alternatives including non-market forms of care such as relative and spouse care would be of great interest. Such a study could further investigate whether parents have chosen their work schedules to accommodate their child care needs (as suggested by Moen's work (1992) or whether parents choose child care options to accommodate their work schedules.

References

Bloom, D. E. & Steen, T. P. (1988). Why child care is good for business. American Demographics, 10(7), 22-27, 58-59.

Children's Defense Fund (1990, January). Child Care: Key Facts. Washington, D.C..

Collier, D. A. (1983). The service sector revolution: The automation of services. Long Range Planning, 16(6), 10-20.

Czeisler, C. A., Moore-Ede, M. C. & Coleman, R. M. (1982). Rotating shift work schedules that disrupt sleep are improved by applying circadian principles. Science, 217(4558), 460-462.

Dawson, D. A., & Cain, V. S. (1990, October 1). Child care arrangements, health of our nation's children, United States, 1988. Advance Data, No. 187.

Folk, K. F. (1991). Use of multiple child care arrangements by mothers of preschool children. In J. W. Bauer (Ed.), Family Economics-Home Management Section of the American Home Economics Association: Conference Proceedings (pp. 89-96). St. Paul, Minnesota: American Home Economics Association.

Folk, K. F. & Beller, A. H. (1993). Part-time work and child care choices for mothers of preschool children. Journal of Marriage and Family, 55, 146-157.

Grieves, R. T. (1988, June 27). And baby makes three. Forbes, pp. 142-143.

Hayghe, H. (1988). Employers and child care: What roles do they play? Monthly Labor Review, 111(9), 38-44.

Hofferth, S. L. (1989). What is the demand for and supply of child care in the United States? Young Children, 44(5), 28-33.

Hyland, S. L. (1990). Helping employees with family care. Monthly Labor Review, 113(9), 22-26.

Kisker, E. E. & Piper, V. (1992b). A profile of child care settings: Home-based programs (Data set 15-16, Lang, E. & Card, J. J., Archivists) [machine-readable data file and documentation]. Mathematica Policy Research, Inc. (Producer). Los Altos, CA: Sociometrics Corporation, American Family Data Archive (Producer & Distributor).

Kisker, E. E. & Piper, V. (1992a). A profile of child care settings: Center-based programs (Data set 17-18, Lang, E. & Card, J. J., Archivists) [machine-readable data file and documentation]. Mathematica Policy Research, Inc. (Producer). Los Altos, CA: Sociometrics Corporation, American Family Data Archive (Producer & Distributor).

Levitan, S. A., Belous, R. A. & Gallo, F. (1988). What's Happening to the American Family? Baltimore, MD: The Johns Hopkins University Press.

Mapes, G. (1990, April 10). Was it an accident Chernobyl exploded at 1:23 in the morning? Wall Street Journal, pp. 1, A16.

Maxwell, N.L. (1987). Influences on the timing of first childbearing. Contemporary Policy Issues, 5(2), 113-122.

McEnroe, J. (1991). Split-shift parenting. American Demographics, 13(2), 50-52.

Mikalauskas, A. (1989). The Determinants of Female Shift Work. Unpublished masters thesis, Cornell University, Ithaca, NY.

Moen, P. (1992). Women's Two Roles: A contemporary dilemma, New York: Auburn House.

Moen, P. & Dempster-McClain (1987). Employed parents: Role strain, work time, and preferences for working less. Journal of Marriage and the Family, 49(August), 579-590.

Presser, H. B. (1989). Can we make time for children? The economy, work schedules, and child care. Demography, 26(4), 523-543.

Riley, D. (1990). Network influences on father involvement in childrearing. In M. Cochran, M. Larner, D. Riley, L. Gunnarsson & C. R. Henderson (Eds.) Extending families: The social networks of parent and their children (pp. 131-153). Cambridge, MA: Cambridge University Press.

United States Department of Labor (1990). Employers and Child Care: Benefiting Work and Family. Washington, DC: Office of the Secretary, Women's Bureau

United States Department of Labor (1992a). News. (Report No. 92-491). Washington, DC: Bureau of Labor Statistics

United States Department of Labor (1992b). Shift work: Data from the May 1991 current population survey, (Unpublished data.) Washington, DC: Bureau of Labor Statistics

United States Department of Labor (1992c). Beginning and ending hours: Data from the May 1991 current population survey, (Unpublished data.) Washington, DC: Bureau of Labor Statistics

Information and The Role of Child Care Resource and Referral Services

Karen Fox Folk, University of Illinois at Urbana-Champaign[1]

This paper uses research on the marketing of services in general as a framework to explain consumer behavior when searching for child care. Child care resource and referral services (CCR&R) were established in many communities to assist parents in the search for child care. Utilization of CCR&Rs and implications for their consumer education programs are discussed in light of consumer responses to child care as a service good.

Introduction

Employed parents searching for substitute child care face information problems common to consumers selecting other services, i.e., the difficulty of judging the quality of an experience good before use (Nelson, 1970). Zeithaml, Parasuraman and Berry (1985) proposed a conceptual framework for analyzing the effects of the unique characteristics of services on consumer behavior. This paper uses that framework and related empirical marketing research to yield insights into research findings on parental behavior in the search for child care arrangements. Other explanations for parental behavior as a response to imperfect information and risk are also discussed. The paper concludes with a discussion of the role of child care resource and referral services in improving information flows in the child care market and consumer education strategies to improve parents' ability to search for quality child care.

Characteristics of Services

Services are characterized by four qualities: 1) intangibility, 2) inseparability of production and consumption, 3) heterogeneity, and 4) perishability (Zeithaml, et al., 1985). Intangibility is the problem of being unable to observe the characteristics of services prior to purchase; inseparability means that the service is produced as it is consumed; heterogeneity means that each service delivery will be a unique interaction between service provider and consumer; and perishability means that it is impossible to stockpile an inventory of services which would allow a quick response to variations in supply and demand. Intangibility and heterogeneity are the two qualities most relevant to consumer behavior, while inseparability and perishability have a greater impact on producers and marketers of services.

Intangibility

Intangibility makes information on salient characteristics difficult or impossible to judge prior to purchase. Empirical studies of a variety of services find that, given these intangible characteristics, consumers rely on personal sources of information, have a greater perceived risk, and use price and physical facilities as indicators of quality (Zeithaml, et al., 1985). Intangibility may decrease the benefits of search for characteristics which can be judged only after experiencing the service. Viewed as responses to dealing with intangibility, parents' documented reliance on both few and informal sources of information in searching for child care are logical efforts to limit search to sources with personal experience with the intangible characteristics of the potential child care provider. Studies using a variety of samples all find that parents looking for child care use informal contacts with relatives, friends, and neighbors as their first and often only source of information on available providers (Bradbard, Endsley & Readdick, 1983; Fuqua & Labensohn, 1986; Hofferth, Brayfield, Deich & Holcomb, 1991; Powell & Widdows, 1987; Walker, 1991).

Another consumer response to intangibility of services documented in empirical marketing studies is the "vividness effect," i.e., the tendency for consumers to give more weight to concrete images, anecdotes, or case histories than to factual comparisons of the tangible characteristics of services (studies reviewed in Drumwright, 1985). Reliance on "vivid" characteristics is hypothesized to reduce the burden of information processing for consumers. Studies of child care selection criteria consistently report that warmth and/or personality of the child care provider is one of the most important characteristics for parents, an intangible characteristic which would be judged at first interview or on the basis of reports from those who know the provider (Bogat & Gensheimer, 1986; Hofferth, et al., 1991). In addition, an ethnographic study reported that low-income mothers relied on instant positive or negative reactions during a visit to a center as the basis for selecting care for their child (Zinsser, 1987).

Heterogeneity

While intangibility complicates the search process, heterogeneity in a provider's services, or the uniqueness of each transaction increases monitoring costs once a provider is selected. All types of child care are subject to "hidden action," in which usual care differs from that given to children when a parent is present (Walker, 1991). The potential for shirking or misrepresentation may be lower for informal caregivers whose habits and caregiving style are known to parents prior to the

---

[1]Division of Consumer Sciences

delivery of child care services, further reinforcing consumer preferences for a search based on information from relatives, friends, and neighbors.

The risk of "hidden action" is highest for infants and very young children who cannot report details of caregiving as older children might. This may partially explain why relative care is both more frequently used and more often cited as the preferred choice of care for very young children than for older preschoolers (Hofferth, et al., 1991; Mason & Kuhlthau, 1989). A preference for caregivers known to the parent may be reinforced by the "vividness effect" in which highly publicized, yet isolated, incidents of abuse in day care centers increase the perceived risk to parents of choosing an unknown caregiver.

Market Structure

Information on availability of child care is also restricted by the structure of the child care market. While most day care centers are listed in the Yellow Pages, few family day care homes are. Less than 10% of family day care providers are licensed or registered and often fill openings through informal and local networks, not through advertising (Walker, 1992). Poor information flows may reduce the effectiveness of consumers' search for child care. One study reported that parents perceived themselves as having few options for care or as unable to obtain their preferred form of care (Shinn, Phillips, Howes, Galinsky & Whitebook, 1991).

In addition, high rates of exit and entry among family day care providers in the child care market mean that information parents gather on available providers is quickly outdated. In one study, 37% of registered family day care providers were no longer registered after 1 year and 63% viewed the work as temporary (Nelson, 1990). High turnover also increases the frequency of searches to replace a current provider who exits the market.

Resource and Referral Services

Child care resource and referral services (CCR&R) have been established by community groups and employers responding to a perceived need to assist parents searching for child care. Additional goals for some CCR&Rs include improving the quality and increasing the supply of child care in local markets. Having a central service which gathers information on child care providers in the community and matches available openings with parents' needs is viewed as a way to improve the efficiency of the child care market (Ferber & O'Farrell, 1991). CCR&Rs have also been the most common employee benefit provided by employers wishing to reduce employee stress caused by difficulties in locating quality child care (Hayghe, 1988).

Resource and referral services have expanded rapidly with the provision of federal funds to

states through the Family Support Act of 1988 and the 1990 Child Care and Development Block Grants. Nine percent of the population in the 1990 National Child Care Survey reported finding their current arrangement through a CCR&R (Hofferth, et al., 1991). In addition, large national employers such as Xerox and NCR who contract with private firms for resource and referral services report that about 5% of their target population utilize this employee benefit ("Supports for," 1988).

While utilization rates may rise as more parents learn of the existence of CCR&R services, consumers may prefer to rely on information from a source with direct experience with the service provider as discussed above. Resource and referral services may be particularly helpful to parents who have less access to word-of-mouth information, perhaps recently moved to the area, or who have needs for child care which is more difficult to find, e.g., for infants, or during evening or weekend hours (Gaumer, 1993). One study which compared users of CCR&Rs to nonusers found that those who contacted a CCR&R had younger children (mean age 2.5 years vs. 4 years for nonusers) and that their children had been in care for longer periods (Fuqua & Schieck, 1989). CCR&R users spent more time on searches and made greater use of written materials describing care. Further research is needed to determine if those using CCR&Rs are a self-selected group of consumers who tend to invest more in search, or, if they have special needs which prevent them from locating care through informal contacts.

In addition to improving the flow of information in the child care market, many CCR&Rs provide consumer education to improve parents' ability to select quality child care. An underlying goal of this consumer education is to raise the overall quality of the child care market based on increased demand for quality (Siegel & Lawrence, 1984).

Duncan and Olshavsky (1982) studied the role of consumer beliefs in the extent of external prepurchase search for television sets. They found that consumers' confidence in their ability to judge differences in goods was positively related to extent of search. Parents might search more if they had received education on which characteristics indicate quality child care. Parents in one study reported not knowing where to look for care and felt that most parents know little about selecting quality child care (Fuqua & Labensohn, 1986). Further research on consumer beliefs about the benefits of wider search for child care, and the characteristics of those likely to search more extensively could provide direction for development of consumer education efforts of CCR&Rs.

Implications for CCR&Rs

Based on the research on marketing of service goods and consumer search for child care reviewed above, CCR&Rs seeking to increase their effectiveness should use techniques which stimulate word-of-mouth referrals. They could add copies of brochures and business cards to the packet of materials sent to users of their service with a note requesting that parents mention their service to others. Personal contact with parents through presentations at PTA meetings, and visits to school secretaries and principals to publicize their service may also be effective. In one study of parents seeking after-school care, 15% of those receiving help in locating care obtained it from the school (Powell & Widdows, 1987). Other techniques which may effectively increase word-of-mouth referrals include contacting local opinion leaders including physicians, educators, and clergy and speaking to civic and neighborhood organizations (Black, Black & McGlashan, 1987).

CCR&Rs designing consumer education materials may increase use and educational impact by considering the problems for parents caused by imperfect information and intangibility of child care services. Bogat and Gensheimer (1986) reported that only half of the well-educated parents in their sample used their checklist for selecting quality child care, but speculated that this may have been related to the length of the 45-item checklist. Consumer education materials could be written to include characteristics identified by research as important to parents as well as characteristics important for child development. Including factors which may cause failure of the child care arrangement such as convenience and payment arrangements on a checklist could reduce turnover due to dissatisfaction and benefit the child.

Ignoring time constraints of parents by setting unrealistic expectations for search in printed materials may result in nonuse of the materials. An example would be recommending personal visits to at least three providers when research shows that parents generally visit one or two providers before selecting care (Bogat & Gensheimer, 1986; Bradbard, et al., 1983; Fuqua & Labensohn, 1986). A more realistic recommendation might be to advise parents to search until they find a provider who meets safety and health standards and whose personality appears compatible with the child. Emphasizing warmth or the nature of caregivers' interactions with children acknowledges the necessity of relying on some intuitive judgment of personality when judging an intangible service. Research comparing the effectiveness of various forms of consumer education materials for parents would be helpful to CCR&Rs in improving parents' ability to effectively select quality child care.

References

Black, C.F., Black, K.U. & McGlashan, R. (1987). Marketing child care in an urban setting. Child & Youth Care Quarterly, 16, 210-211.

Bogat, G.A. & Gensheimer, L.K. (1986). Discrepancies between the attitudes and actions of parents choosing day care. Child Care Quarterly, 15, 159-169.

Bradbard, M.R., Endsley, R.C. & Readdick, C.A. (1983). How and why parents select profit-making day care programs: A study of two southeastern college communities. Child Care Quarterly, 12, 160-169.

Drumwright, M.E. (1985). Processing information regarding service industries. In T.M. Bloch, G.D. Upah, & V.A. Zeithaml (Eds.), Services Marketing in a Changing Environment. Chicago: American Marketing Association.

Duncan, C.P. & Olshavsky, R.W. (1982). External search: The role of consumer beliefs. Journal of Marketing Research, 19, 32-43.

Ferber, M.A. & O'Farrell, B. (Eds.). (1991). Work and family: Policies for a changing work force. Washington, D.C.: National Academy Press.

Fuqua, R.W. & Labensohn, D. (1986). Parents as consumers of child care. Family Relations, 35, 295-303.

Fuqua, R.W. & Schieck, R. (1989). Child care resource and referral programs and parents' search for quality child care. Early Childhood Research Quarterly, 4, 357-365.

Gaumer, N. (1993). Personal communication.

Hayghe, H.V. (1988). Employers and child care: What roles do they play? Monthly Labor Review, 111(9), 38-44.

Hofferth, S.L., Brayfield, A., Deich, S. & Holcomb, P. (1991). National Child Care Survey, 1990. Urban Institute Report 91-5. Washington, D.C.: The Urban Institute Press.

Mason, K.O. & Kuhlthau, K. (1989). Determinants of child care ideals among mothers of preschool-aged children. Journal of Marriage and the Family, 51, 593-603.

Nelson, M.K. (1990). Mothering others' children: The experiences of family day-care providers. Signs: Journal of Women in Culture and Society, 15, 586-605.

Nelson, P. (1970). Information and consumer behavior. Journal of Political Economy, 78, 311-329.

Powell, D.R. & Widdows, R. (1987). Social and economic factors associated with parents' decisions about after-school child care: An exploratory study in a medium-sized community. Child & Youth Care Quarterly, 16, 272-282.

Shinn, M., Phillips, D., Howes, C., Galinsky, E.
& Whitebook, M. (1991). Correspondence
between mothers' perceptions and observer
ratings of quality in child care centers.
Unpublished manuscript.

Siegel, P. & Lawrence, M. (1984). Information,
referral, and resource centers. In J.T.
Greenman & R.W. Fuqua (Eds.), Making day care
better: Training, evaluation and the process
of change (pp. 227-243). New York: Teachers
College Press.

Supports for Child Care: Resource and Referral.
(1988, September). Employee Benefit Plan
Review, 43(3), 31-35.

Walker, J.R. (1991). Public policy and the supply
of child care services. In D.M. Blau (Ed.),
The economics of child care (pp. 51-77). New
York: Russell Sage Foundation.

Walker, J.R. (1992). New evidence on the supply
of child care: A statistical portrait of
family providers and an analysis of their
fees. Journal of Human Resources, 27, 40-69.

Zeithaml, V.A., Parasuraman, A. & Berry, L.L.
(1985). Problems and strategies in services
marketing. Journal of Marketing, 49, 33-46.

Zinsser, C. (1987). Over a barrel: Working
mothers talk about child care. New York:
Columbia University, National Center for
Children in Poverty.

Empirical Analysis of the
Rational Expectations-Life Cycle Hypothesis:
A Panel Data Study

Thomas G. Moehrle, Bureau of Labor Statistics[1]

Recent empirical analyses have repeatedly rejected the implications of the Rational Expectation-Life Cycle Hypothesis. This study re-tests the implications of the hypothesis by examining consumption habits of families participating in the Consumer Expenditure Survey. A generalized method of moments (GMM) estimator is used to obtain estimates of the preference parameters of the Euler equation, and test the implications of the hypothesis.

The theory of intertemporal optimization of consumers' lifetime well being has been the generally accepted explanation for consumer resource allocation since the turn of the century. Barring any constraints limiting the allocation of lifetime income, an individual's consumption decision is conditional on expected lifetime income and not current income. Although changes in current income and other events may cause an optimizing consumer to reevaluate expected lifetime income, the changes in current income will affect current consumption in so much as it affects expected lifetime income. We would then expect temporary or irregular changes in current income to have small effects on lifetime income, and hence little or no effect on current consumption. A permanent income change, however, will trigger a strong effect on lifetime income, and through it, current consumption.

The pioneering work of Hall (1978) has provided the path to re-examine the implications of the LCH by using the stochastic Euler equation approach. Hall's central conclusion was that if a consumer forms her expectations rationally, then prior information should not influence future consumption or its growth. It is this information that would have induced prior period adjustments to consumption.

The assumption of rational expectations is not new to the intertemporal theory, but the Euler equation approach explicitly applies the assumption within the testing methodology. It is then perhaps more appropriate to call the Life Cycle Hypothesis the Rational Expectations-Life Cycle Hypothesis (RE-LCH). From this, we can derive stochastic Euler equations from the first order conditions of optimizing consumers, and test the implied orthogonality conditions. Specifically, the forecast errors of the stochastic Euler equations, resulting from new information, should be orthogonal to observed variables contained within the consumers' information set at the time the consumption decisions were made.

Previous empirical analyses that have rejected the implications of the hypothesis blame imperfect capital markets, and hence binding borrowing constraints for the failures. Given this, I use a split sample technique described by Zeldes (1989) and Runkle (1991) to test for binding borrowing constraints. The technique allows direct testing of the hypothesis when binding borrowing constraints are suspected by splitting the sample between likely constrained and nonconstrained families.

Methodology

The first order conditions derived from the standard optimization problem imply the following Euler equation for period t and t+1:

$$U'_{it} = E_{it}B(1+r_{it})U'_{it+1} \qquad (1)$$

where r_{it} is the real after-tax rate of return for consumer i in period t, B is the subjective rate of discount assumed constant across households, E_{it} is the expectations operator, and U' represents the first order derivatives of the utility function with respect to consumption. At the optimal where the equation holds, a consumer can not do better by transferring her assets between the two consecutive periods. In the event of an inequality, an optimizing consumer, trading within perfectly competitive markets, allocates her assets between the two periods until the equality holds. Taking expectations and rearranging (1), we have

$$(U'_{it}+1/U'_{it})B(1+r_{it}) - 1 = e_{i,t+1} \qquad (2)$$

where $e_{i,t+1}$ is the expectation or forecast error resulting from new information on income, the real after-tax rate of return, or preference shocks.

Applying the rational expectations assumption, the forecast error has the property

$$E_t(e_{it+1}|I_t) = 0, \qquad (3)$$

where I_t is the information set as of period t.

[1]Economist, Division of Consumer Expenditure Surveys.

From this, a set of population orthogonality conditions arises that state the

$$E_t(e_{it+1}z_{it}) = 0 \qquad (4)$$

where z_{it} is a vector of instrumental variables contained within the t-period information set. Since information known at period t have been included in consumption decisions at the point the expectations were made, lagged information should be uncorrelated with the forecast error.

The "pure" RE-LCH assumes consumers are forward-looking agents operating in perfectly competitive capital markets. In a financial environment susceptible to adverse selection and moral hazard, specific groups of individuals may be discriminated against from freely borrowing against future income to smooth consumption. For instance, the unemployed may find it difficult to borrow against expected future earnings, or renters may find it difficult to meet collateral requirements. In turn, these consumers may be forced to accept a consumption level no greater than their current levels of liquid assets and incomes, and hence are unable to adjust consumption to desired levels.

The traditional framework of the LCH does not incorporate such borrowing constraints. If borrowing constraints are suspected, tests of the hypothesis should explicitly account for them. If indeed borrowing constraints are binding for a group within the population, the host of empirical studies rejecting the "pure" RE-LCH is not evidence against the theoretical foundation, but the result of misspecifying the optimizing problem.

Let us now examine what may happen if the perfectly competitive capital market assumption is relaxed, and some consumers face an additional period-to-period net borrowing constraint. Assume that the borrowing constraint is in the form of an exogenous quantity constraint:

$$A_{i,t+k} => 0, \qquad (5)$$

where $k = 0, ..., T - t - 1$. I choose this form of constraint in accord with Zeldes (1989) and Runkle (1991).[1] Note that this quantity constraint can take a variant form. Instead of assets set equal to zero, I allow constrained consumers to hold minimal liquid balances for transactions, and hence the constraint is binding at some prescribed positive level of liquid assets. I use this variant in the sample splitting method discussed later.

If the exogenous quantity constraint is binding, consumers may not be able to intertemporally allocate resources to meet the equality in (1). If a consumer is against the constraint in period t, the left-hand side will be equal to or greater than the right-hand side. Any variable relaxing the constraint, such as an increase in current income, will reduce the inequality. Consequently, the forecast error in

(2) will move with changes in this variable and other liquidity variables. This excess sensitivity of consumption will continue until the constraint is no longer binding.

If low liquid wealth holding families are more likely to be against this constraint than are high liquid wealth families, we can test the RE-LCH contingent on perfectly competitive markets by separating the sample of families between low wealth and high wealth holding families. Indeed, if the data fit the Euler equation for the high income families but does not for the low income families, binding borrowing constraints would be the intuitive explanation. The rejection can appear as a rejection of the overidentifying restrictions of the model, or by economically unreasonable parameter estimates.

Three model fits are made employing a generalized method of moments estimator (GMM). The first consists of fitting the entire sample of selected families to the model. The overidentifying restrictions of the model are examined as well as the parameter estimates. If the "pure" RE-LCH model holds across all families, the overidentifying restrictions of the model should not be rejected. If the instruments, chosen from the information set at the time of the expectation formation, are indeed uncorrelated with the forecast error, then the minimized value of the GMM criterion function is distributed asymptotically as X^2_{q-p}, where q is the number of instruments, and p the number of parameters. The model is accepted with large p-values computed from the X^2 distribution, with q-p degrees of freedom. This is an overall test of the Euler equation fit.

To test for rejection of the model resulting from binding borrowing constraints, I fit the same Euler equation to two subsamples: a liquidity sample and a nonliquidity sample. The overidentifying restrictions can be tested for each of these subsamples as well as the check for the reasonableness of the parameter estimates.

As an additional liquidity test, I test whether lagged liquidity variables are uncorrelated with the forecast error. If these are valid instruments, they should not statistically change the minimized value of the criterion function.[2] The test statistic is computed by the difference between the minimized value of the criterion function with and without the additional liquidity instruments. The test statistic again follows a X^2 distribution with the degrees of freedom equal to the number of additional instruments.[3]

Econometric Model

I make the problem tractable by assuming utility can be specified by a constant relative risk aversion utility function:

$$C^{1-A}/1-A \qquad (6)$$

where A is the coefficient of relative risk aversion, and its reciprocal is the rate of intertemporal substitution. I assume this coefficient is equal across households. Using this preference specification, (2) can be written as

$$(C'_{it+1}/C'_{it})^{-A}B(1+r_{it}) - 1 = e_{i,t+1} \qquad (7)$$

This parameterized stochastic Euler equation is used to fit the data and estimate the preference parameters, A and B. From this, a set of orthogonality conditions is constructed from the instruments observed within the consumer's lagged information set. The GMM estimation procedure then uses these orthogonality conditions as the criterion function which is to be minimized by the selection of the parameter values, A and B. For instance, let z_t represent the vector of observable instruments, then the sample orthogonality conditions are stated as

$$((C'_{it+1}/C'_{it})^{-A}B(1+r_{it}) - 1)z_t = e_{i,t+1} \qquad (8)$$

For this econometric model to be identified, the number of orthogonality conditions must be equal to or greater than the number of parameters of the Euler equation. Obviously, as the number of instruments increases, so do the number of overidentifying restrictions. The test of the overidentifying restrictions discussed in the previous section is a test of how close these sample orthogonality conditions are to zero.

Note that r_{it} may not be known at the time expectations are formed, and hence it may be correlated with the forecast error. Consequently, r_{it} must be instrumented. As discussed below, using two-stage least squares will not produce an efficient estimator.

As Hayashi (1985) and Runkle (1991) have suggested, preference shocks to the utility function or measurement error in consumption growth may produce a composite error. This composite error contains a mean zero component resulting from new information, and a moving average component resulting from either preference shocks or measurement error. Since I am using quarterly expenditures, seasonality of the data will produce such a moving average. Hence, I assume the error in equation (8) is a composite error term containing a moving average process of order 1, MA(1).[4]

Given the MA(1) process, two-stage least squares will not produce efficient estimators of the model.[5] Instead, I use the GMM estimator. This method has a number of benefits. The fundamental benefit is that consistent preference parameters are estimated from the objective function without specifying the closed form solution, or specifying the entire economic environment.[5] For this problem, the GMM estimator is defined as the minimized value of the criterion function,

$$g(b)'Wg(b), \qquad (9)$$

over the parameter space b, where b is the parameter vector of A and B, g(b) represents the sample orthogonality statements of (8), and W is an unobserved weighting matrix that must be estimated from sample data. If W is chosen "optimally," the GMM estimator is efficient within the class of estimators that use only conditional moment restrictions.[7]

Data

Aggregate data studies fail to adequately test the RE-LCH particularly if there are binding constraints present.[7] Panel sets with asset and income information provide the necessary information to split the sample between potential constrained and unconstrained families. This allows a direct test of the RE-LCH with potential binding constraints without an assumption on the income process or an assumption about income measurement error. The quarterly Interview survey of the Consumer Expenditure Survey (CES) available from the Bureau of Labor Statistics provide such data.

Data selection

The data used for the current study are restricted to consumer units interviewed from first quarter of 1990 through first quarter 1991, and who have completed the survey for all four quarters. This selection provides two unique panels. Excluded are consumer units headed by individuals under the age of 25, as well as units who did not provide complete reporting of income. This initial sample consists of 1,518 consumer units. To reduce the effect of reporting errors, 226 units whose reference person was self-employed or received some self-employment income were excluded. Four units were deleted because of nonpositive expenditures.[9] Two final selections were made. Consumer units who had consumption grow by more than 200 percent or fall by more than 50 percent were excluded. Lastly, to assure a balanced panel set after these exclusion criteria, only consumer units who provided all four quarters were kept. This left a full sample size of 1,142 unique families. Therefore, each retained consumer unit provided three growth records to fit the Euler equation.

To perform the split sample tests, the full sample of families must be selected for either the nonliquidity constrained group or the liquidity constrained group. I chose the ratio of liquid assets to normal income to determine which group the family belongs. From the CES, I defined liquid assets as checking and savings account balances, U.S. government bonds, and estimated market value of securities.[10] I define normal income as that part of income that is received regularly. This would include wage and salary, interest and rent income, pension, unemployment and other such incomes.

In order not to violate the assumption of rational expectations, normal income is measured for the 12 month period prior to the consumer's first quarterly interview. If a consumer unit has liquid assets equal to at least one-twelfth of his annual income, he is included in the liquid sample. Otherwise the consumer unit is placed in the nonliquid group. Using this split criterion, 486 unique units were include in the liquid group, and the remaining 656 were placed in the nonliquid group.

Variables of the Orthogonality Conditions

In the previous section, I present the instantaneous utility function with the assumption that consumption is separable among commodities. Here, consumption, within the utility function, is assumed separable between nondurables and services, and durables. If this assumption is valid, I can use expenditures on nondurables and services as the consumption measure in the Euler equation. To classify CES expenditure data as nondurables and services, I use the classifications used within the Personal Consumption Expenditure estimates of the Bureau of Economic Analysis.

As in previous studies, I assume that the subjective rate of discount is constant across households, but I allow the rate of return to vary across time and households. The rate of return may vary across time, but will also vary across households because of differences in marginal tax rates. Measure r as the real after-tax rate of return. I measure this by the nominal rate adjusted by the changes in the Consumer Price Index. This real rate is adjusted by marginal tax rates approximated by family composition, average allowable deductions, and income level.[11] The nominal rate of return is approximated by the three-month Treasury Bill--a risk free security. Given this, the real after-tax rate of return is expressed as

$$r_{it} = (1+R_t)(1-m_t)P_t/P_{t+1} \qquad (10)$$

where R is the risk free nominal rate of interest, m is the marginal tax rate, and P the price level.

The standard instrument list used in the GMM estimation include the number of weeks worked in the prior year and the average hours worked per week for the reference person, and if married, for the spouse.[12] Also included are the age of reference person and the number of persons in the consumer unit. In order not to violate the rational expectations assumption, information collected in the first quarterly interview is used.

To test for significance of liquidity variables, I augment the instrument list by two income measurements: transitory income and normal income. Both are lagged. The transitory income instrument includes lottery winnings, income from sale of assets, tax refunds and alike. I call these transitory amounts because they are irregular income components. Normal income includes wages and salaries, interest and rent income, unemployment and workers' compensation, and other regularly received income components.

Results

Data are fitted to the econometric model of (8). The results from fitting the full sample of data to this model are shown in Table I, and the results from the liquid and nonliquid subsamples are shown in Tables II and III. There are four columns of results for each data set. The first column shows results without the liquidity instruments included. The second through fourth show results after adding the liquidity instruments.

The full sample test is a test of the "pure" RE-LCH. To accept the hypothesis, we should expect a B value close to 1 and A less than zero. Results from the standard list of instruments are shown in column 1. From these results, the data do not appear to fit the model well. The parameter estimates are questionable. For instance, A is positive for all estimates with the standard instrument list. This would be expected if liquidity constraints are present or if consumers are not life cycle savers.

Given more evidence against the model is the high X^2 value. Here, the degrees of freedom represents the number of overidentifying restrictions of the model. The p-value is the probability that a $X^2(DF)$ random variate is greater than the computed value of the test statistic under the hypothesis that the orthogonality conditions (8) hold. The p-value for the standard instrument list is below the 5 percent level.

As a further test for liquidity constraints, the standard instrument list is augmented by liquidity variables: irregular or transitory income (TYI) and normal income (NYI). These results are shown in columns 2, 3 and 4. The overidentifying restrictions reject the hypothesis that these variables are valid instruments, and hence, suggest that the liquidity variables and forecast errors are not orthogonal.

Given the "pure" RE-LCH has been rejected, the two subsamples are fitted to (8). For the liquid subsample, however, the overidentifying restrictions do not give strong evidence to accept the restrictions of (8). Moreover, the parameter estimate for A is questionable. For Table III, the nonliquid families produce parameter estimates that are not justifiable. There seems to be, however, a stronger influence on the liquidity variables in this subsample than the liquid subsample. Here the overidentifying restrictions are strongly rejected when liquidity variables are added to the instrument list.

Summary and Conclusion

Orthogonality conditions implied by the RE-LCH are tested by modeling a rational expectation model of intertemporal consumer behavior. Quarterly Consumer Expenditure Survey data are used to fit orthogonality conditions derived from a stochastic Euler equation. The results are not encouraging

Table 1
Full Sample of Families

	1	2	3	4
A Start value = -0.400	0.3397 (0.2111)	-0.1827* (0.0832)	-0.1647* (0.0829)	-0.1391* (0.0636)
B Start value = 0.999	0.9837** (0.0075)	0.9931** (0.0008)	0.9930** (0.0008)	0.9930** (0.0007)
Chi Square: Overidentifying restrictions	10.5933	63.9648	73.5915	93.7033
Degrees of freedom	4	3	3	2
p-value	0.0315	1.55E-9	1.55E-9	5.15E-18
Liquidity Instruments: NYI	None	TYI	NYI	TYI &
Chi Square: Exclusion restriction	-	53.3715	62.9982	83.1100
Degrees of freedom	-	1	1	2
p-value	-	1.55E-9	1.34E-6	8.97E-19

Table 2
Sample of Liquid Families

	1	2	3	4
A Start value = -0.400	0.1877 (0.1639)	-0.2158* (0.0920)	-0.2132* (0.0912)	-0.2157* (0.0919)
B Start value = 0.999	0.9885** (0.0055)	0.9964** (0.0015)	0.9964** (0.0919)	0.9964** (0.0015)
Chi Square: Overidentifying restrictions	13.1235	18.9509	19.2597	19.0632
Degrees of freedom	4	3	3	2
p-value	0.0107	0.0020	0.0017	0.0041
Liquidity Instruments:	None	TYI	NYI	TYI & NYI
Chi Square: Exclusion restriction	-	5.8274	6.1362	5.9397
Degrees of freedom	-	1	1	2
p-value	-	0.0158	0.0132	0.0513

Table 3
Sample of Non-Liquid Families

	1	2	3	4
A	0.6408	0.4616**	0.4412*	0.3061*
Start value = -0.400	(0.5379)	(0.0420)	(0.2146)	(0.0494)
B	0.9731**	0.9804**	0.9807**	0.9850**
Start value = 0.999	(0.0249)	(0.0016)	(0.0075)	(0.0014)
Chi Square: Overidentifying restrictions	1.4705	446.907	24.8426	260.9610
Degrees of freedom	4	3	3	2
p-value	0.8319	1.55E-9	0.0001	1.86E-53
Liquidity Instruments:	None	TYI	NYI	TYI & NYI
Chi Square: Exclusion restriction	-	445.4365	23.3721	259.4905
Degrees of freedom	-	1	1	2
p-value	-	1.55E-9	1.34E-6	4.49E-57

Standard errors are in parentheses under coefficients.
* and ** indicate significance at the 5 and 10 percent level, respectively.

for the "pure" RE-LCH or for the hypothesis when borrowing constraints are suspected. Because binding borrowing constraints may give a reason to reject the "pure" RE-LCH, the sample of families is split between likely liquid and nonliquid subsamples, and liquidity variables are tested for statistical significance. The model using data from the liquid subsample fits the model weakly. For the nonliquidity subsample, the hypothesis is strongly rejected. Because seasonality may have a strong influence for the quarter-to-quarter changes, future research will explore modeling seasonality directly into the Euler equation, and retesting the hypothesis.

References

Chamberlain, G. (1984). Panel Data. Handbook of Econometrics, 2. Elsevier Science Publishers.

Cumby, R.E., Huizinga, J., & Obstfeld, M. (1983). Two-Step Two-Stage Least Squares Estimation in Models with Rational Expectations. Journal of Econometrics, 21, 333-355.

Flemming, J.S. (1973). The Consumption Function when Capital Markets are Imperfect: the Permanent Income Hypothesis Reconsidered. **Oxford Economic Papers**, 25, 160-172.

Hall, R.E. (1978). Stochastic Implications of the Life Cycle-Permanent Income Hypothesis: Theory and Evidence. Journal of Political Economy, 86, 971-987.

Hansen, L.P. (1982). Large Sample Properties of Generalized Method of Moments Estimators. Econometrica, 50(4), 1029-54.

Hansen, L.P. & Singleton, K.J. (1982). Generalized Instrumental Variables Estimation of Nonlinear Rational Expectations Models. Econometrica, 50(5), 1269-86

Hayashi, F. (1985). The Permanent Income Hypothesis and Consumption Durability: Analysis Based on Japanese Panel Data. The Quarterly Journal of Economics, C(4), 1083-1113.

King, M. (1983). The Economics of Savings. National Bureau of Economic Research, Working Paper 1247.

Mankiw, N.G. (1981). The Permanent Income Hypothesis and the real Interest Rate. Economics Letter, 7, 307-311.

Newey, W.K. & West, K.D. (1987). A Simple Positive Semi-Definite, Heteroskedasticity, and Autocorrelation Consistent Covariance Matrix. Econometrica, 55(3), 707-708.

Runkle, D.E. (1991). Liquidity Constraints and the Permanent-income Hypothesis. Journal of Monetary Economics, 27, 73-98

U.S. Department of Commerce, Bureau of Economic Analysis. Personal Consumption Expenditures, Methodology Papers: U.S. National Income and Product Accounts, BEA-MP-6.

U.S. Department of Labor, Bureau of Labor Statistics. Consumer Expenditure Survey, Interview Survey, 1990.

Zeldes, S.P. (1989). Consumption and Liquidity Constraints: An Empirical Investigation. Journal of Political Economy, 97(2), 305-346.

Endnotes

1. This is, however, not the only type of constraint that a consumer may face. For example, low wealth or low income families may be permitted to borrow, but at a premium rate of interest. The literature refers to these as rate-differential constraints. These two rates converge as the premium on the rate differential approaches infinity. See Flemming (1973).

2. For this test, I use lagged income as the sole liquidity variable. Lagged income is contained within the information set. Note, however, that this is not true for the current period income.

3. See Hansen (1982) for a discussion on the overidentifying restriction tests used in this paper.

4. Seasonal movements in data are macro movements which in panel data may prevent the expectations error from having the property that it has mean zero. Consequently, implied orthogonality conditions may be violated unless the movements are purged or modeled. See Chamberlain (1984).

5. See Cumby, Huizinga, and Obstfeld (1983).

6. See Hansen and Singleton (1982) for a discussion of a GMM estimator.

7. See Hansen (1982) and Chamberlain (1984, 1987). To compute the weighting matrix, given the MA(1), I use the Newey-West method described in Newey and West (1987).

8. A further difficulty with aggregate data studies is the potential of aggregation bias. See King (1983).

9. Because medical expenditures are measured as net out-of-pocket costs, a consumer unit may have zero, or negative expenditures because medical expense reimbursements exceed all other expenditures.

10. Securities include stocks, non-government bonds, mutual funds and other such securities. This liquidity information is collected at the last interview. The respondent is asked to give the account and market values as of the last day of the previous month of interview.

11. Estimated marginal tax rates are provided by adjusted income level from the U.S. Treasury. These marginal tax rates account for filing status, number of exemptions, and average allowable deductions. They account for federal, state and local income tax rates. These rates are assumed constant across the four interview quarters.

12. The reference person is defined as the first member mentioned during the survey when asked to "Start with the name of the person who owns or rents the home."

Spending by Older Consumers:
a Comparison Between 1980 and 1990

Pamela B. Hitschler, Bureau of Labor Statistics[1]

Estimates of expenditure and income suggest that older Americans have benefited from higher preretirement and pension earnings than their 1980 counterparts. This is especially true of those aged 65 to 74 years.

As the century draws to an end, more attention is being focused on the aging of the Nation's population. Persons aged 65 years and older will comprise almost 14 percent of the U.S. population by 2010, and 22 percent by 2030.[1] Today, 1 in 8 consumer units has a household head aged 65 or older.[2] With such a large demographic shift, spending patterns in the economy will change. Over the last 10 years, the population aged 65 and older has grown by 22 percent, compared with 9 percent for those under age 65.[3] Among persons 65 and older, the rate of population increase rises with age. During the 1980's, the population aged 65 to 74 grew by 16 percent, while the numbers of persons aged 75 and older rose 31 percent.[4] The economic consequences of an aging population are being studied closely by economists, sociologists, and policymakers.

An earlier article in the Review, which examined the expenditures of older persons using 1984 data from the Bureau of Labor Statistics Consumer Expenditure Survey, reported distinct differences in spending patterns between persons aged 65 to 74 and those aged 75 and older.[5] In particular, differences were found in expenditures for housing, transportation, and health care. Differences also were found in income. This article updates estimates of expenditures and income for the same two age groups. Consumer units (or "households")[6] whose reference person (or "household head") is aged 65 to 74 are refereed to as the "younger group," while those with reference persons aged 75 and older are termed the "older group."

Table 1 Summarizes the differences in income and spending patterns of the two major subgroups of older Americans between 1980 and 1990. For both groups, the largest expenditures in both years were for housing, followed by food and transportation. (Unless otherwise indicated, all expenditure and income estimates presented in this article are in current dollars.) However, the younger group had higher total expenditures and income than the older group in both 1980 and 1990. Consumer units in the younger group spent, on average, a significantly larger amount on every major expenditure category except housing and health care in both years. They did not spend much more on housing than the older group in 1980, but did in 1990. However, they did spend less on health care. In addition, other important changes occurred in measures for transportation, Social Security and pensions, entertainment, and travel.

Expenditure trends

Housing

Older consumer units benefited from the pos-World War II building boom, during which demand was high, mortgages were obtainable at low interest rates, and tax incentives and other Federal policies designed to promote homeownership were in effect. During the 1960's and 1970's, the highest rate of increase in homeownership was among the group aged 45 through 64.[7] Mortgage interest rates hovered around 6 percent through the mid 1960's, remained below 9 percent until the late 1970's, and then rose sharply, reaching a high of 15 percent in 1982.[8] The low interest rates and home prices of the 1960's and 1970's are reflected in the currently large number of homeowners aged 65 and older who have paid off their mortgages (81 percent).

In the last 10 years, the homeownership rate has continued to increase among both the older and younger groups. It rose from 76 percent in 1980 to 82 percent in 1990 for the younger group, and from 66 percent to 72 percent for older households. As homeownership increased, so did the proportion of those homeowners aged 65 to 74 with mortgages--18 percent in 1980, compared with 27 percent in 1990. The proportion of those aged 75 and older with a mortgage was unchanged, at 8 percent, between 1980 and 1990. Consistent with higher rates of homeownership and higher interest rates are higher mortgage interest expenditures. The younger group spent 4 times more on mortgage interest in 1990 than they did in 1980, and the older group spend twice as much as in the earlier year. Even though mortgage interest payments have increased dramatically, particularly for the younger group, they are still a small proportion of the average

[1]Economist: This article is presented as it appears in Monthly Labor Review, May 1993.

Table 1
Income and expenditure share of the older population 1980 vs. 1990.
Consumer Expenditure Interview Survey.

	Age Group 65-74		t-share 90 vs 80	Age group 75 and older		t-share 90 vs 80
	1980	1990		1980	1990	
Income before taxes	$10,150	$21,501		$8,629	$15,435	
Total expenditures	$10,744	$20,386		$8,984	$15,082	
Shares of total expenditures:						
Food at home	17.5	13.8	-4.09*	16.8	13.7	-2.10*
Food away from home	4.5	4.5	-0.29	3.6	3.6	0.08
Housing	30.0	30.0	0.18	37.3	34.5	-0.83
Transportation	18.4	17.0	-1.02	11.5	14.0	1.10
Health care	8.4	10.0	3.06*	12.8	14.0	0.87
Entertainment	3.0	4.3	3.30*	1.8	2.6	2.34*
Reading	0.8	0.8	-0.88	0.8	0.7	-0.52
SSC, pensions	1.7	3.6	3.94*	0.8	0.9	0.32
Life insurance	1.4	1.7	1.22	0.9	0.9	-0.19
Apparel and services	4.2	3.7	-1.41	2.7	2.9	0.37
Other	10.2	10.3	0.49	11.0	12.2	1.81

NOTE: Asterisk denotes significance at the 95 percent confidence level

total housing budget because of the large number of older consumer units who won homes without mortgages. Utilities(30 percent), property taxes (13 percent), and maintenance, repairs, and insurance (11 percent) still consume the bulk of their housing budgets.

Another component of housing expenditures that grew substantially among the two groups is "other lodging." The younger group's expenditures on other lodging more than tripled since 1980; the older group's more than doubled. Other lodging includes two major components: owned second homes and out-of-town lodging, such as costs for hotels, motels, cottages, and so forth. Most of this increase is included in "lodging while out of town," the largest component of other lodging which will be discussed below under travel.

Health care
More of the total budget of those aged 65 and older now is consumed by out-of-pocket health care expenditures than was the case in the early 1980's. As health care costs rise, older persons are paying higher health plan premiums, deductibles, and copayments, and more older persons are buying commercial supplements to Medicare, which is causing a shift in health expenditure shares from medical services to health insurance for both age groups. Table 2 shows detailed out-of-pocket health care expenditures and shares for older households in 1980 and in 1990.

During the 1980's, out-of-pocket medical service expenditures increased 67 percent for the younger group, and the medical services component of the Consumer Price index for All Urban Consumers rose more than 115 percent.[9] However, while both the level of expenditures and the Consumer Price Index increased, the share of medical service

expenditures in the total health care budget dropped from 44 percent in 1980 to 31 percent in 1990 for those consumer units with heads aged 65 to 74, and from 56 percent to 32 percent for those in the older group.

Contributing to trends in medical costs were the large increases over the last decade in Medicare deductibles and copayments required for hospital stays of more than 60 days. Medicare inpatient hospital deductibles--the share of expenses that must be paid by the patient before Medicare payments kick in--rose from $180 in 1980 to $560 in 1990. Copayments are the share of hospital costs that must be born by the insured after the insurance program has begun to pay its share. These copayments for the 61st through the 90th days rose from $45 in 1980 to $148 in 1990; copayments after 90 days tripled as well.[10]

The seeming inconsistency of a large increase in price and a relatively small increase in out-of-pocket medical service expenditures in partially explained by the tripling of health insurance expenditures by consumers: the increase in Medicare deductibles and copayments, and the general rise in cost for medical services have served as an impetus to acquire more comprehensive health insurance coverage to supplement Medicare. Having more health insurance, covering a wider range of health care needs, reduces out-of-pocket medical service expenditures. Health insurance as a share of total health expenditures expanded from 37 percent in 1980 to 48 percent in 1990 for the younger group, and from 26 percent to 45 percent for the older group.

While increased expenditures for health insurance premiums are seen for all age groups in

Table 2.
Health expenditures by age 1980 and 1990. Consumer Expenditure Interview Survey.

| | Age Group | | | | | |
| | 1980 | | | 1990 | | |
Item	65 and older	65-74	75 and older	65 and older	65-74	75 and older
Total Health Care Expenditures	$992	$899	$1,152	$2,109	$2,102	$2,118
Medical services	487	393	647	663	656	674
Health insurance, total	320	333	298	900	1,014	960
Prescription drugs[1]	145	138	161	395	372	424
Medical supplies	39	35	46	61	60	61
Share of health budget:						
Medical services	49.0	43.7	56.2	31.4	31.2	31.8
Health insurance, total	32.3	37.0	25.9	46.9	48.1	45.3
HMOs, Blue Cross\Blue Shield	9.4	11.0	7.3	13.5	12.8	14.3
Commercial health insurance	7.8	9.1	6.0	7.8	8.8	6.5
Medicare payments	11.4	12.6	9.9	16.5	16.6	16.3
Commercial supplements to						
Medicare, other health insurance	3.7	4.4	2.8	9.2	10.0	8.2
Prescription drugs[1]	14.8	15.4	14.0	18.7	17.6	20.0
Medical supplies	3.9	3.9	4.0	2.9	2.9	2.9

NOTE: Asterisk denotes significance at the 95 percent confidence level
[1] Includes prescription drugs and nonprescription drugs.

the population over the 1980-90 period, they are most dramatic for those over 65. In large part, the greater expenditures indicate an increase in participation in commercial health insurance plans. The proportion of households age 65 to 74 reporting expenditures for commercial supplements to Medicare doubled, from 12 percent in 1980 to 23 percent in 1'990; a similar rise is seen for the older group as well.[11] Another reason why health insurance accounts for a growing portion of the health care budget involves rising premiums for the Government's Medicare Supplementary Medical Insurance for Medicare participants: monthly premiums for this insurance tripled over the decade, from $9.60 per individual in 1980 to $28.60 in 1990.

Transportation

While the share of expenditures accounted for by transportation did not change significantly over the 1980's, more older consumer units owned an automobile in 1990 than in 1980. The percentage of consumer units who owned an automobile increased from 79 percent in 1980 to 87 percent in 1990 for the younger group, and from 55 percent to 67 percent for older households. As a consequence, the share of the transportation budget devoted to vehicle finance charges and insurance increased significantly.

The share attributable to gasoline expenditures declined substantially, in part due to falling oil prices, while the level of such expenditures remained virtually unchanged. In 1980, oil prices were high after the 1979-80 oil shock, but in 1982, the price of gasoline began to decline as the oil supply situation eased. It was not until 1990 that the price of gasoline reached a

level above that of 1980. As measured by the Consumer Price Index for All Urban Consumers, the price of gasoline rose 24 percent from 1980 to 1990.

Retirement, pensions, and Social Security

Share of total expenditures for retirement funds changed significantly for the younger group over the 1980-90 period. (See table 1.) Social Security taxes, the largest component of retirement expenditures, more than tripled for the younger households, rising from $149 in 1980 to $463 in 1990. (Because the older group has fewer earners, they are less affected by changes in Social Security tax rates.) The Social Security tax on wage and salary workers rose from 6.1 percent in 1980 to 7.7 percent in 1990, and that for self-employed persons, from 8 percent to over 15 percent. At the same time, the earnings base to which the Social Security tax is applied was raised from $25,900 to $51,300. Of course, while some of the increase in retirement expenditures is accounted for by changes in Social Security regulations, another contributing factor is higher earnings, which will be discussed in the section below on income.

The second largest component of pensions and Social Security comprises IRA's and Keogh fund contributions, reflecting the readier availability of the plans and the tax advantages of IRA's, which were introduced into the tax code in 1981. Expenditures for tax-deferred saving plans increased from an average of $14 in 1980 to $211 in 1990 for households aged 65 to 74. The percent of consumer units in this age group reporting IRA and Keogh fund expenditures rose from percent to 12 percent over the same period.

Table 3.
Entertainment and travel expenditures by age in 1980 and 1990.   Consumer Expenditure Survey

Item	1980		1990	
	65-74	75 & older	65-74	75 & older
Entertainment, total	$340	$168	$874	$393
Fees and admissions	130	57	330	153
TVs, radios, and				
sound equipment	116	75	316	160
Other entertainment	94	36	229	79
Travel, total	417	235	854	435
Food on trips	114	58	245	120
Lodging on trips	89	62	253	131
Transportation on trips	214	115	356	202
Gasoline	93	34	100	42
Airfare	78	61	175	107
Intercity bus fare	14	5	19	15
Other	29	15	52	38

Entertainment

Both the younger and older group spent a significantly larger share of total expenditures on entertainment in 1990 than they did in 1980 (table 1). Some of this change is due to an increase in fees and admissions expenditures, and part is due to increased TV, radio, and sound equipment expenditures. TV, radio, and sound equipment expenditures tripled for the younger group and more than doubled for the older group (see table 3). The percent of consumer units reporting TV, radio and sound equipment expenditures increased from 30 to 61 percent for the younger group and from 24 to 43 percent for the older group. A large part of this increase is accounted for by a rise in cable TV expenditures. The average annual expenditure for cable TV increased from $20 to $148 for the younger group and from $18 to $91 for the older group. Three times as many of the younger households and twice as many of the older households reported this expenditure in 1990 as in 1980. These increases follow a national trend reflecting the proliferation of home entertainment centers, other sources of entertainment, and the rising cost of cable services.

Travel

Travel expenditures more than doubled from 1980 to 1990 for the younger group and nearly doubled for the older group. Even so expenditures for both groups increased in part due to cheaper airfares due to the deregulation of the airline industry and with cheaper gasoline due to lower oil prices. The components included in travel expenditures are food, lodging, transportation, and entertainment expenditures for out of town trips.[12] Table 3 shows the travel expenditure levels, for 1980 and 1990 for the younger and older age groups. For both age groups and in all categories (food, lodging, and transportation, and entertainment) there were increased expenditures and number of CU's reporting expenditures.

Food expenditures while on out-of-town trips

increased at a slightly faster rate as total trip expenditures for both groups. As a share of the total food away from home, food on trips increased slightly for both groups.[13] Explaining much of this rise is the 5 to 6 percentage point increase in percent of consumer units reporting for both groups, the younger rising from 26 percent to 31 percent and the older from 13 percent to 19 percent.

Lodging expenditures while out-of-town rose as well, although as a share of the total travel budget, they grew more for the younger group (21 percent in 1980 to 30 percent in 1990) than for the older group (26 percent in 1980 to 29 percent in 1990). These increases can be attributed to the increases in the percent of consumer units in these age groups reporting lodging while out-of-town; an increase from 13 to 18 percent for the younger group and from 6 to 10 percent for the older group from 1980 to 1990.

Over the same period, transportation expenditures for travel rose 66 percent for the younger group and 76 percent for the older group. The subcomponents of transportation expenditures on trips included travel fares, vehicle rental, and gasoline. Over the 1980s, travel by air was stimulated by special fares and inducements following the federal deregulation of the airline industry in 1978. Average expenditures on airline fares rose 68 percent for all consumer units, and the age 65 to 74 group showed the largest percentage increase, as airfare expenditures rose 124 percent over the period. The older group's airfare expenditures rose 75 percent. Explaining much of this rise in average expenditure is that more older people (those 65 and over) are traveling via airplane. Both groups, the younger and older, reported similar rises in the percent reporting airline expenditures. In 1980, 5 percent of the younger group and 4 percent of the older group reported airline expenditures but in 1990 these figures rose to 8 percent and 5 percent, respectively.

Over the same period, gasoline expenditures on trips remained almost the same in part due to falling oil prices. Indicating an increase in travel by car, is the rise in percent of consumer units reporting gasoline expenditures on trips. The percent reporting gasoline expenditures for trips increased 2 percentage points for both the younger and the older group (27 percent to 29 percent for the former and 14 percent to 16 percent for the latter).

Income

Changes in expenditures reflect changes in income. The average income for families with reference persons aged 65 or older rose doubled during the 1980's. But his figure masks the diversity of income patterns that exists within the older population. The heterogeneity of the group becomes particularly apparent when one looks at

Table 4.
Income share 1980 vs. 1990. Consumer Expenditure Interview Survey.

	1980			1990		
	Age 65 and older	65-74	75 and older	65 and older	65-74	75 and older
Income before taxes.............$ 9615		$10150	$8629	$18842	$21501	$15465
Share of income:						
Wages and salaries.................18.8		22.8	10.2	18.9	25.3	7.3
Self-employment income..............4.9		5.8	2.9	3.4	4.5	1.4
Social Security railroad retirement income.................42.8		41.2	46.3	44.0	38.2	54.3
Pensions and annuities............13.9		14.6	12.5	17.8	18.4	16.7
Interest and dividends............15.4		11.6	23.7	13.5	11.2	17.6
Other income.......................4.1		4.0	4.4	2.5	2.4	2.6

income sources, levels, shares, and poverty rates. The younger group's income rose faster, increasing 112 percent (in 1990 dollars), versus 79 percent for the older group. (See table 4.) In 1980, the younger group's average income was 18 percent higher than that of the older group, but by 1990, the younger group's income was 39 percent higher. The larger increase in come among the younger households is accounted for by the fact that their lifetime earnings and contributions to Social Security and government or private pensions are greater than those of their older counterparts.[14]

Social Security remained a less important source of income for the younger group than for the older group over the study period. As a proportion of total income, Social Security income decreased for the younger group (41 to 38 percent), and increased for the older group (46 to 54 percent) between 1980 and 1990. However, the current-dollar level of Social Security income increased 96 percent for older households, a substantial rise for both groups, and well above the 58-percent increase in the Consumer Price Index. And, more consumer units from each group reported receiving Social Security income: for the younger group, the percent reporting such income rose from 90 percent in 1980 to 94 percent in 1990, while that for older households was up from 93 percent to 97 percent. This increase could be accounted for by the long-term trend toward earlier retirement, which continued throughout the 1980's for men. Civilian labor force participation rates fell from 19 percent in 1980[15] to 16 percent in 1990 percent[16] for men aged 65 and older.

Wages and salaries remain the second largest source of income for those aged 65 to 74. Wages and salaries more than doubled for the younger group over the 1980-90 timespan, while increasing almost one-third for the older group and a little over two-thirds for all other age groups. For the younger group of persons 65 and older, the proportion of income derived from wages and salaries rose from just under 23 percent in 1980 to slightly over 25 percent in 1990, while the corresponding ratio for the older group decreased from 10 percent to 7 percent. The changes can be accounted for by trends in the number of earners

per consumer unit, specifically, an increase in the number of earners per household in the younger group, from 0.5 to 0.6, compared with a decrease of from 0.3 to 0.2 earners for older households. Additionally, while civilian labor force participation rates fell for older men, those for older women actually rose. The rate of increase in labor force participation among women aged 65 to 74 could account for the rise in the average number of earners per consumer unit in the younger group.[17]

For the older group, a higher percentage of whom are retired, private pensions and annuities remain the second largest source of income. However, pensions and annuities were a more important source of income for both age groups in 1990 than in 1980. Such income rose 167 percent for the younger group and 139 percent for the older group over the study period. As a proportion of total income, pensions and annuities grew from 15 percent in 1980 to 18 percent in 1990 for the younger group, and from 13 percent to nearly 17 percent for older households. Explaining much of this pattern of rise is an increase in the percent of consumer units reporting pensions and annuities: the percent doing so increased faster for the younger consumer units than for the older ones. The share of the younger group reporting such income grew from 35 percent in 1980 to 47 percent in 1990, while the corresponding measure for the older group rose from 29 percent to 40 percent. This phenomenon reflects the increased availability of private retirement funds and tax advantages of certain types of funds, from which the younger group have had more opportunity to benefit than have the older group.

Income from interest and dividends followed a pattern that differed from that of pensions and annuities. The level of income derived from interest and dividends doubled for the younger group, and increased by one-third for the older group over the period 1980-90. However, the share of total income derived from interest and dividends fell from 12 to 11 percent for the younger group and from 24 to 18 percent for older households. The percent of consumer units reporting such income also declined--from 47 to 45 percent for the younger group and from 45 to 43 percent for the older group.

As with income, there are large differences in poverty rates between the age groups. For those aged 65 to 74, the poverty rate fell from 13 percent in 1980 to 10 percent in 1990. For those aged 75 and older the poverty rate fell from 20 percent in 1980 to 16 percent in 1990. The following tabulation shows poverty rates of older persons in 1990 by age:[18]

	1980	1990
Age	Percent in poverty	
Under 65 years	12.3	13.0
65 years and older	15.7	12.2
65 to 74 years	13.1	.9
75 and older	20.1	16.0

The dramatic differences in poverty rates among the groups is partially accounted for by factors such as number and sex of earners in the household. Older groups are characterized by fewer earners and more women. Both men and women have longer life expectancies than they did in 1980, part of a long-term trend explained by improvements in medicine and technology. At 65 years, the average life expectancy was 16.4 years in 1980 and 17.2 years in 1990. But women still outlive men. At age 65, a woman's average life expectancy exceeds a man's by 4 years. Women over the age of 65, who grew up during an era in which fewer women worked outside the home, are less likely to have access to pension and Social Security income in their own names. However, with the increase in the number of women who have entered the labor force over the last 20 years, it is more likely that women over 65 will be entitled to their own pension and social security income in the future.

Conclusion

These findings tend to support the assertions of other analysts that we are seeing a "golden age of the golden year,"[19] in that persons aged 65 years and older have higher expenditures and income than they did 10 years ago. Over the 1980's, the two older groups studies here more or less followed the same trends in terms of home-and vehicle ownership and health, pension, and travel expenditures. The continuing availability of data from the Consumer Expenditure Survey will allow us to follow the economic activities of older person in the future.

Endnotes

1. Gregory Spencer, Projections of Population of U.S., by Sex, Age and Race 1980 to 2080, Current Population Reports, Series P-25, No. 1018. (Bureau of Census, January 1989).
2. Cynthia Taeuber, Sixty-five Plus in American, Current Population Reports, Special Studies P23-178 (Bureau of the Census, 1992).
3. Ibid.
4. Ibid. The population aged 75 to 84 grew by 30 percent. The cohort aged 80 and older grew by 33 percent.
5. Beth Harrison, "Spending patterns of older persons revealed in expenditure survey," Monthly Labor Review, October 1986, pp. 15-17.
6. A consumer unit is either (1) all members of a household who are related by blood, marriage, adoption, or other legal arrangements; (2) two or more persons living together who pool their income to make joint expenditure decisions; or (3) a person living alone or sharing a household with others, or living as a roomer in a private home or lodging house or in permanent living quarters in a hotel or motel, but who is financially independent. A person is considered financially independent if he or she provides the income for at least two of the three major living expenses--food, clothing, and shelter. The terms consumer unit and household are used interchangeably throughout this article.
7. Louise B. Russell, The Baby Boom Generation and the Economy(Washington, The Brookings Institute, 1982), p. 13.
8. Economic Report of the President(Government Printing Office, 1992), table B-69.
9. The health care component of expenditures was unusually large for households headed by persons 75 and older in 1980 due to a few large medical service expenditures. Average medical service expenditures for those 75 and older were $487 in 1981 and $447 in 1982. In 1981, total health care expenditures for those 75 and older was $1,037; health insurance was $388; 47 percent of total health care expenditures went to medical services, and 32 percent to health insurance.
10. Social Security Bulletin, Annual Statistical Supplement, 1991.
11. These estimates are presented at a quarterly rate.
12. See Geoffrey Paulin, "Consumer expenditures on travel, 1980-87," Monthly Labor Review, June 1990, pp. 56-60, for more information on travel expenditures.
13. Food away from home includes meals at restaurants, board, catered affairs, school lunches, and meals as pay.
14. Michael Hurd, "The Economic Status of the Elderly," Science, vol. 244(1989), p. 659.
15. Handbook of Labor Statistics, Bulletin 2340 (Bureau of Labor Statistics, August 1989.
16. Employment and Earnings, January 1991, p. 164.
17. See Murray Gendell and Jacob S. Siegel, "Trends in retirement age by sex, 1950-2005." Monthly labor Review, July, 1992, pp. 22, for a more detailed discussion of these findings.
18. Bureau of the Census "Single Years of Age-Poverty Status in 1990," Table 23, March 1991; and Bureau of the Census, "Single Years of Age - All Persons and Related Children Under 18 by Low-Income Status," Table S-1, March 1981. Unpublished data.
19. See Mark Weinstein, "The Changing Picture in Retiree Economics," Statistical Bulletin (Metropolitan Life Insurance), July-September 988, p. 7.

A Five City Audit of Claims on Product Labels: Study Rationale and Design

Robert N. Mayer, University of Utah[1]
Debra L. Scammon, University of Utah[2]

When the FTC issued its Guides on Environmental Marketing in July, 1992, the Commission called for the Guides to be evaluated in three years. This paper briefly overviews the key features of the Guides and then presents a general rationale and method for evaluating the impact of the Guides. It describes the first phase of a three-year longitudinal study of environmental marketing practices in which environmental claims will be audited in 16 product categories across five geographically distinct markets.

Introduction

In July, 1992, just over a year after it held public hearings on environmental marketing, the U.S. Federal Trade Commission (FTC) issued Guidelines for Environmental Marketing Claims (FTC 1992). Issuance of these Guides quieted but did not eliminate (Fahnline 1992) the call from national marketers for federal guidance on the use of environmental claims, guidance many hoped would preempt state regulations. Their issuance has, however, spurred interest in observing how marketers, and ultimately consumers, respond to environmental claims under these guidelines.

Although the FTC Guides do not have the force of law, the agency hopes that the Guides will provide helpful direction to marketers who have argued that, without some instructions on how and how not to make environmental claims, they will cease making such claims altogether. The trade press has cited opinions and statistics suggesting that the use of environmental claims by consumer goods marketers may be declining (Dagnoli 1992; Lawrence 1992; Reitman 1992). It is not clear, though, whether any decline is attributable to firms' uncertainty over acceptable ways in which to make environmental claims. An equally likely culprit would be the nation's economic recession and its effect on consumer willingness to pay extra for brands/products positioned based on their environmental appeal.

Even with the issuance of the FTC Guides, the regulatory environment for environmental claims remains complex. The FTC Guides are only one of several sets of environmental guidelines covering domestic and/or international marketing. The most notable and stringent of these are statutes passed in the nation's two most populous states, California and New York. In addition, specific claims have frequently been challenged by the state attorneys general and the New York City Department of Consumer Affairs.

The response of firms to the FTC Guides must also be placed in economic as well as regulatory contexts. Quite apart from the effects of a lingering recession, firms making environmental claims do so in an increasingly competitive environment. According to Marketing Intelligence Service (1991), the percentage of new products making "green promises" (referring to either the human body or the environment) increased steadily from 1.1% in 1986 to 13.4% in 1991. Perhaps most vexing to firms wishing to capitalize on the environmental attributes of their products is the gap between the public's stated concern for the environment and its purchase, use and disposition behaviors.

To systematically assess the changing marketplace for brands with environmental appeal, this study provides a baseline audit of current environmental marketing practices. Despite its limitations as a strict form of policy evaluation, the study is intended to be useful in assessing the impact of the FTC Guides and the need for and/or desirability of additional federal action in the area of environmental marketing.

The paper proceeds as follows. We begin by outlining the major provisions of the FTC Guides and highlighting some of the issues in which the FTC is likely to be interested as it evaluates the impact the Guides have on industry practice. Since the Guides could have the effect of shifting the types of claims made, we consider both claims for which the FTC Guides provide guidance and those for which they do not. This is an important component in assessing whether additional action by the FTC may be necessary and/or desirable. In the next section, we discuss our research design for conducting an audit of current (and future) marketing practices in the area of environmental marketing claims. We address the need for and

[1]Professor and Department Chair,
Department of Family and Consumer Studies

[2]Professor and Associate Dean,
College of Business

problems with impact evaluation of the FTC Guides in the context of a marketplace with other rules governing environmental marketing as well as the difficulty of defining what constitutes an environmental claim. Our audit covers five diverse market areas and a set of sixteen non-durable consumer products. We conclude by indicating areas in which we anticipate finding the greatest amount of change between the baseline audit and subsequent audits in the frequency, content, and format of environmental claims.

Content of the Guides

With nearly two decades of experience in case-by-case investigation of the use of environmental claims, insights provided by a host of industry and advocacy groups, and testimony presented at two hearings on environmental marketing (the FTC's hearing in July, 1991 and the EPA's hearing in November, 1991), the FTC chose to issue voluntary guidelines as a means of codifying its interpretations of the laws administered by the FTC as they relate to environmental marketing claims. In so doing, the Commission attempted to strike a balance among various viewpoints. At one extreme, parties asserted that existing laws and regulations covering deceptive advertising were quite sufficient for regulating environmental claims. At the other extreme, the FTC was urged to establish standardized definitions and performance standards for environmental claims.

The overarching theme of the FTC Guides was that sellers are free to say whatever they want as long as their claims are clear, specific, appropriately qualified, and substantiated by competent and reliable scientific evidence. The Guides offer both general and specific guidance, point out the concerns as to potential for deception, and provide examples of what is and what is not acceptable under the Guides.

The examples of acceptable uses of claims are meant to provide a "safe harbor" to sellers who might hesitate in making environmental claims without some assurance that what they do will not be challenged by the FTC. The FTC provides even more security for sellers by assuring them that the examples included in the Guides are not the only permissible uses and qualifications of claims. The hope of the Commission is that the Guides will ease sellers' doubts about their ability to make appropriate environmental claims and, at the same time, provide protection to consumers from those claims most likely to be deceptive and/or misleading.

The general principles expressed in the Guides are: (1) qualifications and disclosures should be sufficiently clear to prevent deception and prominently displayed, (2) claims should specify whether the benefit is for the product or the package, (3) claimed benefits should not be overstated nor should claims imply a benefit if it is only negligible, and (4) comparisons between products should be clear and substantiable. Of these principles, only the second is unique to environmental claims, since it is rare that benefits are claimed for a product's package and even rarer that these benefits would be confused with benefits derived from a product itself.

The Guides follow these general principles with guidance for three types of claims: general environmental benefit claims; claims including several solid waste management terms (degradability, compostability, recyclability, recycled content, source reduction, refillability); and claims regarding impact on the ozone. The Guides do not provide precise definitions of these terms but instead encourage sellers to qualify their claims so that they are accurate given the particular circumstances. Thus, the Guides do not set any minimum standard for the percent of recycled material required before a product can claim to be made from recycled material. They merely require that if such a claim is made, that it be accompanied with a qualification stating the percentage of recycled material contained in the product.

Evaluation Issues

There are a number of questions in which the FTC is likely to be interested as they decide how well their Guides are working over time. At least five specific trends in the marketplace will be relevant in an impact evaluation.

Frequency and Types of Claims. A basic question of concern to the FTC is the frequency with which environmental claims are made. The Guides are designed to encourage claims, so it is important to determine whether claims are increasing or decreasing overall and how this might vary by types of claims. Because the use of various claims may be affected by local or state rules as well as by national guidelines like the FTC Guides, monitoring trends across different market areas will help determine which "level" of guidance is driving actual marketplace practices with regard to environmental claims.

There are a large number of environmental claims that could be made for various brands. Claims that refer exclusively to the impact of a product, package, or production process on the natural environment are of the most relevance in assessing the impact of the Guides. These include claims referring to recyclability, recycled content, degradability, solid waste reduction, and ozone depletion.

Trends in how various types of claim are used as well as shifts from one type of claim to another (e.g., plastic trash bags may shift their claims from "recyclable" claims to "made from recycled material" claims) will be important to identify. For recyclability claims, how "qualified" are claims with respect to the feasibility of recycling in various locations and the overall rate of recycling? How are the mobius loop, SPI code, and other symbols used in claims?

For recycled content claims, to what extent are specific percentages of recycled material given? Is pre-consumer content distinguished from post-consumer content? How frequently is the mobius loop displayed? For degradability claims, given the uncertainty about and manufacturers' lack of control over disposal methods, do manufacturers make claims regarding the degradability of their product/packaging? For ozone claims, do manufacturers who use volatile organic components as propellants continue to use "no CFCs" claims?

Variance Among Claims. Independent of questions about specific types of claims, the degree of heterogeneity among claims made within a given product class will be important to track. If, for example, claims become more homogeneous within product classes this may suggest that they provide less information to consumers (at least with regard to differences between brands). The FTC might then decide that such claims should be avoided because they are not based upon brand uniqueness.

Use of Environmental Seals of Approval. Over the next several years the use of environmental certifications (e.g., Green Cross and Green Seal) is likely to increase as the organizations sponsoring the environmental seals become better established and their methods of and criteria for testing products are further refined. It will be important to monitor how such certifications are used and how, if at all, they are qualified.

Implied Claims. There are a number of ways in which implied claims may be made. For example, environmental terms may be used in brand names (e.g, "Green" or "Nature"), environmental symbols may be used on packages (e.g., trees or globes), and sellers may make exhortations for consumers to take environmental action (e.g., "please recycle"). It will be especially interesting to track the frequency and nature of implied environmental claims since the FTC guidelines mention implied claims but offer few examples for their proper use. Firms may choose to avoid the more regulated area of explicit claims in favor of the less regulated area of implied claims.

In summary, with regard to the content of claims, impact evaluations of the FTC Guides should allow for assessment of the frequency with which various types of claims are made, variance among claims within a specific product class, and the ways in which claims are presented. Evaluations should allow for assessment of both claims covered by the Guides and related claims that are not covered by the Guides. We turn now to a fuller discussion of our evaluation approach.

Research Design

Evaluation Approach

The FTC, at the time of issuing its voluntary guidelines, stated that it would review their effectiveness after three years. There are many possible ways by which the Commission might evaluate the Guides, for example, maintaining records of how often firms need further guidance from the FTC or asking firms to comment on their experience with the Guides. The Commission might also conduct surveys of consumer confidence in and propensity to use environmental claims. We choose to focus, however, on trends in the frequency, content, and format of actual claims as they appear on product labels.

Regardless of the criterion selected, the Guides ideally would be judged in terms of their independent impact on the prevalence and quality of environmental claims, but this is not likely to be possible given the number of other potential influences acting simultaneously with the Guides (e.g., state laws). Nevertheless, evidence of the possible impact of the Guides can be collected and should be as systematic as possible. (See Gray-Lee, Scammon, and Mayer, 1993, for a comparison of the various laws, regulations, and guidelines pertaining to environmental claims.)

Trends in the use of environmental claims have been monitored by the Marketing Intelligence Service since 1986 using the Productscan data base of new product introductions. The major advantage of this data base is that it is national in scope and covers a wide variety of non-durable consumer goods. One of its major disadvantages (besides not being available to academic researchers on limited budgets) is that it is confined to new product introductions. Focusing only on new product introductions may hide minor product modifications as well as changes in claims made during a product's life cycle. For example, the initiation of campaigns will be observable, but it is unclear whether deletion or substitution of claims will be detectable. Additionally, there is some ambiguity regarding how "new" products are defined for inclusion in this data base.

A further problem with the Productscan data is that environmental claims have been defined differently over the years and include claims that might more properly be defined as health claims. In addition, the Productscan data base places claims into a few broad categories (e.g., toxicity; recyclability; recycled content) and does not contain information on the exact wording and placement of an environmental claim.

The evaluation approach we chose was to monitor changes at six-month intervals in the frequency, content, and format of environmental claims. The method used was in-store audits of one large, high volume supermarket in each of five strategically selected locations across the United States--New York City, Champaign-Urbana in Illinois, Salt Lake City, San Diego, and Corvallis, Oregon. Rather than conduct a comprehensive audit of all products available in all five stores (which would have been beyond our resources), we chose to collect data on all brands within sixteen product categories. Specific product classes were selected for inclusion in the study to ensure a reasonable number of claims covering a variety of environmental attributes of products and packages. An additional consideration was including brands marketed at both the national and regional level to account for the possible effects of state-level regulation of claims. The specific product classes and the rationale for their selection are described below.

The study design has the advantage of being based on the actual behavior of firms--both national and regional--operating under a variety of legal and regulatory environments. It also has the advantage of including data collected on a regular basis throughout the post-Guides period. (Ideally, we would have collected data before the Guides were issued, but the FTC had the temerity to issue the Guides without any warning and, worse during our summer vacations.)

The study has obvious limitations as a "true" evaluation study, that is, there is no way to attribute any changes in the frequency, content, or format of environmental claims to the FTC Guides. If some type of "improvement" is observed, it could be attributable to any number of other factors (e.g., motivation of individual firms; growing public interest in environmental claims; court cases involving misleading claims; competing guidelines and laws issued by state, national, and international bodies; long range impact of other government actions regulating environmental claims). If negative change is observed, it could be because of the Guides, or it might be argued that the change would have been even more negative in the absence of the Guides. Nevertheless, this type of "before"-after design can lend credence to certain assessments of the Guides' impact and cast doubt on others (Phillips and Calder 1979).

Further complications might arise from the product life cycle (i.e., history) of various brands. Specifically, some brands might be introduced and others withdrawn during the study period, thereby complicating the task of assessing trends in the use of environmental claims. Despite these problems, the auditing of actual claims made by firms, on a broad geographical and product class basis, seems an appropriate way of assessing the impact of the FTC Guides. And regardless of the ability to strictly evaluate the impact of the FTC Guides, our approach enables one to see what is actually happening in the marketplace and thereby determine whether additional regulatory or self-regulatory action is warranted.

Selection of Product Classes
The main criterion for selecting product classes for inclusion in the study was the likelihood of their making environmental claims covering a variety of environmental attributes of products and packages. In making these selections, we also tried to achieve a balance between product classes where virtually all brands are sold on a

national basis and product classes in which regional and local brands are available. The latter product classes were included in the hope of tapping any state-specific influences on environmental claims. Finally, we did not confine our list of product classes to those in which claims are currently found, for this would blind us to the possibility of manufacturers beginning to make claims in a particular product class. We therefore included three product classes where environmental claims are not yet found but are conceivable in the near future: multi-course TV dinners, plastic soda bottles, and milk containers (plastic and cardboard).

The sixteen product classes were non-durable goods in both the food and non-food categories. (Of course, environmental claims can appear on durable goods as well.) Figure 1 shows the product classes chosen and the major environmental claim(s) they were intended to represent for products and/or packages. We did not attempt to include all potential environmental claims (e.g., compostability; safety for landfill or incineration; preservation of endangered species and locations) in our audit. We opted instead for a few of the most prominent and unambiguous (in terms of their reference to an environmental benefit).

Auditing Procedures and Timing
The auditing procedure was developed to take advantage of the fact that many products are sold on a national basis. Because of this, Salt Lake City was designated "home base" for the study. This meant that the most exhaustive auditing occurred there. The home base auditors recorded (a) which brands were sold and (b) what environmental claims were made, if any, and how. For brands carried both in the home base and at one of the four remote sites, auditors in the remote sites merely noted whether the brand was carried. By doing so, the study assumes national uniformity in the claims being made for nationally distributed brands at a given point in time. (In fact, we uncovered a few discrepancies across study sites as firms were in the process of introducing or modifying environmental claims.) If an auditor at a remote site found a brand not carried in the home base, s/he recorded full information on its environmental claims. Full information consisted of both the content as well as the placement and format of the claims.

After conducting a pretest, a set of instructions was developed for recording the content and prominence of environmental claims. Four of the five audits were conducted during the last week of September and the first week of October, 1992. (The Corvallis audit occurred during the last week of October.) Future rounds of audits will occur at six month intervals. The data collection is being supervised by the authors, Jason-Gray Lee (doctoral student, University of Utah), Brenda Cude (University of Illinois), and James McAlexander (Oregon State University).

Definition of an Environmental Claim

What does and does not constitute an environmental claim on a product label or container? An environmental claim is a voluntary statement on the part of a seller that links (explicitly or by implication) a firm or its products to the well-being of the natural environment. Of greatest interest in this study are claims that characterize the relationship between one or more of a brand's attributes and the well-being of the natural environment. The relevant attribute(s) may refer to the qualities of the product, its packaging, or both. The relevant attribute may involve the presence of a positive feature or the absence of a negative feature. The environmental attribute may refer to the production, distribution, use, or disposition of the product, or at several points in this "economic chain" (Iyer and Banerjee 1992). In terms of its format, the claim may consist solely of text, solely of graphic symbols, or a combination of both.

It might be asked, "Which aspects of the natural environment are relevant to an environmental claim?" The Marketing Intelligence Service, in constructing its Productscan data base, includes claims that mix consumer health and environmental well-being (e.g., no pesticides, organically grown). Similarly, one might consider the claim that brands are "cruelty free" (i.e., involve no animal testing) to refer to the natural environment when, in fact, this brand attribute has little direct relevance to the natural environment. A third problematic type of claim involves energy saving claims, since these may attract buyers independent of any environmental benefit. In this study, product classes were selected to avoid these ambiguous cases. That is, products involving fruits, vegetables, and unprocessed grains were avoided, as were personal care products (e.g., shampoos) and electric appliances.

In addition to claims that refer to a brand's attributes, our definition of an environmental claim also encompasses statements that refer in a more general or indirect way to a firm's environmental commitment. One example might be a statement that a firm contributes 10% of its profits to environmental organizations. Or a label might contain the statement, "We care about the environment."

The thorniest aspect of this broad definition of an environmental claim has to do with implied claims. Several aspects of a brand's packaging and promotion might potentially be construed as environmental claims by at least some consumers. Consider these examples: (1) a brand name containing words like "Green," "Eco," or "Nature"; (2) packages with symbols like a globe or a tree; (3) packages bearing environmental seals of approval like the Green Cross or endorsements like "approved by the Sierra Club"; and (4) statements that it is technologically feasible to do something without a definitive statement that the company is

doing so (e.g., "The technology is currently available to include recycled plastic in soft drink bottles at levels between 25% and 35%."). In all four of these examples, consumers might infer despite the absence of an affirmative claim regarding a product attribute that the brand has certain attributes that are better for (or less damaging to) the environment.

More complicated examples also exist. Think of exhortations to take environmental action, like "please recycle" or "support recycling in your community." Some consumers will no doubt interpret these statements as implying that the brand at hand is itself recyclable; if so, these statements constitute implied claim about brand attributes. Other consumers will interpret these statements as vague expressions of environmental concern on the part of the manufacturer. The links between exposure to these claims and reasons for subsequent consumer behavior are difficult to establish, but they leave open the possibility of implied claims that influence consumer choice.

Consider one final illustration. Suppose a manufacturer provides general environmental information on its package, that is, information with no obvious connection to the brand's attributes. For example, a cereal manufacturer might place the following message on the outside of its package: "Did you know that you use six gallons of water each time you flush the toilet? So flush the toilet only when necessary." By offering this information, the firm is implying (to some consumers, at least) that it is concerned about the natural environment and that this concern is reflected in other aspects of corporate behavior. The latter implication is crucial in creating a perceived link between a firm and the well-being of the natural environment.

Our study is not designed to sort out these questions of consumer perception. Instead, we record any information on a brand's label that might be considered an environmental claim by a reasonable number of consumers--with a few exceptions. First, some beverage containers bear the message that a refund is available in specific states for returning the container. These refunds are generally based on a state-mandated deposit, and notification on the container is generally a matter of law. Hence, we do not consider the message that a refund is available to be an environmental claim in these cases because it lacks the volitional nature of a claim.

Second, many plastic products bear a special code developed by the Society of the Plastics Industry to assist in the separation of plastic for recycling. In cases where state laws require manufacturers to place the codes on their plastic containers, use of the recycling code lacks the volitional character of an environmental claim. Moreover, the behavior of most manufacturers suggests that they do not intend consumers to see the recycling codes, placing them on the bottoms of

Figure 1: Product Classes Studies and Environmental Claims Anticipated for Product and/or Package

PRODUCT	Recyclability	Recycled Content	Degradability	Solid Waste	Ozone	Toxicity
SHAVING CREAM (aerosols)					Package	
DEODERANTS (sprays & pumps)					Package	
TAMPONS (but not pads)		Package				
LAUNDRY DETERGENTS (boxes & plastic bottles)	Package	Package	Product	Package		
LIQUID DISH DETERGENT (plastic bottles)	Package	Package	Product	Package		
FABRIC SOFTENER (refills only)				Package		
PLASTIC TRASH BAGS (kitchen)		Product	Product			
TOILET PAPER		Product				
BATTERIES (size AA)						Product
DISPOSABLE DIAPERS (smallest size diaper)		Product	Product			
JUICES (all except large cans)	Package	Package				
FRESH MILK (cardboard & plastic containers)	Package	Package				
COFFEE FILTERS (cone & basket)		Package				
SODA BOTTLES (plastic)	Package	Package				
FROZEN TV DINNERS (multi-course)	Package	Package				
COLD CEREALS		Package				

containers and merely pressing the code into the plastic without any color differentiation. However, to the extent that manufacturers highlight the codes to increase their visibility to consumers (e.g., place them somewhere other than on the bottom of a plastic container and print them in a color different from the background against which they appears), then we consider the SPI recycling code to be an environmental claim. (This coding decision is consistent with the position taken in the FTC Guides.)

Defining what constitutes an environmental claim is one of the most challenging aspects of this research project. We have adopted a broad definition. Having gathered data based on a broad definition, we can always narrow our definition later if public policy indicates, for example, that implied claims should be treated differently than explicit claims.

Initial Findings

To this point, data have been collected for the baseline audit only. We will eventually provide specific results both within and across the sixteen product classes studied. For instance, of the recycled content claims audited, what percentage provide exact percentages of recycled content and what percentage distinguish between pre- and post-consumer waste? As another example, what percentage of the recyclability claims refer to the feasibility of recycling in the local market where the product was purchased?

We are still in the process of combining and verifying the data obtained in our five research sites. Nevertheless, we have already uncovered a number of claims that are clearly consistent with the FTC Guides as well as some that are not. For example, Final Touch Fabric Softener Refill makes the following: "The Final Touch Refill contains less packaging material than regular Final Touch." While this statement may sound unremarkable by itself, it is superior to that of its competitors Downy and Rinse 'n Soft, neither of which provide a firm basis of comparison for their claims. Ultra Downy Refill makes the claims: "REDUCE Solid Waste in the Environment" and "REUSE your Ultra Downy bottle again and again." Rinse 'n Soft makes the label statement: "Better for Environment--Less Packaging to Throw Away." Less than what? Similarly, both Oxydol and Purex laundry detergents make the claim on their box that "This product requires less energy to produce and deliver." Less energy than what: its previous formulation, competitors, conventional formulations, 1 cup usage detergents? Several other brands in this product class make a similar claim but clarify the basis of comparison.

Another major source of variation has to do with whether claims differentiate pre-consumer and post-consumer recycled content. Recycle 1 plastic trash bags bear the Green Cross seal of approval along with the explanation that the bags consist of

at least 70% recycled plastic. Referring to this recycled content, the package also makes the following informative disclosure: "Not less than 11% is POST-CONSUMER recycled plastic; the remainder is from industrial plastics that would otherwise be landfilled or incinerated. We do not include our own manufacturing scrap in these claims." This level of explanation contrasts with its competitor Renew, which also has the Green Cross on its package, but fails to mention whether its recycled content contains any post-consumer plastic.

For sheer educational value, Rainforest Crisp breakfast cereal deserves mention for its environmental claims. Rainforest Crisp, both through its name and supporting label information, claims to help save the world's rainforests. This goal is accomplished in several ways. First, the nuts in the cereal are purchased from Cultural Survival, a non-profit human rights organization which helps forest residents increase their income by selling shelled rather than unprocessed nuts. The increased revenues are intended to make the trees of the rainforest too valuable to cut down. Second, the makers of Rainforest Crisp "pay a 5% environmental premium over the market price for nuts which helps Cultural Survival continue their good work." Third, at least 7% of the cereal manufacturer's net profits are contributed to ecological causes. In addition to these claims, the cereal box also explains the rationale for saving the rainforests and how to obtain additional information about this important issue. (The cereal's box is also described as recyclable and made of recycled material.)

On the negative side, some claims seem inconsistent with the FTC's directive to "avoid implications of environmental benefits if the benefit is in fact negligible." Consider the case of Glad trash bags. The front, back, and bottom of the Glad package announce "Now with StressFlex II Formula." By reading the package more closely, we learn more about StressFlex II:

> This product is made with a specially formulated plastic which requires less material and provides the same strength as our previous product. GLAD estimates that plastic trash bags account for only about 0.5% of waste in landfills. This product, with less material, will reduce the 0.5% by approximately 2%. Although very small, this reduction is a continuing effort on the part of GLAD to help reduce solid waste.

In other words, if all trash bag manufacturers switched over to StressFlex II, the waste in landfills would be reduced by 0.01%, that is, a one hundredth of one percent. Yes, this reduction would be "very small."

Conclusion

If the FTC is to have a reasonable evaluation of the impact of its Guides three years hence, it is important that the groundwork be laid now for monitoring changes in the ways in which environmental claims are used by sellers. Our data offer several advantages for an impact evaluation. While not covering all product classes, our study includes many of the most important in the area of environmental claims. It provides data from a sample of markets selected to tap the variety of state and local rules that appear to be more stringent that the FTC Guides and thus ultimately may drive marketing practices in the area of environmental claims. Probably the greatest strength of our data is the fact that it contains verbatium records of claims as well as observational data on placement and prominence of claims. With these data we will be able to analyze the frequency of various types of environmental claims within each of our sixteen product classes.

We noted that detection of trends in the use of environmental claims would only be feasible if both claims covered in the Guides and claims not included in the Guides were monitored. In our selection of product classes, we have not focused on all the of the specific claims covered by the Guides (e.g., compostablility) nor all claims that might be considered "environmental claims" (e.g., preservation of endangered species and locations) in our audit. Nor have we deliberated included certain seller statements that combine environmental claims with nutrition claims (e.g., pesticide free) or with money-saving claims (e.g., saves on electricity bills)--although we have recorded such claims when they were observed. We have, however, included observational data on implied claims which are not covered in the Guides. Thus, we will be able to detect any shifts from "covered" claims to those not mentioned in the Guides should such changes occur.

Data from our baseline observations suggest that there are a number of current practices that are not in compliance with the Guides. Most notable is the lack of clarification and specification of terms. Seldom did we find recycled content claims that included specification of the amount of recycled material contained in the product. Rarely did we observe recyclability claims that cautioned consumers that recycling was only possible where facilities exist. We also found general claims that did not specify whether the benefit touted was for the product or its package, and we found claims of "No CFC's" on products that contained other potentially damaging propellants.

Although our analysis is not yet complete, our initial conclusion is that marketers will have to make some changes in their claims and, in the process, show their true environmental colors. We plan to be out there watching the shades of green change.

References

Dagnoli, Judann (1992). Green ads wilt: NAD chief. Advertising Age, 63 (January 6), 4.

Fahnline, Kathy (1992). Telephone conversation regarding petitions and comments submitted to the FTC in response to its Guides for the Use of Environmental Marketing Claims, November 7.

Federal Trade Commission (1991). Public Hearings, Proposed Rule: FTC Petitions for Environmental Marketing and Advertising Guides; Public Hearings. Federal Register, 56 (105, May 31), 24968-82.

Federal Trade Commission (1992). Guides for the Use of Environmental Claims, Washington, D.C., July 28.

Gray-Lee, Jason, Debra L. Scammon, & Robert N. Mayer (1993), A guiding light: Illuminating the green marketing guides. Paper to be presented at the 1993 Marketing and Public Policy Conference.

Green, Mark (1991). Recyclable...or just fraudulent? New York Times, April 21, p. F11.

Iyer, Easwar and Bobby Banerjee (1992). Anatomy of green advertising. Paper presented at the annual meetings of the Association for Consumer Research, Vancouver, British Columbia, October 8-11.

Lawrence, Jennifer (1992). Marketers drop 'recycled.' Advertising Age, 63 (March 9), 1.

Marketing Intelligence Service (1991). The recession Is having a mixed impact on new products. Press release, Naples, New York, December 18.

Mayer, Robert N., Debra L. Scammon, & Cathleen D. Zick (1992), Turning the competition green: The regulation of environmental claims. In Paul N. Bloom & Richard G. Starr, Jr. (Eds.), Proceedings of the 1992 Marketing and Public Policy Conference, Washington, D.C., May 15-16, 152-165.

Phillips, Lynn W. & Bobby J. Calder (1979). Evaluating consumer protection programs: Part I. Weak but commonly used research designs. Journal of Consumer Affairs, 13 (Winter), 157-185.

Reitman, Valerie (1992). Green product sales seem to be wilting. Wall Street Journal, May 18.

The Federal Trade Commission's Environmental Marketing Guidelines: An Academic's Perspective

Brenda J. Cude, University of Illinois at Urbana-Champaign[1]

The Federal Trade Commission issued guidelines for environmental marketing claims in July 1992. This paper reviews some of the history preceding the issuance of the Guides as well as the Guides themselves and offers the perspective of an academic involved in the deliberations leading up to the Guides.

In the last few years, environmental marketing issues have captured the attention of consumers, industry, and government regulators. Much of the activity has focused on environmental marketing claims. Surveys show that consumers increasingly notice such claims but tend to mistrust them (Roper Organization, 1990). As manufacturers continue to reevaluate product and package design with the environment in mind, the number of environmental marketing claims increases each year (Green MarketAlert, 1991). Regulators at all levels have jumped into the fray, proposing and enacting legislation designed to curb the confusion and deception that some environmental claims have generated.

Therefore, environmental marketing claims are an important consumer issue. This paper will examine that issue, primarily focusing on the Federal Trade Commission (FTC) Environmental Marketing Guides issued last year. As background, the first section of the paper reviews some of the regulatory efforts that preceded the issuance of the FTC Guides. The second section outlines the Guides and assesses their potential effectiveness. The final section of the paper offers the personal perspectives of an academic who was involved in the proceedings that culminated in the issuance of the Guides.

Regulation of Environmental Marketing Claims

The increased attention of marketers to environmental issues has meant that consumers have been exposed to a variety of unfamiliar and often ambiguous terms. Biodegradable, compostable, environmentally safe, and the many other environmental claims now relatively common in the market are new to most consumers. At best, many of these claims have no clear meaning and are subject to interpretation; at worst, they are potentially deceptive or misleading. Most consumers lack the scientific background to understand many environmental issues and few have relevant previous experience to guide them in assessing the relative environmental merits of marketplace alternatives. Gray-Lee, Scammon, and Mayer (1993) also note that environmental claims are likely to confuse or mislead consumers because they tend to be credence claims, refer to aspects of the product which are only indirectly associated with the actual use of the product, and are often dependent upon events or situations beyond the control of sellers. As Gray-Lee, et al. correctly note, many consumers cannot evaluate the environmental characteristics of a product before, during, or after using it because they lack the expertise or the means. For example, how could a consumer independently determine if a product were biodegradable? Consumers also find some environmental qualities difficult to assess because they occur before they buy the product (in manufacture, for example) or after disposal. Finally, some environmental claims depend on the actions of others; for example, whether or not a material is recyclable depends, in part, on the existence of a local infrastructure to collect and market recyclable materials. Thus, the potential for consumer fraud and deception in environmental marketing claims is great.

The potentially fraudulent nature of environmental marketing claims has made them a target for the attention of regulators at a variety of levels. Local, state, and federal regulations related to environmental claims have been proposed and enacted both in the U.S. and internationally. In the U.S., numerous states have proposed and at least six have passed legislation defining one or more terms related to environmental claims (Hayes & Woo, 1992). California and New York have been particularly aggressive in regulating environmental marketing. Since 1989, a task force of U.S. Attorneys General has studied environmental advertising claims. The task force has held public forums and issued two reports. In Spring 1990, the National Association of Attorneys General adopted a resolution that called on the federal government to work with the states to develop uniform national standards for environmental advertising (National Association of Attorneys General, 1991). At the regional level, the Northeast Recycling Council, an organization comprised of state environmental officials from ten northeastern states, has developed consensus guidelines for the use of selected claims in environmental labeling (U.S. EPA, 1991).

The Federal Trade Commission (FTC) held hearings in July 1991 to seek guidance as to its

---

[1]Associate Professor, Division of Consumer Sciences

role in regulating environmental claims (FTC, 1991). In July 1992, the agency issued voluntary guidelines (FTC, 1992).

The Environmental Protection Agency (EPA) held hearings in November 1991 and proposed voluntary guidelines on use of the terms recycled and recyclable (U.S. EPA, 1991). However, the EPA's position was primarily advisory to the FTC; EPA has not taken independent regulatory action concerning environmental marketing claims.

Companies that market goods internationally must also be aware of economic regulations in other countries. Those include Canada's Environmental Choice labeling requirements and the International Chamber of Commerce's Environmental Advertising Code (ICC, 1991).

The FTC's Guides for the Use of Environmental Marketing Claims

The FTC's Guides for the Use of Environmental Marketing Claims (FTC, 1992) specifically address the application of Section 5 of the FTC Act to environmental marketing and advertising practices. They are voluntary guidelines and do not have the force or effect of law. However, many expect that most manufacturers will take them seriously (Consumers Digest, 1992).

The Guides apply to advertising, labeling, and other forms of marketing to consumers but do not preempt state or local laws or regulations. The Guides describe various claims, noting those that should be avoided because they are likely to be misleading. They also illustrate the types of qualifying statements that could be added to claims to avoid consumer deception. The claims are followed by illustrative examples. The Guides outline principles that apply to all environmental claims and address the use of eight commonly-used environmental claims. A summary follows.

General Principles
1. Qualifications and disclosures should be sufficiently clear and prominent to prevent deception.

2. An environmental marketing claim should be presented in a way that makes clear whether the environmental benefit refers to the product, package, or both. For example, a claim need not be qualified if an incidental part (such as a bottle cap) is not recyclable while the bottle is.

3. An environmental marketing claim should not be presented in a way that overstates the environmental attribute or benefit. One example in the Guides suggests that labeling a trash bag intended for the landfill as degradable is deceptive because it conveys a benefit when none exists.

4. Environmental marketing claims that include a comparative statement should be presented in a way that makes the basis for comparison clear.

Environmental Marketing Claims
1. It is deceptive to misrepresent that a product or package offers a general environmental benefit. Examples of general claims likely to be considered deceptive include a brand name like "Eco-Safe," a package labeled "environmentally friendly," and a pump spray product that contains chemicals contributing to smog but is labeled "environmentally safe."

2. It is deceptive to misrepresent that a product or package is degradable, biodegradable, or photodegradable. Claims should be substantiated with scientific evidence that the entire product or package will completely break down and return to nature. An example in the Guides of a claim likely to be deceptive is a trash bag that is customarily incinerated or landfilled but claims degradability.

3. It is deceptive to misrepresent that a product or package is compostable. Claims should be qualified if municipal composting facilities are generally not available where the package is sold or the claim misleads consumers about the environmental benefits if the product is not composted. The Guides also suggest qualifying a claim that might mislead consumers to believe the package can be safely composted at home when it cannot.

4. It is deceptive to misrepresent that a product or package is recyclable. Claims should be qualified to the extent necessary to avoid consumer deception about availability of recycling programs and collection sites. The FTC suggests qualifications such as "Check to see if recycling facilities exist in your area" or stating the approximate percentage of communities or the population to whom the programs are available.

5. A recycled content claim may be made only for materials that have been recovered or otherwise diverted from the solid waste stream, either during the manufacturing process (pre-consumer) or after consumer use (post-consumer). To claim pre-consumer content, the manufacturer or advertiser must have substantiation for concluding that the pre-consumer material would otherwise have entered the solid waste stream.

6. It is deceptive to misrepresent that a product or package has been reduced or is lower in weight, volume, or toxicity. Source reduction claims should be qualified to the extent necessary to avoid consumer deception.

7. It is deceptive to misrepresent that a package is refillable. One example in the Guides describes as deceptive a claim about a

container that can be refilled but the manufacturer has no collection program for the container. The other example, a claim that a bottle is a "handy refillable container," is not deceptive because the consumer can purchase a larger container from which to refill the smaller container.

8. It is deceptive to misrepresent that a product is safe for or "friendly" to the ozone layer. A claim that a product does not harm the ozone layer is deceptive if the product contains an ozone-depleting substance.

Likely Impact of the FTC Guides

Janet Steiger, FTC Chairman, stated when she announced the FTC Guides that "Our goal is to protect consumers and to bolster their confidence in environmental claims, and to reduce consumers' uncertainty about which claims might lead to FTC law-enforcement actions, thereby encouraging marketers to produce and promote products that are less harmful to the environment" (FTC News, 1992). Did the FTC achieve that goal?

Response to the Guides has been mixed. Few industry representatives have publicly criticized the Guides even though they failed to achieve one important industry objective-- alleviating the problems created by trying to conform to a patchwork of local and state laws and regulations. Gray-Lee, et al. (1993) compared the Guides to six other environmental guidelines: California's Public Law 17508.5, New York's state statute 6NYCRR Part 368, the recommendations for action included in the state attorneys general's Green Report II, the EPA's proposed guidelines for use of the terms recycled and recyclable and the recycling emblem, the Canadian Environmental Choice guidelines for environmental labeling, and the International Chamber of Commerce's Environmental Advertising Code. The authors note the following about the FTC Guides:

1. They tend to "rely on the argument that the environment will benefit from truthful claims which promote competition with respect to the environmental attributes of brands." This is in contrast to some other guides which are "more direct in their advocacy of improving the environment," by, for example, specifying a minimum recycled content as required to make a recycled content claim.

2. The FTC Guides recognize and are meant to apply to both explicit and implicit references; they are not primarily definitional in nature as are some other guides nor are they limited to explicit claims. The Guides apply to both advertising and labeling; other guides refer only indirectly to labeling.

3. The FTC Guides are quite specific in stating how claims should be presented, requiring, for example, that qualifications should appear in close proximity to the claims they modify and in comparatively consistent type size with the claim.

In summary, Gray-Lee, et al. (1993) conclude that the FTC Guides are "relatively lenient and focused primarily on protecting consumers and ensuring fairness among competitors." Compared to other guidelines, the FTC Guides place less priority on environmental protection, are less likely to set stringent definitions and standards for terms or to ban terms, and as a result offer marketers a "fair amount of leeway in their environmental marketing claims, relying predominantly on affirmative disclosure to ensure clarity of claims." The Guides encourage the use of important and relevant claims, allowing marketers to use most environmental claims that are factually true as long as they also present appropriate disclaimers and qualifiers.

Gray-Lee, et al. (1993) also note some inconsistencies in the Guides. For example, the Guides rely on manufacturers to clarify some claims (recycled content and recyclable) while suggesting the use of common sense standards for others (degradable and compostable).

Richard Denison (personal correspondence, September 1992), a senior scientist with the Environmental Defense Fund (EDF), has also given the Guides a mixed review. While the EDF publicly applauded the FTC for issuing industry guides, it also urged Congress and the EPA to adopt regulatory definitions and standards for terms used in such claims (EDF, n.d.). Denison provided three examples of deceptive claims one could still see under the FTC Guides.

1. A product that is recycled at a national rate of only 1% would be allowed to carry a claim that it is "recyclable" as long as the recycling rate is disclosed.

2. A product made of organic materials would be allowed to carry the claim: "Compostable where municipal solid waste composting facilities exist. There are currently 20 such programs across the country."

3. A product that has been demonstrated to completely break down in a reasonable time after customary disposal could be labeled "degradable," even if it contains a toxic heavy metal pigment that is released upon degradation.

Personal Observations from an Academic

I was personally involved in several dimensions of the activities surrounding the development of the FTC Guides; I talked with FTC staff persons on numerous occasions prior to the FTC hearings, collected data from consumer surveys which were summarized and submitted to the FTC, presented both oral and written testimony to the

EPA, and was frequently interviewed by media once the Guides were issued. What follows are some reflections on the process. The reader should note that they are based on only one experience and discount their generalizability accordingly.

1. **To be involved in policy-making, one has to be able to act quickly.** I learned in February 1991 that the FTC, EPA, and U.S. Office of Consumer Affairs (USOCA) planned to hold hearings on environmental marketing. My initial inquiries to learn the specifics were primarily motivated by an interest in attending the hearings. I contacted all three offices and after much persistent effort finally located two staff members at the FTC who were interested in talking with me. While they didn't have any details about the upcoming hearings, they did have a strong interest in consumer data related to the many questions they had about how "real people" respond to certain types of claims. I had several conference calls with Kathy and Carolyn and they wrote me long, detailed letters outlining their questions about consumer perceptions and why the questions were important. I began to consider the possibility that I might be able to answer some of those questions and proceeded to make plans to collect data through a network of University of Illinois Cooperative Extension professionals. The data collection began in May. The first official details about hearings on environmental marketing were in the Federal Register notice (published May 31, 1991) which announced that comments were due to the FTC by July 17, the hearings were scheduled for July 17 and 18, and those intending to testify were required to notify the FTC by June 20 and submit a copy of the oral testimony of July 12. I was shocked by the short turnaround time. If I had waited for the Federal Register notice, I would have had one month to design a survey instrument, collect and analyze data, and write my oral testimony. I would have had another two weeks to put the finishing touches on a written comment. By beginning data collection prior to the publication of the notice, I ran the risk that my surveys would not correspond to all of the questions or the most important questions identified in the notice. The surveys didn't cover all of the terms identified in the Federal Register notice; however, the additional month for data collection and analysis was a worthwhile trade-off. In hindsight, I believe that my written comment would have been read and considered by FTC staff even if I hadn't submitted it until after the hearings, but I can't be certain of that.

Acting quickly also has costs. To collect and analyze data quickly, one may find it necessary to take shortcuts that may make the research less publishable. And, a quick turnaround time offers little opportunity for the type of reflective thinking that could be valuable when your testimony will be distributed widely.

2. **You can make an impact by submitting only written testimony, if you have information of interest to the agency.** The FTC staff advised me that attending the hearings to testify orally was not required to ensure that my comments would be considered by the staff in their deliberations. And, I am convinced that was true. I didn't attend the hearings but I received numerous phone calls from the FTC staff following the hearings. Most of the calls were wanting more specific information about survey results.

    I did attend the EPA hearings and testified there. I have no sound basis for believing that anyone at EPA ever read my written comments.

3. **Presenting oral testimony may or may not be worthwhile if your goal is increased visibility for your research.** Providing oral testimony was an interesting experience but not without drawbacks. Each person who requested the opportunity to testify was given that chance. The two days of hearings were simply divided up to give everyone an opportunity to make their statements. That meant that each of us had no more than six minutes to comment, a very short time for such a complex subject. Following our comments, the members of the task force (representatives of the FTC, EPA, and USOCA) had the opportunity to ask questions. However, they often asked questions of only the last one to two persons who had testified in that panel.

    Testifying was a sobering experience. My written comments were duplicated and distributed to anyone who entered the room. Forty-three people testified--4 state officials, 26 representatives of trade associations, 8 companies' representatives, 3 representatives of public interest groups (Environmental Defense Fund, National Resources Defense Council, and Recycling Advisory Council), 1 recycling coordinator, and me--the sole voice for the consumer and consumer education. Before the hearings, I could not fathom why some individuals were there to testify--the International Association of Wiping Cloth Manufacturers, for example. After the hearings, I could not imagine how the EPA could ever devise definitional guidelines for recycled and recyclable that would be accepted by even a fraction of those testifying (they didn't).

4. **Attending hearings and presenting oral testimony can be a valuable way to learn more about an issue.** Government agencies are generally unable or unwilling to reimburse the

costs that are associated with collecting data and traveling to Washington, D.C. to testify. Fortunately, my university was willing to support me financially. And, the benefits of participation were many. Because I used the Cooperative Extension network to collect data, we were able to share with people who completed surveys that their responses would be used directly to impact policy. Their excitement that someone finally wanted to know what they thought was contagious. Attending the hearings was like taking an intensive short course on the topic. All (or most) perspectives were represented in the two days of the hearings. Others testifying as well as agency staff were very accessible, so the merits of various viewpoints could easily be discussed with others over lunch or during coffee breaks. Testifying at the hearings also provided the news angle that is often required to get media interested in your research.

References

Consumers Digest. (1992, January/February). Recycled or recyclable?, pp. 10, 12.

Environmental Defense Fund (EDF). (n.d.). EDF applauds issuance of guides on environmental claims by FTC but says regulatory standards must follow from Congress and EPA [News release].

Federal Trade Commission (FTC). (1991, May 31). Petitions for environmental marketing and advertising guides; public hearings; proposed rule. Federal Register, pp. 24968-24982.

Federal Trade Commission (FTC). (1992, August 13). Guides for the use of environmental marketing claims. Federal Register, pp. 36363-36369.

FTC News. (1992, July 28). FTC Chairman Steiger announces national guidelines to prevent misleading environmental marketing claims [News release].

Gray-Lee, J., Scammon, D.L., & Mayer, R.N. (1993, May). A guiding light: Illuminating the green marketing guidelines. Paper presented at the Public Policy and Marketing Conference, East Lansing, Mich.

Green MarketAlert. (1991, January). The majors march into green (ed-up) products, pp. 3-5.

Hayes, A.S. & Woo, J. (1992, February 24). "Green marketing" labeling law piques food industry coalition. The Wall Street Journal, p. B6.

International Chamber of Commerce's Commission on Marketing-Advertising and Distribution (ICC). (1991). Code on Environmental Advertising.

National Association of Attorneys General. (1991,

May). The Green Report II: Recommendations for Responsible Environmental Advertising. Madison, Wis.: State of Wisconsin Department of Justice.

Roper Organization Inc. (1990, July). The Environment: Public Attitudes and Individual Behavior. Racine, Wis.: Author.

U.S. Environmental Protection Agency (EPA). (1991, October 2). Guidance for the use of the terms 'recycled' and 'recyclable' and the recycling emblem in environmental marketing claims; notice of public meeting. Federal Register, pp. 49992-50000.

Improving Basic Taxpayer Literacy
(Workshop Summary)

Jane Schuchardt, U.S. Department of Agriculture[1]
John Clow, State University of New York[2]
Maureen Shaffer, Internal Revenue Service[3]

To improve basic taxpayer literacy, the Internal Revenue Service (IRS) has funded the development of a new adult learner curriculum called Taxes and You. The purpose of the workshop is to introduce consumer educators to this new resource.

The Challenge

Many people, especially young adults who are relatively new to the federal income tax system, pay more taxes than necessary. They misunderstand the tax laws, fail to organize financial records, don't know the difference between legal tax avoidance and illegal tax evasion, and think receipt of a hefty tax refund is good money management.

All too often, paying taxes is viewed only as an April 15th crisis. People fear an audit, worry they did not keep proper records or made mistakes, and brace themselves for owing far more taxes than expected. Understanding how legal tax avoidance, not to be confused with illegal tax evasion, can save tax dollars is basic financial management literacy for all Americans. Education is always more cost effective than ignorance for individuals, families, communities, and our Nation.

The Response

The Internal Revenue Service (IRS) is strongly committed to taxpayer education. Understanding of federal tax laws leads to compliance and reduces the need for tax collection enforcement.

Every State, plus Guam and Puerto Rico, has at least one IRS Taxpayer Education Coordinator. Often these educators are available by phone toll-free. They also are receptive and eager to partner with other educational organizations concerned with improving basic taxpayer literacy.

Many high school educators have used the IRS curriculum Understanding Taxes. The purpose of this educational tool is increase understanding among youth about taxpayer responsibilities, tax forms, how taxes evolve, the impact of taxes, and fairness issues related to taxation.

After experiencing success with this curriculum, the IRS questioned what was needed at the post-secondary level. Specifically, could the high school curriculum be adapted for use with other audiences, what was the extent of taxpayer education currently underway with post-secondary students, and what are the taxpayer educational needs of these students?

With IRS funding, the Joint Council on Economic Education (JCEE) studied these questions via survey in the late 1980s. Findings confirmed the need for a taxpayer education curriculum for post-secondary audiences, especially first-time taxpayers.

In early 1991, the JCEE had convened a design team of educators representing community colleges, business proprietary schools, and the Cooperative Extension System. This group conceptualized the materials, provided technical expertise as needed, and enlisted staff from respective constituency groups to act as reviewers.

The Results

The educational materials, named Taxes and You, and produced by the JCEE and the Agency for Instructional Television, Bloomington, IN, began taking shape. In mid-1991, representatives from each of the constituency groups met for review of the materials. By mid 1992, pilot testing was well underway. Availability of these new tools, all free, is scheduled for mid-summer 1993.

Taxes and You teaches adults how to pay only what they owe. The instructor's resource package includes video programs, a student manual, software tutorials, instructor's guides, and a public information folder to advertise the course.

The software is ideal for use with class lectures or as an independent student tutorial. Updated materials will automatically be sent each year to teachers who ordered the original materials.

[1]National Program Leader,
 Extension Service

[2]Professor of Business Education

[3]"Taxes and You" Project Officer

Taxes and You has two modules. "Economics of Taxation" paints the big picture of how taxes affect people and the economy. Key components are:

- shifting resources to government while affecting economic behavior;

- progressive, regressive, and proportional taxes; and

- criteria for determining tax fairness.

A second module, "Becoming Tax Wise," relates interpreting and preparing tax forms to personal financial management. It explores:

- tax avoidance and sufficient withholding;

- record keeping; and

- tax adjustments, exemptions, deductions, and credits.

Strategies

As the panel interacted with participants, the key point was to use the Taxes and You beyond the traditional classroom. For example, National Coalition for Consumer Education State Coordinators might collaborate with community groups to use the curriculum in non-formal educational settings.

Current International Consumer Issues

Margaret A. Charters, Syracuse University[1]
Jane Kolodinsky, University of Vermont[2]
Carol B. Meeks, University of Georgia[3]
Richard Vosberg, University of Guelph[4]

This panel might well be sub-titled "ACCI Members Abroad" with a focus this year on European visits. The four panelists presented perspectives from visits to the U.K., Germany, Norway and Hungary. The UN and IOCU updates on issues are given by Nancy Hawkins and Robert Kerton. Their reports follow this summary. Ben Beauharnais, a senior Consumer Studies major from Syracuse University, represented American students abroad in a report on his semester in London with S.U.'s Department of International Studies Abroad. This included an internship with The Consumer Association focusing on green marketing. The first 1993 issue of the ACCI International Committee Newsletter was distributed at the session.

Richard Vosberg

Dick Vosberg reflected the perspective of all the panelists with his introductory reminder that a brief visit does not provide for more than impression about the country visited. This is not to put down the value of the impressions or to suggest that he panelists don't know much more than they knew before, but that there is much more to know about the many agencies and organizations involved in various aspects of the marketplace in these countries.

In his report on the State of Affairs in Britain, he observed that British consumer policy, particularly related to the EC, reflects cultural attitudes, current national concerns and some universal interests. He continued noting some lessons to be learned. First, there is some questioning of whether Britain is really part of Europe which colors the U.K. perspective on the EC. Clearly, this ambivalence makes it hard to decide what stand Britain should take on various issues affecting more than the marketplace. The British have a pride in institutions that have done well for centuries and served as the foundation for many other countries. I suspect that this underlying and proper respect for the past may make for some reticence toward change.

Secondly, there is so much bad news from the monarchy to the masses that consumer issues are often shoved out of direct, major concern by people in general and politicians in particular.

Thirdly, my observation (happily supported by senior people at the National Consumer Council and the Consumers' Association, and student experience doing projects for CA) is that the number of consumer agencies is bordering on dysfunctional. For example, there are 157 members of the consumer congress, a collection of "organizations in the consumer movement in the U.K." not including county or regional bodies who are not members. This means it is hard to get a unified agenda. It also means that there are many variations or conflicting views for each topic area or issue. Co-ordination is attempted informally and, thus, is dependent in all the personal, historical, and political influences that go with such relationships.

Common Concerns With Regional Markets

The U.K. is no different than other developed countries entering regional trade agreements. Three traditional consumer affairs functions attract particular attention. Standards are regularly noted concerns, particularly when the British standard is higher than the exporting country standard. The rationale of whatever is acceptable in one country is acceptable in all is problematic. Major consumer education is the least that may be required. Secondly, the availability of information, either on labels or in some other readily accessible form, is a concern. Again, consumer education seems to least of the policy moves that will be required. Finally, redress is seen as potentially inadequate. Language, distance and regulatory differences complicate this area of consumer affairs.

[1]Associate Professor, Director,
   Consumer Studies Program

[2]Assistant Professor, Merchandising,
   Consumer Studies and Design

[3]Professor and Head,
   Housing and Consumer Economics

[4]Professor, Consumer Studies

Two Specific Issues That Strike a Responsive Note to Canadians

Matters related to advertising provide examples of the concern for control outside the U.K. In the first case, pornography beamed into the U.K. shows that regional openness can acerbate what technology creates, namely cross jurisdictional marketing and delivery issues. Coping with a ban on tobacco advertising in the EC calls attention to the problem of rules set outside "our country". Finally, there was concern about the use of quality marks in advertising. The view was that, with more openness, there will be more marks, more claims, and fewer real benefits to consumers due to uncertainty, confusion and the need to learn lessons avoided when there was only one set of marks to learn.

Matters that tie the marketplace to the quality of life, E.G. social support programs or regional development were major concerns. Consumer organizations generally have supported more free trade as a means to lower prices greater choice. The competition that is involved can lead to regional dislocation and changes in the social support systems for a particular quality of life. In recent months, the closing of many mines and the restructuring of the health care system, while perhaps on the national agenda for other reasons, were regarded as linked in part to pressures to be competitive.

So What?

We in North America can learn form the longer and, in some ways, more complicated experience of the EC. For example, it is important to note that labor, small and large business and other special interests are more likely to express themselves early in the process. Consumer matters seem to be taken up much later. Secondly, the resolution of regional consumer difference is more difficult than some other issues in that consumer and lifestyle issues are so intertwined. Some concerns only reflect a simple resistance to change. However, the more legitimate concerns may be for the loss of a decade or more of work by the consumer movement.

Jane Kolodinsky

Jane Kolodinsky next reported on her visit to Germany.

The 17th annual International Federation of Home Economics Congress was held in Hannover, Germany, July 26-31, 1992. Over sixty countries were represented, and several members of ACCI attended and presented papers. The theme of the Congress was "Focusing on Families and Households: Change and Exchange." Two publications resulted: "Abstracts of the Research Presentation at the 17th World Congress of IFHE," and "Families in Transition," Nancy Liedenfrost, editor. These publications are already in print. A third publication has resulted from a pre-conference workshop, "Youth and Households: Options for the Future."

Several of the presentations at the workshop would be of interest to ACCI members: Time Use, Biotechnology, issues of the elderly; housing and technology, health care policy, home based business, consumer influences on business and industry, and research methods. In fact, many of the presentations in these areas could have been easily modified to fit in our own ACCI program, for many of the same topic areas have been focused on at this year's meetings. And, while some of the topics required some broadening to fit within the scope of ACCI, others made the transition easily. For example, one researcher working in Pau Pau New Guinea found that marketers were able to convince native persons that "tinned" fish was better than that caught in the sea.

The meetings were especially useful for networking. I found many persons working in the same area as I, or held similar interests. I also met many persons hungry for information about many of the areas ACCI members conduct research in. Several of these contacts were from former Eastern European countries.

Carol Meeks

Carol Meeks primarily provided A Focus on Norway with her remarks but generalized a little to Scandanavia and Europe in reporting on the two months she spent working for the National Institute of Consumer Research (SIFO) in Oslo in the Physical Science Section.

SIFO conducts consumer research and testing. Its general mission is similar to that of Consumers Union except that it is funded 60 percent by the Norwegian government and 40 percent by commissioned research. The institute cooperates closely with the Consumer Council and the Consumer Ombudsman, two other agencies in the Ministry of Family and Consumer Affairs.

SIFO with a staff of 55 is divided into two divisions: social sciences and physical sciences which includes food/nutrition, textiles/laundering, and technical household appliances and product safety. I worked in the latter group.

A principal objective of SIFO is to increase the competence of the consumer as well as meet the public authorities' need for knowledge, both as a basis for decision making and implementation of various measures but also in connection with efforts to ensure that legislation and regulation function as they were intended.

A major effort of the social science section has been the study of Norwegian households that are experiencing serious debt payment problems. They have developed a computer program for economic planning in the family which is used by consumers, social security offices, schools, and financial institutions.

One of the most important topics in the last

few years has been consumer political issues concerning Norway's relationship to the EEC. Scandinavian and European consumer policy differ both with regard to goals, means and the organization of consumer interests. The benefits of adopting the consumer policy of the EEC for Scandinavian countries is seen as lower prices and more choice but also less safe products, a reduction of consumer influence, and a weakening of legislative protection for consumers.

Norway's rapprochement to the EEC has resulted in increased involvement for SIFO in European work on standardization in the areas of toys, children's care products, playground equipment, textiles, furniture, noise from household equipment, and ergonomics.

SIFO is testing a series of products including children's thermos bottles, toys, combined range- and dishwashers, microwave ovens, washers and detergents.

SIFO has participated in several Nordic projects on product safety which have been conducted. Often testing of products are divided among the laboratories of the different countries based on interest and facilities. In the long term if there is to be a free flow of goods and services with EEC's inner market, there must be a mutual acceptance of test results by all the countries. Therefore testing laboratories in all countries must meet specific requirements. This is being developed (European Standard EN 45001).

SIFO along with several other Norwegian organizations are interested in the well-being of the elderly. The Scandinavian countries have one of the oldest populations in the world. Several projects being conducted relate human factors and ergonomics to design of appliances and housing units to meet the needs of the elderly. A goal is to increase the use of technology so that the elderly could remain independent for a longer time period. I worked on a research project involving technological change and the elderly, including developing a study to increase the use of microwave ovens. Use of computers and sophisticated phone systems were being tested with elderly at different locations. One of the most interesting aspect to me was the cooperation between engineers and social scientists in developing technological solutions and strategies for their adoption.

In Norway, in the past, the support for technological assistance has been provided primarily by the government, on a sliding fee basis. Most elderly paid little for assistance aids or services. As the number of elderly continue to increase and Norway's economy stagnates, this policy may have to be re-examined.

Information on research results is distributed by SIFO to the press, public policy makers, organizations, research groups and schools. Information is communicated to consumers in cooperation with the Consumer Council which publishes a magazine similar to Consumers Reports.

For a very small country (the population of Norway is 2/3 of Georgia's) there was a very high awareness of consumer issues and concern for consumer protection. A major issue is the EEC and its effect on Norwegian consumers. This topic was constantly discussed. Comparisons were made between state and federal regulations in the U.S. In sum, though, consumer concerns receive much more consideration in Norway than in the U.S.

Margaret Charters

Margaret Charters told The Saga of an Eastern European Consumer Magazine based on a visit to Budapest, Hungary by asking the audience to put themselves in the position of an aspiring editor.

Imagine yourself in Hungary, a young economist, Matyas Vince by name, honorary (unpaid) Board member of the new National Consumer Protection Association formed in November 1991, a little more than a year ago. The predecessor of your organization, the National Board of Consumers was founded in the early 60's. It was a semi-government organization attached to the People's Front (Communist Party) which provided its funding.

The political system and the government have changed to a democracy and parliamentary form. You want your new association to be a genuine non-government organization to protect consumers. You have an image problem and a financial problem! Former members were asked if they wanted to join your new group. Two counties said "no". You are left with a nationwide organization 600-700 members strong distributed in local chapters in 17 of the 19 counties of your country. There are no membership fees to date as you are afraid of losing members. Any person or other smaller consumer protection organization can be put on the membership list if they wish to join. So far it is a whole organization of volunteers.

A new Board is formed with very few of the old leadership remaining. Istvan Fodor, who speaks for the non-partisan 8% of the parliament is chairman. One of your goals is to establish a monthly consumer magazine. Its purpose is to create visibility for and establish credibility for your organization as well as to serve consumers. You want to win the broadest possible readership by monitoring the Hungarian markets of goods and services from the consumer perspective, providing comparative tests of products and services , establishing a forum for citizen's rights in a democratic society! Your model is Consumer Reports. However, you have no money. What are the options?

1. Support from the government. You have a small office, 2 1/2 employees, one the Secretary of the Association plus a typist and a general helper. You have had a little help through

government decrees and in June 1992 Finance Ministry passed a budget which has given you minimal support of about $30,000....6 months late , the bank is empty and employees have already accepted a delay in pay.There are four lawyers contracted to handle special cases who either don't bill full hours or handle small things free. Even this amount from the government, although essential, is a barrier to an image of an independent voice. Certainly there is no extra money to start a magazine.

2.   Membership fees. You are afraid these will scare off the members you do have at this stage.

3.   Grants   or   continuous   backing   from institutions, associations or foundations that agree with the aims and principles of the new magazine. In Hungary, you have approached several trade associations, companies and banks have already been approached for seed monies. It has been made explicit that no benefits will be granted to them by the magazine or the association in return for such grants. International aid or assistance from abroad is included.

4.   Advertising in the magazine. This may create a conflict of interest with some of the potential funders such as Consumers' Union and threaten your image of independence.

5.   Subscription and newsstand sales of the magazine. This does not provide seed money for initial startup. Additional contributions will be encouraged from readers once a magazine is launched, perhaps in the form of membership in the National Consumer Protection Association.

In any case it is essential to keep costs to a minimum. One's own testing program is out of the question. The magazine will print the notices and other communications of the state-owned Hungarian quality control organizations, KERMI and MEEI etc. You may be able to phase in some special tests on a contract basis with these quality control organizations as finances improve. Consumer magazines   from   other   countries   may   share comparative test results on products also used in Hungary. Conversations have already taken place with editors of the German magazine Test with good results.

You will be editor-in-chief of the new magazine. As founding editor-in-chief of World Economy Weekly (HVG) which became one of the most renowned weeklies in Hungary, you have plenty of experience. You were also an editor at the World Bank in Washington D.C. between 1988 and 1990.

So, you move ahead with Phase I of the plan for your magazine during 1992. You already run a small publishing company and have set up the Foundation for the Fair Information of Consumers in close cooperation with the National Consumer

Protection Association to get financial support for the launching of the magazine. Phase II will include the publication of a trial issue of the magazine to be called The Magnifier to be distributed nationwide.

Regional meetings in Bled, Slovenia of the Central and Eastern European group of members of IOCU are announced for late 1992. Consumers Union will attend! You will join other editors from Czechoslovakia, Poland, Slovenia and Russia among others for a session scheduled on consumer magazines. Hans van der Molen, IOCU Coordinator for Central and Eastern Europe reported in April that the Magnifier does not exist anymore. Financing was stopped when the publishing house had to wind up several smaller magazines including this one to produce a big weekly. It was replaced by Teszt. It is an A4, 70 page monthly with color cover and looks highly professional. Circulation is about 30,000 issues a month. Six issues have been published to date. It uses advertisements on a fairly large scale. The chief editor Matyas Vince is convinced that in order to survive, income from advertising is still needed.

Consumer Voice in New and International Markets:
The Role of the International Organization of Consumers Union

Robert R. Kerton, University of Waterloo, Canada[1]

There is a compelling need for the consumer voice to be head in emerging market economies. IOCU can play a crucial role by helping to foster local consumer voicing mechanisms. Secondly, early efforts to help Africa and Eastern Europe consist of too much devout worship of the free market when the need is for tool-oriented measures to construct the basic market framework. ACCI represents a prime source of this applied expertise.

I. The Move to the Market in Eastern Europe and Africa

Countries with little or no experience with "the market" are desperately trying to make use of consumer choice. This change occurs at a time when incomes have fallen by more than fifteen percent in Africa, and by even greater amounts in former Soviet countries. Much good may yet come, but at this stage, it is evident that two monumental mistakes are being make in developing the market economy. The first is the use of temporary western expertise which is stronger on market theology than on understanding local institutions. The second is a complete neglect of consumer "voice" in the design and development of the market framework.

The development of successful market economies over the last two centuries is largely explained by the role of consumer voice in reducing abuses like food adulteration, deceptive practices, predatory pricing and so on. The attempt to move to a market-based system (which uses consumer preferences to make allocation decisions) without the input of consumers is fundamentally illogical. Ordinarily, the main thrust for including consumer interests in national decision-making comes from consumer organizations. And, since 1960, the most important resources for assisting local consumer groups has been the International Organization of Consumers Union (IOCU).

II. Consumers in Africa

"It was another ordinary, dreadful month for Nigerian consumers. The month began with the news that Shell Oil operations had produced an oil slick that polluted 34 villages in Rivers State... It ended with the death of four children and the hospitalization of 11 others when a domestic gas cylinder explored... Between these two disasters the telecommunications authorities hiked their international tariffs by 650 percent,... fake drug products were exposed..." (Obading, 1988:8,9).

Abject poverty is on urgent problem, market failure is another. In some cases, more than a third of the products in the market are defective, and the market itself is part of the reason for the decline in the standard of living. Abuses long since banished in many western markets are able to thrive. The Africa Circular Letter of IOCU covers developments in more than 15 African countries. It demonstrates that the initial burst of consumer organization arises from urgent threats to survival: dangerous food, polluted water, life-threatening pharmaceuticals, scandalous dumping of substandard products, especially those affecting food, or drugs (IOCU, 1988). "Choose any subject on consumerism and you will find that Africa suffers most" (J. Okelo, 1988:3). Yet the creation of organizations which could voice the need for change "...had been hampered by a low level of consumer awareness and lack of technical skills and necessary infrastructure, as well as by some national policies that constrain the full realization of consumer aspirations." (Karpatkin, in IOCU, 1988:3,4). "Costs and access have made the right to consumer education a non-starter. The same applies to the right to be informed on a continent with over 160 million illiterates!" (Okello, 1991:3).

III. The U.N. Guidelines

The most constructive policy tool for bringing forward sensible rules has been the United Nations Guidelines for Consumer Protection, available "off the shelf" as a ready-made market framework to be adapted for local use. One important conference of consumer groups (held in Kenya in 1988) led to "The Nairobi Declaration" seeking implementation of the U.N. Guidelines (IOCU, 1988: 30-34, 65-70). Indeed, some countries have already used the Guidelines to start a program of basic protection (IOCU, 1992: 8; 1993: 1-9).

IV. IOCU Office for Africa

In 1993/4 IOCU will establish a regional office for Africa to provide resource support for consumer education and legislative action. Countries which have already participated in IOCU - sponsored training sessions include Benin, Botswana, Burkina Faso, Cote d'Ivoire, Egypt, Gambia, Ghana, Kenya, Mali, Mauritius, Nigeria, Senegal, Tanzania, Uganda, Zambia and Zimbabwe. In 1988 the Council for Communication Education brought together journalists, educators, and consumer leaders (Boafo, 1988). By 1989, Botswana, Ghana, Mauritius, Nigeria, Senegal, South Africa,

---

[1]Professor, Department of Economics

Zambia and Zimbabwe had formal affiliations with IOCU. The effort to address "exploitation by shrewd monopoly", and "the low level of education" intends to shape national economic policies so that "...develop policies had a consumer face." (Okello, 1991:3). Consumer organizations represent one of the only effective voicing agencies available. The task is daunting, but since 1960 IOCU has had a remarkable record of success in assisting consumers in many corners of the world.

V. Consumers in Eastern Europe

Official aid to Eastern Europe has serious shortcomings. Among these is the lack of a consumer focus, and the absence of any consumer participation. But some hope exists in the form of fledgling consumer organizations with local leadership and an ongoing commitment to making the market work. In October of 1992, more than 100 participants from 21 countries met in Bled, Solvenia, under the auspices of IOCU, to share experiences. The conference agreed on the "Bled Declaration" seeking the implementation of the United Nations Guidelines for Consumer Protection. Nothing will be easy, but it is a start.

VI. The Market as Problem and Solution

There are obvious merits of the market system. But the important institutions which guide our markets were won - over time - in two centuries of struggle. Fair trade laws etc., are complementary with economic progress. Needed are the vital institutions which provide the incentive structure that allows superior goods and services to thrive. The very first step toward success must come from the consumers affected. In this regard, the new organizations in Eastern Europe and in Africa are essential for development. After that, institution-building requires a full range of applied skills.

References

Boafo, S.T.K., & Adagala, E. (Eds.) (1991). Mass Media and Consumer Information. Final Report on ACCE/KCO/IOCU Workshop held in Nairobi, Kenya 28-31 October. African Council for Communication Education (ACCE) Box 47495, Nairobi.

International Organization of Consumers Unions (IOCU)(1988). Consumers in Africa: Meeting the Challenge. Proceedings of the IOCU Conference for Anglophone Africa, Nairobi, Kenya, 14-18 June. The Hague.

International Organization of Consumers Unions (1991), (1992), (1993). Africa Circular Letter, Numbers 1,2, and 3.

Obadina, E. (1988). "Marketplace." In Consumers in Africa, A Growing Voice(pp. 8-11). The Hague: IOCU.

Okello, J.A. (1991). Consumer and Media: Issues of Concern in Africa; in Boafo, above.

Report of ACCI NGO Representative to UN Department of Public Information

Nancy Hawkins[1]

The peacekeeping activity of the UN has moved beyond traditional military dimensions to involve no less than the reconstruction of entire societies. An integrated strategy combining operations of UN Development Program, UN Fund for Population Activities and the World Food program would be carried out in each country headed by a UN representative who would be the resident coordinator for the system. The Economic and Social Council (ECOSOC) would provide integrated oversight for all funding for development operations. This is important to consumer organizations that want to integrate consumer issues into development and educational programs and promote adoption of the UN Guidelines on Consumer Protection.

ECOSOC has been instructed by the General Assembly to establish a high level gender-balanced Commission on Sustainable Development to meet June 14-25, 1993. Once the Commission is functioning, issues of sustainable consumption and population will be addressed.

UN Commission on the Status of Women is preparing for the 4th World Conference on Women to be held in Beijing in 1995.

Nancy Hawkins is working with the NGO committee on the Status of Women, Committee on Development for Women. Their findings are to be presented to the UN Commission on the Status of Women in Vienna in March. Their contributions deal with women and children in extreme poverty. Entrepreneurship, consumer and legal education for women are essential as in many countries women are, under the law, legal infants i.e. they have no rights and little education so that when left alone they must depend on sons or family for support. This is a major cause of poverty worldwide.

Elizabeth Dowdeswell of Canada, widely qualified in environment and social issues, is chief of the UN Environment Program (UNEP). This appointment helps bring gender balance in UN policy level positions, a goal to be met by the 50th anniversary of UN in 1995.

---

[1]ACCI Representative to the United Nations

Widening The Crack -- Strengthening Consumer and Family Economics Programs

Edward J. Metzen, University of Missouri[1]

Panelists:
W. Keith Bryant, Cornell University
"Results of a Survey of Consumer Programs Around the Country"
Goon Soog Hong, Purdue University
"The Consumer Affairs Professional Major at Purdue University"
Sherman Hanna, The Ohio State University
"The Financial Planning and Counseling Major at The Ohio State University"
Carol Meeks, University of Georgia
"The Consumer Economics Major at the University of Georgia"
Edward J. Metzen, University of Missouri
"The Consumer and Family Economics Program at the University of Missouri"

This session, generated by Cathleen Zick and Keith Bryant, is one of a series of programs and publications focused on maintaining and enhancing our academic programs and our profession. Bryant and Metzen raised a flag of concern in Advancing the Consumer Interest (Autumn 1991), in a piece entitled "Is the Crack Closing?" The message was that ours is a field which exists in a crack between the basic disciplines and other fields, and that, because of lack of understanding and appreciation of the field by important institutional decision-makers, it is subject to being squeezed when budgetary stringencies develop. That was followed by a session at the 1992 ACCI conference, entitled "A Call To Arms: Maintaining and Strengthening Consumer and Family Economics Programs in the Face of the Budget Stringencies of the 1990s" The concern was also the topic of a session at the 1992 Southeast Regional Home Management-Family Economics Conference. "Turning the Ebbing Tide of Consumer Studies Programs," by Zick and Richard Widdows, appeared in the Fall 1992 issue of Advancing the Consumer Interest. More recently, Zick and Widdows conducted a survey of the condition of academic programs in Consumer and Family Economics in colleges and universities across the country (report under development). Widdows and Bryant have developed a manuscript entitled "Consumer and Family Economics: A Justification" (forthcoming in the Spring 1993 issue of Advancing the Consumer Interest).

The session reported here was planned in the context of various developments affecting Consumer and Family Economics programs, as a contribution to the effort to develop effective responses to the threats to such programs. The purpose of the session was two-fold:

1. To highlight some of the undergraduate programs around the country that have recently made positive curriculum changes.

2. To reflect on factors involved in such positive developments and share ideas for strengthening programs in our field and thus widening the crack in which we exist to a chasm.

Bryant reported preliminary results of the program survey on behalf of Zick and Widdows. The general picture is that, while many programs are under pressure, some have been merged, and others have been eliminated, others have at the same time experienced impressive growth. On average, Consumer and Family Economics programs seem to be faring as well as the others surveyed, Human Development and Family Studies, and Agricultural Economics.

Each of the panelists then presented a description of their program and developments in it, and perspectives on factors that are important to program viability and success. Details of programs are not reported here. What follows is a combination of some commonalities among these programs and a summary of some of factors identified as important to success in maintaining and strengthening programs.

> We must recognize that ours is primarily a professional field, not a discipline; we must therefore be able to show how our programs can contribute the solution of significant problems confronting individuals and families.

> We must have substantive curricula, with well-defined majors which have clear objectives and career potentials for graduates.

> Programs seem be predominantly organized around two foci: some type of Consumer Affairs major, and some type of Personal Financial Management Services major.

> Program identity and visibility, along with relevance and credibility, are important ingredients in gaining program support. We must do well what we do, and we must be able to articulate it clearly to relevant constituencies -- administrators, legislators, prospective employers, students, parents, and others.

---

[1]Chairperson and Recorder

> The best recruiting device for our programs seems to be word of mouth advertising by our students. Effective, committed teaching, advising, and mentoring is essential if our students are to make the program attractive to others.

>Faculty interaction with faculty and student advisors in other programs on the campus is also important in effective student recruitment.

> Potentials for advertising the program include ads in the schedule of courses, campus busses, and bulletin boards around campus, and talks to various student groups (student organizations, dormitories, fraternity and sorority houses).

> Interaction with business, government, and other agencies and institutions which have an interest in hiring our graduates and in the effectiveness of our programs is valuable in terms of keeping our curricula relevant, developing internship and career opportunities for our students and graduates, and generating material and moral support for our programs.

> It is very helpful to a program for faculty to have networks of colleagues on the campus. A particularly effective means for developing these is through service on a variety of campus committees; others include cooperative research endeavors, service on graduate student committees, and other academic interactions.

> Active involvement of faculty in a variety of professional academic, governmental, and public service organizations and activities serves to stimulate dynamism in a program and to generate program visibility and support.

> Internships are a valuable program component, for the experience and the potential career opportunities they afford students, and for the interest and support they generate for the program on the part of supervising firms and agencies.

> We must capitalize upon the excellent contribution to general education of students from every corner of the campus that is afforded by some of the courses in our curricula. While preparing our professional majors, we can at the same time make a important contributions to the general education mission of the institution and concomitantly garner additional interest in and support for our programs.

> An advisory board of prominent individuals from relevant business, government, not-for-profit, and other insitutions and agencies can be a very valuable resource in terms of communicating to the program developments in their areas of expertise and responsibility, providing internship and career opportunities for students, generating contacts with other entities, providing symposia and lectures for the professional and personal development of students, contributing to program visibility among peers in their respective fields, and providing material and moral support for the program.

> An effective, vigorous student organization associated with the program provides valuable opportunities for professional development of students in terms of both expanding subject matter insights and expertise, and gaining experience in organization management; further, it generates cohesiveness, vitality, and support for the program through the student-student and student-faculty interactions that occur through professional and social activities of the organization.

> Maintenance of records on job placement of graduates, and on-going contact with graduates, are helpful in validating need for the program and nurturing program support of former students.

> Teamwork among faculty, and between faculty and students, is a vital ingredient to maximizing success of a program. Combined with effectiveness, an atmosphere of cohesiveness, mutuality, and collective enthusiasm for a common purpose, is a significant factor in achieving a vigorous, successful program.

> If a program is to be merged with another, it is important to both that program and the field at large that whatever the composition or structure of the merged unit, the Consumer and Family Economics component maintain visibility by a title which maintains its identity.

Finally, it was suggested by Scott Maynes that, in a broad, fundamental sense, our programs need to contribute to the consumer movement and the family movement.

It is the hope of the panel that the ideas shared at this session will prove useful in strengthening Consumer and Family Economics programs, and in "widening the crack" to a chasm within which our programs can flourish.

Contemporary Strategies for Effective Teaching
with Applications in the Consumer Area
(Panel Summary)

Douglas Haskell, University of Cincinnati[1]
Janet Koehler, AT&T Universal Card[2]
Marvin Pasch, Eastern Michigan University[3]
Joan Ryan, Lane Community College[4]

To ensure that consumer education is an integral part of the nation's education program, consumer educators need to participate in the current dialogue on instruction and curriculum. Examination of recent educational advances will help to deliver consumer education more effectively. This panel discussion focused on changes in the methodology and technology of teaching and included suggestions on how these developments might be relevant to consumer education applications.

Assessment Approaches

Three views of assessment currently have the greatest effect on how educators develop and change curriculum. The case for the importance of consumer education is easily illustrated in each approach. Authentic or alternative assessment involves the direct examination of student performance on significant tasks that are relevant to life outside the school. Certainly consumer education fits uniquely as a model of authentic assessment.

Theodore Sizer, author of Horace's School: Redesigning the American High School, 1992, suggests that we must restructure high schools around demonstrations of student capabilities to do important real life tasks. He defines the term "exhibitions" as culminating experiences in which students display their grasp and use of important ideas and skills. A "capstone" experience is an exhibition, not to replicate knowledge and skilled behavior but rather to demonstrate a capability to apply them within a set of particular conditions. The school's program would be, to the largest extent possible, the preparation for these exhibitions. If we did so, we could eliminate tremendous amounts of the elaboration and redundancy in the curriculum which prevent students from seeing what is important. With its multidisciplinary foundation, consumer education provides excellent opportunities for Sizer's approach to assessment.

Outcomes-based education (OBE) is another closely allied approach to curriculum assessment. Just as in exhibitions, OBE establishes what are the most important outcomes of schooling, and the curriculum is then restructured to meet those exit competencies or outcomes. William Spady who is most closely identified with this concept suggests that there are three stages to OBE. In a traditional plan, the existing single subject-based curriculum is modified to make it fit more closely with the exit outcomes. In transitional OBE the outcomes become interdisciplinary. Consumer education is a natural example for OBE, since by definition it is a multi-disciplinary field. The ultimate stage is transformational OBE in which the entire school is organized around these major exit outcomes; all the curricula and everything within the school is reformulated to meet these outcomes. At present only a few schools in the country are experimenting with this stage[1].

Exhibitions and outcome-based education fit well together and are more than just assessment. They percolate through the entire structure, staffing, scheduling and certainly the curriculum.

Selection of Learning Activities

To help teachers select learning activities, the following six principles are broad enough to encompass important content and yet are inclusive enough to cover all essential concepts. They can serve both as guides to the development or selection of learning activities and as standards used to judge the appropriateness of the curriculum program[2].

Congruence

One of the two or three most important concepts, the principle of congruence dictates that learning activities must be directly related to the

---

[1]Associate Director, Center for Economic Education

[2]Executive Director, Consumer Affairs

[3]Professor, College of Education

[4]Professor

objectives of the course; they must not be selected simply because they are enjoyable or satisfying to the students. Assessment procedures also must be directly related to both objectives and learning activities.

Organization and Clarity

To achieve organization and clarity, concept maps use brief verbal statements, circles and lines to show the relationship between the major concepts. As an activity for a teacher in curriculum development[3], concept maps can be used to ensure that all of the relationships, the scope and depth of the content are known by the teacher before developing the unit, activities, and evaluation procedures. There is also a feedback path going back to the goals.

Higher-level Learning

An educational program which goes beyond the replication and reproduction of knowledge requires that students demonstrate mastery of the thought processes. To do so, teachers must come up with a novel stimulus in the testing situation; they must force students to apply, analyze and evaluate within a set of conditions which students haven't seen before. Teachers cannot just say "describe the laws of supply and demand"; they must put students in a situation in which they must apply the laws to unfamiliar data or contexts.

Active Processing

Students must be involved in the activity to enable the teacher to check for understanding. Some activities are more appropriate for active processing than others.

Variety

Ideally, an individualized learning program should be developed that would relate directly to each student's learning style. However, variety is the best we can offer. Interviews conducted with urban, rural and suburban teachers over the last two years showed that active processing and variety are the two most important factors explaining a teacher's success with each of the three student groups[4].

Real-life Experience

Any educational objective must be linked to the student's own experience if it is to be internalized and retained. For example, the study of the Civil War must be tied to today's concerns, issues and dilemmas. Clearly, consumer and economic education have a real advantage over other subjects in providing real-life examples.

Economic Thinking and Problem Solving

A structured approach for teaching economic decision-making has powerful implications for teaching in many other areas including consumer economics, social studies, business, etc. Developed for use by the National Council on Economic Education in their Capstone Program, the principles for problem solving provide students with a framework for decision-making.

Six Basic Principles

1. People always want to benefit from their choices. (People economize.)

   People choose to do the things that give them the greatest satisfaction of their wants with the least cost. Everyone expects to benefit from their economic decisions.

2. There is a cost to all choices. (All choices involve cost.)

   When making a choice people experience both costs and benefits. The real cost of a choice is the next best alternative choice. Your choice is always of more value to you than the next best alternative.

3. People like to be rewarded for the things they do. (People respond to incentives.)

   People choose to do things for which they are rewarded. When provided with an incentive, a person's behavior will change in predictable ways.

4. Rules affect people's decisions. (Economic systems influence individual choice and incentives.)

   Rules and values affect how people act and their economic decisions. Our personal decisions are affected by the opinions of others and society.

5. Everyone wants to benefit from a trade. (Voluntary trade creates wealth.)

   When two people voluntarily trade, each person seeks to benefit. When both people benefit, greater wealth is created and they are better off.

6. Only future costs are important. (The consequences of choices lie in the future.)

   People make choices based on expected outcomes. Since we cannot change things that have happened in the past, we should consider only future costs and benefits when making an economic decision.

Benefits to Students

The benefits to students of using this problem solving method based on these six principles follow:

1. Students will be more aware of their choices. A decision-making framework allows them to focus on gathering information about costs and about benefits. It simply makes them more aware of their choices.

2. Students will use a structured approach to

decision-making. They can go through the process constantly going back to this guide for decision-making and figure out "Have I covered all the costs? Have I covered all the benefits?"

3. Students will be more aware of their decisions. They will also acquire better information about alternatives.

4. Students will be empowered to make decisions. In economic terms information is power. Consumer information is market power. Many consumers go into the marketplace believing that they have to pay whatever price is asked. We give students the power to make decisions when we help them to acquire information.

5. Students will feel more in control of their lives. This is a direct result of feeling empowered to make decisions. "At-risk" students in particular benefit from gaining a sense of control which may be lacking in the rest of their lives.

6. Students will be more thoughtful and productive citizens. They will vote with more information, purchase with more information, and produce with more information.

Artificial Intelligence

Expert systems offer much promise in the teaching and application of consumer education topics. An expert system is a new breed of commercial software that is based on the principles of artificial intelligence. These programs emulate the problem solving process of human experts. They are used to help less knowledgeable or less skilled people to benefit from the knowledge of experts without having direct access to those experts.

An Example of an Expert Systems

The most well-known example of an expert system is "Mycin", the infectious disease expert. Developed at the Stanford Medical Center in 1979, Mycin is based on interviews with over 1,000 doctors to enable the projection of a diagnosis within a certain probability based on a serious of questions. The program can also recommend the best antibiotic therapy to maximize the effective coverage of the cause infection while keeping the number, toxicity, and side effects of the drug to a minimum. In addition, the software can be questioned to determine how the diagnosis was arrived at, and to recommend alternative therapy choices. Mycin is used very effectively to recommend emergency treatment at clinics that do not have immediate access to a medical doctor. It is currently available in a consumer version, the Home Medical Advisor, priced at $79.95, that enables you to decide whether or not you should see a doctor.

How does Artificial Intelligence (AI) Work?

AI researchers develop computer programs that emulate the way people use their minds to tackle problems beyond the reach of "ordinary" computers -- they can make decisions with a percentage probability of being correct. Conventional programming uses algorithms such as:

Sales revenue - cost of goods sold = gross profit

AI uses a type of logic called "heuristics" in place of algorithms. All heuristic statements use the "if, then" format; IF a certain situation occurs, THEN a known outcome is likely. For example, if the stock market hits a new high, then it will probably go down the next day as a result of profit taking.

What is an Expert System?

The expert system program can be a software shell purchased on a disk at a computer store. The user simply enters questions -- no programming is needed. Every expert system has a general problem-solving strategy. The user enters knowledge rules through a natural language interface. The program edits the rules and incorporates them into its inference engine. Once the user has specified the rules, the program is ready for use. Then the program asks the user a series questions until it is able to find a pattern that leads to a solution.

Characteristics of Expert System Tasks
* There are many possible solutions. It would take too long to examine each one.
* The problem-solving expertise is conceptual; it cannot be reduced to numbers.
* The information needed is incomplete, uncertain, subjective, inconsistent, and/or subject to change. The program can work with incomplete data.
* The conclusions reached will often be uncertain. The expert system will state it has only a certain level of confidence that its answer is correct. It will rank conclusions by their likelihood of being correct.
* Experts may disagree on how to solve the problem. The task is always changing and evolving. The cost of a poor or late decision is very high.

Steps in Building an Expert System
1. Identify the problem. Make sure it is appropriate for an expert system. Break it down into smaller pieces.

2. Find the key knowledge concepts and problem-solving strategies the experts use. Look at existing programs.

3. Design an overall structure to organize the knowledge for efficient problem-solving.

4. Put the knowledge and problem-solving strategies into rules, and encode them into computer language.

5. Test the prototype expert system against cases

with known outcomes, and refine the rules.

6. Operate the newly graduated expert system on real cases. Users double check the results.

7. Fine tuning, major revisions, and expansion will continue indefinitely. Maintaining the program is essential if it is to remain useful.

Potential Uses in Consumer Education

Potential applications of expert systems in consumer education are very exciting. Fraud prevention and detection systems could be developed by organizations based on previously detected fraudulent schemes and accessed by consumers with touch-tone telephones. Financial planning advice is another application which could be made available to consumers at a low cost and from an independent source which does not also sell one of the financial products. Another application might be whether to purchase a new or a used car and what make and model based on the consumer's preferences, general repair experiences, etc.

For the instruction of consumer education, expert systems could be used to develop plans for teaching a new course by relying upon what has been done successfully rather than by learning through trial and error. In developing a new course, an educator could tap into the expertise of people across the country.

References

Dologite, D.G. (1993). Developing knowledge-based systems. New York, N.Y.: Macmillan Publishing Company.

Van Horn, M. (1986). Understanding expert systems. New York, N.Y.: Bantam Books.

Endnotes

1. Marshall, K.J. & Spady, W.G. (October 1991). Beyond traditional outcomes-based education. Educational leadership, 67-72.

2. Gardner, T.G., Moody, C.D. Pasch, M., Sparks-Langer, G., & Starko, A.J., (1991). Teaching as decision making. White Plains, N.Y.: Longman Publishing Group.

3. Tyler, R.W. (1969). Basic principles of curriculum and instruction. Chicago, Ill: University of Chicago Press.

4. Ilmer, S., Johnson, R., Pasch, M., Pasch, S., Simmons, J. & Stapleton, E. (March 1993). A tale of three cities revisited: Reflections of urban education. Presentation at the Association of Teacher Educators Annual Conference. Los Angles, Calf.

5. Adapted from the "Handy dandy guide" in

Capstone: The nation's economics course, Joint Council on Economic Education (1989).

Home-Based Business and Family Outcomes

Ramona K.Z. Heck, Cornell University[1]
Kathryn Stafford, The Ohio State University[2]
Mary Winter, Iowa State University[3]
Charles B. Hennon, Miami University[4]

A larger household size and the use of child care services were associated with a decrease in the likelihood that the ratio of net home-based business income to total family income was greater than the mean ratio. The likelihood of higher ratios was increased by the presence of children, especially those under 6 years old. Further study and more detailed specification of family characteristics in relation to business outcomes are warranted.

Introduction

Families and businesses are both intense human endeavors. Both absorb our time, energies, money and other human and material resources. Families form, nurture and maintain human resources. Family owned businesses offer important and vital employment alternatives by providing a job base, income generation, and a return to their family owners. But exactly how do these two arenas -- family and business activities -- relate to each other? Do they enhance or detract from each other? How do family demands and outcomes (characteristics) relate to known measures of business activities? Are the respective well-being and stability of each related in either positive or negative ways?

If negative and positive family outcomes or characteristics are combined with negative and positive business outcomes in a two-by-two matrix, four possible combinations result. Both negative family and business outcomes are likely to lead to the dissolution of the family as well as the business. On the other hand, positive outcomes for both the family and business are desirable but may not be common or frequent in occurrence. The final two combinations--positive family outcomes combined with negative business outcomes, and positive business outcomes combined with negative family outcomes--pose real challenges for those families who are engaged in business enterprises.

The purpose of this analysis is to pursue two specific hypotheses concerning family-owned home-based businesses:

H[1]: Families with a greater number of family members are more likely engaged in businesses where the generated net business income represents a high proportion of the family's total income.

H[2]: Families in beginning and ending stages of the family life course are less likely engaged in businesses where the generated net business income represents a high proportion of the family's total income.

Previous Research

There is limited literature on family life and home-based employment. Some studies have concluded that due to flexibility of scheduling and the closeness of one's workplace, working at home enhances the quality of family life. Beach (1985) found that home-based workdays were frequently interrupted by child, family, and household tasks. Women in her sample tended to adjust their paid work to meet the needs of their families. Horvath (1986) has suggested that home-based work allows for more effective combinations of work and family roles. Others have noted an incompatibility between family demands, especially children, and home-based work (Ahrentzen, 1990; Christensen, 1985; McLaughlin, 1981; Olson, 1983).

For all home-based workers in the nine-state research study (i.e., NE-167), their families included a high proportion (61%) of married-couple-with-children and a comparatively small proportion (25%) of adult-only families or with only adult children at home (Rowe & Bentley, 1992). As compared to wage workers, owners of home-based businesses are older, have less education, live in larger households, have lived in their communities longer, and have lower incomes than their wage-earning counterparts (Masuo, Walker, & Furry,

---

[1]Associate Professor, Consumer Economics and Housing

[2]Associate Professor, Family Resource Management

[3]Professor, Human Development and Family Studies

[4]Professor, Family and Consumer Sciences and
    Associate Director, Family and Child Studies Center

1992). The presence of children age 18 or under reduces the number of hours of home-based work; children under age 6 reduces work hours even further (Heck, 1992). Paid child care is less likely for business owners in general and more likely for owners who hired employees or services (i.e., related to larger-scale businesses) (Heck, Saltford, Rowe, & Owen, 1992).

Because important differences have been revealed between home-based wage work and business owners in the nine-state research study, this analysis proposes to delve deeper into the specific relationships between family and household outcomes (characteristics) and one measure of business outcomes.

Data and Methods

The data for the study reported here were from a nine-state project focused on households in which at least one individual generated income by working at or from their home. Thirty-minute telephone interviews were conducted with the household manager in 899 households in which there was home-based employment (Stafford, Winter, Duncan, & Genalo, 1992). The subsample used in this analysis was limited to 670 households who owned a family business. The unit of analysis was the household and the data were weighted by the relative importance in the population of the respective states and the rural/urban areas in the states (Stafford et al., 1992). Descriptive statistics of the various research variables were used to examine selected socio-economic characteristics of the households engaged in home-based businesses that earn a high proportion of the family's total income.

For each home-based business, the proportion or fraction of the net business income to total family income was calculated. The dependent variable was created from this proportion. If the proportion of net business income to total family income was greater than or equal to the mean proportion which was .36, then the dependent variable assumed the value of one. If the proportion was less than the mean of .36, then the dependent variable assumed the value of zero.

A logit estimation was used to examine the factors associated with the likelihood that the net business income represented a greater relative importance of the family's total income than the mean of .36. In most cases, this binary variable represented a greater dependency on the home-based business income or situations where the net home-based business income was the main source of income for the family.

The logit procedure is a nonlinear technique designed for use with dependent variables that are dichotomous variables and other multinomial variables (Kmenta, 1986). When estimated, the logit equation predicts the natural logarithm of the odds ratio of the probability than an event

occurs given the levels at which the independent variables were set. Qualitatively, the interpretation of a logit coefficient is similar to the linear regression model. The logit coefficient is the percentage change in the logarithm of the odds ratio of probabilities, $\ln(P/1-P)$, given a small change in the value of the independent variable and holding all other variables constant (Kmenta, 1986). The sign of the logit coefficient indicates the direction of the effect, and the size of the coefficient indicates the strength of the effect. Therefore, the logit coefficients are associated with the contributions of a particular characteristic of either the household/family, the worker, or the work to the likelihood that the net home-based business income represents a larger proportion (than the mean proportion) of the family's total income.

Research Results

The home-based business owners were examined descriptively and compared to the total sample which also included wage workers. As compared to the total sample, the home-based business owners had slightly larger household sizes, fewer children, higher rates of home ownership and had lived one year longer in their respective communities (Table 1). Business owners were slightly older than the total group of home-based workers including both business owners and wage workers (Table 1). Business owners were more often engaged in seasonal work and worked fewer hours than the total group of home-based workers. About one half of the business owners hired employees or services (Table 1).

The mean net business income of $15,628 was nearly 30% of the mean gross business income of $53,296 and about $8,600 less than net wage income. The mean ratio of net business income to total family income was .36 for the subsample of business owners studied. Forty percent of the businesses earned net business incomes greater than the mean (Table 1).

Logit analysis was used to test the effects of household/family, worker and work characteristics on the relative importance of the net home-based business income to the family's total income. The overall chi-square statistic for the logit equation was significant, indicating that the conceptual model used in this analysis was useful in explaining higher ratios of net home-based business income to total family income.

Five of the seven household/family characteristics were significant but only one variable, years lived in the community, had the expected directional effect. It was hypothesized that households/families with a greater number of members would more likely engage in businesses where the generated net business income represented a higher (than the mean) proportion of the total family's income. A larger household size was associated with a decrease of .3287 in the logarithm of the odds that the net home-based business income to total family income was greater than the mean ratio (Table 2) (Pindyck & Rubinfeld, 1991). This negative sign may indicate that a larger household/family detracts from the home-based business owner's ability to earn a higher level of net business income. As a result, the net business income is lower and less important than other sources or types of income that contribute to the family's total income. It may

Table 1:
Descriptive Statistics for Research Variables[a]

Variable	Business owners	Entire sample
Household/family characteristics		
Household size	3.43[b]	3.35
	1.49[c]	1.49
Children ≤ 18 (proportion)	.54	.55
Children < 6 (proportion)	.27	.28
Used child care services (proportion)	.17	.17
Non-homeowners (proportion)	.11	.13
Years lived in community	20.94	19.84
	15.34	15.47
Towns < 2500, rural areas and farms (proportion)	.47	.46
Worker characteristics		
Male worker (proportion)	.58	.58
Age of worker	44.28	43.57
	12.23	12.30
Years of education	13.72	13.89
	2.34	2.36
Singles (proportion)	.15	.15
Work characteristics		
Years engaged in	9.46	9.13
	8.74	8.80
Seasonality of work (proportion)	.18	.14
Occupational rank	4.87	4.37
	2.44	2.52
Total work hours (annual)	1792.58	1829.14
	1338.89	1319.49
Hired employees and/or services	.52	.39
Income types		
Gross business income (1988 annual)	53,296.00	
	89,244.56	
Net business income (1988 annual)	15,627.85	
	20,505.47	
Net wage income (1988 annual)	24,300.08	
	21,432.01	
Total family income (1988 annual)	42,263.45	
	23,191.06	
Dependent variables		
Business owners	-------	.75

Ratio of net business income to total family income	-------	.36.40

Business owners with higher ratio	.40	-------

Number of observations	670	899

[a]Weighted numbers, percentages, and means in relation to population in the nine states studied. [b]Mean. [c]Standard deviation.

also be the case that the financial demands of larger households/families necessitate income from several sources, thereby, lowering the relative importance or contribution of the net home-based business income to the family's total income.

It was expected that the presence of one or more children age 18 or under, and less than 6 years of age would detract from the intensity of business activities engaged in by the household. Opposite effects were found. The presence of one or more children age 18 or under was associated with a .3995 increase in the logarithm of the odds that the ratio of net home-based business income to total family income was greater than the mean ratio (Table 2). The effect for the presence of one or more children under age 6 was also positive at a higher level of .5495 (Table 2). These positive effects for the variables representing the presence of children may be associated with the financial demands that children place on the household. In other words, the mere existence of children in the household may necessitate having a viable business enterprise and, therefore, a higher than the mean ratio of net home-based business income to total family income. Children may increase the need for more income and, at the same time, complicate the ability of the household to earn this needed income by increasing the time pressures on the family. As a result, the household might intensify its income earning activities in one area, namely a home-based business. Consequently, the relative importance of net home-based business income to total family income would increase as well as the household's dependency on home-based business income as its main source of income.

It was hypothesized that the use of child care services would allow more time and greater efforts to be concentrated toward the family's home-based business. Therefore, the use of child care services was expected to be associated with an increase in the likelihood that the ratio of net home-based business income to total family would be greater than the mean ratio. A negative effect was revealed (Table 2). It may be the case that the use of child care services and their associated costs may compel households to seek more than one source of income. Having other income sources in order to afford child care costs would decrease the ratio of net home-based business income to total family income.

Table 2
Logit Estimates of Research Variables

Variable	Business owners with ratios (greater than mean)
Household/family characteristics	
Household size	-.3287[a] (-3.5203)***
Children ≤ 18	.3995 (1.3065)*
Children < 6	.5495 (1.8318)**
Used child care services	-.5512 (-1.7728)**
Non-homeowners	.2648 (.8723)
Years lived in community	-.0108 (-1.4376)*
Towns < 2500, rural areas, and farms (proportion)	.0827 (.4232)
Worker characteristics	
Male worker	2.0561 (9.2195)***
Age of worker	.0063 (.5671)
Years of education	.1015 (2.1118)**
Singles	-.0250 (-.0870)
Work characteristics	
Years engaged in	.0230 (1.7171)**
Seasonality of work	-.2089 (-.8466)
Occupational rank	-.0028 (-.0682)
Total work hours (annual)	.0006 (7.9805)***
Hired employees and/ or services	.3018 (1.4599)*
Constant	-3.9870 (-3.8791)***

Log-likelihood = -342.02633

Chi-square = 254.95697***

Number of observations = 670

[a]Regression coefficient with t-statistic listed below in parentheses.
*p < .10. **p < .05. *** p < .01.

As expected, the more years lived in a community was associated with a decrease in the likelihood that the ratio of net home-based business income to total family income was greater than the mean ratio (Table 2). This negative relationship may suggest that long-time residents in a community may have access to other employment and income-earning activities that are not home-based business enterprises. Consequently, the ratio of net home-based business income to total family income is decreased.

Two worker characteristics were significant and positive as expected. Home-based business owners who were male and who had more years of education were more likely to produce higher than mean ratios of net business income to total family income (Table 2). Previous research has consistently shown a gender effect relative to the level of earnings from home-based work (Heck, 1992; Loker & Scannell, 1992; Rowe & Bentley, 1992; Rowe, Stafford, & Owen, 1992). Within bivariate and multivariate analyses, males earned higher levels of home-based income than females regardless of family composition, occupational type, ownership status, number of hours worked, and other socio-economic characteristics such as age, education, and marital status.

A higher level of education may be associated with more expertise and skills in running a profitable home-based business. Thus, greater profitability would enhance the relative contribution of the net home-based business income to the family's total income and increase the ratio of these two income measures.

Three work characteristics were significant and had positive effects as expected. These were years engaged in the home-based business, the total annual work hours, and the hiring of employees and/or services (Table 2). If a home-based business owner had been in business longer, the likelihood of having a ratio of net business income to total family income higher than the mean ratio was increased.   This finding suggests that the length of ownership is associated with an increase in profitability and viability of the home-based business.

As expected, the larger the number of total work hours annually was related to higher ratios. Because more hours of home-based work generally generates higher levels of net business income, the ratio of net business income to total family income increases.   As in the case of traditional employment away from the home, greater home-based work efforts by business owners produce monetary returns and enhance the relative importance of the net home-based business income to the family's total income.

Finally, the hiring of employees and/or service by home-based business owners was significant and positive as expected (Table 2).   Such hiring may be associated with larger-scale businesses. In turn, these larger-scale businesses may produce higher levels of net home-based business income.   Thus, the ratio of net home-based business income to total family income would be increased.

Summary and Conclusions

In sum, a larger household size, the use of child care services and the longevity of residency in the community were associated with a decrease in the likelihood that the ratio of net home-based business income to total family income was greater than the mean ratio for all business owners.   The likelihood that this ratio would be greater than the mean was positively associated with the presence of one or more children whose age was 18 years or less, the presence of one or more children whose age was less than 6 years, male owners, higher levels of education, longer periods of business ownership, a greater number of total work hours annually and the hiring of employees and/or services.

Clearly, a number of factors contribute to the relative importance of net home-based income to the family's total income.   However, the effects of these household or family characteristics were not as hypothesized.   A more complete understanding of the mix and interrelationships between family and business activities is yet to be achieved.   This research is preliminary in nature.   Further and more detailed specifications of household and family characteristics in relation to business outcomes are warranted.

References

Ahrentzen, S.B.   (1990).   Managing conflict by managing boundaries: How professional homeworkers cope with multiple roles at home.   Environment and Behavior, 22, 723-752.

Beach, B.   (1985).   Working at home: Family life/work life.   Unpublished doctoral dissertation, The University of Connecticut, Storrs, CT.

Christensen, K.E.   (1985).   Women and home-based work. Social Policy, 15(3), 54-57.

Heck, R.K.Z.   (1992).   The effects of children on the major dimensions of home-based employment. Journal of Family and Economic Issues, 13, 315-346.

Heck, R.K.Z., Saltford, N.C., Rowe, B.R. & Owen, A. (1992).   The utilization of child care by households engaged in home-based employment. Journal of Family and Economic Issues, 13, 213-237.

Horvath, F.W.   (1986).   Work at home: New findings from the current population survey Monthly Labor Review, 109(11), 31-35.

Kmenta, J.   (1986).   Elements of econometrics.   New York: Macmillan.

Loker, S., & Scannell, E.   (1992).   Characteristics and practices of home-based workers.   Journal of Family and Economic Issues, 13, 173-186.

Masuo, D.M., Walker, R., & Furry, M.M.   (1992). Home-based workers: Worker and work characteristics.   Journal of Family and Economic Issues, 13, 245-262.

McLaughlin, M.   (1981).   Physical and social support systems used by women engaged in home-based work.   Unpublished master's thesis, Cornell University, Ithaca, NY.

Olson, M.   (1983).   Overview of work-at-home trends in the United States.   New York: New York University Press.

Pindyck, R.S., & Rubinfeld, D.L.   (1991). Econometric models and economic forecasts.   New York: McGraw-Hill.

Rowe, B.R. & Bentley, M.T.   (1992).   The impact of the family on home-based work.   Journal of Family and Economic Issues, 13, 279-297.

Rowe, B.R., Stafford, K., & Owen, A.J.   (1992). Who's working at home: The types of families engaged in home-based work.   Journal of Family and Economic Issues, 13, 159-172.

Stafford, K., Winter, M., Duncan, K.A., & Genalo, M.A.   (1992).   Studying at-home income generation: Issues and methods.   Journal of Family and Economic Issues, 13, 139-158.

Family Functioning and Home-Based Business:
A Comparison of Statistical Methods

Alma J. Owen, Lincoln University[1]
Kathyn Stafford, The Ohio State University[2]

This paper describes two ways of using data gathered about family functioning from families who run businesses from their homes. The items were designed to measure the ways family members interact in a personal subsystem. An interval level scale, based on factor analysis, was constructed and items were also combined to create a nominally scaled variable of family functioning. When used as dependent variables in separate types of analysis with household management as the dependent variable, each family functioning variable displayed approximately the same explanatory value. However, they offered distinct information about underlying connections between the managerial and personal subsystems of families.

The high start-up and failure rates of small businesses in the United States may be ascribed, in part, to families undertaking businesses that conflict with their composition or interaction style. This study is a preliminary step to research that will assist in educating potential at-home business persons on the benefits and pitfalls of combining work for income and family interaction in a single spatial environment. The scales outlined in this paper are to be used to help families assess the fit between specific demands of occupations and the manner in which family members prefer to engage in day to day activities.

This paper uses data collected for a regional research study of families that had at least one household member who worked at home for income (Stafford, Winter, Duncan, & Genalo, 1992). This regional study of the impact of home-based work on family management, productivity, and stability was funded by the experiment stations of Hawaii, Iowa, Missouri (Lincoln University), Michigan, New York (Cornell), Ohio, Pennsylvania, Utah and Vermont. It sought to provide measures of multiple family concepts and issues to aid in the interpretation of the family and work interface.

Introduction

A central organizing concept for this research was Deacon and Firebaugh's (1981) model for family resource management. In this model, they have defined managerial and personal subsystems that could be used to describe how families accomplish tasks and organize activities. They have specified that these subsystems form an integrated whole within a family's life and have devoted particular attention to the managerial subsystem.

The personal subsystem is only roughly defined; little is done to explicate this subsystem that informs, and is enhanced by, activities in the managerial subsystem. The personal subsystem is the source of values and other intrapersonal attributes which shape the standards that managerial activities are expected to attain as well as, in part, defining the interpersonal conditions under which family managerial activities take place.

The intermingling of business and affective activities is a hallmark of home-based business. Study of such a set of families gives researchers a unique opportunity to explore the factors that portend how family members weigh the importance of these two sets of activities. In this study, measurement of the personal subsystem is achieved through the use of family functioning scales derived from Kantor and Lehr (1975) and Constantine (1986). Development of two variables, an interval and a nominal one, is described. These variables are tested in regression and multiple classification analysis to determine their usefulness in explaining managerial behavior. Finally, implications are drawn on the way these two scales can assist management and family theory to enhance interdisciplinary research with family and consumer studies.

Measurement of Family Functioning Types

To remain consistent with Deacon and Firebaugh's (1981) systems approach to family management, Kantor and Lehr's (1975) theory of family functioning was used. This theory of family functioning was considered to be the most consistent with the systemic foundations of Deacon and Firebaugh's (1981) work. As organized by Constantine (1986), Kantor and Lehr's (1975) systemic theory of family affective functioning also provided information on time perception and space use which supplements the managerial subsystem portion of the research.

[1]Associate Professor and Home Economics Specialist

[2]Associate Professor, Family Resource Management

A Systems Approach to Family Functioning

Kantor and Lehr (1975) have defined three types of family systems: closed, random, and open. Constantine (1986) added a fourth, the synchronous family, and elaborated on how the family types fit together. Kantor and Lehr (1975) and Constantine (1986) have used target and access dimensions to categorize the eight concepts that they observed to differentiate underlying family constructs. Target dimensions were those objectives that a family seeks to attain as a result of members' interaction. They included control, affect (emotional nurturance), content, and meaning. These outcomes are secured through use of the access dimensions of space, time, matter, and energy.

In the development of measurement items, the genuine though subtle difference between closed and synchronous families was determined to be too obscure and unique to be measured in a telephone interview. Thus the research on home-based work studied three of the family types defined by Constantine (1986) as: closed, random, and open. Each of these is described below.

Simply defined, a "closed family" is one that seeks to maintain the status quo. It engages in activities and attends to ideals and values that maintain continuity with the past. Decisions, direction, and roles are delegated based on how things were done in the past and often replay the structures of the families of origin. Analysis of the systems embedded in and around closed families shows that the family, not the individual or the community, is the most distinct unit, that is, the one with the most definite boundary. "Stability through tradition" is Constantine's (1986) phrase for the closed family.

Constantine (1986) has described the "random family" as the antithesis of the closed one. The random family revels in variety and change. It is oriented to the present and seeks a constant influx of new experience. Each member is in charge of his or her own direction and action and usually does not coordinate activities with those of other individual members. The individual has the most distinct boundary and interacts within and outside the family with equal freedom. "Variety through innovation" is the random family's motto.

The "open family" combines aspects of closed and random types. Its members seek to introduce some change into the enduring family unit. In doing so, the open family acknowledges ties with the past and incorporates experiences of the present to build a path to the future. Decisions and direction for the family are negotiated among all members. There is little role delineation inside the family, though some delineation based on age, may exist. Individual members and the family unit have equivalent boundaries. Members consider the family's identity as important as their own and each other's in determining actions and goals. "Adaptability through negotiation" is the hallmark of processes observed in open families.

Kantor and Lehr (1975) and Constantine (1986) have clearly stated that these family types were not absolute. Families display a mix of types in their everyday activities. However, they are expected to display a propensity to one type or another. This propensity may be an overall preference for one type or another; it could also display itself in certain dimensions, such as space use, being rigidly random or closed.

Home-based Business and Family Life

Beach (1989) and Gray and Owen (1986) have conducted qualitative studies of small samples to determine elements that appeared to influence the way families with home-working members met their needs and responsibilities. This paper reports empirical results of scales that measure family affective functioning and the relationship of such functioning to managerial behavior in relation to those determined salient to these researchers.

Methodology and Data

The Data

The data for this study were from a nine-state project focused on households in which at least one individual generated income by working at or from the home. During spring 1989, thirty-minute telephone interviews were conducted with the household manager in 899 households in which there was home-based employment. The unit of analysis was the household and the data were weighted by the relative importance in the population of the respective states and the rural and urban areas in the states. For more information on sampling, methodology, and definitions, see Stafford et al., (1992).

Of the 899 respondents, 69.0% of the weighted sample (70.5% of the unweighted sample) were families who ran a business at or from their homes. This subsample excludes single person households and households consisting solely of unrelated individuals as well as all home-based workers who worked as employees at their homes.

Definition of Research Variables for Family Functioning

Previous attempts to examine and quantify Kantor and Lehr's (1975) theory have concentrated on clinical analysis which presumed assessment of the family's affective functioning style through direct contact with a therapist. In keeping with the telephone interview format of this study, a self-reported measure was used. Three family functioning types were represented: closed, random, and open. The family types were measured by four dimensions conceptualized as being the most discriminating (among the family types) and the least invasive, that is, the ones likely to be answered over the telephone. The dimensions represented were time and space from Kantor and Lehr's (1975) access dimensions. Representing the target dimensions were pattern (or meaning) and decision-making style, referred to by Kantor and Lehr (1975) as control. Wording for these items can be accessed in Owen, Rowe and Gritzmacher (1992).

Previous attempts at quantification of family functioning (Imig & Phillips, 1989) have indicated that families do not sort neatly into the family types postulated by Kantor and Lehr (1975) and Constantine (1986). Rather, the reality of family life was a mix of styles or paradigms. Furthermore, the variation itself reflected different rationales of diversity. For example, a family may vary on their dominant style with respect to different dimensions; members may appear to structure time use randomly but be quite closed in how they use space. For the home-based work study, the researchers expected the same mixture of styles within a family but anticipated that a measurable range of behavior might exist that would inform their study.

Confirmatory Factor Analysis

Principal components analysis was used for confirmatory factor of the twelve family functioning items (Owen et al, 1992). Results reflected certain dominant themes that could inform understanding of the relationship between the family and the home-based business. Owen et al (1992) summarized the family autonomy scale as follows:

> Autonomy of family members is based on Constantine's (1986) conceptualization of closed, random, and open families. The scale reflects a low score for families that combine negotiation and structured collective behavior and high scores for families in which members display a high degree of individualistic, self-reliant behavior (p. 312).

Because the family functioning items displayed a great deal of variance and some items required reverse coding, the items were recoded from a 1 to 5 scale to a 0 to 4 scale with the absolute variance in each item preserved. While this does not change the factor analysis results, the resultant family autonomy score is stronger since there is grater contrast between random family scores and scores for families that show high contrast to this type. A summary of the factor loadings that informed the development of the autonomy scale and the nominally scaled variable discussed in the next section are discussed in Owen, et al (1992).

Nominal Variable of Family Affective Functioning

In addition to the family autonomy scale, the factor analysis confirmed the strength of items combined in other ways as long as items were appropriately reversed and duplicate use of individual items was avoided. To do this the highest loadings of each item were used to develop a categorical scale of family type. A random score

combined the random time and decision-making items with the reverse of the open decision-making and time scores. As discussed by Owen et al (1992), closed time and random pattern display, respectively, functional and societal influences on the open family affective score; they are combined with the open pattern to create the open family score. The closed family score is the sum of closed time and pattern values. Descriptive statistics for the family autonomy score as well as for each of the family type scores (closed, open and random), are displayed in Table 1.

Table 1
Descriptive Statistics for Family Functioning.

Variable	Mean	Standard Deviation
Family Autonomy	6.55	5.84
Random	5.03	1.92
Open	7.98	2.73
Closed	4.90	1.90

In order to convert the scores for each family type into a categorical variable, each of the family scores were recoded into a low and high value for each case. Respondents were then assigned to one of eight categories as shown in Figure 1. The untyped families are those that scored low or high on all three family types. Percentages of families that fell into each category are noted on Figure 2.

Figure 1
Family Functioning and Management

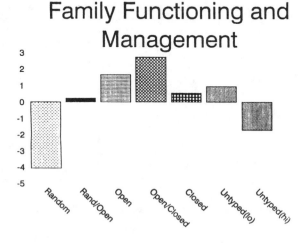

Family Functioning and Management

Figure 2
Family Functioning Types

Family Functioning Types

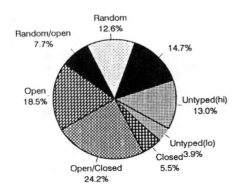

N=620

Analysis of Family Functioning and Management

In order to test the effectiveness of the family functioning interval and categorical scale, each were tested against the family managerial scores of respondents in the home-based business data set. The managerial score is the sum of ten components of managerial activities as defined and explored by Heck, Winter and Stafford (1992). For the 620 businesses used in this analysis, the mean total management score was 37.67 (StD=6.01). Figure 2 is a graphic representation of the managerial score deviations by family functioning category. Regression analysis and multiple classification analysis were run on the interval and categorical scores respectively.

Regression Analysis

Table 2 displays the results of the regression analysis on household management. The R^2 change for family autonomy was significant at .1448, explaining the preponderance of the variance in management. Education of the home based worker also explained a modest amount of variance (R^2 change=.0106). Thus, while education is often used as a proxy for managerial activity (Furtan & Bollman, 1979), for household management, a family's affective style may be more useful in explaining managerial behavior.

Table 2
Regression on Household Management.

Variable	$R^2 \Delta$	Beta	r
Family Autonomy	.172	-.417	-.417
Education	.011	.107	.201
Total R^2	.183		
SigF	.000		

Multiple Classification Analysis

Because family affective behavior can often be observed by estimates of predominant behavior, it is important that any measure of family functioning be convertible to a categorical scale and that scale should display similar results to use of the interval scale. Multiple classification analysis (MCA) was used to determine the effectiveness of the nominally scaled variable. As shown in Table 3, MCA using only the family categories resulted in an R^2 of .151, a stronger explanatory score than the regression analysis produced.

Table 3
ANOVA (MCA) on Household Management.

Category	N	Eta
Random	78	-4.07
Random/Open	48	.01
Open	115	1.64
Open/Closed	150	2.72
Closed	34	.55
Closed/Random	91	-2.12
All Low	24	.95
All High	81	-1.70
R^2		.151

Discussion

While the focus of this study was on household management, family functioning scores can be useful across a range of topics related to family and consumer economics. The family types dictate the manner in which families make purchase decisions, who purchases which items for individual or family use, and the manner in which families allocate other resources. In a random family, consumer information must be delivered to each individual for it to be effective. In a closed family, different members are likely to have different roles that related to purchasing different items; consumer education must appropriately target the proper purchase agent. Only in open families are purchase decision discussed in a manner that would share information within the family so that optimal purchasing may take place.

This paper sought to explore the efficacy of distinct but complementary family functioning variables in the analysis of household management. similar explanatory scores were found for intervally and nominally scaled variables that were based on the same respondent scores. These similarities indicate that either scale can be used with confidence in better understanding the household managerial activities of families. The

360

availability of two different types of scales allows researchers to increased collaboration between family economics and family functioning disciplines as well as provides necessary information on buying behavior.

References

Beach, B. (1989). Integrating work and family life: The home-working family. Albany, NY: State University of New York Press.

Constantine, L. (1986). Family paradigms: The practice of theory in family therapy. New York: Guilford.

Deacon, R., & Firebaugh, F. (1981). Family resource management: Principles and applications. NY: Allyn and Bacon.

Furtan, W H., & Bollman, R. (1979). Returns to operator education in Saskatchewan agriculture. American Journal of Agricultural Economics, 61, 318-321.

Heck, R.K.Z., Winter, M. & Stafford, K. (1992). Managing work and family in home based employment. Journal of Family and Economic Issues, 13, 187-212.

Kantor D., & Lehr, W. (1975). Inside the family: Toward a theory of family process. NY: Harper Colophon.

Owen, A. J., Rowe, B., & Gritzmacher, J. (1992). Building family functioning scales into the study of at-home income generation. Journal of Family and Economic Issues, 13, 299-314.

Stafford, K., Winter, M., Duncan, K.A., & Genalo, M.A. (1992). Studying at-home income generation: Issues and methods. Journal of Family and Economic Issues, 13, 139-158.

Family-Owned Home Businesses and their Economic Outcomes

Barbara R. Rowe, Purdue University[1]
Ramona K.Z. Heck, Cornell University[2]
George W. Haynes, Montana State University[3]
Marion T. Bentley, Utah State University[4]

This study explored the financial success of 620 family-owned home businesses. Characteristics of the home business owner, of the business, and of the owner's managerial practices both within and outside the business arena were evaluated systematically. Dimensions of the business were more powerful in explaining the amount of income generated by the business than personal characteristics of the owner, although both played significant roles.

The family firm has traditionally played a dominant role in the U.S. economy. Over 95% of all businesses in the nation are classified as being family controlled, meaning that management decisions and/or ownership are influenced by a family (Dyer, 1986). These family firms account for about one-half of all the country's jobs and a significant percentage of its gross national product. Therefore, the effectiveness of such companies, the quality of their management, and their level of profitability are clearly significant for the economy and the society.

One measure of business success is the amount of income or profit generated by the enterprise (Aldrich & Weiss, 1981; Kallenberg & Leicht, 1991). While every business owner may not define success in this way, income does provide one indicator of differences in outcome that can be objectively measured.

Previous research suggests three major categories of variables--reflecting either personal or work characteristics--that can affect the amount of income earned from a family-owned home business. First, the more skills and experience an individual brings to the business, the more likely it is that income will be higher (Bender, 1980). Those with money to invest have overcome one of the major obstacles to success--difficulty in securing capital (Aldrich & Auster, 1986). Secondly, personal characteristics such as a strong need for achievement and an internal locus of control appear to be linked to economic success (McClelland, 1961; Mortimer & London, 1984). Another important

personal dimension is the family situation of the owner. Business owners can benefit from the tangible and emotional support of family members (Aldrich, Cater, Jones, & McEvoy, 1983). Alternatively, the difficulties of balancing family and business demands may detract from an owner's ability to devote time and effort to the business negatively thereby impacting sales (Loscocco, Robinson, Hall, & Allen, 1991).

Features of the business itself--reflecting organizational context and structure--is the third major category of key influences on income. Whether the business is service-related or makes a product is one such determinant. Among structural characteristics of the business, the size and number of years in the marketplace have been emphasized as particularly important features of economic outcomes (Aldrich & Weiss, 1981; Humprhreys & McClung, 1981). How the business is promoted and the characteristics of its sales efforts are other important predictors of financial success.

Each of the categories of determinants described above has been offered as a possible explanation for the differences in economic outcomes for small businesses. These explanations place the responsibility for the amount of income generated by small businesses either on the individual owner (human capital, personal attitudes, and family situation) or on the work itself (market and business characteristics). Management theory suggests a fourth predictor: the more intense or numerous the engagement of specified management practices, the more effective the overall management style and the greater the output (i.e., income) from the home-based work.

Accordingly, this study examined those factors which might affect the amount of income generated by family-owned home businesses. The dependent variable for all analyses was net business income ($15,880). The following variables were included: gender, age, and education of the home-business owner; household size, family type and the number of dependents requiring care; rural/urban location and size of the community of residence. Business

---

[1] Associate Professor, Consumer Sciences & Retailing

[2] Associate Professor, Consumer Economics & Housing

[3] Assistant Professor, Agricultural Economics

[4] Associate Professor, Economics

context was tapped by whether the firm produced a product or provided a service, size of the firm as indicated by whether they engaged paid or unpaid help and the numbers of helpers, the numbers of hours worked in the business; by where and how they promoted and marketed the output of the business; and by whether they had to borrow or boot-strap to start the business (possibly incurring debt to be paid off in the start-up years). Based on management theory, net business income was also examined in relation to the owners' scores on a business management scale and on a family management scale.

Methodology and Data

The sample for this study consisted of 899 rural and urban households in nine states. A two-stage area probability sample design was used to identify respondent households: a primary stage sample of rural and urban counties in the participating states followed by a stratified random selection of households within sampled area segments. To qualify for inclusion in the study, a household had to contain at least one member, 18 years or older, who had received income from home-based work in 1988, had engaged in this work for at least 312 hours annually, and had been in business for at least the previous 12 months. The sample contained both home-business owners (home-based workers who owned their own business and were responsible for all the business's activities) and wage workers (individuals who worked at home for piece-rate wages provided by an outside employer). The person interviewed was the household manager--defined as the individual who took care of most of the meal preparation, laundry, cleaning, scheduling of family activities, and child care.

Sample observations were weighted to represent the total number of households in each stratum using the total number of rural-urban households in the stratum in 1985 as estimated by the Bureau of Census. For more information on sampling, methodology, and definitions, see Stafford, Winter, Duncan, & Genalo (1992). The sample for the analyses discussed in this article consisted of 620 households that were self-identified as operating a family-owned home business.

Results

Net business income for all of the family-owned home business in the sample ranged from the 68 respondents who reported no income after expenses to net earnings of $150,000. The amount of income earned from the business was affected by whether or not the business owner was male or female. On average, family firms owned by men were earning $14,082.74 more than women's businesses $F(1, N=620) = 78.6542, p = 000$. In all but two instances, women were realizing significantly less income from their home businesses than men even when they were in the same field.

The age of the owner was significantly related

to the amount of income generated by the business $(r = .xx, p = <.05)$; as did their years of schooling $F(12, N=620) = 4.2788, p = .000$. Although higher incomes tended upward with the number of years of schooling, college graduates with a bachelor's degree earned slightly more than graduates with a postgraduate experience.

Because home-based work is a highly complex entity that intertwines the family and the business within the same physical space it was believed that net business income would vary by such characteristics as household size, family status or type, and the number of dependents needing care. Therefore, a typology of the families in the sample was created based upon the marital status of the household manager and the presence or absence of children in the household. Households were categorized as informal families (where the household manager, male or female, was not married and there were no children in the household but they self-identified as living in a family), single-parent households (where the household manager, male or female, was not married but who lived with one or more children), adult-only households (where couples were married but no children under 18 years old were present), and full-nest households (where couples were married and children under age 18 were present). When households were grouped according to their family type (informal family, single-parent, adult-only or full-nest), 348 home-business owners lived in full-nest families (56%), 226 in adult-only families (36.4%), 24 in single-parent families (3.9%), and 22 in informal families (3.6%).

Household size, family type, and the number of dependents requiring care did not in themselves affect net business income. Only when these characteristics were combined with the gender of the home-business owner was income impacted. Incomes were smallest for single-parent families ($8,283) and largest for adult-only ($16,554) and full-nest ($16,265) families. In all instances, female business owners were realizing less income from their family-owned firm than were men, suggesting that family responsibilities diminish women's relative success as small business owners (see Hisrich, 1989).

To further explore the differences in income from family-owned home businesses, rural/urban location and size of the community of residence were examined. Net business income was over $4,000 higher for firms located in large cities, and varied by as much as $5,000 annually depending upon whether the business was located in a rural or urban location $F(1, N-620) = 10.8141, p = .001$.

One explanation for the amount of income earned from home-based work is the nature of the work itself. The businesses were sorted into nine categories using the Standard Occupational Classification Manual: professional/ technical, marketing and sales, clerical, mechanical/ transportation, crafts and artisans, managers, services, contractors, and agricultural products and sales (U.S. Department of Commerce, 1980). The largest business incomes were made in marketing and sales ($29,748) followed by clerical and administrative support ($25,206), contractors ($19,978), and professional/technical work ($16,397). Agricultural sales ($8,120) and service firms ($4,237) were earning much less than other home businesses. Both male and female business owners were more likely to be working in service-oriented fields (85.7% and 14.3%, respectively) than manufacturing or assembling a product for resale although the net business income for product makers was significantly higher ($13,571 and $29,748, respectively) F (1, N=620) = 49.8921, p = .000.

Home business owners were asked whether anyone besides the owner/manager worker worked for or helped out in the business. This could have been paid or unpaid family members, other relatives, independent contractors, or employees. The majority of these extra workers were paid employees (on average, these businesses employed 3.71 workers). The businesses who did employ help were earning, on average, $19,582 compared to $9,961 for those businesses who did not employ help. Differences in net business income were also reflected in the amount of time spent on the work. The number of hours spent in the business was significantly correlated to household size (r = .23, p <.01).

Most home business owners did not (or could not) borrow money or find an outside investor to begin their enterprise. This finding confirms anecdotal evidence that start-up capital for most business ventures, home-based or main street, must come from the business owner's own savings, family, or friends rather than from formal financial institutions. Four hundred eighty-five business owners (79.2%) funded their business start-up themselves. Although borrowing to fund an enterprise means incurring debt to be paid off in the lean years, the 127 business owners who did borrow money were realizing more income from their venture ($21,223) than those who did not ($14,165) and the difference was significant F(1, N=612) = 12.0208, p = .006.

One of the goals of this study was to be able to measure family and business management practices. To that end, two multiple-item scales were developed (Heck, Winter, & Stafford, 1992). The business management questions were asked only of the 304 household managers in the sample who also were the home-based worker. The family management scale was administered to the entire sample. To be consistent, the management concepts measured by both scales were based on the Deacon and Firebaugh (1988) management framework derived from systems theory.

The leading question asked was "Which number, (1 = not at all; 2 =; 3 = somewhat; 4 =; 5 = exactly) describes how much the statement is like you." Three questions were reverse coded for analysis. Higher scores for each question (after recoding) indicated behavior most closely aligned with better management practices. It was assumed that the more numerous the engagement of these specific management practices, the more effective the overall management style and the greater the output from the home-based work (i.e., profit).

The individual scores for each management item within each scale were totaled for each observation. Thus a total score for both the business management scale and the family management scale were obtained for each household. Mean scores for each question within each scale were computed and an overall mean score of the total scores was computed for each scale. A paired t-test for differences in means was used to discover statistical differences between the mean score for each scale and the average income earned by the family-owned business. Contrary to expectations, there was no significant relationship between the net income earned from the business and the mean total scores of either management scale.

Table 1
Which factors influence net business income

Variables*	Regression Coefficients	SE	pvalue
In-state sales	-12528.23	(2067)	.000
Service/product	14815.99	(1579)	.000
Education	2189.77	(243.6)	.000
Paid/unpaid help	6174.96	(1177)	.000
Family type	-1935.15	(592.6)	.001
Hours worked	1.3114	(.5383)	.015
Rural/urban	-4068.43	(1628)	.013
Business management score	-287.55	(116.6)	.014
Gender of home-based worker	3914.87	(1676)	.020

n = 620 R^2 = .6196   *in order of entry

Summary

The final analysis included almost all the factors through which individual and business characteristics are thought to affect the financial success of a family-owned home business. Using OLS regression in a stepwise procedure, the following variables are listed in order of entry: 1) does the business sell in-state; 2) service- or product-related; 3) education level of the owner; 4) whether the business had paid or unpaid help; 5) the family's structure; 6) number of hours at paid work; 7) rural/urban location; 8) overall business management score; and the 9) gender of the home-based worker/ owner. The results, shown in Table 1, suggest that dimensions of the business were more powerful in explaining the amount of income generated by the business than personal characteristics of the characteristics of the owner/operator or environmental factors although all played significant roles.

Acknowledgement

This paper reports results from the Cooperative Regional Research Project, NE-167, entitled, "At-Home Income Generation: Impact on Management, Productivity and Stability in Rural and Urban Families," partially supported by Cooperative States Research Service, U. S. Department of Agriculture, and the Experiment Stations at the University of Hawaii, Iowa State University, Lincoln University (Missouri), Michigan State University, Cornell University (New York), The Ohio State University, The Pennsylvania State University, Utah State University and University of Vermont.

References

Aldrich, H., & Auster, E.R. (1986). Even dwarfs started small: Liabilities of age and size and their strategic implications. In B.M. Staw & L.L. Cummings (Eds.), Research in organizational behavior (Vol. 8, pp. 165-198). Greenwich, CT: JAI Press.

Aldrich, H., Cater, J., Jones, T., & McEvoy, D. (1983). From periphery to peripheral: The South Asian petite bourgeoisie in England. In I.H. Simpson & R. L. Simpson (Eds.), Research in the sociology of work: Peripheral workers (Vol. 2, pp. 1-32). Greenwich, CT: JAI Press.

Aldrich, H., & Weiss, J. (1981). Differentiation within the United States capitalist class: Workforce size and income differences. American Sociological Review, 46, 279-290.

Bender, H. (1980). Report on women business owners. New York: American Management Association.

Dyer, W.G. (1986). Cultural change in family firms. San Francisco: Jossey-Bass.

Heck, R.K.Z., Winter, M., & Stafford, K. (1992). Managing work and family in home-based employment. Journal of Family & Economic Issues, 13, 187-212.

Humphreys, M.A., & McClung, H. (1981). Women entrepreneurs in Oklahoma. Review of Regional Economics and Business, 6(2), 13-20.

Kallenberg, A.L., & Leicht, K.T. (1991). Gender and organizational performance: Determinants of small business survival and success. Academy of Management Journal, 34, 136-161.

Loscocco, K.A., Robinson, J., Hall, R.H., & Allen, J.K. (1991). Gender and small business success: An inquiry into women's relative disadvantage. Social Forces, 70, 65-85.

McClelland, D.C. (1961). The achieving society. New York: Free Press.

Mortimer, J., & London, J. (1984). The varying linkages of work and family. In P. Voydanoff (Ed.), Work and family: Changing roles of men and women (pp. 20-35). Palo Alto, CA: Mayfield Publishing.

Rosenblatt, P.C., deMik, L., Anderson, R.M., & Johnson, P.A. (1990). The family in business. San Francisco: Jossey-Bass.

Stafford, K., Winter, M., Duncan, K.A. & Genalo, M.A. (1992). Studying at-home income generation: Issues and methods. Journal of Family and Economic Issues, 13, 139-158.

U.S. Dept. of Commerce, Office of Federal and Statistical Policy. (1980). Standard Occupational Classification Manual. Washington, DC: Government Printing Office.

The Gender Factor in Hours Worked and Net Income of Home-Based Business Owners

Rosemary Walker, Michigan State University[1]
Marilyn Furry, Pennsylvania State University[2]
Diane Masuo, University of Hawaii[3]

Are the determinants of work hours and income different for women home-based business owners than for men? The answer is yes. Three variables negatively influenced hours worked of both men and women: age, outside job, and sole owners. Experience had a positive influence on women's hours while being in a female dominated occupation had a positive influence for men. Presence of young children had a negative influence on women's net home-based business income in contrast to a positive effect on men's income. Sole owners, with no effect on men's income had a negative effect on women's incomes.

Increasingly men and women engage in similar patterns of employment activities. However, in the labor force, substantial differences in the occupational distributions and earnings of men and women continue (Blau and Ferber, 1986).

Previous studies have found similar gender differentials among home-based workers. Kraut (1989) found that men home-based workers were more likely to be in professional and technical occupations, worked longer hours, and earned more income from this work than did women home-based workers. Rowe and Bentley (1992) found that regardless of family type, women's home-based work income was considerably less than that of men.

Between 1975 and 1988, self-employment increased steadily in both absolute numbers and as a percent of all workers (Aronson, 1991). The term self-employment is usually synonymous with "small business" and can include organizing as a sole proprietorship, as a partnership, or corporation. Aronson questioned why people become self-employed, since studies show that on average this group works longer hours at lower wages than their employee counterparts. The focus of this study is on how the determinants of hours worked and income earned differ by gender for owners of home-based businesses, a group about which little is known.

The Data

The data are from a nine-state regional research project which focused on 899 households in which at least one individual generated income by working at or from the home. Each household was selected as part of a stratified random sample. Information about the work and the worker was collected by means of a 30 minute telephone interview with the household manager. This study focuses on the 670 owners of home-based businesses. The data were weighted to reflect the relative importance in the population of the respective states and the rural/urban areas of the states. The project was supported by the Agricultural Experiment Stations of the participating states.

Research Variables, Research Hypotheses and Procedures

Control variables in the research model were those characteristics of the home-based worker or work that had been shown to be related to working at home for pay (Heck, 1992; Horvath, 1986). These control variables were age, education, location of residence, seasonality of work, and experience.

Children under 6. Heck (1992) in her sample of business owners and employees found that, independent of gender, the presence of children under 6 had a negative influence on the number of home-based work hours and no effect on work income. Rowe and Bentley (1992) concluded that women in certain family situations choose work with fewer hours and demands in order to better integrate their paid work with high family demands. Young children require much care and represent a large time commitment on the part of adults. If women respond differently than men to the requirements of raising children, it was expected that the presence of young children would negatively affect women's number of hours worked. Furthermore, it was hypothesized that independent of the number of hours worked, the presence of children would negatively affect their net income.

[1]Associate Professor,
  Family and Child Ecology

[2]Assistant Professor,
  Agricultural and Extension Education

[3]Assistant Professor,
  Department of Human Resources

Outside job. Because of the 24 hour time constraint, it was hypothesized that having a job outside the home in addition to the home-based work would negatively influence the number of hours spent on the business. Furthermore, independent of the number of hours worked, owners with an outside job were expected to earn less net home-based business income than those with no outside jobs. The presence of income from another job may reduce the profit motive; additionally, owners with outside jobs may operate less efficiently if a greater proportion of their work time is spent "getting ready" and "cleaning up", two important phases of work which do not necessarily contribute to output and income. The differential effect by gender was not hypothesized.

Sole Owner. Businesses can organize as sole-proprietorships (sole owner), partnerships, or corporations. Owners may incorporate for a variety of reasons, such as to reduce personal legal liability, to lower marginal tax rates, or to make themselves eligible for unemployment insurance. The act of incorporating suggests that the business owner has a certain level of sophistication about the business environment and a seriousness about the profit motive that may not be characteristic of other owners. Partnerships have the possibility of dividing the many responsiblities of ownership (including planning, producing, marketing, selling, distributing, and bookkeeping) between two people. The partners can specialize in specific functions, develop efficient operations, and work fewer hours and produce higher incomes than sole proprietors. Thus it was expected that being a sole owner would increase the hours worked and reduce net business income. The differential effect of gender was not hypothesized.

Female dominated occupation. Blau and Ferber (1986), among others (Bergmann, 1986), have shown that the wage rates of individuals who work in occupations that have mainly female workers are lower than those working in mixed gender or male dominated occupations. It was expected that working in a female dominated occupation would increase the number of hours worked for women (to compensate for lower wage rates) and reduce their net business incomes, independent of the number of hours worked. The effect for men was not hypothesized.

The definitions of the research variables are shown in Table 1. The variable "female dominated occupation" requires further explanation.

Table 1
Definitions of Research Variables

Variable	Definition
Age	years of age of home-based worker in 3 brackets
Education	years of education of home-based worker
Children <6	equals 1 if one or more childrens' age was less than 6 years; equals 0 otherwise
Location (rural)	equals 1 if community lived in was town <2,500, rural area or farm; equals 0 otherwise
Outside job	equals 1 if home-based worker is employed outside the home; equals 0 otherwise
Seasonal	equals 1 if home-based work was seasonal in nature, such as retail farm sales, landscaping services; equals 0 otherwise
Sole owners	equals 1 if business was solely owned by worker; equals 0 if partnership or corporation
Female dominated	equals 1 if workers in the occupation consisted of at least 75% women; equals 0 otherwise
Experience	number of years worker has been doing work covered by survey interview
Hours worked	total number of annual hours of work by one or more worker in household and whose work was covered by the survey interview
Income	total net 1988 annual income earned from the home-based business.

Responses to the question "what does the worker do?" were coded into 20 occupational categories, shown in Table 2. Also shown at the end of each row is the total number of businesses in that occupation. The middle column shows the percent of businesses in each occupation owned by a female. An occupation was considered female dominated if 75 percent or more of the owners were women. Thus it can be seen that the following occupations were female dominated: food service, beautician, human services, other services, service managers, and crafts. Least squares regression was the statistical procedure employed.

Table 2
Occupation by Percentage of Female Owners (n=670)

Occupation	% Female	n
Food Service	100.0	1
Beautician	100.0	26
Human Services	100.0	67
Other Services	90.4	6
Service Managers	85.8	14
Crafts	78.8	68
Agricultural Sales	63.7	16
Sales Agents	63.0	31
Clerical	59.7	22
Teachers	59.0	17
Livestock Sales	55.2	4
Manager of Income	52.9	9
Other Sales	38.6	53
Creators	29.8	31
Shopkeepers	15.0	9
Truck Drivers	14.9	42
Professional	13.8	60
Contractors	6.4	124
Mechanics	0.0	65
Sales Representatives	0.0	5

Results

Descriptors for the research variables are presented in Table 3 for female and male owners. Both groups were predominately in the 35-54 age group and had slightly less than 14 years of education. Almost 30 percent of the female owners had children under 6 compared to 25 percent of the males. About one-third of the males had outside jobs compared to about 23 percent of the females. Almost 60 percent of the women owners were in female dominated occupations compared to 4 percent of the men. Females had owned their businesses about two years less than the males. Females worked fewer annual hours and earned considerably less business income than males.

Table 4 shows the regression results. The overall F statistic was significant for each of the four equations, indicating the model was useful in explaining the variation in female's and male's hours worked and net business income. The highest adjusted R^2, .39, was achieved in the regression on female's net income.

Table 3
Descriptive Statistics For Research Variables[a]

Variable	Female (n=279)	Male (n=391)
Age(%)		
<35	26.1	23.9
35-54	53.9	54.0
55 or more	20.1	22.1
Education	13.9[b]	13.6
	(2.4)[c]	(2.4)
Children <6(%)	29.4	25.5
Location (rural)(%)	49.8	45.7
Outside job(%)	22.9	32.3
Seasonal(%)	15.5	19.5
Sole owners(%)	85.3	80.3
Female dominated occupation(%)	59.2	4.4
Experience(years)	8.4	10.2
	(7.9)	(9.5)
Hours(annual)	1521.78	1963.71
	(1279.23)	(1311.07)
Income(net)	7691.17	21297.94

[a] Weighted percentages and means relative to the population of the nine states.
[b] Mean.
[c] Standard deviation.

Children under 6 had no significant effect on hours worked for either gender group. It had a negative effect of nearly $4,000 on female's income and an opposite, positive effect on male's net business income. Thus holding constant hours worked, the presence of children produced monetary results for women that were far different from those of men. One explanation suggests that, given equal work hours, women with young children may be less productive in their business work than their male counterparts, if they are interrupted by household and family demands. In contrast, in families where business work is synonymous with "male work", the presence of young children may stimulate more intense work and a stronger profit motive.

Table 4
OLS Estimates of Owners' Home-Based Work Hours and Net Business Income[a]

Variable	Hours Worked		Net Business Income	
	Female	Male	Female	Male
Worker Characteristics				
Age group	-566.52[b] (-4.12)***	-183.80 (-1.71)*	-2802.91 (-2.61)***	2500.10 (1.32)
Education	-31.19 (-.96)	15.40 (.55)	1335.46 (5.42)***	3310.54 (6.75)***
Children <6	-121.06 (-.62)	13.41 (.00)	-3972.41 (-2.70)***	7826.93 (2.98)***
Location (rural)	65.46 (.44)	114.39 (.90)	-1458.14 (-1.30)	-3469.47 (-1.54)
Work Characteristics				
Outside job	-466.98 (-2.72)***	-997.19 (-7.04)***	-3491.77 (-2.65)***	-6828.12 (2.58)**
Seasonal	-20.04 (-.10)	-524.91 (-3.34)***	-942.56 (-.62)	-2217.88 (-.79)
Sole owner	-771.01 (-3.62)***	-399.96 (-2.58)**	-11218.28 (-6.74)***	-3649.72 (-1.33)
Female dominated occupation	-123.78 (-.78)	628.45 (-2.07)**	-3805.16 (-3.14)***	-9252.44 (-1.73)*
Experience	33.05 (3.31)***	3.97 (.53)	7.47 (.10)	-20.20 (-.15)
Hours worked	----	----	1.69 (3.66)***	3.50 (3.89)***
Constant	3584.24 (5.18)***	1691.12 (3.22)***	4238.67 (.86)	-34235.36 (3.66)***
F ratio =	5.75***	9.30***	18.6***	10.17
Adjusted R^2	.13	.16	.39	.19
N =	279	391	279	391

[a]   Weighted to represent nine states' population.
[b]   Regression coefficient; t statistic below in parenthesis.
*   Significant at .10 level.
**   Significant at .05 level.
***   Significant at .01 level.

Outside job negatively influenced hours worked and net income for both males and females, as hypothesized. However, the effect was substantially greater for men, a result with no obvious explanation since details about the nature of the job or the hours worked were not available.

Sole owner had a negative effect on females' hours and net incomes and on males' hours. The expectation of a negative effect concerned the possible differences between sole owners and owners who use other forms of business organization, with the focus on entrepreneurial intent and efficiency. The results seen to corroborate these differences in female-owned businesses. The results are mixed for males. While the negative effect prevailed on their hours worked, holding constant hours worked, sole owner did not influence their net incomes.

Female dominated occupation significantly reduced net income for females as expected. It also significantly reduced the hours worked and net income for males.

Hours worked was a significant influence on net business income for both genders; however, the coefficient values were substantially different. An additional hour worked by a male produced more than double the income earned by a female.

Results of Chow tests corroborate that the gender models for both dependent variables are different. Chow test results were: hours worked, $F(10,650) = 4.43$; net business income $F(11,648) = 6.37$. Thus the empirical results indicate that at least some of the influences on business owners' hours worked and net income differ by gender.

Conclusions

It is "old news" to find that some of the major determinants of two important dimensions of work - hours worked and income - are different for women and men. Researchers have been finding this for years in studies of workers. Most of these studies have been samples of employees, however. Similar conclusions related to business owners have been based on sparser evidence (Aronson, 1991; Moore, 1983). What is new here is that, in a random sample of home-based business owners, the gender differences persist.

References

Moore, R.L. (1983). Employer discrimination: Evidence from self-employed workers. Review of Economics and Statistics, 65(3), 496-501.

Rowe, B.R. & Bentley, M.T. (1992). The impact of the family on home-based work. Journal of Family and Economic Issues, 13(3), 279-298.

Aronson, R.L. (1991). Self-employment: A Labor Market Perspective. Ithaca, NY: ILR Press.

Bergmann, B.R. (1986). The Economic Emergence of Women. Basic Books.

Blau, F.D. & Ferber, M.A. (1986). The Economics of Women, Men, and Work. Englewood Cliffs, NJ: Prentice-Hall.

Heck, R.K.Z. (1992). The effects of children on the major dimensions of home-based employment. Journal of Family and Economic Issues, 13(3), 315-346.

Horvath, F.W. (1986). Work at home: New findings from the current population survey. Monthly Labor Review, 109(11), 31-35.

Kraut, R.E. (1989). Telecommuting: The trade-offs of home work. Journal of Communication, 39(3), 19-47.

Implicit Income Generated by Home-Based Employment and Its Impact on Household and Social Welfare

Xiaojing Jessie Fan, The Ohio State University[1]

The purpose of this study was to estimate the implicit income generated from taking care of their own children when working at home and its impact on welfare change both at micro and macro level. The results show that for a typical home-based worker of this kind, the yearly Hicksian compensating and the Hicksian equivalent variation were about $2564.53 and $1651.87, respectively. For the nine states included in the sample, a point estimate of the aggregate Hicksian equivalent variation was about 80.5 million.

As the labor force participation rate of women with young children increased dramatically in the last thirty years, child care as an institution is facing a crisis of funding and recognition. The gap between the demand of paid care giving and child care service supply give at least some households the incentives to work at home and use home-based employment as a solution to the family's needs for child care. For these households, the income earned from home-based employment was twofold. While visible money income was generated from the paid employment, there was a certain amount of invisible income generated from providing child care at the same time. The purpose of this paper was to estimate this invisible income and its impact on welfare change both at micro and macro level. The presented information can help us better evaluate the costs and benefits of home-based employment and its related policy issues.

Theoretical Framework

Assume the household's utility function is $U(X,H)$, where X is a vector of commodities and H denotes the time of paid work. The budget constraint may be written as $PX - wH = m$, where P is a vector of prices of goods X and w is the wage rate. The household's compensated demand function and labor supply function can be derived from the solution to the problem: minimize $PX - wH$ subject to $U(X, H) = u$. By solving the first-order conditions, the compensated commodity demand and labor supply functions (Boadway & Bruce, 1984) may be written as:

$$x_i = x_i(P, w, u) \qquad i = 1, \ldots, n$$
$$H = H(w, P, u).$$

Given the fact that the group of home-based workers generated implicit income by working and providing child care simultaneously, their real wage rate was higher than their visible money wage rate. Denote the visible money wage rate as w', the real wage rate was $w^2 = w' + m'/H$, where m' was the amount of implicit income generated from providing child care. Thus given the labor supply function, if the wage rate were only the visible money wage rate w', their desired hours of working would have been different from what they did under w^2, which was the true wage rate.

The Hicksian compensating variation HC measure of welfare change due to this wage rate change was defined to be the amount of money that could be taken away from the household in the situation with the implicit income in order to leave it as well off as in the situation without the implicit income. Making use of the expenditure function and the Hotelling's lemma, the formula of HC may be written as:

$$HC = m^2 - e(p^2, w^2, u_1) = \int_{w^1}^{w^2} H(w, p, u_1)\, dw \quad (1)$$

Alternatively, we can also use Hicksian equivalent variation HE, which was the amount of income that must be given to the household in the situation without implicit income in order to give the household same utility level in the situation with implicit income:

$$HE = e(p^2, w^2, u_2) - m^1 = \int_{w^1}^{w^2} H(w, p, u_2)\, dw \quad (2)$$

However, empirically, without assuming a specific functional form of the utility function, only the Marshallian uncompensated labor supply function can be estimated from observable data and the Marshallian uncompensated workers surplus can be estimated. Following labor economic theory, labor supply H is a function of prices, wage rate, and exogenous income. Because of the cross-sectional nature of this study, prices can be treated as being constant. Therefore, the uncompensated labor supply function for an individual takes the form:

$$H = H(w, m_0)$$

with m_0 denoting the exogenous income (Ehrenberg & Smith, 1988).

Data and Methods

The data set for this study was a subsample

---

[1]Ph.D candidate,
Family Resource Management

from a 1988-1989 nine-states project on households in which at least one individual generated income by working at or from home (HBW) (Stafford, Winter, Duncan & Genalo, 1992). The subsample used in this study was 351 households with children who needed care on a daily basis.

Another sample was from the National Longitudinal Survey of Youth (NLSY) with 869 households who had child care expenses in 1988.

The methods of the study consisted of the following steps: (1) a OLS regression for estimation of weekly child care expense per child using the NLSY subsample; (2) prediction of the hypothetical child care expenses for the HBW subsample; (3) estimation of the yearly implicit income for each HBW household; (4) a OLS regression for estimation of the labor supply functions for both business owners (n=263) and paid employees (n=88); (5) computation of the Marshallian workers surplus change MM for each observation based on estimated labor supply functions:

$$MM = \int_{w^1}^{w^2} H(w, m_0) \, dw; \qquad (3)$$

(6) estimation of Hicksian compensated welfare change using Willig's approximation formula with η as the income elasticity (Willig, 1976).

$$HC = MM - \frac{1}{2} \frac{\eta MM^2}{m^0}, \quad HE = MM + \frac{1}{2} \frac{\eta MM^2}{m^0}; \qquad (4)$$

(7) estimation of the aggregate welfare change utilizing the sample incidence information.

Selected Empirical Results and Discussion

The sample mean wage rate without implicit income was $14.18 for business owners and $10.42 for paid employees. After adjusting for implicit income, the real wage rate was $15.37 and $11.53, respectively. Selected results of the labor supply equation are presented in Table 1.

Table 1.
Estimated Labor Supply Function (OLS)

Variables	Business owner Coef.	t-value	Paid Employee Coef.	t-value
$LN(w^2)$	-6.62***	-5.130	3.36*	1.816
$LN(m_0)$	-1.04***	-2.747	-1.18**	-1.993
Other controlled variables				
adj. R^2	0.2734		0.4913	

*** statistically significant at 99% level
** statistically significant at 95% level
* statistically significant at 90% level

Based on the results of the estimated labor supply function, household welfare change due to implicit income was calculated using the formulas provided in the data and methods section. The overall weighted mean Marshallian worker's surplus for the whole sample was $2023.32. The corresponding Hicksian compensating variation HC and Hicksian equivalent variation HE were $2564.53 and $1651.87. This means, holding other things equal, assume a typical household in the sample did not generate implicit income from providing child care when working at home, then $1651.87 must have been given to this household to let it attain the utility level with implicit income.

Using the incidence rate information collected in the pilot study of HBW data (Stafford et al, 1992), the estimated population size for household with home-based worker was 1,248,495 for nine states, and the estimated proportion of the subpopulation with at home child care was 0.3904. Thus a point estimate of the total Hicksian compensating variation was about 1.25 billion. For Hicksian equivalent variation, a point estimate was 80.5 million. This means, if these households could not take care of their children when working, 80.5 million must be compensated to them in order to keep them as well off as they could provide child care when working, a number which is too big to be ignored!

Conclusion

The results of this study show that providing child care when working at home did have important welfare impact on the economic status of the households by increasing the household well being both at the individual and aggregate level at a substantial amount. Therefore, when analyzing the welfare status of this group of households either for the purpose of intragroup (group of households with home-based employment) or intergroup comparisons, using only money income will substantially underestimate the true welfare level of this group and influence the goodness of the comparison. Further studies on the determinants of the magnitude of the welfare change will be very useful.

References

Boadway, R.W. & Bruce, N. (1984). Welfare Economics. Basil Blackwell.

Ehrenberg, R.G. & Smith, R.S. (1988). Modern Labor Economics - Theory and Public Policy. Scott, Foresman and Company.

Stafford, K., Winter, M., Duncan, K.A. & Genalo, M.A. (1992). Studying at-home income generation: issues and methods. Journal of Family and Economic Issues, 13(2), 139-158.

Willig, R.D. (1976). Consumer's surplus without apology. The American Economic Review. 66(4), 589-597.

The Benefits of Home-Based Work

Karen A. Duncan, The Ohio State University[1]

Reservation wage rates were estimated using a sample of home-based workers pulled from the 1986 interviewing year of the Panel Study of Income Dynamics. The estimates were calculated by age of youngest child and employment status of the wife. The reservation wage rate estimates were lower than those obtained in previous research which did not separate home-based workers from all other workers

---

In general terms, home-based work is paid work done in or from the home. One of the reasons this type of work continues to gain attention is it's perceived attractiveness as a way for women to balance work and family demands. Home-based may also be more attractive than traditional work settings if people perceive home-based work as a lower cost entry into the labour force.

However, the research on home-based work is more suggestive than definitive of possible benefits and costs of working at home for pay. One notable exception is the work of Kraut and Grambsch (1987) which indicates the importance of fixed costs and controlling for both productivity and tastes and preferences for work. In this study, Heckman's (1976) procedure was used to estimate the reservation wage for home-based work and to compare the estimates to those obtained in previous research.

The reservation wage is the wage one must offer a nonemployed person to induce that person into the labour market, that is, to overcome one's reservations about market work. Thus, any costs associated with employment should raise the reservation wage. If fixed costs are lower for home-based than office-based work, then the reservation wage for home-based work should be lower. This yields the expectation that the reservation wage which must be offered to induce someone to engage in home-based work will be lower than that needed to induce the same person to engage in office-based work.

Data

The 1986 interviewing year of the Panel Study of Income Dynamics (PSID), the most recent year of data which permitted identification of home-based workers, was selected for use in the analysis. The sample was restricted to married, adult women whose spouse was present and employed. Home-based workers were identified as those individuals who were employed but did not report travelling any distance to work. Note that this definition excludes home-based workers such as salespeople, who travel from a home-based office. The

restrictions resulted in a sample of 1,128 women of which 83 were home-based workers and 945 were nonlabour force participants.

Empirical Model

The equation for probability of the wife's labour force participation was specified as:

$$LFP = ED + WKEXP + WKEXP2 + HEALTHLT + OCCUPN + SMSA + HUSBWY + TRANSFY + KIDLT6 + NUMKIDS + UNEMP \quad (1)$$

and estimated using the PROBIT option in Shazam. The inverse mills ration (LAMBDA) was generated in this step and entered as an independent variable in the wage and hours equations. Next, the following empirical specifications of the wage and hours equations were estimated using the OLS option:

$$LNWRATE = a_0 + a_1ED + a_2WKEXP + a_3WKEXP2 + a_4HEALTHLT + a_5OCCUPN + a_6SMSA + a_7UNEMP + a_8LAMBDA \quad (2)$$

$$HRSMKTWK = c_0 + c_1ED + c_2WKEXP + c_3WKEXP2 + c_4HEALTHLT + c_5SMSA + c_6UNEMP + c_7HUSBWY + c_8TRANSFY + c_9KIDLT6 + c_{10}NUMKIDS + c_{11}LAMBDA. \quad (3)$$

The parameters of the reservation wage equation,

$$LNWSTAR = b_0 + b_1ED + b_2WKEXP + b_3WKEXP2 + b_4AREA + b_5HUSBWY + b_6TRANSFY + b_7KIDLT6 + b_8NUMKIDS + b_9HRSMKTWK \quad (4)$$

were calculated from the parameters of equations (2) and (3). Definitions and summary statistics of variables used in the model are presented in the Appendix. The theoretical model upon which the empirical model is based may be found in Heckman (1976).

Results and Discussion

In Table 1, the reservation wage rates calculated from the PSID are compared with those obtained by Zick and Bryant (1983). Regardless of employment status of the wife or age of youngest child, the reservation wage rates for home-based workers were much lower than those obtained for employed women by Zick and Bryant. Presuming few home-based workers were in the NE-113 data used by Zick and Bryant, these results may provide some preliminary indication that reservation wage rates are lower for home-based than office-based work.

---

[1]Graduate Administrative Associate, Graduate School.

That is, lower entry costs may be associated with home-based as opposed to office-based work.

Table 1
Reservation Wage Estimates by Age of Youngest Child and Employment Status of the Wife.

| Age of youngest child | NE-113 data[a] | | NLS data | |
	Employed	Not Employed	Employed	Not Employed
12-17	8.32	7.31	4.13 (n=15)	3.45 (n=97)
6-11	7.75	7.63	4.66 (n=20)	4.17 (n=157)
2-5	7.61	6.88	4.50 (n=12)	3.08 (n=260)
1	8.20	6.99	6.50 (n=12)	2.57 (n=267)
< 1	7.03	6.48	-	-
None	-	-	7.73 (n=24)	3.49 (n=264)
Overall	7.90	7.01	5.70 (n=83)	3.21 (n=1045)

[a]From Zick & Bryant (1983). These numbers have been inflated by the change in the Consumer Price Index (Bureau of the Census, 1990, Table No. 762) between 1977 (when the NE-113 data were collected) and 1985.

Further work needs to be done with the PSID in examining the reservation wage rates for office-based women. If reservation wage rates for office-based work are found to be higher than those for home-based work, it would indicate a perception of lower barriers to entry for home-based work.

In addition, alternative specifications of the wage equation should be explored. The specification used here did not perform well in explaining wage rates. Finally, the possible effect of a household being part of the low income subsample of the PSID should be investigated.

References

Heckman, J. J. (1976). The common structure of statistical models of truncation, sample selection and limited dependent variables and a simple estimator for such models. Annals of Economics and Social Measurement, 5, 475-492.

Zick, C. D., & Bryant, W. K. (1983). Alternative strategies for pricing home work time. Home Economics Research Journal, 12, 133-144.

Appendix

Definitions and Descriptive Statistics of Variables Used in the Model.[a]

Variable	Definition	Mean[b] (std. dev.)
Dependent variables		
LFP	1 = wife is a home-based worker 0 = wife is a full-time homemaker	.07 (.26)
LNWRATE	Natural log of the wage rate	1.26 (.95)
LNWSTAR	Natural log of the reservation wage	
Independent variables		
ED	Wife's years of education	12.50 (1.56)
WKEXP	Wife's years of labour force experience	5.31 (7.88)
HEALTHLT	1 = wife has a health limitation 0 = no health limitation	.14 (.34)
HUSBWY	Income of husband from wages and salary	27,310.00 (26,633.00)
TRANSFY	Income of household from other sources	1,193.80 (3,241.20)
KIDLT6	1 = child under 6 years of age present in household 0 = no child under 6 years of age present	.49 (.50)
NUMKIDS	Number of children under 18 years of age present	1.53 (1.26)
UNEMP	Unemployment rate for county of residence (x.xx%)	6.84 (2.90)
SMSA	1 = rural 0 = urban	.47 (.50)
HRSMKTWK[c]	Weekly hours worked in market by wife during survey week	31.76 (19.53)
LAMBDA	Sample selection correction factor	

[a]N = 1128. [b]Means reported for noncontinuous variables represent the proportion of the sample with a value of 1. [c]For employed wives only.

Health Insurance Coverage of Home-based Workers

Kathryn Stafford, The Ohio State University[1]
Patricia D. Olson, The Ohio State University[2]

The same proportion of home-based workers are covered by health insurance as in the population. Only 12.4 percent of home-based business owners are covered by a policy at least partially paid by the business but 51.8 percent of home-based wage earners are covered by a group policy. Another job is the most frequent means of coverage for the business owners, 54 percent. Income and age of worker were the most influential variables on the odds of being covered. Nonhome-based income had a larger effect than home-based income.

Health insurance coverage is a topic of current debate throughout the country. Major health care reforms are being planned. Advocates for national health care reform often discuss the lack of health insurance for home-based business owners and home-based wage earners. The purpose of this paper is to provide baseline data on health insurance coverage of home-based workers.

The national monthly average proportion of the adult population covered by either private or government health insurance is 87.1 percent, leaving 12.9 percent uninsured at any one point in time (U.S. Bureau of the Census, 1992).

Methods

The sample for this study consisted of the 899 households interviewed by the Iowa Statistical Laboratory for United States Department of Agriculture Cooperative State Research Service Regional Project NE 167 "At-Home Income Generation: Impact on Management, Productivity, and Stability in Rural/Urban Families." The participating states were Hawaii, Iowa, Michigan, Missouri, New York, Ohio, Pennsylvania, Utah, and Vermont. To qualify for inclusion in the study a household had to have at least one adult who worked at least 312 hours the past year earning income at home and had no other office for this work. The sample has been described fully elsewhere (Stafford et al., 1992), but a brief overview of pertinent sample characteristics is provided here in Table 1. One respondent did not reply to questions on insurance so the actual sample size in the study was 898.

Data were collected during 30-minute telephone interviews in the spring of 1989. The self

Table 1
Mean Explanatory Variables

	Mean (Std. Dev.)	Proportion
Home-based income ($ 1989)	$17,918.18 (21,117.02)	
Nonhome-based income ($ 1989)	$24,428.71 (18,437.60)	
Household size	3.35 (1.48)	
Farm		.07
Rural, nonfarm		.197
Small town		.194
Business owner		.74
Age of worker	43.68 (12.54)	
Currently employed outside		.26

identified home manager was the person interviewed. Home-based workers are a "rare" population. The screening questions used to identify qualifying households and the ensuing incidence rate have been described fully in Stafford (1992). All questions about income, hours on the job, and insurance coverage referred to the preceding year, 1988. Income was imputed for households which did not provide that information.

Each respondent was asked, "Is (hbw) covered by health insurance?" If the answer were "Yes," the respondent also was asked, "Who pays for (hbw's) health insurance?" The coded responses to the second question differed slightly for business owners and wage earners. Coded wage earners' responses included several arrangements for splitting the costs between employer and employee (Table 2). The responses to these two questions have been analyzed in the research reported in this article.

To ascertain the proportion of workers covered by health insurance responses to the first question

---

[1]Professor, Family Resource Management Department

[2]Ph.D Student, Family Resource Management Department

were tabulated. Responses to the second question also were tabulated and a chi-square test of independence was run to ascertain whether the means of obtaining health insurance coverage differed between home-based business owners and wage earners. Finally, a logit analysis of the odds of being covered by health insurance was conducted to identify variables which increase the odds of being covered.

Results

Home-based workers have health insurance in similar proportions to the national average. The proportion of home-based workers in this sample covered by health insurance was 89 (s.d.= 31) percent with 89 (s.d.= 31) percent of owners and 92 (s.d. = 28) percent of wage earners covered. Any difference must be in who pays for the health insurance.

Table 2
Who Pays for Health Insurance

	Business Owners	Wage Earners
	Percent	Percent
Business expense	11.9	23.9
Someone else's job	39.0	26.6
Own other job	15.0	8.9
Personal policy	26.1	8.5
Medicare, gov't.	7.4	4.2
Combination	.5	21.2
Group policy		6.7
	n = 594	n = 209

Even a brief perusal of Table 2 leads to the conclusion that business owners and wage earners obtain and pay for their health insurance by different means, and the cursory conclusion is reinforced by the chi-square statistic (7, n = 822) = 245.6, p<.001. Another job is the most frequent means of obtaining coverage for business owners; whereas, the home-based job is the most frequent means of obtaining health insurance for wage earners. Over half of the owners obtain their health insurance via another job. Fifteen percent of them obtain coverage via another job of their own, but 39 percent of the owners obtain health insurance via someone else's job. Indeed, one might conclude an employed spouse is their best asset.

Table 3
Odds of Health Insurance Coverage

		Logit coeff. (std. error)
***	Home-based income	.00003 (8.8 E-6)
***	Nonhome-based income	.00005 (8.88 E-6)
	Household size	.0224 (.0691)
	Farm	-.3734 (.3845)
	Rural, nonfarm	-.3734 (.2590)
	Small town	-.1275 (.2769)
	Business owner	-.0892 (.2650)
*	Age of worker	.0229 (.0092)
	Currently employed outside	-.0239 (.2397)
	Intercept	.2590 (.5837)
	N = 898	

*** p≤.0001
*   p≤.05

The results in Table 3 indicate income and age of worker increase the odds of a home-based worker being covered by health insurance. The coefficients may be interpreted as percentage change in the odds of coverage.

References

Stafford, K., Winter, M., Duncan, K.A., & Genalo, M.A. (1992).   Studying At-Home Income Generations: Issues and Methods. Journal of Family & Economic Issues, 13(2), 139-158.

U.S. Bureau of the Census. (1992).   Health Insurance Coverage: 1987-1990 (CPR Series P-70, No 29). Washington DC: U.S. Government Printing Office.

The Money Attitude Scale: What College Students Think About the Green Stuff

Jan Andersen, Paul Camp, Elizabeth Kiss,
Satomi Wakita, and Jennifer Weyeneth,[1]
with the assistance of Vicki Schram Fitzsimmons[2]
University of Illinois at Urbana-Champaign

College student money attitudes were measured with the Money Attitude Scale (MAS) and compared with attitudes of an adult population. Similarities and differences were found. Factor analysis results showed that college student money attitudes were: Power-Prestige, Complaining-Doubting, and Retention-Time. Multiple regression analysis showed that gender and source of income were determinants of money attitudes.

College students today have a myriad of consumer problems related to money (easy access to consumer credit, premature affluence, increasing costs of tuition, books, room and board, and fewer available low-interest loans). An understanding of how college students view their interactive role with money is a fundamental step towards understanding how they are influenced by money. One method of determining what money means to undergraduate college students is to study their multi-dimensional attitudes toward money.

Background Information

The term attitude is widely agreed to refer to a positive or negative feeling towards a given class of stimuli (Seibold, 1980). Theorists believe attitudes help to organize and structure a rather chaotic world by providing ready aids for sizing up objects and events in the environment (Pieters, 1988). Also, it is believed that attitudes direct behavior. Thus, a knowledge of attitudes is essential to explain, predict, or modify consumer behavior. Attitudes, however, are not static; they evolve over the life cycle.

College students are considered to be transitional consumers in the consumer life cycle framework (Stampfl, 1978). They may be classified as adolescent consumers or early single consumers depending on their age and financial autonomy. Consumer characteristics of these stages that apply to college students include experimentation with life style and consumption, evolving tastes and preferences, and susceptibility to peer pressure.

Garman and Forgue (1991, pp. 74-77) ascribed financial tasks, problems, and challenges to various life cycle stages. College student consumers fit into the singlehood, transitional stage. Some financial management tasks, problems, and challenges in this stage include first time credit use, budget control, recordkeeping, and establishment of financial goals and plans. For many college students money management is a first time experience. College students may have money management problems associated with the learning process and/or the relative freedom of being on their own.

The purpose of this research was to understand undergraduate college student attitudes toward money. Further, the researchers wanted to compare money attitudes between college students and the general adult population.

Related Literature and Hypothesized Relationships

Research on money attitudes has taken a variety of foci. Instrument development was the primary focus of Furnham (1984) and Yamauchi and Templer (1982). Moschis and Churchill (1978) described the process by which young people acquire consumer-related knowledge, attitudes, and skills as consumer socialization. They examined the socializing influences of consumerism on money attitudes and the effect of money attitudes on behaviors. Several studies have investigated gender differences in money attitudes (Bailey & Lown, 1992a; Furnham, 1984; Wilhelm, Fridrich, & Varcoe, 1992). Cross-cultural differences in money attitudes and the influence of money attitudes in the assessment of one's economic well-being were reported by Bailey and Lown (1992a) and Wilhelm and Varcoe (1991), respectively. The dichotomous relationship of attitudes toward spending and saving (Bailey & Lown, 1992b) and the use of the Money in the Past and Future Scale (Bailey & Lown, 1992b; Furnham, 1984) also were explored.

Instrumentation

Yamauchi and Templer (1982) generated an

---

[1] Graduate students; authorship shared equally, and names appear alphabetically.

[2] Associate Professor, Family and Consumer Economics

instrument containing 62 items which reflected security, retention, and power-prestige domains. They administered the instrument to 300 volunteer subjects from the general population of adults living in Los Angeles and Fresno, California. Principal components factor analysis (varimax rotation) with a scree test indicated that the original instrument measured five dimensions of attitudes towards money; however, one dimension, Quality, was omitted from the final scale because it did not seem to be motivationally different from the Power-Prestige factor. The remaining four money attitude factors (Power-Prestige, Time-Retention, Distrust, and Anxiety) were designated the Money Attitude Scale (MAS).

The MAS asks respondents to indicate the frequency with which their actual behavior matches any of several test items designed to reflect the presence of the four separate money attitudes. Power-Prestige refers to the extent to which the individual views money as a means to impress and influence others. Time-Retention measures the extent to which the respondent engages in financial behaviors which require careful planning and preparation for the future. Distrust is an indication of the extent to which the respondent harbors hesitant and suspicious attitudes about money and its use. The final factor, Anxiety, refers to attitudes which reflect anxiety, or conversely, protection from anxiety by the use of money.

Cronbach's alpha coefficients for the four subscales were .80 (Power-Prestige), .78 (Time-Retention), .73 (Distrust), and .69 (Anxiety), indicating good internal consistency (Yamauchi & Templer, 1982). Test-retest reliability (5 weeks after the original administration) yielded coefficients of .95, .92, .87, and .88, respectively.

Yamauchi and Templer (1982) reported that the psychological perceptions of money, as measured by the MAS, were essentially independent of a person's income. Because Yamauchi and Templer failed to investigate any other demographic differences such as age and sex, Furnham (1984) identified this omission as a major shortcoming of Yamauchi and Templer's research. Also, Furnham felt that Yamauchi and Templer had not given enough attention to normal social beliefs and attitudes or to the aetiology of these beliefs.

Furnham (1984) expanded Yamauchi and Templer's (1982) research from the psychological perspective of understanding personality disorders in order to find significant relationships between demographic determinants and money beliefs and behaviors of average people. Furnham created a 60-item inventory to measure money attitudes called the "Money Beliefs and Behavior Scale" (MBBS). The MBBS consisted of three main parts: (a) Yamauchi and Templer's MAS; (b) Goldberg and Lewis' (1979) psychology of money items; and (c) Rubinstein's (1980) Midas Scale items.

Furnham's (1984) results were both similar to and different from Yamauchi and Templer's (1982) study. Using factor analysis, Furnham measured six money attitudes: Obsession, Power/Spending, Retention, Security/Conservative, Inadequacy, and Effort/Ability. Obsession measures an attitude indicating obsession with all aspects of money. Power/Spending refers to gaining power through the use of money. Retention is an attitude of people who use money very carefully. Security/ Conservative identifies an old-fashioned attitude toward money. Inadequate measures I-haven't-got-enough-money feelings. Effort/Ability refers to how money is obtained.

Influences of Money Attitudes

Age was one of the determinants of money attitudes that Furnham (1984) examined which was pertinent to this study. He found that when compared to older people, younger people used money more as a means of power, were less security-minded, and were less careful and retentive with money. Using a sample of 806 12- to 18-year-olds, Moschis and Churchill (1978) also found a significant relation between age and socially desirable behaviors. Thus, for college students, age should have a significant relationship with one or more money attitudes.

Moschis and Churchill (1978) found a significant relationship between social class and economic motivation for consumption. These researchers viewed social class as one of many reference groups with which college students might identify. In the process of developing money attitudes, college students may be influenced by the standards and values of their reference groups. Their reference groups may give them valuable information (Wärneryd, 1988). Further, Moschis and Churchill found that adolescent's consumer affairs knowledge, social motivations for consumption, and level of materialism were related positively to peer communication about consumption. Thus, college students' money attitudes should be influenced by the variables that have reference-group attributes (e.g., persons of the same year in school, persons of the same race, persons from the same neighborhoods, persons of the same sex, persons using the same method to finance their college education).

Another aspect to consider when studying college students is gender differences; the influence of gender role perceptions is important in understanding the behaviors associated with the meaning of money. Several researchers, using money attitude surveys, have found that male respondents tended to be more obsessed with money while female respondents were more conservative and security conscious (Furnham, 1984; Moschis & Churchill, 1978; Wilhelm, et al., 1992). Also, female respondents tended to agree with statements that indicate they use money to buy friendships and as a weapon, possibly to provide a sense of control within interpersonal relationships (Wilhelm, et al., 1992). They tended to have "an unrealistic view of the power and importance of money" and tended to "associate inadequacy of money [worry over finances and comparison with friends in respect to financial success] with the perception or fantasy that if money was available everything would be alright" (Wilhelm, et al., 1992, pp. 176-177). Thus, for college students there should be a significant relationship between gender and money attitudes.

Objectives

The first objective of this research was to examine the money attitudes of college students using the MAS (Yamauchi & Templer, 1982). College student attitudes, then, were compared to the attitudes of the heterogeneous population used in Yamauchi and Templer's study. A second objective of this research was to explore the determinants of money attitudes by analyzing relationships between college students' demographic characteristics and their predominant money attitudes.

Methods

Sample

Total participants in this study were 165 undergraduate students enrolled in two general education courses at the University of Illinois at Urbana-Champaign. Students from one section of introductory geology and political science courses comprised the convenience sample. (A convenience sample was used because this study was partly exploratory and because time and money constraints existed.) Data were collected during one of the regularly scheduled class meetings early in the 1992 fall semester. Nine participants, whose ages exceeded 21, were omitted from further study because it is likely that they are not representative of typical undergraduate college students and that their responses would skew the results. Also, omission of these outliers removed from the sample the only two participants who were married. Final sample size was 156.

Mean age for the sample was 18.9 years (range = 17-21). Fifty-three percent of the students were male, and 47% were female. Most (72%) of the students were underclassmen (freshmen or sophomores), and 28% were upperclassmen (juniors or seniors). Over half of the sample was majoring in either the social sciences (37%) or language and communication (22%). Eleven percent of the sample reported their major as business, 9% as natural or physical science, and 7% as engineering. The remaining participants were listed either as missing or enrolled in pre-professional programs, education, or general majors. Almost all (95%) had never been married. The majority of the sample (58%) were originally from large metropolitan areas including suburbs. The remainder of the sample were divided almost equally between rural (20%) and urban (21%) backgrounds. Caucasian students comprised 78% of the sample; the remainder were Asian (7%), African-American (5%), Hispanic (6%), Native American (1%), Other (2%), and Missing (2%).

Available demographic data for the total undergraduate population at the University of Illinois were limited. However, males comprised 56% of the population, and females 44%. Almost all (98%) undergraduates were single. Thus, marital status and gender were similar in both the sample and the population. The population was divided almost equally between underclassmen (48%) and upperclassmen (50%); the remainder (2%) were classified as other. Thus, the sample overrepresented underclassmen and underrepresented upperclassmen.

Data Collection

The questionnaire consisted of two parts. The first part was a randomized-items version of the MAS. The researchers chose to use Yamauchi and Templer's (1982) MAS instead of Furnham's (1984) MBBS for two reasons. First, the MBBS was designed and tested on a British sample and the MAS was developed using an American sample. Because there might be cultural differences in money attitudes, the MAS seemed better to use with an American college student sample. Second, the MAS consisted of fewer items than the MBBS and, therefore, better fit the instrument administration time constraints of this study. The second part of the questionnaire consisted of demographic questions.

The 29 money-attitude variables were measured by asking respondents to indicate their feelings regarding a variety of money-behavior statements (e.g., "I use money to influence other people to do things for me."). The instrument was scored in 7-point Likert format with the lower and upper endpoints labeled as 'Never' and 'Always' respectively. These endpoints were identical to the ones used by Yamauchi and Templer (1982). Although the intervening points used in this study (seldom, sometimes, occasionally, usually, and most of the time) were not identical to those used by Yamauchi and Templer (very seldom, seldom, sometimes, often, and very often), they were very similar.[1] These 29 variables were subsequently reduced by factor analysis to form the dependent variables.

A total of 14 independent variables were included in the data set. Continuous variables were age, year in school (1 = freshman, 2 = sophomore, 3 = junior, 4 = senior), and weekly number of work hours. Dichotomous variables were gender (0 = male and 1 = female), ethnic heritage (0 = non-white and 1 = white), and location of primary residence while growing up (1 = rural and 2 = urban/metropolitan). Finally, data were collected on the percentage of funding for college expenses from a number of different sources (parents, merit scholarships, need-based scholarships, loan programs, summer employment, on-campus employment, savings, or other non-specified sources). Each was treated as a continuous independent variable.[2]

Statistical Analysis

Statistical analyses were completed using the

SPSS/PC+ software package. All analyses were done on an IBM personal computer.

For the first objective, confirmatory factor analysis was done to determine variable loadings by specifying the extraction of four factors (the number of factors obtained by Yamauchi and Templer, 1982). The 29 money-attitude variables were submitted to principal components factor analysis with varimax rotation. The resulting factors could then be used to make comparisons with Yamauchi and Templer's findings and as dependent variables in the multiple regression analysis for the second objective of this study.

Each factor was examined to ensure that those items with high loadings (an absolute value of .4 or greater) were conceptually related and that their inclusion did not cause large breaks in the distances between variable loadings. Variables meeting these criteria were retained in the factor, and tests for Cronbach's alpha were conducted to determine internal consistency of each factor. A coefficient of .65 was selected as being sufficient to indicate scale reliability. Factor scores were saved for the subsequent multiple regression analysis.

To determine which independent variables had the largest impact on undergraduate money attitudes (objective 2), multiple regression analysis was used. The factors created in objective 1 were the dependent variables. The independent variables were student's age, year in school, gender, and percentage of respondent's funding for college expenses from a number of different sources (parents, merit scholarships, need-based scholarships, loan programs, summer employment, on-campus employment, savings, and other non-specified sources). Standardized beta coefficients were calculated.

Correlation analysis of all independent variables was used to identify problems of potential multicollinearity. Variables correlated at .6 or higher were run in separate regression models. The initial regression analysis results were compared to identify the best model. Adjusted R^2, number of significant variables, and meaningfulness of the highly correlated variables all were considered in choosing the model for the final regression. Following this stage, variables significant at the .10 level or beyond were retained for the final multiple regression analysis.

Results and Discussion

Factor Analysis

Four factors were extracted via principal components factor analysis. Combined, these factors explained 48.7% of the variance. Item means, rotated factor loadings, and Cronbach's alpha coefficients for each of the four factors are presented in Tables 1 through 4.

Table 1

Item Means and Variable Loadings for Factor 1, Power-Prestige, n = 156

Variables	Mean Response	Rotated Factor Loadings
I behave as if money were the ultimate symbol of success.	2.5	.820
I must admit that I purchase things because I know they will impress others.	2.2	.726
In all honesty, I own nice things in order to impress others.	2.6	.722
Although I should judge the success of people by their deeds, I am more influenced by the amount of money they have.	2.6	.708
People I know tell me that I place too much emphasis on the amount of money a person has as a sign of success.	2.0	.667
I use money to influence other people to do things for me.	1.8	.662
I must admit that I sometimes boast about how much money I make.	2.0	.634
I seem to find that I show more respect to people with more money than I have.	2.6	.621
I often try to find out if other people make more money than I do.	2.7	.563

Note. Cronbach's Alpha = .87.

Table 2

Item Means and Variable Loadings for Factor 2, Complaining-Doubting, n = 156

Variables	Mean Response	Rotated Factor Loadings
When I buy something, I complain about the price I paid.	3.0	.728
I argue or complain about the cost of things I buy.	3.7	.665
I hesitate to spend money, even on necessities.	3.3	.659
After buying something, I wonder if I could have gotten the same for less elsewhere.	4.3	.641
I show signs of nervousness when I don't have enough money.	3.9	.633
I show worrisome behavior when it comes to money.	3.9	.553
I worry that I will not be financially secure.	3.7	.541
I automatically say, "I can't afford it," whether I can or not.	2.7	.500
When I make a major purchase, I have the suspicion that I have been taken advantage of.	2.9	.499

Note. Cronbach's Alpha = .81.

The nine variables which loaded on Factor 1 all were positively related to each other. Cronbach's alpha for this factor was .87. Factor 1 was named "Power-Prestige" because items loading on this factor relate to the use of money as a primary measure of success and as a medium with which to impress others. Boasting about personal

Table 3

Item Means and Variable Loadings for Factor 3, Retention-Time, n = 156

Variable	Mean Response	Rotated Factor Loadings
I put money aside on a regular basis for the future.	3.8	.783
I do financial planning for the future.	3.0	.770
I have money available in the event of another economic depression.	3.1	.696
I keep track of my money.	5.1	.641
I save now to prepare for my old age.	2.0	.626
I follow a careful financial budget.	3.9	.602
I am very prudent with money.	3.9	.479

Note. Cronbach's Alpha = .80.

Table 4

Item Means and Variable Loadings for Factor 4, Compulsive-Compensatory, n = 156

Variables	Mean Response	Rotated Factor Loadings
I am bothered when I have to pass up a sale.	3.3	.765
It's hard for me to pass up a bargain.	3.7	.724
It bothers me when I discover I could have gotten something for less elsewhere.	5.1	.577
I spend money to make myself feel better.	3.0	.442

Note. Cronbach's Alpha = .64.

income or prying into another's financial condition are behaviors related to attitudes defining this factor. Thus, compared to low scorers, high scorers on Power-Prestige place a greater value on using money to impress others and using money as a measure of success. Yamauchi and Templer's (1982) "Power-Prestige" factor contained the same nine variables. However, in their study items loaded in a different order and the factor loadings were of smaller magnitudes. Thus, although they were similar, college students appear to differ from the general adult population in the relative importance of the money behaviors which reflect this attitude and in the overall strength of the attitude. This difference may be related to college students' general lack of income. For college students, having money is likely to mean more power than they now have on their limited incomes.

Variables loading on Factor 2 were similar to Yamauchi and Templer's "Distrust" factor. However, one of their items, "it bothers me when I discover I could have gotten something for less elsewhere," did not load high enough in the college student

sample to be included. Also, three items from Yamauchi and Templer's "Anxiety" factor (expressing attitudes of worry or nervousness about money) loaded on Factor 2 for the college student sample. They were, "I show signs of nervousness when I don't have enough money," "I show worrisome behavior when it comes to money," and "I worry that I will not be financially secure."

Thus, Factor 2 in this study can best be described as a hybrid of Yamauchi and Templer's "Distrust" and "Anxiety" factors. Because behaviors related to an attitude of complaining or doubting constituted Factor 2, it was named "Complaining-Doubting." Cronbach's alpha was .81 and all items were positively related. The emergence of this different factor, Complaining-Doubting, appears to identify an attitude held by college students that is not held by the general adult population. High scorers for Complaining-Doubting emphasize money attitudes of suspicion and doubt. They are never quite sure of the appropriateness of their financial transactions and are afraid that they never have enough money. This is not surprising considering college students' transitional stage of the life cycle. Compared with the general adult population, college students have small incomes and little money management experience.

Seven variables loaded on Factor 3. This factor was named "Retention-Time" because each of the statements in Factor 3 had loaded on Yamauchi and Templer's "Retention-Time" factor. However, like the items comprising the "Power-Prestige" factor, the ordering differed between the college student group and the general population. Also, one item, "I put money aside on a regular basis for the future," loaded at a lower magnitude in this study than the same item in Yamauchi and Templer's study. Cronbach's alpha for Factor 3 was .80. Items loading on this factor indicate an emphasis on careful planning for the future as well as the need for careful accounting of funds. Compared to low scorers, high scorers for Retention-Time value being prepared and carefully budget and save for current and future events. Again, this may be related to the college students' small incomes which require them to be more careful in their spending.

Factor 4 had an internal reliability of .64, slightly below the level set for this study. The theme of Factor 4 can best be described as the expression of compulsive and/or compensatory attitudes toward money. The four items reflect a need to participate in sales or other "bargain" activities as well as a tendency to elevate a low mood by spending money. Factor 4 is the least like any of Yamauchi and Templer's factors. The concepts of the items that loaded on this factor seem less related to an overall theme than did items from the other factors. Also, when compared to the other factors, the distances between factor loadings for Factor 4 were large, indicating a less well-defined attitude. Thus, the factor was dropped from further analysis.

Based on the factor analysis results, three factors were retained as dependent variables in the next stage of analysis. These were: Power-Prestige, Complaining-Doubting, and Retention-Time. Factor scores were generated for use in the multiple regression analysis.

Initial Multiple Regression Analysis

Correlation analysis of all independent variables indicated that only the students' age and year in school were correlated at .6 or higher. To avoid possible multicollinearity effects, two models were developed for each dependent variable. Both models contained all 14 independent variables with Model 1 omitting year in school and Model 2 omitting age.

In the initial multiple regression stage, variables significant at $\leq$ .10 were identified. Models 1 and 2 had the same significant variables for Power-Prestige. These were: gender, loan programs, merit scholarships, savings, other, summer employment, need-based scholarships, and parents. Four variables, gender, other, summer employment, and need-based scholarships, were significant in both models for Complaining-Doubting. For Retention-Time, loan programs was significant in both models. Age was significant in Model 1 and year in school was significant in Model 2.

Model 2, with the variable year in school, was chosen for the final multiple regression analysis for three reasons. First, although differences in adjusted R^2 were extremely small, Model 2 yielded the highest adjusted R^2 for two of the dependent variables. Second, for Power-Prestige the adjusted R^2 had a higher significance level (.001) for Model 2 than Model 1 (.01). Finally, the researchers felt that year in school conceptualized a stage in the life cycle more accurately for college students than age did.

Final Multiple Regression Analysis

Variables significantly (p $\leq$ .10) related to each factor (Power-Prestige, Complaining-Doubting, and Retention-Time) in the initial multiple regression analyses were entered into a final equation. The results are shown in Table 5 and are discussed separately by dependent variable.

Power-Prestige. Eight variables, significant in the initial stage, were entered into the final equation for the dependent variable, Power-Prestige; all were significant (p $\leq$ .05) in the final equation. Furthermore, income from parents, need-based scholarships, and savings were significant at the .01 level, and gender was significant at the .001 level. Eighteen percent of the variance in Power-Prestige was explained by the eight variables in the final analysis (adjusted R^2 = 0.175, p $\leq$ .0001). Seven out of the eight independent variables were measures of the

students' income sources; all were negatively related to the Power-Prestige money attitude, with income from parents having the

Table 5

Final Multiple Regression of Selected Variables on Money Attitudes Held by College Students

Independent Variables	Dependent Variables (Beta coefficients)		
	Power-Prestige (n = 125)	Complaining-Doubting (n = 126)	Retention-Time (n = 126)
Income from parents	-0.782**	-	-
Income from merit scholarships	-0.427*	-	-
Income from need-based scholarships	-0.603**	0.184*	-
Income from loans	-0.368*	-	-0.138
Income from summer employment	-0.336**	0.104	-
Income from savings	-0.417**	-	-
Other types of non-specified income sources	-0.256*	0.178*	-
Gender	-0.352****	-0.165	-
Year in school	-	-	-0.186*
Adjusted R^2 =	0.176****	0.059*	0.033*

*p $\leq$ .05. **p $\leq$ .01. ***p $\leq$ .001. ****p $\leq$ .0001.

greatest influence as measured by the beta weight. Thus, students who received less money from parents, need-based scholarships, savings, loans, summer employment, or other non-specified sources tended to have greater scores for Power-Prestige. This is not surprising. College students as a whole have small uncertain incomes. Because money can give power and prestige to an individual, it follows that when an individual has such a small income then Power-Prestige will be lower. The income sources in this study can be classified as small and/or uncertain.

The eighth significant variable was gender. Men had higher Power-Prestige scores than women. This is not surprising since Furnham (1984) and Wilhelm, et al. (1992) concluded that there are gender differences in money attitudes, and one difference concerns power or prestige.

Complaining-Doubting. Four variables significant in the initial multiple regression analysis were entered into a final equation for the Complaining-Doubting dependent variable. Only two of these variables were significant (p $\leq$ .05) in the final regression equation: need-based scholarships and other non-specified income sources. Six percent of the variance was explained by the linear combination of the independent variables (adjusted R^2 = 0.059). Also, the significant variables were positively related to the dependent variable.

The students who received need-based scholarships and other types of non-specified income were more likely to complain or to be suspicious about their financial dealings. This suggests a relationship between lower incomes and the Complaining-Doubting money attitude for college students that was not found in the general adult population studied by Yamauchi and Templer (1982). This is not surprising given the small, uncertain incomes of many college students. Future research might compare college students with low-income adults to see if the same relationships are evident. Whether the other non-specified sources of income are need-based is unknown. However, if they are, this, too, would give additional support for the relationship between low income and Complaining-Doubting.

Retention-Time. Variables representing year in school and income from loans were entered into a final equation for Retention-Time. Year in school was significant at the .05 level, and adjusted R^2 was .033 (p $\leq$ .05). Also, year in school was negatively related to the factor. This suggests that as college students move from freshman to senior they budget and save for current and future events less. This is a surprising result in view of the fact that as college students get nearer to graduation, they are closer to a major life cycle change necessitating planning. On the other hand, graduation hopefully brings a much larger and more stable income which might lessen the perceived need to budget and save in the present. This relationship deserves further study.

Implications for Educators, Counselors, and Researchers

Because college students continue to have easy access to consumer credit, and because they continue to have a variety of money-related problems, it is important to help them develop appropriate strategies to solve their money problems. Because money behaviors are a reflection of money attitudes, the first step in helping students is to gain an understanding of their various money attitudes. Then, consumer educators can design materials that will help college students discover, understand, and modify their money attitudes and consumer behaviors.

Because college students are in a transitional stage of the life cycle and often lack experience in dealing with day-to-day market transactions, all college students need to be aware of how their attitudes toward money influence their marketplace behavior. The Money Attitude Scale offers insight into attitudes which may influence these important consumer matters. For example, educators can have students complete the MAS, then discuss the meanings and implications of the results. Undesirable behaviors related to specific money attitudes can be identified, and suggestions made of strategies for change. This type of activity works best in small groups.

College and university administrators can help encourage students to develop appropriate money attitudes and behaviors by instituting personal and family financial management courses as part of the general education curriculum. Consumer educators and financial counselors also can help students, parents, and financial aid officers to understand the unique financial responsibilities, problems, and challenges which college students face.

An understanding of college students' money attitudes can help financial aid officers and university administrators revise policies regarding financial aid disbursements, direct tuition payments, and student account charges. For example, certain money attitudes might prevent students from saving or budgeting. Lump-sum distributions of financial aid (or any other type of income) might not be wise for these students. They might spend the financial aid quickly and be in a financial bind well before the end of each semester. Other money attitudes might identify students who might not be able to handle the easy access to student credit that the university and other financial institutions allow; these students could charge themselves into financial trouble.

Finally, this study provides the basis for additional research that can, for example, examine other determinants of money attitudes by including subjective variables such as perceptions of relative wealth/poverty in childhood, impressions of parents' money attitudes, and motives behind the uses of money. Because a convenience sample was used in this study that was both similar and different from the University of Illinois population, caution must be taken in generalizing the results of this study beyond the University of Illinois or to the University population in general. Further, it is possible that students from other regions of the United States and in other countries have differing money attitudes. Additional research using random samples of university students would add greatly to knowledge of college student money-attitudes. Further, if the MAS is to accurately measure the same attitudes (e.g., "Anxiety" and "Distrust") in both student and adult populations, the scale needs to be adapted for population differences. Additional research could clarify usefulness of the MAS with a variety of populations.

References

Bailey, W.C. & Lown, J.M. (1992a). A cross cultural examination of the etiology of attitudes toward money. Proceedings of the 1992 Conference of the Southeastern Regional Association of Family Economics/Home Management, 66-74. Columbus, OH: The Ohio State University.

Bailey, W.C. & Lown, J.M. (1992b). Attitudes toward spending and saving: The relationship among these attitudes, and money in the past and future scale. In D.R. Iams (Ed.), Proceedings of the Association for Financial

Counseling and Planning Education, 157-171. Tucson, AZ: University of Arizona.

Furnham, A. (1984). Many sides of the coin: The psychology of money usage. Journal of Personality and Individual Differences, 5, 501-509.

Garman, E.T. & Forgue, R.E. (1991). Personal Finance (3rd ed.). Boston: Houghton Mifflin.

Goldberg, H. & Lewis, L. (1979). Money madness: The psychology of saving, spending, loving and hating money. London: Springwood.

Moschis, G.P. & Churchill, G.A., Jr. (1978). Consumer socialization: A theoretical and empirical analysis. Journal of Marketing Research, 15, 599-609.

Pieters, R.G.M. (1988). Attitude-behavior relationships. In W.F. van Raaij, G.M. van Veldhoven & K.E. Wärneryd (Eds.), Handbook of economic psychology, 147-204. Boston: Kluwer Academic Publishers.

Rubinstein, C. (1980, December). Your money and your life. Psychology Today, 47-58.

Seibold, D.R. (1980). Attitude-verbal report-behavior relationships as causal processes: Formalization, test, and communication implications. In D.P. Cushman & R.D. McPhee (Eds.), Message-attitude-behavior relationship: Theory, methodology, and application, 195-244. New York: Academic Press.

Stampfl, R.W. (1978). The consumer life cycle. Journal of Consumer Affairs, 12, 209-219.

Wärneryd, K. (1988). Social influence on economic behavior. In W.F. van Raaij, G.M. van Veldhoven & K.E. Wärneryd (Eds.), Handbook of economic psychology, 207-247. Boston: Kluwer Academic Publishers.

Wilhelm, M.S. & Varcoe, K. (1991). Assessment of financial well-being: Impact of objective economic indicators and money attitudes on financial satisfaction and financial progress. In S.M. Danes (Ed.), Proceedings of the Association for Financial Counseling and Planning Education, 184-201. St. Paul, MN: University of Minnesota.

Wilhelm, M.S., Fridrich, A.H. & Varcoe, K. (1992). Gender differences in money attitudes: A factor analysis. In D.R. Iams (Ed.), Proceedings of the Association for Financial Counseling and Planning Education, 172-187. Tucson, AZ: University of Arizona.

Yamauchi, K.T. & Templer, D.I. (1982). The development of a money attitude scale. Journal of Personality Assessment, 46, 522-
528.

Endnotes

1. The upper and lower endpoints were indicated in the article by Yamauchi and Templer (1982) which reported their results. The intervening points were obtained through private correspondence with Yamauchi but not until after data for this study had been collected.

2. Because of potential difficulties with a high proportion of zero responses, each variable also was recoded to 0 = no funding received and 1 = funding received. Results of the regression analysis were no different for the two types of coding. For ease in interpretation, the continuous coding was used.

Consumer Economics, A Profession Gone Adrift:
Some Positive Suggestions for Action

E. Thomas Garman, Virginia Tech[1]
William Bailey, University of Arkansas[2]
Margaret Charters, Syracuse University[3]
Robin Douthitt, University of Wisconsin[4]
Roger Swagler, University of Georgia[5]

The panel presented a number of ideas aimed at improving the academic profession of consumer economics and its academic professional association. Key among the more than fifty concrete suggestions were the need: to define the field of consumer economics, the curriculum, and its customers; to redefine the goals of ACCI in an effort to bring other consumer-related professionals into the organization; to increase networking opportunities for professors and students; to focus greater attention on undergraduate programs; and to refocus the topics presented at annual meetings.

The purpose of this panel discussion was to establish a framework and offer a series of concrete ideas to facilitate a serious discussion among members of the American Council on Consumer Interests (ACCI) and the ACCI Board of Directors on what the consumer economics profession in academe must do to survive, and perhaps to prosper. At the outset of the discussion, the following framework was established: an atmosphere of positive thoughts, no one blames anyone else, and everyone makes an effort to keep the discussion upbeat.

Most of the members of the American Council on Consumer Interests are well aware of the several problems facing the organization and the profession. A well-attended panel at the 1992 ACCI meeting in Toronto began to grapple with the broad concerns by identifying some of the problem areas. A year later both the organization and the profession remain in crisis, while additional pertinent issues remain unstated. The time, therefore, is ripe for ACCI consumer economics professors to look forward and take concrete actions to create their own destiny.

One observer has stated that the root of ACCI's evolving dilemma is that as the only academic organization serving professionals in consumer economics in higher education, over the years the group simply has chosen not to provide enough networking opportunities for its members to allow them to develop strong support systems. Others have commented that the professional association may be serving the professors but not the profession. Over time, the consumer economics effort at academic institutions has weakened along with the professional organization itself.

The following provides a brief overview of "the problems," and the great majority of discussion time was aimed at offering some positive suggestions for change. After the panelists made their specific presentations, the audience participated in the discussion.

The Problems . . .

When you look at the confusion in the profession, the declining enrollments in colleges, the poor attendance at ACCI's annual meetings, its dwindling membership numbers, the lack of a national focus on curriculum, the wide range of likely unknown views of others about what should be taught to undergraduates, the general disarray of perceptions about "the problem" or "the solution," and the years-on-end consternation about how things have changed, the solution is obvious: think and take action. Handwringing is the type of non-thinking that got us into this problem, and it is not the type of thinking that will get the consumer economics profession out of difficulty.

Times have changed over the years but, the profession of consumer professors has not changed much. Excluding internal problems of the

[1]Professor of Consumer Affairs and Family Financial Management

[2]Assistant Professor of Home Economics

[3]Associate Professor and Director of Consumer Studies Program

[4]Professor of Consumer Science

[5]Professor of Consumer Economics

professional association, which are probably serious because they have contributed to the current state of affairs, the profession of consumer economics in higher education must face two fundamental questions:

(1) Who are our customers? In other words, who is hiring and promoting our students? Or, perhaps who should be hiring our graduates? The answers to that question should help drive the definitions of the field, the curriculum, the content of courses, the perspectives brought to each course by each professor. Oh, it is fine for a professor to be philosophic and sound to students like one who possesses wisdom every day, but the reality of life--the profession--demands much more. Professors are on notice to get real! Get with the program! Discover the program, please! Get to work as a profession and make it happen your way.

(2) What can we do, as professors, to provide our "customers" (the hiring agencies) with not only the best possible "product" (our students) but also graduates who are likely to be the first promoted because they are not only good, but they also possess that all-important mature vision to be able to see the future, adapt to that future while helping to shape its dimensions, and to help change business, government, their employers, and society to better the level of living for all consumers.

The Challenge . . .

Life in the consumer economics teaching profession will get better, but not before the consumer economics professors change what they can see and take positive actions to create where they are going. In sum, consumer economic professors must have/create "something" that others want-- curriculum, certification, students with competitive abilities, an clear image of a product that fills a need, whatever--or there is no need for the consumer economics profession to exist! The consumer economics profession needs to gather its forces and act; members of ACCI must find the political will to seize the moment, and move forward.

A Sampling of Suggestions for Action . . .

A great number of suggestions for action were offered by the panelists and discussion participants:

1. addressing the historical perspective of ACCI being an exclusive group designed only to serve academics at four-year colleges and universities;
2. addressing the ACCI membership pricing structure that discourages students from joining the organization;
3. establishing a task force to create a list of definitions in the field (including the terms consumer economics, consumer education, and personal finance);
4. establishing a task force to develop a scope and sequence for undergraduate courses in consumer economics;
5. establishing a curriculum committee to develop model course outlines for undergraduate courses in consumer economics and to regularly publish these in the proceedings of the organization;
6. beginning an accreditation program for academic majors in consumer economics in colleges and universities;
7. beginning a registration program for courses of study in consumer economics in universities, colleges and secondary schools;
8. addressing the anti-business and anti-government mentality present during annual meetings;
9. discussing how to attract business people to ACCI;
10. examining how to attract union people and credit union officials to ACCI;
11. examining how to attract more grassroots consumer advocates to ACCI;
12. discussing what to do about ACCI not serving our largest client group, consumer affairs professionals in business and government;
13. discussing what to do about ACCI ignoring the needs of the thousands of consumer affairs professionals employed in hospitals;
14. considering what to do about ACCI not serving the needs of the hundreds of professors in community colleges and technical schools who teach economics;
15. discussing what to do about ACCI ignoring the needs of the thousands of secondary and middle school teachers of consumer economics;
16. examining what to do about the lack of a national internship program;
17. sharply increasing the number of awards given to ACCI members to recognize the quality of their work and provide them with organization support in dealing with their employers;
18. addressing successfully the generational differences between ACCI leaders and the membership of the organization;
19. having annual conference sessions on non-traditional outreach programs in consumer economics;
20. having annual conference sessions on effective extension programs in consumer economics;
21. having annual conferences regularly focus on successful academic programs;
22. having annual conferences regularly focus on successful consumer complaint-handling systems in business;
23. having annual conferences regularly focus on successful consumer complaint-handling systems in the federal government;
24. having annual conference sessions focus on successful consumer complaint-handling systems in local government;
25. having annual conference regularly focus on effective recruitment materials used by universities, colleges, and high schools;
26. having annual conferences regularly focus on teaching excellence;
27. having annual conferences regularly focus on

exchange course syllabi;

28. having annual conferences regularly focus on the sharing of research funding sources;

29. having annual conference presentations by experts in marketing and advertising;

30. having regular annual conference presentations by one of the several consulting firms that consult with businesses and governments on consumer satisfaction/consumer complaint-handling;

31. having annual conference sessions on pertinent public policy questions not solely delivered by the "I-am-right-liberal-left" perspective, but presented in a balanced manner designed to fully illuminate all sides;

32. revisit the ACCI policy of non-voting status for corporate membership, a second-class status;

33. developing a network to list all consumer affairs job openings (education, government, corporate, non-profit, etc.), especially as the bachelor's degree level;

34. establishing a formalized network for linking businesses seeking research, with researchers;

35. improving information sources and networking;

36. moving the curriculum closer to the political process;

37 encouraging new consumer economic programs to be developed in small home economics departments with the strong support of professors at larger universities;

38. having special conferences on applied topics, especially designed to genuinely improve participants' knowledge and skills;

39. sharing recruiting materials and approaches;

40. promoting consumption science and consumer education sections at other professional meetings;

41. promoting co-operative education programs in consumer economics to help students pay for their tuition, that also would enrich classroom discussion, improve communication with industry, and provide credibility to placement opportunity claims;

42. using Hazel Kyrk's perspectives on rethinking our theories and hypotheses and begin to take another look at our "forest";

43. refocusing our efforts toward the undergraduate programs;

44. convening another national conference of directors of consumer economics programs, similar to the one Ron Stampfl had years ago;

45. paying attention to the masters degree programs, especially making efforts to make part-time study for adults a reality;

46. considering the implications of total quality management (TQM) on consumer economics;

47. being certain that students use up-to-date technology;

48. redefining the business that we are in;

49. clarifying the focus of consumer economics to include program delivery activities of state cooperative extension specialists;

50 building partnerships between ACCI and other professional organizations;

51. recognizing that the world has become one of specialists, rather than generalists, and prepare students accordingly;

52. considering professional exchanges between consumer economics professors and people in business, government, and the consumer movement; and

53. expanding the ACCI board to include designated slots for internationals.

Endnotes

1. More than one observer noted that our product is the information, education and values provided to students while our customers are the hiring agencies. Others suggested that the students are our customers.

Expenditure Patterns of
Hispanic versus non-Hispanic Households

Virginia Solis Zuiker, The Ohio State University[1]
Mi Kyeong Bae, The Ohio State University[2]

This paper reviews research on consumption patterns of Hispanics. Both bivariate and multivariate analysis are used with a new dataset created by one of the authors from the 1990 Survey of Consumer Expenditures in an attempt to understand the effects of Hispanic status on expenditures.

"Consumption involves a broad slice of human activity" (Cochrane & Bell, 1956, p.3). Consumption is concerned with all phases of the using up of goods and services. When one is eating food, sleeping on a bed, or visiting the doctor, one is said to be consuming. However, there are other aspects to consumption. The choosing or selecting of particular goods and services is also part of the consumption process which involves acquiring information, participating in transactions and making decisions. Therefore, consumption is concerned with the problem of choice and how choice decisions are made. Why does the consumer choose a particular combination of goods and services, and what would happen if he were to choose some other combination? The economist is interested in the problem of choice only where the number and extent of wants exceed the means of satisfying those wants. Therefore, the consumer must make a choice with respect to the goods and services to be consumed to satisfy those wants (Cochrane & Bell, 1956).

Review of Literature

Characteristics of Hispanic Families

The U.S. Hispanic population constitutes one of the largest minority groups and is predicted to be the fastest growing ethnic group in the country (Wagner & Soberon-Ferrer, 1990). The Hispanic population differs from the general population in terms of income, family composition, characteristics of the household head, and location (Wagner & Soberson-Ferrer, 1990). Hispanic groups tend to share similarities in terms of values, beliefs, and attitudes, culture and self-perception. These similarities distinguish the Hispanic population from other ethnic and consumer groups (Segal & Sosa, 1983)

Differences in Spending Between
Hispanics and non-Hispanics

According to Wagner and Soberon-Ferrer (1990), Hispanic households spend more than other households for food at home. Trager (1986) suggests that Hispanic consumption of processed foods for home consumption is lower than that of the mainstream. Segal and Sosa (1983) stated family-oriented expenditures, such as food, are important among Hispanic households. Pitts (1990) found that Hispanic households spend less on transportation than their counterparts. Additionally, Pitts (1990) found that Hispanics and Blacks spend less in health care than Whites and others. Myers (1991) found that Hispanics, non-Hispanic Blacks, and non-Hispanic Asians spend less on health care than do non-Hispanic whites. Pitts (1990) and Myers (1991) found that Hispanics spend less on reading and education than non-Hispanics.

Analysis

Preliminary Analysis

The 1990 BLS public use tape, EXPN, was used to construct a sample of consumer units with four quarters of 1990 interviews. Details of the methods and assumptions used are in Bae (1992). (Note: for convenience, the term 'household' is used interchangeably with the BLS term 'consumer unit'.) With various exclusions, the sample size was 1,109 consumer units.

The BLS definition of expenditures included Social Security and pension contributions, so the variable "spending" was created by subtracting Social Security and pension contributions. The spending variable was also adjusted for the transportation category, as the BLS includes net vehicle purchases, regardless of how a vehicle was purchased. Net vehicle purchases were subtracted, and annual vehicle loan payments were added, to obtain the spending variable. Households with a reference person listed as Hispanic comprised 4.9% of sample, or 54 households. T-tests were run between Hispanic and non-Hispanic households. The results (in percentage differences between Hispanic and non-Hispanic households) are shown in Table 1 in the column titled 'Actual'. The calculated percentage differences (assuming both groups were identical in terms of all other independent variables) based on the coefficient for Hispanic

---

[1]Ph.D Student, Family Resource Management

[2]Ph.D Student, Family Resource Management

status are shown in Table 1 in the column titled 'Adjusted'.

Table 1
% Difference by Hispanic Status of Reference Person

Category	Hispanic vs non-Hispanic adjusted	actual
Income After Tax & FICA	ⓐⓐⓐ	-13.31%
Total Spending	-13.10%**	-13.05%
Food at Home	13.80%	24.80%**
Food Away From Home	-15.69%	-24.34%
Apparel & Services	1.91%	-22.81%*
Shelter	10.50%	-8.87%*
Transportation	1.82%	-3.84%**
Health Care	-47.07%*	-17.47%**
Utilities	23.88%	-8.99%
Entertainment	-23.19%	-39.63%**
Reading & Education	-61.07%**	-75.34%**
Personal Care	2.03%**	28.46%**
Household Equipment	9.74%	-3.25%
Life Insurance	-43.06%**	-54.46%**
Alcohol	11.83%	-27.98%**
Household Operation	5.35%	-6.20%**
Tobacco	-17.30%	6.71%
Miscellaneous	2.16%	-3.23%**
Cash Contributions	-2.20%	-60.51%**

* Significantly different from base category at the 10% level
** Significantly different from base category at the 5% level

Hispanics spent 24.8% more on food-at-home than non-Hispanics. This finding is consistent with suggestions that reflect food as a family-oriented expenditure of importance among Hispanic households (Segal & Sosa, 1983). Wagner and Soberon-Ferrer (1990) suggest that Hispanics may be less likely to frequent exclusive restaurants where the food is expensive and the atmosphere less conducive to bringing a family due to their strong family orientation.

Hispanic households spent about 28% less on alcohol than non-Hispanic households. This finding is consistent with previous research by Wallendorf and Reilly (1983) on cultural differences in drinking behavior.

In both the adjusted and actual models, Hispanic households spend significantly less on reading and education materials than their counterparts, 61% and 75%, respectively. It is possible that cultural factors and language differences contributed to this phenomenon. Pitts (1990) and Myers (1991) findings also suggests that Hispanics spend less on reading and education than non-Hispanics.

Hispanics spent significantly less in health care than non-Hispanics. Pitts (1990) indicates that Hispanics and Blacks spend less in health care

than Whites and other. Myers (1991) found that Hispanics, non-Hispanic Blacks, and non-Hispanic Asian spend less on health care than non-Hispanic whites.

Implications

The lower total spending of Hispanic households, even after controlling for the effects of other variables, is an intriguing result that merits further investigation. Professionals in the areas of family economics and consumer economics interested in assisting these families can develop programs that teach new American families how to compare brands for quality and find reliable product information (Pitts, 1990). A great deal of work remains to be done before the consumer behavior of this large and rapidly growing segment of the American population will adequately be characterized.

References

Bae, Mi Kyeong (1992). Analysis of household spending patterns, Ph.D. dissertation, The Ohio State University.

Cochrane, W.W. & Bell, C.S. (1956). The economics of consumption. New York: McGraw-Hill Book Company, Inc.

Myers, P.M. (1991). Minority households: A comparison of selected characteristics and expenditures contributing to future economic well-being. Family Economic Review, 4(2), 2-8

Pitts, J.M. (1990). Income and expenditures of Hispanic households. Family Economic Review, 3(2), 2-7.

Segal, M.N. & Sosa, L. (1983). Marketing to the Hispanic community. California Management Review, 26(1), 120-134.

Trager, C.S. (1986). Fast food market is in McDonald's court. Advertising Age, 57.

Wagner, J. & Soberon-Ferrer, H. (1990). The effect of ethnicity on selected household expenditures. The Social Science Journal, 27(2), 181-198.

Wallendorf, M. & Reilly, M.D. (1983). Ethnic migration, assimilation, and consumption. Journal of Consumer Research, 10, 292-302.

New Trends in the Supermarket Business: Shopper's Discount Club Program

Frank F. Chiang[1]

The economic theory of clubs is briefly shown in this paper. The structures of the supermarket's revenues were compared in two different situations, i.e. before and after executing the "Shopper's Discount Club Program". In some cases, customers benefit some discounted value from discounted items, but they may pay higher price for non-discounted items. Overall the consumers' welfare and benefits do not increase.

Recently, "Frequent Shopper Program", "Price Club", or "Shopper's Discount Club Program" are introduced into the supermarket. This successful retailing idea is taking a cue from airlines who provide the "travel mileages" to the airlines' flier members. These new sales promotion strategies have been shown very successful in the supermarket business in the past year. For example, Smitty's Super Value Inc., Phoenix, Arizona, recently introduced a frequent shopper program--a voluntary, no-cost membership that gives discounts when a membership card is scanned at the checkout (Johnson, 1990). What is the economic explanation for using a membership format? This study has three specific research objectives: (1) to show the shopper discount club program and its advantages for supermarkets and consumers, (2) to format the structure of the supermarket's revenues when using a membership format program, and (3) to discuss the impacts of using membership format program on the consumers' welfare and benefits.

The Theoretical Basis of the Shopper Club

The Economic Theory of Clubs

Since this study discuss the member club, it is necessary to look at the economic theory of clubs. One of the most influential article discussing clubs is by Buchanan (1965). He developed an economic theory of the function, size, and internal operations of clubs. He defined a club which has "an infinitely large membership is preferred to all arrangements of finite size". The main question in a theory of clubs is to determine the membership margin based on the size of the most desirable cost and consumption sharing arrangement.

Price Discrimination

Stigler (1961), and Maynes and Assum (1982) shown that a local consumer market is informationally imperfect which charges the different prices for the same quality. Behavior of

this type confirms to Salop's (1977) price discrimination argument. Price discrimination happens in local consumer markets when different prices are charged for the same items, i.e. discounting, sales, and discounted coupons, etc. In Salop's study (1977), he pointed out that people have differences in optimal information-generating processes. There are efficient and less efficient information-gatherers. Those efficient searchers are often obtain better buys on average. For the less efficient information-gatherers will search less and generally pay a higher price than will efficient searchers.

What is the Shopper's Discount Club?

Types of Shopper's Discount Club Program

Rebate points format. Shoppers present their membership cards for scanning at checkout and earn rebate points when they buy participating brands. Members get a monthly tally of their purchases and a certificate for the rebate amounts earned. Shoppers can redeem the earn points via a catalogue for items including jewelry and kitchen appliances at the supermarket.

Cash discount instant format. Shoppers present their scannable membership cards for scanning at the beginning of every transaction. The computer recognizes the customer as a member and gives the shopper a discount on any of the items the supermarket discount at that period.

The Advantages of Shopper Club Program

From the firm's viewpoint, the primary objective of the program is trying to increase the customer count and to foster store loyalty. Generally the increases of customer count will more likely to increase the amounts of sales. The second objective of the program is to provide firms demographic information and purchasing patterns on consumers. Third advantage is easy to communicate with their customers via the direct mail or advertising flier. Fourth advantage is that the firms take less risk in accepting customers' checks and to increase the cash flows. And from the consumer's viewpoint, at no monetary cost to participate the shopper club and lower requirements customers can easily sign up becoming a member. Discounted items are distributed via the advertising fliers or member newsletter to the participating customers periodically. The customers are better informed. The participating customer presents their scannable card at the checkout for cash discount instantly when they

[1]Graduate Student, Consumer Economics and Housing

purchase the discounted items. Overall, the gained benefits for those participating members not only have financial saving but also have time saving. Especially those high cost search customers gain greater benefits than those with lower cost search.

The Structure of the Revenues

Case 1: With Supermarket's Coupon Discount

Supermarket offers coupons to customers for some specific goods in a given period. These supermarket's coupons include the partial price and full discounts for the selected goods under some limitations of the purchased quantity, i.e. price discounting for first quantity and no discount for two or more. Customers clip these coupons through newspaper and supermarket's advertising, etc. Assume there are two types of customer: coupon-insensitive customer and coupon-sensitive customer. Coupon-sensitive customers search coupons in order to obtain the lowest price. As Salop (1977) pointed out that the search techniques and the efficiency among different consumers are not the same. Hence, those consumers who are more efficient information-gatherers and searchers generally obtain better buys. The supermarket's revenue are the sum of the expenditure of the coupon users and non-coupon users. The coupon users have some price discounts on certain goods but the non-coupon user all pay the regular price.

Case 2: With Member Card (Pre-Club Customers)

As supermarket introducing the "Shopper's Discount Club Program", this program serves as a device for separating the customers into two groups: members and non-members. Members present their member card and obtain a discount instantly without clipping the coupons. Hence, this scannable member card not only serves as a "passport" but also represents a "multi-purpose coupon". In this study, we assume that all coupon-sensitive customers will participate the program which is provided the same effect as coupons. Further, this program will attract a portion of the coupon-insensitive customers who is a high cost searchers mostly. Hence, the supermarket's revenue are the sum of the expenditure of the members and non-members.

Case 3: With Member Card (Post-Club Customers)

One goal of the program is to foster store loyalty for the existing customers. The other important purpose is to attract new customers or to "steal" customers from the competitors, in other words. Under this situation, the supermarket's revenue are the sum of the expenditure of the old members, new members and non-members. As in case 2, the members have some price discounts on certain goods but the non-members all pay the regular price.

The Impacts on the Consumers' Welfare

For those consumers participating the shopper's discount clubs obtain the benefits of financial and time savings which is benefitted from the omission of clipping and searching coupons. Consumers are better informed via the member news letters from the supermarket. The searching cost is less than before participating the program. However, if supermarket provides the high portion of the discounted goods which are not urgently preferred by customers, the consumers surplus for the members may be very small. The consumers are still not better off. In most cases, customers benefit some discounted value from discounted items, but they may pay higher price for non-discounted items. Overall the consumers' welfare and benefits do not increase.

Conclusion and Summary

As "Shopper's Discount Club Program" grows, one can expect that it becomes profitable for supermarkets. However, how to attract new customers and keep the existing members are the crucial issues to the supermarket. As described before, the structures of the supermarket's profit functions were compared in two different situations, i.e. before and after executing the "Shopper's Discount Club Program". The participation rate represents the attractiveness of this program. In fact, the "Shopper's Club Program" has different meanings to different types of customers, low search cost vs high search cost consumers. For example, the "noise" form the supermarket will confuse those high search cost consumers and/or the new coming consumers who may pay higher prices for non-discounted goods than some other supermarket where the additional cost will offset the savings from the program. In this situation, the high search cost consumers may not be better off. More further study on this issue is needed to explore especially the empirical analysis and the incorporation of the economic theory of clubs.

References

Buchanan, J. M. (1965). An economic theory of clubs. Economica, 32, 1-14.

Johnson, J. L. (1990). Smitty's combo formula. Discount Merchandiser, 30(11), 22-30.

Maynes, E. S., & Assum, T. (1982). Informationally imperfect consumer markets: Empirical findings and policy implications. Journal of Consumer Affairs, 16(1), 62-87.

Salop, S. (1977). The noisy monopolist: Imperfect information, price dispersion and price discrimination. Review of Economic Studies, 4, 393-406.

Stigler, G. J. (1961). The economics of information. Journal of Political Economy, 69(3), 213-220.

Compulsive-Addictive Buying Behavior: Examining the Effects of Childhood Experiences

Susanne Friese, Oregon State University[1]

The purpose of the study was to examine the effects of childhood family experiences and family types on compulsive-addictive buying behavior. The results indicate that negative childhood experiences such as abuse, parental neglect and family discord contribute to the development of this behavioral trait. The open and random family types may have an advantage over the closed family type, although this advantage may be lost when these families are disrupted by family discord.

Abstract

This exploratory study investigated the probable causes of compulsive-addictive buying behavior. According to Pettit and Brown (1988), childhood experiences, such as feelings and behavior patterns observed by children in the family in which they grew up, influence the children's way of seeing things, solving problems, and coping with life. In addition, poor parental managerial skills, high levels of conflict in families, and other family problems such as alcoholism can cause behavioral difficulties which may continue through adolescents and adulthood (Vernon, 1985). This led to the assumption that the roots of addictive buying behavior may lie in childhood. Previous research supported this assumption. Results showed that addictive buyers experienced a variety of problems during their childhood (Scherhorn, Reisch, & Raab, 1990; Faber, and O'Guinn, 1988).

Childhood family experiences and the ways of solving the problems of family living may differ depending on the family type in which the child is raised. Therefore, the objective of this study was to identify any relationship among consumers who were raised in different types of family organization, their childhood experiences, and their later buying behavior.

The family system's theory, developed by Constantine (1986), was employed as a theoretical framework. Constantine (1986), in his book about family paradigms, distinguished three major types of family organization: closed, open and random. In order to classify consumers according to these three family types, a measuring scale was developed by this researcher. Other scales employed in this study were the Compulsive Buying Scale developed by Valence, d'Astous and Fortier (1988), the Family Discord Scale, and the Psychasthenia Scale. Both of the latter where taken from the Minnesota Multiphasic Personality Inventory (Dahlstrom, Welsh and Dahlstrohm, 1972). Further questions assessed various childhood experiences and the family history of addictive behaviors.

A survey was administered to 52 clients of Consumer Credit Counseling Services in Oregon and Washington. Because of the pilot nature of this study, a purposive rather than a random sample selection was made. Respondents who were likely to fit the target population where selected in the most direct method possible.

Positive relationships were found between five pairs of variables: 1) Negative childhood experiences and family discord, 2) Psychasthenia (i.e., obsessive-compulsive personality traits) and family discord, 3) Psychasthenia and addictive buying behavior, 4) Family discord and addictive buying behavior, and 5) Family history of addictive behaviors and addictive buying behavior.

While no direct relationship was found between family types and addictive buying behavior, some trends emerged. The tendency to be a compulsive buyer was highest for individuals who were raised in a closed family type, and lowest for individuals from a random family type. Holding family type constant, the observed relationship between psychasthenia and addictive buying behavior only held for individuals from a more closed family structure; and the relationship between family discord and addictive buying behavior only held for individuals from a more open family structure. In general, the level of family discord was highest in the closed family type, and there was no difference in the levels of psychasthenia among the three family types. The results indicated that the closed family type may operate in ways which result in less than favorable outcomes with regard to raising children.

In addition, 14 personal interviews were conducted. The interviews were organized around the two main areas of interest, the buying behavior and the family environment of the buying-addicted consumers. The analysis of this data gave insight into the observed relationships between family discord and negative childhood experiences. The interviews revealed that the compulsive buyers often carried an enormous burden of unexpressed feelings. They were also likely to be raised in a dysfunctional family, experiencing neglect, physical, emotional, and/or sexual abuse, or having alcoholic parent(s).

It can be concluded that consumers seeking the gratification of needs in addictive buying behavior are unhappy individuals who are trying to compensate for their feelings of low self-worth and/or a burden of unexpressed feelings. These consumers have most likely been subjected to influences distorting their autonomy, for example, maltreatment and/or negligence by parents. Since the shopping experience has the potential to serve as a source of gratification of needs, the individuals' attempt to cope with the above

---

[1]Doctoral Student,
Social Sciences, Germany

mentioned childhood and family experiences may result in the development of a buying addiction.

Given the constraints of this study, additional research is needed to explore the suggested differences among the closed, open and random family type, and to pinpoint which of the characteristics of a particular family type are most damaging. The results may provide valuable information for consumer therapy, and will be necessary information for taking preventative measures in order to reduce the number of buying-addicted consumers.

References

Constantine, L. L. (1986). Family paradigms. The practice of theory in family therapy. New York: Guilford Press.

Dahlstrom, W. G., Welsh, G. S., & Dahlstrom, L. D. (1972). An MMPI handbook: A clinical interpretation. Minneapolis: University of Minnesota Press.

Faber, R. J., & O'Guinn, T. C. (1988). Compulsive Consumption and Credit Abuse. Journal of Consumer Policy, 11, 109-121.

Pettit, G. S., Dodge, K. A., & Brown, M. M.(1988). Early family experience, social problem solving pattern, and children's social competence. Child Development, 59, 107-120.

Scherhorn, G., Reisch, L., & Raab, G. (1990. Addictive buying in West Germany: An empirical study. Journal of Consumer Policy, 13, 355-387.

Valence, G., d'Astous, A., & Fortier, L. (1988). Compulsive buying: Concept and measurement. Journal of Consumer Policy, 11, 419-433.

Vernon, J. (1985). Children of alcoholics. Kiwanis Magazine, 3, 34-37.

The Effect of Child Support on Educational Attainment of Young Adults: Changes During the 1980s

Pedro M. Hernandez, University of Illinois[1]
Andrea H. Beller, University of Illinois[2]

This paper examines the effects of child support payments on the educational attainment of young adults in the United States over the 1980s. Its major objective is to investigate why child support has such a strong positive effect on children's educational attainment relative to other sources of income.

Details of the Study

According to recent estimates, if present trends continue, six out of every ten children born today will spend part of their childhood in a single--parent family (Norton & Glick, 1986). Too often the children's father provides little or no financial assistance and sees his children infrequently if at all. Increasingly the pubic has come to view child support--that is, regular legally-mandated payments from a noncustodial to a custodial parent--as one of the keys to improving the well-being of children (Beller & Graham, forthcoming).

We compare data from the 1979 and 1988 Current Population Survey (CPS) Child Support Supplements to assess the impact of the improvements in the child support enforcement system, which should have increased the proportion of reluctant payers among fathers paying support over this period.

As a result of new laws and stricter enforcement during the 1980s, it is expected that a somewhat more reluctant group of fathers were paying child support at the end than at the beginning of the 80s. The 1980s provide a natural experiment to investigate where unobservable characteristics of noncustodial fathers who pay support causes both greater payment levels and higher educational attainment of their children.

Following Beller and Chung (1988), we investigate whether child support helps mitigate some of the negative effects on education of living in a female-headed family. However, unlike their study, we also investigate why child support matters.

Hypotheses

We test the hypotheses that both the negative effect of living in a single-parent family and the positive effect of child support income on educational attainment decreased over time.

Data and Sample Characteristics

To study the impact of family structure and child support on children's education, we created a special mother child extract from both the 1979 and 1988 March/April Match File of the CPS. From this match file we were able to extract data on more than 4,000 families for each year containing as least a mother and one own child between the ages of 16 and 19.

Summary

Changes in educational attainment between 1979 and 1988 favor children from intact families. Our educational attainment outcomes are very similar in 1988 and 1979 for children from intact families. For children from non-intact families our educational outcomes are also similar in both years. Compared with 1979, children from non-intact families in 1988 are slightly less likely to have graduated from high school, but they are slightly less likely to have fallen behind in school.

Child Support Income

Table 1, which looks only at the child support population (i.e., 792 and 966 observation in 1979 and 1988, respectively), we compare the effects of child support with all other income. In 1979, increases in the amount of child support received raises general schooling. In addition, child support income has a much larger effect on education than equal increments of other types of income. In 1988, the effect of child support is in the predicted direction (except for high school graduation), but is insignificant.

---

[1]Graduate Student, Division of Consumer Sciences

[2]Professor, Division of Consumer Sciences

Table 1

Effect of Child Support on Child's Education, Age
16-19

	1979	1988
Yrs. of Schooling Completed		
Child Support Income	.025**	.022
Other Family Income	.004*	.005***
% Grad. from H.S.		
Child Support Income	0.95	-0.49
Other Family Income	0.08	0.21**
% Behind in School		
Child Support Income	-2.22***	-1.13
Other Family Income	-0.09	-0.21***

*, **, *** Denote statistically significant differences
from intact families at the 10%, 5%, or 1% levels,
respectively.

The results are partially consistent with our
hypothesis that the effect of child support is
larger in 1979 than in 1988. As a result, we move
on to consider the more complex version of the
hypotheses. In this version, we compare the
coefficients on child support to the comparable one
on family structure and postulate that it is the
ratio of child support to family structure that has
diminished over time. The data are uniformly
consistent with this version of the hypothesis
because in each case, the educational disadvantage
among children receiving child support was larger
in 1988 than in 1979.

We found evidence that indirectly supports the
notion that the effect of child support is
partially due to unobservable characteristics of
father paying support. We find that child support
eliminates a smaller portion of the educational
disadvantage from living in a single-parent family
in 1988 than in 1979.

Conclusions

We can conclude that on average, children who
live with their mother only exhibited lower
educational outcomes (based on our educational
measures). Among children in mother-only families,
those who were eligible for child support tend to
obtain the least schooling. But, among those
eligible for child support, we found that children
who received support from their father obtained
significantly more schooling than those who did not
receive support. In addition, we found that
increases in child support payments appear to have
stronger effects that equal increases in other
sources of income.

Based on our analysis we reject our first
hypothesis, that the negative effect of living in a
single-parent family has diminished over time.
Children from non-intact families in our 1979

sample suffered a smaller disadvantage relative to
those in intact families than those in our 1988
sample.

Our data were consistent with our second
hypothesis, that the proportion of the negative
effect from living in a single-parent family
eliminated by child support declined over time.

Our results if anything suggest that the
former effect became more negative over time
whereas child support income has become less
effective at eliminating this negative effect. Our
findings are consistent with the interpretation
that the impact of child support on children's
educational attainment represents in part
characteristics of the father-child relationship.

Policy Implications

Children in terms of educational outcomes were
better off in 1979 than in 1988. This could mean
that it is not only the amount of child support
that matters, but that there are unobservable
variables that affected our educational measures.

Because of the recent reform in child support
enforcement a higher proportion of eligible
families received support in 1988 than in 1979.
Although child support enhances educational
outcomes for those who received it, the increase in
the number of reluctant payers in 1988 seems to
have decreased the effects of child support income
on their children's educational attainment. This
is not to say that child support income would not
have any positive effect on a child's educational
attainment but, rather the effect may not exceed
that of any other source of income, which, we must
remember is still positive.

References

Beller, A.H., & Chung, S.S. (1988). The effect of
child support payments on the educational
attainment of children. Paper presented at
the Population Association of America Annual
Meeting, New Orleans, April.

Beller, A.H., & Graham, J.W. (forthcoming). Small
change: The economics of child support. New
Haven, CT: Yale University Press.

Norton, A.J., & Glick, P.C. (1986). One parent
famines: A social and economic profile.
Family Relations, 35(1), 9-17.

The Air Pollution Problem

Sharon A. DeVaney, The Ohio State University[1]

The control of pollution is a costly activity. Devoting more of society's scarce resources to controlling pollution means that less is available to do other things that are valued by society.

Economics of Pollution

Ordinarily, pollution results from one of the following factors: (a) the fact that no one has property rights or enforces them in the environment being polluted, or (b) the collectively consumed characteristics of the environment being polluted. If an owner cannot police, or have policed a portion of the environment, then it becomes possible for others to use the area as a disposal for wastes without being charged for dumping. When values cannot be placed on the amounts of environmental services used by any one person, it is difficult to induce people not to pollute by charging them for doing so. At the same time, costs to non-polluters are higher than they would be if there were no pollution. Polluters are induced to overuse environmental services such as water and air while other users are induced to use less of environmental services because of pollution. Thus, pollution involves inefficient use of environmental services among those who use them. Most environmental ills are public problems and cannot be solved through purely private action (Sharp, Register & Leftwich, 1990).

Pollution Control Policies

Benefit-cost analysis is frequently used to evaluate pollution control policies. The benefits of pollution control consist of the increase in the well-being of the members of the society that results from pollution control activities. The basic consideration in costing public-health protection is the value to be placed on an individual (Chambers, 1966). Values in terms of community welfare seem more accessible and more readily shaped to conformity with dollar indices. But, the response to environmental adjustment may become apparent only in future generations.

Mills (1967) argues that, "Any given pollution level should be reached by the least costly combination of means available. The level of pollution should be achieved at which the cost of a further reduction would exceed the benefits" (p. 101). He states that (a) decision-making should be as decentralized as possible, (b) early attempts at abatement should be experimental and flexible, and (c) careful economic research on benefits and costs

should be part of the plan.

Kneese and Schultze (1975) believe that (a) pollution removed at high levels is subject to increasing marginal costs, (b) in reaching any given standard of air quality, the largest reductions should be made by pollution sources whose costs of control are least, and (c) the costs of alternative control measures differ sharply--- the most efficient solution varies with the circumstances. According to Dales (1968), charges related to property rights may be the most beneficial because polluters would have an incentive to find an acceptable way to reduce the amount of waste. Problems which must be overcome before charges are efficient are: (a) the trial and error procedure in finding the right level for the pollution charge, and (b) an estimate of the extent to which existing polluters should reduce their wastes in order to allow new factories to settle in the region without increasing the total amount of waste discharged. Administrative costs for a pollution charge plan may be lower than other methods thus contributing to overall economic efficiency.

Air Pollution Legislation

Pollution control was not an important issue until the mid 1960s; the 1963 Clean Air Act was the first significant clean air legislation. State and local officials were required to develop and implement emission controls on stationary sources. Local governments were given the major authority and the Federal government was primarily a researcher on the nature of air quality. In 1965, the Act was amended to include auto emissions and the Federal government assumed the role of overseer (Benarde, 1973; Jasinowski, 1984).

A regional approach was adopted in 1967 but was abandoned in 1970 when the Clean Air Act Amendments placed control with the Federal government. The establishment of national standards for air quality and research and technical assistance to states were designated as the responsibility of the Federal government. Additional amendments in 1971 further increased the Federal government's role. Amendments in 1977 required the states to survey every major source of emissions within its borders and develop strategies to insure compliance with legislated guidelines; each state plan required the approval of the Environmental Protection Agency (EPA).

Cost-benefit analyses in the 1970s provided conflicting reports on the progress in controlling

---

[1]Graduate student, Family Resource Managment

air pollution. With imprecise monitoring and limited information on the history of exposure of individuals, studies of health effects were subject to criticism. The results of laboratory experiments were not easily extrapolated to the general population. Nonhealth benefits were equally difficult to quantify because the value of clean air is not traded in the marketplace. The impact on marketable crops was perhaps the only effect readily estimated by conventional techniques (Crandall, 1983). On a more positive note, a significant reduction in auto emissions occurred although at a slower rate than originally designated.

A Clean Air Act which was designed to replace the 1977 Act was signed on November 15, 1990. Congress may have approved controls that were tougher and more costly for industry than the administration intended (Pytte, 1990). Experts' opinions vary on the outcomes of the Act. Assessment of costs and benefits in regard to health issues continues to be controversial. Abelson (1990) stated, "The EPA still sets guidelines on carcinogenic risks based on the limited information available during the 1970s" (p. 1497). Blake (1991) believes that the Act is designed to fail because its goals for the environment will always be out of reach. Ayers and Garrison (1991) contend that the Act's failure or success will be determined by the degree of commitment to enforcing the law. Krupnick and Portney (1991) view the attainment of national ambient air quality standards as one of the most difficult problems to solve. Their argument is based on the fact that most pollution control measures were implemented during the last 20 years. Further reduction in emissions is likely to be more expensive than earlier reductions. Cook (1991) predicts higher costs for many utilities and higher rates for the utilities' customers. Howe (1991) stated that established firms liked the biases against new firms that must meet higher pollution standards.

Summary

Extensive research was built into the 1990 Clean Air Act (Raloff, 1990). Planned studies include research on the effects of acid rain on waters in the Adirondack Mountains, a five year investigation of air pollution's contribution to atmospheric haze, and the establishment of a Risk Assessment and Management Commission to study chronic health effects caused by air pollutants. A cost-benefit assessment of compliance by the EPA was scheduled to begin in November 1992. Substantial progress has been made in some areas of pollution control during the first 20 years (1970-1990); some problems were highly visible and the costs of cleaning them up were relatively low. There appears to be general agreement that economic-based incentives hold the most promise for long term growth and development of industry. The writer encourages the consumer to employ a long term perspective in assessing the effectiveness of pollution control policies.

References

Abelson, P. H. (1990, December 14). Incorporation of new science into risk assessment. Science, 250, 1497.

Ayers, R. E. & Garrison, J. R. (1991). Viewpoints: An environmentalist's perspective. EPA Journal, 17(1), 56-58.

Benarde, M. A. (1973). Our precarious habitat. New York: W. W. Norton & Company, Inc.

Blake, F. (1991). Viewpoints: A skeptical observer. EPA Journal, 17(1), 59-60.

Chambers, L. A. (1966). Risks versus costs in environmental health. In Goldman, M. I. (Ed.), Controlling pollution: The economics of a cleaner America. Englewood Cliffs, NJ: Prentice-Hall, Inc.

Cook, J. (1991, March 4). Rain from heaven. Forbes, 147(5), 90-92.

Crandall, R. W. (1983). Controlling industrial pollution. Washington, DC: The Brookings Institution.

Dales, J. H. (1968). Pollution property & prices. Toronto: Toronto University Press.

Howe, C. W. (1991). An evaluation of U.S. air and water policies. Environment, 33, September 10-15.

Jasinowski, J. J. (1984). Improving the balance between jobs and clean air. In J. Sullivan (Ed.), The American environment. New York: The H. W. Wilson Company.

Kneese, A. J. & Schultze, C. L. (1975). Pollution, prices and public policy. Washington, DC: The Brookings Institution.

Krupnick, A. J. & Portney, P. R. (1991, April 26). Controlling urban air pollution: A benefit-cost assessment. Science, 252, 522-528.

Mills, E. S. (1967). Economic incentives in air-pollution control. In Goldman, M. I. (Ed.), Controlling pollution: The economics of a cleaner America. Englewood Cliffs, NJ: Prentice-Hall, Inc.

Pytte. A. (1990, October 27). A decade's acrimony lifted in the glow of clean air. Congressional Quarterly Weekly Report, 48, 3587-3592.

Raloff, J. (1990, November 3). Clean air bill mixes new limits with research and development. Science News, 138, 277.

Sharp, A. M., Register, C. A. & Leftwich, R. H.
    (1990).   Economics of social issues.
    Homewood, IL: BPI Irwin.

Determinants of Households' Asset/Debt Holdings and Debt Burdens

Julie Yu, Purdue University[1]

The correlations between household asset/debt holdings, debt burdens and socioeconomic variables including household size, income, age, education, occupation, sex, race and marital status are examined using 1983 Survey of Consumer Finances. Cross-tabulation and Multiple Regression are conducted. From the findings, suggestions for creditors and financial planners are given.

Introduction

The debt holdings of consumers have been growing tremendously since the end of World War II. The growing consumer credit has had great impact on the economy and society. As a result, consumer credit has become a research issue. On the macro level, considerable research has been done on this level. On the micro level, how consumer credit affects individual consumer's consumption and saving behavior, and how demographic variables affect consumer credit behavior are worthwhile areas of study. Because of the lack of data, not much research has been done to answer these questions. Furthermore, as consumer credit rises dramatically, many people are worried about whether or not consumers are over indebted. Debt measured in dollars can not give an accurate answer to this question. The debt burden can reflect the real financial situation of the household.

The purpose of this study is to examine how the socioeconomic and demographic variables are related to the asset/debt holdings as well as debt burdens of the household.

Review of Literature

Life cycle income hypothesis suggests that income and Age have effects on households' financial situations. (Ando and Modigliani, 1963) Findings using univariate analysis in 1983 Survey of Consumer Finances are reported. (Avery, Elliehausen and Canner, 1984a; Avery, Elliehausen and Canner, 1984b; Avery Elliehausen and Canner, 1988; Bloom and Steen, 1987). Income, age, education, occupation, and race are found to be related to households' asset and debt holdings. Multivariate analysis is also performed. (Bloom and Steen, 1987; Sullivan and Worden, 1986). Education, gender, marital status, income, age, family size are found to have effects on households' finances.

Methodology

Data used are from the 1983 Survey of Consumer Finances. The sample is a "randomly selected, nationally representative, area probability sample of all U.S. households." (Avery and Elliehausen, 1985, p3).

Based on theory, previous studies, and the data, a model is developed. Households' asset holdings, debt holdings, and debt burdens are functions of income, age, sex, race, marital status, education, occupation, and household size.

Results and Discussions

Cross-tabulation is conducted and chi-square values are calculated to see if there is a significant relationship between each of the dependent variable and independent variables. The results verified that there are significant relationships between dependent and independent variables for all the variables.

Multiple regression analysis is also performed. The results are shown in Table 1. Income level is positively related to both assets and debt holdings with a slight downward trend for high-income households reflected by the significantly small negative coefficient of income squared. Surprisingly, income level is not significantly related to debt burden.

As age increases, the asset level rises but the debt level and debt burden decrease. Family size has a significantly positive effect on debt holdings and debt burdens, but not asset holdings. Larger family size might be associated with greater consumption need resulting in more debt. However, larger family size does not mean more income sources or more asset holdings. Marital status of the head has very little effect on family's financial situation after controlling for income and other socioeconomic factors.

Higher education is related to higher levels of assets and debt holdings. This finding indicates that knowledge is an important determinant in family financial situation controlling for income. On one hand, people with higher education are more likely to have higher income and more assets. On the other hand, they have more expensive consumption patterns and more ability to handle debt. In addition, higher income people are more likely to be granted credit. As a result, people with higher education have more

---

[1]Graduate Student, Consumer and Family Economics

asset and debt holdings. After controlling for income, education and other factors in the model, occupation turns out not to be significant. It only has a significant positive effect on debt levels. Part of the occupation effects might have been absorbed by income and education in the analysis.

Table 1.
OLS Regression Coefficients in the Model.

Variables	Asset	debt	ratio
income	3.90***	0.73***	-0.00
	(31.52)[a]	(24.35)	(-0.88)
size	260.03	1768.80***	5.82***
	(0.18)	(5.09)	(3.03)
age	2152.43***	-160.90***	-0.38**
	(18.45)	(-5.74)	(-2.43)
sex	-10526.00*	-989.79	-16.88**
	(-1.72)	(-0.67)	(-2.07)
race	10774.00**	1582.28	-28.70***
	(2.21)	(1.35)	(-4.42)
ms	3925.84	435.33	-14.68*
	(0.63)	(0.29)	(-1.77)
ed	4549.17***	613.85***	0.22
	(6.23)	(3.49)	(0.23)
occp	2953.36	3625.14***	-7.96
	(0.66)	(3.36)	(-1.33)
incomesq	-0.26E-5***	-0.13E-5***	4.38E-10
	(-7.96)	(-15.99)	(0.96)
adjusted R^2	0.53	0.30	0.02

*** significant at 0.01 level.
** significant at 0.05 level.
* significant at 0.10 level.
a t-values in parentheses.

Whites have more assets and less debt burden than non-whites which might be explained by the discriminations against non-whites in the credit market. Male-headed families have less debt burden than female-headed families.

Notice that in cross-tabulation analysis, all the independent variables are found to be significantly related to the dependent variables. However, in multiple regression analysis, some factors become insignificant. For those factors which are significant in the multiple regression results, although they have interactions with income, they can also provide additional information on family's financial situations. For example, education is correlated with income. However, education has a significant effect even controlling for income. This means that education itself can provide information on family's financial behavior. Other factors which are significant in cross-tabulation analysis but not significant in multiple regression analysis have effects that are absorbed by income and other factors in the equation. For example, occupation is related to asset and debt burdens in univariate analysis but not significant in regression analysis. So because occupation interacts with

income and other factors, it does not provide additional information on asset holdings and debt burdens of the family.

The results may give some implications for the credit grantors to target different consumers. It is important for them to be aware of the difference due to the demographic factors which are tested in this study and proved to be significant in OLS analysis. Finally, for financial planners, they should be aware of the difference of their customers. For example, age is an important determinants in asset and debt holdings and debt burdens of consumers. Therefore, they should treat consumers at different age with different advice. As far as the asset holding is concerned, occupation is not a significant determinant. Difference of occupation might have been caused by difference in income and education level. Thus they may be more concentrated in giving advises based on different income and education levels instead of occupation.

Acknowledgement

The author would like to thank the Board of Governors of the Federal Reserve and University of Michigan for providing the data.

The paper was developed when the author was taking two courses from Consumer Sciences & Retailing Dept. of Purdue University. The author is deeply indebted to the instructors of the courses, Dr. Dixie Johnson and Dr. Patrica Titus for their valuable comments in various stages of the study.

References

Ando, A., & Modigliani, F. (1963). The "Life Cycle" hypothesis of saving: aggregate implications and tests. American Economic Review, 53(1), 55-84.

Avery, R. B., & Elliehausen, G. E. (1988). 1983 Survey of Consumer Finance technical manual and codebook. Washington D.C.: Board of Governors of the Federal Reserve System.

Avery, R. B., Elliehausen, G. E., Canner, G. B. & Gustafson, T. A. (1984, September) Survey of Consumer Finances, 1983. Federal Reserve Bulletin, pp. 857-868.

Avery, R. B., Elliehausen, G. E., & Canner, G. B. (1984, December). Survey of Consumer Finance 1983: a second report. Federal Reserve Bulletin, pp. 857-868

Avery, R. B., & Elliehausen, G. E., & Canner, G. B. (1987, October). Changes in consumer installment debt: evidence from the 1983 and 1986 Survey of Consumer Finances. Federal Reserve Bulletin, pp. 761-778.

Bloom, D. E., & Steen, T. P. (1987, October).

Living on credit. *American Demographics*, pp. 22-29.

Sullivan, A. C. and Worden, D. D. (1986). Economic and demographic factors *associated* *with consumer debt use,* (Working Paper, No. 52) W. Lafayette: Credit Research Center, Purdue University.

Innovative Teaching Techniques For Undergraduate Courses

S. H. A. Jafri, Tarleton State University, TX[1]
M. A. Block, Tarleton State University, TX[2]

This paper summarizes the experience of using a class research project as a teaching tool. The methods and procedures are described followed by the results and implications of using this approach.

How do you make an abstract course interesting and also captivate your students? How do you explain economic theories that can be understood, appreciated and applied by undergraduate students? Rather than using the traditional lecture format, a new approach of involving students in a class research project was experimented to meet the stated objectives. In general, undergraduate students are also not exposed to the rigors of research nor are they aware of the procedures in conducting a research project. This approach, therefore, was expected not only to bridge the gap between theory and the "real world" but also to introduce students to an outline of the research process.

Methods and Procedures

A research project "Credit Card Usage by College Students" was designed and implemented in Consumer Economics and Money and Banking classes at Tarleton State University in Spring of 1992. This topic was selected as interest rates and the use of consumer credit are discussed in both classes. As such, the research project became an excellent tool for learning and discussing credit issues. Moreover, papers submitted by students in previous courses suggested that many of them carry a high debt load on credit cards and other forms of installment debt. Our objective for this project was to ascertain if this indebtness was typical of students at our university or if students with high debt represent a small segment of the student population.

A survey instrument was developed and reviewed by the instructors in their respective classes. As several items on the survey instrument represented new information for students, every item was discussed and explained to justify the rationale for its inclusion. Each student in the class was assigned to survey four other students across the campus. In addition, students were expected to summarize two articles related to credit use from professional journals and trade publications. Analysis of data was accomplished through class discussions and also individually by students in the form of a paper. In all, two hundred twenty one students (221) students responded to the survey.

Results

From the surveys collected, it was found that on an average, students had 3.5 cards, carried an outstanding balance of $1000 and were making monthly payments of just $39. About two-thirds of them indicated having no problem in obtaining cards and about 84 percent surveyed were unaware of consumer laws regarding credit card usage.

Conclusions and Implications

Overall, the class research project was a success in meeting the objectives of the project. It was felt by the instructors that students were able to appreciate the issue of debt more realistically and comprehensively by participating in this project than they would have through lecture presentations. Moreover, a research project such as this one is potentially an excellent tool for teaching students about practical problems of field work, data collection methods as well as allowing them to analyze and evaluate concepts from their own experiences. Perhaps the most valuable benefit is making them realize the importance of discovery through research.

As can be imagined, designing, executing and evaluating such projects requires planning, monitoring and guiding groups of students and is indeed very time consuming. If students work in a group, a "free rider" problem may exist. Students withdrawing from the course in the middle of the semester or taking a casual and poor attitude towards the project (thus adversely affecting the data collected) poses additional problems. The opportunity cost of the time involved from the student and the instructor's perspective should be considered as well. Nevertheless, the long term benefits to the students at the conclusion of the project may be worth the cost.

---

[1]Assistant Professor, Economics

[2]Associate Professor, Home Economics